EDUCATION AND PHILOSOPHICAL THOUGHT

second edition

Kingsley Price

The Johns Hopkins University

Boston
Allyn and Bacon

To L.H.P. and J.A.P.

Foreword
to the second edition

In this second edition of *Education and Philosophical Thought* I have endeavored to make good some of the deficiencies of the first. The first edition does not assist the reader in carrying his study beyond the scope of the book. Here, I have added a bibliography at the end of each chapter that enables the reader to look farther into the subject with which the chapter deals. In the first edition as well as this one, many of the passages quoted from philosophers are somewhat opaque—especially for the reader who is just beginning his study of philosophy of education. In this second edition, I have supplied outlines that make those passages more transparent. The first edition does not include passages from numerous important philosophers who have thought about education, and many readers have been kind enough to make gentle complaints at my having neglected this, that, and the other author. It is not possible to include passages from all those who have contributed to my theme. However, in this second edition, I have added a chapter on the work of St. Thomas Aquinas that places it in the Aristotelian tradition, together with a representative passage from his writing about education; and another, on the work of Johann Friedrich Herbart, together with passages from his *General Practical Philosophy* hitherto unavailable in English. I fear that some readers may still lament my neglect of other philosophers, but I hope they will agree that those whose consideration I have added to this second edition are among the most significant of those ignored in the first.

There are many more minor alterations in this second edition. I trust that, together with the other changes mentioned, they will enable the reader to pursue philosophy of education beyond the covers of this volume.

My sincere gratitude goes to Lenore Johnston and Jesse Kalin whose unfailing assistance was irreplaceable in the preparation of this second edition, and to David A. McCullough who labored with great care at the preparation of the bibliographies and who translated the passages from Herbart's *Allgemeine Praktische Philosophie*.

K.P.   Baltimore

Foreword

to the first edition

This book would have been much longer coming to the light without my mother's unstinting assistance in research, and my father's kind willingness to be neglected by her. It would have been difficult to organize without the patient and efficient help of the staff of the library of The Johns Hopkins University—notably of Martha Hubbard, Sue Kemp, Loretta Reinhardt, and Louise Kuethe—and without the critical reading of it by students working in that university for the degree of Master of Arts in Teaching. Its preparation for the press is unimaginable apart from the cheerful competence of V. Monroe, Doris Stude, Mary Gill, Carroll Routh, Elizabeth Hansen, Edith Schell, Roberta Speel, and Donald Reitz. I rest more easy in my mind for having asked Professor James C. Atkinson of the University of North Carolina at Greensboro to read over the hitherto unpublished passage in translation from Rousseau.

My work on the book was supported by the Johnson Fund of the American Philosophical Society, and by the Dean's Research Fund of The Johns Hopkins University.

I wish to thank all those named for generous assistance and support, and to acknowledge the help of many others so numerous as to defy mention—especially several classes of students who bore kindly with the lectures out of which parts of the book grew, and the philosophers whose work I have expounded and drawn upon.

K.P.   Baltimore

CONTENTS

XII

John Dewey 549

XIII

In Retrospect 581

Education
and
Philosophical
Thought

I

INTRODUCTION

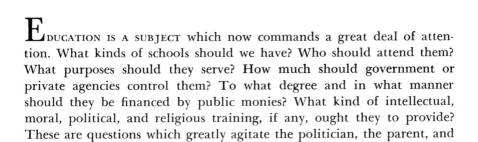

EDUCATION IS A SUBJECT which now commands a great deal of attention. What kinds of schools should we have? Who should attend them? What purposes should they serve? How much should government or private agencies control them? To what degree and in what manner should they be financed by public monies? What kind of intellectual, moral, political, and religious training, if any, ought they to provide? These are questions which greatly agitate the politician, the parent, and the ordinary citizen alike.

Interest in education is more highly concentrated in a special group: thousands of teachers and thousands of others preparing for the teaching profession constitute this group, and for them a more important interest arises. They must ask themselves not only questions such as those listed, but also many others specific to their profession. What is education? Are there any general objectives for us? Are there any universal methods in it? Is there such a thing as the typical child upon whom they may be practiced? — these are some of the more specific questions with which teachers must be concerned.

Many have felt that both these general and specifically professional questions can be dealt with satisfactorily only by bringing a philosophy of education to bear upon them. But the student, the teacher, the politician, the parent, and the ordinary citizen, in many cases possess no ready-made philosophy of education, although they may be interested in trying to work one out for themselves. It is to assist them in this task that the philosophies of education of several celebrated intellects have been examined, and representative passages from their writings have been presented here.

Although many believe that a philosophy of education is necessary to a sensible solution for its problems, they also find a certain unclarity in the idea of such a philosophy, for the philosophy of education is a subject which is not clear and definite in ordinary thought. It will be useful, therefore, to introduce the subject by laying down the boundaries of the field and providing a definition for the phrase.

DEFINITION OF "PHILOSOPHY OF EDUCATION"

How, THEN, CAN WE DEFINE "philosophy of education"? We should begin by noticing that the obscurity of its meaning springs from an obscurity about the meaning of the words "philosophy" and "education." Let us consider the last word first.

OF "EDUCATION"

"Education" is a word to which different meanings have been given. In its broadest sense, John Dewey says, education is the means of "social continuity of life."[1] Others have defined it more narrowly as the process by which a culture is deliberately transmitted from one person or generation to another. The first definition makes education include such activities as tilling the fields, preserving monuments, and governing families. The second excludes from education these somewhat physical and spontaneous activities. It makes "education" refer to the deliberate teaching, learning, and enhancing of attitudes and skills, of arts, sciences, and other elements of a social heritage—to the deliberate transmission of culture. The term "education" will not be used here in either of these senses although it is used in one closely related to the second.

The closely related sense is that in which "education" means the discipline that endeavors to understand the process of deliberate cultural transmission. It makes "education" refer not to the activities of teaching, learning, and improving upon past accomplishments, but rather, to the

[1] John Dewey, *Democracy and Education,* The Macmillan Co., New York, 1923, p. 3.

theory[2] that describes and explains those activities. This discipline concerns itself with three different aspects of the process of transmitting and fostering a culture: instruction, administration of schools, and guidance of students into those professions and occupations best suited to them. With respect to each of these kinds of activity, it makes statements of fact and recommendations. For the making of statements of fact, it draws upon a great number of different sources. History, sociology, psychology, anthropology, and common sense—from all these and other areas as well, information may be gleaned concerning instruction, administration, and guidance. This information is embodied in statements of the form: If people of a certain sort are dealt with in a certain way, then a certain kind of result will follow. Statements of this kind are statements of fact.

We should notice that these statements are accepted as true or false on the grounds that they have been found to be so through empirical investigation. A statement of fact is one we accept or reject either because experience reveals directly the facts to which it refers, or because experience provides some evidence, however indirect, for or against it. The information included in education, then, is embodied in statements of fact.

We should also notice that this rummaging of common sense and science for information concerning the consequences of instructing, administering, and guiding in certain ways may now give very little reliable information to the factual part of education. It is, none the less, the discovery of true or probable information that motivates the person who is genuinely interested in the factual part of education; and to a discipline thus idealized—a discipline whose statements of fact are *supposed* to be true or probable—the word "education" is here used to refer.

To the three subordinate areas of the factual part of education correspond three kinds of statements in the recommending part. The factual part informs us that a certain method will suffice to instruct students of a certain sort in a certain subject; that organizing a school in a certain way will, under certain conditions, maintain it as a going concern; and that guiding persons of a certain kind into a certain area of life will satisfy them adequately. But in no case do whatever reliable statements there may be concerning those subjects tell us that instructors, administrators, and counsellors *ought* to act in the ways described. The recommending part of education involves, therefore, some consideration other than that of facts, and consists of statements which recommend that instructors adopt certain teaching methods, that administrators employ

2 Cf. Kingsley Price, "Discipline in teaching; in its study and in its theory," in *Discipline of Education*, edited by John Walton and James Kuethe, University of Wisconsin Press, Madison, Wisconsin, 1962.

certain administrative techniques, and that counsellors use certain principles for the professional and vocational direction of their charges.

We should notice that recommendations differ markedly from
statements of fact. The latter are seen to be true or false in experience of
the things to which they refer, or of others whose relation to the former
is one of evidence. For recommendations, on the other hand, acceptability
is not determined by experience of the things they are about. Exactly the
same fact may be experienced by one who recommends something concerning it as by one who makes a contrary recommendation. "Men ought
to love one another" certainly does not describe the relations we find to
prevail among them; and the more these relations are characterized by
hatred and violence, the more most of us are inclined to accept the recommendation of love. But one possessed by an evil spirit might, contemplating the same cruelty and selfishness of men, recommend that they endeavor to enhance it as much as possible. Recommending statements urge
that something be done about the things to which they refer, while statements of fact need only be empirically true or false of them.

The factual and the recommending parts of education are related
in a certain way. The factual part is, in all cases, a partial support or justification for the doctrines of the recommending part. It is a *partial* support because it must be supplemented by moral statements in order that
recommendations should be derived from it. Nonetheless, it is in view of
statements taken to embody facts concerning particular kinds of students,
schools, and guidance problems that certain teaching methods, administrative procedures, and guidance principles are recommended. The facts
which education takes itself to find are treated as providing a partial basis
for inference to its recommendations.

We have defined the word "education" to refer, not to the activity
of deliberate transmission of culture, but to the theory concerning it in
order to allow ourselves to speak of certain discernible factors in education, the relation between them and of its relation to philosophy—a difference which we could not speak of if the word were used to refer to the
factual process of deliberate teaching and learning. If the word were used
in that way, then we could not speak of a support given to goals by procedures; we could only describe the ways in which activities do, in fact,
lead to their consequences. As a factual process, education would be simply whatever goes on in the deliberate transmission of culture from one
person to another and in the succession of generations; and the elements
which we wish to get at could not be discriminated within it. Nor could
we speak of the support (or lack of it) that a philosophical theory provides for education. For philosophy, as we shall see, is the activity of endeavoring to find out whether certain statements are true, along with the
doctrines taken to embody such truths; it is not a fact like a thunderstorm

or World War II. And it is not intelligible to speak of the support or lack of it provided by cognitive activities and doctrines for facts. The activity of seeking the truth about a thunderstorm and World War II neither supports nor fails to support these violent events; nor does a statement about storms and wars support or fail to support them although the facts themselves might be so related to the statements. In order to examine what the authors we consider here take to be facts, what they make as recommendations, the relation between them, and the occurrence of the whole in a philosophy of education, we have defined that word as referring not to the process of transmitting culture but to a theory or discipline about its deliberate transmission of the kind described.[3]

Education considered as a discipline is made up of a set of statements of fact and a set of recommendations, where the statements of the former set are viewed as a partial support for those of the latter. In order to explain the meaning of the phrase "philosophy of education," having explained that of the word "education," we must now consider that of the word "philosophy."

OF "PHILOSOPHY"

The word "philosophy" has frequently been used to refer to activities of two different kinds as well as to the doctrines in which they result. The first activity is analysis; and while there is doubt among philosophers as to the nature of analysis, there is little difficulty in recognizing it when it occurs. It is a certain way of trying to understand a word, to clarify an idea, or to comprehend a concept. It is well exemplified in the early parts of Plato's *Republic,* and in *Moby Dick* where Melville is concerned with understanding the concept "whale": ". . . how shall we define the whale . . ." he writes, "so as conspicuously to label him for all time to come. To be short . . . a whale is *a spouting fish with a horizontal tail.* There you have him. However contracted, that definition is the result of expanded meditation."

This "expanded meditation" is analytical activity; and when it succeeds, it affords an understanding of words, of ideas, or of concepts by presenting to us their parts and their relations to one another. Its results are expressed in the statements of the philosophers who perform the

---

[3] The reader may find that I have occasionally strayed from this use, sometimes using "education" to refer to the process of deliberate cultural transmission. He may also find that the phrase "educational theory" sometimes replaces "education" as defined above. The point with which we are concerned, however, is the relation philosophers have thought themselves to find between philosophy and education as the word is defined above, i.e., between philosophy and the theory that describes the deliberate transmission of culture; and this point is independent of the definition given since it can be made in any words whose use is appropriate.

analysis. But it is impossible to lay down any bounds to such statements; for it is impossible to decide, *a priori,* what words, ideas, or concepts we shall find unclear. Plato wished to understand the term "justice" more thoroughly, and Melville, the concept "whale"; but, in advance of the fact, no one could have known that analyses of these terms would be needed. We may, none the less, quite properly hold that analytical philosophy is constituted not only by the activity of analysis, but also by all those doctrines which human beings reach by way of that activity.

The second kind of activity may be more precisely delimited. It need not exclude analysis, but does differ from it. It is the activity of arriving at certain theories—those of metaphysics, ethics, epistemology, aesthetics, and logic.

The activities by which people have sought to answer these questions are extraordinarily diverse. Usually, they have relied in some measure on analysis. Some have borrowed from the empirical sciences. Many have found help in theology and religion. Others have appealed to what they regarded as a peculiarly philosophical insight or peculiarly philosophical method. Still others have supposed that an intuition, in one way or another mystical, lay at the bottom of their answers. However diverse, all these activities have in common the purpose of providing answers to philosophical questions by making reference to the things toward which those questions are directed. In this respect, speculative philosophy differs from analysis. Analysis moves toward the clarification of words, ideas, or concepts by a consideration which does not depart from the terms to be clarified. Speculative philosophy, although it often engages in analysis, seeks the answers to its questions by doing something different—by speculating about the nature of the things which generate those questions.

Metaphysics deals with the question as to the nature of reality, and may be thought of as comprised of all the statements which philosophers have made on that subject. These statements vary. Idealists declare that reality is spiritual; materialists, that it is material; dualists, that it is somehow both; mystics, that it is an unbroken unity incomprehensible to ordinary thought; and there are still other metaphysical theories, some of which are represented in this volume. However metaphysicians differ as to the nature of reality, they agree that it lies behind or above, not in, the observable world. This world is made up of the things we find by the help of sight and touch and the other means of sensory perception, as well as by the methods of the various sciences; and although this world does not reveal the nature of reality, it is thought to be an appearance of it.

The distinction between reality and appearance is one not easily understood in detail; nor is it necessary here to achieve such a perfect understanding. Suffice it to say that as an experience of color is the appearance to some person of light waves vibrating from some object to his eye, so, according to the metaphysician, the world of observable things and of the sciences is throughout an appearance of the reality that lies behind it. The experience of color manifests the physical occurrence, although that occurrence does not appear in the experience; the observable world manifests reality, although reality does not appear in the observable world. If idealism is true, mountains are really mental; if materialism is true, they are really material; if dualism is true, they are really material or, in some way, really both, according to the variety of dualism involved; and if mysticism is true, they are really, one would imagine, illusions of troubled souls. But no matter which is right, or even if none should be, the metaphysician contends that mountains are an appearance of the reality which he believes to exist behind their observable character.

Ethics deals with two questions: "What kinds of things are morally right and good?" and "What is the nature of moral rightness and goodness?" We should notice that the first of these is not the question that it might seem to be. Independently of ethical reflection, we know a good many of the kinds of things that are morally right and good. Alleviating general poverty, refraining from theft, fostering universal peace, we know to be morally right or good in most circumstances without any philosophical reflection on the subject. We might suppose that a list of such kinds of things known to be morally right or good, prior to all reflection on the subject, might constitute an answer to our first question; but this would be a mistake. The first question of ethics does not ask merely for a list of those kinds of things which are morally valuable; it asks, rather, for a list of such things as can be morally *justified*. It requires, that is to say, that what is morally right and good be shown to be so; and lest there be some error in this justification, it works out a theory as to what the justification of a moral judgment is. The first question of ethics thus asks for a list of those kinds of things which can be shown to be morally right or good, and for a description of the kind of reflection in which this justification or showing occurs.

The second question, "What is the nature of moral rightness or goodness?" is closely related to this last endeavor, for no kind of action could be justified as morally right or good unless we knew in what its moral rightness or goodness consisted. A definition of moral value is required to answer the first question of ethics, and a definition for it is what an answer to the second question provides. There are many answers to that question. Some ethical theories hold that moral goodness is a trait accessible only to reason; others, that it is some quality like pleasantness, the possession of which is open to empirical discovery; and still others, that it properly characterizes nothing, being like love or rage, a human response to things although subtly different from these. Similar statements might be made concerning the varying treatments of moral rightness.

In the answer to its second question, ethics professes to clarify and analyze the very traits which everyday moral statements express. One such everyday statement is "Universal peace is good." In the first part of ethics, this statement would receive a justification—the ethical philosopher would show why universal peace is good. In connection with that justification, he would be led inevitably into a theory of what such a justification is and, hence, into an effort to analyze the notion of good employed. If the proper answer to the question "What is the nature of moral goodness?" be that it is pleasure, then universal peace, if it is pleasant, is morally good. Similar statements may be made with respect to other answers to the question about the nature of moral value. These answers require that those things which possess the properties in terms of which moral value is analyzed be good or right. A complete catalogue of what is genuinely good and right would, therefore, at once test every theory as to the nature of goodness and rightness, and show which is true and which false.

Epistemology endeavors to answer two questions: "What is knowledge?" and "What are the methods by which it is secured?" However, a list of the statements known, and a set of descriptions of the ways in which they come to be so, would not answer these questions. To make such a list would be the task of a remarkable encyclopedist; the task of describing the ways we come to know would be performed by psychology, were it sufficiently developed. The first question asks, rather, for an exhibition of the constituents of knowledge, and for a statement of the relationship it requires between the knower and the known. The second asks for a reconstruction of the methods which serve to secure knowledge, so that the critic may be assured that it is not vitiated by errors in the procedures through which it was achieved.

Aesthetics asks, "What things are beautiful or ugly, excellent or deficient in the realm of art and nature?" and "What is the constitution of aesthetic excellence and deficiency?" Logic traditionally conceived asks for the truth determining relations of propositions. The activity of answering these questions—as well as those of metaphysics, ethics, and epistemology—together with the doctrines in which that activity rests, represent the second part of the reference of the word "philosophy."

OF "PHILOSOPHY OF EDUCATION"

The philosophy of education may be understood in relation to the definitions of "philosophy" and "education" made out above. "Philosophy of education," as the phrase is employed here, means an analytical treatment of education together with an attempt to relate it in a certain way to certain parts of speculative philosophy. It should be noted that this way of understanding the phrase conforms to the practice, if not to the explicit formulation, recorded in the literature.[4] It should be noted also that logic and aesthetics are not called upon to provide subdivisions of philosophy of education. Logic is not, because all theories must conform to its requirements; hence, it has no import for education in particular. Aesthetics is not, because even though some recommendations of education may include some which find a foundation in it, they are included not for that reason, but because they are morally justified.

In its first subdivision, analysis, philosophy of education is the activity of clarifying our understanding of those terms in education which need it. In its second subdivision, philosophy of education treats education from the point of view of speculative philosophy. It attempts a metaphysical explanation for the factual part of education; and a certain supplement for it; it finds in ethics a justification and clarification of the recommendations which education includes; and it endeavors to derive a theory of learning from epistemological enquiry. I shall now explain this view of philosophy of education in a little more detail.

Analysis

In the history of civilization, every generation to one degree or other has concerned itself with the transmission and fostering of its culture— of its skills, its arts, its sciences, etc.; and to one degree or other, each has treated of this process in the discipline we call education. Each generation, no doubt, has developed a more or less specific body of thought, words, ideas, or concepts for this purpose. The words, ideas, and concepts that it employs become obscure from time to time. Plato used the phrase "the idea of the good" in stating doctrines of the utmost importance in education as he understood it; St. Augustine used phrases like "interior light" in a corresponding way. These terms cannot be acquitted of the charge of obscurity, and they demand some kind of analysis for those who would understand the educational theory of these two celebrated minds.

In our own day, the number of obscure terms in education has immensely multiplied. They occur both in its factual and recommending parts. Consider, for example, such terms as "integrated," "child-centered," "the whole person," "core curriculum," "on-going process," "experience," "shared experience," "citizenship," "loyalty," "disloyalty," "enrichment," "growth," "need," "meaningful," and "value." It is doubtful that many have a very clear notion as to the use of these terms, and it is certain that some employ them to signal an attack or justify a defense, rather than to

[4] Cf. John Dewey, *Democracy and Education,* The Macmillan Co., New York, 1923, p. 27; and *Modern Philosophies and Education,* edited by Nelson B. Henry, The University of Chicago Press, Chicago, 1955, p. 16.

make clear statements of fact or intelligible recommendations. Yet it is in such terms that entire programs are praised or condemned, and personnel evaluated. Such jargon serves well to rally the faithful and to disperse the enemy; but because of its obscurity, it serves but ill in the statement of educational facts and educational recommendations. Part of the task of a philosophy of education is the analysis of this jargon whenever and wherever it occurs, of the ideas it expresses, or of the concepts whose application its employment constitutes. An understanding, let alone an agreement, among educationists can be accomplished only when such an analysis of obscure terms is provided.

Speculation: Metaphysics

The metaphysical reflection upon education attempts to explain the facts that education states. A statement of fact is a statement, belief in whose truth or probability demands observation of the fact it asserts or of some fact that is evidence for it; and it is often said that no such statement can explain any other. Consider the fact that many adolescents are rebellious. The statement of this fact may be verified by our observation of adolescents; and if to the untutored eye they do not appear so, other statements based on observation may be adduced in support of the first. The psychiatrist, for example, may advance the testimony and behavior of his patients to support it. But, the metaphysician holds, the statements of fact that the psychiatrist might advance, however much his experience warrants them, require for themselves another explanation. Why, it might be asked, should the motives engendered in the young child by his familial context make him rebellious in adolescence? And a similar question might be asked concerning whatever it is that answers this one. In this way, it is contended that no statement of fact can explain any other adequately, for about every statement of fact, a similar demand for explanation may be made. Indeed, were there a statement that truly asserted all observable facts, one might still ask why this particular statement was true and not some other. Thus, it might be argued, while common sense and science give education its facts, a theory of reality is necessary as their ultimate guarantee.

The metaphysical explanation of the facts of education carries within it a second good office, that of guaranteeing the recommendations that education makes. These recommendations are derived, in part, from education's statements of fact. If many adolescents are rebellious, for example, certain procedures of administrators, teachers, and counselors are right, and others wrong; and a guarantee that they are rebellious is a strengthening of our assurance concerning the value of the procedures in question. In this way, metaphysical reflection on education would guarantee both its facts and its recommendations.

Besides explaining the facts and guaranteeing the recommendations of education, metaphysical theories also would supplement the facts in a certain way. Orthodox metaphysical theology throughout Christendom asserts that the person survives death; and orthodox materialism, wherever it occurs, denies it. The assertion of neither theory is a statement of fact in the sense of the phrase employed here; for belief in it need not, and perhaps cannot, depend upon observation. But it is a statement which, nevertheless, supplements the information that common sense and science provide for education. Most metaphysical theories would add to the statements of fact in education some similar statement concerning the persons involved in instruction, administration, and guidance.

The metaphysical supplementation of the facts of education is of great importance, for it provides for education the basis for recommendations of a highly imperative sort. If a man is an immortal being, caught only for a brief span in the web of time, then everything that he undergoes in that web should be subordinated to his larger life, and the objectives of his education should be altered accordingly. The glorification of God and the preparation for eternity should be paramount, while the transmission and fostering of the skills, the arts, and the sciences should be diminished to that degree which his short life here warrants. If he is not immortal, then an education devoted to a diligent increase of secular progress ought to be the goal of education. And according as philosophers of education adopt one or other metaphysical view, they explain the facts of education and guarantee as well as augment its recommendations.

Ethics

What may we say concerning ethics and education? We should remember that ethical theories endeavor to answer two questions: "What kinds of things are morally right and good?" and "What is the nature of moral rightness and goodness?" It might be supposed, first, that ethical reflection on education is what results from a certain way of uniting an ethical theory with education; it might be supposed, that is to say, that ethical reflection on education provides that part of the answer to the first question of ethics, that pertaining to educational recommendations. According to this way of viewing the matter, the recommendations of education are simply a part of a very large collection of statements concerning all the kinds of things that are right and good. But educational recommendations and ethical reflection on education are different things, for there is more to ethics than the simple fact of issuing injunctions and making recommendations.

Secondly, it is often supposed that ethical reflection on education supplies a statement of the objectives educators and others entertain for the programs in which they participate. But this, too, is a mistake, for to state one's intentions is not to produce an ethical theory of any sort, but only to inform others as to what one is about. The stating of intentions, while often described as a philosophical activity, is a very different thing from an ethical theory. Such a theory is motivated by an effort not simply to produce injunctions or reveal intentions, but to justify a judgment that some kind of thing is right or good, or a statement as to the nature of rightness and goodness.

We should emphasize, thirdly, that constructing a theory of this kind is distinct both from making recommendations and from stating intentions. To recommend and to express oneself require little more than the desire to do so. To justify a statement or a judgment of the kind mentioned above, on the other hand, requires the giving of reasons for it. The giving of reasons consists in the endeavor to show that the recommendations we have made or the intentions we have entertained are valid.

Consider the recommendation that children should be allowed to develop their own interests without let or hindrance from the instructor. The repetition of this injunction clearly would not constitute a philosophical or ethical treatment of it, nor would the mere statement that so to proceed is someone's intention. Yet laying down reasons for educational recommendations does not exhaust ethical reflection on education. One who makes the recommendation and advances reasons for it does not, so far, complete an ethical treatment of education. Of course, the question whether this is a valid recommendation is one which we think of as a peculiarly ethical question; what it asks is whether the proposed action actually is a right or good one. But the giving of reasons for a recommendation does not, as such, show that the recommendation is valid, for we might be mistaken in the reasons we propound. Ethical reflection on education demands a theory of the way in which reasons genuinely justify the recommendations of education, together with a list of the recommendations thus shown to be valid.

But there is still more to ethical reflection on education. The endeavor genuinely to justify the recommendations of education cannot succeed without some consideration of the second question of ethics generally taken. We cannot know that some proposed action is genuinely right, or some state of things genuinely good, without having some notion as to the nature of "rightness" or "goodness." For if we were ignorant as to the nature of either, our judgment might assign a moral character to some action or state of things which were undeserving of it; confusion might take the place of understanding. An ethical treatment of education, then, brings forward a general theory of the nature of moral rightness and goodness, a theory of the nature of moral justification, and a use of both to test the validity of the recommendations that education makes, as well as a setting down of those which survive that philosophical ordeal.

In the second part of education there are two distinct kinds of recommendation; and in the ethical treatment of them there is a corresponding division of topics. In education we discover, first, a great many statements to the effect that something should exist. Some of these statements pertain to societies of various sorts; and others, to persons of various sorts. Thus, Plato recommends the existence of an aristocratic state and an aristocratic man; Dewey, the democratic state and the democratic man; and Rousseau, the less corrupted state and the innocent man. These we may call "goal recommendations," for they present certain states of affairs as ideals eminently worthy of our diligent efforts. Statements of the second sort recommend particular procedures in the daily business of instructing, administering, and guiding as methods by which social and personal ideals are realized or at least approximated. Thus, Plato recommends that the young guardians should be made to view battles; Dewey, that school activities should be predominantly cooperative; and Rousseau, that the young gentleman should be long isolated from his fellows. Statements of this sort we may call "subordinate recommendations"; for, since they are thought to further them, they secure their force from the objectives embodied in goal recommendations.

An ethical treatment of education must consider the recommendations of both these kinds; and with respect to each kind, it must consider two questions. With respect to goal recommendations, it must ask whether genuine rightness or goodness, and not some impostor, is attributed to the goals and whether such reasons as may be advanced for them genuinely show them to be right or good. With respect to subordinate recommendations, it must ask similar questions. Thus ethical reflection on education must test, in the light of the general ethical considerations discussed above, both goal and subordinate recommendations in that discipline.

One moral should be drawn from this discussion. It is that, at least in the inception of ethical reflection, there is no such thing as *the* ethical treatment of education. We have seen that there are several different kinds of ethical theory, and we may now add that within each, there is much variation from one particular theory to another. Each particular ethical theory provides us with its own unique way of treating education; for even though there should be one single coherent body of valid educational recommendations, each ethical theory would supplement the statement of those precepts by its unique understanding of the nature of rightness and goodness, and its own theory of the nature of moral justification. In the beginning, at least, the pragmatic or experimentalist treatment of education, for example, is only one among many other such theories. In the end, after careful consideration of the claims of the various theories, one might well offer his allegiance to one as opposed to the rest. To accept one from the outset, however, is a dogmatism against which this moral warns; while to accept one upon reflection, where cognitive superiority manifests itself, is an obligation which philosophy imposes.

Epistemology

In order to understand the relationship between epistemology and education, we must bear in mind that epistemology concerns itself with the nature of knowledge and with the nature of the procedures by which it may be achieved. Of these two parts of epistemology, the second has been thought, primarily, to bear upon education. A considerable number of philosophers have endeavored to make use of their answers to the question "What are the methods by which knowledge may be secured?" for educational purposes. Dewey believed that all knowledge is achieved by engaging in the "scientific method"—apparently the hypothetico-deductive procedure with which we are all familiar; he recommended, accordingly, that instruction be altered to fit that pattern. In this way, some philosophers have derived from epistemological reflection a theory of learning and instruction, and a consequent recommendation of it, from the methods epistemology lays down.

But the answer to the first question of epistemology cannot be completely ignored, for it often determines in part the answer to the second. Plato held that knowledge is reason's illumination of supersensible objects—the "ideas" or "forms"—and he was obliged, consequently, to contend that the method of knowledge is rationalistic in character. While he did not conclude that instruction and learning must pursue such a rationalistic route, what he did contend about the nature of coming to know is different from what it would have been had he believed that the objects of knowledge are, let us say, denizens of the observable world. Epistemological reflection on education attempts to derive from a study of the method of knowledge and its nature a description of the procedures by which learning may be furthered, and a consequent recommendation that such courses be pursued in the schools.

A philosophy of education consists in an analysis of educational terms and in metaphysical, ethical, and epistemological reflections on education—each understood in the fashion made out above. The phrase is used here to refer to any such set of doctrines.

Our definition of "philosophy of education" has proceeded from a definition of the two chief terms contained in the phrase. From the distinction within philosophy between analysis and speculation, a corresponding distinction within philosophy of education was generated. This duality suggests that each of the philosophers of education with whom we are concerned engages either in analysis, in speculation, or in both; it also suggests that his thought may be understood as falling clearly under these categories. This is a mistaken view.

"Philosophy," of course, does refer to analysis and to speculation; and that it does so is a reflection of a certain historical fact. If we wish to define "philosophy" as the term is in fact used, we must look to the work done by those whom we call philosophers. And in the work of the prominent figures in the history of philosophy, both kinds of philosophical activity and statement do occur. But they occur fused and indistinct, or at best, side by side with no explicit boundary to separate them. We cannot understand the reference of the word "philosophy" unless we bear in mind the distinction between analysis and speculation; but since typical philosophers have not explicitly engaged now in the one exclusively, and now in the other, it is futile and misleading to try to catalogue their doctrines neatly and separately under both heads. For a like reason, the work of philosophers of education does not divide itself clearly and neatly into analysis and speculation, even though both may be found in their writings. Having noticed the distinction in order to define "philosophy" and "philosophy of education," we shall, none the less, not often use it in presenting the views of those concerned in this volume.

METHOD OF THE DEFINITION

WE SHOULD NOTICE THAT few authors have explicitly advanced a philosophy of education, taking the phrase in the sense established. Most have been concerned with only a few aspects of the field, and often those who have written on education have been content to assert facts and to draw recommendations from them without attending at all to the bearing philosophy might have upon education.

While much of the literature is incomplete and only implicitly philosophy of education, there are three authors who present doctrines clearly of the kind called to our attention by the phrase. They are Plato, who wrote in Athens in the fourth century B.C., St. Augustine, who died in 430 A.D., and John Dewey, whose work has only recently been completed. Their doctrines have been taken as models for all those to which the phrase "philosophy of education" refers; others are taken as parts of the reference of that phrase even though they fall short of the models in some way. We do not refuse to describe a certain person as a man even though he is misshapen in one way or another, in body or mind or both, so long as deviation from some model case is not great. In the same way, we do not refuse to describe a doctrine as a philosophy of education so long as it is not very unlike those advanced by Plato, St. Augustine, and Dewey. The vagueness of the phrase "philosophy of education"—the vagueness that it ordinarily possesses in the language of educationists, and which we have deliberately endeavored to preserve in our definition of it —will not be troublesome if the models for the doctrines to which it refers are clearly understood; for all others to which it refers may be understood as like or unlike the models in this or that or some other respect.

This vagueness of the phrase "philosophy of education" consists in the absence of a boundary sharply marking off philosophies of education from other theories and it is brought about in either of two ways. First, a philosophy of education may be incomplete in comparison with those of Plato, St. Augustine, and Dewey; an author might discuss, for example, only the relation of ethics to education. Secondly, a philosophy of education may be only implicit. Quintilian, for example, did not make clear the bearing of any philosophy upon the facts he asserted and the proposals he advocated. Any set of doctrines may be a more or less complete and implicit philosophy of education. The more complete and the less implicit it is, the greater its resemblance to those of Plato, St. Augustine, and Dewey; the less complete and the more implicit, the less its resemblance to them. There are, thus, many doctrines clustering around those taken as models, and in the outlying reaches of this body there are doctrines quite unlike the models. But there can be no sharp boundary to the body as a whole. There can be only a more or less wide fringe beyond which there are doctrines that are clearly not philosophies of education, and on the hither side of which doctrines that are sufficiently like the models and therefore philosophies of education even though incomplete or implicit.

Because of this manner of defining "philosophy of education," several of the theories presented in this volume must be regarded as somewhat incomplete and implicit philosophies of the subject. Some will perhaps be thought to come perilously close to the outer edge of the margin of vagueness, and this thought will be correct. But where it is so, the authors have been chosen either because their views typify a certain point of view more clearly than others, or because they have exerted an original influence upon subsequent philosophies of education. In any event, an attempt has been made to avoid those authors whose views are clearly and exclusively educational as well as those whose doctrines are clearly and exclusively philosophical.

II

PLATO

Plato was born to a distinguished Athenian family in 428-7 b.c., and died in 348-7. In his youth, he came under the influence of Socrates whose chief interest was, through discussion and without the exaction of fees, to convince anyone who would listen that conventional opinion on moral topics was mistaken or unfounded, and to direct them into the path by which wisdom might be reached. The position of Plato's family would have made politics his natural career; but political abuses, the disturbances of the Peloponnesian War with the consequent deterioration of the Athenian constitution caused him to refuse that career until a time in which the reforms he envisioned would seem more likely of achievement. This time in Athens never came, although Plato is thought by some to have made unsuccessful efforts at reform at Syracuse in Sicily.[1]

The chief political abuse that turned him from a civic career was the trial and consequent death of Socrates on a charge of impiety and religious corruption of the youth. Plato's conviction was that the charge was false, and the entire procedure a calculated use of political power for the selfish purposes of those whose conventional morality was ruffled by

[1] Belief in Plato's efforts at actual political reform depends, in good measure, upon the account of his life given in the seventh letter attributed to him. Not all agree that this letter is genuine. Cf. Edelstein, Ludwig, *Plato's Seventh Letter*, E. J. Brill, Leiden, 1966.

Socrates' questioning. The trial and death moved him deeply; and his early literary works are thought to be a record of the manner as well as of the content of Socrates' teachings designed to vindicate his master. This manner was that of conversation, and the record took the form of the dialogue. Plato continued to use this literary form in the many works that he composed throughout his long literary career.

Revulsion from the egoism and self-seeking of political life manifested itself in Plato's establishment of the Academy in Athens in 387-6. Through this institution, his teachings concerning the good life for society and for its members could indirectly influence those actual political currents from which he, for the most part, remained aloof. We may infer that the system of higher education outlined in the *Republic* sets forth the ideal that Plato endeavored to achieve in the Academy. In it, he trained young men from many cities in the theory of governing; but the curriculum was not confined to political science. Courses were offered in all branches of knowledge on the ground that they not only were interesting in themselves, but also contributed to the art of ruling.

Aristotle studied in the Academy during the last twenty years of Plato's life; and his work, though different from that of his master in some ways, is an important channel through which Socrates, Plato, and the Academy have determined much that is characteristic of contemporary Western civilization. But Plato had a direct influence as well. Most of his literary work remains for us; and in founding the Academy, he established the first university. It did not always teach Platonic doctrine, but it existed with varying vitality until 529 A.D. In that year, as a pagan institution, it was closed and its property confiscated by the Emperor Justinian.

EDUCATIONAL THEORY

STATEMENTS OF FACT

In developing his educational theory, Plato was chiefly concerned with four kinds of statements of fact: those of psychology which describe the human soul or personality, those which pertain to human society, those which assert the relation between a certain kind of person and a certain kind of society, and those which describe the training that leads to the existence of such persons and societies. We shall outline his psychology first.

The individual

In Plato's day, psychology like all science was not experimental; there was no concerted and serious effort to embody the relation between motives and observable behavior in mathematical formulae, and to attempt, by controlling the conditions of life, to discover how variations of behavior are related to each other and to more hidden springs of action. But psychology was nonetheless empirical. In his attempt to understand personality, Plato relied upon introspection as well as upon common sense observation of others; and he assumed that where differences were observable in either of these ways, different, if more hidden, motives were at work to cause the differences in what was observed.

On the basis of this observation and inference, Plato advanced the view that the soul is composed of three kinds of abilities or faculties of action—reason, spirit, and the appetitive faculty. Reason is that part of the soul which enables us to discover truth and falsehood, and which especially enables us to prove the truth or falsehood of some statements, given that of others. It is the power, for example, which enables us to do geometry. Reason is thus the motive to all knowledge.

The most important kind of knowledge which the activity of reason can yield is wisdom; this is knowledge of the nature of goodness and of those ways of acting which make up the good life for society and for the individual. But reason alone is of no effect in controlling human action. We might know what we ought to do, but nevertheless act differently. Spirit is the power which executes the decisions of reason. It is analogous to the more modern notion of the will; for like the will, it is the power to get things done. But unlike it, where reason decides what is good, spirit always acts in accordance with it. Spirit, thus, is the agency in the soul which translates the knowledge that is wisdom into action which is virtuous.

The appetitive faculty is constituted by all those desires that are closely related to bodily functions; and Plato distinguishes two subordinate kinds of desires, necessary and unnecessary. Necessary desires are those the satisfaction of which is necessary for the maintenance and continuation of life; they are such desires as those of hunger and sex, and that for shelter. Unnecessary desires are those whose realization does not further life, but adorns it, is indifferent to it, or is disruptive of it; and they are illustrated by the desire for elaborate and fancy foods. All desire aims at the securing of personal pleasure; and for this reason, each appetite, in itself, is merely a clamorous urgency toward its own fulfillment. The appetites, consequently, cannot provide an orderly realization for themselves unassisted.

Their assistance comes indirectly from reason, and directly from spirit. For the wisdom which reason may discover concerns the orderly fulfillment of appetites, both necessary and unnecessary; and spirit is the power which puts that wisdom into practice. Plato describes the human soul or person as made up of the powers to secure wisdom through reason, to desire many things, and to order the realization of desires by the action of spirit.

Although every soul contains faculties of these three sorts, the degree to which any one of them is perfectible differs from one person to another. Some are capable of reasoning well, and consequently, apt for the acquisition of knowledge and wisdom. Others possess a low capacity for reasoning, but a high capacity for forceful action; they are able, through the dominance of spirit, forcefully to control the appetites; and they will order them well so long as others direct them in the paths of wisdom. Still others possess little reason and little spirit, their souls being constituted predominantly by the power to desire. In them the appetites are in the ascendancy. They are peculiarly fit for those actions which lead to the satisfaction of desires, but unable to order them well unless both wisdom and authority to enforce it are supplied from without.

Since the faculties vary from one person to another, the economic and professional aptitudes of each also vary. Where reason is strong, the professions which require learning are peculiarly appropriate. Where spirit predominates, the forceful actions of the military, including the police, offer greatest opportunity of success. Where the appetites prevail, the offices of production and distribution of economic goods and services are called for; for these are the pursuits which provide most ample scope for personal pleasure.

In various parts of the *Republic,* Plato advanced a kind of natural history of the soul.[2] At birth its powers are only latent, but after the first few years of life they begin to awaken. Until the age of seventeen or eighteen, reason is incapable of the acquisition of knowledge and wisdom, spirit is still unreliable, and the appetites are possessed of no stable pattern of activity. But during this time the faculties are not entirely inoperative. Reason, while it cannot secure knowledge, can acquire belief; and images of the good, the beautiful, and the true may place before it the good life for society and for the individual which wisdom may later establish. Spirit is still not entirely trustworthy, but it may be habituated into a considerable support of the images which the developing reason contemplates. The appetites do not willingly submit to order, but habituated spirit may still control them in a way suggested by the images of wisdom. After seventeen or eighteen, all the faculties are capable of the highest degree of perfection which a particular soul allows. Reason can acquire knowledge and wisdom, and can substitute it for belief in the images of beauty, truth, and goodness. Spirit can freely support reason, and the appetites submit to its rule. This natural history is an interval only in the

---

[2] Richard Lewis Nettleship, *Lectures on the Republic of Plato,* Macmillan and Co., Ltd., London, 1951, pp. 80ff.

life of the soul. On metaphysical grounds, Plato held that the soul exists eternally, both before birth and after death.

Plato held that the faculties of reason, spirit, and appetite were distributed independently of sex. He held, consequently, that a woman might be as apt for governing, for the military, or for economic activity as might a man.

Another fact must be noticed concerning human beings. This is that no matter what one's capacities and aptitudes may be, no one is able to supply all his own needs adequately. The individual aptitude which each person possesses for some particular kind of work would be wasted if not constantly and appropriately utilized. A division of labor naturally grows up based on the capacities of each person, and on a desire to satisfy the needs of all in the most efficient way. Society presupposes the inadequacy of each individual to meet his own needs and a peculiarly high capacity on his part to contribute in some way toward the satisfaction of the needs of all.

Society

In a part of the *Republic* not included here, Plato suggests that primitive society is chiefly economic in function. Where the tastes of men are simple and undepraved, government and war are not necessary; and men live together spontaneously and peaceably for the sake of such economic benefit as the natural division of labor affords. But in civilized society, originally simple economic needs become elaborate and complex; and while a civilized society must perform the economic function, it must perform others as well. It must enforce its policy abroad by arms, and at home by police; this is its military function. It must determine foreign policy and make laws for governing itself; this is its governmental function. No civilized state can exist which does not, to some degree, accomplish purposes of these three sorts.

The kind of society that Plato envisioned as performing these economic, military, and governing functions was that of the Greek city-state. These states consisted of a relatively small area of land on which food was produced, dominated by a city in which the government was located, and which often acted as a center of internal and external trade. His imagination scarcely enabled him to contemplate imperial states like that of Athens before his time as genuine cohesive societies; and he did not dream of such societies as modern nation-states.

The individual and society

In order that any civilized state should exist, those who perform each of the three functions mentioned must, to some degree, be talented for them. In order to increase the economic life of one's society, the artisan or businessman must desire the pleasure his work affords or the money with which other pleasure may be purchased, and this desire is a part of the natural aptness for productive life of the economic sort. A society whose artisans and traders had no appetites would quickly disappear. Similarly, a society whose armed forces had no ambition for military glory or for internal order brought about by enforcement of the laws would quickly disintegrate; no one would execute the policies that the governors formulated. The intention to enforce them is spirit; i.e., the executive power of the person which causes him to act in the direction of wisdom. Moreover, a society in which those who govern have no reason would also quickly vanish. For reason is required in order even to attempt to discover the good for society, and it is by reference to this good that all laws and policies are formulated. Thus, in every civilized state there is to some degree a recruiting of persons into three social classes: the artisans who serve the economic needs of the community, the auxiliaries who perform the military functions, and the guardians who enact legislation and determine relations with foreign states. So long as a civilized society exists, to some extent those in whom the appetites predominate serve as artisans, those in whom spirit is strongest act as auxiliaries, and those in whom reason has hegemony function as guardians.

Manner of training

On the basis of this psychology and social theory, Plato advanced several statements of fact concerning the manner in which the skills, the arts, and the sciences are transmitted and fostered. We shall outline here those which are central in his educational theory.

The first is that if those in whom reason prevails are dealt with in a certain way, they will become efficient guardians and perfectly just individuals. This "certain way" consists in a training which falls into the following five stages. (1) From birth to 17 or 18. This stage is divided into two periods which in the *Republic* are not clearly demarcated. In the first, the child is reared by experts in common nurseries, and kept in ignorance of his parents. He plays games that will maintain the normal development of the body. The second period begins when the child's mind is sufficiently developed to learn to read and write. In it, he is made to appreciate music, which for Plato includes literature as well as music in the modern sense of the term; he is taught the elements of science; and he is put through gymnastic exercise. Both literature and music are highly censored in content and form. The sciences are not taught in a rigorous mathematical way, but by use of concrete objects and imagery, most suitable to the young. Physical training is subordinated to the nurture of the soul. (2) From 17 or 18 to 20, the youth undergoes an intensive military and physical training. (3) From 20 to 30, training in science occurs. All science, Plato thought, is mathematical in form. In his time it consisted of arithmetic, plane geometry, solid geometry, astronomy, and harmonics. The last was something like the theory of music; it consisted of a physical or acoustical explanation of tone and mode or scale. (4) From 30 to 35, dialectic is engaged in. This is a study carried on by conversation in which the principle from which all the sciences might be derived is sought. As the basis of all knowledge, it provides a systematic understanding of the world. Plato conceived of this principle as a formulation of the nature of goodness, calling it "the idea of the good" or "the essential form of the good." (Different translators use different English expressions.) (5) From 35 to 50, those who were successful in dialectical training assume subordinate posts in government. After fifty, those who were successful in ancillary positions are elevated to full status in the class of guardians.

Plato contended that if those who are predominantly rational are not dealt with in this way, different results will ensue. If they read or recite unwholesome poetry, for example, their characters will be turned into those paths which lead to a life of self-seeking rather than to community service; and if they do not study the sciences, they will not come to know the idea or essential form of the good without knowledge of which no legislation can be known to be useful.

The second statement of fact concerns those in whom spirit is predominant. Plato contended that if they are given as much of the training outlined above as they can profit from, they will become useful auxiliaries, although less perfect in their private lives than those who become guardians. There is apparently some confusion in Plato's thought concerning them, for he defended the view that the military function should be sharply separated from that of the guardian, while he also argued that in the fifth stage of training, those subjected to it would occupy posts both of a military and a governing office. Nonetheless, the predominance of spirit over reason should have led him to hold that at some point in the study of science or dialectic, those in whom this predominance occurs would by virtue of it be relieved of further academic study to assume their military duties. The auxiliaries, thus trained, would lack wisdom; but they would possess a kind of courage which would lead them to accept the rational decisions embodied in the policies of the guardians.

If those in whom spirit prevails are not trained in this way, their ambition for energetic action will cause them to assume political power and to use the latter for personal economic aggrandizement. They will be an ever-present source of danger to a civilized society, and unable to achieve the virtuous life which is appropriate to those strongly endowed with spirit.

The third statement is that if those in whom the appetites prevail are put through the first stage of training, they will become productive members of the artisan class. They will be willing to be ruled by the guardians in company with the auxiliaries. For they will realize their incapacity for reasoning out governmental policy, as well as for enforcing it, and the fictions of their literary studies will make them recognize their peculiar fitness for contributing to the economic life of the state. This is the fitness to produce wealth; and their handling of wealth will be socially and personally temperate.

If they are not trained in this way, their unnecessary desires for pleasure, or the necessary desire for money with which it can be purchased, will be uncontrolled. They will seek to secure political authority or military power in order to insure or to increase the wealth which their desires create. Social order will be destroyed, and their private lives will be chaotic.

Plato contended that if this procedure is followed, each citizen will learn to do what he is best fitted for, he will contribute most effectively to his society, and he will achieve the most orderly personal life. Those most apt for the skills and arts will learn them in a period of apprenticeship apparently following upon the first stage of training; and the transmission of the sciences consists in the elementary teaching of them to all children in the first stage as well as their advanced study by some in the third and fourth. The bequeathing and fostering of the nonphysical possessions of culture may be accomplished by separating out those who are best suited to receive training of each sort after a basis of general culture has been laid throughout the student population, and the purpose of this transmission is the preservation or achievement of a good society.

RECOMMENDATIONS

Upon these statements of fact supplemented by principles drawn from his philosophy of education, Plato recommended certain goals and certain procedures subordinate to their achievement with respect to the transmission and fostering of the skills, the arts, and the sciences. We shall outline them briefly here.

Goal recommendations

The ultimate goal of all human effort, he argued, is a society and a personal life which are harmonious or just. A just society is one in which each of the classes performs its function well without interfering in that of the others; and in parallel with it, a just person is one in whom each faculty of the soul plays its role to perfection without infringing on the provinces of the others. It is the production of such a society made up of such citizens that the skills, the arts, and the sciences serve, and for which they are transmitted and fostered.

Let us consider these ideals in more detail. Plato urged that a just society could occur only if the members of each of its classes acted in a certain way. The guardians must possess wisdom—or knowledge of the nature of goodness—and the means by which a good society may be achieved and preserved. The auxiliaries must be courageous, i.e., must preserve a true opinion about those things which it is right to fear and not to fear. They must, that is to say, fear the refusal to enforce the policies of the guardians, and be ready in all circumstances to support them whether in war abroad or in peace at home. The guardians and auxiliaries must be removed from all temptation to use political and military power for private purposes; and consequently, Plato recommended that they should possess no private wealth, no permanent wives or husbands, and no children identifiable as their own. The members of these classes would live with due ceremony, and in temporary though frequent and highly eugenic marital arrangements. The artisans must be temperate; they must freely submit to control in whatever ways are found necessary by the wisdom of the guardians. They should own the tools by which they ply their trades and till the fields; and this recommendation shows the error of a widespread interpretation of Plato according to which he is alleged to have recommended a communist state. This interpretation is probably based upon a confusion of the ban against private property among the guardians and auxiliaries with a proscription against it for all. It is clear, Plato contended, that a society in which any one of these virtues did not characterize the classes concerned would be to some extent inharmonious or unjust. Unwise laws would lead to disobedience. Defective courage would lead to laxity in enforcement. Intemperance would lead to the intervention of the artisans in ruling or in the military function. Disharmony would result; and a just society requires the other three social virtues.

Justice in the individual soul is the harmony which results from the proper functioning of each of its parts. The soul whose reason is well developed will possess personal wisdom, i.e., knowledge of the nature of goodness and of the pattern of personal life in which it is embodied. Where spirit is well exercised, the soul is courageous, for it fears a failure to support the dictates of reason and brings all its energy to that cause. Where the appetites submit to the rule of reason as enforced by spirit, the soul is temperate. One in whom both reason and spirit are deficient suffers all the disharmony that results when antagonistic claims fall under the authority of no wise judge. The functioning of the three faculties to secure a personal life which is just depends upon the highest development of each of those three powers compatible with that of the other two.

Subordinate recommendations

Recommending the just life for society and for the individual as the goal most worthy of all human effort, Plato went on to recommend the program of training and instruction we have outlined as the means by which it might most nearly be realized. He was not disturbed by the probability that no society or person will ever perfectly embody the life of justice; the latter functioned explicitly in his thought as an ideal, close approximation to which is the best condition for which we can reasonably hope. He advocated the program mentioned as the path by which human life, both social and personal, may come closest to justice even though that path may not bring us directly to it. Moreover, he urged that every person in the state should follow that path as far as the faculty predominant in his soul permits, and this recommendation that all children should take part in school activity constitutes the chief subordinate recommendation in his educational theory. We shall discuss each stage of the program in order.

Plato recommended that children be reared from birth to the time at which they are susceptible of mental training, the period of the soul's latency, in common nurseries in ignorance of their parents. He justified this early training on two grounds: first, that it would make brotherly feeling pervade the entire community; and second, that it would prevent particular familial attachments for the guardians and auxiliaries. Where brotherly feeling was lacking, children might grow into adults who would not perform the duties of the social class to which their abilities destined them. He justified ignorance of parents on the ground that if a child knew his parents, he would be inclined, should he become a ruler, to use his power for the benefit of his family rather than for that of the state as a whole.

Plato recommended the later interval of the first stage as one in which good conduct might be inculcated even though knowledge that it was good could not yet be achieved. In this time, the child's faculties are awakening into activity, and images of the good life can influence imagination and belief. These images, presented in epic poetry, drama, and religious myth purged of the impropriety of much Greek literature, will produce belief as to what is good for society and for man, a diligence for achieving it, and a voluntary, if uninformed, submission of the appetites to its authority. Only that music will be played or sung which produces emotions of loyalty to the ideal of justice to which belief is attached. Plato believed that physical training can influence the soul for good if not engaged in to excess; and during this time, it will be used to supplement literature and music in this regard. His recommendation of elementary science seems to be aimed not at any utility for the life of habitually good conduct, but rather at laying a foundation for the subsequent training of those who have a high capacity for scientific learning.

The second stage is that of intensive military and physical training. Plato advocated that this training should be given only to prospective auxiliaries and guardians. His principle that in society as in the soul each part should do that for which it is best fitted led him to condemn citizen armies as inefficient and wasteful, and to approve a military force made up exclusively of professionals. Guardians must have this training because wise decisions must be made in the light of the capacity of the state to enforce them; the auxiliaries, of course, must have undergone such training. But the artisans ought to terminate their studies with the second interval of the first stage, becoming citizens who, though not well educated, possess that modicum of culture which is the maximum their minds can compass, and the minimum which suffices for social stability.

In the third stage, advanced study of the sciences is carried on; and Plato recommends it for all whom it can benefit. This benefit consists in taking the soul a long way toward wisdom. Plato thought of the various sciences as providing an idealized picture of the world at large, so that the nature of each thing might be understood by comparison with that picture. It could show us what each thing ought to be. Wisdom consisted in knowledge of the nature of goodness, not merely in knowledge as to what things were good. The sciences then could not provide wisdom, and were not in fact, as Plato says, quite properly named.

This stage is also recommended for the direct practical utility of the training it involves. In war and in peace, knowledge may always serve some instrumental function, and Plato was not loath to recommend it for this reason.

The methods of instruction in this stage differ somewhat from those recommended in the last part of the first stage. In the latter, particular figures and images analogous to our blackboard constructions ought to be used for elementary science, and the same concrete objects may be employed in the third stage of training. But their use must be different. In the first, it was to exemplify scientific truths; in the second, it is to refer to the ideas or forms, and to further the deduction of their nature and interrelation. The method of instruction here is thought to be identical with the method of proof. One takes a set of hypotheses or assumptions, deduces conclusions from them, and accepts the latter as true because he accepted the former as such. Thus arithmetic, geometry, and the other sciences severally describe divisions of the realm of ideas; and the character of this domain as well as of its residents can be revealed only to thought in the form of deductive argument. The third stage aids in the development of wisdom by instruction in the sciences which causes the student to follow the deductive course that determines their ideal structure.

The fourth stage is that in which dialectic is studied. In Plato's thought "dialectic" means both a procedure and a goal aimed at. It is a procedure by which some single principle which is self-evident is arrived at, and from which the hypotheses for all sciences may be derived. It is also a name for the knowledge of that principle as well as for all knowledge that it yields. But all knowledge can be derived from that principle, and in the second sense "dialectic" is a name for the system of all truth conceived of as emanating through logical relations alone from a single principle. This single principle Plato referred to as the idea of the good. As a process, dialectic is a search for the idea of the good; as knowledge, it is knowledge of it together with knowledge of all those things which manifest it.

Plato recommended this stage as the completion of a process begun in the third. The third, we saw, took the student a little way toward wisdom, for it made him think his way from hypotheses about things to their precise natures in connection with which their goodness could be understood. In the fourth stage of instruction, this process is completed; for the knowledge of the idea of the good, should it ever be achieved, would show us why everything must have the nature that it has, or fit into the system of ideas just where it happens to do so. The fourth stage, in a system of training which is perfectly successful, will yield graduates who are perfectly wise, courageous, temperate, and just in their personal lives, and who are ready to become just guardians of the welfare of the state.

In the fifth stage this readiness is activated, and the younger guardians temper their knowledge with practical experience of government in subordinate posts. It is recommended as a time of final testing and, apparently, as a way of assuring that the elder guardians are not too much busied about trivial affairs.

Besides the recommendation of these stages of training and instruction, Plato makes others which pertain to administration of the schools and guidance in them. He recommends that, with respect to administration, the schools be publicly owned, publicly controlled, and that attendance be compulsory, although he also urges that training of the mind be made as agreeable as possible. With respect to guidance, he advocates a continual and severe testing of students in order to weed out those who ought not to be advanced. Apparently every citizen would receive the primary training,[3] and this principle included the radical reform—radical for Plato's day as for our own—that treatment of children, as of adults, should be wholly independent of their sex.[4] Those who could not profit from elementary training in music and literature (those who were mentally deficient) and those whose poor health was incurable should be killed or allowed to die; and the determination of those who become

---

[3] But there is confusion here, because Plato speaks of training for the children of the guardians and auxiliaries alone, although he insists that children from all classes of citizens should participate in it if talented accordingly.

[4] Incidental references lead to the conclusion that Plato contemplated the existence of slavery in a just society; and to the conclusion that, not being citizens, the children of slaves would not be taught in the way described here. Presumably they would have a predominantly vocational training.

auxiliaries and guardians is based upon success in the various parts of the stages which follow the first. It is clear that these administrative and guidance proposals are necessary to the success of the program of training as a whole, and that the latter is necessary to the life of justice which Plato urged.

PHILOSOPHY OF EDUCATION

WE SHALL NEXT OUTLINE the central features of Plato's philosophy of education, pointing out some of the more important ways in which it affects his educational theory.

METAPHYSICS AND EDUCATION

In various parts of the *Republic* Plato expounded the view that the observable world is made up of many things. Each of them is particular, confined to one place and spread over a single stretch of time. Each is continually changing its qualities and relations, or moving from one place to another. Each belongs to some natural class. The tree outside the window, for example, is such a thing. It is observable by the senses, distinct from all other things (even from all other trees), continually changing its foliage, continually growing, and a member of the class of plum trees. While such descriptions of perceptible things seem not very remarkable, Plato drew from them some rather interesting conclusions.

Every observable plum tree belongs to the class of such trees, and since this class can be distinguished from all others as one class, Plato argued that there must be one essence or idea which determines that class. The same argument may be repeated for every class of things in the observable world. The idea for any class of things is that which each of its members manifests in common with all the others, and which every thing outside that class must fail to manifest. The idea "plum tree" is thus only one among a large family of such ideas; that family includes the ideas "oak tree," "periwinkle," "kangaroo," "man," "society," and so on through all the natural kinds of particular observable things.

Unlike each observable thing, each idea is universal rather than particular. It has many different manifestations, occurs in many different places, and at many different times. Each is eternal rather than changing. The idea "plum tree," for example, has as many manifestations as there are members of the class of plum trees, although it itself is only one. It must be eternal, for to speak of the idea "plum tree" as changing into something else is to speak without meaning. Particular plum trees are its manifestations, and they change. But the idea itself, as all ideas, must remain unaltered.

The ideas of things are perfect, Plato held, whereas each particular which manifests them is to some degree less so. Every plum tree exhibits some imperfection, some idiosyncracy of shape or structure or blossom or fruit; but the idea "plum tree" which the botanist entertains possesses no flaw. It is that by reference to which the excellence of any particular tree is ascertained. Every idea is the perfection which reason and understanding can discover to lie behind the particular observable things of every kind.

The ideas are related to each other in certain orders. Some of these orders are exhibited in the sciences so far developed, and all would be exhibited if complete scientific knowledge could be achieved. Each idea and the order into which it falls can be imperfectly understood as following from certain principles which Plato called "hypotheses"; and he believed that the order of the ideas of numbers could be understood in this way by arithmetic—that of the ideas of figures by plane and solid geometry, that of the ideas of heavenly motion by astronomy, and that of the ideas of tone by harmonics. Other ideas, he suggested, would be understood and would be seen to fall into certain patterns through other sciences, such as those of sociology and psychology. All these orders of ideas can be perfectly understood by deriving their hypotheses from the idea of the good. This is a principle from which all other ideas may be derived by reason; and the perfection of each idea consists in its relation to the others of its order, and through the latter to the idea of the good. The idea of the good thus provides a system into which all other ideas fall by virtue of being contained in the orders which the various sciences disclose.

The metaphysical theory that Plato advanced is the view that behind the observable world there is a comprehensive system of ideas which explains that world. The latter is made up of changing particulars which themselves are images of the ideas that determine their classes, and whose relations to other things are, in their turn, only somewhat like the relations that their ideas bear to one another. The entire world of nature, the world that we can observe through our senses, is thus portrayed as a faint copy determined, item by item and relation by relation, by the world of ideas. Plato suggested that the ideas have an existence of their own and, consequently, that the world of ideas would exist even though there should be no natural world. But there is such a world, and the important point to notice here is that he explained it on the grounds that it was incapable of being anything but a comprehensive image of the system of ideas.

This metaphysical explanation of the entire observable world carried with it an explanation of the facts in Plato's educational theory.

Thus, it is the idea "man" that Plato found to explain his psychological statements. In order to be a man, anything must possess to some degree the power of reasoning, of forceful action in the direction of reason's decisions, and to be impelled by the appetites. The idea "man" contains these three ingredients; and the empirical facts about human behavior must therefore reflect them. Similarly, the idea "society" includes within it the economic, the military, and the legislative function; consequently, the statements we make about any observable social group must describe the manner in which it behaves in these three ways. Since a society is made up of human beings, the relation between the citizen and the state must be something like that which obtains between the idea "man" and the idea "society." This metaphysical guarantee of Plato's facts gives a force to his educational recommendations which they would lack if men and their societies could be radically different from their ideas.

In other dialogues, and in a part of the *Republic* not presented here, Plato argues that the soul is immortal. One of his arguments is that the soul is like an idea and consequently eternal and incorruptible. This metaphysical argument provides a supplement for his statements of fact, and in view of immortality, he urges that the life of justice be pursued not merely because it is the most valuable of all, both in its social and personal aspects, but as a guarantee that no harm will befall a just man after death.

ETHICS AND EDUCATION

Plato's ethical reflections on education consist in a general theory of the nature of goodness, a general theory of the manner in which ethical recommendations are justified, and justification of his own educational recommendations.

The general theory of goodness depends upon the Platonic metaphysics. We have seen that every observable thing belongs to a natural class which is determined by an idea, and that this idea constitutes the perfection of all the things which exhibit it. No particular thing exhibits it perfectly, but all are more or less like it. Plato's general theory of goodness is that the goodness of each observable thing is the degree to which it exhibits the idea of its class.

Consider the plum tree once again. It is clear, Plato would hold, that we cannot determine its excellence by reference to the pleasure it might cause in some observer, for many are pleased by things which are bad or evil. Nor can we judge it by reference to the idea of oak trees; a plum tree could not possibly possess that cluster of traits whose embodiment are oaks. The goodness of a plum tree is that which is peculiar to such a tree; and while none is perfect, the goodness of this plum tree is the degree of clarity to which it expresses the idea "plum tree as such." So it is for all particular things: their goodness is their expression, however inadequate, of the idea that governs their kind.

That this is the case, Plato thought, is susceptible of a more comprehensive demonstration. Each idea, we have seen, may be deduced from a fundamental principle which Plato called "the idea of the good." He never stated this principle, but from his description of it we may infer that knowledge of it would guarantee the goodness of each thing by showing that the idea which determines its class could not be different from what it is. To give an ethical reason for anything, then, is to show that it is good of its kind, and that the idea for that kind can be logically derived from the idea of the good.

Plato endeavored to establish the ideas of social and personal justice, and to justify them as goals of action. Common to all societies, there must be some feature that marks them off from anarchic collections of individuals as well as from all other things. This feature must be a set of relations between the members of a society which constitutes their performance, to some degree of adequacy, of the three functions we have mentioned; a group of persons that failed to exercise the economic, the military, or the legislative function would be a rabble or a club, perhaps, but not a society. The performance of these functions is justice, and the idea of justice is their perfect and orderly performance. The goodness of a particular society, consequently, is the degree to which it embodies the idea "justice as such."

Analogously, he held that common to all men is some degree of harmony in the exercise of the three faculties which animate them. A creature in whom there was no concordant activity of these three faculties would not be human; and however chaotic the life of each particular man, there must be some degree of harmony in his soul so long as his humanity remains. This harmony between reason, spirit, and the appetites is justice; and perfect harmony between them is the idea "justice." The goodness or justice of any particular life, consequently, is the degree to which it manifests the idea.

The validity of the ideas of personal and social justice, Plato suggested, can be demonstrated by deducing them from the ideas of the good. He believed that ethical justification is a matter of argument like the mathematical; and if this justification is not at present possible, it is only because human knowledge is not far enough advanced.

Plato converted the *idea* of society and of men into *ideals* for social and personal action. This conversion required four steps. First, he asserted as statements of fact the psychology and social theory discussed in the first part of this chapter. Secondly, he maintained, as a statement of fact, that if people were dealt with in the ways discussed in that same section, a certain kind of society and of citizen would in fact result. Thirdly, he maintained that societies and persons of these kinds were the best possible because they were nearest the ideas of society and of humanity, and because these ideas might be derived from the idea of the good. For that reason, fourthly, he recommended that people should be dealt with according to his program of instruction, administration, and guidance in schools. Anyone who could contemplate the ideas of social and personal justice, he contended, would approve his recommendation of them as goals for human conduct; and anyone who would agree that his educational procedures would enhance the possibility of societies and of citizens like them would approve his subordinate recommendation of those procedures.

EPISTEMOLOGY AND EDUCATION

Plato advanced the view that knowledge is a state of mind characterized by certainty as to the nature of its objects. These objects are never things in the observable world. As we have seen, the latter are continually changing, and this trait makes it impossible to be certain about their nature and relations. The world of becoming is something about which we may have opinions; and even though these might be true, their nature, according to Plato, precludes the certainty of those opinions. The objects of knowledge must be, then, the ideas in their systematic connection.

There are two degrees of the certainty of our knowledge; hypothetical and absolute certainty. The statements of the sciences, of arithmetic, geometry, etc., are hypothetically certain; for our assurance as to their truth depends upon our assurance of the truth of the hypotheses from which they are derived. Absolute certainty would attach to our awareness of the idea of the good should we ever achieve it; and this absolute certainty, for those who have it, converts the hypothetical knowledge of the sciences into absolute, since the hypotheses of the sciences may be rigorously derived from that idea. For Plato, knowledge is the awareness of the ideas that the sciences proffer and of the systematic order of all ideas guaranteed by the idea of the good. For him, knowledge consists in seeing that any statement about ideas can be proved either hypothetically or absolutely.

Opinion, Plato suggested, also falls into two parts: conviction and perception. Our views as to the nature and relations of the things of the observable world possess a degree of force, and this force amounts to a strong belief that certain statements are true of them. That there is a plum tree outside the window is a conviction that we cannot help harboring, although no reason can be given sufficient to show that there must be such a tree in that location. But about the things that we merely perceive, such things as shadows and reflections in water and polished surfaces, we can have scarcely any belief at all. One who perceived a shadow and nothing else at all could not, so far, believe that it was a shadow as opposed to a tree that might cast it, as one who perceived merely a reflection could not believe that it was a reflection as opposed to the body it reflected. Within the realm of incertitude, opinions possess two degrees of clarity or force, analogous to the two degrees of certainty in that of knowledge.

Plato held that the methods by which students might be made to contemplate ideas and to possess some hypothetical knowledge concerning them were of various sorts. This is shown by his discussion of the uses made of physical things in both elementary and advanced study of the sciences. He seems to have provided, also, for various devices to be used in the course of dialectic, the objective of which is knowledge of the idea of the good. But he was quite clear that however knowledge might be arrived at, it must, in order to be knowledge, be formulable in a certain way, i.e., in the way known traditionally as rationalistic. All the statements that we can know we can show to be true by deriving them logically from an appropriate set of hypotheses, and these in turn from the idea of the good, the statement of which is self-evident. The methods of learning may, if successful, be replaced by a procedure that is wholly rationalistic. The methods by which knowledge is learned may make use of empirical objects, but the method which assures that what is learned is knowledge requires no reference to anything observable.

Plato argued that learning as opposed to giving the grounds for knowledge ought to follow a certain path. Reason, as we have seen, is latent during the first few years of life; and in the metaphors of the divided line and of the cave, Plato suggested that there is a normal development of it. It begins with perception, proceeds through conviction and what he calls understanding, and achieves its fullest activity in intelligence or reason proper. Plato supposed it could be developed profitably in most persons no further than conviction. Some, however, can arrive at the third stage, and a few at the fourth. The objects that it contemplates in the first two stages are those which constitute the observable world, and Plato believed that most persons could be given the true opinions concerning the constitution of that world, and especially of moral conduct in it, although they could achieve no knowledge of either. The others could be brought to hypothetical and absolute knowledge respectively of the system of ideas that governs and explains the observable world. For most persons, consequently, learning should consist in the inculation of habitual, but true, beliefs about the natural world and about the moral order into which each person fits, while for the others (apparently the guardians), it should be directed toward achieving an understanding, more or less complete, of both as determined by the ideas and their coherent union. Instruction in primary training, then, should be devoted to the dissemination of true convictions in accord with the capacity of each student; on higher levels, it should be devoted to the acquisition of knowledge by those in whom there is a capacity by use of it to create or to maintain a society nearest the ideal.

ANALYSIS AND EDUCATION

In the *Republic,* there is much discussion of an analytical sort. Plato was careful to try to make clear all of the important terms that occur in his educational theory. Pre-eminent among these are "justice," "wisdom," "courage," "temperance," and "education." There is no need here to recapitulate Plato's attempts to clarify these terms, but a brief comment may be made concerning the last.

"Education" here means the process of instruction and training which Plato advocated; and taken as a whole, he argued that it consists in the turning of the soul's eye or reason from the changing world of perception and conviction (what he called "becoming") to a contemplation of the order of ideas (what he called "being"). In dialogues other than the *Republic* Plato argued that this turning consists in coming to remember the ideas and their connection with one another from a life before birth in which the soul, pure and unalloyed with sense, contemplated them clearly and distinctly; this is his famous doctrine of reminiscence. An educated man, then, is one who has gone some way in this revolution, and a fully educated man is one who has come to remember the order in its totality.

Two points should be noticed about this analysis of education. The first is that to understand it fully requires an understanding of Plato's psychological, metaphysical, and epistemological theories. The second is that it implies that a fully educated person possesses not only knowledge but wisdom as well; and that he will see the moral necessity of putting his wisdom and his knowledge of all things to the service of the society in which he lives, the necessity of furthering justice in that society and as a part thereof the just lives of those who live within it.

A Guide to Selections from Plato's *Republic*

In Book II 374–376c,[5] Plato argues that no one can succeed in the exercise of any more than one art or skill. But each person in the state

[5] The numbers used here refer to book and pages in the edition of Plato's *Republic* taken as authoritative. In this volume they are given, as Plato's translator and editor gave them, in the right-hand margin.

should make an informed contribution to it, and consequently, should do so by exercising the one art or skill he possesses. The success of this exercise requires both a talent for the skill concerned and practice and training. The talents required for the art of the guardian are a certain disposition of mind—hostility to enemies and gentleness to friends—which grows out of the proper relative exercise of spirit and reason.

In Book II 376c–Book III 413, Plato holds that the practice in which these talents are developed is education of which the elementary stage (Plato discusses the nursery school elsewhere, Book V 460c, d) consists in the study of music and gymnastic. Music is the arts known to Plato as well as music in the more narrow sense of the term. All parts of music are to be highly censored in order that the child's soul should not be corrupted by imitating models of what is inferior, and in order that destructive emotions not be aroused in it. The business of both music and gymnastic is not to produce practitioners of the fine arts and athletes; but more positively it is to produce beauty in the souls of the children who study them—of those, even, who are unable thoroughly to comprehend the beauty thus revealed to them. This education should produce persons who are able to withstand the temptation of personal advantage in favor of the performance of social obligation.

Book III 414 presents Plato's distinction between the guardians who make the laws and foreign policy and the auxiliaries who enforce both by military means.

In Book III 416e–Book IV 424, the dialogue advances the view that education ought to produce guardians who will achieve and maintain the unity of the state. For that reason they must prevent a sharp cleavage between rich and poor; for it leads to indolence on the part of the wealthy, viciousness on the part of the poor, and a disposition toward revolution in the state. For the same reason, they should make certain that a sufficient number of people are properly trained to perform state functions, and that each performs only that function he can perform best.

In Book IV 427c–434c, Plato argues that there are four virtues or excellencies of a state. Wisdom is knowledge of what is best for the state as a whole, and the guardians have it. Courage is the power to preserve a true opinion about what is to be feared—an opinion taught by the guardians to the auxiliaries. Temperance is the rule of the better part over the worse, of the two higher classes in the state over the artisans, but involves their willing acceptance of that rule. Justice in the state consists in the performance by each class of the purpose appropriate to it alone.

In Book IV 439c–445b, Plato expresses the view that the soul, like the state, has three parts. They are reason, spirit, and the appetites. It has four virtues, wisdom, courage, temperance, and justice, which are relations between its parts of the same kind as the relations which constitute the same virtues of a state. It is obvious now that the just man will be happy and the unjust unhappy.

In Book V 451c–467, Plato treats the question of family arrangements in the guardian class. Marriages should be appointed by the state, temporary, and directed chiefly toward preserving the purity of the hereditary strain. Children and parents should remain unknown to each other, the former being reared in nurseries by trained personnel. The children should be early observers of, and so far as practicable participants in, the duties of their parents, including war.

In Book V 473 to Book VI 505b, there occurs the famous statement that an actual state will most closely approximate the just state or Republic only if philosophers become kings. And to become philosophers, those who have the ability—a strong capacity for reasoning—must undergo rigorous advanced education in order to come to know the Idea of the Good. Only by reference to this idea or form can the state and the person be properly regulated.

In Book VI 509d to Book VII 519b, Plato represents the distinction between knowledge of the ideas or forms and opinion about the natural world in a figure of a divided line. Elaborating the same figure, he represents four different abilities whose exercise enables us to be aware of nature as well as of the supernatural world of the ideas or forms. In these passages, he likens the condition of most men to that of those imprisoned in a cave and able to see only shadows of things which they would, of course, take to be real things cast on its wall by a procession going by its mouth. Education—the process of teaching and learning—is like the process of getting out of the cave; and coming to know is like the discovery that the sun illumines real things, and that shadows are not the real things that cast them. Education is the art of turning the eye of the soul from appearances to ideas or forms.

The passage from Book VII 519b–541c holds that the man who has such an education is a philosopher, and should be a guardian. He should not be content with knowledge for its own sake. He should use it for reform of both societies and persons. In the latter parts of the passage, Plato discusses the higher education that will make a philosopher-king or guardian, the connection of the parts of knowledge, and that of the system they form to appearances or nature. He also discusses the character a guardian should have, and reverts to the organization and curriculum of his training.

SELECTIONS FROM PLATO'S

*Republic**

▸◆◂

Persons of the Dialogue

SOCRATES, *who is the narrator*	CEPHALUS
GLAUCON	THRASYMACHUS
ADEIMANTUS	CLEITOPHON
POLEMARCHUS	

and others who are mute auditors

The scene is laid in the house of Cephalus at the Peiraeus; and the whole dialogue is narrated by Socrates the day after it actually took place to persons who are never named. . . .

Socrates and his friends have discussed and rejected several typical common-sense notions concerning the nature and value of justice or the good life. We break in after Socrates has started to advance a view concerning it to which he is favorably disposed.

BOOK II

. . . The shoemaker was not allowed by us to be a husband- [*374b*] man, or a weaver, or a builder—in order that we might have our shoes well made; but to him and to every other worker was assigned one work for which he was by nature fitted, and at that he was to continue working all his life long and at no other; he was not to let opportunities slip, [*c*] and then he would become a good workman. Now can anything be more important than that the work of a soldier be well done? Or is war an art so easily acquired that a man may be a warrior who is also a husband-man, or shoemaker, or other artisan; although no one in the world would be a good dice- or chess-player who merely took up the game as a recreation, and had not from his earliest years devoted himself to this and nothing else? No equipment will make a man a skilled workman, or athlete, nor be of any use to him who has not learned how to handle it, and has never bestowed sufficient attention upon it. How then will he who takes up a shield or other implement of war become a good fighter all in a [*d*] day, whether with heavy-armed or any other kind of troops?

* Reprinted, with kind permission of the publisher, from *Dialogues of Plato*, Volume II, translated into English by B. Jowett, Fourth edition, 1953, Oxford at the Clarendon Press.

Yes, he said, the tools which would teach men their own use would be beyond price.

And just as the duties of the guardian surpass all others in importance, I said, so does his business require the most skill and practice, [e] as well as undivided attention.

No doubt, he replied.

Will he not also require natural aptitude for his calling?

Certainly.

Then it will be our duty to select, if we can, natures which are fitted for the task of guarding the city?

It will.

It is no light task, then, that we have undertaken, I said; but we must be brave and do our best.

We must.

Do you agree that the noble youth is very like a well-bred [375] dog in respect of guarding and watching?

What do you mean?

I mean that both of them ought to be quick to see, and swift to overtake the enemy when they see him; and strong too if, when they have caught him, they have to fight with him.

All these qualities, he replied, will certainly be required by them.

Well, and your guardian must be brave if he is to fight well?

Certainly.

And is he likely to be brave who has no spirit, whether horse or dog or any other animal? Have you never observed how invincible and unconquerable is spirit and how the presence of it makes the soul of [b] any creature to be absolutely fearless and indomitable?

I have.

Then now we have a clear notion of the bodily qualities which are required in the guardian.

True.

And also of the mental ones; his soul is to be full of spirit?

True again.

But how can these spirited natures fail to be savage with one another, and with everybody else?

A difficulty by no means easy to overcome, he replied.

Whereas, I said, they ought to be dangerous to their enemies, [c] and gentle to their friends; if not, they will destroy themselves without waiting for their enemies to destroy them.

True, he said.

What is to be done, then? I said; how shall we find a gentle nature which has also a high spirit, for the one is the contradiction of the other?

True.

He will not be a good guardian who is wanting in either of these two qualities; and yet the combination of them appears to be impossible; and hence we must infer that to be a good guardian is impossible. [d]

I am afraid that what you say is true, he replied.

Here feeling perplexed I began to think over what had preceded. —My friend, I said, no wonder that we are in a perplexity; for we have lost sight of the image which we had before us.

What do you mean? he said.

It has escaped our notice that there do exist natures gifted with those opposite qualities.

Where?

Many animals, I replied, furnish examples of them, but most of all the dog, to which we compared the guardian: you know the dispo- [e] sition of a well-bred dog, perfectly gentle to its familiars and acquaint-ances, and the reverse to strangers.

Yes, I know.

Then there is nothing impossible or out of the order of nature in our finding a guardian who has a similar combination of qualities?

Certainly not.

Would not he who is fitted to be a guardian, besides the spirited nature, need to have the qualities of a philosopher?

I do not apprehend your meaning.

The trait of which I am speaking, I replied, may be also seen [376] in the dog, and is remarkable in the animal.

What trait?

Why, a dog, whenever he sees a stranger, is angry; when an ac-quaintance, he welcomes him, although the one has never done him any harm, nor the other any good. Did this never strike you as curious?

The point never struck me before; but I quite recognize the truth of your remark.

And surely this instinct of the dog is very charming;—your [b] dog is a true philosopher.

Why?

Why, because he distinguishes the face of a friend and of an enemy only by the criterion of knowing and not knowing. And must not an ani-mal be a lover of learning who determines what is or is not friendly to him by the test of knowledge and ignorance?

Most assuredly.

And is not the love of learning the love of wisdom, which is phi-losophy?

They are the same, he replied.

And may we not say confidently of man also, that he who is likely to be gentle to his friends and acquaintances, must by nature be a [c] lover of wisdom and knowledge?

That we may safely affirm.

Then he who is to be a really good and noble guardian of the State will require to unite in himself philosophy and spirit and swiftness and strength?

Undoubtedly.

Then we have found the desired natures; and now that we have found them, how are they to be reared and eduated? Is not this an inquiry which may be expected to throw light on the greater inquiry which is our final end—How do justice and injustice grow up in States? [d] for we do not want either to omit what is to the point or to draw out the argument to an inconvenient length.

Adeimantus thought that the inquiry would be of great service to us.

Then, I said, my dear friend, the task must not be given up, even if somewhat long.

Certainly not.

Come then, and let us pass a leisure hour in story-telling, and our story shall be the education of our heroes. [e]

By all means.

And what shall be their education? It would be hard, I think, to find a better than the traditional system, which has two divisions, gymnastic for the body, and music for the soul.

True.

Presumably we shall begin education with music, before gymnastic can begin.

By all means.

And when you speak of music, do you include literature or not?

I do.

And literature may be either true or false?

Yes.

Both have a part to play in education, but we must begin [377] with the false?

I do not understand your meaning, he said.

You know, I said, that we begin by telling children stories which, though not wholly destitute of truth, are in the main fictitious; and these stories are told them when they are not of an age for gymnastics.

Very true.

That was my meaning when I said that we must teach music before gymnastics.

Quite right, he said.

You know also that the beginning is the most important part of any work, especially in the case of a young and tender thing; for that is the time at which the character is being formed and the desired im- [b] pression is more readily taken.

Quite true.

And shall we just carelessly allow children to hear any casual tales which may be devised by casual persons, and to receive into their minds ideas for the most part the very opposite of those which we shall wish them to have when they are grown up?

We cannot.

Then the first thing will be to establish a censorship of the writers of fiction, and let the censors receive any tale of fiction which is good, [c] and reject the bad; and we will persuade mothers and nurses to tell their children the authorized ones only. Let them fashion the mind with such tales, even more fondly than they mould the body with their hands; but most of those which are now in use must be discarded. . . .

BOOK III

. . . But shall our superintendence go no further, and are [401b] the poets only to be required by us to express the image of the good in their works, on pain, if they do anything else, of expulsion from our State? Or is the same control to be extended to other artists, and are they also to be prohibited from exhibiting the opposite forms of vice and intemperance and meanness and deformity in sculpture and building and the other creative arts; and is he who cannot conform to this rule of ours to be prevented from practising his art in our State, lest the taste of our citizens be corrupted by him? We would not have our guardians grow up amid images of moral deformity, as in some noxious pasture, and there browse and feed upon many a baneful herb and flower day by day, little by little, [c] until they silently gather a festering mass of corruption in their own soul. Let us rather search for artists who are gifted to discern the true nature of the beautiful and graceful; then will our youth dwell in a land of health, amid fair sights and sounds, and receive the good in everything; and beauty, the effluence of fair works, shall flow into the eye and ear, like a health-giving breeze from a purer region, and insensibly draw the [d] soul from earliest years into likeness and sympathy with the beauty of reason.

There can be no nobler training than that, he [Glaucon] replied.

And therefore, I said, Glaucon, musical training is a more potent instrument than any other, because rhythm and harmony find their way into the inward places of the soul, on which they mightily fasten, imparting grace, and making the soul of him who is rightly educated grace- [e]

ful, or of him who is ill-educated ungraceful; and also because he who has received this true education of the inner being will most shrewdly perceive omissions or faults in art and nature, and with a taste, while he praises and rejoices over and receives into his soul the good, and [*402*] becomes noble and good, he will justly blame and hate the bad, now in the days of his youth, even before he is able to know the reason why; and when reason comes he will recognize and salute the friend with whom his education has made him long familiar. . . .

After music comes gymnastic, in which our youth are next [*403c*] to be trained.

Certainly.

Gymnastic as well as music should begin in early years; the training in it should be careful and should continue through life. Now [*d*] my belief is,—and this is a matter upon which I should like to have your opinion in confirmation of my own, but my own belief is,—not that the good body by any bodily excellence improves the soul, but, on the contrary, that the good soul by her own excellence improves the body as far as this may be possible. What do you say?

Yes, I agree.

Then, to the mind when adequately trained, we shall be right in handing over the more particular care of the body; and in order to avoid prolixity we will now only give the general outlines of the subject. [*e*]

Very good.

That they must abstain from intoxication has been already remarked by us; for of all persons a guardian should be the last to get drunk and not know where in the world he is.

Yes, he said; that a guardian should require another guardian to take care of him is ridiculous indeed.

But next, what shall we say of their food; for the men are in training for the great contest of all—are they not?

Yes, he said.

And will the habit of body of our ordinary athletes be suited [*404*] to them?

Why not?

I am afraid, I said, that a habit of body such as they have is but a sleepy sort of thing, and rather perilous to health. Do you not observe that these athletes sleep away their lives, and are liable to most dangerous illnesses if they depart in ever so slight a degree from their customary regimen?

Yes, I do.

Then, I said, a finer sort of training will be required for our warrior athletes, who are to be like wakeful dogs, and to see and hear with the utmost keenness; amid the many changes of water and also of

food, of summer heat and winter cold, which they will have to en-   [b]
dure when on a campaign, they must not be liable to break down in
health.

That is my view. . . .

The very exercises and toils which he undergoes are in-   [410b]
tended to stimulate the spirited element of his nature, and not to increase
his strength; he will not, like common athletes, use exercise and regimen
to develop his muscles.

Very right, he said.

Neither are the two arts of music and gymnastic really designed,
as is often supposed, the one for the training of the soul, the other   [c]
for the training of the body.

What then is the real object of them?

I believe, I said, that the teachers of both have in view chiefly the
improvement of the soul.

How can that be? he asked.

Did you never observe, I said, the effect on the mind itself of exclusive devotion to gymnastic, or the opposite effect of an exclusive devotion to music?

In what way shown? he said.

The one producing a temper of hardness and ferocity, the   [d]
other of softness and effeminacy, I replied.

Yes, he said, I am quite aware that the mere athlete becomes too
much of a savage, and that the mere musician is melted and softened
beyond what is good for him.

Yet surely, I said, this ferocity only comes from spirit, which if
rightly educated would give courage, but if too much intensified is liable
to become hard and brutal.

That I quite think.

On the other hand the quality of gentleness must come from   [e]
the philosophical part of human nature. And this also when too much
indulged will turn to softness, but if educated rightly will be gentle and
moderate.

True. . . .

And as there are two principles of human nature, one the   [411e]
spirited and the other the philosophical, some god, as I should say, has
given mankind two arts answering to them (and only indirectly to the
soul and body), in order that these two principles (like the strings of an
instrument) may be relaxed or drawn tighter until they are duly har-
monized.   [412]

That appears to be the intention.

And he who mingles music with gymnastic in the fairest proportions and best attempers them to the soul, may be rightly called the true
musician and harmonist in a far higher sense than the tuner of the strings.

You are quite right, Socrates. . . .

Then what is the next question? Must we not ask who are to [*b*] be rulers and who subjects?

Certainly. [*c*]

There can be no doubt that the elder must rule the younger.

Clearly.

And that the best of these must rule.

That is also clear.

Now, are the best husbandmen those who are most devoted to husbandry?

Yes.

And as we are to have the best of guardians for our city, must they not be those who have most the character of guardians?

Yes.

And to this end they ought to be wise and efficient, and to have a special care of the State?

True. [*d*]

And a man will be most likely to care about that which he loves?

To be sure.

And he will be most likely to love that which he regards as having the same interests with himself, and that of which the good or evil fortune is supposed by him at any time most to affect his own?

Very true, he replied.

Then there must be a selection. Let us note among the guardians those who in their whole life show the greatest eagerness to do what they suppose to be for the good of their country, and the greatest repug- [*e*] nance to do what is against her interests.

Those are the right men.

And they will have to be watched at every age, in order that we may see whether they preserve their resolution, and never yield either to force or to enchantment, so as to forget or cast off their sense of duty to the State. . . .

And perhaps the word "guardian" in the fullest sense ought [*414b*] to be applied to this higher class only who both preserve us against foreign enemies and maintain peace among our citizens at home, that the one may not have the will, or the others the power, to harm us. The young men whom we before called guardians may be more properly designated auxiliaries and supporters of the principles of the rulers. . . .

And therefore every care must be taken that our auxiliaries, [*416b*] being stronger than our citizens, may not behave in this fashion and become like savage tyrants instead of friends and allies?

Yes, great care should be taken.

And if they have really received a good education, will not that furnish the best safeguard?

But they have received it, he replied.

I cannot be so confident, my dear Glaucon, I said; but I believe the truth is as I said, that a sound education, whatever that may be, [c] will have the greatest tendency to civilize and humanize them in their relations to one another, and to those who are under their protection.

Very true, he replied.

And not only their education, but their habitations, and all that belongs to them, should be such as will neither impair their virtue as guardians, nor tempt them to prey upon the other citizens. Any man of sense must acknowledge that. [d]

He must.

Then now let us consider what will be their way of life, if they are to realize our idea of them. In the first place, none of them should have any property of his own beyond what is absolutely necessary; neither should they have a private house or store closed against anyone who has a mind to enter; their provisions should be only such as are required by trained warriors, who are men of temperance and courage; they should agree to receive from the citizens a fixed rate of pay, enough to meet [e] the expenses of the year and no more; and they will go to mess and live together like soldiers in a camp. Gold and silver we will tell them that they have from God; the diviner metal is within them, and they have therefore no need of the dross which is current among men, and ought not to pollute the divine by any such earthly admixture; for that commoner metal has been the sources of many unholy deeds, but their own is [417] undefiled. And they alone of all the citizens may not touch or handle silver or gold, or be under the same roof with them, or wear them, or drink from them. And this will be their salvation, and they will be the saviours of the State. But should they ever acquire homes or lands or moneys of their own, they will become householders and husbandmen instead of guardians, enemies and tyrants instead of allies of the [b] other citizens; hating and being hated, plotting and being plotted against, they will pass their whole life in much greater terror of internal than of external enemies, and the hour of ruin, both to themselves and to the rest of the State, will be at hand. For all which reasons may we not say that thus shall our State be ordered, and that these shall be the regulations appointed by us for our guardians concerning their lodging and all other matters? . . .

BOOK IV

I wonder whether you [Adeimantus] will agree with an- [421c] other remark which occurs to me.

What may that be?

There seem to be two causes of the deterioration of the arts. [*d*]

What are they?

Wealth, I said, and poverty.

How do they act?

The process is as follows: When a potter becomes rich, will he, think you, any longer take the same pains with his art?

Certainly not.

He will grow more and more indolent and careless?

Very true.

And the result will be that he becomes a worse potter?

Yes; he greatly deteriorates.

But, on the other hand, if he has no money and cannot provide himself with tools or other requirements of his craft, his own work will not be equally good, and he will not teach his sons or apprentices [*e*] to work equally well.

Certainly not.

Then, under the influence either of poverty or of wealth, workmen and their work are equally liable to degenerate?

That is evident.

Here then is a discovery of new evils, I said, against which the guardians will have to watch, or they will creep into the city unobserved.

What evils?

Wealth, I said, and poverty; the one is the parent of luxury [*422*] and indolence, and the other of meanness and viciousness, and both of a revolutionary spirit. . . .

And yet there might be a danger to the poor State if the [*e*] wealth of many States were to be gathered into one.

But how simple of you to think that the term State is applicable at all to any but our own!

Why so?

You ought to speak of other States in the plural number; not one of them is a city, but many cities, as they say in the game. Each will contain not less than two divisions, one the city of the poor, the other of the rich, which are at war with one another; and within each there [*423*] are many smaller divisions. You would be altogether beside the mark if you treated these as a single State; but if you deal with them as many, and give the wealth or power or persons of the one to the others, you will always have a great many friends and not many enemies. And your State, while the wise order which has now been prescribed continues to prevail in her, will be the greatest of States, I do not mean to say in reputation or appearance, but in deed and truth, though she number not more than a thousand defenders. A single State of that size you will hardly find, either among Hellenes or barbarians, though many that appear to [*b*] be as great and many times greater.

That is most true, he said.

Hence, I said, it can be seen what will be the best limit for our rulers to fix when they are considering the size of the State and the amount of territory which they are to include, and beyond which they will not go.

What limit would you propose?

I would allow the State to increase so far as is consistent with unity; that, I think, is the proper limit. [*c*]

Very good, he said.

Here then, I said, is another order which will have to be conveyed to our guardians: Let them guard against our city becoming small, or great only in appearance. It must attain an adequate size, but it must remain one.

And perhaps, said he, you do not think this is a very severe order?

And here is another, said I, which is lighter still,—I mean the duty, of which some mention was made before, of degrading the offspring [*d*] of the guardians when inferior, and of elevating into the rank of guardians the offspring of the lower classes, when naturally superior. The intention was that, in the case of the citizens generally, each individual should be put to the use for which nature intended him, one to one work, and then every man would do his own business, and become one and not many; and so the whole city would be one and not many.

Yes, he said; that is not so difficult.

The regulations which we are prescribing, my good Adeimantus, are not, as might be supposed, a number of great principles, but trifles all, if care be taken, as the saying is, of the one great thing,—a thing, [*e*] however, which I would rather call, not great, but sufficient for our purpose.

What may that be? he asked.

Education, I said, and nurture: if our citizens are well educated, and grow into sensible men, they will easily see their way through all these, as well as other matters which I omit; such, for example, as marriage, the possession of women and the procreation of children, which will all follow the general principle that friends have all things in [*424*] common, as the proverb says.

That will be the best way of settling them.

Also, I said, the State, if once started well, moves with accumulating force like a wheel. For where good nurture and education are maintained, they implant good constitutions, and these good constitutions taking root in a good education improve more and more, and this improvement affects the breed in man as in other animals. . . . [*b*]

So now the foundation of your city, son of Ariston [Glau-   [*427c*]
con] is finished. What comes next? Provide yourself with a bright   [*d*]
light and search, and get your brother and Polemarchus and the rest of
our friends to help, and let us see where in it we can discover justice and
where injustice, and in what they differ from one another, and which of
them the man who would be happy should have for his portion, whether
seen or unseen by gods and men.

Nonsense, said Glaucon: did you not promise to search yourself,
saying that for you not to help justice in her need would be an im-   [*e*]
piety?

Your reminder is true, and I will be as good as my word; but you
must join.

We will, he replied.

Well, then, I hope to make the discovery in this way: I mean to
begin with the assumption that our State, if rightly ordered, is perfect.

That is most certain.

And being perfect, is therefore wise and valiant and temperate and
just.

That is likewise clear.

And whichever of these qualities we find first in the State, the one
which is not yet found will be the residue?

Very good.   [*428*]

If in some other instance there were four things, in one of which
we were most interested, the one sought for might come to light first, and
there would be no further trouble; or if we came to know the other three
first, we should thereby attain the object of our search, for it must clearly
be the part remaining.

Very true, he said.

And is not a similar method to be pursued about the virtues, which
are also four in number?

Clearly.

First among the virtues found in the State, wisdom comes into
view, and in this I detect a certain peculiarity.   [*b*]

What is that?

The State which we have been describing has, I think, true wisdom.
You would agree that it is a good counsel?

Yes.

And this good counsel is clearly a kind of knowledge, for not by
ignorance, but by knowledge, do men counsel well?

Clearly. . . .

Well, I said, and is there any knowledge in our recently   [*428c*]
founded State among any of the citizens which advises, not about any
particular thing in the State, but about the whole, and considers   [*d*]

how it can best conduct itself in relation with itself and with other States?

There certainly is.

And what is this knowledge, and among whom is it found? I asked.

It is the knowledge of guarding, he replied, and is found in those rulers whom we were just now describing as perfect guardians.

And what is the name which the city derives from the possession of this sort of knowledge?

The name of good in counsel and truly wise.

And will there be in our city more of these true guardians or   [*e*] more smiths?

The smiths, he replied, will be far more numerous.

Will not the guardians probably be the smallest of all the classes who receive a name from the profession of some kind of knowledge?

Much the smallest.

And so by reason of the smallest part or class, and of the knowledge which resides in this presiding and ruling part of itself, the whole State, being thus constituted according to nature, will be wise; and this, which can claim a share in the only knowledge worthy to be called wisdom has been ordained by nature to be of all classes the least.   [*429*]

Most true.

Thus, then, I said, the nature and place in the State of one of the four virtues has somehow or other been discovered.

And, in my humble opinion, very satisfactorily discovered, he replied.

Again, I said, there is no difficulty in seeing the nature of courage, and in what part that quality resides which gives the name of courageous to the State.

How do you mean?

Why, I said, everyone who calls any State courageous or cow-   [*b*] ardly, will be thinking of the part which fights and goes out to war on the State's behalf.

No one, he replied, would ever think of any other.

The rest of the citizens may be courageous or may be cowardly, but their courage or cowardice will not, as I conceive, have the effect of making the city either the one or the other.

No.

The city will be courageous also by one part of herself, in which resides the power to preserve under all circumstances that opinion about the nature and description of things to be feared in which our legis-   [*c*] lator educated them; and this is what you term courage. . . .

You know, I said, that dyers, when they want to dye wool for   [*d*] making the true sea-purple, begin by choosing the white from among all the colours available; this they prepare and dress with much care and pains, in order that the white ground may take the purple hue in full perfection. The dyeing then proceeds; and whatever is dyed in this [*e*] manner becomes a fast colour, and no washing either with lyes or without them can take away the bloom. But, when the ground has not been duly prepared, you will have noticed how poor is the look either of purple or of any other colour.

Yes, he said; I know that they have a washed-out and ridiculous appearance.

Then now, I said, you will understand that our object in selecting our soldiers, and educating them in music and gymnastic, was very [*430*] similar; we were contriving influences which would prepare them to take the dye of the laws in perfection, and the colour of their opinion about dangers and of every other opinion was to be indelibly fixed by their nurture and training, not to be washed away by such potent lyes as pleasure —mightier agent far in washing the soul than any soda or lye—or by sorrow, fear, and desire, the mightiest of all other solvents. And this sort [*b*] of universal saving power of true opinion in conformity with law about real and false dangers I call and maintain to be courage, unless you disagree.

But I agree, he replied; for I suppose that you mean to exclude mere right belief about dangers when it has grown up without instruction, such as that of a wild beast or of a slave—this, in your opinion, is something not quite in accordance with law, which in any case should have another name than courage.

Most certainly. . . .   [*c*]

Two virtues remain to be discovered in the State—first, temperance, and then justice which is the end of our search. . . .   [*d*]

As far as I can at present see, temperance has more of the na- [*e*] ture of harmony and symphony than have the preceding virtues.

How so? he asked.

Temperance, I replied, is the ordering or controlling of certain pleasures and desires; this is curiously enough implied in the saying of 'a man being his own master'; and other traces of the same notion may be found in language, may they not?

No doubt, he said.

There is something ridiculous in the expression 'master of himself'; for the master must also be the servant and the servant the [*431*] master, since in all these modes of speaking the same person is denoted.

Certainly.

The meaning of this expression is, I believe, that there is within the man's own soul a better and also a worse principle; and when the better has the worse under control, then he is said to be master of himself; and this is a term of praise: but when, owing to evil education or association, the better principle, which is also the smaller, is overwhelmed by the greater mass of the worse—in this case he is blamed and is   [b] called the slave of self and dissolute.

Yes, there is reason in that.

And now, I said, look at our newly created State, and there you will find one of these two conditions realized; for the State, as you will acknowledge, may be justly called master of itself, if the words "temperance" and "self-mastery" truly express the rule of the better part over the worse.

On looking, he said, I see that what you say is true.

Let me further note that the manifold and complex pleasures and desires and pains are generally found in children and women and   [c] servants, and the freemen so called who are of the lowest and more numerous class.

Certainly, he said.

Whereas the simple and moderate desires, which follow reason and are under the guidance of mind and true opinion, are to be found only in a few, and those the best born and best educated.

Very true.

These too, as you may perceive, have a place in your State; and the meaner desires of the many are held down by the desires and wisdom of the more virtuous few.   [d]

That I perceive, he said.

Then if there be any city which may be described as master of its own pleasures and desires, and master of itself, ours may claim such a designation?

Certainly, he replied.

It may also for all these reasons be called temperate?

Yes.

And if there be any State in which rulers and subjects will be agreed as to the question who are to rule, that again will be our   [e] State? Do you think so?

I do, emphatically.

And the citizens being thus agreed among themselves, in which class will temperance be found—in the rulers or in the subjects?

In both, as I should imagine, he replied. . . .

What remainder is there of qualities which make a state vir-   [432b] tuous? For this, it is evident, must be justice. . . .

Why, my dear friend, far back from the beginning of our in-   [d] quiry, justice has been lying at our feet, and we never saw her; nothing could be more ridiculous. Like people who go about looking for what   [e] they have in their hands, we looked not at what we were seeking, but at what was far off in the distance. . . .

You remember the original principle which we laid down at   [433] the foundation of the State; we decided, and more than once insisted, that one man should practice one occupation only, that to which his nature was best adapted;—now justice, in my view, either is this principle or is some form of it.

Yes, we did.

Further, we affirmed that justice was doing one's own business, and not being a busybody; we said so again and again, and many others have said the same to us.   [*b*]

Yes, we said so.

Then to attend to one's own business, in some form or another, may be assumed to be justice. Do you know my evidence for this?

No, but I should like to be told.

Because I think that this is the virtuous quality which remains in the State when the other virtues of temperance and courage and wisdom are abstracted; and that this not only made it possible for them to appear, but is also their preservative as long as they remain; and we were   [*c*] saying that if the three were discovered by us, justice would be the fourth or remaining one.

That follows of necessity. . . .

Suppose a carpenter sets out to do the business of a cobbler,   [*434*] or a cobbler that of a carpenter; and suppose them to exchange their implements or social position, or the same person to try to undertake the work of both, or whatever be the change; do you think that any great harm would result to the State?

Not much.

But when the cobbler or any other man whom nature designed to be a trader, having his heart lifted up by wealth or strength or the   [*b*] number of his followers or any like advantage, attempts to force his way into the class of warriors, or a warrior into that of legislators and guardians, to which he ought not to aspire, and when these exchange their implements and their social position with those above them; or when one man would be trader, legislator, and warrior all in one, then I think you will agree with me in saying that this interchange and this meddling of one with another is the ruin of the State.

Most true.

Seeing then, I said, that there are three distinct classes, any meddling of one with another, or the change of one into another, is the greatest harm to the State, and may be most justly termed evil-doing?   [*c*]

Precisely.

And the greatest degree of evil-doing to one's own city would be termed by you injustice?

Certainly.

This then is injustice; and on the other hand when the three main classes, traders, auxiliaries, and guardians, each do their own business, that is justice, and will make the city just. . . .

Now are there times when men are thirsty, and yet unwill- [439c] ing to drink?

Yes, he said, it constantly happens.

And in such a case what is one to say? Would you not say that there was something in the soul bidding a man to drink, and something else forbidding him, which is other and stronger than the principle which bids him?

I should say so.

And the prohibition in such cases is derived from reasoning, whereas the motives which lead and attract proceed from passions [d] and diseases?

Clearly.

Then we may fairly assume that they are two, and that they differ from one another; the one with which a man reasons, we may call the rational principle of the soul, the other, with which he loves and hungers and thirsts and feels the flutterings of any other desire, may be termed the irrational or appetitive, the ally of sundry pleasures and satisfactions?

Yes, he said, we may fairly assume them to be different.

So much, then, for the definition of two of the principles existing in the soul. And what now of passion, or spirit? Is it a third, or akin to one of the preceding? [e]

I should be inclined to say—akin to desire. . . .

And are there not many other cases in which we observe that [440] when a man's desires violently prevail over his reason, he reviles him- [b] self, and is angry at the violence within him, and that in this struggle, which is like the struggle of factions in a State, his spirit is on the side of his reason;—but for the passionate or spirited element to take part with the desires when reason decides that she should not be opposed, is a sort of thing which I believe that you never observed occurring in yourself, nor, as I should imagine, in anyone else?

Certainly not.

Suppose that a man thinks he has done a wrong to another, [c] the nobler he is the less able is he to feel indignant at any suffering, such as hunger, or cold, or any other pain which the injured person may inflict upon him—these he deems to be just, and, as I say, his spirit refuses to be excited by them.

True, he said.

But when a man thinks that he is the sufferer of the wrong, then the spirit within him boils and chafes, and is on the side of what it believes to be justice; and though it suffers hunger or cold or other pain, it is only the more determined to persevere and conquer. Such a [d] noble spirit will not be quelled until it has achieved its object or been slain, or until it has been recalled by the reason within, like a dog by the shepherd? . . .

You remember that passion or spirit appeared at first sight to [e] be a kind of desire, but now we should say quite the contrary; for in the conflict of the soul spirit is arrayed on the side of the rational principle.

Most assuredly.

But a further question arises: Is passion different from reason also, or only a kind of reason; in which latter case, instead of three principles in the soul, there will only be two, the rational and the concupiscent? or rather, as the State was composed of three classes, traders, auxil- [441] iaries, counsellors, so may there not be in the individual soul a third element which is passion or spirit, and when not corrupted by bad education is the natural auxiliary of reason?

Yes, he said, there must be a third.

Yes, I replied, if passion, which has already been shown to be different from desire, turn out also to be different from reason. . . .

And so, after much tossing, we have reached land, and are [c] fairly agreed that the same principles which exist in the State exist also in the individual, and that they are three in number.

Exactly.

Must we not then infer that the individual is wise in the same way and in virtue of the same quality which makes the State wise?

Certainly.

Also that the State is brave in the same way and by the same [d] quality as an individual is brave, and that there is the same correspondence in regard to the other virtues?

Assuredly.

Therefore the individual will be acknowledged by us to be just in the same way in which the State has been found just?

That follows of course.

We cannot but remember that the justice of the State consisted in each of the three classes doing the work of its own class?

I did not think we have forgotten, he said.

We must now record in our memory that the individual in whom the several components of his nature do their own work will be just, [e] and will do his own work?

Yes, he said, we must record that important fact.

First, it is proper for the rational principle, which is wise, and has the care of the whole soul, to rule, and for the spirit to be the subject and ally?

Certainly.

And, as we were saying, the blending of music and gymnastic will bring them into accord, nerving and sustaining the reason with noble words and lessons, and moderating and soothing and civilizing the [442] wildness of passion by harmony and rhythm?

Quite true, he said.

And these two, thus nurtured and educated, and having learned truly to know their own functions, will rule over the concupiscent, which in each of us is the largest part of the soul and by nature most insatiable of gain; over this they will keep guard, lest, waxing great and strong with the fullness of bodily pleasures, as they are termed, the concupiscent soul, no longer confined to her own sphere, should attempt to enslave and rule those who are not her natural-born subjects, and overturn the whole life of man?

Very true, he said.

Both together will they not be the best defenders of the whole soul and the whole body against attacks from without; the one counselling, and the other going out to fight as the leader directs, and courageously executing his commands and counsels?

True.

Likewise it is by reference to spirit that an individual man is [c] deemed courageous, because his spirit retains in pleasure and in pain the commands of reason about what he ought or ought not to fear?

Right, he replied.

And we call him wise on account of that little part which rules, and which proclaim these commands; the part in which is situated the knowledge of what is for the interest of each of the three parts and of the whole?

Assuredly.

And would you not say that he is temperate who has these same elements in friendly harmony, in whom the one ruling principle of reason, and the two subject ones of spirit and desire, are equally agreed that [d] reason ought to rule, and do not rebel?

Certainly, he said, that is a precise account of temperance whether in the State or individual.

And finally, I said, a man will be just in that way and by that quality which we have often mentioned. . . .

And in reality justice was such as we are describing, being [443c] concerned however, not with man's external affairs, but with an in- [d] ner relationship in which he himself is more truly concerned; for the just man does not permit the several elements within him to interfere with one another, or any of them to do the work of others,—he sets in order his own inner life, and is his own master and his own law, and at peace with himself; and when he has bound together the three principles within him, which may be compared to the higher, lower, and middle notes of the scale, and any that are intermediate between them—when he has bound all these together, and is no longer many, but has become one en- [*e*] tirely temperate and perfectly adjusted nature, then he proceeds to act, if he has to act, whether in a matter of property, or in the treatment of the body, or in some affairs of politics or private business; always thinking and calling that which preserves and cooperates with this harmonious condition, just and good action, and the knowledge which presides over it, wisdom, and that which at any time impairs this condition, he will call unjust action, and the opinion which presides over it ignorance. . . . [*444*]

The time has come, then, to answer the final question of the [*445*] comparative advantage of justice and injustice: Which is the more profitable, to be just and act justly and honourably, whether one's character is or is not known, or to be unjust and act unjustly, if one is unpunished, that is to say unreformed?

In my judgement, Socrates, the question has now become ridiculous. We know that, when the bodily constitution is gone, life is no longer endurable, though pampered with all kinds of meats and drinks, and having all wealth and all power; and shall we be told that when the natural health of our vital principle is undermined and corrupted, life is [*b*] still worth having to a man, if only he be allowed to do whatever he likes, except to take steps to acquire justice and virtue and escape from injustice and vice; assuming them both to be such as we have described?

Yes, I said, the question is, as you say, ridiculous. . . .

BOOK V

. . . The drama of the men has been played out, and now [*451c*] properly enough comes the turn of the women, especially in view of your challenge.

For men born and educated like our citizens there can, in my opinion, be no right possession and use of women and children unless they follow the path on which we sent them forth. We proposed, as you know, to treat them as watchdogs of the herd.

True.

Let us abide by that comparison in our account of their birth [*d*] and breeding, and let us see whether the result accords with our design.

How can marriages be made most beneficial?—that is a ques- [*459*] tion which I put to you, because I see in your house dogs for hunting, and of the nobler sort of birds not a few. Now, I beseech you, do tell me, have you ever attended to their pairing and breeding?

In what particulars?

Why, in the first place, although they are all of good pedigree, do not some prove to be better than others?

True.

And do you breed from them all indifferently, or do you take care to breed from the best only?

From the best.

From the oldest or the youngest, or only those of ripe age? [*b*]

From those of ripe age.

And if care was not taken in the breeding, your dogs and birds would certainly deteriorate?

Certainly.

What of horses and of animals in general? Is there any difference?

No, it would be strange if there were.

Good heavens! my dear friend, I said, what consummate skill will our rulers need if the same principle holds of the human species! . . .

Had we not better appoint certain festivals at which we [*459e*] will bring together the brides and bridegrooms, and sacrifices will be offered, and suitable hymeneal songs composed by our poets: the [*460*] number of weddings is a matter which must be left to the discretion of the rulers, whose aim will be to preserve the same total number of guardians, having regard to wars, plagues, and any similar agencies, in order as far as this is possible to prevent the State from becoming either too large or too small.

Certainly, he replied.

We shall have to invent some ingenious kind of lottery, so that the less worthy may, on each occasion of our bringing them together, accuse their own ill luck and not the rulers.

To be sure, he said.

And I think that our braver and better youth, besides their [*b*] other honours and rewards, might have greater facilities of intercourse with women given them; their bravery will be a reason, and such fathers ought to have as many sons as possible.

True.

And the proper officers, whether male or female or both, for offices are to be held by women as well as by men—

Yes.

The proper officers will take the offspring of the good parents [*c*] to the pen or fold, and there they will deposit them with certain nurses who dwell in a separate quarter; but the offspring of the inferior, or of the better when they chance to be deformed, will be put away in some mysterious unknown place, as they should be.

Yes, he said, that must be done if the breed of the guardians is to be kept pure.

They will provide for their nurture, and will bring the mothers to the fold when they are full of milk, taking the greatest possible care that no mother recognizes her own child; and other wet-nurses may be engaged if more are required.   [*d*]

You agree then, I said, that men and women are to have a   [*466c*] common way of life such as we have described—common education, common children; and they are to watch over the citizens in common whether abiding in the city or going out to war; they are to keep watch together, and to hunt together like dogs; and always and in all things, as far as   [*d*] they are able, women are to share with the men? . . .

There is presumably no difficulty, I said, in seeing how war   [*e*] will be carried on by them.

How?

Why, of course they will go on expeditions together; and will take with them any of their children who are strong enough, that, after the manner of the artisan's child, they may look on at the work which they will have to do when they are grown up; and besides looking on they will have to help and be of use in war, and to wait upon their fathers   [*467*] and mothers. . . .

Let me next endeavour to show what is that fault in States   [*473b*] which is the cause of their present maladministration, and what is the least change which will enable a State to pass into the truer form; and let the change, if possible, be of one thing only, or, if not, of two; at any rate, let the changes be as few and slight as possible.

Certainly, he replied.   [*c*]

I think, I said, that there might be a reform of the State if only one change were made, which is not a slight or easy though still a possible one.

What is it? he said. . . .

I said: Until philosophers are kings in their cities, or the kings and princes of this world have the spirit and power of philosophy,   [*d*] and political greatness and wisdom meet in one, and those commoner natures who pursue either to the exclusion of the other are compelled to stand aside, cities will never have rest from their evils,—no, nor the human race, as I believe,—and then only will this our ideal State have a possibility of life and behold the light of day. . . .   [*e*]

BOOK VI

. . . The guardian then, I said, must be required to take the   [*504c*] longer circuit, and toil in learning not less hard than in physical   [*d*] training, or he will never arrive at the highest knowledge which, as we were just now saying, most belongs to him.

What, he [Adeimantus] said, is there a knowledge still higher than this—higher than justice and the other virtues?

Yes, I said, there is. And of the virtues too we must behold not the outline merely, as at present—nothing short of the most finished picture should satisfy us. When things of little value are elaborated with an infinity of pains in order that they may appear in their full beauty and utmost clearness, how ridiculous that we should not think the high-   [e] est truths worthy of the highest accuracy!

A right noble thought; but do you suppose that we shall refrain from asking you what you mean by this highest knowledge and what is its subject?

Nay, I said, ask if you will; but I am certain that you have heard the answer many times, and now you either do not understand me or, as I rather think, you are disposed to make trouble by holding me   [505] back; for you have often been told that the Idea of good is the highest knowledge, and that all other things, justice among them, become useful and advantageous only by their use of this. You can hardly be ignorant that this is what I am about to say, and moreover that our knowledge of the Idea of the good is inadequate. Yet you understand that without this knowledge, no other knowledge or possession of any kind will profit us at all. . . .   [b]

Now take a line which has been cut into two unequal parts,   [509d] and divide each of them again in the same proportion, and suppose the two main divisions to answer, one to the visible and the other to the intelligible, and then compare the subdivisions in respect of their clear-   [e] ness and want of clearness, and you will find that the first section in the sphere of the visible consists of images. And by images I mean, in the first place, shadows, and in the second place, reflections in water   [510] and in solid, smooth and polished bodies and the like. . . .

Imagine, now, the other section, of which this is only the resemblance, to include the animals which we see, and every thing that grows or is made. . . .

Would you [Glaucon] not admit that both the sections of this division have different degrees of truth, and that the copy is to the original as the sphere of opinion is to the sphere of knowledge?

Most undoubtedly.   [b]

Next proceed to consider the manner in which the sphere of the intellectual is to be divided.

In what manner?

Thus:—There are two subdivisions, in the lower of which the soul, using as images those things which themselves were reflected in the former division, is forced to base its enquiry upon hypotheses, proceeding not towards a principle but towards a conclusion; in the higher of the two, the soul proceeds *from* hypotheses, and goes up to a principle which is above hypotheses, making no use of images as in the former case, but proceeding only in and through the Ideas themselves.

I do not quite understand your meaning, he said.

Then I will try again; you will understand me better when I [*c*] have made some preliminary remarks. You are aware that students of geometry, arithmetic, and the kindred sciences assume the odd and the even and the figures and three kinds of angles and the like in their several branches of science; these are their hypotheses, which they and everybody are supposed to know, and therefore they do not deign to give any account of them either to themselves or others; but they begin with them, and go on until they arrive at last, and in a consistent manner, at the solu- [*d*] tion which they set out to find?

Yes, he said, I know.

And do you not know also that although they make use of the visible forms and reason about them, they are thinking not of these, but of the ideals which they resemble; not of the figures which they draw, but of the absolute square and the absolute diameter, and so on—the forms which they draw or make, and which themselves have shadows and [*e*] reflections in water, are in turn converted by them into images; for they are really seeking to behold the things themselves, which can only be seen with the eye of the mind?

That is true.   [*511*]

And this was what I meant by a subdivision of the intelligible, in the search after which the soul is compelled to use hypotheses; not ascending to a first principle, because she is unable to rise above the region of hypothesis, but employing now as images those objects from which the shadows below were derived, even these being deemed clear and distinct by comparison with the shadows.

I understand, he said, that you are speaking of the province of [*b*] geometry and the sister arts.

And when I speak of the other division of the intelligible, you will understand me to speak of that other sort of knowledge which reason herself attains by the power of dialectic, using the hypotheses not as first principles, but literally as hypotheses—that is to say, as steps and points of departure into a world which is above hypotheses, in order that she may soar beyond them to the first principle of the whole; and clinging to this and then to that which depends on this, by successive steps she descends again without the aid of any sensible object, from ideas, [*c*] through Ideas, and in Ideas she ends.

I understand you, he replied; not perfectly, for you seem to me to be describing a task which is really tremendous; but, at any rate, I understand you to say that that part of intelligible Being, which the science of dialectic contemplates, is clearer than that which falls under the arts, as they are termed, which take hypotheses as their principles; and though the objects are of such a kind that they must be viewed by the understanding and not by the senses, yet, because they start from hypoth- [d] eses and do not ascend to a principle, those who contemplate them appear to you not to exercise the higher reason upon them, although when a first principle is added to them they are cognizable by the higher reason. And the habit which is concerned with geometry and the cognate sciences I suppose that you would term understanding and not reason, as being intermediate between opinion and reason.

You have quite conceived my meaning, I said; and now, corresponding to these four divisions, let there be four faculties in the soul— reason answering to the highest, understanding to the second, faith [e] (or conviction) to the third, and perception of shadows to the last—and let there be a scale of them, and let us suppose that the several faculties have clearness in the same degree that their objects have truth. . . .

BOOK VII

And now, I said, let me show in a figure how far our nature [514] is enlightened or unenlightened:—Behold! human beings housed in an underground cave, which has a long entrance open towards the light and as wide as the interior of the cave; here they have been from their childhood, and have their legs and necks chained, so that they cannot move and can only see before them, being prevented by the chains from [b] turning round their heads. Above and behind them a fire is blazing at a distance, and between the fire and the prisoners there is a raised way; and you will see, if you look, a low wall built along the way, like the screen which marionette players have in front of them, over which they show the puppets.

I see.

And do you see, I said, men passing along the wall carrying all sorts of vessels, and statues and figures of animals made of wood and [c] stone and various materials, which appear over the wall? While [515] carrying their burdens, some of them, as you would expect, are talking, others silent.

You have shown me a strange image, and they are strange prisoners.

Like ourselves, I replied; for in the first place do you think they have seen anything of themselves, and of one another, except the shadows which the fire throws on the opposite wall of the cave?

How could they do so, he asked, if throughout their lives they [b] were never allowed to move their heads?

And of the objects which are being carried in like manner they would only see the shadows?

Yes, he said.

And if they were able to converse with one another, would they not suppose that the things they saw were the real things?

Very true.

And suppose further that the prison had an echo which came from the other side, would they not be sure to fancy when one of the passers-by spoke that the voice which they heard came from the passing shadow?

No question, he replied.

To them, I said, the truth would be literally nothing but the [c] shadows of the images.

That is certain.

And now look again, and see in what manner they would be released from their bonds, and cured of their error, whether the process would naturally be as follows. At first, when any of them is liberated and compelled suddenly to stand up and turn his neck round and walk and look towards the light, he will suffer sharp pains; the glare will distress him, and he will be unable to see the realities of which in his former state he had seen the shadows; and then conceive someone saying to him that what he saw before was an illusion, but that now, when he is [d] approaching nearer to being and his eye is turned towards more real existence, he has a clearer vision,—what will be his reply? And you may further imagine that his instructor is pointing to the objects as they pass and requiring him to name them,—will he not be perplexed? Will he not fancy that the shadows which he formerly saw are truer than the objects which are now shown to him?

Far truer.

And if he is compelled to look straight at the light, will he not [e] have a pain in his eyes which will make him turn away to take refuge in the objects of vision which he can see, and which he will conceive to be in reality clearer than the things which are now being shown to him?

True, he said.

And suppose once more, that he is reluctantly dragged up that steep and rugged ascent, and held fast until he is forced into the presence of the sun himself, is he not likely to be pained and irritated? When he approaches the light his eyes will be dazzled, and he will not be [516] able to see anything at all of what are now called realities.

Not all in a moment, he said.

He will require to grow accustomed to the sight of the upper world. And first he will see the shadows best, next the reflections of men and other objects in the water, and then the objects themselves; and, when he turned to the heavenly bodies and the heaven itself, he would find it easier to gaze upon the light of the moon and the stars at [*b*] night than to see the sun or the light of the sun by day?

Certainly.

Last of all he will be able to see the sun, not turning aside to the illusory reflections of him in the water, but gazing directly at him in his own proper place, and contemplating him as he is.

Certainly.

He will then proceed to argue that this is he who gives the seasons and the years, and is the guardian of all that is in the visible world, and in a certain way the cause of all things which he and his fellows have been accustomed to behold? [*c*]

Clearly, he said, he would arrive at this conclusion after what he had seen.

And when he remembered his old habitation, and the wisdom of the cave and his fellow-prisoners, do you not suppose that he would felicitate himself on the change, and pity them?

Certainly, he would.

And if they were in the habit of conferring honours among themselves on those who were quickest to observe the passing shadows and to remark which of them went before and which followed after and [*d*] which were together, and who were best able from these observations to divine the future, do you think that he would be eager for such honours and glories, or envy those who attained honour and sovereignty among those men? Would he not say with Homer,

'Better to be a serf, laboring for a landless master,'
and to endure anything, rather than think as they do and live after their manner?

Yes, he said, I think that he would consent to suffer anything [*e*] rather than live in this miserable manner.

Imagine once more, I said, such a one coming down suddenly out of the sunlight, and being replaced in his old seat; would he not be certain to have his eyes full of darkness?

To be sure, he said.

And if there were a contest, and he had to compete in measuring the shadows with the prisoners who had never moved out of the cave, while his sight was still weak, and before his eyes had become [*517*] steady (and the time which would be needed to acquire this new habit of sight might be very considerable), would he not make himself ridiculous? Men would say of him that he had returned from the place above with his eyes ruined; and that it was better not even to think of ascending; and if anyone tried to loose another and lead him up to the light, let them only catch the offender, and they would put him to death.

No question, he said.

This entire allegory, I said, you may now append, dear Glaucon, to the previous argument; the prison-house is the world of sight, the [b] light of the fire is the power of the sun, and you will not misapprehend me if you interpret the journey upwards to be the ascent of the soul into the intellectual world according to my surmise, which, at your desire, I have expressed—whether rightly or wrongly God knows. But, whether true or false, my opinion is that in the world of knowledge the Idea of good appears last of all, and is seen only with an effort; although, when seen, it is inferred to be the universal author of all things beautiful [c] and right, parent of light and of the lord of light in the visible world, and the immediate and supreme source of reason and truth in the intellectual; and that this is the power upon which he who would act rationally either in public or private life must have his eye fixed. . . .

If I am right, certain professors of education must be wrong [518b] when they say that they can put a knowledge into the soul which was not there before, like sight into blind eyes. [c]

They undoubtedly say this, he replied.

Whereas our argument shows that the power and capacity of learning exists in the soul already; and that just as if it were not possible to turn the eye from darkness to light without the whole body, so too the instrument of knowledge can only by the movement of the whole soul be turned from the world of becoming to that of being, and learn by degrees to endure the sight of being, and of the brightest and best of being, or in other words, of the good. [d]

Very true.

And must there not be some art which will show how the conversion can be effected in the easiest and quickest manner; an art which will not implant the faculty of sight, for that exists already, but will set it straight when it has been turned in the wrong direction, and is looking away from the truth?

Yes, he said, such an art may be presumed.

And whereas the other so-called virtues of the soul seem to be akin to bodily qualities, for even when they are not originally innate they can be implanted later by habit and exercise, the virtue of wisdom [e] more than anything else contains a divine element which never loses its power, and by this conversion is rendered useful and profitable; or, by conversion of another sort, hurtful and useless. Did you never observe the narrow intelligence flashing from the keen eye of a clever rogue [519] —how eager he is, how clearly his paltry soul sees the way to his end; he is the reverse of blind, but his keen eye-sight is forced into the service of evil, and he is mischievous in proportion to his cleverness?

Very true, he said.

But what if such natures had been gradually stripped, beginning in childhood, of the leaden weights which sink them in the sea of Becoming, and which, fastened upon the soul through gluttonous indulgence in eating and other such pleasures, forcibly turn its vision down-   [*b*] wards—if I say, they had been released from these impediments and turned in the opposite direction, the very same faculty in them would have seen the truth as keenly as they see what their eyes are turned to now.

Very likely.

Yes, I said; and there is another thing which is likely, or rather a necessary inference from what has preceded, that neither the uneducated and uninformed of the truth, nor yet those who are suffered to prolong their education without end, will be able ministers of State; not the   [*c*] former, because they have no single aim of duty which is the rule of all their actions, private as well as public; nor the latter, because they will not act at all except upon compulsion, fancying that they are already dwelling apart in the islands of the blest.

Very true, he replied.

Then, I said, the business of us who are the founders of the State will be to compel the best minds to attain that knowledge which we have already shown to be the greatest of all, namely, the vision of the good; they must make the ascent which we have described; but when they   [*d*] have ascended and seen enough we must not allow them to do as they do now.

What do you mean?

They are permitted to remain in the upper world, refusing to descend again among the prisoners in the cave, and partake of their labours and honours, whether they are worth having or not.

But is not this unjust? he said; ought we to give them a worse life, when they might have a better?

You have again forgotten, my friend, I said, the intention of   [*e*] our law, which does not aim at making any one class in the State happy above the rest; it seeks rather to spread happiness over the whole State, and to hold the citizens together by persuasion and necessity, making each share with others any benefit which he can confer upon the   [*520*] State; and the law aims at producing such citizens, not that they may be left to please themselves, but that they may serve in binding the State together.

True, he said, I had forgotten. . . .

And now shall we consider in what way such guardians will   [*521c*] be produced, and how they are to be brought from darkness to light,—as some are said to have ascended from the world below to the gods? . . .

The process, I said, is not the turning over of an oyster-shell, but the turning round of a soul passing from a day which is little better than night to the true day; an ascent towards reality, which we shall affirm to be true philosophy?

Quite so.

And should we not inquire what sort of knowledge has the power of affecting such a change?   [*d*]

Certainly.

What sort of knowledge is there, Glaucon, which would draw the soul from becoming to being? . . .

But what branch of knowledge is there, my dear Glaucon,   [*522b*] which is of the desired nature; since all the useful arts were reckoned mean by us?

Undoubtedly; and yet what study remains, distinct both from music and gymnastic and from the arts?

Well, I said, if nothing remains outside them, let us select something which is a common factor in all.

What may that be?

Something, for instance, which all arts and sciences and intel-   [*c*] ligences use in common, and which everyone has to learn among the first elements of education.

What is that?

The little matter of distinguishing one, two, and three—in a word, number and calculation:—do not all arts and sciences necessarily partake of them?

Yes.

Then the art of war partakes of them?

To be sure. . . .

I should like to know whether you have the same notion which   [*e*] I have of this study?

What is your notion?

It appears to me to be a study of the kind which we are seeking, and which leads naturally to reflection, but never to have been   [*523*] rightly used; for it has a strong tendency to draw the soul towards being. . . .

Do you follow me when I say that objects of sense are of two   [*b*] kinds? some of them do not invite the intelligence to further inquiry because the sense is an adequate judge of them; while in the case of other objects sense is so untrustworthy that inquiry by the mind is imperatively demanded. . . .

When speaking of uninviting objects, I mean those which do not pass straight from one sensation to the opposite; inviting objects are   [*c*] those which do; in this latter case the sense coming upon the object, whether at a distance or near, does not give one particular impression more strongly than its opposite. An illustration will make my meaning clearer:—here are three fingers—a little finger, a second finger, and a middle finger.

Very good.

You may suppose that they are seen quite close: And here comes the point.

What is it?

Each of them equally appears a finger, and in this respect it makes no difference whether it is seen in the middle or at the extremity, [d] whether white or black, or thick or thin, or anything of that kind. In these cases a man is not compelled to ask of thought the question what is a finger? for the sight never intimates to the mind that a finger is the opposite of a finger.

True.

And therefore, I said, there is nothing here which is likely to invite or excite intelligence.

There is not, he said.   [e]

But is this equally true of the greatness and smallness of the fingers? Can sight adequately perceive them? and is no difference made by the circumstance that one of the fingers is in the middle and another at the extremity? And in like manner does the touch adequately perceive the qualities of thickness or thinness, of softness or hardness? And so of the other senses; do they give perfect intimations of such matters? Is not their mode of operation on this wise—the sense which is concerned   [524] with the quality of hardness is necessarily concerned also with the quality of softness, and only intimates to the soul that the same thing is felt to be both hard and soft?

It is, he said.

And must not the soul be perplexed at this intimation which this sense gives of a hard which is also soft? What, again, is the meaning of light and heavy, if the sense pronounces that which is light to be also heavy, and that which is heavy, light?

Yes, he said, these intimations which the soul receives are very   [b] curious and require to be explained.

Yes, I said, and in these perplexities the soul naturally summons to her aid and calculation and intelligence, that she may see whether the several objects announced to her are one or two.

True.

And if they turn out to be two, is not each of them one and different?

Certainly.

And if each is one, and both are two, she will conceive the two as in a state of division, for if they were undivided they could only be conceived of as one?

True.

The eye, also, certainly did see both small and great, but only   [c] in a confused manner; they were not distinguished.

Yes.

Whereas on the contrary the thinking mind, intending to light up the chaos, was compelled to reconsider the small and great viewing them as separate and not in that confusion.

Very true.

Is it not in some such way that there arises in our minds the inquiry 'What is great?' and 'What is small?'

Exactly so.

And accordingly we made the distinction of the visible and the intelligible.

A very proper one.   [d]

This was what I meant just now when I spoke of impressions which invited the intellect, or the reverse—those which strike our sense simultaneously with opposite impressions, invite thought; those which are not simultaneous with them, do not awaken it.

I understand now, he said, and agree with you.

And to which class do unity and number belong?

I do not know, he replied.

Think a little and you will see that what has preceded will supply the answer; for if simple unity could be adequately perceived by the sight or by any other sense, then, as we were saying in the case of the   [e] finger, there would be nothing to attract towards being; but when something contrary to unity is always seen at the same time, so that there seems to be no more reason for calling it one than the opposite, some discriminating power becomes necessary, and in such a case the soul in perplexity, is obliged to rouse her power of thought and to ask: 'What *is* absolute unity?' This is the way in which the study of the one has a power of drawing and converting the mind to the contemplation of true   [525] being.

And surely, he said, this occurs notably in the visual perception of unity; for we see the same thing at once as one and as infinite in multitude?

Yes, I said; and this being true of one must be equally true of all number?

Certainly.

And all arithmetic and calculation have to do with number?

Yes.

And they appear to lead the mind towards truth?   [*b*]

Yes, in a very remarkable manner.

Then this is a discipline of the kind for which we are seeking; for the man of war must learn the art of number or he will not know how to array his troops, and the philosopher also, because he has to rise out of the sea of change and lay hold of true being, or be for ever unable to calculate and reason.

That is true.

But our guardian is, in fact, both warrior and philosopher?

Certainly.

Then this is a kind of knowledge which legislation may fitly prescribe; and we must endeavour to persuade those who are to be the principal men of our State to go and learn arithmetic, and take up   [*c*] the study in no amateurish spirit but pursue it until they can view the nature of numbers with the unaided mind; nor again, like mechants or retail-traders, with a view to buying or selling, but for the sake of their military use, and of the soul herself, because this will be the easiest way for her to pass from becoming to truth and being. . . .

And next, shall we inquire whether the kindred science also   [*526c*] concerns us?

You mean geometry?

Exactly so.

Clearly, he said, we are concerned with that part of geometry   [*d*] which relates to war; for in pitching a camp, or taking up a position, or closing or extending the lines of an army, or any other military manoeuvre, whether in actual battle or on a march, it will make all the difference whether a general is or is not a geometrician.

Yes, I said, but for that purpose a very little of either geometry or calculation will be enough; the question relates rather to the greater and more advanced part of geometry—whether that tends in any degree   [*e*] to make more easy the vision of the Idea of good; and thither, as I was saying, all things tend which compel the soul to turn her gaze towards that place where is the full perfection of being, which she ought, by all means, to behold.

True, he said.

Then if geometry compels us to view being, it concerns us; if becoming only, it does not concern us?

Yes, that is what we assert.   [*527*]

Yet anybody who has the least acquaintance with geometry will not deny that such a conception of the science is in flat contradiction to the ordinary language of geometricians.

How so?

They speak, as you doubtless know, in terms redolent of the workshop. As if they were engaged in action, and had no other aim in view in all their reasoning, they talk of squaring, applying, extending and the like, whereas, I presume, the real object of the whole science is knowledge.

Certainly, he said. [*b*]

Then must not a further admission be made?

What admission?

That the knowledge at which geometry aims is knowledge of eternal being, and not of aught which at a particular time comes into being and perishes.

That, he replied, may be readily allowed, and is true.

Then, my noble friend, geometry will draw the soul towards truth, and create the spirit of philosophy, and raise up that which is now unhappily allowed to fall down.

Nothing will be more likely to have such an effect.

Then nothing should be more sternly laid down than that the [*c*] inhabitants of your fair city should by no means remain unversed in geometry. Moreover the science has indirect effects, which are not small.

Of what kind? he said.

There are the military advantages of which you spoke, I said; and further, we know that for the better apprehension of any branch of knowledge, it makes all the difference whether a man has a grasp of geometry or not.

Yes indeed, he said, all the difference in the world.

Then shall we propose this as a second branch of knowledge which our youth will study? . . .

After the second dimension the third, which is concerned [*528b*] with cubes and dimensions of depth, ought to have followed.

That is true, Socrates; but so little seems to have been discovered as yet about these subjects.

Why, yes, I said, and for two reasons:—in the first place, no government patronizes them; this leads to a want of energy in the pursuit of them, and they are difficult; in the second place, students cannot learn them unless they have a director. But then a director can hardly be found, and even if he could, as matters now stand, the students, who are very conceited, would not attend to him. That, however, would be other- [*c*] wise if the whole State were to assist the director of these studies by giving honour to them; then disciples would show obedience, and there would be continuous and earnest search, and discoveries would be made; since even now, disregarded as they are by the world, and maimed of their fair proportions, because those engaged in the research have no conception of its use, still these studies force their way by their natural charm, and it would not be surprising if they should some day emerge into [*d*] light. . . .

Then assuming that the science now omitted would come into   [e]
existence if encouraged by the State, let us take astronomy as our fourth
study.

The right order, he replied. And now, Socrates, as you rebuked the
vulgar manner in which I praised astronomy before, my praise shall be
given in your own spirit. For everyone, as I think, must see that   [529]
astronomy compels the soul to look upwards and leads us from this world
to another.

Everyone but myself, I said; for I am not sure that it is so.

And what then would you say?

I should rather say that those who elevate astronomy into philosophy treat it in such a way as to make us look downwards and not
upwards.

What do you mean? he asked.

You, I replied, have in your mind a truly sublime conception of
our knowledge of the things above. And I dare say that if a person were
to throw his head back and study the fretted ceiling, you would still   [b]
think that his mind was the percipient, and not his eyes. And you are
very likely right, and I may be a simpleton: but, in my opinion, that
knowledge only which is concerned with true being and the unseen can
make the soul look upwards, and whether a man gapes at the heavens or
blinks on the ground, when seeking to learn some particular of sense, I
would deny that he can learn, for nothing of that sort is matter of science;
and I say that his soul is looking downwards, not upwards, even   [c]
though, in the quest for knowledge he floats face upwards on the sea, or
on the land.

I acknowledge, he said, the justice of your rebuke. Still, I should
like to ascertain how astronomy can be learned in any manner more conducive than the present system to that knowledge of which we are speaking?

I will tell you, I said: The starry heaven which we behold is
wrought upon a visible ground, and therefore, although the fairest and
most perfect of visible things, must necessarily be deemed inferior   [d]
far to the true motions with which the real swiftness and the real slow-
ness move in their relation to each other, carrying with them that which
is contained in them, in the true number and in true figures of every
kind. Now, these are to be apprehended by reason and intelligence, but
not by sight. Do you doubt that?

No, he replied.

The spangled heavens should be used as a pattern and with a view
to that higher knowledge; they may be compared to diagrams which   [e]
one might find excellently wrought by the hand of Daedalus, or some
other great artist. For any geometrician who saw them would doubtless

appreciate the exquisiteness of their workmanship, but he would never dream of thinking that in them he could find the true equal or the true double, or the truth of any other proportion. [530]

No, he replied, such an idea would be ridiculous.

And will not a true astronomer have the same feeling when he looks at the movements of the stars? Will he not think that heaven and the things in heaven are framed by the Craftsman who made them in the most perfect manner in which such things can be framed? But if he finds someone supposing that the proportions of night and day, or of both to the month, or of the month to the year, or of the stellar movements generally to these and to one another, being, as they are, embodied and [b] visible, are eternal and unchanging, and never deviate in any direction, and that it is worth while to investigate their exact truth at any cost—will he not think him a queer fellow?

I quite agree, now that I hear it from you.

Then, I said, in astronomy, as in geometry, we should employ problems, and let the heavens alone if we would approach the subject [c] in the right way and so make the natural gift of reason to be of any real use.

That, he said, is a work infinitely beyond our present astronomers.

Yes, I said; and I think we must prescribe the rest of our studies in the same spirit, if our legislation is to be of any value. But can you tell me of any other suitable study?

No, he said, not without thinking.

Motion, I said, has many forms, and not one only; a wise man will, perhaps, be able to name them all; but two of them are obvious [d] enough even to wits no better than ours.

What are they?

There is a second, I said, which is the counterpart of the one already named.

And what may that be?

It appears, I said, that as the eyes are designed to look up at the stars, so are the ears to hear harmonious motions; and these are sister sciences—as the Pythagoreans say, and we, Glaucon, agree with them?

Yes, he replied.

But this, I said, is a laborious study, and therefore we shall [e] inquire what they have to say on these points, or on any others. For our own part, we shall in all this preserve our own principle.

What is that?

There is a perfection which all knowledge ought to reach, and which our pupils ought also to attain, and not to fall short of, as I was saying that they did in astronomy. For in the science of harmony, as you probably know, the same thing happens. The teachers of harmony [531] compare only the sounds and consonances which are heard, and their labour, like that of the astronomers, is in vain.

Yes, by heaven! he said; and 'tis as good as a play to hear them talking about their close intervals, whatever they may be; they put their ears close alongside of the strings like persons catching a sound from their neighbour's wall—one set of them declaring that they distinguish an intermediate note and have found the least interval which should be the unit of measurement; the others insisting that the two sounds have passed into the same—either party setting their ears before their under-   [b] standing.

You mean, I said, those gentlemen who tease and torture the strings and rack them on the pegs of the instrument: I might carry on the metaphor and speak after their manner of the blows which the plectrum gives, and of accusations against the strings, and of their reticence or forwardness; but this would be tedious, and therefore I will only say that these are not the men, and that I am referring to the Pythagoreans, of whom I was just now proposing to inquire about harmony. For they too are in error, like the astronomers; they investigate the numbers of the harmonies   [c] which are heard, but they never attain to problems—to inquiring which numbers are harmonious and which are not, and for what reason.

That, he said, is a thing of more than mortal knowledge.

A thing, I replied, which I would rather call useful; that is, if sought after with a view to the beautiful and good; but if pursued in any other spirit, useless.

Very true, he said.

Now, when all these studies reach the point of inter-communion and connexion with one another, and come to be considered in their   [d] mutual affinities, then, I think, but not till then, will the pursuit of them have a value for our objects; otherwise there is no profit in them.

I suspect so; but you are speaking, Socrates, of a vast work.

What do you mean? I said; the prelude or what? Do you not know that all these are but preludes to the actual strain which must be learnt? For you surely would not regard those skilled in these sciences as dialecticians?

Assuredly not, he said; apart from a very few whom I have   [e] met.

But do you imagine that men who are unable to give and take a reason will have the knowledge which we require of them?   [532]

Neither can this be supposed.

And so, Glaucon, I said, we have at last arrived at the hymn of dialectic. This is that strain which is of the intellect only, but which the faculty of sight will nevertheless be found to imitate; for sight, as you may remember, was imagined by us after a while to behold the real animals and stars, and last of all the sun himself. And so with dialectic; when a person starts on the discovery of the real by the light of reason only, and without any assistance of sense, and perseveres until by pure intelligence he arrives at the perception of the absolute good, he at last [*b*] finds himself at the end of the intellectual world, as in the case of sight at the end of the visible. . . .

Say, then, what is the nature and what are the divisions of the [*e*] power of dialectic, and what are the paths which lead to our destination, where we can rest from the journey.

Dear Glaucon, I said, you will no longer be able to follow [*533*] me here, though I would do my best, and would endeavour to show you not an image only but the absolute truth, according to my notion. Whether that notion is or is not correct, it would not be right for me to affirm. But that it is something like this that you must see, of that I am confident.

Doubtless, he replied.

But I must also remind you, that the power of dialectic alone can reveal this, and only to one who is a disciple of the previous sciences.

Of that assertion you may be as confident as of the last.

And assuredly no one will argue that there is any other [*b*] method of comprehending by any regular process all true existence or of ascertaining what each thing is in its own nature; for the arts in general are concerned with the desires or opinions of men, or with processes of growth and construction; or they have been cultivated in order to care for things grown and constructed; and as to the mathematical sciences which, as we were saying, have some apprehension of true being—geometry and the like—they only dream about being, but never can they [*c*] behold the waking reality so long as they leave unmoved the hypotheses which they use, and are unable to give an account of them. For when a man knows not his own first principle, and when the conclusion and intermediate steps are also constructed out of he knows not what, how can he imagine that such a fabric of convention can ever become science?

Impossible, he said.

Then dialectic, and dialectic alone, goes directly to the first principle and is the only science which does away with hypotheses in order to make her ground secure; the eye of the soul, which is really buried [*d*] in an outlandish slough, is by her gentle aid lifted upwards; and in this work she uses as handmaids and helpers the sciences which we have been discussing. We have often used the customary name sciences, but they ought to have some other name, implying greater clearness than opinion and less clearness than science: and this, in our previous sketch, was called understanding. But why should we dispute about names when we have realities of such importance to consider?

Why indeed, he said, when any name will do which expresses   [*e*]
the thought of the mind with clearness?

At any rate, we are satisfied, as before, to have four divisions; two
for intellect and two for opinion, and to call the first division science,
the second understanding, the third belief, and the fourth perception of
shadows, opinion being concerned with becoming, and intellect with
being. . . .

And do you also agree, I said, in describing the dialectician   [*534b*]
as one who attains a conception of the essence of each thing? And he who
does not possess and is therefore unable to impart this conception, in
whatever degree he fails, may in that degree also be said to fail in intelligence? Will you admit so much?

Yes, he said; how can I deny it?

And you would say the same of the conception of the good? Unless the person is able to abstract from all else and define rationally the
Idea of good, and unless he can run the gauntlet of all objections,   [*c*]
and is keen to disprove them by appeals not to opinion but to absolute
truth, never faltering at any step of the argument—unless he can do all
this, you would say that he knows neither the Idea of good nor any other
good; he apprehends only a shadow, if anything at all, which is given by
opinion and not by science;—dreaming and slumbering in this life, before
he is well awake here, he arrives at the world below, and has his final   [*d*]
quietus.

In all that I should most certainly agree with you.

And surely you would not have the children of your imaginary
State, whom you are nurturing and educating—if your imagination ever
becomes a reality—you would not allow the future rulers to be mere irrational quantities, and yet to be set in authority over the highest matters?

Certainly not.

Then you will make a law that they shall have such an education
as will enable them to attain the greatest skill in asking and answering
questions?

Yes, he said, you and I together will make it.   [*e*]

Dialectic, then, as you will agree, is the coping-stone of the sciences,
and is set over them: no other study can rightly be built on and above
this, and our treatment of the studies required has now reached its end?

I agree, he said.

But to whom we are to assign these studies, and in what way   [*535*]
they are to be assigned, are questions which remain to be considered.

Yes, clearly.

You remember, I said, the character which was preferred in our
former choice of rulers?

Certainly, he said.

I would have you think that, in other respects, the same natures must still be chosen, and the preference again given to the surest and the bravest, and, if possible, to the fairest; but now we must look for something more than a noble and vile temper; they should also have the [b] natural gifts which accord with this higher education.

And what are these?

Such gifts as keenness and ready powers of acquisition; for the mind more often faints from the severity of study than from the severity of gymnastics: the toil is more entirely the mind's own, and is not shared with the body.

Very true, he replied.

Further, he of whom we are in search should have a good memory, and be an unwearied solid man who is a lover of labour in any line; [c] or he will never be able, besides enduring some bodily exercise, to go through all the intellectual discipline and study which we require of him.

He will not, he said, unless he is gifted by nature in every way. . . .

Although in our former selection we chose old men, we [536c] must not do so in this. Solon was under a delusion when he said that [d] a man when he grows old may learn many things—for he can no more learn much than he can run much; youth is the time for great and frequent toil.

Of course.

And, therefore, calculation and geometry and all the other elements of instruction, which are to be a preparation for dialectic, should be presented to the mind in childhood; not, however, under any notion of forcing our system of education.

Why not?

Because a freeman ought not to acquire knowledge of any [e] kind like a slave. Bodily exercise, when compulsory, does no harm to the body; but knowledge which is acquired under compulsion obtains no hold on the mind.

Very true.

Then, my good friend, I said, do not use compulsion, but let early education be a sort of amusement; you will then also be better able to find out the natural bent. [537]

There is reason in your remark, he said.

Do you remember that the children were even to be taken to see the battle on horseback; and that if there were no danger they were to be brought close up and, like young hounds, have a taste of blood given them?

Yes, I remember.

The same practice may be followed, I said, in all these things—labours, lessons, dangers—and he who is most at home in all of them ought to be enrolled in a select number.

At what age?

At the age when the necessary gymnastics are over: the period   [b] whether of two or three years which passes in this sort of training is useless for any other purpose, for sleep and tiring exercise are unpropitious to learning. Moreover the trial of their quality in gymnastic exercises is one of the most important tests to which our youth are subjected.

Certainly, he replied.

After that time those who are selected from the class of twenty years old will be promoted to higher honour than the rest, and the sciences which they learned without any order in their early education   [c] will now be brought together, and they will be able to see the natural relationship of them to one another and to true being.

Yes, he said, that is the only kind of knowledge which, in a few fortunate persons, takes lasting root.

Yes, I said; and the capacity for such knowledge is the great criterion of dialectical talent: the comprehensive mind is always the dialectical.

I agree with you, he said.

These, I said, are the points which you must consider; and   [d] those who have most of this comprehension, and who are most steadfast in their learning, and in their military and other appointed duties, when they pass the age of thirty will have to be chosen by you out of the select class, and elevated to higher honour; and you will have to prove them by the help of dialectic, in order to learn which of them is able to give up the use of sight and the other senses, and in company with truth to attain absolute being. . . .

Suppose, I said, the training in logic to be continued dili-   [539d] gently and earnestly and exclusively for twice the number of years which were passed in equivalent bodily exercise—will that be enough?

Would you say six or four years? he asked.   [e]

Say five years, I replied; at the end of the time they must be sent down again into the cave and compelled to hold any military or other office which young men are qualified to hold, so that they may not be behind others in experience of life, and here again they must be tested, to show whether, when they are drawn all manner of ways by temptation, they will stand firm or flinch.

And how long is this stage of their lives to last?   [540]

Fifteen years, I answered; and when they have reached fifty years of age, then let those who still survive and have distinguished themselves in every action of their lives and in every branch of knowledge be brought at last to their consummation: the time has now arrived at which they must raise the eye of the soul to the universal light which lightens all things, and behold the absolute good; for that is the pattern according to which they are to order the State and the lives of individuals, and the remainder of their own lives also; making philosophy their chief [b] pursuit, but, when their turn comes, toiling also at politics and ruling for the public good, not as though they were performing some heroic action, but simply as a necessity; and when they have brought up in each generation others like themselves and left them in their place to be governors of the State, then they will depart to the Islands of the Blest and dwell there; and the city will give them public memorials and sacrifices and honour them, if the Pythian oracle consent, as demigods, but if not, as in any case blessed and divine.　　　　　　　　　　　　　　　　　　　　[c]

You are a sculptor, Socrates, and have wrought statues of our governors faultless in beauty.

Yes, I said, Glaucon, and of our governesses too; for you must not suppose that what I have been saying applies to men only and not to women as far as their natures can go.

There you are right, he said, since we have made them to share in all things like the men.

Well, I said, and you would agree (would you not?) that what [d] has been said about the State and the government is not a mere dream, and although difficult not impossible, but only possible in the way which has been supposed; that is to say, when true philosophers are born in the reigning family in a State, one or more of them, despising the honours of this present world which they deem mean and worthless, esteeming above all things right and the honour that springs from right, and regarding justice as the greatest and most necessary of all things, whose [e] ministers they are, and whose principles will be exalted by them when they set in order their own city?

How will they proceed?

They will begin by sending out into the country all the inhabitants of the city who are more than ten years old, and will take posses- [541] sion of their children, who will be unaffected by the habits of their parents; these they will train in their own habits and laws, which will be such as we have described: and in this way the State and constitution of which we were speaking will soonest and most easily attain happiness, and the nation which has such a constitution will gain most.

Yes, that will be the best way. And I think, Socrates, that you [b] have very well described how, if ever, such a constitution might come into being.

Enough then of the perfect State, and of the man who bears its image—there is no difficulty, I suppose, in seeing how we shall describe him also.

There is no difficulty, he replied; and I agree with you in thinking that nothing more need be said.

Bibliography

LODGE, RUPERT CLENDON, *Plato's Theory of Education*, London, K. Paul, Trench, and Trubner, 1947.

NETTLESHIP, RICHARD LEWIS, *The Theory of Education in Plato's Republic*, London, Oxford University Press, 1935.

WOODBRIDGE, FREDERICK JAMES EUGENE, *The Son of Apollo*, Boston and New York, Houghton Mifflin, 1929. (Cf. esp. the chapter "On Education.")

.   .   .

FIELD, GUY CROMWELL, *Plato and His Contemporaries*, London, Methuen, 1930.

FRIEDLAENDER, PAUL, *Plato,* translated by Hans Meyerhoff, New York, Pantheon Books, Vol. I, 1958, Vol. II, 1964. (*Platon,* Berlin and Leipzig, W. de Guyter and Co., 1928–30. Second revised and expanded edition, Berlin, 1954.)

GULLEY, NORMAN, *Plato's Theory of Knowledge,* London, Methuen, 1962.

NETTLESHIP, RICHARD LEWIS, *Lectures on the Republic of Plato,* edited by G. R. Benson, Lord Charnwood, London and New York, Macmillan, 1901; New York, St. Martin's Press, 1961.

ROSS, SIR WILLIAM DAVID, *Plato's Theory of Ideas,* Oxford, Clarendon Press, 1951.

TAYLOR, A. E., *Plato: the Man and His Work,* London, Methuen, 1955 (6th edition); also in Meridian paperback.

III

QUINTILIAN

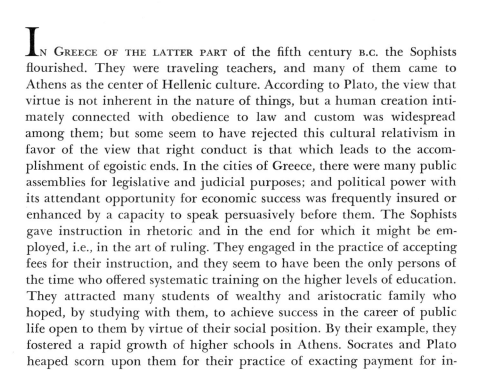

In GREECE OF THE LATTER PART of the fifth century B.C. the Sophists flourished. They were traveling teachers, and many of them came to Athens as the center of Hellenic culture. According to Plato, the view that virtue is not inherent in the nature of things, but a human creation intimately connected with obedience to law and custom was widespread among them; but some seem to have rejected this cultural relativism in favor of the view that right conduct is that which leads to the accomplishment of egoistic ends. In the cities of Greece, there were many public assemblies for legislative and judicial purposes; and political power with its attendant opportunity for economic success was frequently insured or enhanced by a capacity to speak persuasively before them. The Sophists gave instruction in rhetoric and in the end for which it might be employed, i.e., in the art of ruling. They engaged in the practice of accepting fees for their instruction, and they seem to have been the only persons of the time who offered systematic training on the higher levels of education. They attracted many students of wealthy and aristocratic family who hoped, by studying with them, to achieve success in the career of public life open to them by virtue of their social position. By their example, they fostered a rapid growth of higher schools in Athens. Socrates and Plato heaped scorn upon them for their practice of exacting payment for instruction, and combatted their views concerning morality; but the Academy as well as other Athenian schools might have been longer delayed had the Sophists never taught. They succeeded in rendering the Sophist movement inoperative by developing more carefully the inquiry which the Sophists stimulated and by providing permanent places for instruction.

Isocrates, who had close affinities with the Sophists, established a school in Athens in 390 B.C. It was attended by students from many cities as well as from Athens, and it seems that they were required to have a general training in literature and music. In it, Isocrates prepared them for public life by instructing them in the theory of debate, by requiring their practice of it, and by indoctrinating them with a common sense view as to the uses to be made of political authority. His school achieved considerable success. It is to be distinguished from the Academy in the emphasis it placed upon the art of public speaking, in the relative paucity of the curricular offerings, and in the belief that inspired it—the belief that detailed knowledge of the sciences and minute reflection upon virtue were not necessary to the good life for society and for the individual.

The rhetorical tradition of the Sophists did not die out when the Platonic Academy, the school of Aristotle, that of the Stoics, and that of the Epicureans, assumed responsibility for higher education in Athens. To some degree, they absorbed rhetoric; and the art of public persuasion continued to be taught as useful for those in public life. When Rome began its ascent to political hegemony, it borrowed many ingredients of Greek education; and in accord with its ingrained distrust of too much learning, it took over the Sophistic tradition rather than the Platonic, i.e., the practice of stressing oratory as a means to practical success in the forum and before the bar together with a general education in literature and law, rather than that of painstaking reflection in order to insure that a course embarked upon is a right one. Quintilian called Isocrates "the prince of instructors"; and he epitomizes the Roman attitude toward education.

During the period of its rise to greatness, Rome was a republic; consequently, in the senate and in related institutions, there was considerable opportunity for persons of energy to ascend to positions of power in the state. In these institutions, oratory was an extremely important means to such power, and training in it may have been a part of the education native to Rome. In any event, Greek theory and practice of rhetoric was borrowed by the Romans in the earlier part of the third century B.C.; and the study of it along with that of Greek poetry and drama as well as of Roman literature, translated from or patterned on the Greek, and of Roman law, became the chief content of higher education despite the considerable opposition of people like Cato more conservatively inclined. By the middle of the first century B.C., the theory and practice of rhetoric was well established as a preparation for those who would enter public life in politics and in the practice of law.

A little before the beginning of the Christian era, after a period of internal violence, the Republic expired and the Empire took its place. Under relatively peaceful conditions, the emperors, for some time, governed a tremendous region extending from Britain to Asia Minor, and from the Danube to the Mediterranean coasts of Africa, and embracing populations of most diverse cultural origins. This task required a large number of governmental administrators, and the imperial policy of preserving a considerable amount of local autonomy required that these administrators be acquainted with the theory of law and with its practice in the courts. The senate retained many of the forms connected with legislating, and continued to function as an organ for the expression of aristocratic opinion. The actual needs of governing and the participation of prominent persons in institutions like the senate supported the continuance of training in rhetoric; skill in oratory was socially useful in governmental affairs and personally so in public debate. The general training in literature afforded content for the art of speaking as did also that in jurisprudence; and the advanced training of Roman youth did not alter notably with the change from Republic to Empire.

Like several of the great Roman writers, Marcus Fabius Quintilianus was born in Spain. By this time Roman culture with its borrowings from the Greek had succeeded in transforming many parts of the Empire into its own likeness; and Quintilian grew up as a Roman rather than as a Spaniard. As a young man, he went to Rome, and worked as an assistant to Domitius Afer, a well-known lawyer. He probably returned to Spain about 60 A.D., and taught rhetoric for about ten years. In the neighborhood of 70 A.D., he was appointed to the first publicly supported chair of rhetoric by the Emperor Vespasian. For a period of about twenty years he taught rhetoric in Rome and practiced law as well. His students came from leading families, some from the imperial family itself; and some of his clients appear to have been equally prominent. He became very wealthy and was granted the privileges of the rank and name of consul. He was born about 35 A.D., and died not long after the year 90.

Quintilian intended his chief work, the *Institutio Oratoria,* written near the end of his life, primarily for the use of those who would bring up and instruct Geta, the son of his friend Marcellus Victorius, as well as the elder of his own two sons. Of course he expected others to read it since he published it. His elder son died during its creation while the younger as well as the young mother of both had died not long before its inception. Quintilian was haunted by the fear that he would die before his elder son; and his primary intention together with his fear may help to explain a certain characteristic of the book. Its objective is to outline the best training for an orator—an important task in Rome of the first century; but it is characterized by an almost complete absence of reflective consideration of the recommendations that it embodies and of the facts upon which those recommendations might be thought in part to rest. Perhaps Quintilian relied upon knowledge among his associates as to his philosophical views, supposing that they would be taken for granted, and regarding publication only as a kind accommodation to a public clamorous after his latest thoughts. Perhaps the fear of leaving his work unfinished drove him to the superficiality that it betrays. Perhaps he was afraid of being caught philosophizing, a mode of thought very dangerous at the time because many professors of philosophy publicly opposed the dynastic ambitions of the emperors. Perhaps Quintilian was simply too shallow a mind to engage in careful thought, or to feel the need for justifying the recommendations he offered by anything other than his own position of social and educational eminence. But whatever the explanation, Quintilian's philosophy of education falls well within the fringe of doctrines, discussed in Chapter I, about any one of which it is somewhat arbitrary to say either that it is or that it is not a philosophy of that subject.

Nonetheless, because the *Institutio Oratoria* represents an important point of view with respect to the objectives of training and instruction, we shall endeavor to state the facts upon which Quintilian's recommendations depend so far as he expressed them, to set down the main features of the recommendations he advanced, and to winnow out of a rather long work such philosophical theories as it is reasonable to suppose Quintilian thought relevant to his educational mission.

EDUCATIONAL THEORY

STATEMENTS OF FACT

Like most of those who have written on education and who are regarded as philosophers of that subject as well, Quintilian expressed opinions as to the facts out of which his recommendations grew; but his statements of fact were few, undeveloped, and scattered. They suggest views of a psychological sort.

The psychology suggested is that every human being harbors three kinds of capacity: that for impulsive behavior, that for passive cognition, and that for reasoning. The capacity for impulsive action is simply the power of acting in this way or that; and Quintilian's work suggests that, initially, the human being is a reservoir of energy capable of being channeled in any direction whatever.[1] The activation of the power of passive cognition determines the direction that impulsive energy assumes. Through the senses, various objects and actions are brought into awareness. They are retained there by memory, repeated in imitation, and mixed and elaborated by imagination. Upon some of these objects and actions, impulse focuses; and the result is desire which varies from one time and person to another. Reason is the power to discover what is true and good, and its office is actively to govern the desires that result from a cooperation between the passive power and the impulsive energy of human nature. The result is a character or personality, i.e., a certain pattern of impulses, enduring through life, and established by reason.

Although every human being harbors these capacities, the degree of excellence to which they may develop varies from one person to another. Some have greater and some less impulsive energy; the powers of some for sensory discrimination, for remembering, for imitation, and for imagination are unusually active or dull; and the capacity for reason is high in some and low in others. Each capacity may vary in degree on a scale running continuously from high to low. Those persons, however, whose capacities fall at the lower end of one or all of these dimensions are rare; and those in whom a balanced character, formed out of a normal or high functioning of capacities, cannot be developed are very few.

The capacity for normal or superior development seems to have been regarded by Quintilian as independent of sex. He argued that if a child is to be reared well, the nurse must be a philosopher or something like one, and both parents well educated. He cites instances of women who rose to great heights of eloquence and who assisted in the training of their sons. It should be noted that it was not altogether unusual for women to be highly trained in Rome, and that the cultivated Roman lady was much less rare than her counterpart in the Athens of Plato. Quintilian, however, made no explicit provision for the training of girls.

The normal or superior character develops, Quintilian seems to have believed, through three stages. For several years after birth, the child is chiefly an impulsive being, the passive powers of cognition remaining unorganizable and reason inoperative. During this time, the child's mind is pliable and easly moulded;[2] and this pliability consists in the failure of impulse to have selected its own objectives for action and the possibility that a wide variety of these may be supplied from without by deliberately offering them to the mind through the senses.

The second stage begins some little time before the age of seven. In it the power of fixing objects of sense begins to awaken. This fixation consists in memory of what has been perceived and imitation of actions ob-

[1] Quintilian, *Institutio Oratoria*, Book I, Chapter XII, § 10.
[2] *Ibid.*, I, XII, 10.

served. In the first stage, of course, many objects and actions will have been noted; and unsystematic impulse will have directed the child toward avoiding or securing some of the objects and toward repeating some of the actions. But when memory awakens, it may be "quick to take in and faithful to retain impressions of what it receives";[3] and this power to remember enables the exercise of the power to imitate. Actions which the child remembers and on which he places a positive value, impulse will direct him to reproduce; and this imitation offers the possibility of learning.

In the third stage, imagination first, and then reason come into play.[4] The power to remember and to reproduce is coupled with the power to mix and to combine what is passively admitted to the mind, and the result for the normal boy is a somewhat wild and exuberant imagination. Images are summoned up of things which never existed, and actions are engaged in which were never observed. But with time, the wild growth is pruned by reason; the "critical faculty" distinguishes between good and bad images, good and bad actions, and between true and false statements. At the end of this stage, the person is mature; an enduring and coherent set of impulses has been established by providing for native energy a clearly understood set of goals together with knowledge of the ways in which they may be realized.

There is no single passage in the *Institutio Oratoria* where this course of personal development is set down. A few scattered statements describe the child at different periods of his life, but that this is the normal pattern of development is as much suggested as it is stated by Quintilian. Notwithstanding, one opinion sometimes attributed to him,[5] the opinion that the child is simply an imperfect adult, was not precisely his own. ". . . a child fully formed in every limb," he said, "is likely to grow up a puny weakling. The young should be more daring and inventive and should rejoice in their inventions, even though correctness and severity are still to be acquired. Exuberance is easily remedied, but barrenness is incurable, be your efforts what they may. To my mind the boy who gives least promise is one in whom the critical faculty develops in advance of the imagination. I like to see the first fruits of the mind copious to excess and almost extravagant in their profusion."[6]

Quintilian's book was intended to outline the training of a man who would engage in public life; and it is not unremarkable that there

---

3 *Ibid.*, I, ɪɪɪ, § 1.

4 *Ibid.*, II, ɪv, § 6.

5 William Boyd, *The History of Western Education*, Adam and Charles Black, London, 1947, Fourth Edition, p. 73.

6 *Institutio Oratoria*, II, ɪv, §§ 6–7.

is no explicit discussion of the nature and problems of society and of the individual's relation to it. His interests were apparently closely bound up with those of the ruling class in Rome, and he may have feared that such a discussion would be thought subversive. His pupils were destined to occupy positions in the Roman ruling class, or in a corresponding class in the provinces; and no doubt, he intended to develop in them that sort of character which would enable them to fit comfortably into their administrative, juridical, or ornamental posts.

These posts were in Rome; but they were also in cities from the Rhine to the deserts of Africa and from London to the Euphrates. The Roman nobility exercised ownership over immense tracts of land, which were tilled by many slaves and freemen who worked for hire. There was much commerce also dependent upon slavery; and into the coffers of the Roman nobility immense revenues poured, while a commercial class of great wealth flourished there as well. Beneath the noble and commercial classes, thousands of impoverished citizens lived idly on the public dole of bread, watched the games provided for their amusement and their favor, and loitered in the many public baths. Political authority emanated from the imperial office; governors with large staffs of bureaucrats were appointed to the various regions which the city ruled. In these regions, considerable bodies of local law and custom remained unaltered. By no means were all the people of these regions Roman citizens. Imperial courts were introduced, using Roman law to settle controversies between Roman citizens, and local laws for controversies involving persons who could not claim the rights attaching to that citizenship. There must have been many legal problems rising out of the juxtaposition of local and Roman law. The emperor continued to observe the ancient forms of senatorial power, receiving or exacting the senate's approval of his possession of the office; but the *de facto* source of imperial power was the army. Its allegiance was bought with money and lands and transferred to others by larger offers of the same. The empire paid taxes relatively easily during a considerable period of prosperity, and supported a wild growth of luxury, refinement, and vice in the wealthy classes of the imperial city.

On the grand scale, life in the empire during Quintilian's time was peaceful; no serious wars with peoples beyond its borders threatened. The administration earlier established by Augustus worked well. But internally, the life of the empire was subject to much disturbance. In Rome, many felt that they should wear the purple, and this feeling constantly threatened authority in the army and the security of imperial power. Consequently, when there were not revolutions, there were assassinations to prevent them. And the entire empire was covered by a system of informers whose profit it was, especially when the emperor might confiscate the fortunes of wealthy but condemned suspects, to render the lives of the innocent and the guilty as circumspect, and in many cases as short, as possible.

Quintilian seems not to have questioned the economic and political structure of the empire. Presumably, his students presented cultivated speeches in the forum, before the senate, played a part in the administration of imperial institutions, and in the courts dealt with the many legal problems which arose out of the geographical overlapping of Roman and local law as well as the usual problems of economic and social life. But nowhere does Quintilian discuss Roman or imperial institutions; they simply loom in the background as the life into which he knew his orator would be absorbed.

RECOMMENDATIONS

The goal which Quintilian recommended to teachers of rhetoric was the creation of a certain type of character. He saw about him in Rome many persons who enjoyed all the privileges of wealth and nobility in a completely cosmopolitan city, and who used those privileges for refined and elaborate but often shallow and vicious purposes. The emperor Vespasian under whom he first received his academic appointment sprang from a rural family and endeavored to render the tastes and activities of Roman life more simple. This effort was supported by a faction of the aristocracy which had not ceased to hope that the republic with its more austere tastes and less complex manner of living might be re-established. Many of the rural gentry were ennobled, and sat in the senate. Quintilian shared their admiration for the simpler life, and may have been appointed to a position of educational influence in order to further Vespasian's aim. The kind of man he hoped to create by his training was "a good man skilled in speaking."[7]

Skill in speaking is required in order that any good man should be effective in governmental administration, in the courts, or in public assemblies. But this skill must be accompanied by virtue if it is to be anything more than the art of the demagogue. Virtue consists in doing one's duty, and in maintaining internal balance in a world as insecure as was that of Quintilian. But both duty and equanimity required much knowledge, and a good man skilled in speaking was also well informed.

Quintilian argued that a good orator must necessarily be a good man. First, nature does everything for the best; and since she has provided speech for man, she must have provided good speech for good men and only the good. Secondly, to be a good orator one must be intelligent; and no intelligent man would fail to use his gifts for good rather than evil

[7] *Ibid.*, XII, i, § 1.

purposes. Thirdly, it takes so much time to become a good orator that there will have been no time for evil designs. Moreover, fourthly, a good man will be more convincing in his presentation to a judge or any other audience even though he may say what is false—something which may be necessary in defending the innocent as well as those whose guilt is offset by a greater virtue.

Quintilian commends the good man skilled in speaking as the ultimate goals of the activities of those who read his book; and subordinate to this, he advances a procedure by which that goal might be accomplished. The procedure is a course of training, beginning at birth and running to manhood. There are four stages in it, and two aspects of it— that of method and that of curriculum.

The first period covers the first several years of life. During it, the child should be surrounded by beneficent influences. His parents, his nurse, his companions, and his pedagogue (a person, often a slave, charged with general supervision of the child) should be a good character. The child is primarily a bundle of dynamic but, as yet, unformed impulses; and lest evil should receive early encouragement, good objects and actions alone should be presented as targets for his aims. The method of training is to provide a good environment in which unformed energies may develop.

The child should be taught to speak Greek first, and Latin along with it only a little later. Since Latin literature is derived from the Greek, Latin will be picked up spontaneously in any case. All who surround the child should speak well lest inadequate speech become ingrained and native habit.

The second period begins some little time before the age of seven in most children. It commences when the senses, memory, and the power of imitation become alert. The teacher should be of good character for the same reason as before. He should devote careful attention to the individual child in order not to tax his powers so highly as to prevent learning; and the process of learning should be made attractive and pleasant in every possible way. Flogging, a practice common in Roman schools, Quintilian strongly censures, and for reasons that are correct.

During this period, the child should learn to read and write the languages that he began to speak in the first. The alphabet should be taught by use of ivory letters because they are attractive; and learning to write should be facilitated for the child by his running a pen through the shapes of letters cut into a board. Reading should be steady but not hurried because undue haste taxes the child beyond his capacities. Some say that elementary arithmetic should be taught at this period,[8] but Quintilian makes no mention of it in the *Institutio Oratoria*. Time would be

[8] Cf. William M. Smail, *Quintilian on Education*, Oxford, The Clarendon Press, 1938, p. xxiv.

devoted to games because relaxation helps study, and because play reveals character and capacity to the discerning eye. Reading, writing, and more formal games can be learned at this period because the senses can discriminate objects, memory can fix them in mind, and the power to imitate enables the child to reproduce them.

The method of administering this education should be that of a school. Quintilian does not say so; but a chapter advocating the latter as opposed to private tutoring at home immediately follows a chapter concerning the second period. Moreover, it was the practice in Rome to send children to a school at about the age of seven. A school, Quintilian argued, has all the advantages that a home education might offer, and more besides.

In the third period, the child studies chiefly grammar. The practice in Rome was to engage in this study in the school of the grammarian, separate from the elementary school, and entered at the age of thirteen or fourteen. Quintilian mentions no separate school,[9] and complains that advanced training in the school of rhetoric, a third school in Roman practice, begins too late. It began at about the age of sixteen. He seems to have intended to telescope the elementary and grammatical training, and this suggests that he may have considered combining the elementary and the secondary schools.

In Quintilian's time, the word "grammar" referred not only to the study of the history and nature of language as it does today, but also to literature; and the chief content of study during the third period is Greek and Latin poetry. It would be dealt with in the way a modern grammarian and philologist would handle it, but also in the manner of a critical interpreter. The poetry considered in class ought to be carefully censored in order to provide only images of good character and noble deeds for the developing interests of the child to fix upon. The active memory and power of imitation should be used to the full.

The methods of instruction ought to be those of the lecture combined with questions from students and discussion with them, and of recitation, oral reading, exercise in literary composition, practice of music, and gymnastic. Careful attention should be devoted to the individual student to discover his peculiar interests and capacities, and to cope with his peculiar problems; and competition should be employed as a stimulus to excellence of performance. The objective of these procedures is to lay a foundation for clear and eloquent expression in oratory.

Although poetry is the chief study, other subjects must be included in the third period. These are philosophy, music, mathematics, and physical training. Philosophy is necessary for the interpretation of poetry.

[9] Quintilian promises to tell us at what age each subject should be commenced (I, III, § 18), but he does not make his promise good.

Much of the latter, Lucretius for example, is the poetic expression of philosophical doctrine, and cannot be correctly interpreted unless it is understood as such.

Music must be studied because it relieves mental stress, improves the voice of the speaker, and enables the understanding of meter and accent in poetry. All weak and effeminate strains must be excluded from the curriculum. Quintilian seems to have intended the performance of vocal and instrumental music rather than the study of its theory.

Mathematics included arithmetic, geometry, and astronomy. The orator must be able to speak on all subjects, and he may very well be obliged to calculate. Geometry will be useful in dealing with boundary suits, in sharpening the mind, and in developing the ability to create rigorous and conclusive arguments. Astronomy will show the student that celestial events are governed by law, and will enable the orator to dispel public panics caused by eclipses.

Physical training, kept well short of athleticism, will lay a foundation for poise of the public speaker and for good gesture.

In the fourth period of training, rhetoric is studied. Quintilian speaks of this period as if it were to be spent in a separate school,[10] and urged that it be initiated not at a fixed age, but when the child is ready. He might still be in need of training by the grammarian; and although Quintilian jealously argued that the duties of the rhetor and the grammarian be sharply distinguished and that overlapping be rigidly precluded, he provided for such a child distinct hours for continued training in grammar and the new training in rhetoric. Boys and young men (Roman youth matured early) must sit apart, and Quintilian recognized the problems of discipline that come with classes of different age groups. The child is ready for training in rhetoric when the development of his imagination suits him for literary composition and for public rhetorical performance, and when his reason begins to be competent for exercising personal criticism of ideas found in literature. The methods of training in the rhetorical school are those of reading and composition, practice in declamation and debate, and lectures with questions and discussion from the floor. There is the usual advocacy of consideration for the individual student, the awakening of his interests in the subject-matter rather than use of compulsion, and kindly but reserved treatment of him. All these methods, however, must be accompanied by common sense; and in developing the individual bent, the teacher must remember that a successful orator must learn many things which he will find initially tedious, difficult, and dull.

Rhetoric is the art of speaking well, and the whole of life provides

[10] *Institutio Oratoria,* I, Preface, § 21.

its subject-matter since one may need to speak well about any topic whatever. Consequently, training in rhetoric must provide a general, but not necessarily a detailed knowledge about all important aspects of human existence. These constitute the themes of great literature both ancient and contemporary with Quintilian. In it, the wisdom of the past and of the present is elucidated and distilled; consequently, training in rhetoric is not merely training in speech, but a study of all the important phases of human life in order that that speech, however artful, should proceed toward good objectives.

The curriculum of the rhetorical school should be broad. It should include an advanced study of poetry and drama; of prose including history; of the orators, especially the legal; of law, of philosophy, and of the theory of rhetoric.

In those who have the capacity, the four periods of training and instruction, Quintilian contended, will develop the type of the orator, the man skilled in speaking who must be a good man, i.e., who will surely put his gifts to work for the public service and be able to retain his equanimity in that service and in retirement. The conduct of study, requiring affection for the child, awakening of native interest, individual consideration, and stimulation of moderate competition between students, will develop the orator in those for whom it is possible; and in those for whom it is not, it will foster the maximum development of their "weaker understandings." In each stage, the methods of instruction will be geared to the awakening powers of the child as will the content of instruction also. In this way, Quintilian urged the creation of orators and recommended the means thereto.

PHILOSOPHY OF EDUCATION

WE MUST NOW CONSIDER Quintilian's philosophy of education as opposed to his educational theory. We have pointed out that there is little philosophy of education in Quintilian's *Institutio Oratoria*. It remains to indicate the respects in which his doctrine is incomplete or inadequate, as well as those in which it seems to be, more properly speaking, philosophical.

ANALYSIS AND EDUCATION

Quintilian seems to have felt no need whatever for an analysis of the ideas he employed in his educational theory. It is difficult to believe that there were not many which were obscure for the thinkers of his day.

"Wisdom," "courage," "temperance," "equity," "justice," "virtue"—all these terms and many like them are used by Quintilian to describe subjects of the curriculum and to set forth the nature of the orator he would create; but surely, in a time and place as corrupt as his own, there must have been a considerable uncertainty or unclarity as to the meaning of terms like these. His words at times suggest that virtuous conduct implies knowledge of the virtue it exhibits; but beyond this there is not even a suggestion as to the meaning of the various ethical terms in his educational theory. He held that dialectic, one of the areas of philosophy as it was divided in his day, consisted in the definition of words and the clarification of ideas, and that very little was necessary to the skill of the orator. He was an orator and engaged in very little of it. Doubtless, he was not capable of minute reflection when he wrote the *Institutio Oratoria,* and the absence of analytical thought is a chief ingredient in the shallowness that is the most salient feature of Quintilian's book for the careful reader.

METAPHYSICS AND EDUCATION

Quintilian apparently entertained some metaphysical views. In several places, his words suggest that there is, behind the observable world, a principle of order that governs and controls the latter. There is no argument for this view but only a suggestion of it. There is the further suggestion that the principles of ethics depend upon metaphysics, i.e., upon what Quintilian refers to as physics. Together, these suggestions imply that from the nature of reality, the world of fact can be explained, and the nature of moral value as well as the things that possess it derived. This would be an important doctrine in Quintilian's thought if he actually worked it out, for it would provide a metaphysical explanation of education. But he never worked it out, and it is not even clear that his words do not merely suggest it.

ETHICS AND EDUCATION

There is a corresponding lack of explicit ethical discussion in the *Institutio Oratoria.* In Book XII, Chapter II, we are informed that the orator must read philosophy—apparently a reinforcement of the recommendation that it be included in the third and fourth stages of training; and the chief ground is that the main topic of philosophy is the good life for man. No particular school should be adhered to, all ethical philosophies having something important to contribute to the formation of the orator's character. This view, however, amounts to a recommendation that ethical philosophy be included in the training of the orator, not to an ethical discussion of doctrines in educational theory. But it does suggest an ethical position with regard to the objective of his educational theory.

The type of character that Quintilian wished to create is that of the person acquainted with all the traditions of his culture, developed as far as his capacities will allow in all directions, of use as an orator to society, and possessed of inner resources which render him, notwithstanding, to some extent independent of that society. The negative side of this emphasis is seen in his rejection of detailed philosophical or scientific knowledge as fostering an attitude of withdrawal from social responsibility—an attitude widely attributed in his day to professional philosophers. The ideal character that motivates his educational theory is largely that now called "humanistic," and is an inherent part of the tradition stemming from the Sophists and Isocrates. Like Plato, Quintilian believed that the ultimate objective of training is the creation of a good man; but like Isocrates, he contended that virtue depended not upon detailed scientific knowledge of the nature of things (a Platonic view), but upon general knowledge of humanity—something incorporated in literary tradition by his time, and embodying not only the insights into human life afforded by more ancient Greek writers, but also those of subsequent Greek and Roman thinkers as well.

Although this is the ethical ideal that lies behind his work, Quintilian nowhere explicitly endeavored to establish it. The entire enterprise of justifying ethical statements, of showing what an ethical justification is, and of providing a statement of the nature of goodness and rightness seems foreign to his interests and to his capacities. His work suggests an ethical view of education that is inadequate and incomplete. It asserts that the supremely good life, the one recommended in his educational theory, is that of the humane man; but it is incomplete and inadequate because it offers no justification, and no definition of ethical terms which would elucidate the statement of the humanist goal.

EPISTEMOLOGY AND EDUCATION

There is even less reason to attribute to Quintilian an epistemological treatment of education. In the *Institutio Oratoria* there is no discussion of the nature of knowledge and of the criteria for it. Consequently, there is no derivation from views on either of these subjects of a theory of learning. There is much discussion, and some of it very valuable, of the conditions under which learning may most readily occur; but this is psychology rather than epistemology.

There is nonetheless a suggestion of a criterion of knowledge. Quintilian's practice is to appeal to authority in support of many of his assertions. An authority is a person agreement with whose utterances guarantees the truth of one's own, and Quintilian often refers to Cicero among others for support. This practice suggests the view that however knowledge may be arrived at, its justification lies in the discovery that an authority has supported the statements it involves. That this is a criterion of knowledge fits well with the emphasis on literary tradition—as opposed to painstaking scientific and philosophical thought—embodied in Quintilian's recommendations.

It should be noted that although Quintilian's work contains little philosophy of education, it has had a considerable influence in the development both of educational theory and of the philosophy of that subject. Until the collapse of the Western Empire, the *Institutio Oratoria* was widely influential as a textbook in education. The Middle Ages possessed no complete version of it and strayed far from the ideal that inspired it. But near the beginning of the fifteenth century, a complete text was discovered in the monastery of St. Gall; and the *Institutio Oratoria* became one of the important factors in the reconsideration of the purposes of education, and the revival of the humanistic ideal, in the Renaissance.

A Guide to Selections from *Institutio Oratoria*

In the excerpts from Book I, Quintilian argues that a school education, from about the age of seven, is more effective than a private education at home. The former is administered through fairly large classes while the latter assumes the form of tutorial conferences. His particular arguments all conclude that the environment of the school is more likely to produce an orator than is that of the home. They turn on the view that the successful orator must have achieved adjustment to other persons and a competence in literary and humanistic studies. Hence, they can be viewed as relevant to these objectives of education as well as to the now somewhat obsolete goal of success in rhetoric.

In the excerpts from Book II, Quintilian describes the curriculum offered by the teacher of rhetoric. He distinguishes three kinds of narration; and by showing that two occur in literature while the third occurs in history, and by asserting that the student of the rhetorician should first read history, he provides a continuity between the elementary study of literature and the more advanced study of rhetoric. He presents several methods for teaching oratory, and describes the subject matter of that art as anything upon which the orator is required to speak. Since the orator may be required to speak on anything whatever, it follows that he should learn everything; but the universal knowledge thus demanded of him need extend only to the general features of all the branches of knowledge, not to their details. Quintilian's work is influenced by the notion of the liberal arts formulated by Varro in the first century B.C.—a conception of the curriculum which included the general features of the sciences as they were then conceived, as well as of the arts.

In Book XII, Quintilian describes the concept of an orator, argues that an orator must be a good man, and defends the view that an education of the kind he has described will produce one. His argument for the view that an orator must be a good man seems strained and artificial because the question is now of little importance; but it can be read in light of an analogous modern question, namely, whether a schooling which brings about social adjustment to his fellows and a general knowledge of the humanistic subjects—of the sciences as well as of the arts—will produce a person who does what he ought. Put simply, it is the question whether bringing a person to a general knowledge of things is sufficient to assure his possession of a good character.

SELECTIONS FROM

*Institutio Oratoria**

▬◄◆►▬

BOOK I

II.   But the time has come for the boy to grow up little by little, to leave the nursery and tackle his studies in good earnest. This therefore is the place to discuss the question as to whether it is better to have him educated privately at home or hand him over to some large school and those whom I may call public instructors. . . .

It is above all things necessary that our future orator, who   [*18*] will have to live in the utmost publicity and in the broad daylight of public life, should become accustomed from his childhood to move in society without fear and habituated to a life far removed from that of the pale student, the solitary and recluse. His mind requires constant stimulus and excitement, whereas retirement such as has just been mentioned induces languor and the mind becomes mildewed like things that are left in the dark, or else flies to the opposite extreme and becomes puffed up with empty conceit; for he who has no standard of comparison by which

* Reprinted by permission of the publishers and the Loeb Classical Library, from *The Institutio Oratoria of Quintilian,* translated by H. E. Butler, Cambridge, Mass.: Harvard University Press. Footnotes omitted.

to judge his own powers will necessarily rate them too high. Again when the fruits of his study have to be displayed to the public gaze, our re- [19] cluse is blinded by the sun's glare, and finds everything new and unfamiliar, for though he has learnt what is required to be done in public, his learning is but the theory of a hermit. I say nothing of friend- [20] ships which endure unbroken to old age having acquired the binding force of a sacred duty: for initiation in the same studies has all the sanctity of initiation in the same mysteries of religion. And where shall he acquire that instinct which we call common feeling, if he secludes himself from that intercourse which is natural not merely to mankind but even to dumb animals? Further, at home he can only learn what is taught to himself, while at school he will learn what is taught others as well. He will hear many merits praised and many faults corrected every day; he will derive equal profit from hearing the indolence of a comrade rebuked or his industry commended. Such praise will incite him to emulation, he will think it a disgrace to be outdone by his contemporaries [22] and a distinction to surpass his seniors. All such incentives provide a valuable stimulus, and though ambition may be a fault in itself, it is often the mother of virtues. . . .

Further while emulation promotes progress in the more ad- [26] vanced pupils, beginners who are still of tender years derive greater pleasure from imitating their comrades than their masters, just because it is easier. For children still in the elementary stages of education can scarce dare hope to reach that complete eloquence which they understand to be their goal: their ambition will not soar so high, but they will imitate the vine which has to grasp the lower branches of the tree on which it is trained before it can reach the topmost boughs. So true is this that it is the master's duty as well, if he is engaged on the task of training un- [27] formed minds and prefers practical utility to a more ambitious programme, not to burden his pupils at once with tasks to which their strength is unequal, but to curb his energies and refrain from talking over the heads of his audience. . . . It is a good thing therefore that a boy [29] should have a companion whom he will desire first to imitate and then to surpass: thus he will be led to aspire to higher achievement. I would add that the instructors themselves cannot develop the same intelligence and energy before a single listener as they can when inspired by the presence of a numerous audience.

For eloquence depends in the main on the state of the mind, [30] which must be moved, conceive images and adapt itself to suit the nature of the subject which is the theme of speech. Further the loftier and the more elevated the mind, the more powerful will be the forces which move it: consequently praise gives it growth and effort increase, and the thought that it is doing something great fills it with joy. The duty of stoop- [31]

ing to expend that power of speaking which has been acquired at the cost of such effort upon an audience of one gives rise to a silent feeling of disdain, and the teacher is ashamed to raise his voice above the ordinary conversational level. Imagine the air of a declaimer, or the voice of an orator, his gait, his delivery, the movements of his body, the emotions of his mind, and to go no further, the fatigue of his exertions, all for the sake of one listener! Would he not seem little less than a lunatic? No, there would be no such thing as eloquence, if we spoke only with one person at a time. . . .

IV.   As soon as the boy has learned to read and write without difficulty, it is the turn for the teacher of literature. My words apply equally to Greek and Latin masters, though I prefer that a start should be made with a Greek: in either case the method is the same. This profession [2] may be most briefly considered under two heads, the art of speaking correctly and the interpretation of the poets; but there is more beneath the surface than meets the eye. For the art of writing is combined with that of speaking, and correct reading precedes interpretation, while in [3] each of these cases criticism has its work to perform. . . . Nor is it sufficient to have read the poets only; every kind of writer must be carefully [4] studied, not merely for the subject matter, but for the vocabulary; for words often acquire authority from their use by a particular author. Nor can such training be regarded as complete if it stop short of music, for the teacher of literature has to speak of metre and rhythm: nor again if he be ignorant of astronomy, can he understand the poets; for they, to mention no further points, frequently give their indications of time by reference to the rising and setting of the stars. Ignorance of philosophy is an equal drawback, since there are numerous passages in almost every poem based on the most intricate questions of natural philosophy, while among the Greeks we have Empedocles and among our own poets Varro and Lucretius, all of whom have expounded their philosophies in verse. No small powers of eloquence also are required to enable the teacher [5] to speak appropriately and fluently on the various points which have just been mentioned. For this reason those who criticise the art of teaching literature as trivial and lacking in substance put themselves out of court. Unless the foundations of oratory are well and truly laid by the teaching of literature, the superstructure will collapse. The study of literature is a necessity for boys and the delight of old age, the sweet companion of our privacy and the sole branch of study which has more solid substance than display. . . .

X.   There are other subjects of education which must be studied [2] simultaneously with literature. These being independent studies are capable of completion without a knowledge of oratory, while on the other hand they cannot by themselves produce an orator. The question has consequently been raised as to whether they are necessary for this purpose. What, say some, has the knowledge of the way to describe an equi- [3] lateral triangle on a given straight line got to do with pleading in the law-courts or speaking in the senate? Will an acquaintance with the names and intervals of the notes of the lyre help an orator to defend a criminal or direct the policy of his country? They will perhaps pro- [4] duce a long list of orators who are most effective in the courts but have never sat under a geometrician and whose understanding of music is confined to the pleasure which their ears, like those of other men, derive from it. To such critics I reply, and Cicero frequently makes the same remark in his Orator, that I am not describing any orator who actually exists or has existed, but have in my mind's eye an ideal orator, perfect down to the smallest detail. . . .

So too the teacher of geometry, music or other subjects which [6] I would class with these, will not be able to create the perfect orator (who like the philosopher ought to be a wise man), but none the less these arts will assist in his perfection. . . .

Timagenes asserts that music is the oldest of the arts related [10] to literature, a statement which is confirmed by the testimony of the greatest of poets in whose songs we read that the praise of heroes and of gods were sung to the music of the lyre at the feasts of kings. Does not Iopas, the Vergilian bard, sing, "The wandring moon and labours of the Sun" and the like? Whereby the supreme poet manifests most clearly that music is united with the knowledge even of things divine. . . .

As regards geometry, it is granted that portions of this science [34] are of value for the instruction of children: for admittedly it exercises their minds, sharpens their wits and generates quickness of perception. But it is considered that the value of geometry resides in the process of learning, and not as with other sciences in the knowledge thus acquired. Such is the general opinion. But it is not without good reason that [35] some of the greatest men have devoted special attention to this science. Geometry has two divisions; one is concerned with numbers, the other with figures. Now knowledge of the former is a necessity not merely to the orator, but to any one who has had even an elementary education. Such knowledge is frequently required in actual cases, in which a speaker is regarded as deficient in education, I will not say if he hesitates in making a calculation, but even if he contradicts the calculation which he states in words by making an uncertain or inappropriate gesture with his fingers. Again linear geometry is frequently required in cases, as in lawsuits [36] about boundaries and measurements. But geometry and oratory are related in a yet more important way than this. In the first place logical [37] development is one of the necessities of geometry. And is it not equally a necessity for oratory? Geometry arrives at its conclusions from definite premises, and by arguing from what is certain proves what was previously uncertain. Is not this just what we do in speaking? Again are not the problems of geometry almost entirely solved by the syllogistic method, a fact which makes the majority assert that geometry bears a closer resemblance to logic than to rhetoric? But even the orator will sometimes, though rarely prove his point by formal logic. . . .

But geometry soars still higher to the consideration of the sys-   [46] tem of the universe: for by its calculations it demonstrates the fixed and ordained courses of the stars, and thereby we acquire the knowledge that all things are ruled by order and destiny, a consideration which may at times be of value to an orator. . . .

BOOK II

IV.   I shall now proceed to indicate what I think should be the first subjects in which the rhetorician should give instruction, and shall postpone for a time our consideration of the art of rhetoric in the narrow sense in which that term is popularly used. For in my opinion it is most desirable that we should commence with something resembling the subjects already acquired under the teacher of literature.

Now there are three forms of narrative, without counting the   [2] type used in actual legal cases. First there is the fictitious narrative as we get it in tragedies and poems, which is not merely not true but has little resemblance to truth. Secondly, there is the realistic narrative as presented by comedies, which, though not true, has yet a certain verisimilitude. Thirdly, there is the historical narrative, which is an exposition of actual fact. Poetic narratives are the property of the teacher of literature. The rhetorician therefore should begin with the historical narrative, whose force is in proportion to its truth . . . it should be neither dry nor jejune (for why spend so much labour over our studies if a bald and naked   [3] statement of fact is regarded as sufficiently expressive?); nor on the other hand must it be tortuous or revel in elaborate descriptions, such as those in which so many are led to indulge by a misguided imitation of poetic license. Both these extremes are faults; but that which springs from   [4] poverty of wit is worse than that which is due to imaginative excess. For we cannot demand or expect a perfect style from boys. But there is greater promise in a certain luxuriance of mind, in ambitious effort and an ardour that leads at times to ideas bordering on the extravagant.   [5] I have no objection to a little exuberance in the young learner. Nay, I would urge teachers too like nurses to be careful to provide softer food for still undeveloped minds and to suffer them to take their fill of the milk of the more attractive studies. For the time being the body may be somewhat plump, but maturer years will reduce it to a sparer habit. Such

plumpness gives hope of strength; a child fully formed in every limb   [6]
is likely to grow up a puny weakling. The young should be more daring
and inventive and should rejoice in their inventions, even though correctness and severity are still to be acquired. Exuberance is easily remedied,
but barrenness is incurable, be your efforts what they may. To my mind
the boy who gives least promise is one in whom the critical faculty   [7]
develops in advance of the imagination. I like to see the first fruits of the
mind copious to excess and almost extravagant in their profusion. The
years as they pass will skim off much of the froth, reason will file away
many excrescences, and something too will be removed by what I may
perhaps call the wear and tear of life, so long as there is sufficient material
to admit of cutting and chiselling away. And there will be sufficient, if
only we do not draw the plate too thin to begin with, so that it runs the
risk of being broken if the graver cut too deep. Those of my readers who
know their Cicero will not be surprised that I take this view: for does   [8]
he not say "I would have the youthful mind run riot in the luxuriance of
its growth"?

   We must, therefore, take especial care, above all where boys are
concerned, to avoid a dry teacher, even as we avoid a dry and arid soil
for plants that are still young and tender. For with such a teacher   [9]
their growth is stunted and their eyes are turned earthwards, and they
are afraid to rise above the level of daily speech. Their leanness is regarded as a sign of health and their weakness as a sign of sound judgment,
and while they are content that their work should be devoid of faults
they fall into the fault of being devoid of merit. So let not the ripeness of
vintage come too soon nor the must return harsh while yet in the vat; thus
it will last for years and mellow with age.

V.   I will speak of the theory of declamation a little later. In the
meantime, as we are discussing the elementary stages of a rhetorical education, I think I should not fail to point out how greatly the rhetorician
will contribute to his pupils' progress, if he imitates the teacher of literature whose duty it is to expound the poets, and gives the pupils whom he
has undertaken to train, instruction in the reading of history and still
more of the orators. I myself have adopted this practice for the benefit of
a few pupils of suitable age whose parents thought it would be useful.
But though my intentions were excellent, I found that there were   [2]
two serious obstacles to success: long custom had established a different
method of teaching, and my pupils were for the most part full-grown
youths who did not require this form of teaching, but were taking my
work as their model. However, the fact that I have been somewhat late
in making the discovery is not a reason why I should be ashamed to   [3]
recommend it to those who come after me. I now know that this form of
teaching is practised by the Greeks, but is generally entrusted to assistants,

as the professors themselves consider that they have no time to give indi- vidual instruction to each pupil as he reads. And I admit that the form of lecture which this requires, designed as it is to make boys follow   [4] the written word with ease and accuracy, and even that which aims at teaching the meaning of any rare words that may occur, are to be re- garded as quite below the dignity of the teacher of rhetoric. On the other hand it is emphatically part of his profession and the under-   [5] taking which he makes in offering himself as a teacher of eloquence, to point out the merits of authors or, for that matter, any faults that may occur; and this is all the more the case, as I am not asking teachers to undertake the task of recalling their pupils to stand at their knee once more and of assisting them in the reading of whatever book they may select. It seems to me at once an easier and more profitable method   [6] to call for science and choose some one pupil—and it will be best to select them by turns—to read aloud, in order that they may at the same time learn the correct method of elocution. The case with which the speech selected for reading is concerned should then be explained, for if this   [7] be done they will have a clearer understanding of what is to be read. When the reading is commenced, no important point should be allowed to pass unnoticed either as regards the resourcefulness or the style shown in the treatment of the subject: the teacher must point out how the orator seeks to win the favour of the judge in his *exordium*, what clear- ness, brevity and sincerity, and at times what shrewd design and well- concealed artifice is shown in the statement of facts. . . .

It will, however, be the duty of the rhetorician not merely to   [13] teach these things, but to ask frequent questions as well, and test the critical powers of his class.

XXI.   As to the material of oratory, some have asserted that it is speech, as for instance Gorgias in the dialogue of Plato. If this view be accepted in the sense that the word "speech" is used of a discourse com- posed of any subject, then it is not the material, but the work, just as a statue is the work of the sculptor. For speeches like statues require art for their production. If on the other hand we interpret "speech" as indi- cating the words themselves, they can do nothing unless they are related to facts. Some again hold that the material consists of persuasive argu- ments. But they form part of the work, are produced by art and require material themselves. Some say that political questions provide the ma- terial. The mistake made by these lies not in the quality of their   [2] opinion but in its limitation. For political questions are material for elo- quence but not the only material. Some, on the ground that rhetoric is a virtue, make the material with which it deals to be the whole of life.   [3] Others, on the ground that life regarded as a whole does not provide material for every virtue, since most of them are concerned only with de- partments of life (justice, courage and self-control each having their own duties and their own end), would consequently restrict oratory to one particular department of life and place it in the practical or pragmatic department of ethics, that is to say the department of morals which deals with the business of life. . . .

But this material, as we call it, that is to say the things brought [7] before it, has been criticised by some, at times on the ground that it is limitless, and sometimes on the ground that it is not peculiar to oratory, which they have therefore dubbed a *discursive* art, because all is grist that comes to its mill. I have no serious quarrel with these critics, for they [8] acknowledge that rhetoric is concerned with every kind of material, though they deny that it has any peculiar material just because of that material's multiplicity. But in spite of this multiplicity, rhetoric is not unlimited in scope, and there are other minor arts whose material is characterised by the same multiplicity: such for instance is architecture, which deals with everything that is useful for the purpose of building: such too is the engraver's art which works on gold, silver, bronze, iron. As for sculpture, its activity extends to wood, ivory, marble, glass [9] and precious stones in addition to the materials already mentioned. . . .

Again, the objection that to discourse of what is good, ex- [12] pedient or just is the duty of philosophy presents no difficulty. For when such critics speak of a philosopher, they mean a good man. . . . Why then should I feel surprised to find that the orator whom I identify with the good man deals with the same material? There is all the less reason, [13] since I have already shown in the first book that philosophers only usurped this department of knowledge after it had been abandoned by the orators: it was always the peculiar property of rhetoric and the philosophers are really trespassers. Finally, since the discussion of whatever is brought before it is the task of dialectic, which is really a concise form of oratory, why should not this task be regarded as also being the appropriate material for continuous oratory?

There is a further objection made by certain critics, who say [14] "Well then, if the orator has to speak on every subject, he must be the master of all the arts." I might answer this criticism in the words of Cicero, in whom I find the following passage:—"In my opinion no one can be an absolutely perfect orator unless he has acquired a knowledge of all important subjects and arts." I however regard it as sufficient that an orator should not be actually ignorant of the subject on which he has to speak.

BOOK XII

I. The orator then, whom I am concerned to form, shall be the orator as defined by Marcus Cato, "a good man, skilled in speaking." But above all he must possess the quality which Cato places first and which is in the very nature of things the greatest and most important, that is, he must be a good man. This is essential not merely on account of the fact that, if the powers of eloquence serve only to lend arms to crime, there can be nothing more pernicious than eloquence to public and private welfare alike, while I myself, who have laboured to the best of my ability to contribute something of value to oratory, shall have rendered the worst of services to mankind, if I forge these weapons not for a soldier, but for a robber. But why speak of myself? Nature herself will have proved [2] not a mother, but a stepmother with regard to what we deem her greatest gift to man, the gift that distinguishes us from other living things, if she devised the power of speech to be the accomplice of crime, the foe to innocency and the enemy of truth. For it had been better for men to be born dumb and devoid of reason than to turn the gifts of providence to their mutual destruction. But this conviction of mine goes further. For I [3] do not merely assert that the ideal orator should be a good man, but I affirm that no man can be an orator unless he is a good man. For it is impossible to regard those men as gifted with intelligence who on being offered the choice between the two paths of virtue and of vice choose the latter, nor can we allow them prudence, when by the unforeseen issue of their own actions they render themselves liable not merely to the heaviest penalties of the laws, but to the inevitable torment of an evil con- [4] science. But if the view that a bad man is necessarily a fool is not merely held by philosophers, but is the universal belief of ordinary men, the fool will most assuredly never become an orator. To this must be added the fact that the mind will not find leisure even for the study of the noblest of tasks, unless it first be free from vice. The reasons for this are, first, that vileness and virtue cannot jointly inhabit in the selfsame heart and that it is as impossible for one and the same mind to harbour good and evil thoughts as it is for one man to be at once both good and evil: and secondly, that if the intelligence is to be concentrated on such a [5] vast subject as eloquence it must be free from all other distractions, among which must be included even those preoccupations which are free from blame. For it is only when it is free and self-possessed, with nothing to divert it or lure it elsewhere, that it will fix its attention solely on that goal, the attainment of which is the object of its preparations. . . .

. . . There is nothing so preoccupied, so distracted, so rent and torn [7] by so many and such varied passions as an evil mind. For when it cherishes some dark design, it is tormented with hope, care and anguish of spirit, and even when it has accomplished its criminal purpose, it is racked by anxiety, remorse and the fear of all manner of punishments. Amid such passions as these what room is there for literature or any virtuous pursuit? You might as well look for fruit in land that is choked with thorns and brambles. Well then, I ask you, is not simplicity of life essential if [8] we are to be able to endure the toil entailed by study? What can we hope to get from lust or luxury? Is not the desire to win praise one of the strongest stimulants to a passion for literature? But does that mean that we are to suppose that praise is an object of concern to bad men? Surely every one of my readers must by now have realised that oratory is in the main concerned with the treatment of what is just and honourable? Can a bad and unjust man speak on such themes as the dignity of the subject demands? Nay, even if we exclude the most important aspects of the [9] question now before us, and make the impossible concession that the best and worst of men may have the same talent, industry and learning, we are still confronted by the question as to which of the two is entitled to be called the better orator. The answer is surely clear enough: it will be he who is the better man. Consequently, the bad man and the perfect orator can never be identical. For nothing is perfect, if there exists some- [10] thing else that is better. However, as I do not wish to appear to adopt the practice dear to the Socratic of framing answers to my own questions, let me assume the existence of a man so obstinately blind to the truth as to venture to maintain that a bad man equipped with the same talents, industry and learning will be not a whit inferior to the good man as an orator; and let me show that he too is mad. There is one point at [11] any rate which no one will question, namely, that the aim of every speech is to convince the judge that the case which it puts forward is true and honourable. Well then, which will do this best, the good man or the bad? The good man will without doubt more often say what is true and honourable. But even supposing that his duty should, as I shall show may sometimes happen, lead him to make statements which are [12] false, his words are still certain to carry greater weight with his audience. On the other hand bad men, in their contempt for public opinion and their ignorance of what is right, sometimes drop their mask unawares, and are impudent in the statement of their case and shameless in their assertions. . . .

However, let us fly in the face of nature and assume that a bad man has been discovered who is endowed with the highest eloquence. I shall none the less deny that he is an orator. For I should not allow that every man who has shown himself ready with his hands was necessarily a brave man, because true courage cannot be conceived of without the accompaniment of virtue. Surely the advocate who is called to de- [24] fend the accused requires to be a man of honour, honour which greed cannot corrupt, influence seduce or fear dismay. Shall we then dignify the traitor, the deserter, the turncoat with the sacred name of orator? But if the quality which is usually termed goodness is to be found even in quite ordinary advocates, why should not the orator, who has not yet existed, but may still be born, be no less perfect in character than in excellence

of speech? It is no hack-advocate, no hireling pleader, nor yet to use   [*25*]
no harsher term, a serviceable attorney of the class generally known as
causidici, that I am seeking to form, but rather a man who to extraordi-
nary natural gifts has added a thorough mastery of all the fairest branches
of knowledge, a man sent by heaven to be the blessing of mankind, one
to whom all history can find no parallel, uniquely perfect in every detail
and utterly noble alike in thought and speech. How small a portion of all
these abilities will be required for the defence of the innocent, the   [*26*]
repression of crime or the support of truth against falsehood in suits involving questions of money? It is true that our supreme orator will bear
his part in such tasks, but his powers will be displayed with brighter
splendour in greater matters than these, when he is called upon to direct
the counsels of the senate and guide the people from the paths of error
to better things. . . .

. . . Again, will not this same man, whom we are striving to form,   [*28*]
if in time of war he be called upon to inspire his soldiers with courage for
the fray, draw for his eloquence on the innermost precepts of philosophy?
For how can men who stand upon the verge of battle banish all the
crowding fears of hardship, pain and death from their minds, unless those
fears be replaced by the sense of the duty that they owe their country, by
courage and the lively image of a soldier's honour? And assuredly the
man who will best inspire such feelings in others is he who has first   [*29*]
inspired them in himself. For however we strive to conceal it, insincerity
will always betray itself, and there was never in any man so great eloquence as would not begin to stumble and hesitate so soon as his words
ran counter to his inmost thoughts. Now a bad man cannot help   [*30*]
speaking things other than he feels. On the other hand, the good will
never be at a loss for honourable words or fail to find matter full of
virtue for utterance, since among his virtues practical wisdom will be one.
And even though his imagination lacks artifice to lend it charm, its own
nature will be ornament enough, for if honour dictate the words, we
shall find eloquence there as well. Therefore, let those that are   [*31*]
young, or rather let all of us, whatever our age, since it is never too late
to resolve to follow what is right, strive with all our hearts and devote
all our efforts to the pursuit of virtue and eloquence; and perchance it
may be granted to us to attain to the perfection that we seek. For since
nature does not forbid the attainment of either, why should not someone succeed in attaining both together? And why should not each of us
hope to be that happy man? But if our powers are inadequate to   [*32*]
such achievement, we shall still be the better for the double effort in proportion to the distance which we have advanced toward either goal. At
any rate let us banish from our hearts the delusion that eloquence, the
fairest of all things, can be combined with vice. The power of speaking is

even to be accounted an evil when it is found in evil men; for it makes its possessors yet worse than they were before. . . .

II.   Since then the orator is a good man, and such goodness cannot be conceived as existing apart from virtue, virtue, despite the fact that it is in part derived from certain natural impulses, will require to be perfected by instruction. The orator must above all things devote his attention to the formation of moral character and must acquire a complete knowledge of all that is just and honourable. For without this knowledge no one can be either a good man or skilled in speaking. . . .   [2] I will proceed to my next point, that no one will achieve sufficient skill even in speaking, unless he makes a thorough study of all the workings of nature and forms his character on the precepts of philosophy and the dictates of reason. For it is with good cause that Lucius Crassus, in the third book of the *de Oratore,* affirms that all that is said concerning   [5] equity, justice, truth and the good, and their opposites, forms part of the studies of an orator, and that the philosophers, when they exert their powers of speaking to defend these virtues, are using the weapons of rhetoric, not their own. But he also confesses that the knowledge of these subjects must be sought from the philosophers for the reason that, in his opinion, philosophy has more effective possession of them. And it is   [6] for the same reason that Cicero in several of his books and letters proclaims that eloquence has its fountain-head in the most secret springs of wisdom, and that consequently for a considerable time the instructors of morals and of eloquence were identical. Accordingly this exhortation of mine must not be taken to mean that I wish the orator to be a philosopher, since there is no other way of life that is further removed from the duties of a statesman and the tasks of an orator. For what philos-   [7] opher has ever been a frequent speaker in the courts or won renown in public assemblies? Nay, what philosopher has ever taken a prominent part in the government of the state, which forms the most frequent theme of their instructions? None the less I desire that he, whose character I am seeking to mould, should be a "wise man" in the Roman sense, that is, one who reveals himself as a true statesman, not in the discussions of the study, but in the actual practice and experience of life. But inasmuch   [8] as the study of philosophy has been deserted by those who have turned to the pursuit of eloquence; and since philosophy no longer moves in its true sphere of action and in the broad daylight of the forum, but has retired first to porches and gymnasia and finally to the gatherings of the schools, all that is essential for an orator, and yet is not taught by the professors of eloquence, must undoubtedly be sought from those persons in whose possession it has remained. The authors who have discoursed on the nature of virtue must be read through and through, that the life of the orator may be wedded to the knowledge of things human and   [90 divine. But how much greater and fairer would such subjects appear if those who taught them were also those who could give them most eloquent expressions! O that the day may dawn when the perfect orator of our heart's desire shall claim for his own possession that science that has lost the affection of mankind through the arrogance of its claims and the vices of some that have brought disgrace upon its virtues, and shall restore it to its place in the domain of eloquence, as though he had been victorious in a trial for the restoration of stolen goods! And since philosophy falls into three divisions, physics, ethics, and dialectic, which, [*10*] I ask you, of these departments is not closely connected with the task of the orator?

Let us reverse the order just given and deal first with the third department which is entirely concerned with words. If it be true that to know the properties of each word, to clear away ambiguities, to unravel perplexities, to distinguish between truth and falsehood, to prove or to refute as may be desired, all form part of the functions of an orator, who is there that can doubt the truth of my contention? . . . And just as the trainers of the wrestling school do not impart the various *throws* [*12*] to their pupils that those who have learnt them may make use of all of them in actual wrestling matches (for weight and strength and wind count for more than these), but that they may have a store from which to draw one or two of such tricks, as occasion may offer; even so the science of dialectic, or if you prefer it of disputation, while it is often useful [*13*] in definition, inference, differentiation, resolution of ambiguity, distinction and classification, as also in luring on or entangling our opponents, yet if it claim to assume the entire direction of the struggles of the forum, will merely stand in the way of arts superior to itself and by its very subtlety will exhaust the strength that has been pared down to suit its limitations. . . .

Proceeding to moral philosophy or ethics, we may note that it [*15*] at any rate is entirely suited to the orator. For vast as is the variety of cases (since in them, as I have pointed out in previous books, we seek to discover certain points by conjecture, reach our conclusions in others by means of definition, dispose of others on legal grounds or by raising the question of competence while other points are established by syllogism and others involve contradictions or are diversely interpreted owing to some ambiguity of language), there is scarcely a single one which does not at some point or another involve the discussion of equity and virtue, while there are also, as everyone knows, not a few which turn entirely on questions of quality. Again in deliberative assemblies how can we [*16*] advise a policy without raising the question of what is honourable? Nay, even the third department of oratory, which is concerned with the tasks of praise and denunciation, must without a doubt deal with questions of right and wrong. For the orator will assuredly have much to say on [*17*] such topics as justice, fortitude, abstinence, self-control and piety. But the good man, who has come to the knowledge of these things not by mere hearsay, as though they were just words and names for his tongue to employ, but has grasped the meaning of virtue and acquired a true feeling for it, will never be perplexed when he has to think out a problem, but will speak out truly what he knows. . . .

For mere garrulity that is ignorant of all such learning must needs go astray, since its guides are either non-existent or false.

Physics on the other hand is far richer than the other branches of philosophy, if viewed from the standpoint of providing exercise in speaking, in proportion as a loftier inspiration is required to speak of things divine than of things human; and further it includes within its scope the whole of ethics, which as we have shown are essential to the very existence of oratory. For, if the world is governed by providence, it [*21*] will certainly be the duty of all good men to bear their part in the administration of the state. If the origin of our souls be divine, we must win our way towards virtue and abjure the service of the lusts of our earthly body. Are not these themes which the orator will frequently be called upon to handle? Again there are questions concerned with auguries and oracles or any other religious topic (all of them subjects that have often given rise to the most important debates in the senate) on which the orator will have to discourse, if he is also to be the statesman we would have him be. And finally, how can we conceive of any real eloquence at all proceeding from a man who is ignorant of all that is best in the world? . . .

. . . there is no need for an orator to swear allegiance to any one philosophic code. For he has a greater and nobler aim, to which he directs [*27*] all his efforts with as much zeal as if he were a candidate for office, since he is to be made perfect not only in the glory of a virtuous life, but in that of eloquence as well. He will consequently select as his models of eloquence all the greatest masters of oratory, and will choose the noblest precepts and the most direct road to virtue as the means for the formation of an upright character. He will neglect no form of exercise, but will devote special attention to those which are of the highest and fairest nature. For what subject can be found more fully adapted to a rich [*28*] and weighty eloquence than the topics of virtue, politics, providence, the origin of the soul and friendship? The themes which tend to elevate mind and language alike are questions such as what things are truly good, what means there are of assuaging fear, restraining the passions and lifting us and the soul that came from heaven clear of the delusions of the common herd.

But it is desirable that we should not restrict our study to the [*29*] precepts of philosophy alone. It is still more important that we should know and ponder continually all the noblest sayings and deeds that have been handed down to us from ancient times. And assuredly we shall nowhere find a larger or more remarkable store of these than in the records of our own country. Who will teach courage, justice, loyalty, self- [*30*] control, simplicity, and contempt of grief and pain better than men like Fabricius, Curius, Regulus, Decius, Mucius and countless others? For if the Greeks bear away the palm for moral precepts, Rome can produce more striking examples of moral performance, which is a far greater thing. But the man who does not believe that it is enough to fix his eyes [*31*] merely on his own age and his own transitory life, but regards the space allotted for an honourable life and the course in which glory's race is run as conditioned solely by the memory of posterity, will not rest content with a mere knowledge of the events of history. No, it is from the thought of posterity that he must inspire his soul with justice and derive that freedom of spirit which it is his duty to display when he pleads in the courts or gives counsel in the senate. No man will ever be the consummate orator of whom we are in quest unless he has both the knowledge and the courage to speak in accordance with the promptings of honour. . . . *XI.*   Wherefore let us seek with all our hearts that true majesty [*30*] of oratory, the fairest gift of god to man, without which all things are stricken dumb and robbed alike of present glory and the immortal record of posterity; and let us press forward to whatsoever is best, since if we do this, we shall either reach the summit or at least see many others far beneath us.

Such, Marcellus Victorius, were the views by the expression of [*31*] which it seemed to me that I might, as far as in me lay, help to advance the teaching of oratory. If the knowledge of these principles proves to be of small practical utility to the young student, it should at least produce what I value more,—the will to do well.

Bibliography

COLSON, FRANCIS HENRY, *M. Fabii Quintiliani Institutionis Oratoriae*, Liber I, Cambridge, Cambridge University Press, 1924. ("Introduction" and commentary in English.)

GWYNN, AUBREY OSBORN, *Roman Education from Cicero to Quintilian*, Oxford, Clarendon Press, 1926.

SMAIL, WILLIAM M., *Quintilian on Education*, Oxford, Clarendon Press, 1938. (Introduction and translations.)

WILKINS, A. S., *Roman Education*, Cambridge, Cambridge University Press, 1905.

IV

ST. AUGUSTINE

AURELIUS AUGUSTINUS WAS BORN in Tagaste, a town in what is now Algeria, in 354. His mother, Monica, was a devout Christian and his father, almost all his life, a pagan. Monica worried much over the paganness of her husband and that of her son during his early life. Through her efforts, the former was converted to Christianity shortly before his death; and while Augustine's Christianity grew out of a very complex internal struggle, Monica's efforts certainly played an important part in the conversion of her son as well.

St. Augustine received a typical Roman education. His elementary training occurred in Tagaste and in Madaura which was near by. His family sent him to Carthage to study rhetoric. Shortly before his departure for that city in company with "a gang of youthful good-for-nothings,"[1] and for the joy of sheer mischief, he rifled a neighbor's pear tree; and the vivid impression of the evil of this act was, apparently, never absent from his mind. He became a professor of rhetoric, practicing in Carthage, Rome, and Milan, an important city where the Western emperor often resided.

[1] St. Augustine, *Confessions*, translated by Vernon J. Bourke, Fathers of the Church, Inc., New York, 1953, p. 40.

In Carthage he took a mistress who bore him a son, Adeodatus. This union greatly troubled him, not because it was extralegal but because it was based upon lust rather than on the intent of progeny. In Carthage, also, he became closely associated with the Manichean sect, a cult centering around Manes, a Persian religious leader. In Milan, at the behest of his mother, St. Augustine proposed marriage to another woman, sent his mistress to whom he had always been faithful back to Africa, postponed his marriage for two years, and took another mistress for the intervening period. He came under the influence of several Christian friends, listened to the sermons of St. Ambrose, bishop of the city, read Neo-Platonic and Christian literature, and was converted to Christianity in 387. He withdrew from academic life and made plans to return to Africa. At Ostia, while awaiting his ship, Monica died. St. Augustine returned to Africa; and before many years became bishop of Hippo, now the city of Bona in Algeria. He died in the year 430 while the Vandals were besieging the city.

St. Augustine gave all his great talent to the young movement of Christianity. He occupies, now, a position both as father and as doctor of the Church. He served the Roman Catholic Church by contributing in large measure to the formulation of its theology, by combatting various factions that sprang up immediately after establishment was achieved, by determining the heretical nature of several prevalent opinions in the course of that combat, thus aiding in the delimitation of true belief, and by providing as much of a philosophy of education as has ever been developed within Catholic thought. St. Thomas, of course, commented on education; but his contributions to the philosophy of that subject, as we shall see,[2] are of a narrower compass than St. Augustine's and consist chiefly in a different support for much the same conception of teaching and learning as was arrived at by his great predecessor.

EDUCATIONAL THEORY

ST. AUGUSTINE WROTE voluminously from the age of twenty until his death.[3] In no single work is his entire philosophy of education set down; and as a consequence, a view of it can be arrived at only by bringing together doctrines from many separate books or passages. Moreover, his opinion on many topics changed throughout the course of his writing; and with respect to some important and many less significant details, one can un-

[2] Cf. Chapter 5.
[3] His works (not all of them are extant), together with the index, occupy Vols. 32–47 in the *Patrologie Latine*, Librairie Garnier Frères, Paris, 1841–1908.

doubtedly find incompatible tenets in his thought. Here, the most characteristically Christian views have been taken to compose his philosophy of education with a clear awareness that on some points one might find other positions in his writings difficult to reconcile with those attributed to him. But although diffuse and unsystematic, his work reveals an acute intellect, profound learning, and a wide range of interests. We shall begin the study of it in the usual way with a discussion of his educational theory.

STATEMENTS OF FACT

The statements of fact in Augustine's educational theory are a little unlike those involved in the theories discussed in the preceding chapters. Augustine's assertion of them involves something other than observation or inference made from observation. It relies upon the authority of Scriptural texts. It might be argued that belief in these texts is something wholly different from belief in statements of fact, that faith is something to which observation of the world or inference from it is altogether irrelevant. On the other hand, it might also be contended that the veracity of Scripture is guaranteed by the witness of miracles or by the appearance of God or his angels to holy men; so that belief in them stems from observation of the miracles or of utterances made to prophets and seers. In any case, the statements concerned are about things such as the creation of Adam, and the Fall, which could have been observed had anyone been in the immediate neighborhood. Since they are very much like statements of fact, and since the arguments for and against their being so are subtle and remote from our purposes, we shall treat them here as if they were statements of fact.

Augustine's statements of fact are of two kinds: psychological and historical. We shall begin with the first.

Psychology

Augustine describes the human personality, in general, as consisting in a combination of body and soul. The body is derived, according to biological principles, from Adam, whom God created, and Eve, whom He fashioned of a bone taken from Adam's side.[4] It endures throughout life and in a dispersed condition after death. At the resurrection, its parts are reassembled by God to provide an eternal body for the surviving soul. The body performs all corporeal actions and is acted upon by the soul in certain ways.

The soul's action upon the body consists in its utilization of it in psychic functions which are not purely mental. These functions stem from

---

4 *The City of God,* XII, xxii, xxiii.

sensation and do not exhaust the soul's activity. It performs many actions, as well, which are purely mental. The soul was created by God and endures continuously throughout life and after life eternally. The human person is, thus, a union of body and soul, and this union consists in the soul's utilization of the body for its own purposes.

The soul's purposes are its activities, and these may be classified under the three headings which, in a later time, became traditional, viz., knowing, feeling, and willing.

There are four ways of knowing in which the soul engages, and they differ according to differences in the soul's activity, and according to the objects its activity reveals.[5] The first is knowledge by sensation. The soul obtains knowledge of this sort by centering its activity in the body's organs of sense, and this utilization of those organs yields knowledge of external bodies. Thus, when the soul attends to the deliverances of vision as opposed to mere acquiescence in them, it is aware of all those things which fall within the reach of the eyes; and so it is for all other knowledge by sensation.

The second way of knowing is remembering.[6] In the awareness of a tree, the tree is directly present to us; but an image of it is immediately taken and stored in memory. It is the image of the tree we have in our minds when we remember it; but in order to know by remembering, much more than the presence of an image must occur. We have many images of things which we do not remember. To know by means of an image, to be aware of the tree when the image of it occurs, the image must not occur merely. The mind must also be aware of it, and must recognize it as an image of the tree. Knowing by remembering requires consciousness of images, and the activity of recognizing them as such.[7] When the soul remembers, its activity consists in recognizing an image; and many of the objects memory reveals are the external bodies of which images have been stored in the mind.[8] But there are other objects of memory. The

[5] Frederick Copleston, *A History of Philosophy*, Vol. II, The Newman Press, Westminister, Maryland, 1950, pp. 56–60.

[6] Augustine speaks of all knowledge other than that of sense as remembering *(memoria)*. This manner of speaking is probably a result of Plato's theory of reminiscence. Augustine suggests that nothing can be known in any way except for the way of sensation, unless it is in the mind; and that to be in the mind is to be remembered. It is clear that even though one should hold this view, one should still distinguish between what is ordinarily called "memory," and what is ordinarily called "reasoning," "scientific knowing," and the like. Here we have endeavored to free Augustine's views concerning knowing from their involvement with his doctrine of memory. For the latter, cf. especially *Confessions*, Book X.

[7] Cf. *Confessions*, X, VIII, XVIII.

[8] The effort deliberately to remember as opposed to memory by recognition is the process now often referred to as "recall." Involuntary memories often frustrate this effort and Augustine's discussion of them suggests the process of association as a hindrance to thought analogous to its treatment by Hobbes and Locke.

deliberate activity of recall as well as that of recognition sometimes reveals the soul in its past actions, its acts of knowing, of willing, and of feeling; and these events as well as physical bodies are known by memory, i.e.,
by the consciousness of images of them.[9]

The third way of knowing is reasoning. It consists in the activity of
discovering certain things, and of relating these things in a certain way.
Reason discovers logical principles, numbers and their relations, perfect
beauty, and moral worth. None of these can be found in sensation; for if
they could, they would be visible or sounding, gustatory, odorous, or
tangible. But it is clear that they can exhibit no such features.[10] They are
not found in the observable world; they are found in the mind where they
"lie haphazard in many wondrous and separate compartments."[11] But
reason is not only the discovery of these things; it is also the activity of
ordering them in such a way as to enable us to distinguish and connect
them. Thus, when the soul reasons, it discovers the principle of contradiction, the principle that nothing can both be and not be, together with
other logical principles. These principles, it distinguishes and connects in
an order which yields the systematic understanding of relations of truth
and falsehood between statements. It also discovers such things as the
numbers two and three. These, it clearly distinguishes from one another
and connects in certain orders. In this way, reason yields the truth that
two plus three equals five. It discovers beauty and virtue, and subsequently distinguishes them and connects them in an order of value. The
third way of knowing is, thus, the discovery of certain kinds of objects,
and the production of systematic knowledge concerning their relations—
the knowledge of logic, of mathematics, and of value.

This third kind of activity yields purely rational knowledge. The
systems of logic and mathematics, of beauty and morality describe nothing
sensible. They provide us with standards for evaluating sensible things;
consequently they cannot be taken as descriptions of those things. That
these two things and those three things equal five things is a statement
which truly describes a sensible fact; but it can be seen to be true only
by use of the arithmetical law that two plus three equals five, although
this law describes nothing sensible. Reasoning, as such, is the activity
which provides knowledge of something other than the sensible world.

There is a fourth way of knowing which is a combination of the
other three. It is the soul's activity of applying purely rational principles
to the things knowable by sensation. To know that these two chairs together with those three make five chairs, the soul ordinarily does four
things: it perceives the chairs, remembers them from moment to moment,

---

[9] Cf. *Confessions*, X, xiv.
[10] Cf., *ibid.*, X, x–xii.
[11] Cf. *ibid.*, X, viii–x, xv.

knows rationally the truth that two plus three equals five, and perceives a congruence between this arithmetical law and the collection of chairs before it.[12] Similarly, when the soul knows that some sensible thing is beautiful or some sensible action good, it is because it has observed it, has in reasoning recalled the nature of beauty and of goodness, and has applied them to the things perceived. The object of this fourth way of knowing is the entire sensible world, and the statement of such knowledge is what we would now call natural and social science, æsthetic criticism and applied ethics.

The second major activity in which the soul engages is that of feeling. There are four different ways of feeling out of which all others may be derived: desiring, enjoying, fearing, and sorrowing. These are all mental activities; and desires, joys, fears, and sorrows, immediately upon their enactment by the soul, are swallowed up by memory as a stomach admits food taken in through the mouth.[13] The question whether they exist in memory as ideas is a difficult one for they return upon recall, make reference to their original occurrence, but seem to possess no emotional quality,[14] so that it appears to Augustine that feelings remembered both are and are not images of the original mental occurrences. He suggests, finally, that the way in which feelings can be remembered is inscrutable to man but does not doubt that it occurs.

Each of the four fundamental ways of feeling is directed upon some object about which knowledge also may occur. To desire in any way is to desire some thing, and what one desires is, as such, a candidate for the knowing activity as well. Similarly, to feel joy or fear or sorrow is to take them in an object or condition; and these objects or conditions may be known as well as felt toward. To feel and to know are, alike, activities of the soul.

The third major function of the soul is willing. This activity Augustine regards as that of deliberate choice. It is unlike desire, for desire is a simple urge. In a certain sense it governs desire, for it may choose which of two or more desires it may realize. It is capable of error; and when the soul commits an error of will, it chooses to realize a desire for a worse condition or thing as opposed to one for a better.

Every soul is endowed with these three powers, the power to know, to feel, and to will. But the extent to which each may exercise these powers varies from one person to another. Some persons are capable of a high degree of reasoning, some are predominately passionate, and some

[12] But (cf. *Confessions*, X, viii) Augustine suggests that where no sensible objects are immediately perceived, as in knowledge of the past and future, their images function in their stead; so that the fourth way of knowing sometimes does not involve the first.
[13] Augustine wavers between the view that mind and memory are identical and the view that memory is to the mind as a stomach is to a mouth.
[14] *Confessions*, X, xvi.

are possessed of energetic and active wills. Augustine contended that for purposes of training, the important difference between persons is that between those who are capable of much knowledge and those who are not.

Universal history

There is no time after which the universe began to exist, for time is the duration of the universe. But there is a first moment of time; and in it, there occurred all the stuff out of which the universe developed. The development of the universe is the moving actualization of what was present in the first moment. This is the germ of Augustine's view concerning universal history.

In the first moment of history, the entire universe came into existence. Of course it was not all actually there; for the very notion of history is the notion of things happening, of new occurrences, of events which cannot be repeated. But in the first moment, there came into existence a condition of things within which there were all the possibilities, the realization of which constitutes the development of the corporeal and the social realms of history. In that condition, there was a certain spatial arrangement of the physical elements; and from this arrangement, according to law, the subsequent vicissitudes and moving appearances of the corporeal universe take their origin. Within that condition, also, there were the seeds (*rationes seminales*) of all forms of organic life, none of which was actually there present, and each of which developed at various later times. These seeds were not seeds in the ordinary sense of the term; they were the invisible possibilities which must be present in things in order that each species of plants and animals might arise.

The development of the corporeal universe, both inanimate and animate, may be understood by use of two concepts, that of relative density or weight of elements, and that of law. The stuff of which bodies are composed is of four kinds: earth, water, air, and fire.[15] Any body may harbor stuff of all four kinds; and from one body to another, we find the four elements combined in varying proportions. But earth is heavier or more dense than water, water than air, and air than fire. Consequently, those bodies in which earth predominates will be nearer the center of the universe than will those in which another element is the chief ingredient; and similarly, for other bodies in which other elements prevail. There is, in this way, a place for each body determined by the proportion of its different elementary constituents; earthy bodies near the center, the watery next above them, the airy next, and the fiery highest of all.[16]

However, the concept of elementary weight is not adequate for the understanding of the corporeal universe; for if we were to think by use of

15 Cf. *City of God*, XXII, XI.
16 But Augustine felt some doubts about this view. Cf. *ibid*.

this concept alone we would be obliged to conceive the corporeal world merely as a static, spatial arrangement of things. In fact, it is a history, or more properly, a complex of histories. It consists in many different things moving constantly, and changing with respect to their qualities. Stars revolve, plants run through their life cycles, and animals grow and decay. These changes of place and of quality always happen according to law; and in order to understand the history of the corporeal universe we must think of it not merely as made up of things with different elementary constitutions but of these things changing according to invariable laws. It is by law that: ". . . all the world maintains, as far as this world of sense allows, the wondrous stability of things by means of the orders and recurrences of seasons. . . ."[17] It is by virtue of law as well as the proportion of elementary constituents that a thing finds its place. Birds, though chiefly made of earth, dwell in the air; and the corporeal universe must be understood as moving according to laws which are manifested in different ways according to the elementary constituents of different bodies.

Augustine closely identifies the concepts "law," "order," "justice," and "peace." The laws that govern change assign to each thing a place in an order, and this place is "proper" to it.[18] When a thing acts according to law, when it is in its proper place in an order, its behavior is just; for since justice is giving each thing its due, it prevails when a thing is in its proper place. Moreover, each thing seeks to find its proper place; and we may say that a thing is at peace when it acts according to law. Augustine regards all the corporeal universe, animate as well as inanimate, as a collection of things of divergent elementary constitutions governed by law, order, justice, and peace.[19]

At the center of this universe there is the earth with its numerous species of organic life covered largely by water, the element most heavy next to earth. Above the water there is air, the atmosphere which surrounds earth. Above the air there is the lightest of elements, fire—manifested in the moon, the stars, and especially the sun. These fiery bodies move around the earth in circular orbits. The history of inanimate things is their movement from the beginning of time according to law upon and above the earth. The history of life is the development at prearranged times and according to law of its various species, the seeds of which all were present in the first moment.

Within the corporeal order, and intertwined with the history of corporeal things, there is the history of rational beings, of angels and of men. The angels came into existence in the first moment, about six

[17] Cf. *Soliloquies, The Fathers of the Church, Writings of St. Augustine,* Cima Publ. Co., translated by Thomas F. Gilligan, O.S.A., New York, 1948, I, I.
[18] Cf. *City of God,* XIX, XIII.
[19] Cf. *ibid.,* XIX, XII.

thousand years before Augustine. Not long afterward, a group of them led by Lucifer revolted against the authority of God and set out on a career of personal aggrandizement in opposition to His will.

Adam was fashioned out of earth, a soul breathed into him, and, for a companion, Eve formed out of his rib. Adam and Eve were endowed with free will. They could have disobeyed the commands of God, but they did not do so. Their desire spent itself in the fulfillment of divine law, and their joy was found wholly in its realization. They loved God, and each other in Him. All of the activities of their bodies were voluntary; and their souls used their bodies as instruments for the purposes of divine obedience. Procreation was possible for them; but had it occurred, it would not have been caused by lust. Since there were no involuntary actions, the emotions that follow upon them did not exist. As yet, there was neither fear nor sorrow. They were immortal; and their life was one of perfect happiness.

Shortly, Lucifer in the guise of a serpent persuaded Eve, and she Adam, to violate a command of God. Subsequently, their bodies came to act independently of their souls. They demanded sexual union independently of reason; and the result of a freely chosen disobedience was that the soul of each was filled with the irrepressible clamor of personal and bodily self-seeking. This unending misery is part of the punishment for sin; the rest of that punishment is God's abandonment of them, the taking away of their immortality. From their lustful union, other bodies arose; and a soul was provided for each. But the original sin of choosing badly and the consequent control of the body over the soul was transmitted to each generation. The punishment also was transmitted; and the first parents of all the tribes of men bequeathed to them their sin, their unhappiness, and their death.

The social life of the descendants of Adam is carried on in four communities which are related in a hierarchical way. A community is ". . . a multitude of reasonable beings voluntarily associated in the pursuit of common interests."[20] The smallest community is the family. The next largest is the city, composed of families, but extending the interests of its citizens to goals more comprehensive than those of family life. Thirdly, there is the world-wide community whose objectives embrace those of the city, but extend over problems which no smaller community can solve. This community, in Augustine's day, was typified by the Roman Empire, and in other times by other imperial organizations. Lastly, there is the cosmic community embracing all men who live upon the earth, as well as angels both fallen and unfallen who dwell either on the earth or above it to the outermost limits of the universe. In it, evil men

[20] Cf. *ibid.*, IX, XXIV.

and angels strive for evil purposes; this activity is seen in pagan worship. In it also good men and good angels work for good purposes; and this activity is seen in Christianity.

The pursuit of common interests within each of these communities is highly imperfect because of the distortion of the human soul by original sin. Before the Fall, Adam and Eve lived joyously because their wills directed their behavior in the paths laid down by God's law; their common desire was that of obedience. When they willed to disobey God, the desire to give free reign to the appetite of lust came to dominate all others; and joy in its satisfaction all other joys. Sorrow at its absence came into existence, and the fear of death could be exploited in order to assure its satisfaction. The soul of every member of each family is, thus, continually under the sway of forces that strive against a continued pursuit of common goals. Originating in lust, the family is pervaded by jealousy and hatred. For the same reason, the city, which is made of families, is rent by lawsuits and seditions; the world community, by language-barriers and warfare; and the cosmic community, by the conniving of deceptive demons and gullible men. The meanness of men makes all community of interests, at best, short-lived. The disobedience of the angels and that of the first men has thus saddled human activity in each of its four areas with strife and discord; and human history consists largely in the follies and misfortunes consequent upon the crimes of Eden.

These earthly misfortunes are not the only punishment for sin. The other is death, the eternal punishment of the surviving soul and body. All men are equally guilty; consequently, there is no reason for remitting the punishment of any. Nonetheless, in his mercy, God entered the world in the body of Christ in order to persuade men to repent of their sin in order that they might return to the immortal blessedness which Adam and Eve once enjoyed.[21] A considerable time after the Crucifixion,[22] Christ will return, and the Last Judgment, consigning those who have "sought the things which are above" to eternal bliss and those who have "sought the things which are on the earth" to eternal torment, will be pronounced.[23] The world will be destroyed by fire, and the history of human life, as all time itself, will cease.

Augustine supplements his doctrine of salvation with the doctrine of grace. All men are equally guilty, and equally deserving of punishment. Nonetheless, in His grace, God saves all who repent. In the beginning, as we have seen, men come into existence in potentiality; and consequently,

---

21 Cf. *ibid.,* IX, xv; also XV, I.
22 Perhaps the period was a thousand years, but this is not altogether clear. Cf. *ibid.,* XX, VII.
23 Cf. *ibid.,* XX, IX.

each life with its free decision to repent or not to repent was present. Moreover, this free decision is a part of God's knowledge; and in this way, God foreknows which way each man will decide. The decision for or against repentance divides the race into two groups: those whose repentance brings them salvation through grace, and those whose failure to repent does not. The sin of the first parents and the grace of God determine human life to proceed in a course marked off by three events: the original sin, the incarnation, and the last judgment. "Thus, from a bad use of free choice, a sequence of misfortunes conducts the whole human race, excepting those redeemed by the grace of God, from the original canker in its root to the devastation of a second and endless death."[24]

In this life, human activity, however much it is doomed to an ultimate perdition, must proceed in the four communal spheres described above; but the existence of two groups, those predestined to salvation and those marked off for endless death, makes for two other communities which cut across these four. In each family and city, in the world-wide community and in the cosmic, there are some whose fate is different from that of others. Those who will be saved repent of sin; preferring the commands of God over the importunities of the self, they love Him, and one another in Him. Those who will be lost do not repent; preferring to realize their personal desires over obedience to God, they love themselves and others only so far as they are useful to their secular inclinations. The former are humble before God; the latter, proud. Each group is made up of those who voluntarily cooperate in the pursuit of common interests; and each is a community. The former is the City of God; the latter, the city of the earth. The City of God is made up chiefly of members of the Catholic Church, although some of its citizens are not communicants. The Church typifies the City but is not identical with it. The city of the earth is made up chiefly of non-Catholics, although some members of the Church may belong to it; it is typified by the Roman Empire although not identical with it. These two cities often are in opposition as in the persecution of the heavenly by the earthly power. But they need not always be so; and there are many objectives, those of the humanization of earthly life, in the pursuit of which they both may and should cooperate. For although the chief objective of the City of God is immortal blessedness, and its members merely pilgrims through life toward that goal, there is every reason why the gloom of life should be dissipated as much as possible. Since the objective of the earthly city is secular and individual aggrandizement and its members dwellers in this world, there is every reason why it should wish for personal and social improvement.

24 *Ibid.*, II, xiv. For a discussion of God's foreknowledge and the free decision to repent (the problem of predestination) cf. V, ix, x.

EDUCATIONAL RECOMMENDATIONS

The Augustinian psychology and universal history lead to the following description of human life.

First, the history of man, whether conceived of as that of the four-fold community or as that of the two cities, exhibits a single order; for everything has existed from the first moment. The love and peace of the Heavenly City as well as the strife and discord of the terrestrial, the cooperation of each of the four communities as well as their conflict, all were present in potentiality when things first began; and human life is the development according to order of the seeds of society. This orderly development is one in which everything that happens betrays a kind of justice, and in which ultimately everything finds its peace. The occurrence of slavery is the orderly, lawful, just, and peaceable punishment of sin committed by the bondsman, warfare occurs only where the order of things requires; and the last judgment upon the wicked as upon the virtuous is no more than peace in the cancellation of sin by punishment and the reward of virtue by eternal bliss. Human life, like animate and inanimate nature, constitutes a pattern of events which makes their occurrence just and peaceful. Bad as it is, the history of man is the best life possible for him.

Secondly, the soul of every member of the human race, while engaging in this life, is disorted from the order proper to it. The soul's proper order is the way in which it functioned in Adam and Eve before the Fall. Subsequently, the will first, and then the emotions and the intellect became infected. In some measure, all must will to disobey God, to prefer themselves over God, and to use others for egoistic purposes. In some measure, desire involuntarily seeks fulfillment in sexual satisfaction and in the mundane pursuits ancillary to it. In some measure, joy must be felt at the satisfaction of these ambitions; fear, at the possibility of its diminution or loss in death; and sorrow, at the actual event. In some measure, reason is inevitably employed to secure knowledge of the way in which the secular will and emotions may find their terrestrial satisfaction. But the outcome of this restless infection is continued sorrow and fear. The joy that is sought is happiness in what cannot remain; and the pursuit of which, if it occupies life exclusively, must be suffused with misfortune and must terminate in eternal torment.

Thirdly, the only way in which the misery of earthly life can be alleviated and the happiness enjoyed by Adam and Eve assured, lies through repentance. This consists in the decision of the will to live, as far as possible, according to the commands of God, and the working out, in some measure, of the consequences of that decision. These are constituted by the love of God and of other persons, and the rejection of objectives which are merely secular. Repentance is manifested by conversion to the Catholic faith. Such is the condition and the prospect of man. In view of it, how should he be trained?

The objective of all training, according to Augustine, is conversion to Christianity. This conversion terminates in the awareness of God together with the possession of a Christian character. To be aware of God is to love Him; and this love is the greatest good man can achieve. From it issues a Christian character, for whoever loves God respects His law. God's law requires that one should willingly fit into His order, and treat others in the manner which their place in that order demands. Thus one who loves God will fulfill all his duties toward himself and toward others, and will exhibit all the Christian virtues both private and public. Augustine recommends the love of God and a life according to the Christian interpretation of Him as the ultimate goal of all teaching.

Conversion may be accomplished in two ways; and there are, consequently, two recommendations subordinate to the ultimate goal. The work of conversion should proceed both through the Church and through the instrumentalities of academic training. The Church ought to propagate the Gospel through society at large. Except for its work, no one can come to be aware of God and of His law. But conversion ought also to be sought in the teaching of youth, for the study of the liberal arts as well as of philosophy and theology lends itself readily to this purpose. The first method Augustine advocated more by example than by precept. He spent much of his time preaching and administering ecclesiastical affairs in Africa, and he must have regarded this actvity as a kind of instruction which, by spreading Christian doctrine, would bring men to the love of God and their neighbors in Him. The second method, the use of the curriculum of the schools as well as of informal study, he recommends in his formal statement concerning the content of courses of study.[25]

The liberal arts, according to Augustine's explicit statement, consist in grammar, dialectic, rhetoric, music, geometry, and astronomy;[26] but he probably intended to include arithmetic as well. These subjects constitute what came to be known as the Seven Liberal Arts; and while this course of study had its beginning in Plato's *Republic,* Augustine borrowed the concept quite fully developed from Varro whose work on the subject is not extant.[27] Augustine's point is that the study of these

25 *De Ordine,* sometimes translated by *Divine Providence and The Problem of Evil.* In his book *De Doctrina Christiana,* Augustine treats of the training of the clergy. That book is not considered here in any detail because it is a highly technical discussion of a highly technical training.
26 At the time no sharp distinction was drawn between astronomy and astrology.
27 Cf. William Boyd, *The History of Western Education,* Third Edition, A. & C. Black Limited, London, 1932, p. 73. The title of Varro's work is *Disciplinorum libri novem.* Varro discussed nine disciplines, including medicine and architecture.

arts reveals to the student that divine law or order of both the physical and social world, conformity to which is necessary for virtuous conduct, and awareness of which is of assistance in coming to know God.

After the liberal studies, those students who are well endowed with reason should study philosophy and theology. These subjects, never clearly distinguished, require the use of mathematics and dialectic, or *a priori* reasoning. Augustine suggests that *a priori* mathematical thought is one instance of the search for unity, as love and friendship are other instances of it. This kind of thinking concerning the soul will unify the latter; and when it is thus organized, "then will it venture to see God."[28] Augustine wonders, however, whether this "seeing" can occur in this life.

The method by which the liberal arts are to be taught has both a negative and a positive aspect. The negative aspect is expressed in Augustine's injunction to beware the dangers of sense. The student's energy would naturally expend itself in unprofitable play, on lascivious literature, or on sex; and the teacher must, so far as possible, prevent that energy from flowing in its natural course. Augustine seems to disapprove of flogging, but apparently would approve censorship in the curriculum.

The positive aspect of the method by which the liberal arts are taught should be that of authority. As we have seen, some excel in reason while others do not. But Augustine recommends that all be taught to believe before any are encouraged to understand.[29] The teacher should simply inform the student; he should not bring him to that clear acquaintance with truth which his possession of reason would make possible. He argues, however, that teachers who use this method must, themselves, know how to prove the doctrines they transmit; he in no way advocates the propagation of mere dogma.

For the purpose of training members of the clergy, he urges the use of books in which facts are collected and summarily described. Such textbooks would save much time and labor.[30] One may suppose that he would recommend their use by all students of the liberal arts. The objective of this method is correctly to inform the student concerning nature and society, the providential order which both exhibit, the nature and existence of God, and of the student's duties as determined by the foregoing. But the student must be content to believe this information rather than to know it. The success of this procedure is true belief concerning God, a consequent love for Him, and a disposition to live in accord with His law which that belief engenders.

---

28 *De Ordine,* II.
29 *Ibid.;* also *De Utilitate Credendi,* X.
30 Cf. *De Doctrina Christiana,* II. This suggestion reflected, but also intensified, the contemporary practice, and was instrumental in preserving as much knowledge as Europe had during the Middle Ages.

The method of instruction in philosophy and theology is that of reason. The few who study these subjects possess the capacity to understand clearly their own ideas, to compare and order them in a rational way, and to order the items of experience in accord with them. The teacher of these advanced courses is charged with the task of developing wisdom in the student, i.e., of bringing him to a rational assurance concerning the existence and nature of God and his own soul, of mathematics and logic, and of the fundamental standards of morality and of art. Further, it is his task to foster in the student an application of this higher knowledge to the world of sense, an application which eventuates in useful information concerning the order of nature and society and concerning his own place with respect to each. Success in this instruction is knowledge of God, knowledge of one's self, a rigorous effort to will obedience to God's laws, and happiness in that volition and in the possession of God. It is also wisdom, i.e., the direction of both will and feeling upon the objects that knowledge reveals; and these objects, God, the order of nature and society including the soul, are those things concerning which, earlier, belief was instilled. The man who can reason should know what he, along with others, must first believe. He lives as much in harmony with God and His providential order as knowledge of both will allow to a creature of original sin.

PHILOSOPHY OF EDUCATION

AUGUSTINE'S PHILOSOPHICAL treatment of his theory of education may be dealt with under four headings: the analysis of the concept, "teaching," the metaphysical support of the theory, the ethical justification of its primary recommendation, and the epistemological treatment of it. Let us discuss these in order.

ANALYSIS OF TEACHING

In his *De Magistro, Concerning The Teacher,* Augustine presents an analysis of the fundamental concept of all educational theory, i.e., the concept of teaching. In what, he asks, does teaching consist? It is a familiar view that teaching consists in the use of language for the purpose of increasing knowledge. The one who uses the language teaches; the one whose knowledge would be increased learns. If the teacher succeeds in his use of language, the student learns something; his knowledge is increased. If the teacher fails, the student learns nothing; his knowledge is not increased. Teaching, thus, consists in a situation in which there is a teacher, a student or learner, and a use of language by the former, the purpose of which is to increase the knowledge of the latter.

Augustine's analysis of "teaching" seems to support the familiar view; but his treatment of the notion "use of language" is sufficiently unlike one common understanding of it to lend his analysis of "teaching" an appearance remarkably unlike one which it easily assumes at first. A common interpretation of the phrase "use of language" is that it applies, properly, to the giving of information by one person to another. Using language is analogous to giving a gift; in each case, what one person has, he conveys to another. The speaker gives his information to the hearer; the giver gives his gift to the recipient. On this view of the use of language, teaching appears to consist in the teacher's taking from his own mind and presenting to the learner knowledge which the latter does not already possess. Augustine argues that this is an altogether inaccurate way of understanding the notion. We can begin to understand his view by setting down the main features of his doctrine concerning language.

Language, Augustine contends, is made up of words; and words are signs.[31] A sign is a noise, a mark, or some other thing which refers to something else as the noise or mark "John Jones" refers to the man.[32] Language thus is composed of names; and of names, there are two sorts. Some are proper names, and they name individuals. Others, conjunctions, prepositions, common nouns, verbs, adjectives, etc., name universals. Thus "Ananias" ("Shadrack") names one and only one individual, while the words "boy," "furnace," "fire," and "injure" name universals, i.e., severally name something which, in each case, may be exhibited by many different individuals. Names compose sentences, and sentences are themselves names. They name combinations of those things to which their constituent signs each severally refer. "The fire did not injure Ananias," for example, names the fact of Ananias' miraculous invulnerability to fire; and what fact it names is determined, in part, by the reference of "fire," "injure," "Ananias," etc.

One of the uses of language is intimately connected with this view of it. One use of signs or names taken separately is that of referring to the things they name. We use "Ananias" to refer to the youth; and we use "fire" to refer to the universal of which we find examples in furnaces. We use sentences to refer to the facts they name. We use "the fire did not injure Ananias" to refer to Ananias' invulnerability. The referring use of

31 *De Magistro,* II.
32 For the purposes of this discussion, we speak only of spoken language. For the most part, Augustine follows this procedure. But what is said about spoken language applies to writing and other linguistic forms as well.

language is that of identifying for ourselves and for those to whom we speak the things we have in mind.[33]

We cannot use language in this referential way unless we have before our minds the things for which its parts are names; we cannot employ one thing to refer to another unless that other is known to us. There are for Augustine, it will be recalled, four ways in which we bring things before our minds as well as four kinds of things which, in knowledge, become present to us. The senses give us an acquaintance with sensible objects. In memory we are aware of objects formerly perceived through sense. Reason yields awareness of the objects of logic and mathematics as well as the standards of beauty and morality; and through a cooperation of sense, memory, and reason, the mind confronts the empirical world, both natural and social. We may use names, then, to identify for ourselves sensible objects present when the use occurs, things remembered when their ideas are present, things rational after reason has revealed them, and things of the natural and social order when the products of reasoning have already been imposed upon the deliverances of sense interpreted in the light of the "documents of memory." But no name can be used to refer to any of these things unless they are present in the mind of the user. One can use language referentially for himself, both particular words as well as sentences, only if he knows the things or combinations of them which he identifies in his speech.

Others understand our referential use of language only if the things we name are present to their minds. Clearly, those who hear our language will not understand it rightly unless they use its names to refer to those things for whose identification we, ourselves, employ it; but where those things are absent from their minds, no such naming use of language can occur. Thus, one who is not acquainted with Ananias cannot understand the use of the noise to name him; nor can one who, by the use of reason, has never become acquainted with the number three understand the naming use of "three." One would speak to him in vain of Ananias and of the three boys who were unhurt by fire.[34] For although he might know from what he heard that there was some person so delivered from peril, he could not identify who it was, nor understand the number of the youths thus rescued. When we communicate with others, we tell them nothing which they did not know before; for if they understand our words, they know already what our language names.

---

[33] The view that language is made up of signs or names seems to preclude a distinction between language and its referring use; for it appears that no noise or mark or other thing could be a name unless it were, in fact, used to refer. Augustine does not notice this difficulty.

[34] *De Magistro,* XI.

Our referential use of language, then, cannot increase the knowledge of those to whom we speak; teaching does not consist in the teacher's conveyance to the learner of knowledge which the latter does not possess. For if the learner understands the teacher's language, he already knows the things to which the teacher refers; and if he does not understand them, he learns nothing from the teacher's talk.[35] To give is to present to another something which he did not formerly possess, but to teach and to give are activities totally unlike. For although the former is to use language for the increase of knowledge in the learner, that use cannot consist in delivering to him what he did not know before.

Increase of knowledge proceeds from within; and there are four kinds of knowledge upon whose increase learning depends. In his treatment of the concept, "teaching," Augustine concerns himself with only three of these.[36] Our knowledge of sensible or "carnal" things is increased by increased sensation; our knowledge of remembered things, by an increase in the recognition or recall of their images. Visible things can be known through sensation only if they are illumined for us; and they can be remembered only because once they were thus illumined. Our reason reveals to us the objects of mathematics and logic; and we construct systems of these objects in which they are organized according to relations they bear to one another. By the use of reason, also, we come to know the principles of art and morality, according to which we can compare and order those things which are beautiful and those actions which are right. Thus we know that two plus three equals five, that a building whose windows are symmetrically placed is more beautiful than one whose windows are not, and that to love God is the best of all actions. Augustine argues that reason can reveal these things to us only because its objects are illumined for us in a way analogous to the way in which visible objects are made known. There is an "interior light,"[37] analogous to the exterior, which illumines for the "inner man" the numbers, the ideas of the windows and the building, and all actions in such a way that he sees the relations they bear one another with complete certainty. The fourth way of knowing, Augustine might have said, since it consists in the perception of a congruence between objects of reason and of sense and memory, requires both exterior and interior light. To know is to be certain, and the number of things of which we are certain is increased by an increase in the number of things in both ways.

Increase of knowledge is thus a movement that cannot be compelled from without. The one whose knowledge is increased must experience and remember and reason for himself; for no one can give him an

35 *Ibid.*, x.
36 *Ibid.*, xii.
37 *Ibid.*

experience of sensible things, a memory of them, or the insight in which successful reasoning eventuates. The amount of knowledge each person may acquire is limited, but increase of knowledge within this limit is determined only by will or resolution on the part of him who would know.[38]

Knowing depends upon an act of will, and the act concerned is that of "consulting" what is found within the mind. To acquire knowledge of sensible things is to attend to that which the senses deliver to consciousness. To know by memory is to consult the images of sensible things. To know the things of reason and of the natural and social sciences is to consult the truths revealed by the interior light in conjunction with the truths of sense and memory. Augustine describes the truths of reason as presided over by the "guardian truth within the mind"; and this guardian "who is said to reside in the interior man is Christ, that is, the unchangeable excellence of God and His everlasting wisdom, which every rational soul does indeed consult."[39] It is the interior light which Christ or God causes to illumine the things of reason's realm which enables us, by consulting Him, to see what they are and how they are related to each other, and to apply them to the natural and social world. To know, thus, is to become aware of internal truths and to perceive their congruence with external things, and revelation of the objects of knowledge depends upon divine illumination. Increase of knowledge is knowing more than one did before.

Increase of knowledge, then, depends upon activity internal to the knower and upon divine illumination of the contents of his mind. Yet one human person can teach another. For the use of language to name things we know independently of that use is not its sole employment. We also employ language as an instrument to prompt others to know—to direct their attention to sensible objects, to activate their memories and their processes of reasoning, and to bring about their perception of truths concerning nature and society. Teaching is this instrumental use of language. Those persons who teach employ language in this way to increase the knowledge of others. But they do not by their speech convey knowledge to anyone. They prompt others only to knowledge which they must come by through a consultation of their own inner experience. The human teacher prompts his student to increase his knowledge, and such an increase can occur only as a result of consulting the inner truth. It is learning provided that it results from prompting, and that the person whose knowledge is increased ". . . considers within himself whether what has been explained has been said truly. . . ."[40] i.e., that he sees with the

---

38 *Ibid.,* XI.
39 *Ibid.*
40 *Ibid.,* XIV.

help of the interior light that words heard outwardly are true of things seen inwardly. Thus, teaching consists in the teacher's use of language to increase the knowledge of the learner. But the use is an instrumental one; the learner must be engaged actively; the help of God is presupposed; and the learner learns not through but because of the language employed.

It should be noted that while Augustine usually speaks of teaching as the prompting to certain knowledge, there is a secondary kind of teaching which eventuates in belief. We cannot, however rational, know individuals whose existence lies beyond our reach in space or time; consequently, since we cannot know them, we cannot name them. About them, however, assertions can be made. Since we have experienced universals, we can name them by their names; and although we have not experienced a particular individual, we can refer to facts in which it occurs by use of a sentence composed of universal names, substituting for the individual name a phrase which, without identifying the individual, enables us to describe it. Thus, although never acquainted with him, we can believe that Ananias was invulnerable to fire. For we have experienced the universals, "invulnerable" and "fire"; and we can substitute for "Ananias" phrases like "the first youth named in the story, the companion of Azarias and Misael," etc.[41] We cannot be completely certain that such statements are true, for we cannot know the individuals about whom they are made. Nonetheless, we can believe that such statements are true, and this belief is that which legitimate authority inculcates in the lower curriculum and in religious instruction outside the school. It is the belief that underlies our acceptance of Biblical stories, history, and all statements about individual things beyond our ken. These statements we take on faith, and it is good that we should do so; for at least in matters of theology and philosophy, it is necessary that one should believe before he can know.

METAPHYSICS

In the first moment of history, as we have seen, all things are present—some of them actually so, the others potentially. From this matrix spring all those beings, both physical and psychical,[42] whose order con-

[41] *Ibid.*, xi. In this passage, St. Augustine prefigures a distinction with its corresponding doctrine made prominent in contemporary analytical philosophy by Bertrand Russell. The distinction is that between knowledge by acquaintance and knowledge by description. The doctrine is that where knowledge cannot be secured through acquaintance it frequently may be achieved through description. Cf. Bertrand Russell, "On Denoting," *Mind*, vol. XIV, no. 56 (October, 1905), pp. 479–93; also, "Knowledge by Acquaintance and Knowledge by Description," in *Mysticism and Logic and Other Essays*, George Allen and Unwin, Ltd., London, 1917, pp. 209–32.

[42] But there is a difficulty about souls. Augustine holds each of them is created by God; but he also suggests that each of them is derived ultimately from Adam, apparently in order to account for the inheritance of Adam's sin. Cf. Copleston, *op. cit.*, II, vi.

stitutes the world. In this order, each being arises, endures, and vanishes from the scene according to law; and in it, each has its proper place. Thus, one who knew the laws of the order and the state of the original matrix could predict the character and the occurrence of each being. Despite this fact, every being in the order "tends to nothingness."[43] We can imagine that it should not exist, and we can imagine that its characters should be other than they are. That there is a tree here is a proposition which could be false even when it is true;[44] and that the ordinance and course of the moon should be different from what it is, requires only an alteration of God's will concerning it or the sudden operation of some hidden natural cause.[45] Although the order of the world is lawful, each thing in it might not have occurred and might have been different.

This "tendency to nothingness" gives rise to a question whose answer constitutes Augustine's metaphysical theory. If each being in it might not have existed or might have existed with different properties, why should the order have arisen in the first place? Another order of existing things might have been in the place of this one. Why, then, is it not? There might have been no order at all. Why, then, is there this one?

Augustine's answer seems to be something like the following.[46] There are two kinds of truths of which knowledge is composed: those which are necessary and those which are not. Necessary truths are those which are "eternal and unchangeable"; and since they are discovered by reason, we may conclude that their necessity consists in the fact that their denial is or involves a contradiction. They are the truths which reason in its mathematical, logical, moral, and æsthetic activities yields.[47] Truths that are not necessary are those concerning sensations, and those concerning the corporeal world. Their denial, it appears, does not involve contradiction. One who perceives a color may know that it is true he perceives it, but he might have perceived some other color or none at all.[48] Similarly, as we have seen, that this is a tree and that the moon follows a certain course are propositions that are true; but the will of God or the sudden operation of some hidden natural cause might at any moment

[43] *De Libero Arbitrio,* II, XVII.
[44] *Soliloquia,* I, xv.
[45] *Ibid.,* I, III.
[46] Augustine's clarity of exposition fails him in his metaphysical project. He confuses "truth" as a word for a certain property of sentences or of propositions with truth as a property of things, e.g., *Soliloquia,* I, xv, §28, and II, II, §2. Further, he seems to identify the relation between the "universal truth" and its instances with the relation between that which makes a sentence or proposition true and the truth of the sentence or proposition, e.g., the same passages. The result of this confusion and identification is a snarl of ideas which it would be impracticable to endeavor to disentangle in this place. I have attributed to Augustine a metaphysical theory which his work strongly suggests, and which Copleston, whose work has been very helpful to me, finds in his writings. Cf. Copleston, *op. cit.,* v.
[47] Cf. *De Libero Arbitrio,* II, VIII, IX.
[48] Cf. *Ibid.,* II, III, VII.

make them false.[49] But the truths that are necessary apply to the order of the world as well as to the objects of mathematics, logic, morals, and æsthetics; for no existing thing, whether sensory or corporeal, can violate mathematics and logic, or correct the principles of morality and æsthetics.[50] Propositions that describe sensations and corporeal things *need* not be true, although they may in fact be true; but those which assert mathematical, logical, moral, and æsthetic properties to the things are necessary. Nonetheless, truths of all kinds are "superior to the mind," i.e., they cannot be altered by our will;[51] ". . . there is an unchangeable truth which contains everything that is unchangeably true. You will never be able to say that it belongs particularly to you or to me or to any man, for it is available and offers itself to be shared by all who discern things immutably true, as if it were some strange mysterious and yet public light."[52] It is from this source that both necessary and nonnecessary truths are derived.

One can interpret Augustine's argument for the existence of this source of truth as showing that there is an agent external to the order of the world which called it into existence. We can imagine many different worlds, many sequences of events occupying the whole of time, which are in some or many ways different from that which prevails. These are the worlds some one of which might exist if truth were "inferior to the mind"; and they differ from the actual world with respect to the nonnecessary truths that would describe them.[53] Each of them, together with the actual world, is expressed in a system of propositions some of which are necessary and others of which are nonnecessary, and each of these systems expresses a world that is possible. Only one, however, is true, i.e., there is only one world whose existence makes one of these systems true and all the others false. Truth, as Augustine says, is "superior to the mind."[54] Considered in themselves, however, all of the systems of propositions, taken severally, are equally capable of being true; and the explanation for the actual truth of one alone must lie in the activity of some agency which created the world that makes that system true, and failed to create a world that, had it existed, would have made some other so. Were there not some such agency, all things would remain suspended in the limbo of mere possibility, even the original matrix itself; and nothing would exist at all.

The agency that created the world may be described further. The various systems of possible truths, one of which alone is actually true, are not independent of this agency. Each of them, rather, is a system of ideas;

49 Cf. *Soliloquia*, I, xv, III.
50 Cf. *De Libero Arbitrio*, II, x, xi.
51 Cf. *Ibid.*, II, xii.
52 Cf. *Ibid.*, II, xii, §33.
53 Cf. *Ibid.*, II, xii.
54 Cf. *Ibid.*, II, xiii.

and the agency that made one system true entertains them all as possible. The agency is not unthinking; it is a mind. Augustine's argument for a ground of all truth is for him a proof that God exists.

The system of propositions which God made true sets forth the model he used in creation, and his creation consists in providing the world about which that system is true. It should be noted that God provided it in its entirety. Each being in the existent order, and each collection of beings related in a certain way is like some idea or several of them which the system of true propositions expresses; each is the material embodiment of some part of that system. But God's creative act does not consist in his imposition of forms or universals on some pre-existent material; it consists rather in the establishment in one act of material things with their forms. The material of the world was created out of nothing and the exemplars used to fashion that material into the various beings which the world can boast are the ideas of that world in the mind of God.

This argument for the existence of God and for His relation to the world is, as Copleston points out,[55] the dominant argument in Augustine's writings. Copleston notes, however, that the argument from design, the argument from universal consent, and the argument from the ever-present possibility of nonexistence, the "tendency to nothingness," also make their appearance although they are less well worked out. While there are various grounds offered for it, then, we may conclude that Augustine's metaphysical theory is the view that God exists and that He is the reality which underlies the actual world, i.e., the world observable by human kind.

ETHICS

"The Supreme Good beyond all others," Augustine writes, "is God."[56] By this statement, recurring frequently throughout his writings, Augustine seems to mean, first, that God is perfectly good, and secondly, that the goodness of every other thing is derivative from His. Augustine nowhere defines "perfect goodness" conceived as a term by which we refer to an attribute of God. His failure in this particular is demanded by the description of God as a being perfectly simple and unitary. For if that description were true, it would be impossible to select from the others one of God's attributes for consideration; yet this selection and consideration would be required in order to make plain to what divine trait "per-

---

55 Cf. Copleston, *op. cit.*, v–vi.
56 Cf. *De Natura Boni,* i, translated, *The Nature of the Good,* in The Library of Christian Classics, *Augustine's Earlier Writings,* translated by John H. S. Burleigh, The Westminster Press, Philadelphia, Pa., 1953.

fect goodness" refers. It is, nonetheless, quite clear that there is only one perfectly good being and that that one is God.

"Goodness" as a term by which we refer to some feature of created things, however, is not incapable of definition within Augustine's system; and a definition of it results from a consideration of the view that the goodness of every created thing is derivative from that of God. We have seen that God entertains all possible worlds; that he created only one; and that in the actual world, each being was fashioned after its exemplar in the system of propositions which God's creation made true. The goodness of each created thing is its likeness to its exemplar, and the word "goodness" means this likeness. This definition, however, presupposes the goodness of the exemplars which, clearly, cannot be defined in the same way, and their goodness presupposes the perfection of God. While "goodness" with respect to created things may be defined, its definition borrows all its force and propriety from the perfect goodness of God, the term which cannot be defined. This is the sense in which the excellence of created things is derivative from the supreme goodness of God.

Augustine offers a criterion for the goodness of created things, i.e., a set of traits from whose presence we may with perfect certainty infer the goodness of anything that possesses them. Anything, he says, which has measure, form, and order, is also good.[57] The measure of a thing is, apparently, that about it which admits of quantitative determination, e.g., its size, its weight, and the number and proportion of its parts.[58] The form of a thing is the pattern it exhibits, i.e., the character it must possess by virtue of its exemplar. The order of a thing is the interrelation of its parts and its relations to other beings. An ape has some size, a character determined by the exemplar for apes, and a certain internal organization and external connection with its natural environment. According as the measure, form, and order of a thing are more like its exemplar in the system of divine thought which God made true, the thing is better, for it has more goodness. According as its measure, form, and order are less like that exemplar the thing is worse. An ape four and a half feet high, exhibiting well its form and lacking no vital organ and no vital connection with its jungle is quite a good ape; but one twelve feet high, possessed of short arms, bereft of legs and ill-adjusted to the jungle is a poor one. The measure, form, and order are so deficient as to make it little like the exemplar for apes.[59]

This criterion can never be absent from any created thing. A natural being which could not be measured, which had no form, or which betrayed no internal and external order, would be nothing at all. Every-

[57] Cf., *Ibid.,* III.
[58] Cf., *Ibid.,* VIII, XXI.
[59] Cf. *Ibid.,* XV.

thing that satisfies the criterion of goodness, therefore, exists; and every part of creation possesses some degree of goodness. Augustine regards the entire created world as a system of beings, ranging from the inanimate through the vegetative, the sentient, the embodied rational, and the purely spiritual but mutable, determined by the degree of goodness possessed by each being.

Standing over this system as its creator is God. He cannot be said to be good in the way in which created things are, nor even to exist after their fashion; for the criterion for both is inapplicable to Him. Measure, form, and order issue from His power for use in our judgment of created things;[60] and as a consequence these traits can apply to Him in no way at all. It is nonetheless by reference to Him that Augustine hits upon the nature of the goodness of created things; and by use of this notion, together with that of the criterion of goodness and of existence, he shows that every created thing, angelic, human, sentient, vegetative, and inanimate, is genuinely good—a view that supports the pre-ethical belief expressed in his universal history that everything has its law and, as a consequence, its "proper" or "just" place in the order of the world.

Although everything is good, the goodness for each particular thing, considered concretely, differs from that of many others; for exemplars, likeness to which constitutes the goodness of particular things, vary from species to species. Let us ask, then, what is good for man.

The good for man, according to Augustine, is an existence in conformity with the exemplar for the human species. For a short time, this exemplar had its most perfect embodiment in Adam and Eve; and it is their life of innocence which is most like it. In it, these earliest members of the human species found a life well measured, formed, and ordered. Their faculties, reason, feeling, and will were correctly measured. Each was present, and its proportion to the others was as it should be. Through reason, Adam and Eve knew God intimately. Their sole desire was for possession of Him. They willed to obey His commands. Their lives were very nearly perfectly formed; for their knowledge of God, their love for Him resulting from their desire, and their will to obey the laws which their knowledge revealed, constituted an almost exact likeness of the idea in whose image God created them. Their lives also were well ordered; for their bodies were subservient to their wills, their wills to their reasons, and their feelings to both. To this internal order there corresponded a set of external relations which constituted perfect adjustment to life in the Garden. Well measured, formed, and ordered, their lives were very good; and their great likeness to the exemplar amounted to nearly unblemished joy. Neither fear nor sorrow stained this happiness. It was

---

[60] Cf. *Ibid.,* III.

merely threatened by the possibility of voluntary disobedience, a possibility that stemmed from God's gift to their wills of freedom in choice. Although they shortly abandoned their human excellence, it remains as the best instance of human goodness or the happy life.

All men desire happiness. To be happy is to have what one wants at the time when the wish for it occurs.[61] Moreover, what is wanted and possessed must be perfectly good; otherwise, some degree of wretchedness rather than joy pervades the satisfaction of the wish.[62] What makes one happy, then, "must ever remain, independent of all fate and mishap"; if it did not, it might not exist when it was wanted.[63] The object upon which the desire for happiness focuses must be what is eternal and perfectly good; and this is God. Only a life in union with God can satisfy the desire for happiness in which all men share; and all those who think they find their happiness in activities of other kinds mistake a spurious representation of it for the good life.

In the genuinely happy life, two elements may be distinguished: one is obedience; the other, realization. In his creation God established the model for all conduct of his human creatures; and it is His command that men should live according to it. To act rightly is to obey this command; and one who acts rightly throughout all his life may be happy.

In His creation, God also gave to man the desire to obey His laws. The will of Adam and of Eve was, latterly, exercised in such a way as to frustrate this desire. But since all men wish for and seek genuine happiness, even though they have never achieved it, Augustine argues that the image of the beatific life and the wish to realize it is in their minds, perhaps as a racial inheritance from the early experience of Adam.[64] One who acts rightly, then, and realizes his desire to do so, will live as God commands; he will realize that desire for union with, or possession of divinity in which the highest human joy is found. The measure, form, and order of his activities will be much like that of life before the Fall.

There is a negative as well as a positive import of the command and the desire to measure up well against the exemplar for humanity. All secular pursuits must be reduced to a minimum, i.e., the minimum required for reproducing the race, for bringing it to the Christian insight, and for living with one another in that respectful communion which God's laws require and which is part of the love of God and of one another in Him. Chastity, except for begetting, abstinence from the pleasure of the palate, rejection of knowledge and the arts as pleasures but not as channels to beatitude, repudiation of wealth and secular power, except

[61] Cf. *De Beata Vita;* also *Confessions,* X.
[62] Cf. *De Beata Vita.*
[63] Cf. *Ibid.*
[64] Cf. *Confessions,* X.

as means for advancing Christianity, provide the theme for Augustine's other-worldly morality.

What remains is the duty to further Christianity through religion and education. For despite the inheritance of sin, all men desire beatitude and the possession of Him "whom to know and to love is the blessed life which, though all claim to seek it, few indeed may rejoice that they have found." [65]

EPISTEMOLOGY

We have seen in the discussion of his psychology that Augustine asserts four ways of knowing, together with four different kinds of knowledge resulting therefrom. In his answer to the question, "What is knowledge, and how is it secured?," that is, in his theory of knowledge, Augustine accounts for these four ways of knowing as well as for their products. Let us begin with the first part of the question.

Augustine seems never to have departed from the view that knowledge consists in a certain relation between the soul and an object, and that this relation is such that the soul is completely certain as to the object of which it is aware. Anything else is mere belief, awareness in which we might be mistaken about the object present to us. But the objects of knowledge consist of two kinds: those which are private to each soul, or subjective, and those which are publicly accessible to all, or objective. Those which are private include idiosyncratic deliverances of sense; ". . . one man can both see and hear what another does not see or hear, and with any of the other senses can perceive what another does not perceive." [66] Awareness of such deliverances consists in their presence to sense, and this presence consists merely in a confrontation of the soul by a sharply delimited sensory element. Whenever one is aware of such an object, one can know it; for while its mere presence would carry with it no information (as may be the case with brutes), man's reason guarantees that, however private, it must appear to be what it genuinely is to the sense concerned. If it did not, it would be other than it is. Of such objects, we can know that they are what they seem; and ". . . all in the act of knowing which does not come from sense-perception is provided by reason, to which are reported and referred all external circumstances. Thus sense-data can be accepted—but strictly within their own limits—and can be comprehended not by sense only but also by knowledge." [67] Error con-

---

[65] Cf. *De Magistro*, xiv.

[66] Cf. *Augustine: Earlier Writings, De Libero Arbitrio*, translated by John H. S. Burleigh, The Library of Christian Classics, The Westminster Press, Philadelphia, 1953, II, vii, §15.

[67] Cf., *Ibid.*, II, iii, §9.

cerning idiosyncratic sensations consists not in a mistake as to their character, but in a mistake as to their source or origin, i.e., in supposing that they are public or objective.

Introspection as well as idiosyncratic sensation yields objects that are private. The consciousness of our own acts of reasoning, of feeling, of willing, and of remembering, as well as those of the various kinds of imagining, is the consciousness of things which cannot fail to be what they appear; and although no one else can perceive our feelings, our willings, our imaginings, and our memories, we ourselves cannot doubt that introspection reveals them without error. In the case of memory, as we have seen, there must be recognition of the image as an image of something sensed before; and Augustine treats this recognition as infallible although he does not explain its infallibility.

Objects that are public are those which all men may come to know; and of them, there are six important kinds: the principles of logic together with what they yield, the objects of mathematics, the laws of æsthetics, the standards of morality, the physical and social order, and God. The first four are discovered, in part, by introspection. An inward turning of the soul finds the basic principles concerned; and from these inward truths, reason's activity of ordering and correcting develops systems of logic and mathematics, of æsthetics and morality. As we have seen, these objects of reason must be mental, at least in the sense that they cannot be derived from sensory observation.[68] But although they are either introspected or derived from those which are, they are not private.[69] For all men find the same objects by introspection; and since reason is identical throughout the human species, its working upon them yields results which are identical for all. As a consequence, a single body of logical and mathematical, of æsthetic and moral truths is valid for all men; and relativity in these matters cannot be countenanced.

Each being in the natural and social world, as well as that entire order itself, is an object public to all knowers; and its publicity is of two different sorts. First, there is the publicity of a part of its sensible character; the qualities of things revealed through sight, through hearing, and through touch are open to public observation. That they are so is guaranteed in part by knowledge of idiosyncratic sensations. All men can observe that a given object is red or sounding or rough, for one man's perception of it does not preclude another by altering or destroying it. But smell and taste are always directed toward different things, and always involve an alteration or destruction of the thing smelled or tasted. Smells and tastes consequently, are private. "It is . . . evident that things which we perceive with the bodily senses without causing them to change are by

68 Cf. *Confessions,* X.
69 Cf. *De Libero Arbitrio,* II, VIII, IX.

nature quite different from our senses, and consequently are common to us both, because they are not converted and changed into something which is our peculiar and almost private property."[70] The logical, mathematical, æsthetic, and moral properties of things are not observable by sense. A thing's identity with itself, the number of its parts and proportion of its sides, its beauty, or its moral worth, we cannot perceive. Yet these properties are public; and Augustine finds a second factor in the publicity of the items in the natural and social order which follows from the fact that they provide instances of the truths discovered by reason. Knowledge of the external world, of nature and of man, consists in sensory observation of visible, audible, and tangible objects ordered, arranged, and evaluated according to the truths of reason.

Knowledge of the external world involves, then, truths of two different sorts. First, it involves the truths of reason which, earlier, we saw to be necessary in the sense that their denials involved contradiction. These are the truths which no possible world could violate; and they consist of the logical and mathematical, the æsthetic and moral laws that would govern any possible order. Secondly, there are truths that are not necessary; and of these, there are also two kinds, i.e., those which assert the visible, audible, and tangible qualities of things, and those which assert their rationally discoverable properties. Those of the first kind, that is, the truths of reason, we cannot be mistaken about even though the objects they describe might not have existed; for the sensible characters presented to us are evidently what they are. They are instances of the "knowledge of sense comprehended by reason." Those of the second kind, similarly, we cannot be mistaken about although they need not be true. That this red square has equal diagonals we can be utterly certain of since it is evidently a red *square*. But it need not have been so, and the truth of which we are completely certain is not a necessary one. These nonnecessary truths which describe the external world are those statements at least some of which would be false if another world had existed; and they consist of truths which describe visible, audible, and tangible objects as well as those which state that these objects manifest certain laws. The fifth object of knowledge, public to all, is the natural and social world, and it is described in a body of truths made up of some which are necessary and some which are not.

The sixth object public to all knowers is God. As we have seen, reason, which is universal to man, can prove His existence and at least, in part, His character. This proof, of course, involves a similarly public relation of God to the order of the world. So long as our reasoning is correct, then, our awareness of God cannot be mistaken.

---

[70] Cf. *Ibid.*, II, vii, §19. It is not clear why Augustine uses the word "almost."

Augustine's two claims—the one, that we can know sensations as well as memories, feelings, acts of will, and images, which are confined to ourselves, and the other, that our awareness of logic and mathematics, of æsthetics and morals, of the external world and God amounts to knowledge—allow for one strong objection. Both claims involve the existence of the self, i.e., the existence of a knower who engages in sensation and introspection, and from whose activity rational and empirical knowledge results. If it cannot be shown beyond the possibility of doubt that the self or soul exists, his claims simply cannot be made. In his answer to the question how knowledge may be secured, the second question of epistemology, Augustine provides a method by which the existence of the self or soul is assured, and as a consequence, the answer to the first question of epistemology.

My own existence, Augustine says, is something about which I might be deceived; but if I might be deceived about it, I must exist since the deception of a nonexistent person is incomprehensible. I know, then, that I exist, and from this knowledge it is manifest that I am alive. It is equally manifest from my knowledge of both facts that I am an intelligence.[71] We may substitute any name for the pronoun "I"; and whenever such an argument is made, the existence, the life, and the intelligence of the arguer is guaranteed against all doubt. It is this existence, life, and intelligence which is required in order to support the claims to knowledge which Augustine makes; and in arguing that we know it, Augustine engaged in the method of initial doubt, the procedure of questioning everything in order to see what can be known, whose authorship is often attributed to Descartes. This pre-Cartesian method is, however, a method of reason, for it depends upon the irrationality of denying the existence of the self.

The existence of the soul is guaranteed in another way, and this other way is introspection. In Book Ten, Chapter 8, of the *Confessions*, Augustine gives an account of the things and activities he can know when he comes "into the fields and broad palaces of memory." "Memory" is used as a synonym for "introspection." One of the many things and activities he discovers is "the seat of my very mind";[72] and this seat seems to be the self or soul in its activities of reasoning, including imagination; feeling, including sensation; and willing. What is revealed in this way we can be completely certain of, for the denial that it is before our mind, when it is so, would amount to a contradiction. Augustine does not formally advance introspection as one way of securing knowledge; but in fact, he supplements reason's guarantee of the self with introspective knowledge.

71 *Ibid.*, II, III.
72 *Confessions*, X, §25.

Introspection, also, assures us that the things or contents of our minds, images, memories, feelings, and acts of will are what they appear to it to be; but this assurance is enhanced by reason's guarantee that each one could not be different.

Further, it is by introspection that we discover the principles of logic and mathematics, of æsthetics and of morals. Augustine clearly holds that these principles are discovered within ourselves, even though they possess universal validity. Once introspection has done its work, reason takes over to develop the systems to which these principles lead.

Knowledge of the order of the world may be secured by a method which combines observation with reason. The senses must tell us what visible, audible, and tangible objects surround us, and also what visible, audible, and tangible relations, in fact, sensible objects bear to one another. But reason provides the laws to which these sensible objects are subordinated in our knowledge of the external world.

Our knowledge of idiosyncratic sensations, likewise, is secured through observation and through reason. Observation tells us that we have them and that others do not. Reason assures us that they are what they appear, and even, perhaps, what the laws are by which they are produced.

The existence of God is guaranteed by reason. We have seen that the dominant argument in Augustine's thought is the argument from the necessity of a ground for the truths, both necessary and nonnecessary, which describe the order of the world; but the need for such a ground rests upon the irrationality of there being none. The dominant argument for God's existence contains, however, one element which relies upon observation, namely, the premise that one particular world exists, the one which we find about us. Our knowledge of this statement, as we have seen, depends upon observation as well as upon reason.

Despite the rational and empirical argument, Augustine is not always satisfied that reason and observation can provide knowledge of God. Our observation of our friends gives us only a very superficial acquaintance with them, and our intellect provides no more adequate knowledge of them.[73] What we desire is a knowledge of them which is so thoroughgoing and joyous that observation and reason seem inadequate ways of achieving it. Augustine suggests that the method by which a conclusive knowledge of God may be achieved is like the method which we would follow if we could arrive at this profound knowledge of our friends or even of ourselves;[74] but he says that this method is unknown. For it must be a method that leads to an awareness of God which is not

---

[73] *Soliloquia,* I, III.
[74] Despite the assertions of knowledge, Augustine also doubts that we can know ourselves. Cf. *ibid.*

infallible merely, but suffused with perfect joy as well—a joy much more perfect than that which would accompany a complete knowledge of our friends. Neither reason, observation, nor introspection lead to this beatitude;[75] and Augustine suggests that some method different from one or all of these is required to provide that knowledge of God which is both certain and superlatively good, although he also wonders if this is not a matter rather of the object known than of the path to be pursued.

One might suppose that Augustine wishes to supplement faith in God with an intimate acquaintance with Him analogous to the acquaintance which, in *De Magistro,* he contends we can have with individuals present to us but not with those who never have been present. Of the latter, we can have knowledge only by description; we can know only that they fall under certain universals. Consequently, our awareness of them always falls short of that fullness which direct acquaintance affords. Augustine argues, in this vein, that Plato and Plotinus may have spoken truly and at length about God, and yet have known Him not. But this interpretation of the method for knowing God must be rejected because, Augustine argues, that method is quite unlike observation. Whatever the method, we must start with faith or belief in God as revealed in the Scriptures, with hope that we can come to know Him, and with earnest love of Him. Given these three things, the method by which knowledge of God is secured will be one in whose success faith becomes knowledge, and hope unbroken possession. Love will remain unaltered because its object never can again be lost.

There is a tendency in Augustine's thought toward mysticism, i.e., toward the view that God can be known by no ordinary method, that the method for knowing Him cannot be completely formulated, and that the adorable nature of deity is itself incapable of rational formulation. This tendency is subordinated to the dominant argument. But even when it is present, faith, hope, and love still are necessary; and at times Augustine's words suggest that reason and observation can prepare us for the earthly knowledge that we cannot know God fully here,[76] and for a mystical union with Him after death.

SUMMARY AND CONCLUSION

In his analysis of the concept "teaching" Augustine arrives at the conclusion that teaching consists in the teacher's use of language to prompt the student to his own activity of learning, and that learning involves the student's seeing by divine illumination that the statements he learns are true. This analysis of "teaching" depends upon the existence of

[75] Cf. *Ibid.,* I, v.
[76] Cf. *De Ordine,* II.

God, the source of inner illumination. It would be nonsensical were there no such source, for it would amount to the assertion that teaching which does occur consists in something which does not. Augustine's metaphysics presents a proof that God, the source of inner illumination, does exist. It supplements his analysis of "teaching" by providing a reference for one of the terms into which that concept is analyzed.

The metaphysical theory also explains the psychology and universal history upon which Augustine bases his educational recommendations. God, the creator, explains the psychological statements of fact employed; for His endowing the original parent with a perfect life as well as with a free will accounts for the present degenerate state of the soul together with its desire for perfect happiness. Both these are known by observation, but why they must be as they are observed to be is explained by their divine but unobservable source. Moreover, the history of nature and of man which might analogously be assigned a basis in empirical evidence appears as a necessary consequence of God's omniscient intellect and omnipotent will. Further, the metaphysical theory supplements the statements of fact which Augustine draws from his psychology and universal history; for it shows that the person described by that psychology and whose fortunes and destiny are set forth by that history is immortal.[77] Both faith and reason give assurance that God created man immortal. The Scriptures say it, and reason demonstrates it.

The metaphysical explanation for and supplement of statements of fact serve to strengthen both the goal and subordinate recommendations of Augustine's educational theory. The objective of education is conversion to Christianity and willing obedience to God's law as a consequence of love for Him. But the recommendation of this goal for teaching would be pointless without some assurance that God exists; it appears to have been more urgent for Augustine because of the punishment in immortal life of those who do not achieve conversion and do not manifest repentance. The metaphysical theory provides assurance of God and of His power to reward and to punish; and by strengthening the goal of teaching, it also reinforces the recommendations subordinate thereto, i.e., propagation of Christianity through the Church and the course of study in the schools.

Augustine's ethical theory offers an analysis of generic goodness, of human goodness and rightness, and a statement as to what things possess these traits. In this way, it affords a justification of the view that obedience to God's law is right, and that a life of blessedness, much like that of Adam and Eve, is the best for man. But it is clear that the justification

---

[77] The argument for immortality is both scriptural and dialectical. I have omitted it here because the space required for its explanation is too great. Cf. Saint Augustine, e.g., *Soliloquia, De Immortalitate Animae,* and *De Civitate Dei.*

that is proffered is based on the metaphysical theory, for the view that acting rightly is obeying God's law, and that the good life is one in which secular desires are subordinated to the will to obey the law, would collapse into emptiness in the absence of that theory.

Augustine's theory of knowledge, his account of its nature and method, may be regarded as assuring the propriety of the methods of instruction recommended in his educational theory. We have seen that he recommends authoritative instruction in the earlier stages of education; this method, used in teaching the liberal arts, and designed to foster belief or faith rather than knowledge, is suited to those incapable of careful introspection and highly rationalized procedures and devoid of a wide and cumulative experience of the sensible world. He suggests that, in the more advanced educational stages, what authority teaches may, for the highly reasonable, be converted into knowledge. This conversion requires the introspection of, and logical operation upon those truths which divine illumination reveals, and their application to sensible objects of which discriminating observation has built up a large body of memories or experience in the learner's mind.

From Augustine's writings, two sets of passages have been selected: the first from *De Magistro, The Teacher;* the second, from *De Ordine, Divine Providence and the Problem of Evil.* Both works are dialogues. The persons of *The Teacher* are Augustine and his natural son, Adeodatus, aged fifteen. Augustine tells[78] us that all the views in it expressed by Adeodatus were his own; and quite justly, he says that Adeodatus's talent was a matter of awe. The boy died not long after the conversation.

A Guide to Selections from *The Teacher*

In the excerpts from *The Teacher,* Chapter I, Saint Augustine holds that language serves two purposes. It expresses thought and feeling as in the case of prayer, but it also teaches others. Teaching is bringing others to know something; and Saint Augustine asks how, in view of the nature of language as he understands it, it is possible that we should succeed in teaching by using language for that purpose.

In Chapters II, III, and VIII, Saint Augustine presents the chief points in his theory of language. A sign is a noise, a mark, a gesture, or what not, which directs the attention of its user to its meaning—the physical object, the state of mind, or, generally, the thing signified. Words, the parts of language, make up one class of signs. A sentence is a collection of words, ordered according to the rules of its language, that signifies that

[78] Cf. *Confessions,* IX, VI.

group of things, each member of which is the meaning of one of its words.

At first, Saint Augustine and Adeodatus believe that teaching others requires the use of language; for it seems that directing someone's attention to a thing, i.e., bringing him to know it, can occur only by uttering the word that names it. Then, they notice that since words as noises or marks are different from their meanings, one must discover those meanings, one must come to know the things signified, independently of the words for them. One can never learn a thing by use of its word. For if he understands the word, he already confronts the thing it signifies; if he does not understand the word, he does not have its meaning before him. In neither case does the use of a word bring another person to attend for the first time to the thing it names—to knowledge of it.

In Chapters VIII, X, XI, XII, and XIV Saint Augustine argues that one man can never teach another in the sense of providing him with new information. For when he utters a sentence to another, the other does not understand it at all, or understands either that it is false or that it is true. In the first case, no information is provided; in the second and third cases, the sentence embodies information the other has; but it is not new information since he must have had it in order to understand the sentence—in order to find it meaningful.

In these chapters, Saint Augustine argues that God and nature provide men with new information that comes in through the senses, through introspection, and through rational reflection—all of which is retained in the memory. He holds also that God, or Christ the Teacher, illumines for each man, in accordance with his capacities, the connections between the bits of information thus provided and retained. The discovery of information is a performance, supervised and made possible by God, that each man must engage in for himself. Thus, the tutorial use of language can never consist in bringing others to possess information they do not possess independently of that teaching; it is, rather, at most, the reminding of another of what he has already learned with the help of divine illumination from the observation of nature, and from reflection upon and reasoning about the principles he finds within himself.

SELECTIONS FROM

The Teacher*

⟶◆⟵

CHAPTER I

The purpose of speech

AUGUSTINE. What do you think we propose to do when we speak?

ADEODATUS. As far as occurs to me at this moment, we intend either to teach or to learn.

AUG. One of these is clear to me, and I agree with you: obviously, when we speak we do wish to teach. But as to learning—how does that enter in?

AD. Well, how do you think, but by asking questions?

AUG. Even in that case, as I understand it, we intend to do nothing else than to teach. For, I ask you, do you put questions for any other reason than to teach the one you interrogate, what it is you wish to know?

AD. You are right.

AUG. So you see that our purpose in speaking is solely to teach.

AD. No, that is not clear to me. For if speaking is nothing more than uttering words, I notice we do that when we sing. And since we often sing when we are alone, with no one present to learn, I do not think that we wish to teach anything.

AUG. Yes, but I think there is a kind of teaching which functions by reminding—an important kind, indeed, as the theme of our discussion will bring out. But if you do not think that we learn when we remember and that one does not teach when he reminds, I make no objection; and let me agree, for the present, to two reasons for speaking: either to teach, or to remind others or ourselves; and the latter is what we do even when we sing, do you not think so?

AD. Not entirely. For it is very seldom that I sing to remind myself; I do so only for the pleasure I get out of it.

* The selections that follow are taken from *Ancient Christian Writers*, No. 9, Saint Augustine, *The Teacher (De Magistro)*, edited by Johannes Quasten, S.T.D., and Joseph C. Plumpe, Ph.D., translated and annotated by Joseph M. Colleran, C.SS.R., Ph.D., published by the Newman Press, Westminster, Md., 1950, and Longmans, Green & Co., Limited, London. Reprinted with the kind permission of the publishers. Footnotes omitted.

AUG. I see your point. But you are, of course, aware that what pleases you in song is a certain rhythm of sound. Since this can be added to words or taken from them, is not speaking one thing, and singing another? Song, as you know, is produced by flute and harp; again, the birds sing; and sometimes we, too, hum musical sounds without words, which can be called song, but not speech. Is there anything here you would take exception to?

AD. No, nothing.

2. AUG. You hold, then, that speech originated for the sole reason of teaching or reminding?

AD. So I would hold, did it not strike me that when we pray, we certainly do speak; and—there is the rub—it is not right to think that God should be taught by us or that we should remind Him of anything.

. . .

AUG. . . . Wherefore, there is no need of speech—that is, of vocalized words—when we pray, except perhaps to manifest the mind, as the priests do, not that God may hear, but that men may hear and, by being reminded, may with one accord dedicate themselves to God. Or do you regard this differently?

AD. I am in complete agreement.

. . .

AUG. . . . I believe you notice at the same time that even when a person merely strains his mind toward something, although we utter no sound, yet because we ponder the words themselves, we do speak within our own minds. So, too, speech serves us only to remind, since the memory in which the words inhere, by recalling them, brings to mind the realities themselves, of which the words are signs.

AD. I understand and follow you.

CHAPTER II

Words are signs. Can meanings of words be
shown only by using words?

3. AUG. Do we agree then, that words are signs?
AD. Yes.
AUG. Now, can a sign be a sign unless it signifies something?
AD. No.
AUG. How many words are there in this verse:
    If nothing from this great heaven-doomed city remain?
AD. Eight.
AUG. Then there are eight signs?
AD. Yes.

AUG. I presume you understand this verse.

AD. Quite well, I think.

AUG. Tell me what each word signifies.

AD. I see what "if" signifies, but I find no other word to indicate its meaning.

AUG. Whatever the word signifies—do you at least know where it exists?

AD. It seems to me that "if" signifies doubt, and where is doubt but in the mind?

AUG. I grant that for now. Go on to the rest.

AD. "Nothing" can signify only what does not exist.

.   .   .

AUG. What are we to do, then? Shall we, instead of saying that this word signifies a thing which does not exist, rather say that it signifies some state of mind when it sees no reality, yet finds, or thinks that it finds, that the reality does not exist?

AD. That may be precisely what I was struggling to explain.

.   .   .

AD. The third is the proposition "from," for which we can, I think, say "of."

AUG. I am not asking you to substitute for one word quite familiar another equally familiar having the same meaning—if, indeed, it has the same meaning—but let us grant that for the present. Undoubtedly, if the poet had said, not "from this great city," but "of this great city," and if I asked you what "of" means, you would say "from," since here you would have two words, that is, signs, signifying, as you think, the same thing. But what I am looking for is that one single thing, whatever it is, which is signified by those two signs.

AD. It seems to me that some sort of separation from a thing in which something had been, is signified; and that this is said to be "from" the former, be it that that former thing no longer remains, as in the present verse where a city no longer remains, though some Trojans could be "from"that city; or be it that it does remain, for instance, when we say that traders "from" Rome are in Africa.

AUG. Granted that this is so, and let me not enumerate how many exceptions to this rule of yours can be found: just the same, you can readily see that you have explained words by words—that is, signs by signs—and what is quite familiar by what is equally familiar. But I would like you to show me, if you can, the realities themselves of which these are signs.

CHAPTER III

Can anything be made known without a sign?

5.   AD. I am astonished that you do not know, or rather pretend not to know, that what you wish cannot be accomplished at all by any replies of mine. For we are holding a discussion, and in so doing we cannot give answers except in words. But here you are looking for realities which, whatever they may be, certainly are not words, and yet you yourself, too, are using words to ask for them. Therefore, you must first ask for them without words, if you want me to answer on the same terms.

AUG. You are within your rights, I admit. Yet if I should ask you what the three syllables signify when the word *paries* ["wall"] is pronounced, could you not point it out with your finger, so that, by your showing me and without your using any words, I could directly see the thing itself of which this three-syllable word is a sign?

AD. I admit that can be done, but only in regard to nouns that signify bodies, and when those bodies are present.

AUG. We do not call color a body, do we? Do we not rather call it a quality of a body?

AD. Yes.

AUG. Why, then, can it, too, be pointed out with the finger? Or do you also add to bodies the qualities of bodies, so that the latter, when they are present, can be manifested equally well without words?

AD. When I mentioned bodies, I meant all corporeal things; that is, everything in bodies that can be known by the senses.

AUG. But think this over—should you not also make some exceptions here?

AD. Good advice! For I should have said, not all corporeal things, but all visible things. I admit, of course, that sound, odor, savor, weight, heat and other properties that pertain to the senses other than sight, although they cannot be known by the senses unless they are in bodies, and therefore are bodily, nevertheless cannot be indicated by pointing the finger.

AUG. Have you never seen people holding a sort of conversation with deaf persons by means of gestures, and the deaf themselves also using gestures to ask questions or to answer them, to communicate or indicate most, if not all, of their wishes? When this is done, surely not only visible objects are manifested without words, but also sounds and savors and all the other things of this sort. Yes, actors in the theatres, too, present and enact entire stories, for the most part by employing pantomime without words.

AD. I have nothing to say against that, except that not only I but even the pantomimist himself would be unable to show you, without using words, what that "from" means.

6.   AUG. Perhaps you are right. But let us suppose that he can. You do not doubt, I presume, that whatever that action of the body would be by which he would try to show me the reality that is signified by this word, it would not be the reality itself, but a sign of it. Therefore, he, too, though not using a word for a word, will still be indicating a sign by a sign—meaning that the monosyllable "from" and the gesture will signify some one thing, which is what I would like to have shown me without a sign being made.

AD. How, I ask you, is it possible to do what you want?

AUG. In the same way that it was possible with regard to the wall.

AD. Not even that, so our step-by-step reasoning has made clear, can be shown without a sign. For obviously the pointing of the finger is not the wall, but a sign by means of which the wall can be seen. I see nothing, therefore, that can be made known without signs.

AUG. What if I were to ask you what walking is, and you were to get up and walk? Would you not be using the reality itself, rather than words or any other signs, to teach me?

AD. I admit that is so, and I am ashamed that I did not see what is so evident. From this thousands of other things now occur to me, which can be shown directly and not through signs, such as eating, drinking, sitting, standing, calling, and countless other things.

AUG. Well, tell me now, if I, completely ignorant of the meaning of this word, were to ask you what walking is, while you were walking, how would you teach me?

AD. I should walk somewhat faster, so that following your question some new element would suggest it to you; and at the same time I would be doing only what had to be shown.

AUG. Do you not know that walking and hurrying are two different things? One who walks does not by that fact hurry. And one who hurries does not necessarily walk; for we speak of hurrying in regard to writing and reading, and countless other things. Hence, if after my question you were to do more hurriedly what you happened to be doing, I would think walking is the same as hurrying, for that is the new element you would have added; and I would for this reason be misled.

AD. I admit that we cannot manifest a thing without a sign, if we are asked about it while we are in the act of doing it. For if we add nothing, he who puts the question will think that we are unwilling to show him, and that, ignoring him, we are merely continuing to do what we were doing before. Should he, however, ask about things that we are able to do, but does not ask while we are actually doing them, we can, by doing it after he puts his question, show what he is asking about, by means of the reality itself rather than by a sign—unless he chances to ask me what speaking is, while I am speaking. For then, whatever I should say to teach him—speak I must; and pursuing my course from there, I shall teach him until I make plain to him what he wants to know, without departing from the reality itself which he asked to have shown him, and without looking for signs to manifest it, other than speech itself. . . .

CHAPTER VIII

*The practical value of such discussion. The necessity
of directing attention to realities signified.*

• • •

22.   AUG. Very well, let us then, consider that division in which signs signify not other signs, but those things we call signifiable. And first tell me whether man is man.

AD. But now you are perhaps joking.

AUG. Why so?

AD. Because you think it necessary to ask me whether man is anything but man [homo].

AUG. I suppose you would think that I was again poking fun at you if I should also ask whether the first syllable of this noun is other than *ho-* and the second other than *-mo*.

AD. I certainly would.

AUG. But when those syllables are joined, you have *homo*—or will you deny that?

AD. Who could deny that?

AUG. I ask you, then, whether you are these two syllables conjoined?

AD. Not at all. But I see what you are driving at.

AUG. Tell me, then, to save me from appearing offensive to you.

AD. You think the inference is that I am not a man.

AUG. Well, do you not think so too, since you grant the truth of everything we have said before, from which this follows?

AD. I shall not tell you what I think until I first hear from you whether in your question about man being man you were asking about those two syllables or about the reality itself which they signify.

AUG. Do you rather answer in what sense you have taken my question. For if it is ambiguous, you should have guarded against that first, and not answered until you found out in what sense I put the question.

AD. But why should this ambiguity embarrass me, when I have given the answer to both questions? For man is certainly man: obviously, those two syllables are nothing more than those two syllables; and that which they signify is nothing but what it is.

. . .

AD. Nothing could be more true. Why, then, should the mind take offense when someone says, "So, you are not 'man'," since, according to what we granted nothing truer could be said?

AUG. Because as soon as those words are pronounced, I cannot but think that the conclusion has reference to what is signified by these two syllables, and that by reason of the rule which naturally has dominance, namely, that when signs are heard the attention is directed to the realities signified.

AD. I agree with you.

CHAPTER X

*Is teaching possible without signs? Words themselves
do not make us know realities.*

29. AUG. Do you think that all actions which we are able to perform the moment we are asked about them, can be manifested without a sign, or would you make any exception?

AD. Considering this whole class over and over again, I still find nothing that can be taught without signs, except perhaps speaking, and possibly teaching, if someone should inquire what teaching itself is. For I see that whatever I may do, following his inquiry, to make him learn, he does not learn from the reality itself which he desires to have shown to him. For example, if anyone should ask me what walking is, while I am not, as was said, engaged in anything or while I am doing something else, and I should try to teach him what he is asking about, without a sign, by promptly starting to walk, how am I to avoid having him think that just the amount of walking I have done is walking? And if he should think that, he will be deceived: he will decide that anyone who walks a longer or shorter distance than I have walked, is not walking. And what I have said about this one word applies to all the things which I had agreed can be shown without a sign, save those two which we have excepted.

30. AUG. Very well, I accept that. But does it not seem to you that speaking is one thing, and teaching another?

AD. It certainly seems so. For if they were the same, no one would teach except by speaking; but since we also teach many things by means of other signs besides words, who can doubt that there is a difference?

AUG. Well, then, are teaching and signifying the same? Or is there some difference?

AD. I think they are the same.

AUG. Is he not right who says that we signify in order to teach?

AD. Absolutely right.

AUG. What if another should say that we teach in order to give signs? Would it not be easy to refute him by the norm we established before?

AD. Yes.

AUG. Wherefore, if we give signs in order to teach, but do not teach in order to give signs, teaching and signifying are two different things.

AD. You are right, and I was wrong in answering that both are the same.

AUG. Now answer this: does he who teaches what teaching is, do so by giving signs or in some other way?

AD. I do not see how he can do it otherwise.

AUG. Therefore, it is incorrect to say what you said a while ago, that in the case of the question what teaching is, the reality in question can be taught without signs. For we see that not even this can be done without giving signs, since you have granted that signifying is one thing, and teaching another. Now, if they are different, as they appear to be, and the latter cannot be manifested except by the former, then certainly it is not manifested by itself, as you thought. Consequently, we have as yet found nothing which can be manifested by itself, except speech, which also signifies itself along with other things. Still, since speech itself is also a sign, it is not yet entirely clear that anything can be taught without signs.

AD. I have no reason for not agreeing.

.   .   .

AUG. . . . Suppose, for example, someone who is unfamiliar with the art of snaring birds, which is done with reeds and birdlime, were to meet a fowler equipped with his instruments, though not actually fowling but just walking along. On seeing him, he hurries to catch up with him and, as is natural, reflects and asks himself in his astonishment what the man's equipment means. Suppose that the fowler, when he sees the other man's attention riveted on himself, wishing to show off, disengages the reeds and with his rod and his hawk intercepts, subdues, and captures some little bird he happens to observe close by: would he not, I ask you, teach that spectator of his what he wanted to know, not by signifying, but by means of the reality itself?

AD. I am afraid we have here a repetition of what I said of the man who asks what walking is: again I fail to see that the whole art of fowling has been manifested in this case.

AUG. It is easy to relieve you of that misgiving. Let me add that we do not suppose him to be intelligent enough to understand all the details of the art from what he sees. It is sufficient for our point that it is possible to teach at least some men some matters, though not all, without signs.

AD. To that I can also add this: if he is really intelligent, he will grasp all there is to walking, when walking is demonstrated by a few steps.

AUG. So far as I am concerned, you may add that; and I not only do not object, but I am partial to it. You see that actually both of us have come to the conclusion that some people can be taught certain things without signs and that it is false that, as we thought a little while ago, absolutely nothing can be manifested without signs. Indeed, these examples suggest not one or the other, but thousands of things which are manifested by themselves, without any sign being given. Why, then, I ask you, should we doubt this? For, not to mention the countless performances of men in all the theatres who give exhibitions of things directly as they are without signs, does not God, and does not nature exhibit and manifest directly to the gaze of all, this sun and the light that bathes and clothes all things present, the moon and the other stars, the earth and the seas, and all the countless things that are begotten in them?

33.   Now, if we consider the matter more diligently, perhaps you will find that there is nothing that is learned by signs proper to it. For when a sign is presented to me, if it finds me ignorant of the reality of which it is a sign, it cannot teach me anything; but if it finds me knowing the reality, what do I learn by means of the sign? Thus, when I read: *And their saraballae were not altered,* the word *saraballae* does not manifest to me the reality which it signifies. If it is head-coverings of some sort that are called by this name, did I upon hearing this learn either what a head is or what coverings are? These I had known before; and my knowledge of them was gained not when they were called such by others, but when they were seen by myself. The first time the two syllables *cap-ut* ["head"] struck my ears, I was just as ignorant of what they signified as when I first heard or read *saraballae.* But when "head" was repeatedly expressed, noting and observing when it was used, I discovered that it was the word for a thing which was already most familiar to me from sight. Before I made that discovery, this word was a mere sound to me; but I learned it was a sign, when I found of what thing it is the sign; and I had learned that reality, as I said, not by any signifying, but by seeing it. Therefore, it is a case of the sign being learned from the thing cognized rather than that the thing is learned from a given sign.

34.   That you may understand this more clearly, suppose that we now hear the word "head" spoken for the first time, and, not knowing whether

it is only a vocal sound or whether it also signifies something, we ask what "head" is. (Remember, we wish to acquire knowledge not of the reality which is signified, but of the sign itself, which knowledge we of course lack as long as we do not know of what it is the sign.) If, then, when we put the question, the reality itself is pointed out to us, we learn the sign which we had only heard and not yet understood, by seeing this reality. But since there are two elements in that sign—the sound and the signification—we certainly perceive the sound not by means of the sign, but by the simple fact that the sound strikes the ear. We learn the signification, however, by seeing the reality which is signified. For that pointing of the finger cannot signify anything else than what the finger points out; and it indicates not the sign, but the member which is called "head." Therefore, by means of the pointing I cannot learn either the reality—since I already knew it—or the sign, for the finger was not pointed at that.

But I am not stressing the pointing of the finger; because it seems to me that it is only a sign of the indication itself, rather than of any realities indicated. It is just like the adverb "look!" [*ecce*]. In fact, we are accustomed to point the finger even when we use this adverb, lest one of them would not be a sufficient sign of the indication. What I am above all striving to convince you of, if I can, is that we do not learn anything by means of the signs called words. For, as I have said, we learn the meaning of the word—that is, the signification that is hidden in the sound—only after the reality itself which is signified has been recognized, rather than perceive that reality by means of such signification.

CHAPTER XI

We learn, not through words sounding in the ear,
but through truth that teaches internally.
Christ the Teacher.

36.   As we have seen them so far, the import of words—to state the most that can be said for them—consists in this: they serve merely to suggest that we look for realities. These they do not exhibit to us for our knowledge. On the other hand, a person teaches me something who presents to my eyes or any other bodily sense or even to my mind itself what I desire to know. By means of words, therefore, we learn nothing but words; in fact, only the sound and noise of words. For if things which are not signs cannot be words, then, even though I have already heard a word, I do not know it is a word until I know what it signifies. Consequently, with the knowledge of realities there also comes the knowledge of the words, whereas when words are heard, not even the words are learned. In fact, the words we do know we do not learn; and those we do

not know we cannot but acknowledge that we learn them only on perceiving their meaning; and this occurs not by hearing the vocal sounds
uttered, but by knowing the realities signified. It is indeed purest logic
and most truly said that when words are uttered we either know what they
signify, or we do not know. If we know, we recall rather than learn; but
if we do not know, we do not even recall, though perhaps we receive the
impulse to inquire.

37.   Now, should you say: granted that—unless we see them, we cannot
establish what those head-coverings are whose name we recognize only as
a sound, and we are in no better position regarding even the name, unless
the objects themselves are recognized. Yet we do accept the story about
those boys, how they triumphed over the king and the flames by their
faith and religion, what praise they sang to God, what honors they received even from their enemy himself. Have we learned these things otherwise than by means of words? I answer that we already knew everything
that is signified by those words. For instance, what three boys are, what
a furnace is, what fire is, what a king is, and finally, what it means to be
unharmed by fire, and whatever else those words signify, I already knew.
But Ananias, Azarias, and Misael are as unknown to me as the *saraballae;*
and these names did not help me at all to know them, nor could they help
me. Yet, that all the events which we read about in that account, actually
happened at that time and in the manner described, is something that I
admit I *believe* rather than *know*. And here we have a difference of which
those whom we believe were not unaware; for the Prophet says: *Unless
you believe, you shall not understand.* He certainly could not have said
that if he thought there is no difference between the two. Wherefore,
what I understand I also believe. Again, everything I understand, I know;
but I do not know all I believe. But I am not for that reason unaware how
useful it is to believe also many things which I do not know; and in this
usefulness I also include the account of the three boys. Hence, although
the majority of things cannot possibly be known by me, yet I know how
very useful it is to believe them.

38.   Regarding, however, all those things which we understand, it is
not a speaker who utters sounds exteriorly whom we consult, but it is
truth that presides within, over the mind itself; though it may have been
words that prompted us to make such consultation. And He who is consulted, He who is said to *dwell in the inner man,* He it is who teaches—
Christ—that is, *the unchangeable Power of God and everlasting Wisdom.*
This Wisdom every rational soul does, in fact, consult. But to each one
only so much is manifested as he is capable of receiving because of his own
good or bad will. And if one sometimes falls into error, that does not
occur by reason of defect in the Truth consulted, any more than it is a defect of the light which is outside us that the eyes of the body are often

deceived. And this is a light which we acknowledge that we consult in regard to visible things, that it may manifest them to us to the extent that we are able to perceive them.

CHAPTER XII

Internal light, internal truth.

39. Now, if regarding colors we consult light; and regarding the other sensible objects we consult the elements of this world constituting the bodies of which we have sense experience, and the senses themselves which the mind uses as interpreters to know such things; and if, moreover, regarding those things which are objects of intelligence we consult the truth within us through reasoning—then what can be advanced as proof that words teach us anything beyond the mere sound which strikes the ears? For everything we perceive, we perceive either through a sense of the body or by the mind. The former we call sensible, the latter, intelligible; or, to speak in the manner of our own authors, we call the former carnal, and the latter spiritual. When we are asked concerning the former, we answer, if the things of which we have sense knowledge are present; as when we are looking at a new moon we are asked what sort of a thing it is or where it is. In this case if the one who puts the question does not see the object, he believes words; and often he does not believe them. But learn he does not at all, unless he himself sees what is spoken about; and in that case he learns not by means of spoken words, but by means of the realities themselves and his senses. For the words have the same sound for the one who sees the object as for the one who does not see it. But when a question is asked not regarding things which we perceive while they are present, but regarding things of which we had sense knowledge in the past, then we express in speech, not the realities themselves, but the images impressed by them on the mind and committed to memory. How we can speak at all of these as true when we see they are false, I do not know— unless it be because we report on them not as things we actually see and perceive, but as things we have seen and perceived. Thus we bear these images in the depths of memory as so many attestations, so to say, of things previously perceived by the senses. Contemplating these in the mind, we have the good conscience that we are not lying when we speak. But even so, these attestations are such for us only. If one who hears me has personally perceived these things and become aware of them, he does not learn them from my words, but recognizes them from the images that are stored away within himself. If, however, he has had no sense knowledge of them, he clearly believes rather than learns by means of the words.

40.   Now, when there is question of those things which we perceive by the mind—that is, by means of the intellect and by reason—we obviously express in speech the things which we behold immediately in that interior light of truth which effects enlightenment and happiness in the so-called inner man. And at the same time if the one who hears me likewise sees those things with an inner and undivided eye, he knows the matter of which I speak by his own contemplation, not by means of my words. Hence, I do not teach even such a one, although I speak what is true and he sees what is true. For he is taught not by my words, but by the realities themselves made manifest to him by God revealing them to his inner self. Thus, if he were asked, he could also give answers regarding these things. What could be more absurd than to think that he is taught by my speech, when even before I spoke he could explain those same things, if he were asked about them?

As for the fact that, as often happens, one denies something when he is asked about it, but is brought around by further questions to affirm it, this happens by reason of the weakness of his vision, not permitting him to consult that light regarding the matter as a whole. He is prompted to consider the problem part by part as questions are put regarding those same parts that constitute the whole, which originally he was not able to see in its entirety. If in this case he is led on by the words of the questioner, still it is not that the words teach him, but they represent questions put to him in such a way as to correspond to his capacity for learning from his own inner self.

To illustrate: if I were to ask you whether it is true that nothing can be taught by means of words—the very topic we are discussing now—you would at first think the question absurd, because you could not see the problem in its entirety. Then I should have to question you in a way adapted to your capacity for hearing that Teacher within you. So I should say: "Those things which I stated and you granted as true, and of which you are certain and which you are sure you know—where did you learn them?" You would perhaps answer that I had taught them to you. Then I would rejoin: "Let us suppose I told you that I saw a man flying. Would my words give you the same certitude as if you heard that wise men are superior to fools?" You would, of course, answer in the negative and would tell me that you do not believe the former statement, or even if you did believe it, that you did not know it; whereas you knew the other statement to be absolutely certain. Certainly, the upshot of this would be that you would then realize that you had not learned anything from my words; neither in the case where you were not aware of the thing that I affirmed, nor in the case of that which you knew very well. For if you were asked about each case, you would even swear that you were unaware of the former and that you did know the latter. But then you would actually be admitting the entire proposition which you had denied, since you would now know clearly and certainly what it implies: namely, that whatever we say, the hearer either does not know whether it is true, or knows it is false, or knows that it is true. In the first of these three cases he either believes, or has an opinion, or is in doubt; in the second, he opposes and rejects the statement; in the third, he bears witness to the truth. In none of the cases, therefore, does he learn. The obvious reason is that the one who on hearing my words does not know the reality, and the one who knows that what he has heard is false, and the one who, if he were asked, could have answered precisely what was said, demonstrate that they have learned nothing from my words.

.   .   .

CHAPTER XIV

Christ teaches within the mind. Man's words are
external, and serve only to give reminders.

Teachers do not claim, do they, that their own thoughts are perceived and grasped by the pupils, but rather the branches of learning that they think they transmit by speaking? For who would be so absurdly curious as to send his child to school to learn what the teacher thinks? But when they have explained, by means of words, all those subjects which they profess to teach, and even the science of virtue and of wisdom, then those who are called pupils consider within themselves whether what has been said is true. This they do by gazing attentively at that interior truth, so far as they are able. Then it is that they learn; and when within themselves they find that what has been said is true, they give praise, not realizing that they are praising not so much teachers as persons taught— provided that the teachers also know what they are saying. But people deceive themselves in calling persons "teachers" who are not such at all, merely because generally there is no interval between the time of speaking and the time of knowing. And because they are quick to learn internally following the prompting of the one who speaks, they think they have learned externally from the one who was only a prompter.

46.   But at some other time, God willing, we shall investigate the entire problem of the utility of words, which, if considered properly, is not negligible. For the present, I have reminded you that we must not attribute to words more than is proper. Thus we should no longer merely believe, but also begin to understand how truly it has been written on divine authority that we should not call anyone on earth a teacher, since *there is One in heaven who is the teacher of all.* What "in heaven" means He Himself will teach us, who has also counselled us through the instru-

mentality of human beings—by means of signs, and externally—to turn to Him internally and be instructed. He will teach us, to know and love whom is happiness of life, and this is what all proclaim they are seeking, though there are but few who may rejoice in having really found it.

A Guide to Selections from *De Ordine*

In Book II, Chapters VII and VIII, Saint Augustine asserts that we can know that all things, even those acknowledged to be evil, fall within God's province, and that acquisition of this knowledge requires two procedures. The first is to live a life according to the Christian moral code—a life animated by faith, hope, and love, and dominated by the worship of God. The second is to pursue a certain course of studies. The rest of the passages given here are devoted to describing that course.

In Chapter IX, Saint Augustine describes the method for instructing beginners as authoritarian, but as based on the non-authoritarian knowledge—knowledge grounded in reason and experience if not mystical intuition—of the instructor. In Chapter XI, he asserts that appeal to the student's reason is the method of instruction for those few who should study on an advanced level—those few who are able to advance to knowledge, as opposed to belief, of God, of the soul, and of the Divine Providence in all things.

In Chapter XI, Augustine also analyzes the notion of reason, holding that the word refers to a certain faculty or capacity in the mind, and that its cognates—"reasonable," "rational," etc.—refer to that feature of a thing which depends upon its having been constructed or ordered by reason. The faculty is what makes us seek for, or impose measure, harmony, or order upon things. The feature they possess in relation to reason, their reasonableness, is this measure, harmony, or order. The demand that things be reasonable, the operation of the faculty of reason, expresses itself historically in the development, first, of language for communication of thought and feeling; and then in the liberal arts, and in philosophy and theology, viewed as a path to the discovery of the greatest rationality—the utter and pervasive reasonableness of the universe according to which every event, including the evil and the misfortune, appears as demanded by the measure, harmony, or order that God's reason imposes on it. Subsequent chapters trace this historical development, and treat it as a guide to one's studies of the liberal arts, of philosophy, and of theology.

Chapters XII and XIII deal with the demand that sensible things be reasonable, showing how grammar arises from the ordering of sounds in language, dialectic from the effort to explain this order of words and sentences, and rhetoric from the demand that men's actions be ordered by the rules appropriate to human conduct. In Chapter XIV, reason is presented as endeavoring to escape from the senses by taking their materials, speech and sound, and ordering them in such a way as to make them represent what is not sensible. It gives rise to the art of music. In Chapter XV, geometry, astrology (or astronomy), and arithmetic appear as other ways in which reason demands that we escape from the senses into a realm of purely rational things arranged in an intelligible order. In Chapters XVII, XVIII, and XIX, philosophy and theology give a culmination to this process by revealing the nature of the soul and of God, and of His providential relation to the universe.

SELECTIONS FROM

*De Ordine**

━◄◆►━

Augustine appears as a narrator as well as a participant in De Ordine. *The latter is a series of conversations between Augustine and a circle of close friends, including his mother, Monica. At the beginning of the part reproduced here the persons of the dialogue, which is being recorded as it progresses, are seated on the lawn in the gardens of the villa, Cassiciacum, not far from Milan.*

BOOK II

CHAPTER VII

(24) '. . . Yet, there is a certain exalted branch of learning which is far removed from even the surmise of the generality of mankind, but, to zealous minds that love only God and souls, it promises to show that even all the things which we acknowledge to be evil are still not outside the divine order—and to show this so clearly that even in the addition of numbers we could not have greater certitude.'

---

* The selections that follow are taken from *The Fathers of the Church*, Volume V, *The Writings of St. Augustine*, Volume I, translated by Robert P. Russell, New York: Cima Publishing Company, 1948, and the Catholic University of America Press, Washington, D.C. (title translated as: "Divine Providence and the Problem of Evil"). Footnotes omitted.

CHAPTER VIII

(25) 'Now, this science is the very law of God, which ever abiding fixed and unshaken with Him, is transcribed, so to speak, on the souls of the wise, so that they know they live a better and more sublime life in proportion as they contemplate it more perfectly with their understanding and observe it more diligently in their manner of living. Accordingly, this science imposes a twofold order of procedure on those who desire to know it, of which order one part pertains to the regulating of life, and the other pertains to the directing of studies. Youths devoted to this science ought so to live as to refrain from all wantonness, from the enticements of gluttony, from excessive care and adornment of the body, from silly practices of games, from the dullness of sleep and sloth, from jealousy, detraction, and envy, from the ambition for honor and power, and also from the unrestrained desire for praise. Let them be convinced that love for money is an unfailing poison for all their hopes. Let them do nothing half-heartedly, nothing rashly. In case of faults of their associates, let them either cast out all anger, or so restrain it that it will be like anger dismissed. Let them hate no one. Let them not be unwilling to correct vices. Let them take care especially not to be excessive in vengeance or stinting in forgiveness. Let them punish only what can be improved, and favor nothing that may become worse. Let them regard as their own fellow men all those over whom authority has been given to them. Let them be so obedient that it would be embarrassing to give them commands, and let them rule so considerately that it becomes a pleasure to obey them. Over the faults of others, let them not be troublesome to one who is reluctant. As for enmities, they are to avoid them most carefully, bear them most patiently, and end them most speedily. In every covenant and dealing with men it is enough to observe this one familiar proverb: *Let them not do to anyone what they would not have done to themselves.* Let them not wish to undertake the administration of the State unless they are matured, but let them hasten to become mature either within the senatorial age, or certainly before middle-age. And whoever turns himself to these studies late in life, let him not think himself bound by no precept: in fact, he will all the more easily observe those things in mellowed age.

'Furthermore, in all circumstances of life, in every place and at all times, let them have friends or earnestly seek to have them. Let them be well disposed toward the deserving, even toward those who do not look for it. For the proud, let them be less concerned; and by no means are they to become proud themselves. Let them live in a fitting and decent manner. Supported by faith, hope, and love, let them have God the object of their worship, their thinking, and their striving. Let them desire tranquillity and a definite course for their own studies and for those of all their associates; and for themselves and for whomsoever else such things are possible, a good mind and a quiet life.'

CHAPTER IX

(26) 'It remains for me to declare how instruction is to be imparted to the studious youths who have resolved to live after the manner described above. Likewise, with regard to the acquiring of knowledge, we are of necessity led in a twofold manner: by authority and by reason. In point of time, authority is first; in the order of reality, reason is prior. What takes precedence in operation is one thing; what is more highly prized as an object of desire is something else. Consequently, although the authority of upright men seems to be of the safer guide for the uninstructed multitude, reason is better adapted for the educated. Furthermore, since no one becomes learned except by ceasing to be unlearned, and since no unlearned person knows in what quality he ought to present himself to instructors or by what manner of life he may become docile, it happens that for those who seek to learn great and hidden truths authority alone opens the door. But, after one has entered, then without any hesitation he begins to follow the precepts of the perfect life. When he has become docile through these precepts, then at length he will come to know: (a) how much wisdom is embodied in those very precepts that he has been observing before understanding; (b) what reason itself is, which he—now strong and capable after the cradle of authority—follows and comprehends; (c) what intellect is, in which all things are, or rather, which is itself the sum total of all things; (d) and what, beyond all things, is the source of all things. To this knowledge, few are able to arrive in this life; even after this life, no one can exceed it.'

'As to those who are content to follow authority alone and who apply themselves constantly to right living and holy desires, while they make no account of the liberal and fine arts, or are incapable of being instructed in them—I know not how I could call them happy as long as they live among men. Nevertheless, I firmly believe that, upon leaving the body, they will be liberated with greater facility or difficulty according as they have lived and the more virtuously or otherwise.'

(27) 'Authority is, indeed, partly divine and partly human, but the true, solid and sovereign authority is that which is called divine. In this matter there is to be feared the wonderful deception of invisible beings that, by certain divinations and numerous powers of things pertaining to the senses, are accustomed to deceive with the utmost ease those souls that are engrossed with perishable possessions, or eagerly desirous of transitory power, or overawed by meaningless prodigies.'

'We must, therefore, accept as divine that Authority which not only exceeds human power in Its outward manifestations, but also, in the very act of leading a man onward, shows him to what extent It has debased Itself for his sake, and bids him not to be confined to the senses, to which indeed those things seem wondrous, but to soar upward to the intellect. At the same time It shows him what great things It is able to do, and why It does them, and how little importance It attaches to them. For, it is fitting that by deeds It shows Its power; by humility, Its clemency; by commandment, Its nature. And all this is being delivered to us so distinctly and steadily by the sacred rites into which we are now being initiated: therein the life of good men is most easily purified, not indeed by the circumlocution of disputation, but by the authority of the mysteries.

'But human authority is very often deceiving. Yet it rightly seems to show itself at its best in those men who propose various proofs for their teachings, insofar as the mind of the unlearned can grasp them, and who do not live otherwise than how they prescribe that one ought to live. If certain goods of fortune accrue to these men, they reveal themselves great men in the use of those things, but still greater in their contempt of them; and then it is most difficult to lay blame on anyone who puts trust in those men when they enunciate principles of right living.' . . .

CHAPTER X

(30) 'Reason is a mental operation capable of distinguishing and connecting the things that are learned. But, only a rare class of men is capable of using it as a guide to the knowledge of God or of the soul; either of the soul within us or of the world-soul. This is due to nothing else than the fact that, for anyone who has advanced toward objects of sense, it is difficult to return to himself. Wherefore, although men strive to act entirely within reason in those things which are liable to deceive, yet only a very few know what reason *is,* or what its qualities are. This seems strange, but that is how the matter stands. For the present, however, it is enough to have said that much, for, even if I should wish to expound the matter to you as it should be understood, my incompetence would be equalled by my arrogance if I should profess that I myself have grasped it already. Nevertheless, insofar as reason has deigned to reveal itself in the things that appear familiar to you, let us examine it to the best of our ability, in accordance with the demands of the discussion we have undertaken.'

(31) 'And first of all, let us see in what connection this word which is called *reason* is wont to be used. Of particular interest to us ought to be the fact that man has been defined thus by the ancient philosophers: *Man is an animal, rational and mortal.* In this definition, when the genus

which is called animal has been given, then we notice that two distinguishing notes are added. And by those distinguishing notes, man, I believe,
was to be admonished both whither he is to return and what he ought to
flee, for, just as the soul's forward movement has fallen down to the
things that are mortal, so ought its return be to reason. By the one term,
rational, man is distinguished from brute animals; by the other term,
mortal, he is distinguished from God. Therefore, unless it holds fast to the
rational element, it will be a beast; unless it turns aside from the mortal
element, it will not be divine.

'But, because very learned men are wont to distinguish keenly and
ingeniously between the rational [*rationale*] and the reasonable [*ration-
abile*], such distinction is by no means to be ignored in view of what we
have undertaken. They designate as *rational* whatever uses reason or possesses the faculty of reasoning, but, whatever has been done or spoken
according to reason, *that* they call *reasonable*. Accordingly, we could call
these baths or our discourse *reasonable;* but him who constructed the
baths, or ourselves who are now discoursing, we could term *rational*. Reason, then, proceeds from a rational soul into reasonable things which are
done or spoken.'

(32) 'I see, therefore, two things wherein the faculty and power of reason can even be brought before the senses: namely, the works of man
which are seen and his words which are heard. In each case the mind uses
a twin messenger, the eye and the ear, according to the needs of the body.
Thus, when we behold something formed with well-fitting parts, not
absurdly do we say that it appears reasonably [fashioned]. In like manner,
when we hear a melody harmonize well, we do not hesitate to say that it
sounds reasonably [harmonized]. But, anyone would be laughed at if he
should say that something smells reasonably or tastes reasonably or is
reasonably tender, unless, perchance, in those things which for some purpose have been contrived by men so to smell, or taste, or glow, or anything
else. For instance, if someone, considering the reason why it was done,
should say that a place whence serpents are put to flight by pungent
odors emits smells reasonably; or that a potion which a physician has
prepared is reasonably bitter or sweet; or that the bath which he ordered
regulated for a sickly person is reasonably warm or tepid. But no one,
entering a garden and lifting a rose to his nose, would venture to say:
"How reasonably sweet it smells!" No, not even if a physician should
order him to smell it—indeed in that case, it is said to have been prescribed or offered reasonably, but not to smell reasonably—and still not,
because that odor is a natural one. And, even though food be seasoned by
a cook, we still may say that it is reasonably seasoned. But, in accordance
with accepted usage, it is not said to taste reasonably, whenever without
any extrinsic cause it satisfies a momentary craving. But, if he to whom a

physician has given a potion should be asked why he ought to think it sweet, then something else is implied as the reason for his thinking so, namely, the nature of his illness, which is not in the sense, but is otherwise present in the body. On the other hand, if one is licking something because he is incited by the stimulus of the palate—if he should be asked why it is sweet, and if he should reply: "Because it is pleasant" or "Because I like it," no one will call it reasonably sweet unless, perhaps, its delight is necessary for something, and what he is chewing has been sweetened for that very purpose.'

(33) 'In so far as we have been able to investigate, we now detect certain traces of reason in the senses, and, with regard to sight and hearing, we find it in pleasure itself. Other senses, however, usually demand this attribute, not because of the pleasure they afford, but because of something else, for a purposeful act is the characteristic of a rational animal. With regard to the eyes, that is usually called *beautiful* in which the harmony of parts is wont to be called reasonable; with regard to the ears, when we say that a harmony is reasonable and that a rhythmic poem is reasonably composed, we properly call it *sweet*. But, we are not wont to pronounce it reasonable when the color in beautiful objects allures us or when a vibrant chord sounds pure and liquid, so to speak. We must therefore acknowledge that, in the pleasure of those senses, what pertains to reason is that in which there is a certain rhythmic measure.'

(34) 'Wherefore, considering carefully the parts of this very building, we cannot but be displeased because we see one doorway, toward the side and another situated almost, but not exactly, in the middle. In things constructed, a proportion of parts that is faulty, without any compelling necessity, unquestionably seems to inflict, as it were, a kind of injury upon one's gaze. But, the fact that three windows inside, one in the middle and two at the sides, pour light at equal intervals on the bathing place—how much that delights and enraptures us as we gaze attentively is a thing already manifest, and need not be shown to you in many words. In their own terminology, architects themselves call this *design*, and they say that parts unsymmetrically placed are without *design*.

'This is very general; it pervades all the arts and creations of man. Who, indeed, does not see that in songs—and we likewise say that in them there is a sweetness that pertains to the ears—rhythm is the producer of all this sweetness? But when an actor is dancing, although a certain rhythmic movement of his limbs may indeed afford delight by that same rhythm, yet, since to the attentive spectators all his gestures are signs of things, the dance itself is called *reasonable*, because it aptly signifies and exhibits something over and above the delight of the senses. And, even if he should represent a winged Venus and a cloaked Cupid, how skillfully so ever he may depict it by a wonderful movement and posture of the body, he does not seem to offend the eyes, but through the eyes he would offend the mind, to which those signs of things are exhibited. The eyes would be offended if the movements were not graceful, for that pertains to the sense, in which the soul perceives delight precisely because it is united with the body.

'Therefore, delight *of* the sense is one thing; delight *through* the sense is something else. Graceful movement delights the sense, but the timely import of the movement delights the mind alone through the sense. This is more easily noticed in the case of hearing: whatever has a pleasing sound, that it is which pleases and entices the hearing itself. What is really signified by that sound, that is what is borne to the mind, though by the messenger of our hearing. And so, when we hear these lines—*"Why do the suns in the winter rapidly sink in the ocean? What is the hindrance that holds back late-coming nights in the summer?"*—our praise of the meter is one thing, but our praise of the meaning is something else. Neither is it in the same sense of the term that we say: "It sounds reasonable" and "It is spoken reasonably."

CHAPTER XII

(35) 'There are, then, three classes of things in which that "something reasonable" is to be seen. One is in actions directed toward an end; the second, in discourse; the third, in pleasure. The first admonishes us to do nothing without purpose; the second, to teach correctly; the last, to find delight in contemplation. The first deals with right living; the other two, with those branches of learning which we are now considering. Now, that which is rational in us, that which uses reason and either produces or seeks after the things that are reasonable—saw that names, or meaningful sounds, had to be assigned to things, so that men might use the sense almost as an interpreter to link them together, inasmuch as they could not perceive one another's minds. For reason was held fast by a certain natural bond in the fellowship of those with whom it possessed reason as a common heritage, since men could not be most firmly associated unless they conversed and thus poured, so to speak, their minds and thoughts back and forth to one another. But, they could not hear the words of those not present. Therefore, reason, having carefully noted and discriminated all the sounds of the mouth and tongue, invented letters. But, it could have done neither of these, if the vast number of things seemed to extend endlessly without any fixed limit. Therefore, the great utility of enumerating was brought to mind by its very necessity. When these two discoveries had been made, then arose the profession of copyists and calculators—the infancy of grammar, so to speak, which Varro calls *literatio*. What it is called in Greek, I do not recall just now.'

(36) 'When reason had gone further, it noticed that, of those oral sounds which we used in speaking and which it had already designated by letters, there were some which by a varied modulation of the parted lips flowed clear and pure from the throat without any friction; that others acquired a certain kind of sound from the diversified pressure of the lips; and that there were still other sounds which could not issue forth unless they were conjoined with these. Accordingly, it denominated the letters in the order of their exposition: vowels, semivowels, and mutes. In the next place, it took account of syllables. Then, words were grouped into eight classes and forms, and their entire evolvement, purity and articulation were skillfully and minutely differentiated. Furthermore, not unmindful of numbers and measure, it directed the mind to the different lengths of vocal sounds and syllables, and thereby it discovered that of the time-intervals through which the long and the short syllables were extended, some were double and others were simple. It noted these points as well, and reduced them to fixed rules.'

(37) 'The science of grammar could now have been complete. But, since by its very name it proclaims that it knows letters—indeed on this account it is called "literature" in Latin—it came to pass that whatever was committed to letters as worth remembering necessarily pertained to it. And in this way history was added to this science. For, its name is one, but its subject matter is undefined and many-sided, and is filled more with cares than with enjoyment or truth, and more burdensome to grammarians than to historians themselves. Who, indeed, would tolerate the imputing of ignorance to a man who has not heard that Daedalus flew, and not the imputing of mendacity to the man who invented the fable; folly to anyone who believed it, and impudence to him who questions anyone about it? Or the case in which I always feel great pity for those of our household who are accused of ignorance if they cannot answer what the name of the mother of Euryalus was, since they, in turn, would not dare to call their questioners vain, absurd, or unduly inquisitive?'

CHAPTER XIII

(38) 'When the science of grammar had been perfected and systematized, reason was then reminded to search out and consider the very power by which it produced art, for, by definition, division, and synthesis it not only had made it orderly and syntactical, but also had guarded it against every subtle encroachment of error. How, therefore, would it pass on to other discoveries, unless it first classified, noted, and arranged its own resources—its tools and machines, so to speak—and bring into being that discipline of disciplines which they call *dialectics?* This science teaches both how to teach and how to learn. In it, reason itself exhibits itself, and

reveals its own nature, its desires, its powers. It knows what knowledge is; by itself, it not only wishes to make men learned, but also can make them so. Yet because in the pursuit of the things which are rightly commended as useful and upright, unwise men generally follow their own feelings and habits rather than the very marrow of truth—which indeed only a very exceptional mind beholds—it was necessary that they not only be taught to the extent of their ability, but also frequently and strongly aroused as to their emotions. To the portion of itself which would accomplish this—a portion more replete with lack than with enlightenment, its lap heaped high with charms which it would scatter to the crowd so that the crowd might deign to be influenced for its own good—to this portion, it gave the name of *rhetoric.* And so, the part which is called reasonable in discourse has been advanced to this point by the liberal arts and disciplines.'

CHAPTER XIV

(39) 'From this point, reason wished to be straightway transported to the most blessed contemplation of things divine. But, lest it fall from on high, it sought steps of ascent and devised an orderly path for itself through the slopes it had already won. It longed for a beauty which it alone could behold by itself without these eyes of ours; but it was impeded by the senses. Therefore, it turned its gaze slightly toward those senses, for they, shouting with noisy importunity that they possessed truth, kept calling it back when it fain would fasten to other things. And it began with the ears, because they claimed as their own the very words from which it had fashioned grammar, dialectic, and rhetoric. But reason, being endowed with the keenest powers of discernment, quickly saw what difference there was between sound itself and that of which it was a symbol. It saw that to the jurisdiction of the ears pertained nothing more than sound, and that this was threefold: sound in the utterance of an animate being, or sound in what breath produces in musical instruments, or sound in what is given forth by percussion. It saw that to the first class pertained actors of tragedy and comedy or stageplayers of this kind, and in fact all who give vocal renditions; that the second class was restricted to flutes and similar instruments; and that to the third class were attributed the cithara, the lyre, cymbals, and everything that would be tonal on being struck.'

(40) 'Reason saw, however, that this material was of very little value, unless the sounds were arranged in a fixed measure of time, and in modulated variation of high and low pitch. It realized that it was from this source that those elements came which it called *feet* and *accents,* when, in grammar, it was treating of syllables with diligent consideration. And, be-

cause in words themselves it was easy to notice the syllabic *longs* and *shorts,* interspersed with almost equal frequency in a discourse, reason endeavored to arrange and conjoin them into definite series. At first it followed the sense of hearing itself in this, and superimposed measured link-units, which it called *segments* and *members.* Then, lest the series of feet be carried further than its discernment could continue, it set a limit at which *reversion* to the beginning should be made, and, precisely on this account, called it *verse.* But, whatever was not restricted by a definite limit, and yet ran according to methodically arranged feet—that, it designated by the term *rhythm.* In Latin this can be called nothing other than *number.* Thus, poets were begotten of reason. And, when it saw in them great achievements, not in sound alone, but in words also and realities, it honored them to the utmost, and gave them license for whatever reasonable fictions they might desire. And yet, because they took origin from the first of the liberal disciplines, it permitted grammarians to be their critics.'

(41) 'Reason understood, therefore, that in this fourth step of ascent—whether in particular rhythm or in modulation in general—numeric proportions held sway and produced the finished product. With the utmost diligence it investigated as to what their nature might be, and, chiefly because by their aid it had elaborated all the aforesaid developments, it concluded that they were divine and eternal. From then onwards, it most reluctantly endured their splendor and serenity to be clouded by the material stuff of vocal utterances. And, because whatever the mind is able to see is always present and is acknowledged to be immortal, numeric proportions seemed to be of this nature. But, because sound is something sensible, it flows away into the past and is imprinted on the memory. By a reasonable fiction it was fabled that the Muses were the daughters of Jupiter and Memory. Now, with reason bestowing its favor on the poets, need it be asked what the offspring likewise contained? Since this branch of learning partakes as well of sense as of the intellect, it receives the name of *music.*

CHAPTER XV

(42) 'From this stage, reason advanced to the province of the eyes. Scanning the earth and the heavens, it realized that nothing pleased it but beauty; and in beauty, design; and in design, dimensions; and in dimensions, number. It asked itself whether any line or curve or any other form or shape in that realm was of such kind as intelligence comprehended. It found that they were far inferior, and that nothing which the eyes beheld could in any way be compared with what the mind discerned. These

distinct and separate realities it also reduced to a branch of learning, and called it *geometry*.

'The movement of the heavens also aroused and invited reason to consider it diligently. And there, too, because of the most constant alternations of the seasons, as well as the fixed and unerring courses of the stars and the regulated spacing of distance, it understood that nothing other than dimension and number held sway. Linking these, also, into an orderly whole by definition and division, it gave rise to astrology—a great subject for the God-fearing, but a torment for the curious.'

(43) 'In all these branches of study, therefore, all things were being presented to reason as numerically proportioned. And they were all the more clearly visible in those dimensions which reason, by reflection and contemplation, beheld as most true; but it used to recall rather the shadows and vestiges of those dimensions in the things that are perceived by the senses. Then, reason gained much courage and preconceived a great achievement; it ventured to prove the soul immortal. It treated diligently of all things. It came to feel that it possessed great power, and that it owed all its power to numerical proportions. Something wondrous urged it on. And it began to suspect that it itself was perhaps the very number by which all things are numbered, or if not, that this number was there whither it was striving to arrive. And he of whom Alypius made mention when we were treating of the Skeptics, grasped with all his might—as if Proteus were in his hands—this number which would be the disclosure of universal truth. But, false images of the things which we number drift away from that most hidden something by which we enumerate, snatch our attention to themselves, and frequently make that hidden something slip away even when it has been already in our grasp.'

CHAPTER XVI

(44) 'If a man does not yield to these images, and if he reduces to a simple, true, and certain unity all the things that are scattered far and wide throughout so many branches of study, then he is most deserving of the attribute *learned*. Then, without being rash, he can search after things divine—not merely as truths to be believed, but also as matters to be contemplated, understood, and retained. But, whoever is still a slave to his passions, or is keenly desirous of perishable goods, or even though he flee from these and live a virtuous life, yet if he does not know what pure nothing is, what formless matter is, what a lifeless unformed being is, what a body is, what species in a body is, what place and time are, what *in a place* and *at a time* signify, what local motion is, what non-local motion is, what stable motion is, what eternity is, what it is to be neither

in a place nor nowhere and nowhere not to be, what it is to be never and never not to be—anyone who does not know these matters, and yet wishes to question and dispute about even his own soul—let alone investigating about the Most High God, who is better known by knowing what He is not—such a one will fall into every possible error.

'But then, whoever has grasped the meaning of simple and intelligible numbers will readily understand these matters. Furthermore, anyone of good talents and leisure—through the privilege of age or any kind of good fortune—if he be eagerly devoted to study and if he follow the above-mentioned order of studies in so far as is required, will certainly comprehend such numbers. But since all the liberal arts are learned partly for practical use and partly for the knowledge and contemplation of things, to attain the use of them is very difficult except for some very gifted person who even from boyhood has earnestly and constantly applied himself.'

CHAPTER XVII

(46) 'And, of course, I could say this also about the other studies of this kind. And if, perchance, you despise them completely, I advise you—in so far as I may, as your son, presume to do so, and to the extent that you permit—to preserve steadfastly and carefully that faith of yours, of which you have a mental grasp through the sacred mysteries; furthermore, I advise you to continue in this way and habit of life with constancy and vigilance. But, concerning matters that are most abstruse, and yet pertain to God—(a) how so many evils come to pass, although God is omnipotent, and effects nothing evil; (b) for what purpose did He make the world though He had need of nothing; (c) whether evil always was, or began in time; (d) and if it always was, then was it under God's control; (e) and if it was, then whether this world also, wherein that evil is curbed by divine order, always was; (f) but if the world had a beginning sometime, how was evil held in check by divine power before that time; (g) what need was there to construct a world in which evil, which divine power had already controlled, was included for the punishment of souls; (h) if, however, there was a time when evil was not under God's dominion, what suddenly happened which had not happened before throughout the eternal years? Now it would be most absurd—to say nothing about the impiety of it—to assert that in God there has ever been a change of mind. But, if we say that evil had been troublesome and, as it were, antagonistic to God—as very many think—no learned man will repress his laughter, and every learned man will be indignant. What harm, indeed, could that indescribable nature of evil do to God? If they say that it could do none, then there will be no reason for the creation of the world, but if they say

that it could do some—why, it is an inexpiable crime to maintain that God is subject to injury, or that He has not at least provided by His power that His nature should suffer no injury. In fact, they acknowledge that a soul suffers punishments here, although they would have it that there is absolutely no difference between the substance of God and that of the soul. But, if they say that this world was not made, to believe this would involve both impiety and ingratitude, lest this consequence ensue: that God has not made it. So, any investigation concerning these and similar matters is to be made according to that order or not at all.'

CHAPTER XVIII

(47) 'And, lest anyone think that we have embraced something very extensive, I say this plainly that in a few words: that no one ought to aspire to a knowledge of those matters without that two fold science, so to speak —the science of right reasoning and that of the power of numbers. And, if anyone thinks that this is indeed a great deal, let him master either numbers alone or only dialectics. But, if even this seems limitless, let him merely get a thorough understanding of what unity in numbers is, and what its import is—not yet in that supreme law and order of all things, but in the things that we think and do here and there every day. The science of philosophy has already adopted this learning and has discovered in it nothing more than what unity is, but in a manner far more profound and sublime.

'To philosophy pertains a twofold question: the first treats of the soul; the second, of God. The first makes us know ourselves; the second, our origin. The former is the more delightful to us; the latter, more precious. The former makes us fit for a happy life; the latter renders us happy. The first is for beginners; the latter, for the well instructed. This is the order of wisdom's branches of study by which one becomes competent to grasp the order of things and to discern two worlds and the very Author of the universe, of whom the soul has no knowledge save to know how it knows Him not.'

(48) 'The soul, therefore, holding fast to this order, and now devoted to philosophy, at first introspects itself; and—as soon as that mode of learning has persuaded it that reason either is the soul itself or belongs to it, and that there is in reason nothing more excellent or dominant than numbers, or that reason is nothing else than number—soliloquizes thus: "By some kind of inner and hidden activity of mine, I am able to analyze and synthesize the things that ought to be learned; and this faculty of mine is called reason." As a matter of fact, what ought to be analyzed except what is reputed to have unity, but either has no unity whatever or has less of it than it is believed to have? And, likewise, why must some-

thing be synthesized, unless in order that it become *one,* in so far as it is capable? Therefore, both in analyzing and in synthesizing, it is oneness that I seek, it is oneness that I love. But when I analyze, I seek a homogeneous unit; when I synthesize, I look for an integral unit. In the former case, foreign elements are avoided; in the latter, proper elements are conjoined to form something united and perfect. In order that a stone be a stone, all its parts and its entire nature have been consolidated into one. What about a tree? Is it not true that it would not be a tree if it were not *one?* What about the members and entrails of any animate being, or any of its component parts? Of a certainty, if they undergo a severance of unity, it will no longer be an animal. And, what else do friends strive for, but to be *one?* The more they are one, so much the more are they friends. A population forms a city, and dissension is full of danger for it: to dissent [*dis-sentire*]—what is that, but to think *diversely?* An army is made up of many soldiers. And is not any multitude so much the less easily defeated in proportion as it is the more closely united? In fact, the joining is itself called a coin, a co-union, as it were. What about every kind of love? Does it not wish to become one with what it is loving? And, if it reaches its object, does it not become one with it? Carnal pleasure affords such ardent delight for no other reason then because the bodies of lovers are brought into union. Why is sorrow distressful? Because it tries to rend what used to be one. Therefore, it is troublesome and dangerous to become one with what can be separated.'

CHAPTER XIX

(49) 'Out of several pieces of material hitherto lying around in scattered fashion and then assembled into one design, I can make a house. If, indeed, I am the maker and it is made, then I am the more excellent, and the more excellent precisely because I am the maker. There is no doubt that I am on that account more excellent than a house. But, not on that account am I more excellent than a swallow or a small bee, for skillfully does the one build nests, and the other construct honey-combs. I am, however, more excellent than they because I am a rational creature.

'Now, if reason is found in calculated measurements, does it follow that the work of birds is not accurately and aptly measured? Nay, it is most accurately and aptly proportioned. Therefore, it is not by making well-measured things, but by grasping the nature of numbers, that I am the more excellent. What then? Have the birds been able to build carefully constructed nests without knowing it? Assuredly, they have. How is this shown? By the fact that we, too, accommodate the tongue to the teeth and palate by fixed measurements, so that letters and words rush forth from the mouth, and, when we are speaking, we are not thinking of the oral movement by which we ought to do that. Moreover, what good singer, even though he be unskilled in the art of music, would not, by that same natural sense, keep in his singing both the rhythm and the melody known by memory? And what can become more subject to measure than this? The uninstructed man has no knowledge of it. Nevertheless, he does it by nature's doing. But, why is man superior to brute animals, and why is he to be ranked above them? Because he understands what he does. Nothing else ranks me above the brute animal except the fact that I am a rational animal.'

(50) 'Then, how is it that reason is immortal, and I am defined as something both rational and mortal at the same time? Perhaps reason is not immortal? But, one to two, or two to four, is a ratio in the truest sense. That ratio was no truer yesterday than today, nor will be truer tomorrow or a year hence. Even if the whole world should fall in ruins, that ratio will always necessarily be: it will always be such as it is now. Contrariwise, what the world has today it did not have yesterday and it will not have tomorrow. In fact, not even for the course of an hour during this very day has it had the sun in the same position. And so, since nothing in it is permanent, it does not have anything in the same way for even the shortest interval of time.

'Therefore, if reason is immortal, and if I who analyze and synthesize all those things am reason, then that by which I am called mortal is not mine. Or if the soul is not the same as reason, and I nevertheless use reason, and, if through reason I am superior, then we ought to take flight from the lesser good to the greater, from the mortal to the immortal. The well-instructed soul tells itself all this and more besides, and ponders over them. But I prefer to attend to them no further now, lest, while I am longing to teach you order, I myself should exceed moderation, the parent of order. Indeed, it is not by faith alone, but by trustworthy reason, that the soul leads itself little by little to most virtuous habits and the perfect life. For, to the soul that diligently considers the nature and the power of numbers, it will appear manifestly unfitting and most deplorable that it should write a rhythmic line and play the harp by virtue of this knowledge, and that its life and very self—which is the soul—should nevertheless follow a crooked path and, under the domination of lust, be out of tune by the clangor of shameful vices.'

(51) 'But, when the soul has properly adjusted and disposed itself, and has rendered itself harmonious and beautiful, then will it venture to see God, the very source of all truth and the very Father of Truth. O great God, what kind of eyes shall those be! How pure! How beautiful! How powerful! How constant! How serene! How blessed! And what is that which they can see! What is it? I ask. What should we surmise? What should we believe? What should we say? Everyday expressions present

themselves, but they have been rendered sordid by things of least worth. I shall say no more, except that to us is promised a vision of beauty—beauty through whose imitation all other things are beautiful, and by comparison with which all other things are unsightly. Whosoever will have glimpsed this beauty—and he will see it who lives well, prays well, studies well—when will it ever trouble him why one man, desiring to have children, has them not, while another man casts out his own off-spring as being unduly numerous; why one man hates children before they are born, and another man loves them after birth; or how is it not absurd that nothing will come to pass which is not with God—and, there-fore, it is inevitable that all things come into being in accordance with order—and nevertheless God is not petitioned in vain?

'Finally, how will any burdens, dangers, scorns, or smiles of fortune disturb a just man? In this world of sense, it is indeed necessary to ex-amine carefully what time and place are, so that what delights in a portion of place or time may be understood to be far less beautiful than the whole of which it is a portion. And furthermore, it is clear to a learned man that what displeases in a portion displeases for no other reason than because the whole, with which that portion harmonizes wonderfully, is not seen, but that, in the intelligible world, every part is as beautiful and perfect as the whole.

'These matters will be discussed at greater length if, as I earnestly advise and hope, your zeal will have decided to follow either that order mentioned by us or perhaps another order more concise and appropriate —but, at any rate, a right order—and will have seriously and consistently held it.'

Bibliography

BATTENHOUSE, ROY WESLEY, editor, *A Companion to the Study of St. Augustine,* New York, Oxford University Press, 1955. (Cf. esp. "Christian Instruction," by T. S. K. Scott-Craig.)

BOURKE, VERNON JOSEPH, *Augustine's Quest of Wisdom: Life and Philosophy of the Bishop of Hippo,* Milwaukee, The Bruce Publishing Co., 1945. (Science and Culture Series.)

D'ARCY, MARTIN C., *A Monument to St. Augustine: Essays on Some Aspects of his Thought Written in Commemoration of his Fifteenth Centenary,* London, Sheed and Ward, 1930.

GILSON, ETIENNE H., *The Christian Philosophy of Saint Augustine,* translated by L. E. M. Lynch, New York, Random House, 1960. *(Introduction à l'étude de saint Augustin,* Paris, J. Vrin, 1929.)

GREENWOOD, DAVID, *St. Augustine,* New York, Vantage Press, 1957.

VAN DER MEER, F., *Augustine the Bishop,* translated by B. Battershaw and G. R. Lamb, London and New York, Sheed and Ward, 1961. *(Augustine de Zielzorger,* Utrecht and Brussels, Uitgeverij het Spectrum.)

V

SAINT THOMAS

S AINT AUGUSTINE'S WORK played a decisive role in formulating the belief about man, nature, and God upon which Christianity is founded. He worked them out from his understanding of Scriptural revelation interpreted in the light, no doubt, of his own philosophical and religious insight. But while these were their decisive sources, his beliefs flowed from another as well—the writings of pagan authors, most notably of Plato and Plotinus. In his time, the philosophical foundation and the administrative organization of the Christian religion were still somewhat precarious. More ancient pagan creeds still offered alternatives to Christian thought, and the cults based upon them still appeared to many as ways of life that might compete with Christianity. This insecurity engendered a debate within the Church over the role that pagan thought should play in supporting beliefs based upon Scriptural revelation, and Saint Augustine took the side that favored use of the pagan heritage. "Moreover, if those who are called philosophers, and especially the Platonists, have said aught that is true and in harmony with our faith," he wrote,[1] "we are not only not to shrink from it but to claim it for our own use

---

[1] *On Christian Doctrine* in *Great Books of the Western World, 18, Augustine,* translated by J. F. Shaw, William Benton, publisher, *Encyclopedia Britannica, Inc.,* Chicago, 1952, Book II, Chapter 40.

from those who have unlawful possession of it." After Augustine's time, this tolerant use of non-Christian thought to support Christian belief was largely checked or forgotten; and the knowledge and appreciation of the work of pagan authors was greatly diminished throughout Europe by a rising tide of ascetic monasticism.

Within a century after the death of Saint Augustine, Christianity had prevailed over the older religions. It enjoyed an increasing security as the Church that embodied it succeeded in controlling for its own purposes the political ruins of the Roman Empire in the West. In the twelfth century, the security of Christianity and the increasing availability of ancient books permitted a renewal of interest in non-Christian thought. Pagan literature was translated from Greek and Arabic into Latin—the learned language of Europe. By the beginning of the thirteenth century, most of the works now attributed to Aristotle, who had never become completely unfamiliar to European scholars, had been translated along with many of those of his Greek, Arabic, and Jewish commentators. Works of his followers and even of Plotinus were confused with his own. Nonetheless, the clarity and power of his thought concerning man, nature, and God had become apparent to many. The times were right for a reconsideration of the heritage of the past, and for a second and more deliberate use of its non-Christian philosophy to support Christian revelation in a synthesis of both systems. The naturalism of Aristotelian thought made it, for certain influential elements in the Church, an object of suspicion; but its comprehensiveness made it for others a likely candidate for that synthesis.

Chief among those who were interested in presenting Christian belief within the frame of Aristotle's system was Thomas, son of the Count of Aquino. He went to school in the Monastery of Monte Cassino, attended the University of Naples, joined the Dominican Order, studied under Albertus Magnus, taught theology at the University of Paris and in Rome and Naples, and lived a life crowded with lectures and sermons, with advice to Popes and kings, and with the writing of books of philosophy and theology so comprehensive as to develop all the chief if not most of the minor themes that run through human existence. He was born ca. 1225 and died in 1274. He was canonized in 1323; and in 1879, Pope Leo III in his encyclical letter, *Aeterni Patris*, admitting that scholastic doctors might be mistaken in several ways, nonetheless, exhorted his brethren of the Catholic hierarchy to restore the wisdom of Saint Thomas, to propagate it for the good of the Catholic faith and of society, and to teach and defend it in the academies already founded and in those that might be established in the future.[2]

2 Leo XIII, *The Great Encyclical Letters of Pope Leo XIII*, edited by Rev. John J. Wynne, S.J., Benziger Brothers, New York, 1903, p. 56.

The need to establish Christianity more firmly helps to explain the considerable attention given to education by Saint Augustine. Teaching the young is an effective way of enhancing the growth of institutions into which they may be inducted, and Christianity, in Augustine's time, needed this enhancement. But in the thirteenth century, it dominated Europe through the Catholic Church. Membership in it was almost a natural consequence of being born. This changed position of Christianity helps to explain the less explicit discussion given to education by Saint Thomas. He says almost nothing about the ultimate goal of training and no more about the curriculum and the administration that might lead to it, apparently taking for granted the validity of current practice. His discussion of teaching limits it to the development of reason rather than that of will and desire; and his treatment of the latter—of education for character—is oblique and almost casual. But his great scholarship, enormous intellectual power, and enduring influence give his explicit discussion of teaching and his oblique remarks about character education, a great importance, however narrow their compass.

Saint Thomas' complete system of thought will not be discussed here at length. It is too comprehensive and too detailed to allow of a short exposition, and many elements of it that bear upon his theory of education resemble Augustinian doctrine sufficiently to render a statement of them largely repetitious. Both authors were Christian after all; and Saint Thomas inherited the work of Saint Augustine in interpreting the texts from which Christian belief takes its origin, and in finding philosophical support for that belief independent of these texts. Still, Saint Thomas did make more explicit use of certain metaphysical and ethical ideas than did Saint Augustine. They are a little foreign to the ideas we now ordinarily employ, and he found them in Aristotle.

We shall depart from our usual procedure, and discuss his metaphysical, psychological and ethical doctrines, making reference to their Aristotelian source, before turning to a statement of his views concerning education.

METAPHYSICS: ARISTOTELIAN THOUGHT

Aristotle and his followers made much of the distinction between *potentiality* and *actuality*. These are different ways in which a thing exists. All things in nature change. Clouds become rain; the plum tree blossoms in the Spring; the infant grows into the man. In the final stage of these changes, something exists in actuality—the rain, the blossoming tree, and the adult; but that which exists in these final stages was present in the earlier—the rain in the clouds, the blossom in the barren branch, and the man in the child. Of course, the way in which a thing exists in the final stage of its career is not the way in which it exists before that stage is reached. Clouds are not rain; barrenness shows no blossoms; the infant is not the man. But the way in which a thing ultimately exists must be present somehow in the way it exists from the beginning. The clouds must contain the potentiality or possibility of rain; the unclad tree, of blossoms; and the child, of the man. If this were not true, clouds might turn to sunshine, the winter tree to one of autumn, the child to an elephant or dog. All natural things are caught up in uniform changes; and this uniformity consists, in part, in their transition from the merely potential existence of something to its existence in actuality. This metaphysical doctrine of change results from one use Aristotle and his followers made of the distinction between potentiality and actuality.

Aristotelian thought employed a second distinction—the distinction between *matter* and *form*. The matter of a thing is that of which it is constituted. Marble is the matter of the statue; tone, the matter of the melody. The form of a thing is the pattern assumed by the matter in it, and each form is universal as Plato said. The Venus in marble may appear, as well, in bronze; and the melody of a violin may be played, also, on a flute. Every natural thing is matter in which form resides. The change that each natural thing undergoes is the passage of its matter actually patterned by one form, but potentially by another, to a later stage in which its matter is actually patterned by that other. An actual cloud is water whose form is a certain distribution of it; actual rain is the same water whose form is a quite different distribution. The change of clouds to rain is the transition from water with the first, to the same water with the second form; and clouds change to rain rather than to sunshine because water distributed in the way of rain exists potentially in the actual clouds while rays of light distributed in the way of sunshine do not. All natural things exhibit matter and form; and their change is the transition of their matter arranged by one form to their matter arranged by another—a change rendered uniform throughout nature by the potential existence, in every case of the first stage, of what actually exists in every case of the later.

Aristotle's conception of change as the development into actuality of what was potentially present before, and of development as the overt manifestation of forms always inherent in the matter that comes to exhibit them, amounts to the view that all change is purposeful. The answer to the question 'why does so and so happen?' is a statement of the purpose for the sake of which it happens; and that purpose or 'final cause' of the change is the manifestation of the form that was present in the changing thing as a mere potentiality. Clouds become rain because it is their purpose to do so; plum branches blossom because it is their destiny; the child becomes the man because being the latter is the goal of his existence.

The uniform change all natural things live through is purposeful, and its purposefulness consists in the tendency of each thing actually to exist at a later time in a way in which it potentially exists at an earlier time.

While each thing in nature develops toward its goal, nature as a whole also develops in that way. As a whole, it exhibits an order of things arranged on different levels, differing according as the things on each are more or less removed from the purpose toward which all strive. On the lowest level dwell inanimate things—those composed simply of earth, air, fire, and water, together with a potentiality of existence on another level. That other level supports animate things of a vegetative sort; and when the potential existence of plants gives place to their actual existence, matter actually patterned by the forms of inanimate elements comes actually to be ordered by vegetable forms—earth changing to grass and trees. But in vegetables inheres the potential existence of animals. When devoured, grass becomes the body of a cow. Its destiny is fulfilled, and its goal attained. In animals, men exist potentially; and as grass realizes its purpose in cattle, so theirs is achieved in man. On the level of humanity, too, there is a striving toward something higher; and this higher existence is God. Thus, through all of nature, from inanimate beings through man, there is a tendency toward realization in a single and Divine existence; and the purposefulness of the change in which this tendency is found may be described as actualization on a higher level of potentiality on a lower—the assumption on a higher level by matter of a form whose presence was implicit in that matter on a lower level.

The Aristotelian vision of nature is that of a purposeful hierarchy of things, bounded at the bottom by pure or prime matter, and at the top adorned by God. We cannot avoid thinking of pure or *prime matter* below the hierarchy. But no actual thing is composed of it alone; every such thing, rather, is matter patterned by some form. Still while no thing in the hierarchy of nature can consist in nothing but matter, we must think of the entire hierarchy as resting upon it—upon pure potentiality as its logical foundation.

At the top stands *God*; and while we can think of each lower level as finding the goal for its potentiality on a higher where it assumes a different form, we must think of God as mere form alone. Since He is at the top, nothing can dwell above Him; so that He can contain potentiality for no other existence whatever. In His form, everything potential is actualized and everything imperfect perfected. Containing no potentiality whatever, He does nothing; He neither creates nor in any way alters the world. Being perfect, He contains no matter; and Aristotle identifies this perfect form with thought which, concerned about nothing, having no matter, thinks about itself. Nonetheless, since all change—all motion and alteration—is caused by its purpose, God is the first cause of all motion and alteration. He makes everything happen, not by an act of creation, but simply by being aimed at; not as the player causes the ball to roll, but as the goal post draws the runner.

SAINT THOMAS

Saint Thomas espouses this Aristotelian metaphysical picture, but he makes some significant alterations in it in order to account for the Christian revelation. With Aristotle, he holds that the change undergone by natural things must be understood in terms of the development into actuality of pre-existing potentiality; and this development, in terms of the exhibition by matter in later stages of forms inherent in it in earlier. With him, he holds that each change can be understood only as directed towards its final cause or purpose, and that the whole of nature strives toward its perfection in God.[3] But Saint Thomas holds that God created the universe out of nothing, while Aristotle holds that it is eternal. His creation consists, according to Saint Thomas, in bringing into existence matter with all the forms it will ever exhibit already potential in it; but these forms, God takes from the exemplar forms or ideas that are the objects of his thought,[4] a view Aristotle denies in his rejection of Plato's theory that the forms of things exist independently of them. The change of each thing, thus, is its striving toward a perfection found in God's mind; and the whole of nature endeavors, as well, to conform to the system of exemplars found there. God, for Aristotle, is indifferent to the universe; but Christian revelation interpreted in light of the Platonic theory of forms or ideas in its Augustinian guise required Saint Thomas to hold that God is intimately concerned with his creatures, and that in His Providence He deals with them as a father with his children.

Psychology

Following Aristotle, Saint Thomas classifies the activities that men engage in under three headings. Some of them, he describes as vegetative. They are bodily processes of growth and reproduction; and they are vegetative because, while men share them with animals, they are not unlike the activities that both share with plants.

Men share with animals but not with vegetables, activities of sensation and two others that center in them. Activities of sensation fall into two subordinate kinds. The five senses—those of sight, hearing, touch, taste, and smell—make us aware of colors, sounds, textures, tastes, and odors. Thus conceived, the activities of external sensation do not

---

[3] *Summa Theologica*, P. I, Q. lxvi, A. 1.
[4] *Ibid.*, P. I, Q. xv, A. 1.

enable us, by themselves, to be aware of external objects. They give us only their characteristics—their colors, sounds, etc.; by themselves, they do not give us ideas of the things that possess these characteristics.

The activities of internal sensation, when added to those of external sensation, provide this awareness. They are operations of the mind performed upon the colors, sounds, etc., delivered in external sensation. They consist in mental activities of four kinds: activities of combining the deliverances of external sense into ideas of objects, of retaining in imagination images of ideas thus formed, of using such images in remembering that we formerly experienced external objects (had ideas of them), and of finding that external objects possess certain characteristics that the external senses cannot discover—characteristics like utility which cannot be seen, heard, or touched. In this way, the activities of sensation enable both men and animals to be aware of external objects.

Centering in activities of sensation are two others somewhat different from them. Men desire to possess or to avoid some of the objects of which sensation gives them ideas; and they move themselves accordingly toward or away from them. Because of their affinity with sensation, Saint Thomas classifies the activities of desire and of locomotion under that heading.

The third kind of activities in which men engage, they share neither with plants nor animals. It is made up of activities of reasoning, and all these activities consist in making judgments. The idea of a plum tree, animals can share with man; but unlike men, animals can make no judgment upon the tree. They cannot judge, correctly or incorrectly, that it is a tree, that it is a plum, or that it is in leaf. They can be aware of external things; but possessing no ability to judge, they can know nothing to be true or false about them. In so far as men engage in activities of sensation only, they confront the objects of sense in the same judgmentless awareness as do animals; but in so far as they engage in reasoning, they use the ideas provided by sensation to make judgments about the things those ideas reveal. Thus, they use the idea of a plum tree and of 'thing in leaf' to describe the state a plum tree is in when spring comes upon it.

The making of a judgment consists in holding that something is true—in recognizing a fact. Some judgments express a recognition of facts which does not depend upon recognition of any others. They are obvious or self-evident. In other cases, we make judgments that result from arguments—judgments arrived at by inference from other judgments or evidence. But in the latter as well as in the former case, our reasoning or judgment consists in recognizing either that things exhibit certain forms, or that they are related by certain relations—themselves a kind of forms.[5]

5 *Summa Theologica,* P. I Iae, Q. lxxix, A. 2, 3.

Reasoning falls into two kinds. Some of it is theoretical and some of it is practical. When we endeavor merely to find out what is true—when we passively accept a fact or try, by considering the evidence, whether we can accept it—our activity is theoretical; we are interested simply in knowing what there is. When we endeavor to alter things in order to realize some purpose—when we use our judgments about facts in order to achieve our goals—our activity is practical. The activities of reasoning are all ways of discovering truth. But some of them are ways of discovering truth regarded as important for its own sake, while others are ways of discovering it where its importance rests, as well, upon its utility to practical life.[6]

Sharing in some measure the characteristics of desire and of reason are the activities of volition. To engage in an act of will is to desire something judged to be good. Thus, an act of will, although allied with, is different from one of desire. Men desire some things about whose value they are ignorant, and they desire others when they know them not to be good. But when they will something, they desire it because they judge it to be so—because reason judges, correctly or incorrectly, that fulfillment of the desire considered is what they should endeavor. One may desire to injure a person because of hatred for him; but if he judges that men ought to love their neighbors, he cannot will the injury. On the other hand, if a surgeon judges that an injury will lead to benefit of his patient, he will deliberately inflict it. Thus, activities of will are exerted upon those of desire, but presuppose activities of reason by reference to whose judgments desires are regulated.[7]

The chief kinds of human activities, vegetation, sensation, and reason, Saint Thomas explains by reference to faculties or abilities to engage in them. However, he divides each of these, in turn, into subordinate faculties. The faculty of vegetation includes the abilities to grow and to reproduce; that of sensation is constituted by the abilities to engage in both external and internal sensation as well as in desire and locomotion; the faculty of reason breaks up into those of theoretical and practical reason; and the faculty of will occupies a place closely related both to that of reason and that of desire.

All these faculties belong to the human person; but we must guard against misconceiving the nature of humanity. The person is not the same as the soul. The latter is a form—the form of humanity. Since the form is the same for all men, the individual person cannot be identified with his soul. Nor can he be identified with the matter to which the soul gives form, for matter constitutes his body, and it would be patently erroneous to identify the person with his body. Hence the person can be conceived

[6] *Ibid.,* P. I Iae, Q. lxxix, A. 11.
[7] *Ibid.,* P. I Iae, Q. lxxxi, A. 1–3.

neither as a soul nor as the matter (or body) that soul gives form to. Rather, the human person must be conceived as a unity of soul and body. It is this unity that possesses the faculties of vegetation, sensation, reason, and will, although it possesses them only by virtue of the presence in it of the human soul.

Saint Thomas held, of course, that the human soul is immortal. It cannot be corrupted by the corruption of the matter in the human body to which it gives form, because it is not material. And although it can be destroyed by God as can everything else, since God does not intend to destroy it, the soul is immortal. Moreover, since it is the person to whom immortality is guaranteed by the Scriptures, and not merely the soul; and since the person is a unity of soul and body, immortal existence must be of both—of the human person as a whole.

Ethics

To the extent that they are governed by reason or will, Saint Thomas holds, all men desire to be happy. Their happiness does not consist in being delighted or pleased, although delight or pleasure accompanies it. Rather, it consists in the possession or enjoyment of something that lends its goodness to all their other goals. Of course, men desire many things; but the realization of each desire would be quite unsatisfactory if it were not good. To eat one's dinner would not make one happy unless the eating of it were also good. But the goodness of any goal achieved cannot consist in its conduciveness to the realization of most other desires. The goodness of hunger satisfied cannot consist in its enabling the satisfaction of the desire for health since health is good only to the extent that it enables something else. There must be, therefore, some ultimate good from which the goodness of all other goals is borrowed. Thus, every desire of a rational being is twofold—a desire for what is ultimately good (Saint Thomas calls it "the last end"), and a desire for some particular objective regarded as conducive to it. Happiness consists in the possession of the ultimate good as a consequence of realizing those desires that lead to it; and when men use their faculties well—when reason shows them what the ultimate good is, and when they will to order their desires and their actions in such a way as to achieve it—what they desire their happiness, is a direct vision of God, and such other activities as enable or further that vision.[8]

This direct vision is perfect happiness; and in it, human nature is perfectly realized. But it is not possible in this life, nor by use of natural powers merely. Here, moral virtue—the habitual and temperate expression of bodily desires—may embody practical reason, and by satisfying

[8] *Ibid.,* P. II Iae, Q. i, A. 2, 4, 5, 6, 7.

those desires, may facilitate the realization of theoretical reason in knowledge. This knowledge consists in discoveries about nature and God, and faith can make more vivid the knowledge of God thus achieved. Still, our terrestrial view of God is distant, remote, and at best analogical; and the exercise in this life of practical and theoretical reason, however successful in achieving moral virtue and in securing a contemplation of nature and divinity, leads to a happiness which must remain imperfect. Perfect happiness is the direct vision of God—a vision which eliminates the distance from its object required by the use of symbols and of argument. It can be achieved only with His help, and after death.[9]

Not all men know that their happiness consists in this vision and in those moral virtues. Still, none would be contented with realizing a desire that was not good; and after learning that God exists and what His relation to men is, anyone will see that happiness lies in a direct encounter with Him.

Two goals inherent in man's nature govern all his conscious action —perfect happiness or the vision of God, imperfect happiness or the combination of moral virtue together with rational, but remoter knowledge of Him. Two social institutions serve these two objectives. The state, supplemented by the family, assists the realization of terrestrial objectives. Acting through the prince or sovereign, it assures peace at home and protects citizens against foreign enemies. When necessary, it enforces the law of God. By its action, moral virtue and the pursuit of knowledge of nature, conceived as the effect of God's creativity and consequently of God also, is assured. The Church presides over man's effort to secure perfect happiness. His natural powers of reason cannot assure to him the direct vision of God, but God's help can. Good works and the observances of religion merit this divine assistance, and it comes to each man through the Church established for that purpose. Thus, while Saint Thomas recognizes the state as an institution independent of the Church, he must regard the former as subordinate to the latter, as imperfect happiness is subordinate to perfect. As the happiness man may secure on earth is a means to the happiness he may secure afterward, so the state is an instrument for securing the purposes of the Church.

EDUCATION

RECOMMENDATIONS

Saint Thomas discusses education briefly in three of his books: in *Summa Contra Gentiles,* in *Summa Theologica,* and in *De veritate* (trans-

---

9 *Ibid.,* P. II Iae, Q, iii, A. 1, 2, 4, 5, 8; Q. iv, A. 1–4; Q. v, A. 3, 5 6.

lated as *Truth*). In the first,[10] he recommends that parents provide education for their children, and he has in mind elementary education. In *Summa Theologica*,[11] and in *Truth*,[12] he asserts that teaching has both a theoretical and a practical aspect. The teacher knows the subject matter; this is the theoretical aspect of teaching. But he also endeavors to bring about acquaintance with it in his students. This endeavor is practical activity; and Saint Thomas suggests, in *Truth* especially, that the reason for engaging in it is to 'help our neighbor'. We may suppose that this 'help' consists in enabling the neighbor to achieve those ends that are conducive to the vision of God—that terrestrial happiness made up of moral virtue and of the remoter knowledge of God that makes for perfect happiness.

A n a l y s i s

In the longest of his brief treatments of education, however, Saint Thomas presents not so much recommendations concerning it as an analysis of one of its chief constituents—the notion of teaching.[13] Teaching consists, he tells us, in assisting someone else to come actually to know or to believe something. Thus, the concept applies to a situation in which there is a person, the teacher, who actually possesses knowledge and another, the student, who actually possesses neither knowledge nor belief about the matter concerned; and the analysis is a statement as to what the assistance offered by the teacher to the student in such a situation consists in.

Saint Thomas finds an important likeness between teaching and two other activities.[14] These two are the activities of bringing forms into existence in things, and of instilling moral virtues, dispositions of right conduct, in persons. Teaching resembles them in a way that must be understood by use of three distinctions. Two of them, we have already examined. They are the distinctions between matter and form, and between potential existence and actual existence. The third marks a difference between two kinds of propositions—general and particular. A proposition is anything that is true or false. A general proposition is one whose subject is accompanied by the word "all", and whose predicate, consequently, applies to every member of the group referred to by the subject.[15] 'All plum trees bear fruit' is a general proposition since the property 'bearing fruit' is applied, in it, to every member of

[10] Etienne Gilson, *The Christian Philosophy of St. Thomas Aquinas*, Random House Inc., New York 1956, pp. 281–2; also, Saint Thomas, *Summa Contra Gentiles*, III, 122–6.
[11] *Summa Theologica*, P. II IIae. Q. clxxxi, A. 3.
[12] *Truth*, Q. xi, A. 4.
[13] *Ibid.* Q. xi, A.
[14] *Ibid.*, Q. xi, A. 1.
[15] Or it is a proposition which can be transformed into one that fits this description. 'No man is immortal' can be transformed into 'all men are mortal'.

the class of plum trees. Particular propositions are those whose subjects are not accompanied by the word "all";[16] and the properties referred to by their predicates, consequently, are attributed by the proposition to some (not to all) the members of the class referred to by their subject terms. 'Some plum trees bear fruit' is a particular proposition.

The likeness between teaching, bringing forms into existence, and instilling moral virtue may be misconceived in two ways. All three activities may be thought of as imposition by the Supreme Power, the First Cause, or God—as His imposition of the awareness of true propositions on reason, of forms on matter, and of right or virtuous dispositions on desire. This view presupposes that reason, as such, lacks knowledge; that matter, as such, lacks form; and that the desires, as such, lack the virtues. It consists in the inference that the Supreme Power must make good these deficiencies. The second way of misconceiving the likeness is to think of all three activities as transitions, wholly confined to the things concerned, from the potential existence of something to its actual existence: of teaching, as the student's actualization of knowledge he already possesses potentially; of bringing forms into existence, as the actual exhibition by matter of forms potentially present in it all along; and of instilling virtue, as allowing the manifestation of dispositions latent in the person before he was improved. Viewing the likeness in this way is holding that activities of all three kinds are cases of development from within—development to which positive external agency is irrelevant.

The view that teaching, bringing forms into existence, and instilling virtue are all cases of God's imposition of one thing upon another, and the opposed view that they are all cases of internal development are both mistaken. The first disregards 'proximate causes'. God did not impose form upon matter since he created matter with form potential in it; and in creating the entire universe He created causal chains that link each particular event to the original act of creation. The link nearest the learning of a truth, the acquisition of form, and the manifestation of a virtuous disposition, therefore, exercises some influence in bringing each about. The second way of viewing the likeness also disregards 'proximate causes'. All teaching, bringing of forms into existence, and moral improvement does consist, of course, in the development into actuality of what formerly existed potentially; for as creator of everything, God created matter with all its forms potentially present in it. But while 'proximate causes' cannot bring about the development, they do enable it by removing obstructions to it. Teaching, bringing forms into existence, and improving character are not cases of imposing one thing on another, and are also not cases of development that is wholly internal. Hence, teaching

[16] Or which cannot be transformed into such propositions.

is neither the imposition by God of the subject matter of instruction on the student, nor the student's development of the subject matter for himself.

What teaching is, Saint Thomas discovers by finding the right way of conceiving the likeness it bears to bringing forms into existence, and to improving character. In a person who is ill, the form of humanity is not clearly present; and his restoration to health consists in bringing that form clearly into existence in him. But the work of the physician neither imposes the form, nor does the patient arrive at health with no assistance whatever—at least in many cases. Achieving health is the fulfillment of wholly natural processes; but the work of the physician consists in measures that enable nature to achieve its own end—the form of humanity clearly exhibited in a healthy person. Analogously, acting rightly does not result from an imposition on desires of some external form; nor in the development by the person alone, of virtues inherent in his desires. Rather, it results from an arrangement of the environment that enables a person to develop by practice those habitual actions that embody ends potentially present in his desires. In both cases, nature is assisted in making actual what was formerly potential—health in the patient, and virtue in the natural inclinations of man. These processes owe their outcomes to God since He is their creator; but in each case, human persons assist them by removing obstructions to their natural fruition.

Teaching, like medicine and character improvement, must be understood as the removal of obstructions that preclude the fulfillment of a natural process. This is the process of filling out the knowledge of general propositions with knowledge of particular propositions. Inherent in the human soul, are certain 'inborn', general principles. They contain potentially all knowledge of the particular propositions that men can acquire. Coming to know consists in perceiving the self-evident truth of these general principles, of perceiving particular things, and of seeing that propositions about those particulars follow from the general principles. Thus, coming to know is a process which runs from the awareness that premises are true, to the awareness that their conclusions are; and Saint Thomas regards this process as one of bringing into actual existence the knowledge of particular things that exists potentially in general principles.

In different persons, this potential knowledge exists in different ways. In some, no assistance from other persons is required to make that knowledge actual. They have within their own power the means of applying the general, 'inborn' principles—the opportunity to observe particulars, to consider how they should be described, to reflect on the general principles that may apply to them, the acuity to perceive that they do apply, etc. Such persons make independent discoveries; they follow out, in independence of others, the deductive path that leads from self-evident, general premises in which particular knowledge exists potentially, to the conclusion in which that knowledge exists actually. In other persons, the potential existence of knowledge of particular propositions is 'incomplete'. Although they possess the potential knowledge of particulars, they lack the means for making it actual—the means for applying it to particular cases. They cannot make independent discoveries; they must learn through instruction from others.

Saint Thomas analyzes the concept, teaching, with the help of this distinction between discovery and instruction; but this distinction, in turn, he understands by use of the three we have discussed. To discover is to come to know without the aid of other human beings. It is to see, without their aid, that an inborn general principle is self-evidently true, that it contains the potential existence of knowledge about some particular, that the matter of that particular contains a form made explicit by the general principle, and that the general principle functions as a premiss to a proposition about that particular thing. To be instructed is also to come to know; but besides the processes just described, it includes another as well.

In the situation where instruction is possible, the teacher alone possesses actual knowledge. Either through his own discovery or through instruction from some earlier teacher, he has seen that the general inborn principles are self-evident, and that particular propositions must be true because they follow from these general propositions. The student possesses only potential knowledge—the inborn general principles in light of which all particular things can be known. The teacher's instruction of the student consists in using 'signs' or language—lectures, discussions, etc.—with the intent to show him the reasoning he must go through to arrive for himself at the conclusion being considered. Instruction of one human being by another is the teacher's use of language to help the student to come to know for himself what the teacher formerly discovered or learned by instruction from someone else. To teach is to instruct; to learn through instruction is to come to know by following the path marked out by one's teacher. This is what Aristotle meant when he said: "Demonstration is a syllogism which makes someone know." [17]

The inculcation of belief or faith is enough like teaching to be given the same name. There is a general inborn principle which tells us that whatever neither follows necessarily from, nor is contrary to a self-evident principle may itself be true. We can find no reason for such a proposition; we cannot come to know it. But this general principle al-

[17] *Ibid.*, Q. xi, A. 1; Aristotle, *Posterior Analytics,* I, 1 (71a 1).

lows us to believe it. Where we propose such things to others and try to secure their acceptance of them, we are teaching them to believe, but not to know. We are instructing them in faith, but not in knowledge.

The human teacher knows the truths he helps others to come to know only in the light of reason. This is the light that enables him to see the truth of self-evident, inborn general principles; and in which he sees that particular conclusions follow from those general principles or are not incompatible with them. God is the source from which it flows. But if the student succeeds in knowing or believes the subject matter taught, it is because he sees, with the teacher's help, those general principles and their particular conclusions in the same divine illumination. Since knowledge and genuine belief are the awareness of truth and since achieving it presupposes that light, all human teaching and learning requires the divine illumination of the subject matter.

Saint Augustine holds that human teaching consists in reminding others of what they must come to know independently of it, and Saint Thomas holds that teaching consists in showing others the path to knowledge along which they must make their way quite independently as well. But Saint Thomas agrees with Saint Augustine, although he uses an analogy characteristically Aristotelian, that ". . . God alone teaches interiorly and principally, just as nature alone heals interiorly and principally." [18]

As we have seen, Saint Thomas contrasts teaching with the activity of acquiring virtue. And since he excludes character improvement from teaching, one might suppose that he regards it as no proper part of education. This supposition is mistaken.

Saint Thomas means by "virtue" habitual activity that is good, and he means by "good" conformity to a rule whose rightness is guaranteed by reason. Virtue, then, is habitual activity that conforms to a rule of reason, and the rule to which it conforms asserts that all activity ought to fall at the mean between excess and defect. There are three kinds of virtues: theological, intellectual, and moral. The theological virtues—faith, hope, and charity—are habitual ways of acting that enable us to look forward to the vision of God. They are granted men by God only, and human education by itself is powerless to produce them. The intellectual virtues—typified by wisdom and prudence—are good habits in which reason engages. They are developed by performing those acts that express them. By acting as if we were wise and prudent, we come actually to possess those good habits themselves. Saint Thomas thought of teaching, we may suppose, as consisting in the teacher's bringing the student to engage in those acts that enable him to see a truth with suf-

[18] *Truth,* Q. xi, A. 1.

ficient frequency that discerning self-evident propositions and making correct inferences from premises to conclusions comes to be habitual with him.

The view that the moral virtues are habits of acting in conformity with the rule of reason is more easy to understand. These virtues are habitual activities that express the desires, and it is clear enough what excess and defect in such activities come to. The desire for food is expressed excessively if one eats at every opportunity; it is expressed deficiently if one eats very seldom. The habit of acting toward the first extreme is the vice of gluttony; the habit of acting toward the second is that of undue fasting. Temperance in diet—only one form of that virtue which applies to many desires—is the habit of acting at the mean that falls between the two extremes. The moral virtues of temperance, fortitude, justice, etc. are all habitual activities that fall, thus, at the mean. They constitute the actualization of activities potentially present in desires, and they can be realized or acquired as can all habits, by acting as if we already possessed them. We acquire both intellectual and moral virtues by performing the acts that manifest them until those performances become habitual with us. Saint Thomas speaks of teaching as presiding over the process of acquiring intellectual virtue only, he quite clearly thinks of education, more generally conceived, as presiding over character improvement or the instilling of moral virtue as well.

A Guide to Selections from *Truth*

In the thirteenth century, student debates constituted an important part of university instruction. On certain days questions clustering around a particular topic were presented, and the affirmative and negative answers were argued for. On the day following such a disputation, the master replied, explaining his decision in favor of one side or the other. St. Thomas' book, *Truth,* grows out of a long series of such 'disputed questions' at the University of Paris; and its style reflects the procedure by which the disputations were organized. Each 'question' is divided into subordinate parts called "articles". Each article represents a debate. The question is stated, one side is argued for in a section called "difficulties" and the other in a section called "to the contrary". The third and fourth sections, the "reply" and "answers to difficulties", represent St. Thomas' decision concerning the student disputation.

In the passage reproduced here—*Question Eleven, Article I*—most of the arguments in "Difficulties", all of those in "To the Contrary", and most of those in "Answers to Difficulties" have been omitted. The "Reply" is presented in its entirety since it embodies St. Thomas' own thought about teaching. The arguments reproduced from "Difficulties" and "Answers to Difficulties" represent the influence of the Scriptures and of ancient literature on philosophical thought in the thirteenth century, and the influence in particular of the sacred writings, St. Augustine, and Aristotle—often called "the Philosopher"—on St. Thomas.

SELECTIONS FROM

*Truth**

QUESTION ELEVEN

The Teacher

━━◄◆►━━

ARTICLE I

*The Question Treats of the Teacher, and in the First
Article We Ask: Can A Man or only God
Teach and Be Called Teacher?*

Difficulties:

It seems that only God teaches and should be called a teacher, for

1.   In St. Matthew (23:8) we read: "One is your master;" and just before that: "Be not you called Rabbi." On this passage the *Gloss* comments: "Lest you give divine honor to men, or usurp for yourselves what belongs to God."[19] Therefore, it seems that only God is a teacher, or teaches.

2.   If a man teaches, he does so only through certain signs. For, even if one seems to teach by means of things, as, when asked what walking is, he walks, this is not sufficient to teach the one who asks, unless some sign be added, as Augustine proves.[20] He does this by showing that there are many factors involved in the same action; hence, one will not know to what factor the demonstration was due, whether to the substance of the action or to some accident of it. Furthermore, one cannot come to

* Reprinted, with kind permission of the publisher, Henry Regnery Company Chicago, from *Truth*, Vol. II, Q. xi, A. 1, translated from the definitive Leonine text by Robert W. Mulligan, S.J., 1952. Abbreviations in the footnotes for these selected passages are explained on the last page of this chapter.

19 *Glossa interlinearis,* super Matt. 23:8 (V:71r).
20 St. Augustine, *De magistro,* III (*PL* 32: 1198) X (*PL* 32: 1214–15).

a knowledge of things through a sign, for the knowledge of things is more excellent than the knowledge of signs, since the knowledge of signs is directed to knowledge of things as a means to an end. But the effect is not more excellent than its cause. Therefore, no one can impart knowledge of anything to another, and so cannot teach him.

3.   If signs of certain things are proposed to someone by a man, the one to whom they are proposed either knows the things which the signs represent or he does not. If he knows the things, he is not taught them. But if he does not know them, he cannot know the meanings of the signs, since he does not know the things. For a man who does not know what a stone is cannot know what the word *stone* means. But if he does not know the meaning of the terms, he cannot learn anything through the signs. Therefore, if a man does nothing else to teach than propose signs, it seems that one man cannot be taught by another.

4.   To teach is nothing else than to cause knowledge in another in some way. But our understanding is the subject of knowledge. Now, sensible signs, by which alone, it would seem, man can be taught, do not reach the intellective part, but affect the senses only. Therefore, man cannot be taught by a man.

5.   If the knowledge is caused by one person in another, the learner either had it already or he did not. If he did not have it already and it was caused in him by another, then one man creates knowledge in another, which is impossible. However, if he had it already, it was present either in complete actuality, and thus it cannot be caused, for what already exists does not come into being, or it was present seminally (*secundum rationes seminales*). But such seminal principles cannot be actualized by any created power, but are implanted in nature by God alone, as Augustine says.[21] So, it remains true that one man can in no way teach another.

Reply:

There is the same sort of difference of opinion on three issues: on the bringing of forms into existence, on the acquiring of virtues, and on the acquiring of scientific knowledge.

For some[22] have said that all sensible forms come from an external

---

[21] St. Augustine, *De genesi ad litteram*, VII, 22 (*PL* 34: 367).

[22] Alexander, etc., cf. above, Q, x, A. 8, n. 34. (Note 34 follows).

[34] Alexander of Aphrodisius, *De intellectu et intellecto* (*TH* 76); Averroes, *In De Anima*, III, comm. 18 (VI2; 161E); Avicenna, *De anima*, V, 5 (25r); *Metaph.*, IX, 3 (104r). Cf. St. Thomas, *De unitate intellectus*, V, 54 (*PERR* 119). This doctrine appeared in Christian philosophy under a different form, which made God the agent intellect. This is found in William of Auvergne, Roger Bacon, Adam of Marsh, John Peckham, and Roger Marston. For a discussion of this see Gilson, "Pourquoi St. Thomas a critiqué St. Augustin," *AHDLM*, I (1926–7), 80 ff., and Gilson, "Roger Marston, un cas d'augustinisme avicennesant," *AHDLM*, VIII, 37 ff.

agent, a separated substance or form, which they call the giver of forms or agent intelligence, and that all that lower natural agents do is prepare the matter to receive the form. Similarly, Avicenna says[23] that our activity is not the cause of a good habit, but only keeps out its opposite and prepares us for the habit so that it may come from the substance which perfects the souls of men. This is the agent intelligence or some similar substance.

They also hold that knowledge is caused in us only by an agent free of matter. For this reason Avicenna holds[24] that the intelligible forms flow into our mind from the agent intelligence.

Some[25] have held the opposite opinion, namely, that all three of those are embodied in things and have no external cause, but are only brought to light by external activity. For some have held that all natural forms are in act, lying hidden in matter, and that a natural agent does nothing but draw them from concealment out into the open. In like manner, some[26] hold that all the habits of the virtues are implanted in us by nature. And the practice of their actions removes the obstructions which, as it were, hid these habits, just as rust is removed by filing so that the brightness of the iron is brought to light. Similarly, some[27] also have said that the knowledge of all things is con-created with the soul and that through teaching and the external helps of this type of knowledge all that happens is that the soul is prompted to recall or consider those things which it knew previously. Hence, they say that learning is nothing but remembering.

But both of these positions lack a reasonable basis. For the first opinion excludes proximate causes, attributing solely to first causes all effects which happen in lower natures. In this it derogates from the order of the universe, which is made up of the order and connection of causes, since the first cause, by the pre-eminence of its goodness, gives other beings not only their existence, but also their existence as causes. The second position, too, falls into practically the same difficulty. For, since a thing which removes an obstruction is a mover only accidentally, as is said in the *Physics*,[28] if lower agents do nothing but bring things from concealment into the open, taking away the obstructions which concealed the forms and habits of the virtues and the sciences, it follows that all lower agents act only accidentally.

[23] Avicenna, *Metaph.*, IX, 7 (107c).
[24] Avicenna, *De anima*, V, 6 (25r).
[25] Anaxagoras and the Stoics. On the former, see Aristotle, *Physica*, I, 4 (187a 29); on the latter, see Chalcidius, *In Timaeum*, 309 (*DD* 247).
[26] This opinion and the following (n. 27) are attributed to Plato. See *S.T.*, I, 48, 1; I, 84, 3, obj. 3; and *Q. D. de pot.*, 3, 8. For an explanation of this position see St. Albert the Great, *In Eth.*, I, tr. 7, c. 4 (*BO* VII: 112). Plato gives his position in *Meno*, 82 B; *Timaeus*, 44 A; *Phaedo*, 67 D; 92 A. See Cicero, *Disp. Tuscul.*, I, 31.
[27] *Ibid.*
[28] Aristotle, *Physica*, VIII, 5 (256a 4ff., 256b 3ff.).

Therefore, in all that has been said we ought to hold a middle position between these two, according to the teaching of Aristotle.[29] For natural forms pre-exist in matter not actually, as some have said, but only in potency. They are brought to actuality from this state of potency through a proximate external agent, and not through the first agent alone, as one of the opinions maintains. Similarly, according to the opinion of Aristotle,[30] before the habits of virtue are completely formed, they exist in us in certain natural inclinations, which are the beginnings of the virtues. But afterwards, through practice in their actions, they are brought to their proper completion.

We must give a similar explanation of the acquisition of knowledge. For certain seeds of knowledge pre-exist in us, namely, the first concepts of understanding, which by the light of the agent intellect are immediately known through the species abstracted from sensible things. These are either complex, as axioms, or simple, as the notions of being, of the one, and so on, which the understanding grasps immediately. In these general principles, however, all the consequences are included as in certain seminal principles. When, therefore, the mind is led from these general notions to actual knowledge of the particular things which it knew previously in general and, as it were, potentially, then one is said to acquire knowledge.

We must bear in mind, nevertheless, that in natural things something can pre-exist in potency in two ways. In one, it is in an active and completed potency, as when an intrinsic principle has sufficient power to flow into perfect act. Healing is an obvious example of this, for the sick person is restored to health by the natural power within him. The other appears in a passive potency, as happens when the internal principle does not have sufficient power to bring it into act. This is clear when air becomes fire, for this cannot result from any power existing in the air.

Therefore, when something pre-exists in active completed potency, the external agent acts only by helping the internal agent and providing it with the means by which it can enter into act. Thus, in healing the doctor assists nature, which is the principle agent, by strengthening nature and prescribing medicines, which nature uses as instruments for healing. On the other hand, when something pre-exists only in passive potency, then it is the external agent which is the principal cause of the transition from potency to act. Thus, fire makes actual fire of air, which is potentially fire.

Knowledge, therefore, pre-exists in the learner potentially, not, however, in the purely passive, but in the active, sense. Otherwise, man

[29] *Ibid.,* I, 8 (191b 10ff.).
[30] Aristotle, *Ethica Nicomachea,* II, 1 (1003a 24). Cf. *ibid.,* VI, 11 (1143b 6); VI, 13 1144b 5).

would not be able to acquire knowledge independently. Therefore, as there are two ways of being cured, that is, either through the activity of unaided nature or by nature with the aid of medicine, so also there are two ways of acquiring knowledge. In one way, natural reason by itself reaches knowledge of unknown things, and this way is called *discovery;* in the other way, when someone else aids the learner's natural reason, and this is called *learning by instruction.*

In effects which are produced by nature and by art, art operates in the same way and through the same means as nature. For, as nature heals one who is suffering from cold by warming him, so also does the doctor. Hence, art is said to imitate nature. A similar thing takes place in acquiring knowledge. For the teacher leads the pupil to knowledge of things he does not know in the same way that one directs himself through the process of discovering something he does not know.

Now, in discovery, the procedure of anyone who arrives at the knowledge of something unknown is to apply general self-evident principles to certain definite matters, from these to proceed to particular conclusions, and from these to others. Consequently, one person is said to teach another inasmuch as, by signs, he manifests to that other the reasoning process which he himself goes through by his own natural reason. And thus, through the instrumentality, as it were, of what is told him, the natural reason of the pupil arrives at a knowledge of the things which he did not know. Therefore, just as the doctor is said to heal a patient through the activity of nature, so a man is said to cause knowledge in another through the activity of the learner's own natural reason, and this is teaching. So, one is said to teach another and be his teacher. This is what the Philosopher means when he says: "Demonstration is a syllogism which makes someone know." [31]

But, if someone proposes to another things which are not included in self-evident principles, or does not make it clear that they are included, he will not cause knowledge in the other but, perhaps, opinion or faith, although even this is in some way caused by inborn first principles, for from these self-evident principles he realizes that what necessarily follows from them is to be held with certitude, and that what is contrary to them is rejected completely, and that assent may be given to or withheld from whatever neither follows necessarily from nor is contrary to self-evident principles. Now, the light of reason by which such principles are evident to us is implanted in us by God as a kind of reflected likeness in us of the uncreated truth. So, since all human teaching can be effective only in virtue of that light, it is obvious that God alone teaches interiorly and principally, just as nature alone heals interiorly

[31] Aristotle, *Analytica posteriora,* I, 2 (71b 18).

and principally. Nevertheless, both to heal and to teach can still be used in a proper sense in the way we have explained.

Answers to Difficulties:

1. Since our Lord had ordered the disciples not to be called teachers, the *Gloss*[32] explains how this prohibition is to be understood, lest it be taken absolutely. For we are forbidden to call a man a teacher in this sense, that we attribute to him the pre-eminence of teaching, which belongs to God. It would be as if we put our hope in the wisdom of men, and did not rather consult divine truth about those things which we hear from man. And this divine truth speaks in us through the impression of its likeness, by means of which we can judge of all things.

2. Knowledge of things is not produced in us through knowledge of signs, but through knowledge of things more certain, namely, principles. The latter are proposed to us through signs and are applied to other things which were heretofore unknown to us simply, although they were known to us in some respect, as has been said. For knowledge of principles produces in us knowledge of conclusions; knowledge of signs does not.

3. To some extent we know the things we are taught through signs, and to some extent we do not know them. Thus, if we are taught what man is, we must know something about him beforehand, namely, the meaning of animal, or of substance, or at least of being itself, which last concept cannot escape us. Similarly, if we are taught a certain conclusion, we must know beforehand what the subject and predicate are. We must also have previous knowledge of the principles through which the conclusion is taught, for "all teaching comes from pre-existing knowledge," as is said in the *Posterior Analytics.*[33] Hence, the argument does not follow.

4. Our intellect derives intelligible likenesses from sensible signs which are received in the sensitive faculty, and it uses these intelligible forms to produce in itself scientific knowledge. For the signs are not the proximate efficient cause of knowledge, but reason is, in its passage from principles to conclusions, as has been said.

5. In one who is taught, the knowledge did not exist in complete actuality, but, as it were, in seminal principles, in the sense that the universal concepts which we know naturally are, as it were, the seeds of all the knowledge which follows. But, although these seminal principles are not developed to actuality by any created power, as though they were infused by a created power, that which they have in a primitive way and virtually can develop into actuality by means of the activity of a created power.

---

[32] *Glossa interlinearis,* super Matt. 23:8 (V: 71r).
[33] Aristotle, *Analytica posteriora,* I, 1 (71a 1).

Abbreviations

AHDLM   *Archives d'histoire doctrinale et littéraire du moyen âge.*

BO   St. Albert the Great. *Opera omnia.* Ed. A. Borgnet. Paris, Vives, 1890-99. 38 vols.

DD   Chalcidius. *Timaeus ex Platonis dialogo et in eundem commentarius,* in *Fragmenta philosophorum graecorum.* Ed. G. Mullachius. Paris, Firmin-Didot, 1867-69.

PERR   *Opuscula omnia Sancti Thomae Aquinatis.* Ed. John Perrier, O. P. Paris, Lethielleux, 1949——.

PL   *Patrologiae cursus completus.* Series latina. Ed. J. P. Migne. Paris, 1844-55. 218 vols.

TH   Alexander of Aphrodisias. *De intellectu et intellecto.* Ed. G. Théry, O. P. In *Autour du décret de 1210,* II. Alexandre d'Aphrodise. Le Saulchoir, 1926. Bibliothèque Thomiste, VII.

Bibliography

GULLEY, REV. ANTHONY D., *The Educational Philosophy of Saint Thomas Aquinas,* New York, Pageant Press, 1961.

MAYER, MARY HELEN, *The Philosophy of Teaching of Saint Thomas Aquinas,* Milwaukee, Bruce Publishing Co., 1929.

. . .

COPLESTON, FREDERICK C., S.J., *Aquinas,* Penguin Books (Pelican Philosophy Series), 1955.

D'ARCY, MARTIN C., *Thomas Aquinas,* Boston, Little, Brown, 1930.

GILSON, ETIENNE H., *The Christian Philosophy of St. Thomas Aquinas,* translated by L. K. Shook, New York, Random House, 1956. Also, *The Philosophy of St. Thomas Aquinas,* "authorised translated from the third, revised edition of *Le Thomisme,*" translated by Edward Bullough and edited by Rev. G. A. Erlington, Cambridge, W. Heffer and Sons, Ltd., 1924; (second revised and enlarged edition 1929).

Also translated by L. E. M. Lynch, New York, Random House, 1960, *Le thomisme* (Strasbourg, A. Vix & Cie., 1919; revised and enlarged, Paris, J. *Vrin,* 1922).

MARITAIN, JACQUES, *St. Thomas Aquinas,* originally entitled *The Angelic Doctor,* translated by J. F. Scanlan, New York, Dial Press, 1931. Also translated by Joseph W. Evans and Peter O'Reilly, New York, Meridian, 1958. (*Le docteur angelique,* Paris, 1930.)

VI

COMENIUS

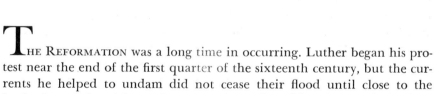

THE REFORMATION was a long time in occurring. Luther began his protest near the end of the first quarter of the sixteenth century, but the currents he helped to undam did not cease their flood until close to the beginning of the eighteenth century. Into the midst of the political turmoil, religious warfare, intellectual antagonism, and educational controversy which Luther helped to start, John Amos Comenius (Komenský) was born in 1592. His family was Protestant in sympathy; and his long life was, from an early period, constantly troubled and pervasively determined by the social turbulence of the times. He died in 1670, still believing that all of Europe could be separated from the Roman Church.

Comenius' native country was Moravia, a vassal state together with Bohemia of the Hapsburg dynasty, and with a center of Protestant revolt against that Catholic line, stemming from the activities of Huss. A little older than most students, he attended a typical Latin school where he was vividly impressed with the ineffectual methods of its traditional books and teaching as well as the arid poverty of the content of its curriculum. At the University of Herborn, Nassau, he prepared himself for ordination in the dominant Protestant sect of his native region, The Bohemian Brethren. In 1618 the Thirty Years War broke out; and its intense destructiveness for the states of central and eastern Europe was nowhere more evident than in Moravia and Bohemia. This war was part of the Reformation turmoil; and in these countries, it resulted from conflict between the Catholic power supported by the Hapsburgs, the Inquisition, and the Jesuits, and the Protestant objection to it fostered by local nobles, merchants, and others involved in the rising nationalisms. Comenius found himself a citizen of a devastated country, and a pastor in a persecuted sect which, while it aspired to freedom of worship if not to the status of a religion established by an independent national government in Moravia and Bohemia, was early in the conflict exiled from its native land. After the Peace of Westphalia Comenius continued to avow a view that he, along with many other Protestants throughout Europe, had held for a long time—the doctrine of chiliasm. This is the view that Jesus will appear on earth a second time, and reign over the world for one thousand years of peace prior to the Day of Judgment. Comenius seems not to have doubted that during this time Protestantism would be tolerated; nor, perhaps, that the Bohemian Brethren would be recognized as the proper religion in Moravia and Bohemia.

Comenius spent much time working out a theory of education to be applied to the schools of a Protestant country together with a philosophical justification of it. For several years he was a teacher in and administrator of schools; and his educational theory no doubt both influenced and was influenced by these activities. He was acquainted with many of the ideas advanced by philosophical writers of the Renaissance, especially the more fantastic ones; and the philosophy that he applied to his educational ideas is an unstable compound of Platonic, Aristotelian, mystical, empirical, rational, and Scriptural elements.

But the philosophy, the theory, and the practice of education by no means exhausted his energy and his time. He was greatly interested in language, working for years on a dictionary for the Czech vernacular, devising theories as to the nature of language in general, and in light of it, writing texts for the teaching of language, especially Latin. These texts were at once enormously successful. They made Comenius one of the most sought-after educators in Protestant Europe, and were used widely into the eighteenth century.

But the writing of textbooks was, for Comenius, always of subordinate importance to the cause of Protestantism and to the working out of those philosophical theories which, he thought, could justify the procedures from which the textbooks grew. In his later life as its bishop, he conducted the affairs of the exiled and almost utterly decimated Bohemian Brethren; but he continued to work on his philosophical books despite the arduousness of his executive post. Many of them were destroyed during a Reformationist battle in 1658, as some had been thirty-seven years before;

and this destruction of a lifetime of writing was a blow that added greatly to the sorrow of a wandering exiled life.

Comenius, from an early age, had been impressed with prophets, especially those who foretold the destruction of the Catholic power and the emergence of Moravia and Bohemia as Protestant countries. Toward the close of his life, he published his opinions, staunchly supporting the views of a famous seer named Drabik whose visions guaranteed that the Catholic Hapsburg emperor would be overthrown by the Protestant sympathizer, Rakoczy, Prince of Transylvania; that Comenius would anoint the latter King; that the Turks (still a very present threat to Europe) would convert *en masse* to Christianity and join forces with Rakoczy and the Swedish king to put an end to Roman Catholicism. Among Protestants, Drabik had a large number of followers throughout Europe although he was a patent fraud; but this fancy on the part of a man of great international reputation for pedagogical sagacity, philosophical competence, and wide learning brought upon Comenius the obloquy of men of good sense throughout Europe—obloquy which would have been the greater if he had lived a few months longer to witness Drabik's conversion to Roman Catholicism.

Comenius died full of sorrows, widely reputed for his textbooks, and embarrassed by his prophets. His biographer, Keatinge, suggests that his association with obvious quacks is the reason for the two centuries of twilight enjoyed by all his writings other than the textbooks. There is little question that these texts are the products of somehing like genius; but there is also little question that the more philosophical books are the products of a mind devoted to philosophy, but quite uncritical of its contents and procedures. Comenius is probably the leading Protestant writer in the philosophy of education, and certainly one of the great reformers in the practice of education. But his contributions to these subjects may stem more from his gentle, humane, and Christian character than from his philosophical acumen.

EDUCATIONAL THEORY

STATEMENTS OF FACT

The statements of fact upon which Comenius rests the recommendations in his educational theory do not always live up to his own requirements. He insists, frequently, that all statements can be validated only by observation; but he fails, on many occasions, to support his claims, either by observation of the facts to which they look or by observation of others which might be evidence for them. His interpretation of Scripture, rather than empirical investigation, provides the basis for many of the assertions involved in his educational theory. In this exposition these statements, nonetheless, will be counted as genuine statements of fact. They are of three kinds; those concerning human nature, those concerning universal history, and those concerning the condition of the schools.

H u m a n   n a t u r e

The nature of every human being, Comenius holds, is threefold. The activities of each person differ enormously from one to another. Nonetheless, they fall into three main kinds. Every person nourishes himself and grows through a certain cycle; every person senses and feels toward things in certain ways; and every person is intellectual to some degree. Relying on doctrines that flow from ancient Greek and Roman sources, Comenius advances the view that the reason why human beings behave in these three ways lies in their being governed by three distinct principles or souls; namely, the vegetative, the animal, and the intellectual soul. The first is that in us which enables our bodies, by using the environment appropriately, to nourish themselves and to grow; it is found alike in all animals and vegetables. The animal soul is that in us which enables us to be aware of things through our sense organs and to move of our own accord; it is found alike in all men and lower animals. The intellectual soul is that which enables us to know truths about the things we sense as well as those we do not, to will to act in certain ways, and to discriminate as better and worse between the objects upon which we direct our desires and emotions; it is found in all men but not in brutes. Man's nature is thus vegetative, animal, and intellectual.[1]

The intellectual soul, since it distinguishes men from other animals, merits more detailed attention. It possesses three powers: reason, will, and the power to feel emotions; and they fall in a certain order. Reason is the power to name all things; and by putting names together to make and to support judgments concerning the characteristics and relations of the things named.[2]

The will is the power to act in one way as opposed to another. The power to feel emotion toward things makes us desire each of them. In a perfect human being, reason provides knowledge of all things, and consequently, of those things which are better than others. The emotions, however, make us desire things regardless of their superior or inferior value. The will directs our actions toward securing what is best—some-

[1] John Amos Comenius, *The Great Didactic,* translated by M. W. Keatinge, Adam and Charles Black, London, 1896, p. 179.
[2] *Ibid.,* p. 188.

thing which it could not do if reason did not discover many things and our emotions make us desire at least some of them. Thus, in a perfect human being, there is a harmony of the three parts of the intellectual soul which consists in the fact that since the perfect man knows what is best among all things, and although his emotions focus upon many things, his will endeavors to secure the most valuable as opposed to the rest.

Before the Fall, the lives of Adam and Eve exhibited this harmony; but since that time no one has achieved it. The vegetative and the animal souls of men have directed their attention away from the pursuit of knowledge; and their emotions, unenlightened by reason, have marked off a field of inferior objectives for will to choose from. This is the source, if not the very nature, of that corruption—the warfare, greed, and unthinking cruelty—which has characterized human history from the Fall to the present time.

Amid this corruption, however, lie the "seeds" or possibilities of improvement.[3] The intellectual soul is submerged by the flood of unconsidered self-seeking that wells from the animal and vegetative souls, but it is not destroyed. Erudition (knowledge) remains a possible achievement of reason; virtue (life according to moral law), a possible goal for the will; and piety (union with God), a possible objective for the emotions and desires or affections. These three ways of life—erudition, virtue, and piety—are desired by all men even though all fall short of their achievement.

The "seeds" of improvement do not develop properly apart from society and from religious teaching. Independently of society, children do not learn to speak, as the discovery of wild children shows;[4] and consequently, are unable to reason and to judge the value of things. This ability to reason and to judge is guaranteed in human company; but a failure in religious teaching may, as it in fact has, permit futile speculation to occur where erudition should have place, and vice and irreverence to supplant virtue and piety. Religion must be added to human society if the possibilities of human nature which grow out of the intellectual soul are to run toward their proper objectives. If a person experiences human society, and if in that society he is provided with religious teaching, he will become as learned, as virtuous, as pious, as the vegetative and animal parts of his nature permit.

Within such a society there is a natural course of development for each individual. During the first six years of his life, his sense organs develop, making possible sensory knowledge of the environment. During the next six, the abilities to imagine and to remember what has been

3 *Ibid.*, v.
4 *Ibid.*, pp. 206–7.

sensed come into existence. During the third period of six years, the ability to judge the characteristics and relations of things sensed, imagined, and remembered—the ability to reason—emerges in its full power. During the period from eighteen to twenty-four, the will becomes strong, enabling the harmonization of desires for those things toward which we feel emotion, and consequently, the self-direction of one's life.[5] Throughout the first twenty-four years of life, the natural course of development proceeds toward the domination of the intellectual over the other souls; and the maturity that one achieves after that time consists in a love of God, a will to manifest it despite the clamor of opposing impulses, and the knowledge of erudition on which such a love and will can rest.

But no matter what the learning, the morality, or the piety of a man, he can never achieve complete perfection in this life. His desire for union with God can never be fully satisfied; his obedience to the moral law cannot be complete; his knowledge cannot be exhaustive. This shows that the goal of human development, although it guides the natural course of human life, can be achieved completely only in some other life —that man's "ultimate end is beyond this world." [6]

Universal history

Universal history must provide an account of the development of two things: of the world of nature, and of the human race. God created all of nature at a certain time in the past, but it did not spring forth immediately in all its fullness. Relying upon the Bible, Comenius tells us that God created pure matter first. Pure matter is that which possesses characteristics, not something with its characteristics. On his view, the pure matter of a blade of grass is not the green leaf; it is what possesses the greenness, the blade-shape, etc. The pure matter that underlies the world of nature existed in many bits or atoms;[7] and these pervaded the "abyss" or space. Into them, God breathed the spirit of life and the seeds of all things. The bits of pure matter assumed different qualities; and the four elements, earth, water, air, and fire, emerged as a consequence. Earth and water came to the center of the abyss; and air and fire took up, respectively, the more outward regions. The earth and heavenly bodies came into existence, and began to move according to the Ptolemaic picture. In due course, plants and animals, as the result of the operation of the spirit of life, developed out of the seeds which God had scattered.

---

5 *Ibid.*, pp. 408–9.
6 *Ibid.*, II.
7 John Amos Comenius, *The Way of Light,* translated by E. T. Campagnac, Liverpool, The University Press, Hodder and Stoughton, Ltd., London, 1938, Chapter IX, p. 58.

Comenius holds that each thing in nature is governed by a certain order. This order is determined by God as the Creator of the universe; and observation shows that it consists in two factors, namely, the internal purposeful development of each thing, and its relations to other things. All change advances toward some result. This is true even for inorganic nature. For example, the movement of each heavenly body is of such a kind as to preserve a uniform path; and the relation of each such path to others is of such a kind as to accomplish an orderly motion of all round the earth—the motion of the sun and other bodies which gives rise to the seasons, to growth and nutrition of plants and animals, and to the life of man.[8]

In organic nature, everything develops in a purposeful way. Comenius takes, as his chief example, the change of an egg into an adult bird; and tells us that the change of all organisms, with the exception of human beings, resembles the development of birds. First, the development of an egg terminates in something, a fowl, which was present in general outline in the egg. From the beginning, the embryo exhibits the form of a bird; and its development is the filling in of that outline. This characteristic of organic change is what Comenius describes as development from "universal to particular."[9] Secondly, this development takes place from within, i.e., nothing external to it can, alone, cause the change of an egg into a fowl. Thirdly, this internal development is the change of the matter in the egg into a concrete (particular) manifestation of the form (universal) which the matter embodied in its initial stage. Fourthly, the development proceeds continuously toward its goal, the adult bird. There are no gaps. Fifthly, there is no stage in the process which does not contribute to what follows it, no part of the adult fowl which does not perform a function necessary to its life, and nothing in the entire development which is not useful to it. Sixthly, each bird of any given species, e.g., each chicken, results from a development of the same sort as do the rest. These six characteristics of organic development are what Comenius calls the "methods of nature." He states them with lamentable confusion of thought, as if each pointed to some distinct fact about growth, in twenty-nine principles.[10]

Individual organisms, developing in this way, are related to each other in an orderly fashion; and so long as that order is maintained, organic nature is stable. The adult bird warms the egg, protects the young, maintains the brood, and contributes to the nourishment of men and the adornment of human life. Similarly, other organisms, fostering

[8] *The Great Didactic*, XIII.
[9] *Ibid.*, XVI, p. 263.
[10] *Ibid.*, XVI, XVII, XVIII.

their young, contribute to the life of birds. Inorganic and organic nature, where each thing develops according to its purpose, exhibit a comprehensive order which makes for their preservation.

But this order is not constantly present. Throughout the universe, from one time to another, order and disorder alternate; thus, calm alternates with stormy weather, good conditions of growth with flood and drought. This alternation, however, is governed by law and harmony, and it will continue for a few thousand years at which time nature (the visible universe) will be destroyed.

The history of the human race begins with the creation of Adam and Eve. It is punctuated by their fall, the advent of Christ, and the Day of Judgment which will occur a few millenia after the first parents.

The history of man, from beginning to end, is an alternation of good and evil. Many forms of natural and social security and insecurity—peace and war, toleration and persecution, feast and famine, nourishing rain and destructive flood—constantly attend their lives. The sin of Adam and of Eve was inherited by their children; and as a result, they are naturally corrupt. Their corruption consists in an inability persistently to choose those objectives which are good. The fluctuation of their wills leads to the alternation of social good and evil; and together with God's intent to punish evil and to exact obedience, to the alternation of natural fortunes and misfortunes.

In this alternation of opposites there is a kind of progress. It is intellectual progress; and it consists in the fact that in each stage of history more men know more about more things than in any preceding stage. In the first, that occupied by him alone, Adam knew only what his senses showed him; his knowledge was what Comenius calls by the strange name "autopsy." With Eve, language began as the male reader might expect; and through informal conversation, the first parents and their immediate successors supplemented the meager knowledge that each secured through autopsy. In the third stage, people assembled in groups, and formal instruction increased the extent and diffusion of knowledge. Reading and writing, along with schools to teach them, were invented in the fourth; and knowledge was transmitted from one generation to another in a way that provided a basis for its increment. In the fifth, printing scattered knowledge even farther than had writing; and in the sixth, new aids to navigation, such as the compass, made for the discovery of hitherto unknown parts of the world, and the diffusion of knowledge as well as its extension throughout all peoples and languages of the globe. There will be a seventh stage of perfect knowledge in which, from all the various languages and peoples, it will be brought together, and through concerted effort, extended to all things. This will occur in the final period of terrestrial history; and at that time, complete knowledge, fully pervading the human race, will make a perfect, if brief, early existence.[11]

The condition of schools

The chief instruments for this climax in human history will be the schools; but at present, they suffer from many deficiencies which must be removed before they can play their role. These deficiencies are of three broad kinds: those of administrations, of methods of instruction, and of curriculum.

The administration of schools does not provide adequately for the health of students. It does not require exercise; it does not assure adequate food; and it compels too many hours of study per day with too few intermissions. But if the body is not healthy, the student cannot learn efficiently.[12] Moreover, students are permitted much irregularity in their attendance, and the dull are frequently excluded altogether from the benefits of schooling.[13] But irregularity in attendance hampers learning; and the dull can acquire as much erudition, virtue, and piety as accords with their ability. Besides, only a few children, and those chiefly of wealthy parents, attend school even irregularly.

Methods of instruction are deficient in three respects. First, in languages, letters, and science, they consist largely in memorizing by rote, and in mechanical drill. But the memorizing of rules and principles, and drill in syntax and vocabulary cannot advance understanding. If one is to learn, he must be interested in doing so; only then can he be brought to learning by the devices of pedagogy.

Secondly, teachers introduce the elements of particular courses in an order that makes their teaching ineffective. In the arts, they endeavor to develop skills before the student has been shown the nature of the materials upon which he will exercise them. In languages, a new one is not developed by reference to that which is native to the student, his vernacular; but Latin is taught by use of Latin, Greek by Greek, etc. Moreover, definitions of words and grammatical rules for their combinations are taught before the students become acquainted with the things and their combinations to which we refer when we use the words and obey the rules concerned. In mathematics and science, teachers try to teach principles and laws before they acquaint the student with the things which those principles and laws would explain and describe; and the details of theories are presented before a general outline of all knowledge.

11 *Ibid.*, xiii.
12 *Ibid.*, xv.
13 *Ibid.*, xvi, §55, p. 24.

Thirdly, there is frequently no language common to all the students and teacher; so that, no matter what the skill of the teacher, learning is made frequently very difficult for all. It must be remembered that Comenius wrote at a time when Europe was divided into relatively small political units, many with their own native languages or vernaculars; and when Latin, which was still a fairly widespread language for the educated, was nevertheless artificially taught rather than naturally acquired.

The deficiencies of curriculum are of two sorts. First, the materials for use in schools are, for the most part, nonexistent; and where they occur, they are of inferior quality. Few schools possess an adequate supply of books, maps, pictures, diagrams, and the like; and those which are so fortunate as to possess a few have books usually ill-written, and other materials poorly contrived for the purposes they should serve.

Secondly, the subjects studied are not geared to the development of the student, i.e., to the four-stage development described earlier. Rather, within each day and each larger unit of time, subjects are taken up haphazard; and students of varying ages, with differing powers of sensory discrimination, of imagination and memory, of reason, and of will, are jumbled together in the same class. The curriculum is disordered, so that a general outline of knowledge is not presented in the earliest stage of the schooling of each student, and so that the later stages do not consist in filling in that outline as opposed to adding at various points subjects that are radically novel. In short, the curriculum is not arranged so that, in accord with the psychological and physiological development of students, success in earlier studies facilitates learning in later subjects.

Comenius spent a good deal of time teaching in and administering schools; and we may assume that his indictment of their administration, instructional methods, and curriculum is based upon that experience.

RECOMMENDATIONS

Goal recommendation

All human beings, according to Comenius, ought to endeavor to achieve a twofold goal: an immortal life of blessedness, and a terrestrial existence of civic welfare and international peace. The former is the objective inherent in human nature, the end which "lies beyond this life." [14] The latter, civic welfare and international peace, he seems to regard as a necessary part of immortal bliss; for he seems to hold that it is by advancing welfare, both material and spiritual, and by abolishing war that men may come to merit the fulfillment of their natures after death.

---

[14] But note that Comenius does not consistently maintain this view, since he also holds that some men are predestined for immortal suffering.

Accomplishing this twofold objective consists in giving to human life the order which pervades nature. That order is the contribution of each thing to the stability of the whole of nature, and stems from the internal development of each item toward its specific goal. The order of human life is that system of relations between persons through which each contributes to the stability of the whole, and this order is achieved to the degree that each individual realizes the nature that he shares with all others. This social order is the concord of nations and of individuals within them; and it is achieved to the degree that each individual acquires the learning, virtue, and piety whose possibilities make up our common human nature. Thus, to the degree that men are genuinely human, terrestrial life will be ordered as is nature; and to the degree that this order pervades individual persons, they will merit eternal bliss. Realizing the goal that Comenius recommends, then, requires imposing on human life that order which we read in the nature that surrounds it. Education is this imposition.

Subordinate recommendations

The recommendations subordinate to the goal set forth in Comenius' educational theory appear as requirements of education thus understood. They are of three sorts: those concerning administration, methods of instruction, and content and arrangement of curriculum. The chief recommendations of these three kinds will be discussed here; many details will be deliberately overlooked.

CONCERNING ADMINISTRATION. Education ought to be universal, uniform, and through the lower schools, compulsory. Each child embodies inclinations of two kinds. Some represent original sin, and direct him away from terrestrial and immortal happiness. Others flow from his human nature, and incline him toward that blessedness. But all men ought to achieve the latter; and contrary inclinations ought, so far as possible, to be thwarted. But to thwart them is to order the life of those who harbor them so that only peculiarly human tendencies are realized. This ordering is education; and therefore, all human beings, including women, should be educated.

In the lower schools, all students should receive an education of the same sort. Human nature is identical in all persons; and the process through which it is realized also does not differ significantly from one to another. Consequently, the methods, materials, and content of instruction ought to be uniform.

In the lower schools, all students should receive an education of the same sort. Human nature is identical in all persons; and the process through which it is realized also does not differ significantly from one to another. Consequently, the methods, materials, and content of instruction ought to be uniform.

Education ought to be compulsory. Since the Fall, human beings have been torn between inclinations of the two kinds described above. All too frequently, the desires which disrupt society and alienate men from their proper ideal have dominated their lives; and their failure to realize the better inclinations results from a lack of schooling or from subjection to incompetent instruction. Consequently, all children ought to be compelled to attend school.

Comenius insists that despite common human nature, children differ in the degree to which they can realize it. Consequently, he urges that higher education be forced on no one, and offered only to those who can benefit from it. Those suffering from extreme sensory privation, or from mental or physical deficiency, ought not to be required to attend schools. He seems to envision the support of schools by public treasuries, although he also seems to identify the latter upon occasion with the private coffers of those who would be willing that the tutor of their children should teach a poor child or two at the same time free of charge.

The health of the student ought to be provided for by limiting the number of hours of instruction per day, and by assuring exercise, regular holidays, and a nutritious diet. This provision is necessary because it takes a good deal of time to earn salvation, and because there are many influences which make for early death.

CONCERNING METHODS OF INSTRUCTION. Comenius advocates many changes in methods of instruction, and argues that each is dictated by its own principle. These principles are by no means so numerous as he supposes. Here, they have been reduced to six because, although the reduction might be carried farther, the six in question call attention to the more significant recommendations he makes concerning teaching methods.

First, the teaching of all subjects ought to proceed by appeal to the interest of the student. The development of a bird is not brought about by external agencies alone as we have seen; and the acquisition of erudition, virtue, and piety ought not to be enforced from without. Indeed, it can be the result only of internal development.

Secondly, the teacher ought to provide, at the beginning of each course of study, a general outline of what is to be learned; and ought to proceed by filling in that outline rather than by introducing points that are entirely new. The embryo bird is, in fact, a general outline (a form) of which the adult fowl is a concrete specification (a particular bird); consequently, the teacher ought to establish in the infant a general outline of the fully educated or specified human being.

Thirdly, the teacher ought to prepare the student for the general outline of each subject before teaching it, and to ready him for new stages within each subject before he enters upon them. The classroom ough to be filled with pictures, maps, mottos, and the like, which intimate the general outline of what is to be learned; and each new stage in the study of a subject should be described before it is carried through. Parent birds carefully warm the eggs, feed the young, and assist in the preliminaries of flight.

Fourthly, the teacher ought to make instruction continuous. The school day ought to be marked off in periods each of which is regularly devoted to a single subject; and the study of each subject should be divided into stages each of which is determined by a goal subordinate to that of learning the entire subject, and explained to the student beforehand. The articulation of the teaching day makes for continuity within the study of each subject; and the division of each study into stages clearly demarcated makes for continuous development of the knowledge of its general outline toward increasingly detailed comprehension. An egg develops into a bird of the appropriate species without wavering in other directions, and the development of each part is marked off into stages of accomplishment subordinate to the development of the whole. Teaching ought to proceed analogously.

Fifthly, everything which the teacher does ought to contribute to the development of human nature; and the student should be shown the practical importance of erudition, virtue, and piety. The energies of parental birds, when dealing with their young, are devoted exclusively to promoting the development of the latter; and each act which they perform improves the practical skill of the members of the brood. It is not clear, incidentally, that Comenius believes that showing the student the practical value of what he does is involved in his analogy.

Sixthly, instruction in the same subjects should be provided for all; and apart from unusual conditions such as the need for severe discipline, all students ought to be instructed in the same fashion. The goal of teaching—erudition, virtue, and piety—is the same for all; and each learns most efficiently in the same way as others. Parental birds, in fact, teach their young the same things and in the same ways.

CONCERNING CURRICULUM. Studies ought to be ordered in four separate schools: the mother-school, the vernacular-school, the Latin-school, and the university. This division is based upon the psychological development of the child described earlier. To the age of six, only the sense organs function at the height of their capacity; and through them, the child may begin his acquaintance with the contents of the world. During this period, the mother (the term "mother-school" refers to the family) should habituate the child in the correct use of his vernacular language, in good social conduct, in religious belief, and in the elements of the arts, primarily music and poetry. The first involves teaching him to use the words for such common-sense phenomena as counting, and referring to light and darkness or apparent largeness and smallness. The second involves showing him how to act rightly, the everyday requirements imposed by society. The third consists chiefly in revealing the religious status of things in a sensory medium, in the catechism, religious ritual, and the like. The fourth amounts to learning simple songs and verses. The materials employed are a handbook telling the mother when to do what and how, as much of the physical world and family environment as the mother can show the child, and a picture-book which supplements and reinforces this showing. The picture-book will begin the child's lessons in reading, for the name of each object pictured will accompany its picture. Comenius' place in the history of education is assured by his publication of such a book—the famous *Orbis sensualium pictus;* for he was the first systematically to employ pictures in books for pedagogical purposes.

Instruction by use of these materials should appeal to the child's interest. He is naturally interested in what he can perceive, and the picture-book should be amusing and charming. His use of language should embody the most general outline of knowledge. Comenius seems to identify understanding simple operations upon things such as those of arithmetic and moral habituation, and the words for things, with the general outline of metaphysics, science, ethical theory, and the like. This is a mistaken identification; and in fact his recommendations for the mother-school amount, in this connection, to urging that at an early age the child be acquainted with those aspects of things for which philosophy, science, and theology give an account, and of which the arts provide embodiments.

From six to twelve, the child ought to attend a vernacular school. In this school, there should be six classes, one for each year; and in each, he should use only one book. In each book, that amount of erudition, virtue, and piety should be presented which is compatible with the emerging powers of imagination and memory. Each of these books should incorporate a little encyclopedia of all knowledge—scientific, moral, theological, and artistic—and in each class an increasingly detailed knowledge of the natural and social world, of morality, of God, and of the arts ought to be advanced. Comenius wrote such books; and his *Orbis sensualium pictus* was used for a long time in elementary schools. In these books, pictures of facts should be presented to enable learning what they are, and the vernacular language used for referring to them.

The subject to be studied is the vernacular language of the area;

but through its study all fields are investigated. For in learning it, the student will come to master the skills of reading, writing, and arithmetic, along with the elements of the natural and social sciences, morals, religion, and the arts.

Comenius believed that all men should speak a single language. He thought Latin unsuited for this purpose; and he recommended the creation of such a language and its propagation through the schools. He does not tell us in which school it should be learned;[15] but it would be necessary, apparently, to teach it in the vernacular, since all should learn it, and not all should attend higher schools.

In the third stage of life, from twelve to eighteen, many will take up their trades and vocations; but those who are fitted for it, or who can afford further training, ought to attend the Latin school. At this time, reason emerges in its full power; and the subjects offered are determined by this new ability.

There should be six classes, one year for each; and the first year ought to be devoted to learning Latin which becomes the vehicle for future study. But from the outset, the learning of it is combined with the study of Latin literature and, in general, the seven liberal arts. This ancient body of studies, reinvigorated by the literary discoveries of the Renaissance, ought to be supplemented with study of subsequent additions to it in the natural and social sciences, theology, and the arts. The result will be a man well versed in humanistic learning, but also cognizant of modern science, religious truth, and artistic accomplishments.

The materials used in the Latin school ought, like those of the preceding, to include pictures of things and picture-like reference to them, e.g., maps and diagrams. For the learning of Latin, Comenius provided such a book—his famous *Janua linguarum*. It is only a short step to the use of such supplements of language in studying all aspects of the world —a short step which Comenius takes when he advocates the use of a model (a skeleton tricked out with imitation organs) in the study of anatomy.

The use of pictures in learning a language is required by the very nature of language, and by the narrowness of human observation. Using a language consists in referring to things. Consequently, we cannot learn a language unless we are first acquainted with the things about which we would talk in its use. But there are more things than we can ever bring under direct observation. Acquaintance must, therefore, be achieved frequently in an indirect manner, i.e., by providing the student with pictures of the things which he cannot observe directly.

Comenius tells us little about the books to be used in the Latin school other than those for teaching Latin. The student should learn his

15 *The Way of Light,* XIX.

vernacular, Greek, and Hebrew as well as the language of Rome; and for this purpose, the books employed should incorporate the principles of picturing, and of embodying in the language study an encyclopedic knowledge of the sciences and arts.[16] Each class should include a study of history, different in each year, and this study should be carried on by the use of handbooks, presenting selected aspects of human and of national development. One may infer from his great enthusiasm for them that many of the books employed would be accounts of literature, books about great books of science, and summaries of the ideas advanced in the different fields of intellectual endeavor rather than the original documents themselves.

From eighteen to twenty-four, those students who are fitted for it should attend a university. At this time, the will emerges; and consequently, the university should offer the young scholar a chance to decide what specialized knowledge he will acquire, or to endeavor to encompass all knowledge. The purpose of a university is to carry on research, to increase specialized knowledge and knowledge of the interconnections of the various special fields, and to train for the professions of medicine and law. Consequently, many courses of varying kinds should be available.

Although censorship in favor of morality and religion should characterize earlier schooling, the university student should be denied no book which interests him. However, since no one can read everything, the books chiefly used in the various formal courses should be of an encyclopedic summary sort. They should be three in number;[17] and Comenius supplies a name for each: Pansophia, Panhistoria, and Pandogmatia. Pansophia should be a statement of the most general truths of nature, man, and God presented in a deductive system. There can be only one such book because there can be only one such system of truths. In it, the student will find a section devoted to the general truths of each particular field of study in its connection with all others. Panhistoria should include all the particular truths which manifest and give evidence for the general truths of Pansophia. Pandogmatia should embody all the opinions true and false which have been published concerning the topics discussed in Pansophia. It would be an introduction for research into the ideas that have occupied the mind of man. Each course would make use of such parts of these books as are relevant; specialized study would of course involve original documents and actual observations if not experiments.

---

16 *The Great Didactic*, xxx.

17 Comenius discusses these three books in complete separation from his discussion of a university. The latter is chiefly in *The Great Didactic*, Chapter xxxi; the former, in *The Way of Light*, Chapter xvi. I have inferred that he designed them for university use; he does not say in which school they should be employed.

Needless to say, Pansophia would be a very difficult book, and Pandogmatia would be a very long one. Comenius apparently endeavored to write Pansophia—but the manuscript was lost in the conflagration of Lisa, 1658, inspired by Catholic-Protestant hatred. We can see, under this rather fantastic guise, an impulse in Comenius toward what we might think of as the unification of the sciences, or an inclusive discipline growing out of their cross-fertilization.

The fourfold education that Comenius recommends for those who can benefit from it in all the stages of personal development does not include one recommendation for which he is well known; namely, his insistence on the College of Light. This would be an international re-search institution in which scientific research of a more or less modern empirical sort would be carried on, but which would thrive side by side with philosophical and theological speculation. Its purpose would be to bring the best minds of the globe to bear in a cooperative way upon the problems whose solution would improve the lot of all mankind, in both the material and spiritual dimensions. It would consist in a community of scholars, but would always boast, presumably, a body of young grad-uates of the universities just entering upon independent research. This idea Comenius developed out of similar proposals on the part of Bacon (*The New Atlantis*) and Campanella (*The City of the Sun*).

Unlike his textbooks, Comenius' pedagogical writings exerted in their own time little influence on thought about education. They were almost unknown and almost completely forgotten for nearly two centuries after his death. Nonetheless, we should note that the schools of our own time have resulted from reforms very similar to those advocated in *The Great Didactic, The Way of Light,* and similar products of Comenius' active, if somewhat uncritical, pen.

PHILOSOPHY OF EDUCATION

As if they could be supported by observation, Comenius advances the following points: (1) human behavior must be understood by refer-ence to three principles, the vegetative, the animal, and the intellectual souls; (2) inanimate nature, from the first to the last moment of time, exhibits an order which makes it stable; (3) order results from the realization by each item in nature of the purpose or goal appropriate to it; (4) from one moment to another, although the order of the whole remains, there is an alternation of order and disorder resulting from recurrent inability on the part of some items to realize their goals; (5) each human being has a goal—perfect erudition, virtue, and piety—which he can realize, and which is a concrete specification of the nature common to all humanity; (6) because of original sin—i.e., the corrupting influence of the vegetative and animal souls together with a will too weak to assure consistently right action—men do not always endeavor to achieve their proper objectives; (7) human history exhibits an alternation of social order and disorder, reflecting the fluctuation of the wills of men toward and away from their proper endeavors; (8) this fluctuation will terminate in a terrestrial paradise immediately preceding the Day of Judgment in which each man will come very close to achieving the end of human nature; (9) the administrative, methodological, and curricular reform of schools, described above, is the means by which this ideal social order will be realized, and by which men will be prepared, so far as that is possible, for eternal happiness.

METAPHYSICS

Comenius' metaphysical theory is scattered, scanty, naïve, fantastic, and frequently incoherent. We have nonetheless advanced it in the best light that we can find.

The proposition fundamental to all Comenius' metaphysical reflections is that God exists. He does not argue for this proposition; he accepts it on faith and because of the inspired character and literal truth of the Scriptures.

By use of this fundamental proposition, Comenius explains his doctrine of human nature. As the creator of the universe, God created men; and He created them, according to the Biblical account, in His own image. He is omniscient, omnipotent, and perfectly disposed toward all good things. As images of Him, men cannot fail to exhibit these properties to some lesser degree; and these properties are assured to them by their possession of the intellectual soul. Their vegetative and animal characteristics, of course, have no counterparts in God; in these respects, men are not images of Him. But to be motivated by the vegetative and animal souls is necessary to a created being; just as being capacitated for knowledge, for deliberate action, and for love of the good is a part of an image of God.

By reference to the existence of God, Comenius also endeavors to explain all the points he makes concerning order in the natural and social world. The universe, both physical and human, must exhibit the order that we find in it; for it was created by God according to a pattern which that order reflects.

The paradoxical assertion that within the stable order of nature and of human life there is an alternation of order and disorder, Comenius explains by appeal to the particular manner of God's creation. God loosed light upon matter. This force generated an opposing force, that of darkness.[18] The action of these two forces upon matter resulted in the four elements, earth, air, fire, and water; but since light and darkness are at war with each other, the proportion and arrangement of the elements is continually changing. Comenius seems to identify order with the dominance of light, and disorder with the dominance of darkness.[19] The dominance of darkness explains the disorder which is corruption, sin, and failure to realize goals; that of light explains perfection, blessedness, and success. Since light and darkness struggle continually for domination over matter, there is a corresponding alternation of order and disorder.

This fluctuation, however, corresponds to God's thought of the world as a whole, i.e., as a place in which there is struggle; and it fits into the pattern that he ordains for it. It is comprehended within a greater order; namely, that design of inanimate nature which makes it serve the animate, and that comedy of human history in which it terminates in a Utopian social order leading to the Day of Judgment. Reformed education as the means of terrestrial and eternal salvation is explained as the final conquest of light over darkness.

The result of this conquest is an immortal life of complete knowledge, utterly right conduct, and union with God—the achievement of the end inherent in man's nature. It would be folly to hold this view if there were no life after death, and Comenius advances an argument for this conclusion. In this world, no man can achieve complete knowledge, unwavering virtue, or piety unsullied by occasional lapse. The clamors of the vegetative and animal souls prevent unwavering pursuit of knowledge, unfaltering moral conduct, and deviating union with God's purposes. But we ought to achieve this threefold goal, and what one ought to do one is able to do. Consequently, there is a life of the intellect free from the exigencies of vegetative and animal life, and unaffected by the procession of time. Reason itself dictates that man "is destined to a higher end than all other creatures, that of being united with God, the culmination of all perfection, glory, and happiness, and of enjoying with Him absolute glory and happiness forever."[20]

Comenius' metaphysical reflection is designed to accomplish two things: first, to explain the nature of human beings and the order of the

---

[18] Comenius may have taken this notion from a mystic poetic writer of the seventeenth century, Jakob Boehme. At times, he seems to identify the force of light with fire (*The Way of Light*, p. 160); and at other times, to identify light and darkness with heat and cold and expansion and contraction. These latter ideas he probably borrowed from Telesio or Campanella.

[19] Comenius suggests (*The Way of Light*, p. 7) that his explanation of things in terms of light and darkness is a fable or a picture of the truth, but the best disposed of readers must admit that his fable soon becomes a reality for him.

[20] *The Great Didactic*, II, p. 179.

universe; and secondly, to show that the souls of men are immortal. His argument for the second point is commonly credited to Immanuel Kant, a later and much more celebrated philosopher.

ETHICS

Comenius' ethical reflection on the statements and recommendations of his theory of education are quite as casual as are his metaphysical thoughts concerning that subject. As with the latter, however, I shall deal with them as seriously as his discussion permits.

With respect to the ethical question, "What things are morally good?" Comenius gives a clear and short answer. It is that a certain kind of personal life, and a certain kind of social existence, are morally good. The best possible personal life is one of immortal blessedness, i.e., the achievement of the goal which he attributes to all persons. In eternity, the surviving intellect knows everything there is to be known (possesses perfect erudition), does everything that it ought to do (possesses virtue), and lives in the happiness of complete union with God (exhibits complete piety). The next to the best personal life is that existence in this world which is characterized by some lesser degree of achievement of this three-fold perfection; it is one in which, according to his abilities, one has acquired some measure of learning, virtue, and piety. The world, Comenius is fond of saying, is the school of God's wisdom.

A personal life that is good is also one that is happy. Happiness is pleasure, but not the pleasure that arises from the satisfaction of vegetative and animal needs and desires. It consists, rather, in the intellectual pleasure that arises from knowing what the world contains, acting rightly, and finding God.[21] This happiness, in the immortal life, is unsurpassable because the achievement is perfect; in terrestrial existence, it varies with the degree to which the human end is attained.

The second thing that is morally good is a social order of a certain kind. It is one in which there are definite classes, in which each man keeps to his proper place, and in which there is a minimum of greed, intolerance, and political abuse. The welfare of each person depends on the welfare of all.[22] Comenius seems to have supposed that the best society is a monarchy, whether absolute or limited by a constitution. A well-conducted monarchy will cooperate with other states rather than make war upon them. For Comenius, the best social order is simply that of most of the European states of his time, but a little more Christian.

Comenius' writings suggest an answer to a second question of ethics, i.e., to the question, "What is the meaning of the moral terms, 'good,'

21 *Ibid.*, p. 225.
22 *The Way of Light*, pp. 128–31.

'ought,' and the like?" To say that something is good is to say that it realizes God's intention in creating it;[23] God intends that men should be learned, virtuous, and pious. He makes them in His image; and an image of God must have these traits to some degree since it must mirror His wisdom, perfection, and harmonious life. It is conformity to God's will which constitutes the goodness of the end inherent in human nature.

To say that something ought to be done, according to Comenius, is to say that doing it is conducive to what is good, i.e., to realizing the goal that God's intention assigns to some thing. It is good for men to be learned, virtuous, and pious; and what men ought to do, *inter alia,* is to teach themselves and others according to the principles we have examined. Our obligation to do this consists in the fact that such teaching is conducive to the good life for man.

Comenius makes a few comments on what, in general, is involved in justifying moral recommendations. A recommendation always tells us that some action ought to be performed; and we have seen that, for Comenius, this means that the action enjoined is conducive to some goal assigned by God. The action would not be needed if its goal would be realized without it; and to perform the action is, in Comenius' words, to "remedy the defects of nature." To show why we ought to perform a particular action, then, requires showing that it will be such a remedy; and the knowledge required is the knowledge of natural processes other than, but analogous to, the one whose goal the action enjoined will help to realize.

Right action is a kind of art, the art of creating a good social and personal life; and the practices constituting this art are justified when based upon an inference from analogous natural processes. In each of the latter, there are stages ordered in such a way as to realize God's purpose for the individual concerned; and we can justify the recommendation that a certain action be performed provided that its performance would give to human life an order more like that of the natural process attended to than its nonperformance allows. Thus, in order to justify a moral recommendation, we must first know that some natural process exhibits a certain orderly realization of its goal, that it is partly analogous to the development of human life toward the realization of its purpose, and that the performance of the action recommended would make the order of human life more like that of the natural process than would its nonperformance. To justify a moral recommendation is to show that acting upon it will enable the human beings concerned to realize more fully the purpose of human life, i.e., to achieve greater erudition, virtue, and piety; and we show this by showing that acting upon it will give to the

---

23 *The Great Didactic,* p. 192.

careers concerned an order more like that of some natural process than would a failure to do so. The art of moral conduct, Comenius writes, "can do nothing unless it imitate nature"; and "if we wish to find a remedy for the defects of nature, it is in nature herself that we must look for it. . . ."[24]

For Comenius, administering, teaching in, and arranging the curriculum of the schools is an art, if not *the* art of moral action, and he presents elaborate justifications for his particular recommendations concerning these activities. They all exhibit this pattern: parental birds order the lives of their young in certain ways which enable the latter to realize their proper objective, i.e., to be adult birds of the species of their parents; the development of the human infant into an adult, i.e., towards his objective, exhibits an order which, in part, deviates from that of the development of birds. Therefore, human educators (including parents) ought to rectify the order through which human infants develop so that it more closely resembles that of birds, i.e., is in accord with the subordinate recommendations described above. For example, Comenius tells us that the development of an egg into a bird is constituted by the orderly filling in of the outline of an adult which is present in the egg from conception —an orderly filling in that is managed by parental activity. The child, however, is not first acquainted with the outline of all knowledge, i.e., of all erudition, virtue, and piety; so that his learning is not constituted by an orderly filling in of such an outline even though his development is like that of a bird in many respects. Consequently, educators ought to present a general outline of everything to be learned at the outset of the process of schooling; and they ought to make all the rest of that process a filling in of details.

THEORY OF KNOWLEDGE

Comenius' reflection upon the nature of knowledge and the method by which it is secured is a little more extended than that concerning moral and metaphysical subjects. It is not, however, much more systematic. I shall make his epistemological ideas as precise and systematic as I can, but the reader should always remember that Comenius' writing displays a strong color of metaphor and of religious emotion which subjects to it differing interpretations.

Comenius begins with an assertion concerning our capacity for acquiring knowledge. "It is evident," he writes, "that man is naturally capable of acquiring a knowledge of all things. . . .[25] Since man is an image of God, and since God is omniscient, man must be at least capable

24 *Ibid.*, p. 250.
25 *Ibid.*, p. 193.

of omniscience himself. Shortly, however, this assertion of capacity becomes one of achievement. We, in fact, know all the things there are. Man "inwardly comprehends all the elements that are spread far and wide through the macrocosm, or world at large. . . ."[26] The mind contains reflections of all things in the universe as a spherical mirror contains reflections of all things in the chamber where it is suspended. Thus, from a metaphysical proposition about God and His relation to men, Comenius first derives a harmless statement about the latter, and then an astounding one about their achievement. We shall return to his statement that we know all things after we examine his notion of knowledge and the kinds of things we know.

Comenius nowhere gives us a definition for the word "knowledge." He seems to have regarded such a procedure as unnecessary. Nonetheless, it is quite clear from his writings that he conceives of knowledge as the mind's comprehension of something, as a comprehension in which we cannot be mistaken about what we comprehend.

There are three kinds of knowledge. They are distinguished from each other by reference to three kinds of objects that we comprehend. Knowledge of the first kind is knowledge of individual things or events. These are all discoverable through one or several of the sense organs. The senses are like scouts which, being sent out by the mind in all directions, return to it with information of the existence and sensible characteristics of all individual things or events.[27] Each bit of sensory knowledge contains two factors: an inner mental event caused by nervous impulses culminating in the brain, and an outer thing or event. Some sensory items, those of sight and hearing, contain a third—a medium (light or air) through which disturbances originating in the external thing or event are transmitted to the sense organ and thence to the brain. But in all cases of sensory knowledge, the mental event is, thus, knowledge of the external thing or event which causes it.[28] The first kind of knowledge is sensation; and since the physical universe (Comenius sometimes calls it "the visible universe") is made up of things or events that are sensible in character, our knowledge that they exist and exhibit certain traits is the sensory comprehension of them which they cause.

The second kind of knowledge is of a totally different sort. It is knowledge yielded by a different faculty from that of sensation, namely, by the faculty of understanding. Comenius says that ". . . the understanding . . . is an empty form, like a bare tablet . . ."[29] and it is not a mistake, perhaps, to interpret this saying to mean that the understanding is what

[26] *Ibid.*, p. 194.
[27] *Ibid.*, p. 195.
[28] *The Way of Light*, p. 182.
[29] *The Great Didactic*, p. 206.

enables us to be aware of the forms in which individual things or events may occur, i.e., the relations or orders in which they can stand. The understanding provides notions of the ways in which individuals can be related to each other; they ". . . . are applied as Norms for whatever the world contains. . . ."[30] Eve, who was innocent of experience, understood in what ways individuals might be related, but it required sensory experience before she knew that a serpent could be related to her as a deceiver to his victim.[31] This shows that the notions that we get by understanding are notions of the relations or orders in which things can stand, not knowledge that certain individuals are related in those ways. Comenius does not give a list of these notions; but his writings suggest[32] that such a list would include the ideas that individual things or events come before and after one another in time, are greater or less in quantity, possess parts which may be numbered, exhibit degrees of value or are worse or better relatively, have causes and effects, and are caused by God.

The notions that understanding gives us, Comenius says, are common to all human beings.[33] Consequently, all human beings have the same ideas as to the ways in which individual things or events can be related or ordered. Moreover, he describes these notions as innate.[34] The roots of the word "innate" suggest that whatever it truly describes is possessed by us from birth onward; and Comenius says as much when he writes that our common notions are present in our minds when they enter the world.[35] But he says a good deal more. Since the common notions are innate, we cannot base our acceptance of them as true on sensation. We accept them independently of what sensation reveals; and besides, sensation shows us only things or events, not the relations in which they can stand. Moreover, in describing them as innate, Comenius seems to imply that we accept some because they are self-evidently true; and all others, because we can prove them to be so by deriving them from those which are self-evident. In the book that he proposed to write, *Pansophia,* all the common notions would be expressed; and his description shows that he regarded the notions as limiting the possible orders or arrangements into which individual things may fall, as knowable independently of experience, and as constituting a deductive system of theorems and self-evident premises for their derivation.[36] The innateness of the common notions of the understanding consists in their being inborn, in their being true

---

30 *The Way of Light,* Dedication, §7, p. 7.
31 *The Great Didactic,* p. 206.
32 *Ibid.,* XIII, where he discusses order, and p. 258 where he speaks of the intellect as ordering the materials provided by sense.
33 *The Way of Light,* Dedication, p. 6.
34 *Ibid.*
35 *The Great Didactic,* p. 194.
36 *The Way of Light,* pp. 145–46, 148–49.

about the possible relations of things, in the independence of their truth from that of sensory knowledge, and in their constituting a deductive system.

Comenius suggests that there is a third kind of knowledge, i.e., an assurance neither of individual things or events, nor of the merely possible ways in which they are related. This is assurance of the facts[37] that constitute the entire universe. Facts are not individual things or events; they are arrangements of them. That wind is an individual event; and this tree is another. But this tree blown down by that wind, i.e., related to it in a certain way, is a fact—the fact that it was blown down by that wind. Such a fact cannot be known by sensation; the latter can reveal only a prostrate tree, a falling tree, or a wind. Nor do we know it by understanding alone. The latter gives us such empty notions as that if there be any events, each of them has a cause. It is through the combined activity of sensation and understanding that we are assured that the tree was blown down by the wind. Sensation shows us the prostrate tree, the falling tree, and the wind; understanding tells us that every event is caused. Together, they tell us that this tree was caused to fall by that wind. Our knowledge of facts, Comenius says, results from the filling up by sensation of the empty forms of the understanding, the application of common notions to the materials of experience, or what experience inscribes upon the bare tablet of the understanding.

We now return to the astounding statement that we know everything. Sensory knowledge consists in the mind's being aware of inner, mental events (sensations) caused by external individual things or events; and as the metaphor of the spherical mirror suggests, we have sensations caused by every individual "element in the world at large." Our innate common notions, we constantly employ to order sensations so that they constitute facts. But not all the sensations continually caused in our minds by all external things or events are clearly present in consciousness. Although he has them, the infant is consciously aware of very few; and the heavy sleeper is consciously aware of none. We possess all knowledge, i.e., we "inwardly comprehend everything in the world at large"; but our knowledge of most of it is not conscious. When we learn something, we make clear to ourselves what would have been, in any case, unconsciously present to us. This is, perhaps, the proper interpretation of the astounding statement: we have within our own minds that which, when we make it clearly conscious, constitutes infallible assurance about every fact, i.e., about the entire universe.

Comenius' statement presupposes the view made famous a little later by the celebrated philosopher, Leibniz, that each man contains within his own mind the entire universe, and amounts to the view that

---

[37] *Ibid.*, pp. 144–45.

the way to acquire knowledge of the world is to make clear to ourselves those facts which we cannot help but harbor. It raises a knotty problem: if we can be aware only of inner sensations which we ourselves arrange according to the forms that our understandings show, how can we possibly claim to know facts in a world beyond our minds? Comenius marvels at the inscrutable wisdom and power of God in having created our minds. "In truth our mind is greater than the universe, since that which contains is necessarily greater than that which is contained."[38] But to regard the mind as harboring the universe in the way that Comenius suggests, a way that extends its roots at least as far as Saint Augustine, is to deliver to philosophy a problem that has not ceased to baffle the lesser wisdom and power of its human practitioners.

The second question of theory of knowledge concerns the methods by which knowledge is secured. With respect to it, Comenius says one negative thing very clearly, and several positive things in a more obscure fashion. We cannot, he tells us, acquire knowledge by appeal to authority. This is the chief method in which ". . . the world hitherto used to acquiesce, though unwillingly, and with occasional revolts and with longing to break through the barriers of its servitude."[39] It is bound to fail. To know by authority is to accept something for true because some other person has said it, and presumably has said it with good reason. But ". . . knowledge . . . is to know a thing as it is in itself and not as it is reputed to be."[40] Consequently, to know by authority is not knowledge of what the authority asserts; at best, it is belief, i.e., the belief that someone else, the authority, has seen or experienced what he reports.[41] It is not knowledge of what is reported. For the authority might be mistaken; and any assurance based upon his report cannot be knowledge since the latter cannot be in error. Comenius, exhibiting his prominent place in the Protestant movement, writes vigorously against the notion that knowledge of God required for piety and virtue, as well as knowledge of facts in nature, can be achieved by reliance upon the words of other men. In order to know something, each man must, for himself, confront it, or find compelling reasons for his being able to do so.

Comenius' positive assertions concerning the methods for securing knowledge are set forth in a way that is obscure, oblique, and frequently confused. He tells us that ". . . before definite knowledge is attained we

38 *The Great Didactic,* p. 198.
39 *The Way of Light,* p. 134.
⸕ 40 *Ibid.*
41 Perhaps Comenius intends to say that what appears to be knowledge by authority of some fact, e.g., the assassination of Julius Caesar, must come, for those who accept the authority, to knowledge of something else, namely, knowledge that the authority said that Julius Caesar was assassinated; and to belief that Julius Caesar was assassinated since the authority may provide some evidence for our accepting the statement about the assassination as true.

get a confused knowledge, before clear knowledge a shadowy knowledge; and so at length through its proper stages of development knowledge shines out in its fullness."[42] All this seems to amount to the statement that coming to know is making clear to ourselves what is implicit in our minds; but the ways by which we clarify our mental possessions are left very dark. Comenius suggests that sensory knowledge is acquired by attending carefully to our sensations[43]—a comment that is not very remarkable; but also, that it is achieved by presenting to our sense organs the sensible facts wherever possible, and describing them in words where it is not[44]—a remark that seems incompatible with the notion that learning is making clear what we unconsciously already possess. He suggests that knowledge of the forms that the understanding yields is achieved by logical derivation from self-evident premises.[45] He suggests that our knowledge of the physical universe can be secured only by a combination of sensation and reason, that experiment alone can show that some set of relations or order which the understanding may derive from self-evident premises is filled by sensory material. This is the suggestion that we can know the physical universe only if we make, within some framework, hypotheses as to how the items that compose it are related; and it is a kind of empirical view about the method of knowledge.

But all these are more suggested than stated by Comenius. While it is correct to attribute to him an interest in finding out what he world is like independent of authoritative statement, it is incorrect to suppose that he was a clear-minded advocate of the notion, in his day being established by the founders of modern science, that the way to find out what things are like is to alter them in accord with some hypothesis or guess, and to observe the results—i.e., to experiment upon them.

Whatever the methods of knowledge, there can be no doubt that Comenius regarded their goal as infallible assurance as to the existence and character of individual things or events, the possible orders in which they might be ranged, and the facts that they constitute as ranged in the orders they actually exhibit. He seems to have supposed that on our knowledge of facts, our knowledge of the nature and locus of virtue must be based. He certainly believed that we can achieve knowledge of the existence and nature of God, however ill it may fit into the analysis of knowledge and the schemes for knowing we have discussed.

We may add that, according to Comenius, knowledge is made possible by two abilities or faculties of the intellectual soul: that of looking in, so to speak, upon the sensations that the animal soul permits us to

42 *The Way of Light,* p. 79.
43 *Ibid.,* pp. 75–77.
44 *Ibid.,* pp. 133–34.
45 *Ibid.,* pp. 133, 145–46.

have; and that of understanding, of presenting to itself the "empty forms" which it also gives to the sensations delivered to it by the animal soul. Thus knowledge appears, in Comenius' thought, as an achievement of reason.

LANGUAGE

Whatever the methods and the faculties whose exercise originally brings us knowledge, its transmission, teaching, and learning proceed through rational discourse. To engage in the latter ". . . is to name all things, and to speculate and reason about everything that the world contains . . .";[46] and to succeed in it is to be able, by using language, to state the properties of all things. Success in teaching and learning, therefore, depends upon success in the use of language. We may discover the conditions for successful teaching and learning by discovering the conditions for a perfect language.

A perfect language is one in which one's thoughts about things can be communicated with no danger, springing from the language itself, that others will have difficulty in understanding.[47] In a perfect language, first, each sensible thing would have no more than one name; a plurality of names for one thing leads to hesitancy and confusion of thought. Secondly, no name would be applied to more than one sensible thing; such an application is ambiguity. Thirdly, every sensible thing would have a name; this condition would permit everything to be discussed. Fourthly, each name would resemble the thing it names; thus, one could see immediately from the language itself what things were being talked about. Fifthly, in a perfect language, the names would be ordered in sentences so that the latter would exhibit a structure identical with the structure of things in the fact to which the sentence refers; this condition would prevent misunderstanding as to what fact one talks about when he uses a particular sentence.

Let us illustrate these five conditions for a perfect language. One of the facts in the world is that Cleopatra loved Caesar. In a perfect language, there would be one name and only one name for Cleopatra, for loving, and for Caesar; this illustrates the first and second conditions stated above. Every other thing (or event) would have one and only one name—the third condition mentioned. But this feature of a perfect language, it is clear, cannot be illustrated in any but a remarkably long book and perhaps not even in it since names would possess names which, in turn, would possess them *ad infinitum*. Moreover, the names "Cleopatra," "love," and "Caesar," together with all other names, would have counter-

46 *The Great Didactic*, p. 188.
47 *The Way of Light*, xix.

parts that resemble more nearly Cleopatra, love, Caesar, etc.; this illustrates the fourth condition. Lastly, in a perfect language, the sentence that would be the counterpart of our sentence, "Cleopatra loved Caesar," would show us what sensible things (or events) its user refers to; and it would show us which of the facts the user is discussing when he employs it. It would show that he is referring to Cleopatra's loving Caesar, for example, not to Caesar's loving Cleopatra. This ordering of the names in a sentence so that its syntactical structure is the same as the structure of the fact involved may be either a temporal and spatial ordering, or it may be one brought about by inflection of the names. The first way of presenting a syntactical structure which is also that of a fact is represented by most English sentences; we must say "Cleopatra loved Caesar," and must not say (speaking of the same fact) "Caesar loved Cleopatra." But in highly inflected languages like Latin the temporal and spatial order plays no role in determining the syntactical structure formed by the names in a sentence; and consequently, no role in the sentence's reflecting the structure of its fact. Comenius does not say which of these devices a perfect language should employ.

Existing languages fall short with respect to the first four conditions. Each existing language contains a plurality of names for a given thing; and the fact of many different languages is, in part, the fact of many pluralities of names for given things. This linguistic failure has characterized the history of men since the sad events at Babel; and since it makes different nations misunderstand each other, it fosters international warfare. It is clear that all existing languages contain much ambiguity; and that lacking names for many things, they are also inadequate for communicating knowledge of them. It is obvious, moreover, that most of our names do not resemble the things they are names for. What could be less like a rhinoceros than the word "rhinoceros"? Apparently, Comenius believed that the sentences we can form in existing languages exhibit a syntax that does not adequately reflect the structure of their facts; but he does not elaborate his complaint on this score.

Foregoing any critical examination of Comenius' views about a perfect language, we shall note only that on his view, the only difference between perfect languages could be that of devices for showing syntactical structure since all plurality of names is excluded; and that his perfect language could be learned with great dispatch and facility not by all, as he thought, but only by those who can remember all the names there are in the language, which must be as many as all the things or events. This would require a very considerable feat of memory if it is not impossible altogether.

To the degree that knowledge is transmitted, the teacher succeeds in communicating to the student what he knows about the properties of things; and this communication occurs through language. Consequently, before knowledge can be transmitted, the learner must be taught the names of things, and the ways of putting them together into sentences whose synactical structure coincides with that of the facts. The first, Comenius insists, ought to be done (but usually is not) by presenting to the student the actual things to be named, or pictures of them where their presentation is not feasible; there is no other way conceivable for teaching names. Its failure makes teaching of languages in the schools a waste of time. He says nothing about the way in which syntactical ordering of words ought to be learned. Once the student has learned names and syntax, i.e., language, the rest of teaching consists in its use for two purposes. The first is to enable the student to clarify for himself the forms of the understanding. These Comenius seems to identify with the general outline of knowledge we have discussed under the heading, "Recommendations." The second is to present to the student or to enable him to clarify for himself the sensations that fill in those forms.

But so long as languages are numerous and therefore imperfect, teaching must remain less than completely effective; and not until a single perfect language is spread throughout mankind can education bring men to perfect knowledge, to the perfect virtue and piety that it makes possible, and to the blessed immortal life that, if God wills, is the inheritance of an ideal earthly existence.

A Guide to Selections from *The Great Didactic*

In Chapter II, Comenius advances unity with God as the proper end of man's life, and holds that it is achieved in an immortal existence. This immortal existence is made to follow from the three-fold nature of the human being, and the impossibility of perfecting the intellectual part in this life.

In Chapters IV, V, and VI, Comenius represents reason as enabling man to achieve erudition, virtue, and piety; and ultimate happiness or unity with God appears as the final stage of a process in which these three aspects of reason are gradually made more perfect—a process starting in this life and ending in immortal blessedness. These three rational powers he attributes to all men, and discusses some of the conditions that impede and further their development. He asserts that experience is necessary to the development of these powers and holds that it is best provided by communication with others through the use of language and the imposition of other social institutions.

In Chapters IX, X, XIII, XIV, XVI, and XVII, he advocates universal schooling, universal instruction, and exact order in all things. He holds that the order followed in instruction should be patterned after that of the development of the young in plants and animals; and he states the principles which govern that order.

SELECTIONS FROM

The Great Didactic*

━━◄●►━━

CHAPTER II

The Ultimate End of Man Is Beyond This Life

1.   Reason itself dictates that such a perfect creature is destined to a higher end than all other creatures, that of being united with God, the culmination of all perfection, glory, and happiness, and of enjoying with Him absolute glory and happiness for ever. . . .

4.   Our nature shows that this life is not sufficient for us. For here we live a threefold life, the vegetative, the animal, and the intellectual or spiritual. Of these the action of the first is confined to the body, the second can extend itself to objects by the operation of the senses and of movement, while the third is able to exist separately, as is evident in the case of angels. So that, as it is evident that this, the last stage of life, is greatly overshadowed and hindered in us by the two former, it follows of necessity that there will be a future state in which it may be brought to perfection.

5.   All our actions and affections in this life show that we do not attain our ultimate end here, but that everything connected with us, as well as we ourselves, has another destination. For whatever we are, do, think, speak, contrive, acquire, or possess, contains a principle of gradation, and, though we mount perpetually and attain higher grades, we still continue to advance and never reach the highest.

For in the beginning a man is nothing, and has been non-existent from eternity. It is from his mother's womb that he takes his origin. What then is a man in the beginning? Nothing but an unformed mass endowed

* The passages that follow have been taken from *The Great Didactic of John Amos Comenius,* translated by M. W. Keatinge. Reprinted by kind permission of the publishers, Adam and Charles Black, London, 1896. This edition includes an extensive account of the writings of Comenius as well as a very careful biography. All footnotes have been omitted.

with vitality. This soon assumes the outlines of a human body, but has, as yet, neither sense nor movement.

Later on it begins to move and by a natural process bursts forth into the world. Gradually the eyes, ears, and other organs of sense appear. In course of time the internal senses develop and the child perceives that he sees, hears, and feels. Then the intellect comes into existence by cognising the differences between objects; while, finally, the will assumes the office of a guiding principle by displaying desire for certain objects and aversion for others. . . .

CHAPTER IV

There Are Three Stages In the Preparation for Eternity:
To Know Oneself (and, with Oneself All things); to Rule
Oneself; and To Direct Oneself To God. . . .

3.   To be a rational creature is to name all things, and to speculate and reason about everything that the world contains, as we find it in Gen. ii. 19, or, in the words of Solomon (Wisdom vii. 17), to know how the world was made and the operation of the elements; the beginning, ending, and midst of the times; the alterations of the turning of the sun, and the change of seasons; . . . For thus, if he know the properties of all things, will he be able to justify his title of "rational being."

4.   To be the lord of all creatures consists in subjecting everything to his own use by contriving that its legitimate end be suitably fulfilled; in conducting himself royally, that is, gravely and righteously, among creatures (adoring only one above him, his Creator; . . .) . . .

5.   Finally, to be the image of God is to represent the perfection of his Archetype, who says Himself "Ye shall be holy, for I the Lord your God am holy" (Lev. xix. 2).

6.   From this it follows that man is naturally required to be: (1) acquainted with all things; (2) endowed with power over all things and over himself; (3) to refer himself and all things to God, the source of all.

Now, if we wish to express these things by three well-known words, these will be:

(i)   Erudition.
(ii)   Virtue or seemly morals.
(iii)   Religion or piety.

Under Erudition we comprehend the knowledge of all things, arts, and tongues; under Virtue, not only external decorum, but the whole disposition of our movements, internal and external; while by Religion we understand that inner veneration by which the mind of man attaches and binds itself to the supreme Godhead.

7.   In these three things is situated the whole excellence of man, for they alone are the foundation of the present and of the future life. All other things (health, strength, beauty, riches, honour, friendship, good-fortune, long life) are as nothing, if God grant them to any, but extrinsic ornaments of life. . . .

9.   It follows, therefore, that we advance towards our ultimate end in proportion as we pursue Learning, Virtue, and Piety in this world. . . .

CHAPTER V

The Seeds of These Three (Learning, Virtue, and Piety)
Are Naturally Implanted In Us. . . .

2.   By the voice of nature we understand the universal Providence of God or the influence of Divine Goodness which never ceases to work all in all things; that is to say, which continually develops each creature for the end to which it has been destined. For it is a sign of the divine wisdom to do nothing in vain, that is to say, without a definite end or without means proportionate to that end. Whatever exists, therefore, exists for some end, and has been provided with the organs and appliances necessary to attain to it. It has also been gifted with a certain inclination, that nothing may be borne towards its end unwillingly and reluctantly, but rather promptly and pleasantly, by the natural instinct that pain and death will ensue if any obstacle be placed in the way. And so it is certain that man also is naturally fitted for the understanding of facts, for existence in harmony with the moral law, and above all things for the love of God (since for these we have already seen that he is destined), and that the roots of these three principles are as firmly planted in him as are the roots of any tree in the earth beneath it. . . .

4.   It is evident that man is naturally capable of acquiring a knowledge of all things, since, in the first place, he is the image of God. For an image, if it be accurate, necessarily reproduces the outlines of its archetype, as otherwise it will not be an image. Now omniscience is chief among the properties of God, and it follows that the image of this must be reflected in man. And why not? Man, in truth, stands in the centre of the works of God and possesses a lucid mind, which, like a spherical mirror suspended in a room, reflects images of all things that are around it. All things that are around it, we say; for our mind not only seizes on things that are close at hand, but also on things that are far off, whether in space or in time; it masters difficulties, hunts out what is concealed, uncovers what is veiled, and wears itself out in examining what is inscrutable; so infinite and so unbounded is its power. If a thousand years were granted to man, in which, by grasping one thing after another, he might con-

tinually learn something fresh, he would still find some spot from which the understanding might gain fresh objects of knowledge.

So unlimited is the capacity of the mind that in the process of perception it resembles an abyss. The body is enclosed by small boundaries; the voice roams within wider limits; the sight is bounded only by the vault of heaven; but for the mind, neither in heaven nor anywhere outside heaven, can a boundary be fixed. It ascends as far over the heavens above as below the depths beneath, and would do so if they were even a thousand times more vast than they are. . . .

5.   Philosophers have called man a Microcosm or Epitome of the Universe, since he inwardly comprehends all the elements that are spread far and wide through the Macrocosm, or world at large; a statement the truth of which is shown elsewhere. The mind, therefore, of a man who enters this world is very justly compared to a seed or to a kernel in which the plant or tree really does exist, although its image cannot actually be seen. This is evident; since the seed, if placed in the ground, puts forth roots beneath it and shoots above it, and these, later on, by their innate force, spread into branches and leaves, are covered with foliage, and adorned with flowers and fruit. It is not necessary, therefore, that anything be brought to a man from without, but only that that which he possesses rolled up within himself be unfolded and disclosed, and that stress be laid on each separate element. Thus Pythagoras used to say that it was so natural for a man to be possessed of all knowledge, that a boy of seven years old, if prudently questioned on all the problems of philosophy, ought to be able to give a correct answer to each interrogation; since the light of Reason is a sufficient standard and measure of all things. Still it is true that, since the Fall, Reason has become obscure and involved, and does not know how to set itself free; while those who ought to have done so have rather entangled it the more.

6.   To the rational soul, that dwells within us, organs of sense have been supplied, which may be compared to emissaries and scouts, and by the aid of these it compasses all that lies without. These are sight, hearing, smell, sound, and touch, and there is nothing whatever that can escape their notice. For, since there is nothing in the visible universe which cannot be seen, heard, smelt, tasted, or touched, and the kind and quality of which cannot in this way be discerned, it follows that there is nothing in the universe which cannot be compassed by a man endowed with senses and reason. . . .

18.   That the roots of piety are present in man is shown by the fact that he is the image of God. For an image implies likeness, and that like rejoices in like, is an immutable law of nature (Eccles. xii. 7). Since, then, man's only equal is He in whose image he has been made, it follows that there is no direction in which he can be more easily carried by his

desires than towards the fountain whence he took his origin; provided that he clearly understand the conditions of his existence. . . .

21.   It must be confessed that the natural desire for God, as the highest good, has been corrupted by the Fall, and has gone astray, so that no man, of his strength alone, could return to the right way. But in those whom God illumines by the Word and by His Spirit it is so renewed, that we find David exclaiming: "Whom have I in heaven but thee? And there is none on earth that I desire beside thee. My flesh and my heart faileth, but God is the strength of my heart and my portion for ever" (Psalm lxxiii 25, 26). . . .

CHAPTER VI

If A Man Is To Be Produced, It Is Necessary
That He Be Formed By Education

1.   The seeds of knowledge, of virtue, and of piety are, as we have seen, naturally implanted in us; but the actual knowledge, virtue, and piety are not so given. These must be acquired by prayer, by education, and by action. He gave no bad definition who said that man was a "teachable animal." And indeed it is only by a proper education that he can become a man. . . .

5.   It is evident, too, that even before the Fall, a school in which he might make gradual progress was opened for man in Paradise. For, although the first created, as soon as they came into being, lacked neither the power of walking erect, nor speech, nor reason, it is manifest, from the conversation of Eve with the serpent, that the knowledge of things which is derived from experience was entirely wanting. For Eve, had she had more experience, would have known that the serpent is unable to speak, and that there must therefore be some deceit.

Much more, therefore, in this state of corruption must it be necessary to learn by experience, since the understanding which we bring with us is an empty form, like a bare tablet, and since we are unskilled to do, speak, or know anything; for all these faculties do but exist potentially and need development. . . .

6.   Examples show that those who in their infancy have been seized by wild animals, and have been brought up among them, have not risen above the level of brutes in intellect, and would not have been able to make more use of their tongues, their hands, and their feet than beasts can, had they not once more come into the society of men. I will give several instances. About the year 1540, in a village called Hassia, situated in the middle of a forest, a boy three years of age was lost, through the carelessness of his parents. Some years afterwards the country people saw a strange animal running about with the wolves, of a different shape, four-footed, but with a man's face. Rumour of this spread through the district, and the governor asked the peasants to try to catch it alive and bring it to him. This they did, and finally the creature was conveyed to the Landgrave at Cassel.

When it was taken into the castle it tore itself away, fled, and hid beneath a bench, where it glared fiercely at its pursuers and howled horribly. The prince had him educated and kept him continually in men's society, and under this influence his savage habits grew gentler by degrees; he began to raise himself up on his hind-legs and walk like a biped, and at last to speak intelligently and behave like a man. Then he related to the best of his ability how he had been seized and nurtured by the wolves and had been accustomed to go hunting with them. The story is found in M. Dresser's work on *Ancient and Modern Education,* and Camerarius, in his *Hours,* mentions the same case, and another one of a similar nature (bk. 1, ch. 75). . . .

CHAPTER IX

All the Young of Both Sexes Should be Sent to School. . . .

2. In the first place, all who have been born to man's estate have been born with the same end in view, namely, that they may be men, that is to say, rational creatures, the lords of other creatures, and the images of their Creator. All, therefore, must be brought on to a point at which, being properly imbued with wisdom, virtue, and piety, they may usefully employ the present life and be worthily prepared for that to come. . . .

3. Now we do not know to what uses divine providence has destined this or that man; but this is certain, that out of the poorest, the most abject, and the most obscure, He has produced instruments for His glory. . . .

4. Nor is it any obstacle that some seem to be naturally dull and stupid, for this renders more imperative the universal culture of such intellects. The slower and the weaker of the disposition of any man, the more he needs assistance, that he may throw off his brutish dulness and stupidity as much as possible. Nor can any man be found whose intellect is so weak that it cannot be improved by culture. A sieve, if you continually pour water through it, grows cleaner and cleaner, although it cannot retain the liquid; and, in the same way, the dull and the weak-minded, though they may make no advance in letters, become softer in disposition and learn to obey the civil magistrates and the ministers of the Church. There have, besides, been many instances in which those who are naturally stupid have gained such a grasp of the sciences as to excel those

who were more gifted. As the poet truly says: "Industry overcomes all obstacles." Again, just as some men are strong as children, but afterwards grow sick and ailing, while others, whose bodies are sickly and under-sized in youth, develop into robust and tall men; so it is with intellects. Some develop early, but soon wear out and grow dull, while others, orig-inally stupid, become sharp and penetrating. In our orchards we like to have not only trees that bring forth early fruit, but also those that are late-bearing; for each thing, as says the son of Sirach, finds praise in its season, and at length, though late, shows that it has not existed in vain. Why, therefore, should we wish that in the garden of letters only one class of intellects, the forward and active, should be tolerated? Let none be excluded unless God has denied him sense and intelligence.

5.   Nor can any sufficient reason be given why the weaker sex (to give a word of advice on this point in particular) should be altogether ex-cluded from the pursuit of knowledge (whether in Latin or in their mother-tongue). They also are formed in the image of God, and share in His grace and in the kingdom of the world to come. They are endowed with equal sharpness of mind and capacity for knowledge (often with more than the opposite sex), and they are able to attain the highest posi-tions, since they have often been called by God Himself to rule over nations, to give sound advice to kings and princes, to the study of medi-cine and of other things which benefit the human race, even to the office of prophesying and of inveighing against priests and bishops. Why, there-fore, should we admit them to the alphabet, and afterwards drive them away from books? Do we fear their folly? The more we occupy their thoughts, so much the less will the folly that arises from emptiness of mind find a place. . . .

CHAPTER X

The Instruction Given In Schools Should Be Universal

1.   We have already shown that every one ought to receive a uni-versal education, and this at school. But do not, therefore, imagine that we demand from all men a knowledge (that is to say, an exact or deep knowledge) of all the arts and sciences. . . .

It is the principles, the causes, and the uses of all the most impor-tant things in existence that we wish all men to learn; all, that is to say, who are sent into the world to be actors as well as spectators. For we must take strong and vigorous measures that no man, in his journey through life, may encounter anything so unknown to him that he cannot pass sound judgment upon it and turn it to its proper use without serious error. . . .

7. The soul in its essential elements consists of three potentialities, which recall the uncreated Trinity, and these are the intellect, the will, and the memory. The province of the intellect is to observe the differences between things, even down to the smallest details. The will concerns itself with choice—that is to say, with the choice of things that are advantageous and the rejection of those which are not. The memory stores up for future use all the things with which the intellect and the will have been busied, and reminds the soul of its dependence on God and of its duty; in which aspect it is also called conscience.

In order, then, that these faculties may rightly fulfill their offices, it is necessary that they be furnished with such things as may illumine the intellect, direct the will, and stimulate the conscience, so that the intellect may be acute and penetrating, the will may choose without error, and the conscience may greedily refer all things to God. Therefore, just as these faculties (the intellect, the will, and the conscience) cannot be separated, since they constitute the same soul, so it is impossible to separate those three ornaments of the soul, erudition, virtue, and piety.

8. Now, if we consider why we have been sent into the world, it will be evident from two points of view that the object is threefold, namely, that we may serve God, His creatures, and ourselves, and that we may enjoy the pleasure to be derived from God, from His creatures, and from ourselves.

9. If we wish to serve God, our neighbours, and ourselves, it is necessary for us to possess, with respect to God, piety; with respect to our neighbors, virtue; and with respect to ourselves, knowledge. These principles, however, are intimately connected, and a man, for his own advantage, should be not only learned, but also virtuous and pious; for that of his neighbour, not only virtuous, but also learned and pious; and for the glory of God, not only pious, but also learned and virtuous. . . .

14. Delight in God is the highest point to which pleasure can attain in this life, and is found when a man, feeling that God is eternally gracious to him, exults in His fatherly and immutable favour to such a degree that his heart melts with the love of God. He desires to know or to do nothing further, but, overwhelmed by God's mercy, he rests in peace and tastes the joys of eternal life. . . .

CHAPTER XIII

The Basis of School Reform must be Exact Order in All Things

1. We find on investigation that the principle which really holds together the fabric of this world of ours, down to its smallest detail, is none other than order; that is to say, the proper division of what comes before and what comes after, of the superior and the subordinate, of the large and the small, of the similar and dissimilar, according to place, time, number, size, and weight, so that each may fulfill its function well. Order therefore, has been called the soul of affairs. For everything that is well ordered preserves its position and its strength as long as it maintains its order; it is when it ceases to do so that it grows weak, totters, and falls. This may be seen clearly in instances taken from nature and from art.

2.   Through what agency, I ask, does the world maintain its present condition? what is it that gives it its great stability? It is this, that each creature, obeying the command of nature, restrains its action within the proper limits; and thus, by careful observation of order in small details, the order of the universe is maintained. . . .

15.   The art of teaching, therefore, demands nothing more than the skilful arrangement of time, of the subjects taught, and of the method. As soon as we have succeeded in finding the proper method it will be no harder to teach school-boys, in any number desired, than with the help of the printing-press to cover a thousand sheets daily with the neatest writing. . . .

CHAPTER XIV

*The Exact Order of Instruction Must be Borrowed From Nature,
and Must be of Such a Kind that No Obstacle Can Hinder It.*

1.   Let us then commence to seek out, in God's name, the principles on which, as on an immovable rock, the method of teaching and of learning can be grounded. If we wish to find a remedy for the defects of nature, it is in nature herself that we must look for it, since it is certain that art can do nothing unless it imitate nature.

CHAPTER XVI

*The Universal Requirements of Teaching and of Learning; That is to
say, A Method of Teaching and of Learning with such Certainty
that the Desired Result Must of Necessity Follow. . . .*

5.   Since this basis can be properly laid only by assimilating the processes of art as much as possible to those of nature (as we have seen in the 15th chapter), we will follow the method of nature, taking as our example a bird hatching out its young; and, if we see with what good results gardeners, painters, and builders follow in the track of nature, we shall have to recognize that the educator of the young should follow in the same path. . . .

7. *Nature observes a suitable time.*

For example: a bird that wishes to multiply its species, does not set about it in winter, when everything is stiff with cold, nor in summer, when everything is parched and withered by the heat; nor yet in autumn, when the vital force of all creatures declines with the sun's declining rays, and a new winter with hostile mien is approaching; but in spring, when the sun brings back life and strength to all. Again, the process consists of several steps. While it is yet cold the bird conceives the eggs and warms them inside its body, where they are protected from the cold; when the air grows warmer it lays them in its nest, but does not hatch them out until the warm season comes, that the tender chicks may grow accustomed to light and warmth by degrees. . . .

19. *Deviation.*—In direct opposition to this principle, a twofold error is committed in schools.

(i)   The right time for mental exercise is not chosen.

(ii)   The exercises are not properly divided, so that all advance may be made through the several stages needful, without any omission. As long as the boy is still a child he cannot be taught, because the roots of his understanding are still too deep below the surface. As soon as he becomes old, it is too late to teach him, because the intellect and the memory are then failing. In middle age it is difficult, because the forces of the intellect are dissipated over a variety of objects and are not easily concentrated. The season of youth, therefore, must be chosen. . . .

10. *Rectification.*—We conclude, therefore, that

(i)   The education of men should be commenced in the springtime of life, that is to say, in boyhood (for boyhood is the equivalent of spring, youth of summer, manhood of autumn, and old age of winter).

(ii)   The morning hours are the most suitable for study (for here again the morning is the equivalent of spring, midday of summer, the evening of autumn, and the night of winter).

(iii)   All the subjects that are to be learned should be arranged so as to suit the age of the students, that nothing which is beyond their comprehension be given them to learn.

11. *Nature prepares the material, before she begins to give it form.*

For example: the bird that wishes to produce a creature similar to itself first conceives the embryo from a drop of its blood; it then prepares the nest in which it is to lay the eggs, but does not begin to hatch them until the chick is formed and moves within the shell. . . .

13. *Deviation*—Against this principle schools are offenders: firstly, because they take no care to prepare beforehand the mechanical aids such

as books, maps, pictures, diagrams, etc., and to have them in readiness for general use, but at the moment that they need this or that, they make experiments, draw, dictate, copy, etc., and when this is done by an unskilled or careless teacher (and their number increases daily), the result is deplorable. . . .

14. Secondly, because even in school-books the natural order, that the matter come first and the form follow, is not observed. Everywhere the exact opposite is to be found. The classification of objects is unnaturally made to precede a knowledge of the objects themselves, although it is impossible to classify, before the matter to be classified is there. I will demonstrate this by four examples.

15. (1) Languages are learned in schools before the sciences, since the intellect is detained for some years over the study of languages, and only then allowed to proceed to the sciences, mathematics, physics, etc. And yet things are essential, words only accidental; things are the body, words but the garment; things are the kernel, words the shells and husks. Both should therefore be presented to the intellect at the same time, but particularly the things, since they are as much objects of the understanding as are languages.

16. (2) Even in the study of languages the proper order is reversed, since the students commence, not with some author or with a skilfully-compiled phrase-book, but with the grammar; though the authors (and in their own way the phrase-books) present the material of speech, namely words, while the grammars, on the other hand, only give the form, that is to say, the laws of the formation, order, and combination of words.

17. (3) In the encyclopedic compilations of human knowledge, the arts are always placed first, while the sciences follow after; though the latter teach of the things themselves, the former how to manipulate the things.

18. (4) Finally: it is the abstract rules that are first taught and then illustrated by dragging in a few examples; though it is plain that a light should precede him whom it lights.

19. *Rectification.*—It follows, therefore, that in order to effect a thorough improvement in schools it is necessary:

(i) That books and the materials necessary for teaching be held in readiness.

(ii) That the understanding be first instructed in things, and then taught to express them in language.

(iii) That no language be learned from a grammar, but from suitable authors.

(iv) That the knowledge of things precede the knowledge of their combinations.

(v) And that examples come before rules. . . .

Fourth Principle

26. *Nature is not confused in its operations, but in its forward progress advances distinctly from one point to another.*

For example: if a bird is being produced, its bones, veins, and
nerves are formed at separate and distinct periods; at one time its flesh
becomes firm, at another it receives its covering of skin or feathers, and at
another it learns how to fly, etc. . . .

30. *Deviation.*—Confusion has arisen in the schools through the endeavour to teach the scholars many things at one time. As, for example,
Latin and Greek grammar, perhaps rhetoric and poetic as well, and a
multitude of other subjects. For it is notorious that in the classical schools
the subject-matter for reading and for composition is changed almost
every hour throughout the day. If this be not confusion I should like to
know what is. It is just as if a shoemaker wished to make six or seven new
shoes at once, and took them up one by one in turn, only to lay them aside
in a few minutes; or as if a baker, who wished to place various kinds of
bread in his oven, were to take them out again immediately, removing
one kind as he put in another. Who would commit such an act of folly?
The shoemaker finishes one shoe before he begins another. The baker
places no fresh bread in the oven until that already in it is throughly
baked.

31. *Rectification.*—Let us imitate these people and take care not to
confuse scholars who are learning grammar by teaching them dialectic,
or by introducing rhetoric into their studies. We should also put off the
study of Greek until Latin is mastered, since it is impossible to concen-
trate the mind on any one thing, when it has to busy itself with several
things at once. . . .

32. Schools, therefore, should be organized in such a manner that the
scholar shall be occupied with only one object of study at any given time.

Fifth Principle

33. *In all the operations of nature development is from within.*

For example: in the case of a bird it is not the claws, or the feathers,
or the skin that are first formed, but the inner parts; the outer parts are
formed later, at the proper season. . . .

36. *Deviation.*—It is on this point that those teachers fall into error
who, instead of thoroughly explaining the subjects of study to the boys
under their charge, give them endless dictations, and make them learn
their lessons off by heart. Even those who wish to explain the subject-
matter do not know how to do so, that is to say, do not know how to
tend the roots or how to engraft the graft of knowledge. Thus they fatigue
their pupils, and resemble a man who uses a club or a mallet, instead of
a knife, when he wishes to make an incision in a plant.

37. *Rectification.*—It therefore follows

(i) That the scholar should be taught first to understand things, and then to remember them, and that no stress should be laid on the use of speech or pen, till after a training on the first two points.

(ii) That the teacher should know all the methods by which the understanding may be sharpened, and should put them into practice skilfully.

Sixth Principle

38.   Nature, in its formative processes, begins with the universal and ends with the particular.

For example; a bird is to be produced from an egg. It is not the head, an eye, a feather, or a claw that is first formed, but the following process takes place. The whole egg is warmed; the warmth produces movement, and this movement brings into existence a system of veins, which mark in outline the shape of the whole bird (defining the parts that are to become the head, the wings, the feet, etc.). It is not until this outline is complete that the individual parts are brought to perfection. . . .

43.   Deviation.—From this it follows that it is a mistake to teach the several branches of science in detail before a general outline of the whole realm of knowledge has been placed before the student, and that no one should be instructed in such a way as to become proficient in any one branch of knowledge without thoroughly understanding its relation to all the rest.

44.   It follows also that arts, sciences, and languages are badly taught unless a general notion of the elements be first given. I remember well that, when we began to learn dialectic, rhetoric, and metaphysics, we were, at the very beginning, overburdened with long-winded rules, with commentaries and notes on commentaries, with comparisons of authors and with knotty questions. Latin grammar was taught us with all the exceptions and irregularities; Greek grammar with all its dialects, and we, poor wretches, were so confused that we scarcely understood what it was all about.

45.   Rectification.—The remedy for this want of system is as follows: at the very commencement of their studies, boys should receive instruction in the first principles of general culture, that is to say, the subjects learned should be arranged in such a manner that the studies that come later introduce nothing new, but only expand the elements of knowledge that the boy has already mastered. . . .

(i) Each language, science, or art must be first taught in its most simple elements, that the student may obtain a general idea of it. (ii) His knowledge may next be developed further by placing rules and examples before him. (iii) Then he may be allowed to learn the subject systematically with the exceptions and irregularities; and (iv), last of all, may be given a commentary, though only where it is absolutely necessary. For he who has thoroughly mastered a subject from the beginning will have little need of a commentary, but will soon be in the position to write one himself.

Seventh Principle

46.   Nature makes no leaps, but proceeds step by step.

The development of a chicken consists of certain gradual processes which cannot be omitted or deferred, until finally it breaks its shell and comes forth. When this takes place, the mother does not allow the young bird to fly and seek its food (indeed it is unable to do so), but she feeds it herself, and by keeping it warm with her body promotes the growth of its feathers. When the chick's feathers have grown she does not thrust it forth from the nest immediately and make it fly, but teaches it first to move its wings in the nest itself or perching on its edge, then to try to fly outside the nest, though quite near it, by fluttering from branch to branch, then to fly from tree to tree, and later on from hill to hill, till finally it gains sufficient confidence to fly right out in the open. It is easy to see how necessary it is that each of these processes should take place at the right time; that not only the time should be suitable but that the processes should be graduated; and that here should be no graduation merely, but an immutable graduation. . . .

49.   Deviation.—It is an evident absurdity, therefore, if teachers, for their own sake and that of their pupils, do not graduate the subjects which they teach in such a way that, not only one stage may lead on directly to the next, but also that each shall be completed in a given space of time. For unless goals are set up, means provided for teaching them, and a proper system devised for the use of those means, it is easy for something to be omitted or perverted, and failure is the result.

50.   Rectification.—It follows therefore

(i)   That all studies should be carefully graduated throughout the various classes, in such a way that those that come first may prepare the way for and throw light on those that come after.

(ii)   That the time should be carefully divided, so that each year, each month, each day, and each hour may have its appointed task.

(iii)   That the division of the time and of the subjects of study should be rigidly adhered to, that nothing may be omitted or perverted.

Eighth Principle

51.   If nature commence anything, it does not leave off until the operation is completed.

If a bird, urged by the impulse of nature, begin to sit on eggs, she does not leave off until she has hatched out the chickens. . . .

56.   Rectification.—It follows therefore

(i) That he who is sent to school must be kept there until he becomes well informed, virtuous, and pious.

(ii) That the school must be situated in a quiet spot, far from noise and distractions.

(iii) That whatever has to be done, in accordance with the scheme of study, must be done without any shirking.

(iv) That no boys, under any pretext whatever, should be allowed to stay away or to play truant. . . .

CHAPTER XVII

The Principles of Facility in Teaching and in Learning. . . .

Ninth Principle

43.   Nothing is produced by nature of which the practical application is not soon evident.

For example, when a bird is formed it is soon evident that the wings are intended for flying and the legs for running. In the same way every part of a tree has its use, down to the skin and the bloom that surround the fruit.

Therefore. . . .

45. Those things only should be taught whose application can be easily demonstrated.

A Guide to Selections from *The Way of Light*

In these passages, Comenius argues that knowledge, as opposed to belief, must be based on personal experience, not on the testimony of authorities. He suggests that much of it demands empirical observation. He holds that a perfect language should be constructed, that it should be taught to all, that books embodying all knowledge should be widely circulated, and the entire race brought, in this way, to the possession of all knowledge.

SELECTIONS FROM

The Way of Light*

——◄♦►——

CHAPTER XIV

The threefold end of the way of Universal Light (namely, that in it all things be made manifest to all men in all their fullness) is more fully set forth....

20.   And this result will be attained if they are taught first things first, and the better things in preference to others, and all things by direct sight and by personal experience, constant and practical. First things first —that is, step by step, by raising themselves from the first and lowest through the intermediary to the final and highest things. For so at last all things will become clear, as they proceed fluently and spontaneously from each other; and all things will become strongly established as they rest one upon another. And they must be taught the better things in preference: by not allowing those that are less necessary to cause delay or to steal the place of those which are more necessary, but arranging that the lighter matters be dealt with in a lighter fashion, and the more serious in a more serious fashion, with an unwavering regard for the more important ends. And when we say that men must learn by their own direct vision, we mean that we must impose the necessary things upon men by knowledge and not by authority (for knowledge is a liberal thing and loves to flow into liberal minds): and we must not only provide them in words however precise and carefully chosen, but present the facts themselves to the senses directly as far as that is possible, so that all men will see by exercising their own eyes, and feel with their own senses and know of their own knowledge everything as it really is. For knowledge in effect is to know a thing as it is in itself and not as it is reputed to be. To know a thing through the reasoning of another person is not knowledge, but belief: just as masticating with another person's mouth is not masticating, but witnessing the process of mastication. I do not taste the cake which you eat or the wine which you drink; a blind man does not see the picture which a man with sight tells him that he himself can see; and

* The materials here presented have been taken from *The Way of Light* translated with introduction by E. T. Campagnac, Liverpool, The University Press, London, Hodder and Stoughton, Ltd., 1938. Footnotes omitted.

similarly if another man tells me that he knows, has seen, read or experienced, that affords me no ground for claiming to know, but only for believing that he has seen, read or experienced. And it was in knowledge very much of this sort (knowledge which consists in loyal acceptance of the authority of the teachers and in an intellectual process not its own but of other people) that the world hitherto used to acquiesce, though unwillingly, and with occasional revolts and with longing to break through the barriers of its servitude. For, indeed, most things which have been transmitted to us from those earlier ages have been of this character, dark and confused. But the time is come for us to rise from the rudiments to completeness of knowledge, no longer to be like children tossed hither and thither by the waves, or permit ourselves to be blown about by every wind of doctrine, but to have such knowledge as befits grown men, so that no one can justly charge our knowledge with emptiness or obscurity or any other harmful defect. . . .

CHAPTER XV

For the Universal Light there are four requisites: Universal Books; Universal Schools; a Universal College; a Universal Language. . . .

4. Now we are quite confident that all these things will be obtained by the means which we have mentioned. For if Universal books (embracing all things that we need know, in a form true, compact and clear) are set up, the result will be that he who reads these and understands them cannot possibly be ignorant of anything which is necessary. But that these books can be read and understood by all men Schools will be able to provide, if they are really universal, that is of a kind in which all our young people can be liberally taught, and enticed and prepared by lesser and introductory books (by little books, I mean, suitable for the earlier years) both to read and to understand all the greater and more important matters. And again, that Schools of this kind shall be set up in every part of the world will be the task of that College of good and learned men, concentrating their common efforts upon this end and spreading themselves in ever-increasing numbers from people to people. And it is a Common language which will make it possible for these wise men to fulfil their task by exchanging ideas and thoughts among themselves from whatever people they may have been drawn and whatever their nature and peculiar speech. . . .

CHAPTER XIX

The Scheme of a Universal Language. . . .

4. Now, therefore, when we are seeking and hoping for the Reform of the whole world we must necessarily have recourse to the aid of languages, i.e., either those who are to spread this light of wisdom must have the gift of speaking in any and every tongue, or else there must be one common language for all peoples. Each of these alternatives may well seem to be beyond attainment: yet the second is easier to secure than the first. For it is easier for all men to learn one language than for one man to learn all—if painstaking and industrious preparation is made. . . .

9.   With him (Luis Vives) we agree so far as to hold that one common language for the whole world is needed, and that, if another cannot be found, Latin should be assigned to this purpose rather than any of the rest. But since our speculations now take a higher flight, we cannot but counsel the making of an entirely new language. And our reasons for this proposal are the following:

10.   First of all in a Universal Language provision should be made impartially for all men. In the Latin language we should be providing preferentially for ourselves, to whom it is already known, and not with equal fairness for uncivilised peoples (though for them we ought to have a larger consideration in this matter since they make the larger part of the world). And to them Latin is as little known as other languages—indeed, it is less known; and it is also equally difficult. It needs the diligent attention and the concentrated study of many years, as our young men know by experience, and as the very structure of the language proves. For (1) it is full of variety in the case of nouns, (2) in the moods and tenses of verbs, (3) in its syntactical constructions; (4) it overflows with innumerable instances of all these anomalies. The Italians, in removing these irregularities in large measure from their own language, may seem to have corrupted Latin: but they have at any rate achieved this result, that not only almost all the peoples of Europe, but the Arabs, Turks, Tartars and other barbarians are not indisposed to learn their language, though it is still full of thorny difficulties,—I mean, it still suffers under a load of anomalies. How great, then, might be our hope, if a language still easier were provided, a language absolutely regular and straightforward in its course through all forms of speech.

11.   In the second place, a universal language ought to be the richest and most copious of all, for the proper and precise expression of all subjects, and entirely adequate for the easy rendering of all conceptions of the mind. And Latin must openly confess that it has not these qualities, for it is poor in composite words, and far from fortunate in its derivations. . . .

12.   Finally this is of the chief importance, a universal language ought to be a universal antidote to confusion of thought. And it can only be that if its course is parallel with the course of thoughts, that is, if it contains neither more nor fewer names than there are things; and joins words to words with the utmost precision as things are joined to each

other, by constantly expressing the nature of the things with which it deals by the very sounds which it uses, and so presenting them to the mind. And in this Latin has as little felicity as any language which could be mentioned. For the men of earlier ages, the authors of that language which has been handed down to us, were not so accurate in their investigation of things as to remark all their peculiar qualities and differentiae, and so to express them in exact and appropriate terms: they were content if they were able to set forth the qualities which met the eye at once. Indeed, very many of their words were brought into being by mere chance and applied upon no principle so as to mean definitely this or that—the same or a similar sound was used for contrary things, and contrary sounds for the same thing. And so all their speech was full of homonyms, synonyms, paronyms, tropes, figures, periphrases, that is in effect, of ambiguities, redundancies and confusions. Whenever they had to speak with comparative precision about things, either they were driven to making perpetual definitions and to repeating over and over again what was meant by this or that word, or else in the very course of their speech they found themselves obliged to be for ever making exceptions, distinctions, limitations, more often ignorantly or sophistically than with regard to the truth. And thus uncertainty and error are always pressing in, since thought itself is never sufficiently free from confusion.

13.   Hence it is that the peoples of the world are all of them still building a Babylon, and never properly understand themselves and each other in their conduct or their speech—and this is true not only of men of different tongues, but of those who use the same idiom. For while words are attached to things without regard to the nature of the things themselves, and the basic qualities of things are not revealed either by the habit of speech or by the reciprocal harmony between things and names, the result is that whenever any dispute arises about things men strive on this side and on that and achieve nothing but a medley of words. For since their words are not exactly commensurate with things, they are unable to form concepts in exact fitness to the things (of which they speak). And so for all the noise of doctrines and discussions we scarcely advance an inch in the study of wisdom: because we speak words, not things.

14.   We may conclude, then, that for the manifold delays and confusions in human intercourse which spring from the number, the difficulty and the imperfection of languages, we can find no more potent remedy than the fashioning of a new language, which in comparison with all those that are now known will be (1) easier, so that it can be learnt without expense of time or substance; (2) pleasanter, so that it will be delightful in the process of learning and when it has been mastered; (3) and more perfect (as perfect, indeed, as may be in the nature of the case and considering our own imperfection in this earthly school) so that to be skilled in it shall greatly help us towards the understanding of things themselves.

15. So, then, we conceive and pray for a language which shall be (1) Rational, having nothing which does not bear a meaning whether in its matter or in its form, and conforming to this rule in its finest and least points: (2) Analogical, containing no anomaly in any matter: (3) Harmonious, bringing no discrepancies between things and the concepts of things, in as much as by its very sounds it would express the essential qualities and characteristics of things—a language which for that very reason would be as it were a funnel through which wisdom would flow. If such a language could be accepted by the common consent of mankind, all men would delightedly recognize that it would be the most appropriate means for reconciling them to each other and their concepts of things to the truth. Then at last that age of illumination and of peace would have dawned and could be proclaimed, an age in which there would be light and quiet in things, in the concepts of things, and in words which are the vehicles of concepts. . . .

Bibliography

LAURIE, SIMON SOMERVILLE, *Studies in the History of Educational Opinion from the Renaissance,* Cambridge, Cambridge University Press, 1903. Chapter XI.

MONROE, WILL SEYMOUR, *Comenius and the Beginnings of Educational Reform,* New York, Charles Scribner's Sons, 1900.

MUNROE, JAMES PHINNEY, *The Educational Ideal: an Outline of its Growth in Modern Times,* Boston, D. C. Heath and Co., 1911. Chapter IV.

. . .

KOŽIK, FRANTIŠEK, *Johan Amos Comenius,* translated by Sylvia E. Fink-Myhre, Prague, SNTL, 1958.

LAURIE, SIMON SOMERVILLE, *John Amos Comenius, Bishop of the Moravians: His Life and Educational Work,* Cambridge, Cambridge University Press, 1904 (sixth edition). Originally published 1887.

VII

LOCKE

J OHN LOCKE LIVED during the revolution against Charles I, the Protectorate of Cromwell, the Restoration of Charles II, and the accession of William and Mary. His life extended over one of the more turbulent and decisive periods in the history of England, and was not far removed from some of its more critical events. He was born in Somersetshire, England in 1632. He died in 1704.

Locke received his early education at home under the supervision of his father; but in 1646, he left home for Westminster School. In 1652, he became a student at Christ Church, Oxford. There he did some experiments in chemistry and read Descartes, a relatively recent and exciting philosopher. In 1660, he was tutoring in Christ Church in Greek, rhetoric, and philosophy. He thought of a clerical career, but studied medicine. During his lifetime, he practiced this art a little, but only on his friends.

Locke maintained his studentship in Christ Church until 1684, living there upon occasion. His political associations, as we shall see in a moment, could not make him a great friend of the Crown; and informers in the college, although apparently unable to learn that he was engaged in anything like treason, nonetheless regarded him with suspicion. In 1684 the Crown informed the dean of the college that it had received information of the "factious and disloyall behaviour of Locke." It asked that he be removed from his studentship and deprived of the rights and advantages pertaining to it.[1] The dean acceded to the request, and Locke's connection with Oxford was severed in November while he was absent from England.

In 1667, Locke became secretary to Anthony Ashley Cooper, later the first Earl of Shaftesbury. Shaftesbury was a prominent politician of the day who was frequently in and out of favor during his lifetime, both with the revolutionary regime and that of Charles II. Locke was closely associated with the Earl until near the end of his checkered career. In 1675 he followed Shaftesbury into exile in France, and returned to England in 1679 when Shaftesbury regained power. The politician fell from favor again; and as part of his effort to extricate himself from his plight, he engaged in very devious politics, some of which seems to have been treasonous. He escaped to Holland in 1682 where, after a few months, he died. Pressure against Locke because of his association with the Earl caused his withdrawal to Holland in 1683. There he became acquainted with William and Mary; after the Glorious Revolution established them as joint monarchs, he returned to England under their protection. He then began to publish his books on political philosophy, theory of knowledge, education, religion, and theology, several of which had been started long before. The last years of his life were spent in semi-retirement in the country, in comfortable government posts, and in reflection upon religious and theological questions.

As secretary to the first Earl of Shaftesbury, Locke perhaps gave medical care as well as political counsel. But the Earl valued Locke for other reasons. Not long after making his acquaintance he put his son into Locke's care; and according to his grandson, the famous and literary third Earl of Shaftesbury, Locke was charged with the education of the grandchildren as well. His interest in education led him to act as tutor to several other families; and he gave much advice concerning the rearing of their offspring to his friends, some of which, first written down as letters, became his treatise on education. Education loomed large in Locke's mind along with politics, philosophy, and theology.

EDUCATIONAL THEORY

THE DIFFERENT PARTS of Locke's educational theory are dispersed throughout his writings. Most of its recommendations occur in *Some Thoughts*

1 Thomas Fowler, *Locke,* Harper & Brothers, New York, 1880, p. 41. From letter quoted there to John Fell, Dean of Christ Church, from Lord Sunderland, writing by his Majesty's command.

Concerning Education; but the statements of fact upon which the recommendations are based are found partly in that book, in *The Conduct of the Understanding, An Essay Concerning Human Understanding,* and the *Second Treatise of Civil Government.* Here we shall bring the parts of the theory together.

STATEMENTS OF FACT

The statements of fact involved in Locke's theory pertain to things of four kinds: human nature, the family, the school, and the development of society. This discussion of human nature amounts to a description of the capacities innate in and common to human beings, and of the adult human being together with the societies he forms viewed as the natural outcome of developing those capacities. His discussion of the family and of the school is incidental to his description of the way in which innate capacities are channeled. He insists that all of his statements either are or could be borne out by observation; and although he does not say so, we may suppose that many of them rest upon his experience as tutor or advisor to the several children in whose rearing he took part.

Human nature

In our study of preceding authors, we have come upon the view that the human being is a combination of two substances: one mental, the other physical; one the mind, the other the body. This view is characteristic of Christian thought. Descartes and his followers helped to establish it as a part of modern philosophy and psychology. A strong tendency in Locke's thought leads to questioning it; but in fact, so far from denying it he suggests that it is a probable view.[2]

Locke devotes most of his attention, however, to the mind. One of the chief objectives of his thought is to make out the nature and extent of human knowledge; but a necessary part of achieving this objective is a description of the mind which harbors that knowledge and holds sway over that extent. This description concerns itself with the innate powers of the mind, with the material upon which those powers exercise themselves, and with the outcome of their exercise on those materials. In order to make Locke's view of human nature clear we must explain these powers and materials.

THE UNDERSTANDING. "The two great and principal actions of the mind which are most frequently considered and which are so frequent that every one that pleases may take notice of them

---

[2] John Locke, *An Essay Concerning Human Understanding,* Book II, Chapter XXVII, §25; cf. also *Some Thoughts Concerning Education,* §§1, 2.

in himself are these two: perception or thinking, and volition or willing." The power of thinking is called "the understanding," and the power of volition is called "the will."[3]

In this passage, Locke tells us that everything which occurs in our minds is either perceived or willed by us, and that we must therefore be endowed with powers to perceive and to will. "To perceive," it should be noted, covers a great many different activities for Locke. Knowing, believing, reasoning, sensing—all these and others, too, are cases of perceiving. "To perceive" means to receive impressions from without or from within ourselves or, in more modern language, to be aware of our ideas in some way or other. The understanding enables us to perceive[4] or to be aware of ideas.

But to understand is not to exercise merely the power to perceive; this power, as Locke says, is only "the first capacity of human intellect."[5] Perceiving itself requires the exercise not only of the power to perceive, but also of several other powers. In order to perceive or to be aware of an idea, we must also distinguish it from other things, retain it before our minds, combine it with still others, abstract others from it, and use a sign to refer to it. The understanding is not a single power but a group of them—the power to perceive along with the powers to engage in these other activities.[6]

Consider the perception of the plum tree in the garden, and remember that this perception need not be a sensory observation but may be only a thought of the plum tree there. In order that such a perception should occur in our minds, we must be aware of the idea of the tree in the garden; the power to perceive must be activated. But secondly, we would not perceive this idea unless we also distinguished it from the ideas of other denizens of the garden, retained it in our minds by attention or memory, compared it with those ideas and united it with them to form the idea of the tree in the garden, recognized it as a general idea of a plum tree, and used this idea of it to refer to the tree itself in the garden itself.

In addition to all these powers, Locks suggests[7] that another is required. The plum tree in the garden is external to the mind, but our perception of it is not. It is evident to Locke that in order that the perception should occur in the mind there must be something there which represents the plum tree in the garden. This is an *idea* of the plum tree in the garden, and we use it as a representative of that external plum tree, in the garden, as a sign for it. Our using the idea as a sign shows that

---

[3] *Essay*, II, vi, §2.
[4] *Ibid.*, II, i, §24; II, ix, §1.
[5] *Ibid.*, II, i, §24.
[6] *Ibid.*—power of distinguishing, II, xii, §1; of retaining, II, x, §1; of combining, II, xi, §§4–6 and II, xii, §1; of abstracting, II, xi, §9; of using signs, II, xi, §8.
[7] *Ibid.*, II, xi, §8.

we possess the *power* to do so. Locke also suggests that we would not use the idea of the plum tree in the garden as a sign for the latter unless we could use the phrase "plum tree in the garden" as a sign for the idea in question. In the case of many ideas, it is using words that signify them that brings them before our minds, and is essential, therefore, for using the ideas to signify external things.[8]

Understanding, for Locke, consists of the six mental powers we have described; and of these, the last five seem to represent themselves as necessary to the exercise of the power to perceive.

IDEAS. When the mind exercises its power to perceive it becomes aware of something; and that of which it is aware is an idea. The word "idea" is, Locke says, the ". . . term which, I think, serves best to stand for whatsoever is the object of the understanding when a man thinks. . . ."[9] There are, according to this definition, two features that all ideas must possess: first, they must be things perceived or thought about; and secondly, they must be capable of being used as signs, i.e., of being employed to stand for things not present in our awareness when the ideas of them are so.

Locke classifies ideas in several ways, and we must notice one of the classifications now. Some ideas, he tells us, come to us from sensation, others, from reflection.[10] Through the sense organs, some object acts upon the nervous system, setting up in it a train of neurological events which terminates in the brain, and whose terminal event causes an idea of the object that initiated the train. The action of a piece of gold upon the retina and optic nerves leads to a brain event which causes our idea of something gold in color, which we use to stand for the piece of metal. It is clear that similar statements could be made for things that act upon the ear, the skin, and other organs of sense. Ideas of sensation are given to us by the action of objects on our senses. Ideas of reflection are found not through sensation, but through introspection. When the mind looks within itself, it finds operations of various kinds in which it is engaging; and these mental operations are ideas of reflection. By looking within, we find the perceiving, the remembering, the reasoning, the doubting, the willing, or whatever other mental action we happen at the moment to be performing. Everything that the understanding can reveal is an idea; and ideas are the materials upon which the powers of understanding always are exercised.[11]

---

8 *Ibid.,* II, xi, §8; III, v, §§10–15.
9 *Ibid.,* I, i, §8.
10 *Ibid.,* II, i, §§3–4.
11 *Ibid.,* II, i, §24. Locke suggests here that all ideas of reflection, all operations of the mind, are directed upon ideas got by sensation, i.e., that all the activities of the mind are either those of sensing or others such as remembering objects sensed, which take their objects or materials from the activity of sensing.

DESIRE. Locke treats desire not as an activity that manifests a faculty different from understanding but, rather, as one kind of idea of reflection. Let us explain this view.

First, one cannot desire to do what he is in fact doing. One cannot desire to be in London when one is in fact in that city. To say that we desire to do what we are in fact doing is a misleading way of saying that we desire to do in the future what we are in fact doing in the present.[12]

Secondly, a desire always *involves* doing something in the future although it must *be* something which, in fact, presents itself to us now. To desire to be in London is to have present to our minds something which involves our going there at some future time; but this something cannot be our being in London since we are not being in London when we desire to be there. The something present to our minds in desire is something which prompts us to some future action.[13]

Thirdly, the something which is thus present in desire is an idea. A person who understands (perceives, believes, supposes, etc.) that he is in New York has the idea of his being there before his mind; and he has the same idea before his mind when he desires to leave New York. One could not desire to leave the latter city without the idea of his being there. The understanding that one is in New York and the desire to leave it (without some concrete terminus for one's journey) involves the same idea, that of being in New York. On the other hand, the person who is in New York, but desires to be in London, understands (perceives, believes, supposes, etc.) a more complex idea—one made up of the idea of his being in New York together with that of his being in London. Such a person, however, will have the same idea in mind if he does not desire to be in London, but understands merely that he is in New York although he might betake himself to the former city. Understanding something and desiring it contain the same idea. How, then, do they differ?

Fourthly, desiring something is painful, while understanding it, merely, is not. Any idea, Locke tells us, may be pleasant or painful.[14] Its pleasantness consists in its delightfulness; its painfulness in its uneasiness. The pleasantness and the painfulness of an idea may depend upon it alone or upon its comparison with some other idea.[15] The idea of poor health is pleasant in comparison with that of severe illness since it is less

---

12 *Ibid.*, II, xxi, §39.
13 *Ibid.*
14 *Ibid.*, II, vii, §2. Locke does not clearly distinguish between two possible views of pleasure and pain: first, that they are experiences separate from, but produced by, those things which are pleasant or painful; secondly, that they are qualities (not separate experiences) of the things which are pleasant or painful, i.e., that each is a form of Hedonic tone. Cf. II, vii, §§2–3; II, xx, §§1, 15–16. We shall treat the latter as his view on this subject.
15 *Ibid.*, II, xx, §16.

painful; the idea of reading this book is painful in comparison with the idea of a walk in autumn because it is less pleasant.

Now Locke's point is that the idea of being where we are, say in New York, may be a painful one; and it may be painful independent of other ideas or its painfulness may depend upon our comparing it with those others, and finding it less pleasant. In the first case, we desire to be in any place whatever other than New York; in the second case, if the comparison be between New York and London, we desire to be in London. The same idea is involved in both cases. But when we want to leave New York simply, the idea of being in New York is painful without respect to any other; while when we desire to be in London, the idea of being in New York is not independently painful, but painful in relation to the idea of being in London.

Fifthly, "to be good" means to be pleasant, while "to be bad" means to be painful; and a thing is pleasant or painful either in itself or because of the pleasantness or painfulness of its consequences.[16] Something may thus be good even though we are not at the moment finding it pleasant. It is good, we may say, not merely in case someone now finds it pleasant, but also in case someone would find it pleasant were he to experience it. But something which is good in either way may not exist when we think of it. Eating tonight's dinner, although thought of now, does not now exist. Where what we think of is good but not now existent, the idea by which we think of it is painful; and a painful idea of a nonexistent good is the desire for that good thing of which it is the sign. A desire, Locke remarks, "is an uneasiness in the want of an absent good. . . ."[17]

Sixthly, it is the painfulness or uneasiness of desires which prompts us to act. We must rid ourselves of pain; and where the idea of some nonexistent good is painful, we rid ourselves of painfulness by acting to establish the existence of that which the idea represents, thus disposing of the idea of its nonexistence. The desire to be in London is made of two parts: the idea of being somewhere else, say New York, and the idea of being in London. This complex idea is painful because part of it represents a nonexistent pleasure—living in London. Its painfulness causes us to take steps to substitute a life in London for one in New York.

Desires are a kind of idea, those which are painful by virtue of being representative of absent goods. They prompt to action, but are not themselves species of activity. They are revealed by the exercise of the powers of understanding and require no separate mental power.

KINDS OF DESIRE. All desires, all painful ideas of absent goods, fall under two kinds: desires of fancy, and desires of

---

[16] *Ibid.,* II, xx, §2.
[17] *Ibid.,* II, xxi, §31.

nature.[18] The latter are those desires which reason alone cannot prevent, which must be satisfied if life is to proceed, and which are not learned.[19] Hunger, thirst, and the desire for sleep are examples. Desires of fancy are either capable of being prevented by reason alone, unnecessary to life, or learned. The desire for apple pie when hungry, for lemonade when thirsty, or for a soft bed when fatigued are examples.

There are several kinds of ideas which, without any learning on our part, prompt us to establish the existence of what they represent, are necessary to life, and are incapable of being prevented by reason alone.[20] They are desires; and since the good things that they represent are not learned to be so, they may be described as natural, or in more modern language, instinctive. Moreover, since they prompt us to action, i.e., to actions that would make those good things exist which they represent, the infant who harbors them brings to his environment certain ways of acting which that environment does not create, however it may alter them.

The natural desires are seven in number. First, we desire to secure bodily pleasure and to avoid bodily pain.[21] Secondly, we desire to be free, i.e., to be the authors of our "own good actions."[22] Thirdly, we desire power; and power consists in two[23] things—in control over others, and in possession of material things. Fourthly, we desire to secure for ourselves the approbation of others, and to avoid their disapprobation.[24] Fifthly, we desire after a long continued activity to engage in one of a different kind; we need not learn, that is to say, to desire recreation.[25] Sixthly, we desire to secure knowledge and to avoid ignorance; this desire is simple curiosity.[26] We should note that Locke sometimes treats curiosity as a desire of fancy, seemingly because it is not necessary to life. Seventhly, we naturally desire (Essay II, xxi, §41) to be happy, i.e., to fulfill as many of our desires as are compatible with each other.

At birth we are endowed with that group of powers which Locke calls "the understanding." The materials upon which we exercise these powers are ideas that represent external things, ideas of sensation, and other ideas which are the operations of our minds, ideas of reflection. When these ideas represent something good as absent or nonexistent, they

[18] *Some Thoughts Concerning Education,* §107. Locke distinguishes here between wants of fancy and wants of nature. But his "want" in the *Thoughts* seems to be used in the same way as his word "desire" in the *Essay;* and we have treated the phrase "wants of fancy and wants of nature" as referring to the same distinction as the phrase "learned desires and natural desires."
[19] *Ibid.*
[20] *The Conduct of the Understanding,* §4; also, *Thoughts,* §102.
[21] *Thoughts,* §4.
[22] *Ibid.,* §73.
[23] *Ibid.,* §§103–5.
[24] *Ibid.,* §§56–58.
[25] *Ibid.,* §108.
[26] *Ibid.*

are desires, prompting us to establish the existence of what they represent. There are seven kinds of things, those enumerated above, which are naturally desirable, and therefore seven kinds of natural desires. The manner in which these natural desires are developed largely determines the adult personality. But before investigating the latter, it is necessary to say something about the will.

THE WILL AND LIBERTY.   According to Locke, we frequently engage in mental actions that involve a preference for one thing over another. We prefer to center attention on the duties of the moment rather than the delights of the approaching holiday; we prefer to walk through the deepening snow rather than drive in the car. The first is a mental action directed upon ideas; the idea of present duties rather than that of future delights. The second is a mental action directed upon one kind of physical motion, walking, as opposed to another. Acts of preferring Locke calls "volitions."[27] Volitions occur when we exercise the will. The latter is the "power which the mind has . . . to order the consideration of any idea, or the forbearing to consider it; or to prefer the motion of any part of the body to its rest, and vice versa, in any particular instance. . . ."[28] Or as Locke says more succinctly elsewhere, ". . . the will, in truth, signifies nothing but a power or ability to prefer or choose."[29]

The will is not the same thing as desire. To desire something, as we have seen, is to entertain a painful idea of the nonexistence of something which prompts us to establish its existence. Frequently, we entertain conflicting desires, but choose to realize one as opposed to the other. We desire both to walk and to drive, but we prefer the former. Our preference cannot be a desire, for a third desire would increase rather than resolve the conflict. This shows that an act of will is different from desire; it is a volition, not a desire in which we choose between conflicting desires. The will is the power to prefer or choose, and acts of volition or willing are actual preferences, choices, or decisions.[30]

Although the will is not the same thing as desire, it is intimately connected with it. When we exercise the will, we choose between two or more competing desires. We prefer realizing the desire to walk rather than the desire to drive. What causes us to engage in this preference? Locke argues that when we prefer to realize one desire rather than another, it is because the present idea of one goal or absent good is more painful than that of the other. We prefer to walk rather than to drive because it is more painful to think of missing the invigorating walk than it is to think of

27 *Ibid.,* II, xxi, §5.
28 *Ibid.*
29 *Ibid.,* II, xxi, §17.
30 *Ibid.,* II, xxi, §30.

missing the indolent drive. What determines us to exercise our wills by preferring one desire to another is "the greatest present uneasiness."[31] Without it, there would be only the contemplation of several absent goods; and this passive contemplation would never cause us to decide in favor of one over the others.[32]

The will is closely associated in Locke's thought with another power of the mind which he calls "liberty." An act of preference, a volition, is wholly within a man's own mind. In order that it should be carried out, we must exercise another power. We may decide to think about present duties or to walk through the deepening snow, but we may find that future delights occupy our minds or that we take the car. In order to realize our preferences we must be able to do so; and doing so is an exercise of our liberty. It is ". . . the power in any agent to do or forbear any particular action, according to the determination or thought of the mind, whereby either of them is preferred to the other. . . ."[33] Our will enables us to prefer one thing to another; our liberty, where we possess it, enables us to realize our preference in further action—either mental or corporeal.

Exercising our liberty takes the form of a suspension of desires, and a calculation of the consequences of acting upon them,[34] as well as that acting itself. Although a desire prompts us to establish the existence of its goal, the absent good, it does not always cause us to do so forthwith. Before walking through the snow, we can consider doing so, and use what knowledge we possess to foresee what consequences it involves. Judgment can show us whether what appears to be an absent good is as good or pleasant as it actually appears; and in showing us this, foresight of consequences can actually diminish or increase the urgency of desire. A desire may become less painful when our judgment tells us that realizing it will lead to less pleasure than we had thought; and it will become more painful if we see that establishing the existence of what it represents will involve more pleasure than we had earlier supposed.[35] Not all desires can be suspended. Bodily torments are desires for relief;[36] and preferring to avoid them cannot be stopped. Moreover, although realizing the natural desires can be delayed, ultimately they cannot be denied. Some desires cannot be prevented from receiving immediate preference, and many cannot be suspended altogether. But it is within our power to suspend some—to determine their relative importance, and to make informed

[31] *Ibid.*, II, xxi, §§40, 36, 71.
[32] *Ibid.*, II, xxi, §34.
[33] *Ibid.*, II, xxi, §§8, 15, 55a, 71.
[34] *Ibid.*, II, xxi, §34.
[35] *Ibid.*, II, xxi, §§46, 69.
[36] *Ibid.*, II, xxi, §57.

judgment the basis both of our volitions and of following out the promptings of those desires upon which we decide.

By virtue of the will, we engage in acts of preference. By virtue of
our liberty, we determine in many cases which desires are most painful,
and consequently, which among alternative desires shall determine our
volition as well as the action it permits.

PRINCIPLES OF PERSONALITY DEVELOPMENT. In all persons the understanding reveals ideas,
some of which are desires; and in all, the will prefers and liberty executes some desires rather than others. Moreover, in all persons, natural
desires that cannot be indefinitely suspended prompt similar actions.
Yet, one person varies enormously from another. The reason is twofold:
first, that the environment in which a person grows up offers some ideas
to his understanding and withholds others; and secondly, that the ideas
upon which his understanding fixes and the ways in which his natural
desires develop are determined by practice and by habit.[37] One who lives
in the environment of a college desires to read history and poetry, having
become familiar with them; while one who grows up on the farm, never
having encountered them, harbors very different ideas and desires. Even
while a "ploughman" or a "country hedger" may, upon occasion, become aware of Rome or Hamlet, the habits of his life usually crowd them
out. Moreover, while all persons naturally desire food when hungry, practice and habit make some desire sauces and others plain cooking. The
kinds of things we can understand and desire are determined by the ideas
that our environment offers us, and by the habits of thought and of volition we acquire. We all possess the powers to understand and to will, but
our habitual ways of exercising these powers, together with the materials
upon which we exercise them, make for considerable differences from
one person or group to another.

However we differ one from another, we develop from infancy to
maturity according to certain general principles. These principles describe
the ways in which natural desires come to limit each other, i.e., the ways
in which the ideas of some absent goods become more painful than those
of others, and consequently determine our preference for the actions that
would establish their existence over the actions that would establish the
existence of other absent goods. They are principles that explain the
development of habitual forms of preference and of action.

These principles are six in number. First, we have seen that by
nature we desire to secure for ourselves the approbation of others and
to avoid their disapprobation. Consequently, the idea of doing something

[37] *Conduct,* §4.

of which others would approve, before we have decided to do it, is more painful or urgent to us than the idea of doing something else in its stead; and the more painful idea determines us to prefer the action that would incite the approbation of others over those which would not. For example, the idea of giving to another something that he needs when such a giving would be approved by others is more painful to us than the idea of keeping the thing for ourselves when that keeping would be disapproved by others. The giving is an absent good whose nonexistence calls urgently for remedy; the keeping is an absent good whose clamor for realization is less urgent. We prefer, therefore, giving to those who are in need over retaining things for ourselves. The first principle of individual development is that if an action is consistently approved or disapproved by others, in certain circumstances, any agent will prefer to do or to refrain from doing that action, in those circumstances.[38]

The second principle is that rewarding people with bodily pleasure and punishing them with bodily pain neither establishes the actions rewarded nor disestablishes those punished.[39] All persons naturally desire to secure bodily pleasure and to avoid bodily pain; consequently, they desire to do those actions which are themselves corporeally pleasant, and to refrain from those which are themselves corporeally painful. But when bodily pleasure or pain is externally attached to an action, it is because it is immediately involved in one action, when that action is conjoined with another. This external attachment occurs in reward and punishment. •When a child is rewarded with candy, eating it accompanies another action—the one rewarded. When a child is punished by corporeal pain, one action, e.g., submitting to a flogging, accompanies or follows another —the action punished. When corporeal reward and punishment occur, a person does not learn to prefer doing the action rewarded or to refrain from doing the action punished; rather, he learns merely to secure the pleasure and to avoid the pain. Moreover, since this can be done by seeming to deserve the reward or not to deserve the punishment, bodily rewards and punishments generate deceit quite as much as they generate the activity that they would instill. What we are likely to come to prefer by the use of bodily rewards and punishments is not so much the activities that these are supposed to foster as it is whatever activities will secure the pleasure and avoid the pain.

The third principle is that we prefer to do those actions with respect to which we are free over those with respect to which we are compelled.[40] By nature, we desire to be free. The idea of an independent action not yet done is more painful or urgent to us than one of an action imposed upon us by others; consequently, we prefer to perform the

---

[38] *Thoughts*, §§56–58.
[39] *Ibid.*, §§47–48, 50, 52.
[40] *Ibid.*, §73.

former rather than the latter. We learn better if learning is not imposed from without, but freely accepted from within.

The fourth principle is that if all of the desires expressed by children are given satisfaction they will become overly aggressive and incapable of socialized behavior.[41] By nature, we desire power or control over others; and a pampering fulfillment of every request of the child develops a habit of ordering others about, which makes him overbearing if it succeeds and socially disruptive if it does not. If the adult is to be modest, submissive, and forebearing, the child's requests for assistance must have been satisfied only when they expressed natural desires, not when they expressed desires of fancy. This denial makes for an adult who will prefer to act cooperatively rather than aggressively.

The fifth principle is that if we are to continue to prefer doing something, we must have occasional relief from it in the form of an activity of some other kind.[42] By nature, we all desire recreation. After a certain interval, any activity becomes boring, and its continuation less desirable than some other. Consequently, if we are to continue to prefer doing something, we must have occasional change from it.

The sixth principle is that if we are to know something we must have been curious about it, i.e., have desired to know it.[43] By nature, we are curious about everything. But other desires are stronger, e.g., that of avoiding public disapprobation; and the natural desire to know, as well as some of the other natural desires, can be smothered by disapproval of the questions that express it. If the child's questions are always honestly attended to, his curiosity will be encouraged; and he will be more likely to prefer trying to acquire knowledge since the motive for doing so—curiosity—remains.

PERSONALITY. The nature of all human beings results from the exercise upon ideas of the powers of the understanding and of the will. Their exercise is determined by habits of thought and of volition. These habits reflect the culture and the history of each of us; and our personality is (if it is no more than this) those ideas which our powers of understanding provide, occurring in patterns of volition and in patterns of those actions to which they lead when we are at liberty. However each person differs from others, the habitual organization of ideas in each conforms to the principles of development stated above.

The family

The statements of fact which Locke makes concerning the family are few, and they may be dealt with briefly.

41 *Ibid.,* §§103–105, 107.
42 *Ibid.,* §108.
43 *Ibid.*

Adam was significantly unlike all his descendants. He had no childhood. He was created with full powers of understanding and of will; and from the first moment of his existence, he was fully equipped to care for himself and others. He knew both the objective of that care, life according to the laws of nature, and the means by which it might be achieved, the ways in which things behave. He needed no education.

All the descendants of Adam are unlike him because their maturity, if they reach it at all, occurs after a stage of immaturity. They are children before they are adults. During the earlier period, although they are possessed of the power of understanding and will, they have not yet been able through practice to develop for the expression of these powers a systematic program of preferences. Their reason has not yet come to maturity; and they cannot yet be aware either of the objective of their lives or of the means to secure it. During this period others must understand and will for them. They are in need both of protection and of education.

The parents provide protection and education during the period of immaturity. If they did not understand and will for the child, he would die for want of food, shelter, and the like; and the race would not continue. If they did not understand and will for him, his actions, not yet capable of obeying or breaking the laws of nature, would nevertheless fail to conform to them, thus fostering the habit of disregard for those laws. The family performs the function of protecting the child, both in his bodily and spiritual aspects, during the period of inexperience; and provides for him that practice for his powers of understanding and of will which is required for establishing the stable patterns of desire, volition, and action in which a personality consists. The parents educate the child.[44]

The school

Educating is a function that parents can, and frequently do, transfer to others. Where the latter are tutors, education is not far removed from parental protection, but where they are persons charged with the care and instruction of "three or four Score Boys lodg'd up and down,"[45] they are schools—more particularly, private boarding schools. Where they are persons who teach skills by the day only, they are vocational or "working schools."

Locke thought that parental and tutorial instruction provides the condition under which a young gentleman learns what he should know most efficiently. In the private boarding school, an English institution well established in Locke's day, the child acquires some learning, but at

[44] Locke, *Second Treatise of Civil Government,* VI, §§56–58, 69.
[45] *Thoughts,* §70.

the cost of virtue and good breeding. In such schools, the masters are able to teach a little Greek and Latin; but because of the large number of students given into their care, they cannot teach virtue. To make a boy good requires individual attention; and the overworked master, even though he might be acquainted with virtue, does not have enough time to convey it to his charges. Education in a boarding school provides the children with self-confidence, but at a greater price—that of corrupting character.[46]

Children of the unemployed poor between the ages of three and fourteen will learn most effectively to assume their position in society if they are compelled to go to vocational day schools. These schools can improve them by teaching them some skill involved in the wool business or some other industrial or agricultural pursuit. In them, children can be fed and sent to church. Also these schools can operate as shops, the sale of whose products will more than reimburse the local government's expenses in running them, and as sources of apprentices for farmers, craftsmen, and businessmen. These working schools provide a place, moreover, where adults can learn a new trade or skill.[47]

The state of nature

During the time of their innocence, Adam and Eve lived under circumstances of ease. If they harbored desires they were immediately satisfied. Labor was unnecessary for them.

Nonetheless, they possessed the capacity for labor. One who possesses the power to understand is able to see the relation between his own actions and their consequences. Where some of these consequences are pleasant, the idea of their not yet existing is painful or uneasy. It is a desire for them; and it runs, naturally, into an action which will establish them. One who possesses the power to will is able to prefer the realization of one desire over that of another; and one who possesses liberty in a relevant respect, is able to institute the action to which the preferred desire leads. To labor is to prefer to realize one desire over another, to engage in the action which the preferred desire leads to, and to find that action as well as the desire for its consequences disagreeable and painful.

---

46 *Ibid.*

47 Locke, *On Education* (editor's title) edited by R. H. Quick, Cambridge University Press, London, 1913. Appendix A, "Working Schools," pp. 189–91. Locke's proposal of working schools appears in suggestions he made to the Board of Trade, of which he was a member, for solving widespread problems of unemployment and pauperism. His recommendations were rejected by the Board. They include penalties for those involved in begging, such as the removal of ears, transportation to the colonies, incarceration at hard labor, and "sound whippings" for children. Despite the Board's rejection, Locke hoped that Parliament would enact them into law. Parliament did nothing of the kind, according to Cranston, until the Poor Law Reforms of 1834. Cf. Maurice Cranston, *John Locke, A Biography,* The Macmillan Co., New York, 1957, pp. 424–26.

Adam and Eve possessed the capacity for labor because they possessed the powers of understanding, of will, and of liberty; and by virtue of these innate powers, all their descendants possess it as well.[48] Since the Fall, it has been necessary for all men to exercise the capacity for labor.[49]

Beginning with Adam and Eve,[50] men lived for some time in a state of nature. This was a condition of human life in which there was society, but no political society. Political power is the right of making laws directed toward the public good, with penalties of death, and consequently all lesser penalties; and of employing the strength of the community as a whole for their enforcement.[51] A political society is one which possesses a government endowed with the right and the strength to make laws and to punish their violation by death. Where there is no political society, men live in groups to be described shortly; and while in these the strength of some is employed to injure or kill others, its employment cannot be the exercise of political power. There is no right on the part of such groups to make laws, and no enforcement by the strength of the group as a whole.

The nonpolitical societies that characterize the natural condition of men grow out of two facts concerning them. First, men have a natural desire for social life, and a need for it brought about by the sex instinct and the long period of care that the human offspring requires.[52] Secondly, each man is incapable of so much, and of such varied labor as is necessary to support himself. Exercising his capacity for work does not prevent his being unable, without assistance, to satisfy his own needs.[53] Noticing these two facts shows that there can be no human life without society.

At first, societies were primarily familial in character. Each person played a role in the economy. Soon, they were enlarged by adding the master and servant relation to that of blood. Later fathers and masters of such extended families became monarchs.

In the state of nature, there is no enacted law. Independently of the punishment of death, all other sanctions become null and void. A society does not possess the right to impose this punishment; it possesses no right whatever to command individuals. In the state of nature there is no social sanction for anyone's commands, and therefore no civil law.

Nonetheless, in the state of nature there is the law of nature. To understand this law, we must understand three things about men in non-

[48] *Essay*, II, xxi, §§34, 36, 37. Also, *Second Treatise*, v. §32.
[49] *Second Treatise*, v, §32.
[50] Locke, *First Treatise of Civil Government*, iii, §16; vi, §67.
[51] *Second Treatise*, i, §3. Locke's elaborate definition mentions, also, employing the force of the community for defense, and seems to identify public good with the regulation and preservation of property.
[52] *First Treatise*, vi, §54; *Second Treatise*, vii, §77.
[53] *Second Treatise*, ii, §15.

political societies. First, each of them is subject to God's will. By virtue of his liberty, man is *able* to flout that will, as Adam and Eve did in the garden; but he is not *free* to do so since divine sanctions attach to violations of it. Man's natural freedom—his freedom in the state of nature, which differs from his liberty—is not the absence of any constraint over his activities; it is the absence of any legitimate *human* constraint. So far as other men are concerned, he may do anything he sees fit.

Secondly, this natural freedom is the basis for natural equality. In His creation of them, God gave natural freedom to all men; and this likeness with respect to natural freedom is their natural equality.[54]

Thirdly, man's natural freedom and equality are closely connected, in Locke's thought, with property. "Property in a thing" means the right to exclude all other persons from the use or control of it.[55] It is clear that one who possesses natural freedom also possesses property in his own person, for no human being can legitimately impose his will upon him. His natural freedom consists in "ordering his actions and disposing of his possessions and person as he sees fit."[56] The equality of men guarantees that all possess property in their persons.

The law of nature is what God wills with respect to human life. It may be put briefly as the command that each man should respect the property rights of all others, i.e., should refrain from interference, in Locke's language, with their lives, liberties, and estates or legitimate possessions.[57]

In the state of nature, society does not possess the right to enforce the law of nature. If it did, it would be a political society, and the law a civil law. The right of enforcement, rather, lies in the hands of each individual. Each person has the right to punish invasions of property, even by death, since such interventions are threats against the very life of the person involved.[58]

Before the necessity for human labor, all things were held in common. There was no private property. But when the race began to labor, private property in land and other possessions came into existence. As we have seen, everyone has property in his own person, and everyone possesses the capacity for labor. We may now notice that the "great common of the world" could not have supported human life if the capacity for labor had not been exercised upon various parts of it. The race could not have been sustained if land had not been fenced and plowed, its ores smelted, and so on. Men mixed their persons in the form of labor with communal possessions, and the property right of each in his person and

---

54 *Ibid.*, II, §4.
55 *Ibid.*, V, §27.
56 *Ibid.*, II, §4.
57 *Ibid.*, II, §6; VII, §87.
58 *Ibid.*, II, §7.

labor extended to the products of the latter. This property in the products of one's labor was further extended by societies, so that ownership by other means such as inheritance came to be established. The story of human life is largely that of the conversion of communal possession into private property.[59]

A nonpolitical society, or the state of nature, is a society of free and equal owners of property. In it, men lived in groups determined by familial and economic relations, supplying the economic insufficiency of each, respecting for the most part one another's property rights, and possessed of the right to punish their infringement as violations of the law of nature. This nonpolitical society has characterized much of human history.

The social contract, and the political state

In the nature of man there is a condition that enables him to form political societies. All men are endowed with the powers of understanding, of volition, and of liberty. The first includes the power to use signs; and since promise-keeping and truth-telling are ways of using signs, these activities belong to "men as men, and not as members of political societies."[60] The understanding also includes the power to perceive, and the power to desire to avoid that which is painful. The power to will enables one to prefer realizing the desire for a political state over realizing the desire for the state of nature. The power of liberty enables one to act upon his preferences, i.e., to try to do what is required to realize the desire preferred as opposed to one which is not.

In the state of nature, there is a circumstance which, in conjunction with human nature, leads to its transformation into political society. Naturally, as we have seen, all men desire power which comes through control over others or through possession of material things. In the state of nature, this desire leads to much insecurity. In it, there is no binding civil law regulating nature, and no sure way of imposing punishment—the effectiveness of individual punishment being a matter of the strength of the person aggrieved.[61] The natural desire for power and the merely individual right to punish violations of the law of nature generate insecurity in the enjoyment of property for those who live in the state of nature.

A nonpolitical society is transformed into a political one when people in it use their natural powers to recognize this insecurity, and to deal with it in a certain way. First, they understand that the insecurity of their property arises from the absence of any civil law, and from the partiality of the individual judges and executioners of the law of nature.

59 *Ibid.,* v, §§25, 26, 27, 32, 45.
60 *Ibid.,* ii, §14.
61 *Ibid.,* viii, §95.

Secondly, they desire to live in the state of nature, and also to live in political society. Thirdly, they prefer the latter to the former, security to insecurity of property. Fourthly, they act to embody this preference by promising each other to surrender to the community their natural rights, to punish violations of the law of nature, and to live according to laws which the community makes for the regulation and preservation of property, i.e., for advancement of the public good.[62] This promising is the act of consent; and it is the consent of its members, one to all the others, which makes a society political, i.e., one endowed with the right to make laws with penalties of death, directed toward the public good, and to enforce them with the strength of the community. It is the promise to obey the enacted law and the judges who interpet it.

The mutual consent or agreement on the part of its members to surrender to the community their individual rights to punish violations of the law of nature by death is the social contract. Its consequence is that society acquires political power and the ability to enforce its laws by the strength of the community as a whole. It did not establish society, for that existed in the state of nature. Rather, it established the political state.

Not all scholars accept this interpretation of Locke's social contract theory. Some hold that the state of nature is a completely nonsocial condition, and that the contract establishes society for the first time as an aspect of human life.[63] Locke's language is frequently unclear, and he may well have entertained contradictory views on this subject. But his explicit effort is to explain how political or civil society came into existence, not to explain the establishment of society as such; and most if not all his statements clearly support the interpretation of the state of nature and of the social contract given above, i.e., the view that in the state social contract is that act on the part of each member of agreeing with all the others to render the society a political or civil one by authorizing it to employ the right to punish, possessed by each in the state of nature.[64]

RECOMMENDATIONS

Goal recommendation

Locke recommends the happiness or "welfare and prosperity of the nation"[65] as education's ultimate goal. Happiness is the continuing satisfaction of desires, but not of all of them. The happiness of an individual

[62] *Ibid.*, VII, §87; VIII, §95.
[63] Cf. Ernest Barker, *Social Contract*, "Introduction," Oxford University Press, London, 1960, pp. xiii, xxiii.
[64] Locke, *Social Contract*, VII, §§77, 89–90.
[65] *Thoughts*, "Epistle Dedicatory," ed. by R. H. Quick, Cambridge University Press, London, 1913, p. lxiii.

person cannot be the satisfaction of all his desires because some conflict with others. Similarly, the nation's happiness cannot consist in the satisfaction of all the desires of all its members because what some men desire is precisely what others also want. In society, both natural and political, controversies over property are settled by denying the claim of at least one of the disputing parties. These settlements consist in frustrating the desires of those whose claims are invalidated. The happiness of the nation is a harmony of individual happinesses in which some desires of some individual persons are curtailed or altogether suppressed. It is this harmony of individual happinesses which education ought to help to bring about.

Although the nation's happiness does not guarantee total satisfaction for every person, ordinarily each citizen should have some share in it. The goal recommendation of education, consequently, requires that each citizen be capacitated for at least some measure of enjoyment. This capacitation cannot be identical in all persons since the role of a citizen differs from class to class and individual to individual. It is nonetheless true that education ought to establish those habits and dispositions which, when activated, will lead each citizen to do those things which the nation's happiness requires.[66]

Subordinate recommendations

EDUCATING THE GENTLEMAN. The most important part of the means for achieving national welfare and prosperity is the preparation of the children of gentlemen for their role in the state. "For if those of that Rank are by their Education once set right, they will quickly bring all the rest into Order."[67] The gentleman's children thus set right may be trusted to act in political life and elsewhere in such a way as to insure the national welfare. How can the children of gentlemen be best equipped for enjoyment of their own lives as well as for social usefulness?

PHYSICAL TRAINING. If the happiness of the gentleman and the welfare and prosperity of the nation are to be secured, one must develop in gentlemen's children habits of three kinds: of physical hardiness, of good character, and of sufficient learning. First, they must be inured to physical hardships such as wet feet, and habituated to health by exercise, plenty of sleep, few medications, simple diet, loose garments, and early rigorous toilet training.[68]

---

[66] *Ibid.*, §§31, 198, 217; also Appendix A, "Working Schools," pp. 189–91.
[67] *Ibid.*, "Epistle Dedicatory," p. lxiii.
[68] *Ibid.*, §§1–30. Locke's discussion of toilet training is based on experiments that he performed upon himself and others. He says he could find nothing on the subject in books. It has an amusing as well as a sensible side.

Secondly, the gentleman's child must acquire those habits which make him virtuous, wise, and well-... cluster of habits, including religious piety, courage, ...aturedness, and the like. Wisdom is the ability to man-... this world with foresight. Breeding (more properly good breeding) is the habit of thinking meanly neither of ourselves nor of others; it expresses itself in actions that are neither bashful and withdrawn, nor aggressive and inconsiderate. Anyone in whom these habits are well established is of good character, himself happy, and able to contribute to the happiness of society as a whole.

ITS METHODS. There are two methods that are useless for the formation of the habits of good character. First, it is futile to require that the child memorize rules of conduct. The success of this method lies not in virtuous, wise and well-bred behavior, but rather in the ability to repeat a rule.[70]

Secondly, it is futile to impose bodily pleasure and pain as a method of instruction. There is a natural desire to secure the first and avoid the second; but this procedure encourages the very opposite of good character. As we have seen while considering the principles of individual development, rewarding will teach the child to do anything that secures the pleasure, while punishing will teach him to do anything which avoids the pain. Corporeal discipline cannot serve the purposes of education,[71] and should not be resorted to except as a way of avoiding extreme difficulties.

Locke makes three positive points concerning the methods of moral training. First, as in all training, one must discover the relative strengths of natural desires.[72] This should be done by observing the child at play when he believes he is not being watched by adults, and therefore is concealing nothing.

Secondly, one must frustrate those desires which are incompatible with good character. Habitual virtue, wisdom, and good breeding require an ability to deny some of one's own desires, following out only those which make part of happiness, while all vice springs from an indulgence in present bodily pleasure and avoidance of bodily pain.[73] Consequently, good character can be formed only by curbing the natural desire for those activities which give a present bodily pleasure or avoid a similar pain. The ability to curb this natural desire may be established by frustrating the wants of fancy which embody it (all of them do except for curiosity),

---

69 *Ibid.*, §§134–47.
70 *Ibid.*, §§64, 165, 175, 185.
71 *Ibid.*, §§47–52.
72 *Ibid.*, §102.
73 *Ibid.*, §§33, 48.

and the child's expression of any such want ought to be sufficient reason for preventing its fulfillment.[74] But this denial is not enough. The approbation of others must be attached to foregoing present personal pleasures, and of withstanding similar pains.[75] Thus, the natural desires for power, for control over others and of possessions, should be limited by satisfying another natural desire, that for approbation. Disapprobation of cruelty, and approbation of sharing and helpfulness—this procedure will establish habits of cooperation and of justice which otherwise might be prevented by the desire for power.[76] Similarly, protecting children from early frights and accustoming them gradually to fear and pain will instill habits of courage; and this procedure involves a large measure of approbation for courageous behavior, and disapprobation of its opposite.[77] Moreover, obedience to the commands of God, the laws of nature, often involves foregoing our own pleasures; and this piety, again, is instilled by approval of the activities that manifest it. The habits of virtue, wisdom, and breeding lead to happiness; and since the gentleman ought therefore to possess them, the tutor should curb the child's natural desire for bodily pleasure and aversion to bodily pain, together with his natural desire for individual power, by making use of his equally natural desire for the approbation of others and aversion to their disapprobation.

An important aspect of the second step in successful moral training is the use of rational procedures. There is a natural desire for freedom, to carry out for ourselves in action those desires which we prefer or will to realize; and there is a principle of individual development according to which the free practice of an action is the most efficient way to acquire the habit of performing it. All moral training involves the supervision of the child by a teacher, but it does not preclude the child's doing freely what the teacher wishes. This will happen, in most cases, if the teacher talks with the child and points out to him the probable consequences of the different actions possible for him. Children are capable of reasoning, of using language for understanding things, much earlier than many have supposed; and it ought to be the way in which moral training is carried on except in cases of extreme obstinacy.[78]

Thirdly, although moral training must frustrate the natural desire for bodily pleasure, it cannot dispense with pleasure of all kinds. The habits of virtue, wisdom, and good breeding cannot become established unless the actions which manifest them are pleasant for the agent. But they will be so if they are made always to satisfy two other natural desires —the desires for approbation and for freedom.

[74] *Ibid.*, §§38–9, 107.
[75] *Ibid.*, §§109, 110, 116.
[76] *Ibid.*, §§109, 110.
[77] *Ibid.*, §115.
[78] *Ibid.*, §§73, 77, 81, 96.

... English languages and literatures, the specula-
tive and empirical beginnings of modern social and natural sciences. For
him, to be learned was of less importance than to be of good character.
Learning can be used to any purpose, good or bad; and it serves purposes
of the first kind only in those whose character is good independently of
it.[79] Moreover, it is not even learning itself toward which the intellectual
training of the gentleman should be directed. One can never tell whether
a child or youth will find any use in the future for what he is being
taught. Consequently, his time should not be wasted in acquiring a detailed and precise knowledge of anything. Rather, he should acquire a
"love and esteem of knowledge," and "the right Way of knowing and
improving himself when he has a Mind to it."[80] This love and esteem,
and this way of improving oneself are habits—habits of valuing and of
coming to know something, rather than the things valued and known.
Intellectual training, like moral training, amounts to the formation of
habits; although their formation requires the compassing of at least some
knowledge of the subjects concerned.

The general method used for intellectual training consists of two
parts. The first depends upon the truth that ". . . where there is no desire,
there will be no industry";[81] and it amounts to the manipulation of non-
intellectual desires in such a way as to make them express themselves in
habits of loving and esteeming, and securing when so minded, the insights
in which learning consists. The child who shows no desire to learn a
given subject matter possesses, nonetheless, the natural desires for recreation, freedom, approbation, and understanding strange things (curiosity).
The desire to "saunter' time away in play, the disposition to idleness, may
be employed for learning in two ways: by treating the opportunity to
learn as a recreation from play, and by compelling the child to play
while presenting the opportunity to learn as an alternative, a fulfillment
for his desire to be free.[82] Also, the desire to learn may be grafted to the
desire for social approbation, especially where approbation flows from
older children or from parents in the form of affection.[83] Again, the desire to learn a given subject may be awakened by introducing strange

[79] Ibid., §147.
[80] Ibid., §195. Also The Conduct of the Understanding, 21st edition of essay, publisher
Bye and Law, §§12, 19.
[81] Thoughts, §126.
[82] Ibid., §§74, 124.
[83] Ibid., §§74, 57.

objects involved in the subject to the student, thus appealing to his curiosity.[84] Where natural desires afford no basis for the habits of learning, those which have been acquired may serve as well, but some desire must be present, frequently other than the desire to learn the subject taught, in order that the student should be taught anything whatever.

The second part of the general method of intellectual training depends upon Locke's theory as to the nature of the subject matter to be learned. This subject matter, however it differs in detail from one time to another, is always a set of ideas. In order to learn it, i.e., to become aware of it, one must be perfectly clear about the component ideas and about their relations, one to another. In order to teach it, therefore, the tutor must divide it into its component parts, find a least one with respect to which the learner is perfectly clear, add others to it by the closest steps possible until the entire set has been presented, and make each idea and each relation perfectly clear to the learner as he goes along.[85] Thus, for example, in teaching the geography of England, one should find some English region with which the learned is clearly acquainted, make him clear about adjacent places and about the relations to that region which make them adjacent, and so on, step by step, until the idea of England as a whole emerges. In teaching history a similar procedure should be followed, except that the ideas concerned will be related in the order of time as well as space. In teaching mathematics, analogously, the ideas should be added in a logical order, i.e., the order of premises and conclusion; and as in the other cases, the additions should always be as small as possible.

The general method of intellectual training consists in appealing to desire in order that the subject matter should be kept up by the student on his own volition, and in presenting ideas to him in such a way and in such an order that while each is clear and distinct to the learner, they also constitute together a unified whole. There are details of the method of intellectual training that will be stated in connection with Locke's recommendations concerning the curriculum.

ADMINISTRATION. As we have seen, Locke held the view that schools provided an environment that made it difficult to give moral training. He recommended, therefore, that the children of gentlemen be kept at home. Their teachers should be tutors and parents —apparently and primarily the former.

Although Locke talks almost always about boys, he argues that education should be administered to girls as well. ". . . where the difference of sex requires different treatment, 'twill be no hard matter to distin-

84 Ibid., §121.
85 Ibid., §§180, 195.

says nothing concerning the latter. Consequently, he does not recommend an arrangement of subjects that corresponds to it. He recommends, rather, a set of subjects ordered in such a way that those which rely upon others will come after them in the course of study. The order of studies, which is given below, is appropriate to Locke's thought, although not clearly evident in it. The specific objectives assigned by Locke are mentioned.

MORAL SUBJECTS. The habits in which virtue consists, Locke seems to say, will be best furthered by examples. He has in mind not merely the virtuous behavior of tutor and parents, but chiefly the moral behavior of historical characters found especially in the Bible. A little religion will help, but a deep study of theology is of very little use in improving the character of the young gentleman. After the correct habits are established, one might well learn rules and study systems of morality such as that of Tully.[87] Wisdom, the "ability to manage one's business in this world with foresight," is furthered by the study of history and by bookkeeping.[88] Dancing, fencing, reading, gardening, woodworking, and travel, early or late but not at the usual age of sixteen—these will make for the habits of good breeding.[89] Very likely Locke thought that all the subjects recommended for the young gentleman would improve his moral character, but those listed above seem to be of immediate relevance to it.

INTELLECTUAL SUBJECTS. The following is a list of subjects that Locke recommends for intellectual training. Speaking English, reading English, writing English, drawing, shorthand, French, Latin, arithmetic, geography, Copernican astronomy, chronology, anatomy, history, Latin grammar, political theory (civil and natural law), English law, rhetoric, logic, natural philosophy, and speculative philosophy.

Locke makes detailed recommendations concerning the method for teaching some of these subjects. Reading should be taught by making it a game, e.g., that of recognizing which letter turns up on the face of a die; writing by tracing over red letters with black ink; French and Latin, by

[86] *Ibid.,* §6.
[87] *Ibid.,* §§82, 185.
[88] *Ibid.,* §§182, 210.
[89] *Ibid.,* §§196, 198, 199, 204, 212.

conversation and by reference to real things rather than by studying grammar and by reading books; geography and history, by use of globes and maps as well as books; and natural philosophy by the writings of Boyle and Newton among others, the first of whom made "rational experiments and observations," while the latter has shown some important truths about "particular provinces of the incomprehensible universe."

There is an order of learning into which these subjects seem to fall.[90] Speaking is the fundamental form of language; consequently, learning to read cannot occur before, and should immediately follow, speaking. For similar reasons writing should be studied after reading. French and Latin should be taught as soon as the child knows how to speak English. Latin grammar should follow the active use of Latin since one cannot understand linguistic rules unless he is acquainted with that to which they apply. Rhetoric should follow the study of grammar since rhetorical language must be highly polished, and grammar helps to that end. The learning of French and Latin should include the study of things that we can observe through our senses, e.g., history and geography; and Locke recommends that much teaching of other subjects should be done in the process of learning those foreign languages. The study of spirit should precede the study of body. The child should study spirit in a brief history of the Bible before he goes on to learn about the physical world; and this study of spirit should be extended into youth, when he can examine the proofs for the existence of the self and of God offered by natural and speculative philosophy.

Certain of the intellectual subjects are given detailed justification.[91] Drawing enables one to remember his travels vividly and to express himself quickly and precisely. Shorthand enables dispatch and secrecy. Latin and most of the literature of philosophy are necessary to good breeding; and in the study of French and Latin, the tutor should take pains to inculcate habits of good character.

While gentlemen's children need study no subject in great detail, there are certain subjects that ought to be excluded altogether.[92] Greek is one. It should be pursued, if at all, only after maturity, and by one who is minded to be a scholar. Music, painting, and poetry should be excluded and the tendencies toward them stifled, for those who create as well as those who enjoy works of art destroy health, fall into odd company, and waste or at best fail to increase their property; ". . . it is very seldom seen, that anyone discovers mines of gold or silver in Parnassus. 'Tis a pleasant air, but a barren soil. . . ."[93] As opposed to translation, composition and

[90] *Ibid.*, §§148, 160, 162, 163, 166, 167, 168, 178.
[91] *Ibid.*, §§161, 164, 166, 178.
[92] *Ibid.*, §§161, 164, 166, 178.
[93] *Ibid.*, §§169–71, 188.

declamation in Latin are useless. They prepare one to speak to, o.
for, the Romans. Moreover, they do not succeed; Latin themes and
teach one sheer invention, not the Latin tongue. Locke gave the fine
no proper role in education nor, for that matter, in life generally.

Certain subjects should be greatly de-emphasized.[94] Religion shou
be taught early; but the study should not be minute, for God is inscr
table, and an early discovery of this fact may lead as well to scepticism as
to virtue. Logic and rhetoric should be studied a little; they are ingredients in polished manners. But the rules of rhetoric do not make one
speak well, as those of logic do not insure good reasoning. It is better to
read those who have done both well.

It should be added that Locke presents his thoughts concerning
the method of teaching gentlemen's children and the subjects they should
be taught only as guides for that education, arguing that particular adaptation of them should be made in the light of each individual's needs,
together with sex and class status.[95]

EDUCATING THE POOR.   Locke devoted most of his thought concerning
education to the problems involved in rearing
gentlemen. We have seen, however, that the need for training children of
the poor did not escape his notice altogether. He recommended the establishment of working schools throughout the realm of the crown for all
children from three to fourteen, whose parents "demand relief of the par-
ish"; and these schools should embody the kind of training which he
thought appropriate to children of laborers—the training referred to in
the preceding section of this chapter. The subjects taught would be the
elements of religion, vocational skills such as those of the "woolen manu-
facture" and agriculture, and presumably "the three R's." The latter
receive no explicit mention, however, in the passage concerning working
schools quoted by Quick in an appendix to his edition of the *Thoughts*.
Unemployed adults ought also to be allowed to attend these working
schools.

PHILOSOPHY OF EDUCATION

EPISTEMOLOGY

Locke holds the view, as we have seen, that the desire for happiness
and the desire to know, curiosity, are widespread throughout mankind.
The objective of education, both of gentlemen and of working people, is

[94] *Ibid.*, §§136, 188.
[95] *Ibid.*, §§6, 217.

the provision for them of those habits of conduct which enable satisfaction of the first of these desires. Education cannot hope to provide, however, so thoroughgoing a means for fulfillment of the need to know. Although the human mind can encompass as much as is necessary for happiness, it is not capable of knowing a very great deal. Locke presents a support for this claim in his epistemology, and we must now examine that theory in order to understand its supporting role.

The nature of knowledge

Knowing consists in a certain exercise of the understanding's powers to combine and to distinguish. In sensation and reflection, the mind is presented with ideas, some of which are perfectly simple—with ideas of colors and tastes, of perceiving and willing.[96] Complex ideas result from our combining these simple ideas in various ways, and from our distinguishing or separating some of these complexes from others. The idea of an oak leaf, for example, results from our combining the simple ideas of a certain colored surface, a certain texture, etc., into the idea of the leaf, and from our distinguishing or separating the idea of the rest of the tree from that of the leaf. Knowing something, however, does not consist in having a complex idea of it; the idea of an oak leaf stands for the leaf but is not knowing about it. Knowing is not harboring a complex idea; it is, rather the making of one by joining or separating ideas in a certain way.

Now the ideas upon which the mind operates in knowing either agree or disagree with each other. The idea of whiteness and that of color agree, while the idea of whiteness and that of taste disagree. The idea of a tree and that of a plant agree, while the idea of a tree and that of a stone disagree. Consequently, when we join ideas, we may join ideas that agree or disagree; and when we separate one idea from others, we may separate ideas that agree or disagree. But it seems perfectly clear that joining ideas that disagree, and separating ideas that agree, cannot be what knowing consists in. "Whiteness is a taste" expresses our joining of ideas that disagree, and "a tree is not a plant" expresses our separating of ideas that agree. But this joining and separating of ideas is not knowing; it is making a mistake. In what does such a mistake consist?

Every idea, it will be recalled, is a sign for something; and the things signified agree and disagree with each other in a way parallel to the way in which their ideas do. Trees agree with plants in the sense that they constitute a class included in the class of plants, and disagree with stones in an analogous way. Consequently, the operation of separating the idea of a tree from the idea of a plant is a false proposition about them—

---

96 *Essay*, II, II, §1; II, VI, §§1–2.

the proposition that a tree is not one; and joining the two ideas is a true proposition—the proposition that a tree is a plant. Locke seems to use the word "proposition" to mean any claim that something is true; and he tells us that "proposition consists in joining or separating signs" while a true proposition "consists in the putting together or separating those signs, according as the things, which they stand for, agree or disagree."[97] A false proposition presumably consists in putting together or separating signs according as the things signified do not agree or disagree. Being mistaken consists in making a proposition that is false.

Knowing, therefore, requires the joining or separating of ideas according as they agree or disagree, for their agreement or disageement reflects the same relation between those things which the ideas represent. But this "right joining or separating" does not exhaust the idea of knowing; for one might join or separate ideas rightly without seeing that they agree or disagree. Reflection upon the mental operation of knowing shows that it consists in being aware of the agreement or disagreement of the ideas joined or separated, i.e., that the joining or separating is right, or that the proposition we make is true. "Knowledge then seems to me to be nothing but the perception of the connexion and agreement, or disagreement and repugnancy, of any of our ideas. . . . Where this perception is, there is knowledge; and where it is not, there, though we may fancy, guess, or believe, yet we always come short of knowledge."[98]

According to this notion, knowing consists in being completely certain about something. This is so because of the nature of agreement and disagreement. These are relations of a very special kind. Some relations do not need to hold between some things. Henry VIII and Catherine of Aragon were related by marriage, but this relation need not have related them. Either might have married someone else, or no one at all. On the other hand, some things are related by relations that could not fail to relate them. "Two plus two" is related by equality to four. This must be so, for if it were not, at least one of the qualities would not be the quality it is—a feat that is very difficult for any quantity to perform. Now agreement and disagreement of ideas are necessary relations. The idea of a tree agrees with the idea of a plant; if it did not, either the first would not be the idea of a tree, or the second would not be the idea of a plant. So also for disagreement. The idea of a tree cannot fail to disagree with the idea of a stone. If it did so fail, one of the ideas would not be the idea it is, but some other instead. The idea of a tree would be, for example, the idea of a boulder. Where agreement and disagreement hold, they could not fail to do so; they are necessary relations. If we join or

---

[97] *Ibid.,* IV, v, §5, also IV, iv, §3.
[98] *Ibid.,* IV, i, §2.

separate ideas according as they do not agree or disagree, we make a proposition that is necessarily false; and we are necessarily mistaken. We would never do this, of course, if we perceived the agreement or disagreement in question. If we join or separate ideas according as they do agree or disagree, and perceive that agreement or disagreement, we are completely certain about it. Knowing is the act of joining or separating ideas according as they, and what they stand for, agree or disagree, where this act is suffused with a perception of that agreement or disagreement; and since these relations are necessary, every act of knowing is a certainty that some proposition (the one in which it consists) is true.

Locke immediately modifies this view concerning the nature of knowledge. There are, he tells us,[99] two kinds of knowledge: actual and habitual. Actual knowledge is all those mental acts of knowing referred to above. But one who has once actually known something knows it still, unless he has forgotten it; and this kind of knowing is habitual. A habit is a power ". . . of doing anything, when it has been acquired by frequent doing the same thing. . . ."[100] When we have actually joined or separated ideas upon several occasions in such a way as to know the proposition thus constructed, we know it habitually even when not constructing it, i.e., given the appropriate occasion we will actually know it again. One who knows a proposition of geometry is not always proving it; but unless he forgets, he is always able to do so at need. It is clear that habitual knowledge must be understood in terms of actual knowledge, and that whatever we actually know, we may come to know habitually.

Locke holds that there are very few things that we can actually know; and therefore very few that we can know in any way whatever. Each man can know to be true the proposition "I exist," together with others that proclaim the occurrence and nature of his ideas.[101] Such propositions are the joining or separating of ideas whose agreement or disagreement can be immediately seen or intuited. We can also know to be true or false any proposition that ascribes a sensible character to a particular object affecting our senses when we make that proposition, or that embodies a memory of such a particular object, present when we make it.[102] These propositions about particular sensible objects are not known to be true by intuition. We cannot extend our minds beyond our ideas to see whether the particular objects concerned do actually possess those features the ideas of which we join or separate. Consequently, perceiving the agreement or disagreement of the latter is not sufficient to assure the truth of the propositions we construct. But Locke thinks there

99 *Ibid.*, IV, I, §§8–9.
100 *Ibid.*, II, XXII, §10.
101 *Ibid.*, IV, IX, §3.
102 *Ibid.*, IV, II, §14; IV, III, §5; also IV, XI, §11.

are other reasons, such as their unalterability at will, which assure us that our sensations provide us with some knowledge of sensible objects. Moreover, we can know the proposition that God exists; and we can also know all the general propositions in which are embodied the truths of ethics and of mathematics.[103] Propositions of both these kinds we know by demonstration, i.e., a series of intermediate intuited ideas linking two ideas whose agreement or disagreement cannot be immediately perceived. But for reasons to be mentioned in the section of ethics, Locke argues that the propositions of ethics and mathematics do not apply to things in the mental and physical world. It follows that even if our knowledge were as perfect as possible we could know nothing of the physical world beyond the narrow circle of our present sensory experience and its memory, nothing of the future or remoter past, and nothing of the existence or character of minds other than our own and God's.

Although we can know only a very few propositions to be true, there are a great many that we judge to be true. Judging consists in presuming that the ideas joined or separated in a proposition agree or disagree. But many may be joined or separated. Why do we accept the propositions that some compose and reject others? We accept those which conform to our own experience, or to that of others expressed in their testimony.[104] It is such a conformity to experience which supports our judgment that a particular man, not observed by us, walked upon the river in freezing weather. This conformity provides evidence for any propositions we make about things which, although not experienced, could be observed by us. There are other propositions, such as those about the minute parts of matter, which concern areas totally incapable of being observed. For these we can find evidence only to the degree that they are analogous to propositions true or probable about what we do experience. We observe the conditions under which heat occurs among sensible bodies, and we infer that they are similar for heat in the minute parts of matter, i.e., their rapid motion. Probable judgment is belief about many things, those beyond our own experience, whose behavior impinges upon our practical activities; it therefore supplements our knowledge, although it is quite different from it.[105]

There is another attitude toward propositions which supplements knowledge. Some propositions are made of ideas whose agreement or disagreement can be neither perceived nor judged to be probable; yet we accept them as true. These are propositions whose truth is revealed by

103 *Ibid.*, IV, x; IV, xII, §8.
104 *Ibid.*, IV, xv, §4. It is a little hard to see how we could accept the testimony of others as making a judgment probable. Locke has said that we cannot know that other minds exist.
105 *Ibid.*, IV, xIv; and IV, xv, §12.

God, and they pertain to such unexperienceable things as the early history and ultimate destiny of men, the existence of angels, and so forth. God cannot deceive, and revelation is a convincing ground for unqualified assent or faith.[106]

Our knowing, Locke argues, can penetrate only a very little way into the world about us. Our curiosity, the desire that is satisfied by knowing, is therefore destined to large-scale disappointment. The desire for happiness, also, cannot be assured success; knowledge of the means to its fulfillment, knowledge of those paths which would lead us to it, cannot be achieved. Here, we must rely upon probable judgment which grows from fallible experience, and upon the propositions of faith guaranteed by the benevolence of God. Locke does not doubt that where knowledge fails, curiosity should be content; and that although happiness cannot be assured by knowledge it will be granted nonetheless through the judicious use of evidence and of faith.

Language and cognition

Making propositions—i.e., knowing, judging, and having faith—can be improved by clarifying the ideas we join or separate. This clarification enhances our knowledge, for we can be certain about agreement and disagreement only where the ideas they relate are clear to us. It also enhances judgment and faith, for it shows us more precisely what it is we judge to be probable and believe to be true. The clarification of the ideas in mental propositions is furthered by a clarification in our language. Every mental proposition has or may have a verbal counterpart that expresses it, and clarifying this verbal proposition also clarifies the mental. In order to understand this view, we must say something briefly about language.

Words, Locke contends, are of two kinds. Those of the first kind name ideas in the mind of the person who uses them.[107] Of these, some name ideas of substances.[108] The word "Bossie," for example, names the idea of a particular cow; and this idea, as we have seen, represents Bossie herself. Other words name general ideas.[109] The word "cow," for example, names not the idea of Bossie, but the idea that represents all the cows with which we have been acquainted. This latter idea is a complex of the ideas of those particular cows, from which we have abstracted all those elements which differ from one particular idea to another, e.g., ideas of their places and times, their colors, and so on. The general idea "cow," therefore, contains as a part the idea of each cow we have experienced; and since each of these represents its own cow, the complex they form

106 *Ibid.*, IV, xvi, §14.
107 *Ibid.*, III, i, §2; III, ii, §2.
108 *Ibid.*, III, iii, §5, III, iv, §2, III, vi, §42.
109 *Ibid.*, III, iii, §6.

together represents all the cows we have ever known. So for all general ideas except for those of ethics and mathematics. These will be discussed later. Words of the first kind name either particular ideas or general ones.

Words of the second kind name nothing; rather, they show one or other of three kinds of activities going on in our minds when we make propositions. Sometimes they "signify the connexion that the mind gives to ideas . . . one with another."[110] The "is" in "Bossie is a cow" shows our joining the ideas of Bossie and of a cow. Secondly, they show the posture of our mind with respect to the proposition it makes.[111] The "is" in the verbal proposition above may show the belief that the ideas we connect agree with each other. Thirdly, they show in verbal discourse how we connect whole mental propositions.[112] Such words are conjunctions like "and" and "but." This entire class of words Locke calls "particles."

Locke says nothing about the clarification of particles, but words of the first kind may be made clear by discovering what ideas they name. Simple words must be treated differently from complex ones. The former we make clear to ourselves either by acquiring, through sensation or reflection, the simple ideas they name and realizing that they do name them, or if we have already acquired the ideas, by discovering what words signify them. Thus the word "indigo" is made clear by looking at something with that color and realizing that the name names the color; or if we have experienced indigo before under some other name, by realizing that "indigo" is a synonym for that other word. The meaning of simple words is clarified either by showing their ideas or by the help of synonyms.[113]

Words that name complex ideas are made clear by definition.[114] This is the activity of providing other words that name the simple ideas composing the complex one named by the word defined. We should notice that proper names and general names name complex ideas, and that clarifying them consists in defining them at least, although it may consist in more. We should also notice that success in defining presupposes clarity as to the simple words employed. Both "Bossie" and "cow" name complex ideas; and understanding them clearly requires understanding the simple words like "here," "there," "red," "white," and "moo" involved in their definitions.

It is obvious that getting clear about the ideas that are the parts of our mental propositions helps to clarify the latter. But why is it necessary, in order to accomplish this purpose, to make an excursion into words? Locke's point seems to be that something other than the ideas themselves

---

[110] *Ibid.*, III, vii, §1.
[111] *Ibid.*, III, vii, §3.
[112] *Ibid.*, III, vii, §§1, 5.
[113] *Ibid.*, III, xi, §14.
[114] *Ibid.*, III, xi, §§15, 19, 24.

is required to hold them clearly before our minds.[115] Ideas are ethereal and fugitive. Words whose use is clear serve to fix them and to fence them off from one another. The clarification of words captures the ideas they name and reveals them clearly to us. Verbal clarity causes mental clarity, and thus improves cognition.

Our own verbal propositions record our mental propositions because the words in them name our own ideas and show our own activities. But about our verbal propositions we make two important suppositions.[116] We suppose that other people who speak our language use the same words in the same ways with respect to their own ideas and mental activities, and we suppose that every verbal proposition whose ideas represent external things refer to a group of them related to each other in a way like the agreement or disagreement between their ideas. Unless the first supposition were true, there could be no communication by language; and unless the second were true, we could not talk about the world outside our minds. Locke insists, nonetheless, that there are *suppositions* for the use of language—not *parts* of its use—and that what words are properly used to stand for or to show is always something in our own minds.

Epistemology and education

Let us ask, now, for the bearing of Locke's epistemology upon his educational theory. The latter consists of statements concerning the nature of human beings, the family, the school, and society, and of others concerning the ways in which gentlemen and working people should be trained in order to realize the general welfare. This includes the happiness of each person sometimes limited, however, by that of others. Subordinate to it is the personal happiness as well as the social usefulness of the gentleman.

What is the bearing of Locke's epistemology on his views concerning the training of gentlemen? It seems to be threefold. It provides a way of justifying the objective of their moral training, an illumination of the objective of their intellectual training, and a part of the method for both.

The immediate objective of moral training is the establishment of habits which, when activated, exercise themselves in acts of virtue, wisdom, and good breeding. In order to foster such habits, it is obviously useful to know that the actions that manifest them are genuinely right. Locke's epistemology assures us that we can be certain on this score. It is possible, for example, to demonstrate that the ideas of truth-telling and of rightness agree, and that those of cruelty and of rightness disagree. Moral propositions are capable of demonstration even though no one

---

115 *Ibid.,* IV, xɪɪ, §14.
116 *Ibid.,* III, ɪɪ, §§4, 5.

has yet provided such a demonstration, and this possibility shows how the objectives of the moral training of the gentleman can be justified.

The immediate objective of intellectual training is the establishment in the pupil of the love of knowledge. This love is a desire that realizes itself in actually knowing when the occasion arises. It is the habit of knowing. But a habit is a power of doing something acquired by doing that thing several times; and it is clear that the love of knowledge cannot be acquired unless one has, on some occasions, actually come to know something. Locke's view concerning actual knowledge shows us what ought to be furthered in the student's mind in order that he should acquire an habitual love of knowledge; and his view concerning habitual knowledge shows us what that love consists in. This is an illumination of the objective of intellectual training, and it has a practical value. Judgment, revelation, faith, superstition, and error—all these make claim to being knowledge; and one who sees with clarity what knowing consists in will not mistake the spurious for the genuine claimant.

The methods of both moral and intellectual training seem to owe something to Locke's theory of knowledge. The latter, first, tells us that all ideas are simple or complex, that the simple ones must originate in sensation or reflection, and that all cognition depends upon perceiving relations that are relations of agreement or disagreement between the ideas. Locke argues that examples of moral action and real objects as well as representations of them, such as moral tales, globes, and maps, should be employed in moral and intellectual training. The reason seems to be that in this way those simple ideas out of which habits and thoughts may be constructed are provided for the student in sensation and reflection. Secondly, Locke recommends, as we have seen, that reasoning be used with children; and by "reasoning" he means, at least, the use of language. This recommendation seems to amount to the assertion that as one should clarify his own ideas by clarifying his words, so the teacher should establish as well as clarify ideas in the mind of the student by the procedure of definition. Moreover, thirdly, he recommends that the student be brought to knowing things as well as to judging them upon evidence by the teacher's making clear to him what he knows already by intuition, and by proceeding "to that which lies next, and is coherent to it, and so on to what he aims at, by the simplest and most uncompounded parts he can divide the matter into." [117] The methods of cognition, intuition and demonstration for knowing, and finding evidence for judgment Locke uses as if they also were methods of instruction.

The training of the poor is designed to make them thrifty and economically independent members of the community. Locke says nothing by way of justifying this objective. Presumably, however, he would argue

[117] *Thoughts,* §195.

that a life of independent respectability for working people is their part in the general welfare, and something that the gentleman will assure from his position of political power.

Locke's theory of knowledge gives a way of justifying the moral objective of the gentleman's training; certain habitual actions are demonstrably right. It provides an analysis of knowledge, judgment, and faith, and consequently, of the objective of intellectual training. It provides a method of teaching, that of the rational use of language, and of the intuition and demonstration of truths. But while it shows that we can know what the gentleman should be made into, it cannot assure us that its methods will achieve its goal. For that they will do so is a proposition about much more than the relations of ideas of present or remembered sensible events whose agreement or disagreement can be perceived. It also cannot assure us that the well-formed gentleman will, in fact, make himself the protector of the general welfare; for his doing so is, again, something which falls beyond the extent of our certainty. Locke's strong belief that training the gentleman according to his recommendations will make him personally happy and socially useful must be, according to his own theory of knowledge, just that—a matter of judgment that pedagogical activities will have in the future the effects we have observed in the past, and of faith that God has made the world in such a way that they can be effective at all.

ETHICS

Locke's ethical reflections concern two topics: the nature and justification of propositions of morality, and the kinds of personal and social conduct which ought to occur. These two topics are quite separate in his writing; but here we shall give them a connection proper to them.

What is the nature of propositions of morality? We should remember, first, that each moral proposition, like all others, has two forms: its verbal form or sentence, and its mental form or that complex of ideas which the sentence represents. We shall be concerned primarily with mental propositions of morality.

Secondly, consider the proposition that "all men are obliged to love their neighbors." This is a proposition of morality; but as such, its moral point is not to inform us concerning the behavior of men. Each of the ideas in it, to be sure, represents something: the idea of men, the race; the idea of "obliged to love their neighbors," a certain kind of behavior. But the mental proposition, the combination of these ideas, does not profess to inform us of anything true or false about men. We accept it quite independently of the way in which they actually deal with one another. Indeed, it would be true even if there were no men at all. A proposition of morality is one which does not inform us as to the *de facto* condition of whatever its ideas may represent.[118]

Thirdly, a proposition of morality is one whose subject is a general idea, and whose predicate is altogether different from its subject. The idea of men is a general idea, and it is clearly altogether different from the idea "obliged to love their neighbors." When we join them by the activity that is exhibited by the verb "to be" we form the proposition we have been considering. "All men are obliged to love their neighbors" is our combination of a general idea with another totally different from it. All propositions of morality are of this kind; one is concerned with the idea of a particular thing.[119] We should notice that the ideas joined in moral propositions, barring some mistake in making them, agree with one another, i.e., are necessarily connected.[120]

Fourthly, the propositions of morality express rules for the guidance of life. A rule says what we ought to do in certain circumstances. "All drivers are obliged to stop at red lights" says what drivers ought to do in the circumstances of the road. In the same way, "all men are obliged to love their neighbors" says how men ought to act in the circumstance of having neighbors. So it is for all propositions of morality.[121]

But, fifthly, the propositions of morality are not merely rules for the guidance of life; each contains, as well, the command that its rule be obeyed. A command is an order given by someone to someone else, and its force lies in the power of the one who issues the command to compel obedience. This compulsion depends upon the reward attached to obedience, and the punishment attached to disobedience. A command that could not be enforced by reward and punishment would not be a command; at best, it would be merely a suggestion. Reward consists in the happiness or pleasure given to obedience by the commander, not in the naturally pleasant consequences of obedience; punishment similarly consists in the pain or unhappiness given to disobedience by the commander, not in the misfortune that may naturally follow upon disobedience. "All men are obliged to love their neighbors" says not merely what men ought to do in certain circumstances; it commands them to do it with the reward of happiness and the punishment of unhappiness. So it is for all propositions of morality. What distinguishes them from all other propositions is that each commands that its rule of conduct be obeyed.[122] Moral propositions thus are laws.

Moral laws are of three kinds: natural, civil, and customary. Natu-

---

118 *Essay*, III, xi, §§16–17; IV, xii, §8.
119 *Ibid.*, III, xi, §18.
120 For the sake of brevity, we disregard negative propositions, i.e., those like "all men are obliged not to murder each other," in which the ideas necessarily disagree.
121 *Ibid.*, II, xxviii, §4.
122 *Ibid.*, II, xxviii, §5.

ral laws are the rules obedience to which is commanded by God; they are summarized in the proposition that all men are obliged to respect one another's property, i.e., not to encroach, except by consent, upon the life, liberties, and legitimate possessions of others. Civil laws are the rules enacted by governments in civil societies to assure the impartial enforcement of natural laws. Customary rules govern conduct that falls in the jurisdiction neither of natural nor of civil law. They express group habits of approval and disapproval.[123]

There are conflicting propositions that appear to embody laws of these three kinds. Customary rules differ from one sector of society to another; opposing civil laws are decreed from one time to another or even at the same time by different parts of a government; and opposing claims may be advanced as to God's intent concerning property and encroachment upon it. How can we know which claimant is the legitimate moral rule? How can we know what command to follow? What is the true law? This is the question of justification.

According to Locke, to justify a law is to show that it is true, i.e., to come actually, and therefore habitually, to know it. To know a moral rule is not to perceive its agreement with human behavior; it is to perceive a necessary connection (or separation in the case of negative propositions) between the ideas that compose it. This we accomplish either by intuition or by demonstration. Intuition is having two ideas perfectly clearly before our minds; entertaining them in this way makes their necessary relations unmistakably evident to us. In this way we perceive that three is necessarily related to two by the relation "greater than." Some propositions contain ideas whose necessary relations are perceived, but not perceived by intuition. They are ideas whose connections can be discovered by interposing others between them. They are known by demonstration. Thus, for someone who is backward we might demonstrate that three is greater than two. Three equals two plus one, and two plus one is greater than two; therefore, three is greater than two. Here, we have interposed the idea, "two plus one" between three and two, and have demonstrated that three is greater than two.

Locke holds that although it has not been worked out, there is a deductive system of moral rules, and that being in this system makes a rule a moral rule, while exclusion from it nullifies its moral force. By intuition we can perceive what rules God commands us to obey. Entertaining the idea of God and the idea of man—the idea of an omniscient, omnipotent, benevolent being, and the idea of a finitely intelligent, voluntary, free, imperfect creature of that being—enables us to perceive a necessary relation between them, namely, the connection expressed in the proposition that man is obliged to obey God. By further investigation

---

[123] *Ibid.,* II, xxviii, §§7, 11. Also *Second Treatise,* ii, §6; vii, §87.

of the idea of God, one can discover his intentions toward the individuals he has created, and toward the ways in which they should deal with one another. The success of such investigation is the discovery of natural law. Civil laws are no more than specific ways, variant from one set of circumstances to another, in which natural laws are embodied. Analogously, customary laws are also ancillary to the fulfillment of natural and civil laws. Locke suggests that from an intuition of the relation between the idea of God and the idea of man, one can demonstrate what rules are natural for mankind, from these what rules ought to be enacted by governments, and from both, what parts of customary codes are legitimate.[124]

So much for the nature and justification of the propositions of morality. From our discussion of these topics, Locke's understanding of one of the chief terms of ethics becomes clear. To say that one ought to do something is to express a proposition embodying a universal rule which commands a kind of conduct. That "one ought to love his neighbors" means that conduct of this kind is commanded. To say "one does what he ought to do" means that his conduct does in fact conform to the rule that commands it. Obligation is conformity to moral law.

Let us ask, now, what kinds of conduct persons and societies ought to engage in. Consider, first, persons living in a state of nature, i.e., apart from government. Here, there can be no civil law; and consequently, disregarding custom, the only moral laws governing conduct are natural. These are summed up in the rule ordained by God that each person should refrain from infringing upon the life, liberty, and legitimate possessions of others, i.e., their property. It is right or obligatory that men should behave in this way. Each is the creature and therefore the property of God; and as such, God has exclusive control over each. He has made each person free and equal to all others, and delegated His control to each man to be exercised at His pleasure, i.e., for the time God has assigned him for life in this world. Consequently, it is a violation of God's property right to infringe upon the life, liberty, and estate of others. One's right to control his own life, liberty, and estate is inalienable from him because it is a part of his being a creature of God; and that one possesses this right is the view that respect for others is the obligation of natural law.[125] Apart from government each man ought to establish property by controlling his own destiny and creating usable commodities (his private possessions) out of the common store of materials which God provides; this is to say that each man has the natural right to prevent others from controlling his life, liberty, and estate. This natural right presupposes natural liberty of action, i.e., each man's ability, having made a decision concerning action, to put that decision into effect.

---

124 *Essay,* II, xxviii, §19; III, xi, §16; IV, iv, §7; IV, iv, §8; IV, vii, §8; iv, xiii, §3.
125 *Second Treatise,* ii, §6; iv, §23.

In the state of nature, however, it is impossible for each person always to know how he ought to act. The discovery of natural laws requires the correct exercise of acute reason, and most men are not capable of such reflection. Conflicting claims to property arise; and as we have seen, obedience to natural law can be assured only where there is civil law that embodies the natural. In order to avoid conflict, political society is instituted. What kinds of conduct ought the governments of such societies to engage in?

First, no group can legitimately exercise the powers of government unless each of those whom it would govern consents to its control. Natural rights include the right to punish those who interfere with one's property, even by death. Discovering the difficulties of the state of nature, men delegate this right of punishment to others; and the latter, then possessing political power, constitute government. Since the rights whose exercise it would regulate are inalienable, it cannot control those who have not consented to such intervention. Governments ought to exercise their power only over those who have agreed to it.[126]

Secondly, the laws and other actions of government should always be approved by a majority of the citizens. Each person has contracted with the others to set up a community and government by delegating his right of punishment; but where the majority disapproves an action the community and its governments each would be dissolved if the action were carried out. The disapproval is the withdrawal of the delegated right of punishment. This withdrawal on the part of the majority leaves a lesser right of punishment in the hands of what would be the community and its government. This lesser power amounts to the incapacity of both to exercise political power and their consequent destruction. Locke does not assert that democracy is the only legitimate form of government, but his insistence that the majority ought to approve governmental action gives to all legitimate governments this democratic feature.[127]

Thirdly, the laws and other actions of government should always be designed to make for the general welfare. This purpose, however, restricts rather than extends the scope of government. Without government control, men come very close to achieving the public good. Their labor converts natural materials into usable property; the device of money enables the distribution of these economic goals; and their uncontrolled interests come close to realizing themselves in the general happiness. They fail to achieve it, independently of government, only because of conflict over property rights. The laws and other actions of government should preclude this conflict; but any more governmental activity could only

---

[126] *Ibid.*, II, §15; VIII, §§95–96.
[127] *Ibid.*, VIII, §96; X, §132.

lessen the public good. In the state of nature, the exercise of natural liberty goes a long way toward happiness; and the freedom that government assures to men ought to be only as much less than natural liberty as is required to avoid conflict.[128]

By reference to obligation and to the kinds of things men ought to do, Locke determines the nature of moral good and the things that exhibit it. The word "good" means pleasant or productive of pleasure; and in this sense, a great many things are good. But the phrase "morally good" means something much more restricted. A morally good life, as such, is not one full of pleasures; rather, it is one in which there is that pleasure which is the reward attached to obedience to moral law. One need not obey such laws; his natural liberty as well as his social freedom is his ability to disobey them. But his life will be morally good if he does, since he will enjoy the rewards of moral obedience. Moreover, it is possible that men are immortal, and consequently, that an immortal bliss is given as reward to those who obey God's law. It is prudent to act as one ought since acting in this way assures the reward in this life of obedience to civil law, and infinite happiness if there be an immortal existence.[129]

We should notice that Locke does not argue that a morally good life, one of genuine happiness, is necessarily one of obedience to civil law. Governments do not always act upon the law of God; consequently, obedience to their decrees is not always a guarantee of genuine happiness. Indeed, it is sometimes wrong to obey their laws; and sometimes, therefore, immoral to enjoy their rewards. In such cases, revolution is justified. Locke applied this ethical doctrine to the Glorious Revolution, with which he had some connection.

Locke's ethical theory presupposes the existence of God; and in the *Essay*, Book IV, Chapter x, we find an argument for it. It is an important chapter. The entire system rests upon the validity of natural law, and this law consists in the rules God commands us to obey. But for the sake of brevity, I have not discussed it.

Ethics and education

Locke's ethical reflection bears upon his educational theory in two very different ways. First, it enables him to discover and justify moral rules in education not included in the system of general moral propositions. Secondly, it shows how the goal and subordinate objectives of education are justified.

First, Locke holds that there is a valid moral rule governing the relations between parents and children. It is the duty of parents to educate their children and the right of children to be educated by them. It is the

---

128 *Ibid.,* ix, §§124–26, 131.
129 *Essays,* II, xxviii, §5; II, xxi, §70.

duty of children to obey their parents and the right of parents to be obeyed and respected by their children. These duties and rights attach also to those who play the roles of parents and children, e.g., to tutors and foster children. These duties and rights may be summarized in the following moral rule: Parents ought to educate their children and children ought to obey their parents.

Locke discovers and justifies this rule by considering four ideas: the ideas of God, of man, of parents, and of children. He holds, as we have seen, that considering the first two ideas carefully shows us by intuition that man, the creature of God, ought to obey His commands. This consideration also assures Locks that man is God's property. A similar examination of the ideas of parents and of children reveals maturity of understanding and of will on the part of the former, and a lack of both on the part of children, but it does not show that children are the property of their parents despite this lack. Since both parents and children are men, and since men are God's property, parents and children are as well.

By examining these four ideas Locke arrives at the following demonstration of the rule given above. All men ought to obey God, and God commands that his property be respected. Children are God's property. Therefore children should be respected. The way to respect God's property is, where appropriate, to enable it to achieve its purpose. The purpose of man is to live according to natural law, and this is achieved only by an informed understanding and will. Children lack both and parents possess both. Therefore parents ought to educate their children, and children, in order to receive education, ought to obey parents.[130]

The effect of this moral rule is to locate responsibility for education. It lies with the parents or in tutors. Locke does not discuss with any care the education of the poor. He says, however, that it is the responsibility of the community to provide a very elementary education for them; and he would probably hold that where parents cannot educate their children, the duty to do so devolves upon the community.

The system of general propositions of morality justifies the goal objective of education. This is the general happiness which is a moral good, and it ought to be brought into existence because natural law of which it is the reward ought to be obeyed. The subordinate objective of education, the moral and intellectual training of gentlemen, is justified on the ground that gentlemen, thus trained, will conduct public affairs in such a way as to embody natural in civil law, thus assuring to all citizens the possibility of obeying legitimate regulations. The habits of good character instilled in gentlemen assure the possibility of correct moral decisions in legislation and civil administration. Their intellectual training, including a study of the jurists who write on natural law, will reveal

---

[130] *Second Treatise*, VI, §§55–59, 63–69.

the standards by which the moral excellence or deficiency of civil law should be estimated.

According to Locke, the propositions of morality, including those concerning the duties and rights of parents and children, are rules, obedience to which is commanded ultimately by God. They do not describe what men actually do. Their truth is not a truth about facts. Rather, it is a necessary connection discovered by intuition or demonstration between the ideas that compose them. This truth makes the propositions of morality appear in Locke's philosophy as a model after which human life in its personal and social dimensions should be fashioned. These dimensions intersect in that formation of physical, moral, and intellectual habits in the young which constitutes education; and while Locke's epistemological reflection helps to elucidate the nature of education, his ethical reflection provides a locus for and a justification of its objective, and a considerable part of its curriculum.

A Guide to Selections from *Some Thoughts Concerning Education*

In early sections omitted here, Locke makes various recommendations designed to establish a sturdy health in the body. This is the regime of 'hardening' for which he is famous; and of which the most celebrated component, perhaps, is his recommendation that children be made accustomed to wet feet in order that they should not be subject to the catarrh.

In Section 31, Locke argues that the excellence of the body, its vigor and strength, is its service to the mind, and that the virtue of the mind consists in its disposition to consent only to what is suitable for a rational creature. In Section 33, he argues that this virtue—this disposition to do only what is reasonable—requires the ability to thwart one's own desires since they are often contrary to reason.

Locke argues in Sections 38, 56, 57, and 58 that the following measures will bring about the ability to act reasonably: withholding from a child what he cries for, publicly approving his doing what he ought, and publicly disapproving his lapse. In Sections 73 and 74, he insists that teaching should occur only when the child is favorably disposed toward learning the subject matter; if he is not, the effort is useless. In Sections 81 and 102, treating the child as reasonably as possible in all circumstances is recommended; and observing him when he is acting spontaneously, in order to find out how to treat him so.

In Sections 103-106, Locke holds that since children naturally desire to dominate others and to possess things, they should be given only what they need. Still, their desire for liberty of expression should not be impeded; and (Section 108) their curiosity and need for recreation should always be satisfied. In Section 109, Locke insists that domineering children should always be made to fail in their efforts at aggrandizement; and in Section 126, he asserts that laziness can be cured by making work a condition for the child's getting what he wants.

In Section 195 Locke holds that learning any subject is an easy matter if the proper method is pursued. The student should be taught the principles of right inference from particular to general propositions and from general to particular propositions. He should always be taught to proceed from what he knows to what he does not know by the simplest and easiest steps.

Locke says at the end (Section 217) that the reader should remember that each child is unique, and use his own judgment in deciding how to apply the principles that have been set forth.

SELECTIONS FROM

Some Thoughts Concerning Education*

——◄●►——

MIND

S. 31 Due Care being had to keep the Body in Strength and Vigour, so that it may be able to obey and execute the Orders of the Mind; the next and principal Business is, to set the *Mind* right, that on all Occasions it may be dispos'd to consent to nothing but what may be suitable to the Dignity and Excellency of a rational Creature. . . .

S. 33 As the Strength of the Body lies chiefly in being able to endure Hardships, so also does that of the Mind. And the great Principle and Foundation of all Virtue and Worth is plac'd in this: That a Man is able to *deny himself* his own Desires, cross his Inclinations, and purely follow what Reason directs as best, tho' the Appetite lean the other Way. . . .

CRAVING

S. 38 . . . If therefore I might be heard, I would advise, that, contrary to the ordinary Way, Children should be us'd to submit their Desires, and go without their Longings, even *from their very Cradles*. The first Thing they should learn to know, should be, that they were not to have any Thing because it pleas'd them, but because it was thought fit for them. If

---

* The following passages are taken from *Locke on Education,* edited by R. H. Quick, M.A., Cambridge at the University Press, 1913, London. All footnotes omitted.

Things suitable to their Wants were supply'd to them, so that they were never suffer'd to have what they once cry'd for, they would learn to be content without it. . . .

REPUTATION

S. 56 . . . *Esteem* and *Disgrace* are, of all others, the most powerful Incentives to the Mind, when once it is brought to relish them. If you can once get into Children a Love of Credit, and an Apprehension of Shame and Disgrace, you have put into 'em the true Principle, which will constantly work and incline them to the right. But it will be ask'd, How shall this be done?

PRAISE

S. 57   First, Children (earlier perhaps than we think) are very sensible of *Praise* and Commendation. They find a Pleasure in being esteem'd and valu'd, especially by their Parents and those whom they depend on. If therefore the Father *caress and commend them when they do well, shew a cold and neglectful Countenance to them upon doing ill,* and this accompany'd by a like Carriage of the Mother and all others that are about them, it will, in a little Time, make them sensible of the Difference; . . .

S. 58   But *Secondly,* To make the Sense of *Esteem* or *Disgrace* sink the deeper, and be of the more Weight, *other agreeable or disagreeable Things should constantly accompany these different States;* not as particular Rewards and Punishments of this or that particular Action, but as necessarily belonging to, and constantly attending one, who by his Carriage has brought himself into a State of Disgrace or Commendation. By which Way of treating them, Children may as much as possible be brought to conceive, that those that are commended, and in Esteem for doing well, will necessarily be belov'd and cherish'd by every Body, and have all other good Things as a Consequence of it; and on the other Side, when any one by Miscarriage falls into Disesteem, and cares not to preserve his Credit, he will unavoidably fall under Neglect and Contempt; and in that State, the Want of whatever might satisfy or delight him will follow. In this Way the Objects of their Desires are made assisting to Virtue, when a settled Experience from the Beginning teaches Children that the Things they delight in, belong to, and are to be enjoy'd by those only who are in a State of Reputation. . . .

TASK

S. 73   1. None of the Things they are to learn, should ever be made a Burthen to them, or impos'd on them as a *Task.* Whatever is so propos'd, presently becomes irksome; the Mind takes an Aversion to it, though before it were a Thing of Delight or Indifferency. Let a Child but be order'd to whip his Top at a certain Time every Day, whether he has or has not a Mind to it; let this be but requir'd of him as a Duty, wherein he must spend so many Hours Morning and Afternoon, and see whether he will not soon be weary of any Play at this Rate. Is it not so with grown Men? What they do chearfully of themselves, do they not presently grow sick of, and can no more endure, as soon as they find it is expected of them as a Duty? Children have as much a Mind to shew that they are free, that their own good Actions come from themselves, that they are absolute and independent, as any of the proudest of you grown Men, think of them as you please.

DISPOSITION

S. 74 2. As a Consequence of this, they should seldom be put about doing even those Things you have got an Inclination in them to, but when they have a Mind and *Disposition* to it. He that loves Reading, Writing, Musick, etc. finds yet in himself certain Seasons wherein those Things have no Relish to him; and if at that Time he forces himself to it, he only pothers and wearies himself to no purpose. So it is with Children. This Change of Temper should be carefully observ'd in them, and the favourable *Seasons of Aptitude and Inclination* be heedfully laid hold of: And if they are not often enough forward of themselves, a good Disposition should be talk'd into them, before they be set upon any thing. . . .

REASONING

S. 81 It will perhaps be wonder'd, that I mention *Reasoning* with Children; and yet I cannot but think that the true Way of dealing with them. They understand it as early as they do Language; and, if I mis-observe not, they love to be treated as rational Creatures, sooner than is imagin'd. 'Tis a Pride should be cherish'd in them, and, as much as can be, made the greatest Instrument to turn them by.

But when I talk of *Reasoning*, I do not intend any other but such as is suited to the Child's Capacity and Apprehension. No body can think a Boy of three or seven Years old should be argu'd with as a grown Man. Long Discourses, and Philosophical Reasonings, at best, amaze and confound, but do not instruct Children. When I say, therefore, that they must be *treated as rational Creatures,* I mean, that you should make them sensible, by the Mildness of your Carriage, and the Composure even in your Correction of them, that what you do is remarkable in you, and useful and necessary for them; and that it is not out of *Caprichio,* Passion or Fancy, that you command or forbid them any thing. This they are capable of understanding: and there is no Virtue they should be excited to, nor Fault they should be kept from, which I do not think they may be convinced of; but it must be by such *Reasons* as their Age and Understanding are capable of, and those propos'd always *in* very *few and plain Words.*

S. 102 Begin therefore betimes nicely to observe your Son's *Temper;* and that, when he is under least Restraint, in his Play, and as he thinks out of your Sight. See what are his *predominate Passions* and *prevailing Inclinations;* whether he be fierce or mild, bold or bashful, compassionate or cruel, open or reserv'd, etc. For as these are different in him, so are your Methods to be different, and your Authority must hence take Measures to apply itself different Ways to him. These *native Propensities,* these Prevalencies of Constitution, are not to be cur'd by Rules, or a direct Contest, especially those of them that are the humbler and meaner Sort, which proceed from Fear, and Lowness of Spirit; though with Art they may be much mended, and turn'd to good Purposes. But this, be sure, after all is done, the Byass will always hang on that Side that Nature first plac'd it: And if you carefully observe the Characters of his Mind, now in the first Scenes of his Life, you will ever after be able to judge which Way his Thoughts lean, and what he aims at even hereafter, when, as he grows up, the Plot thickens, and he puts on several Shapes to act it.

DOMINION

S. 103 I told you before, that Children love *Liberty;* and therefore they should be brought to do the Things are fit for them, without feeling any Restraint laid upon them. I now tell you, they love something more; and that is *Dominion:* And this is the first Original of most vicious Habits, that are ordinary and natural. This Love of *Power* and Dominion shrews itself very early, and that in these two Things.

S. 104 1. We see children, as soon almost as they are born (I am sure long before they can speak) cry, grow peevish, sullen, and out of Humour, for nothing but to have their *Wills.* They would have their Desires submitted to by others; they contend for a ready Compliance from all about them, especially from those that stand near or beneath them in Age or Degree, as soon as they come to consider others with those Distinctions.

S. 105 Another Thing wherein they shew their Love of Dominion, is their Desire to have Things to be theirs: They would have *Propriety* and Possession, pleasing themselves with the Power which that seems to give, and the Right they thereby have, to dispose of them as they please. He that has not observ'd these two Humours working very betimes in Children, has taken little Notice of their Actions: And he who thinks that these two Roots of almost all the Injustice and Contention that so disturb human Life, are not early to be weeded out, and contrary Habits introduc'd, neglects the proper Season to lay the Foundations of a good and worthy Man. To do this, I imagine these following Things may somewhat conduce.

CRAVING

S. 106 . . . It is fit that they should have Liberty to declare their Wants to their Parents, and that with all Tenderness they should be hearken'd to, and supply'd, at least whilst they are very little. But 'tis one Thing to

say, I am hungry, another to say, I would have Roast-Meat. Having de-
clar'd their Wants, their natural Wants, the Pain they feel from Hunger,
Thirst, Cold, or any other Necessity of Nature, 'tis the Duty of their
Parents and those about them to believe them: But Children must leave it
to the Choice and Ordering of their Parents, what they think properest
for them, and how much; and must not be permitted to chuse for themselves, and say, I would have Wine, or White-bread; the very naming of
it should make them lose it. . . .

S. 108 . . . they should always be heard, and fairly and kindly answer'd,
when they ask after any Thing they would *know,* and desire to be inform'd about. *Curiosity* should be as carefully *cherish'd* in Children, as
other Appetites suppress'd.

RECREATION

However strict an Hand is to be kept upon all Desires of Fancy,
yet there is one Case wherein Fancy must be permitted to speak, and be
hearken'd to also. *Recreation* is as necessary as Labour or Food. But because there can be no *Recreation* without Delight, which depends not
always on Reason, but oftner on Fancy, it must be permitted Children
not only to divert themselves, but to do it after their own Fashion, provided it be innocently, and without Prejudice to their Health; and therefore in this Case they should not be deny'd, if they proposed any particular kind of *Recreation.* . . .

S. 109 2. Children who live together, often strive for Mastery, whose
Wills carry it over the rest: Whoever begins the *Contest,* should be sure to
be cross'd in it. But not only that, but they should be taught to have all
the *Deference, Complaisance,* and *Civility* one for the other imaginable.
This, when they see it procures them Respect, Love and Esteem, and
that they lose no Superiority by it, they will take more Pleasure in, than
in insolent Domineering; for so plainly is the other. . . .

S. 126 If some Defect in his Constitution has cast a Damp on his Mind,
and he be naturally listless and dreaming, this unpromising Disposition
is none of the easiest to be dealt with, because, generally carrying with it
an Unconcernedness for the future, it wants the two great Springs of
Action, *Foresight* and *Desire;* which how to plant and increase, where
Nature has given a cold and contrary Temper, will be the Question. As
soon as you are satisfied that this is the Case, you must carefully enquire
whether there be nothing he delights in: Inform your self what it is he
is most pleased with; and if you can find any particular Tendency his
Mind hath, increase it all you can, and make use of that to set him on
Work, and to excite his Industry. If he loves Praise, or Play, or fine
Clothes, etc. or, on the other Side, dreads Pain, Disgrace, or your Displeasure, etc. whatever it be that he loves most, except it be Sloth (for that
will never set him on Work) let that be made use of to quicken him, and

make him bestir himself. For in this *listless Temper,* you are not to fear an Excess of Appetite (as in all other Cases) by cherishing it. 'Tis that which you want, and therefore must labour to raise and increase; for where there is no Desire, there will be no Industry. . . .

S. 195 Order and Constancy are said to make the great Difference between one Man and another: This I am sure, nothing so much clears a Learner's Way, helps him so much on in it, and makes him go so easy and so far in any Enquiry, as a good *Method.* His Governor should take Pains to make him sensible of this, accustom him to Order, and teach him *Method* in all the Applications of his Thoughts; shew him wherein it lies, and the Advantages of it; acquaint him with the several sorts of it, either from General to Particulars, or from Particulars to what is more general; exercise him in both of them, and make him see in what Cases each different *Method* is most proper, and to what Ends it best serves.

In History the Order of Time should govern, in Philosophical Enquiries that of Nature, which in all Progression is to go from the Place one is then in, to that which joins and lies next to it; and so it is in the Mind, from the Knowledge it stands possessed of already, to that which lies next, and is coherent to it, and so on to what it aims at, by the simplest and most uncompounded Parts it can divide the Matter into. To this Purpose, it will be of great Use to his Pupil to accustom him to distinguish well, that is, to have distinct Notions, whereever the mind can find any real Difference; but as carefully to avoid Distinctions in Terms, where he has not distinct and different clear Ideas. . . .

CONCLUSION

S. 217 Tho' I am now come to a Conclusion of what obvious Remarks have suggested to me concerning Education, I would not have it thought that I look on it as a just Treatise on this Subject. There are a thousand other Things that may need Consideration; especially if one should take in the various Tempers, different Inclinations, and particular Defaults, that are to be found in Children, and prescribe proper Remedies. The Variety is so great that it would require a Volume; nor would that reach it. Each Man's Mind has some Peculiarity, as well as his Face, that distinguishes him from all others; and there are possibly scarce two Children who can be conducted by exactly the same Method. Besides that, I think a Prince, a Nobleman, and an ordinary Gentleman's Son, should have different Ways of Breeding. But having had here only some general Views in Reference to the main End and Aims in Education, and those designed for a Gentleman's Son, whom, being then very little, I considered only as white Paper, or Wax, to be moulded and fashioned as one pleases; I have touched little more than those Heads which I judged necessary for the Breeding of a young Gentleman of his Condition in general; and have now published these my occasional Thoughts with this Hope, that tho' this be far from being a complete Treatise on this Subject, or such as that every one may find what will just fit his Child in it, yet it may give some small Light to those, whose Concern for their dear little Ones makes them so irregularly bold, that they dare venture to consult their own Reason in the Education of their Children, rather than wholly to rely upon old Custom.

A Guide to Selections from *An Essay Concerning Human Understanding*

In the passages taken from Book I, Locke defines the key term "idea," analyzes the ideas of good and evil into those of pleasure and pain, and explains desire as the idea of an absent good.

In the passages selected from Book II, Locke discusses the idea of power. He uses it to explain the idea of will. He holds that liberty or freedom consists in the comparison of desires to see which one leads to the best consequences, and asserts that it belongs to the person rather than to his will. He considers the relation between a man's desire for the general good, for his own happiness, and the requirement of obedience to moral rules.

He holds that right or obligatory actions are those that conform to these rules, and that they instruct one in securing good and evil, reward and punishment. There are different sanctions for obeying them. For some the sanction is God; for others civil society; and for others still, public opinion. The proper objective of conduct appears, thus, to possess two factors: the pleasure of consequences desired, and the rightness of obedience to rules.

In the passages from Book III, Locke describes most language in terms of sounds and marks, and the ideas they call up in our minds. Some of these ideas are general, and others particular. He explains general ideas as developed by abstraction from particular ideas. He argues that words refer to realities, as well as to the ideas they call up in our minds. But he says that there are some words that neither call up ideas nor refer to realities. Particles like 'but' express mental actions and do not refer to things. They express the mental action of joining words and propositions.

In the passages from Book IV, Locke argues that knowledge is about our ideas, that it consists in perceiving their agreement or disagreement, and that it is either actual or habitual. He holds that although it is only about ideas, we are entitled to apply it to things as well, in those cases in which our ideas agree with things. He discusses the relevance of mathematical and moral knowledge to reality. He explains the nature of truth, of propositions to which truth belongs, and argues that we can perceive the truth of universal propositions about our abstract ideas, but not that of propositions about substances. He adds that we are not warranted in generalizing from any particular propositions even though we know them to be true.

He argues that rational procedures may give us general truths in mathematics and in morals, that we can know very little by empirical procedures, and that the only substances about which we can be certain are God and ourselves. He concludes, however, that this is knowledge enough.

SELECTIONS FROM

An Essay Concerning Human Understanding

—◄◆►—

BOOK I

CHAPTER I

Introduction

S. 8   . . . I must here in the entrance beg pardon of my reader for the frequent use of the word "idea," which, I think, serves best to stand for whatsoever is the object of the understanding when a man thinks; I have used it to express whatever is meant by phantasm, notion, species, or whatever it is, which the mind can be employed about in thinking; and I could not avoid frequently using it.

I presume it will be easily granted me, that there are such ideas in men's minds; every one is conscious of them in himself, and men's words and actions will satisfy him that they are in others. . . .

CHAPTER XX

Of Modes of Pleasure and Pain

S. 1   Amongst the sample ideas which we receive both from sensation and reflection, pain and pleasure are two very considerable ones. For as in the body, there is sensation barely in itself, or accompanied with pain or pleasure; so the thought, or perception of the mind is simply so, or else accompanied also with pleasure or pain, delight or trouble, call it how you please.

S. 2   Things then are good or evil, only in reference to pleasure or pain. That we call good, which is apt to cause or increase pleasure, or diminish pain in us; or else to procure, or preserve, us the possession of any other good, or absence of any evil. And on the contrary, we name that evil, which is apt to produce or increase any pain, or diminish any pleasure in us; or else to procure us any evil, or deprive us of any good. By pleasure and pain, I must be understood to mean of body or mind, as they are commonly distinguished; though, in truth, they be only different constitutions of the mind, sometimes occasioned by disorder in the body, sometimes by thoughts of the mind.

S. 3   Pleasure and pain, and that which causes them, good and evil, are the hinges on which our passions turn; and if we reflect on ourselves, and observe how these, under various considerations, operate in us; what modifications or tempers of mind, what internal sensations (if I may so call them), they produce in us, we may thence form to ourselves the ideas of our passions. . . .

S. 6   The uneasiness a man finds in himself upon the absence of any thing, whose present enjoyment carries the idea of delight with it, is that we call desire, which is greater or less, as that uneasiness is more or less vehement. Where, by the by, it may perhaps be of some use to remark, that the chief, if not only spur to human industry and action, is uneasiness. For whatsoever good is proposed, if its absence carries no displeasure or pain with it; if a man be easy and content without it, there is no desire of it, nor endeavour after it; . . .

BOOK II

CHAPTER XXI

Of Power

S. 1   The mind being every day informed by the senses of the alteration of those simple ideas it observes in things without, and taking notice how one comes to an end and ceases to be, and another begins to exist, which was not before; reflecting also on what passes within itself, and observing a constant change of it, ideas, sometimes by the impression of outward objects on the senses, and sometimes by the determination of its own choice; and concluding from what it has so constantly observed to have been, that the like changes will for the future be made in the same things, by like agents, and by the like ways; considers in one thing the possibility of having any of its simple ideas changed, and in another the possibility of making that change; and so comes by that idea which we call power. Thus we say, fire has a power to melt gold, i.e. to destroy the consistency of its insensible parts, and consequently its hardness, and make it fluid;

and gold has a power to be melted; that the sun has a power to blanch wax, and wax has a power to be blanched by the sun, whereby the yellowness is destroyed, and whiteness made to exist in its room. In which, and the like cases, the power we consider is in reference to the change of perceivable ideas: for we cannot observe any alteration to be made in, or operation upon, any thing, but by the observable change of its sensible ideas; nor conceive any alteration to be made, but by conceiving a change of some of its ideas. . . .

S. 5 This at least I think evident, that we find in ourselves a power to begin or forbear, continue or end, several actions of our minds, and motions of our bodies, barely by a thought or preference of the mind ordering, or, as it were, commanding the doing or not doing, such or such a particular action. This power which the mind has thus to order the consideration of any idea, or the forbearing to consider it; or to prefer the motion of any part of the body to its rest, and *vice versa*, in any particular instance, is that which we call the will. The actual exercise of that power, by directing any particular action, or its forbearance, is that which we call volition or willing. The forbearance of that action, consequent to such order or command of the mind, is called voluntary. And whatsoever action is performed without such a thought of the mind, is called involuntary. The power of perception is that which we call the understanding. . . .

S. 8 All the actions that we have any idea of, reducing themselves, as has been said, to these two, viz., thinking and motion; so far as a man has power to think, or not to think; to move, or not to move, according to the preference or direction of his own mind; so far is a man free. Wherever any performance or forbearance are not equally in a man's power; wherever doing, or not doing, will not equally follow upon the preference of his mind directing it, there he is not free, though, perhaps, the action may be voluntary. So that the idea of liberty is the idea of a power in any agent to do, or forbear any particular action, according to the determination or thought of the mind, whereby either of them is preferred to the other; where either of them is not in the power of the agent to be produced by him, according to his volition, there he is not at liberty; that agent is under necessity. So that liberty cannot be where there is no thought, no volition, no will: but there may be thought, there may be will, there may be volition, where there is no liberty. . . .

S. 9 A tennis-ball, whether in motion by the stroke of a racket, or lying still at rest, is not, by any one, taken to be a free agent. If we inquire into the reason, we shall find it is because we conceive not a tennis-ball to think, and consequently not to have any volition, or preference of motion to rest, or *vice versa;* and, therefore, has not liberty, is not a free agent; but all its both motion and rest come under our idea of necessary, and are so called. Likewise, a man falling into the water (a bridge breaking under him,) has not herein liberty, is not a free agent. For though he has volition, though he prefers his not falling to falling; yet the forbearance of that motion not being in his power, the stop or cessation of that motion follows not upon his volition; and, therefore, therein he is not free. . . .

S. 16 It is plain then, that the will is nothing but one power or ability, and freedom another power or ability; so that to ask, whether the will has freedom? is to ask, whether one power has another power, one ability another ability? a question at first sight too grossly absurd to make a dispute, or need an answer. For who is it that sees not that powers belong only to agents, and are attributes only of substances, and not of powers themselves? so that this way of putting the question, viz. whether the will be free? is, in effect, to ask, whether the will be a substance, an agent? or at least to suppose it, since freedom can properly be attributed to nothing else. . . .

S. 31 To return them to the inquiry, What is it that determines the will in regard to our actions? And that, upon second thoughts, I am apt to imagine is not, as is generally supposed, the greater good in view; but some (and for the most part the most pressing) uneasiness a man is at present under. This is that which successively determines the will, and sets us upon those actions we perform. This uneasiness we may call, as it is, desire, which is an uneasiness of the mind, for want of some absent good. . . .

S. 35 . . . good, the greater good, though apprehended, and acknowledged to be so, does not determine the will, until our desire, raised proportionably to it, makes us uneasy in the want of it. . . .

S. 36 If we inquire into the reason of what experience makes so evident in fact, and examine why it is uneasiness alone operates on the will, and determines it in its choice, we shall find, that we being capable but of one determination of the will to one action at once, the present uneasiness that we are under does naturally determine the will, in order to that happiness which we all aim at in all our actions; forasmuch, as whilst we are under any uneasiness, we cannot apprehend ourselves happy, or in the way to it: . . .

S. 42 Happiness then in its full extent is the utmost pleasure we are capable of; and misery the utmost pain: and the lowest degree of what can be called happiness, is so much ease from all pain, and so much present pleasure, as without which any one cannot be content. Now because pleasure and pain are produced in us by the operation of certain objects, either on our minds or our bodies, and in different degrees; therefore what has an aptness to produce pleasure in us, is that we call good, and what is apt to produce pain in us, we call evil, for no other reason, but for its aptness to produce pleasure and pain in us, wherein consists our happiness and misery. Farther, though what is apt to produce any degree of pleasure be in itself good; and what is apt to produce any degree of pain, be evil; yet it often happens, that we do not call it so, when it comes in competition with a greater of its sort; because when they come in competition, the degrees also of pleasure and pain have justly a preference. So that if we will rightly estimate what we call good and evil, we shall find it lies much in comparison: for the cause of every less degree of pain, as well as every greater degree of pleasure, has the nature of good, and vice versa.

S. 43 Though this be that which is called good and evil; and all good be the proper object of desire in general; yet all good, even seen and confessed to be so, does not necessarily move every particular man's desire; but only that part, or so much of it, as is considered, and taken to make a necessary part of his happiness. All other good, however great in reality or appearance, excites not a man's desires who looks not on it to make a part of that happiness wherewith he, in his present thoughts, can satisfy himself. . . .

S. 44 This, I think, any one may observe in himself and others, that the greater visible good does not always raise men's desires in proportion to the greatness it appears, and is acknowledged to have: though every little trouble moves us, and sets us on work to get rid of it. The reason whereof is evident from the nature of our happiness and misery itself. All present pain, whatever it be, makes a part of our present misery: but all absent good does not at any time make a necessary part of our present happiness, nor the absence of it make a part of our misery: if it did, we should be constantly and infinitely miserable; there being infinite degrees of happiness, which are not in our possession. . . .

S. 45 The ordinary necessities of our lives fill a great part of them with the uneasiness of hunger, thirst, heat, cold, weariness with labour, and sleepiness, in their constant returns, etc. To which, if, besides accidental harms, we add the fantastical uneasiness (as itch after honour, power, or riches, etc.) which acquired habits by fashion, example, and education, have settled in us, and a thousand other irregular desires, which custom has made natural to us, we shall find, that a very little part of our life is so vacant from these uneasinesses, as to leave us free to the attraction of remoter absent good. . . .

S. 47 There being in us a great many uneasinesses always soliciting, and ready to determine, the will, it is natural, as I have said, that the greatest and most pressing should determine the will to the next action; and so it does for the most part, but not always. For the mind having in most cases, as is evident in experience, a power to suspend the execution and satisfaction of any of its desires, and so all, one after another, is at liberty to consider the objects of them, examine them on all sides, and weigh them with others. In this lies the liberty man has; and from the not using of it right comes all that variety of mistakes, errors, and faults which we run into in the conduct of our lives, and our endeavours after happiness, whilst we precipitate the determination of our wills, and engage too soon before due examination. . . .

S. 54 From what has been said, it is easy to give an account, how it comes to pass that though all men desire happiness, yet their wills carry them so contrarily, and, consequently, some of them to what is evil. And to this I say, that the various and contrary choices that men make in the world, do not argue that they do not all pursue good: but that the same thing is not good to every man alike. This variety of pursuit shows that every one does not place his happiness in the same thing, or choose the same way to it. Were all the concerns of man terminated in this life, why one followed study and knowledge, and another hawking and hunting; why one chose luxury and debauchery, and another sobriety and riches, would not be because every one of these did not aim at his own happiness; but because their happiness was placed in different things. . . .

CHAPTER XXVIII

Of Other Relations. . . .

S. 4 *Fourthly.* There is another sort of relation, which is the conformity or disagreement men's voluntary actions have to a rule to which they are referred, and by which they are judged of; which, I think, may be called moral relation, as being that which denominates our moral actions, and deserves well to be examined; there being no part of knowledge wherein we should be more careful to get determined ideas, and avoid, as much as may be, obscurity and confusion. Human actions, when with their various ends, objects, manners, and circumstances, they are framed into distinct complex ideas, are, as has been shown, so many mixed modes, a great part whereof have names annexed to them. Thus, supposing gratitude to be a readiness to acknowledge and return kindness received; poligamy to be the having more wives than one at once; when we frame these notions thus in our minds, we have there so many determined ideas of mixed modes. But this is not all that concerns our actions; it is not enough to have determined ideas of them, and to know what names belong to such and such combinations of ideas. We have a farther and greater concernment, and that is, to know whether such actions, so made up, are morally good or bad.

S. 5   Good and evil, as hath been shown, Book ii, chapter 20, S2, and chapter 21, S42, are nothing but pleasure or pain, or that which occasions or procures pleasure or pain to us. Moral good and evil, then, is only the conformity or disagreement of our voluntary actions to some law, whereby good or evil is drawn on us by the will and power of the law-maker: which good or evil, pleasure or pain, attending our observance or breach of the law, by the decree of the law-maker, is that we call reward and punishment.

S. 6   Of these moral rules, or laws, to which men generally refer, and by which they judge of the rectitude or pravity of their actions, there seem to me to be three sorts, with their three different enforcements, or rewards and punishments. For since it would be utterly in vain to suppose a rule set to the free actions of man, without annexing to it some enforcement of good and evil to determine his will, we must, wherever we suppose a law, suppose also some reward or punishment annexed to that law. It would be in vain for one intelligent being to set a rule to the actions of another, if he had it not in his power to reward the compliance with, and punish deviation from his rule, by some good and evil, that is not the natural product and consequence of the action itself: for that being a natural convenience, or inconvenience, would operate of itself without a law. This, if I mistake not, is the true nature of all law, properly so called.

S. 7   The laws that men generally refer their actions to, to judge of their rectitude or obliquity, seem to me to be these three: 1. The divine law. 2. The civil law. 3. The law of opinion or reputation, if I may so call it. By the relation they bear to the first of these, men judge whether their actions are sins or duties; by the second, whether they be criminal or innocent; and by the third, whether they be virtues or vices.

BOOK III

CHAPTER I

Of Words or Language in General

S. 1   God having designed man for a sociable creature, made him not only with an inclination, and under a necessity, to have fellowship with those of his own kind; but furnished him also with language, which was to be the great instrument and common tie of society. Man therefore had by nature his organs so fashioned, as to be fit to frame articulate sounds, which we call words. But this was not enough to produce language; for parrots, and several other birds, will be taught to make articulate sounds distinct enough, which yet, by no means, are capable of language.

S. 2   Besides articulate sounds, therefore, it was farther necessary that he should be able to use these sounds as signs of internal conceptions; and to make them stand as marks for the ideas within his own mind, whereby they might be made known to others, and the thoughts of men's minds be conveyed from one to another.

S. 3   But neither was this sufficient to make words so useful as they ought to be. It is not enough for the perfection of language, that sounds can be made signs of ideas, unless those signs can be so made use of, as to comprehend several particular things: for the multiplication of words would have perplexed their use, had every particular thing need of a distinct name to be signified by. To remedy this inconvenience, language had yet a farther improvement in the use of general terms, whereby one word was made to mark a multitude of particular existences: which advantageous use of sounds was obtained only by the difference of the ideas they were made signs of: those names becoming general, which are made to stand for general ideas; and those remaining particular, where the ideas they are used for are particular. . . .

S. 5   It may also lead us a little towards the original of all our notions and knowledge, if we remark, how great a dependence our words have on common sensible ideas; and how those, which are made use of to stand for actions and notions quite removed from sense, have their rise from thence, and, from obvious sensible ideas, are transferred to more abstruse significations; and made to stand for ideas that come not under the cognizance of our senses: v.g. to imagine, apprehend, comprehend, adhere, conceive, instil, disgust, disturbance, tranquility, etc. are all words taken from the operations of sensible things, and applied to certain modes of thinking. Spirit, in its primary signification, is breath: angel, a messenger: and I doubt not, but if we could trace them to their sources, we should find, in all languages, the names which stand for things that fall not under our senses, to have had their first rise from sensible ideas. . . .

CHAPTER II

Of the Signification of Words. . . .

S. 4   But though words, as they are used by men, can properly and immediately signify nothing but the ideas that are in the mind of the speaker; yet they, in their thoughts, give them a secret reference to two other things.

First, They suppose their words to be marks of the ideas in the minds also of other men, with whom they communicate: for else they should talk in vain, and could not be understood, if the sounds they applied to one idea were such as by the hearer were applied to another; which is to speak two languages. . . .

S. 5   *Secondly,* Because men would not be thought to talk barely of their own imaginations, but of things as really they are; therefore they often suppose their words to stand also for the reality of things. But this relating more particularly to substances, and their names, as perhaps the former does to simple ideas and modes, we shall speak of these two different ways of applying words more at large, when we come to treat of the names of mixed modes, and substances, in particular; though give me leave here to say, that it is a perverting the use of words, and brings unavoidable obscurity and confusion into their signification, whenever we make them stand for any thing but those ideas we have in our own minds.

CHAPTER III

Of General Terms. . . .

S. 6   The next thing to be considered, is, how general words come to be made. For since all things that exist are only particulars, how come we by general terms, or where find we those general natures they are supposed to stand for? Words become general, by being made the signs of general ideas; and ideas become general, by separating from them the circumstances of time, and place, and any other ideas that may determine them to this or that particular existence. By this way of abstraction, they are made capable of representing more individuals than one; each of which having in it a conformity to that abstract idea, is (as we call it) of that sort.

CHAPTER VII

Of Particles

S. 1   Besides words, which are names of ideas in the mind, there are a great many others that are made use of, to signify the connexion that the mind gives to ideas or propositions one with another. The mind, in communicating its thought to others, does not only need signs of the ideas it has then before it, but others also, to show or intimate some particular action of its own, at that time, relating to those ideas. This it does several ways; as, is, and is not, are the general marks of the mind, affirming or denying. But besides affirmation or negation, without which there is in words no truth or falsehood, the mind does, in declaring its sentiments to others, connect not only the parts of propositions, but whole sentences one to another, with their several relations and dependencies, to make a coherent discourse.

BOOK IV

CHAPTER I

Of Knowledge In General

S. 1 Since the mind, in all its thoughts and reasonings, hath no other immediate object but its own ideas, which it alone does or can contemplate, it is evident, that our knowledge is only conversant about them.

S. 2 Knowledge then seems to me to be nothing but the perception of the connexion and agreement, or disagreement and repugnancy, of any of our ideas. In this alone it consists. Where this perception is, there is knowledge; and where it is not, there, though we may fancy, guess, or believe, yet we always come short of knowledge. For when we know that white is not black, what do we else but perceive, that these two ideas do not agree? When we possess ourselves with the utmost security of the demonstration, that the three angles of a triangle are equal to two right ones, what do we more but perceive, that equality to two right ones, does necessarily agree to, and is inseparable from, the three angles of a triangle? . . .

S. 8 There are several ways wherein the mind is possessed of truth; each of which is called knowledge.

First, There is actual knowledge, which is the present view the mind has of the agreement or disagreement of any of its ideas, or of the relation they have one to another.

Secondly, A man is said to know any proposition, which having been once laid before his thoughts, he evidently perceived the agreement or disagreement of the ideas whereof it consists; and so lodged it in his memory, that whenever that proposition comes again to be reflected on, he, without doubt or hesitation, embraces the right side, assents to, and is certain of, the truth of it. This, I think, one may call habitual knowledge: and thus a man may be said to know all those truths, which are lodged in his memory by a foregoing clear and full perception, whereof the mind is assured past doubt, as often as it has occasion to reflect on them. For our finite understandings being able to think clearly and distinctly but on one thing at once, if men had no knowledge of any more than what they actually thought on, they would all be very ignorant; and he that knew most, would know but one truth, that being all he was able to think on at one time.

CHAPTER IV

Of the Reality of Knowledge . . . .

S. 1   I doubt not but my reader by this time may be apt to think that I have been all this while only building a castle in the air; and be ready to say to me, "To what purpose all this stir? 'Knowledge,' say you, 'is only the perception of the agreement or disagreement of our own ideas;' but who knows what those ideas may be? . . . Or if there be a sober and a wise man, what difference will there be, by your rules, between his knowledge, and that of the most extravagant fancy in the world? They both have their ideas, and perceive their agreement and disagreement with one another. If there be any difference between them, the advantage will be on the warm-headed man's side, as having the more ideas, and the more lively. And so, by your rules, he will be the more knowing. If it be true, that all knowledge lies only in the perception of the agreement or disagreement of our own ideas, the visions of an enthusiast, and the reasonings of a sober man, will be equally certain. . . ."

S. 2   To which I answer, That if our knowledge of our ideas terminate in them, and reach no farther, where there is something farther intended, our most serious thoughts will be of little more use than the reveries of a crazy brain; and the truths built thereon of no more weight than the discourses of a man who sees things clearly in a dream, and with great assurance utters them. But I hope before I have done to make it evident that this way of certainty, by the knowledge of our own ideas, goes a little farther than bare imagination; and I believe it will appear, that all the certainty of general truths a man has lies in nothing else.

S. 3   It is evident the mind knows not things immediately, but only by the intervention of the ideas it has of them. Our knowledge therefore is real only so far as there is a conformity between our ideas and the reality of things. But what shall be here the criterion? How shall the mind, when it perceives nothing but its own ideas, know that they agree with things themselves? This, though it seems not to want difficulty, yet I think there be two sorts of ideas that we may be assured agree with things.

S. 4   *First,* The first are simple ideas, which since the mind, as has been shown, can by no means make to itself, must necessarily be the product of things operating on the mind in a natural way, and producing therein those perceptions which, by the wisdom and will of our Maker, they are ordained and adapted to. From whence it follows, that simple ideas are not fictions of our fancies, but the natural and regular productions of things without us, really operating upon us, and so carry with them all the conformity which is intended, or which our state requires: for they represent to us things under those appearances which they are fitted to produce in us; . . . .

S. 5   *Secondly,* All our complex ideas, except those of substances, being archetypes of the mind's own making, not intended to be the copies of any thing, nor referred to the existence of any thing as to their originals, cannot want any conformity necessary to real knowledge. For that which is not designed to represent any thing but itself, can never be capable of a wrong representation, nor mislead us from the true apprehension of any thing, by its dislikeness to it: and such, excepting those of substances, are all our complex ideas: which, as I have shown in another place, are combinations of ideas, which the mind, by its free choice, puts together, without considering any connexion they have in nature. And hence it is, that in all these sorts the ideas themselves are considered as the archetypes, and things no otherwise regarded, but as they are comformable to them. So that we cannot but be infallibly certain, that all the knowledge we attain concerning these ideas, is real, and reaches things themselves; because in all our thoughts, reasonings, and discourses of this kind, we intend things no farther, than as they are conformable to our ideas. So that in these we cannot miss of a certain and undoubted reality.

S. 6   I doubt not but it will be easily granted, that the knowledge we have of mathematical truths, is not only certain, but real knowledge; and not the bare empty vision of vain insignificant chimeras of the brain; and yet, if we will consider, we shall find, that it is only of our own ideas. The mathematician considers the truth and properties belonging to a rectangle or circle, only as they are in idea in his own mind. For it is possible he never found either of them existing mathematically, i.e. precisely true, in his life. But yet the knowledge he has of any truths or properties belonging to a circle, or any other mathematical figure, are nevertheless true and certain, even of real things existing: because real things are no farther concerned, nor intended to be meant by any such propositions, than as things really agree to those archetypes in his mind. Is it true of the idea of a triangle, that its three angles are equal to two right ones? It is true also of a triangle, wherever it really exists. Whatever other figure exists, that is not exactly answerable to the idea of a triangle in his mind, is not at all concerned in that proposition: and therefore he is certain all his knowledge concerning such ideas, is real knowledge; . . . .

S. 7   And hence it follows, that moral knowledge is as capable of real certainty, as mathematics. For certainty being but the perception of the agreement or disagreement of our ideas; and demonstration nothing but the perception of such agreement, by the intervention of other ideas, or mediums; our moral ideas, as well as mathematical, being archetypes themselves, and so adequate and complete ideas; all the agreement or disagreement which we shall find in them, will produce real knowledge, as well as in mathematical figures. . . .

CHAPTER V

Of Truth in General. . . .

S. 2   Truth then seems to me, in the proper import of the word, to signify nothing but the joining or separating of signs, as the things signified by them, do agree or disagree one with another. The joining or separating of signs here meant, is what by another name we call proposition. So that truth properly belongs only to propositions; whereof there are two sorts, viz. mental and verbal; as there are two sorts of signs commonly made use of, viz. ideas and words.

S. 3   To form a clear notion of truth, it is very necessary to consider truth of thought, and truth of words, distinctly one from another; but yet it is very difficult to treat of them asunder: because it is unavoidable, in treating of mental propositions, to make use of words; and then the instances given of mental propositions cease immediately to be barely mental, and become verbal. For a mental proposition being nothing but a bare consideration of the ideas, as they are in our minds stripped of names, they lose the nature of purely mental propositions, as soon as they are put into words.

CHAPTER VI

Of Universal Propositions, Their Truth and Certainty

S. 1   Though the examining and judging of ideas by themselves, their names being quite laid aside, be the best and surest way to clear and distinct knowledge; yet through the prevailing custom of using sounds for ideas, I think it is very seldom practised. Every one may observe how common it is for names to be made use of, instead of the ideas themselves, even when men think and reason within their own breasts; especially if the ideas be very complex, and made up of a great collection of simple ones. This makes the consideration of words and propositions so necessary a part of the treatise of knowledge, that it is very hard to speak intelligibly of the one, without explaining the other. . . .

S. 6   On the other side, the names of substances, when made use of as they should be, for the ideas men have in their minds, though they carry a clear and determinate signification with them, will not yet serve us to make many universal propositions, of whose truth we can be certain. Not because in this use of them we are uncertain what things are signified by them, but because the complex ideas they stand for are such combinations of simple ones, as carry not with them any discoverable connexion or repugnancy, but with a very few other ideas. . . .

S. 11 Had we such ideas of substances, as to know what real constitutions produce those sensible qualities we find in them, and how those qualities flowed from thence, we could, by the specific ideas of their real essences in our own minds, more certainly find out their properties, and discover what qualities they had, or had not, than we can now by our senses; and to know the properties of gold, it would be no more necessary that gold should exist, and that we should make experiments upon it, than it is necessary for the knowing the properties of a triangle, that a triangle should exist in any matter; the idea in our minds would serve for the one, as well as the other. But we are so far from being admitted into the secrets of nature, that we scarce so much as ever approach the first entrance towards them. For we are wont to consider the substances we meet with, each of them as an entire thing by itself, having all its qualities in itself, and independent of other things; over-looking, for the most part, the operations of those invisible fluids they are encompassed with; and upon whose motions and operations depend the greatest part of those qualities which are taken notice of in them, and are made by us the inherent marks of distinction, whereby we know and denominate them . . . .

S. 16 To conclude: general propositions, of what kind soever, are then only capable of certainty, when the terms used in them stand for such ideas, whose agreement or disagreement, as there expressed, is capable to be discovered by us. And we are then certain of their truth or falsehood, when we perceive the ideas the terms stand for, to agree or not agree, according as they are affirmed or denied one of another. Whence we may take notice, that general certainty is never to be found but in our ideas. Whenever we go to seek it elsewhere in experiment, or observations without us, our knowledge goes not beyond particulars. It is the contemplation of our own abstract ideas, that alone is able to afford us general knowledge. . . .

CHAPTER IX

Of Our Knowledge of Existence

S. 1 Hitherto we have only considered the essences of things, which being only abstract ideas, and thereby removed in our thoughts from particular existence (that being the proper operation of the mind, in abstraction, to consider an idea under no other existence but what it has in the understanding), gives us no knowledge of real existence at all. Where, by the way, we may take notice that universal propositions, of whose truth or falsehood we can have certain knowledge, concern not existence; and farther, that all particular affirmations or negations, that would not be certain if they were made general, are only concerning existence; they declaring only the accidental union or separation of ideas in things existing, which, in their abstract natures, have no known necessary union or repugnancy.

CHAPTER XII

Of the Improvement of Our Knowledge

S. 1   It having been the common received opinion among men of letters, that maxims were the foundation of all knowledge; and that the sciences were each of them built upon certain *praecognita,* from whence the understanding was to take its rise, and by which it was to conduct itself, in its inquiries into the matters belonging to that science; the beaten road of the schools has been, to lay down in the beginning one or more general propositions, as foundations whereon to build the knowledge that was to be had of that subject. These doctrines, thus laid down for foundations of any science, were called principles, as the beginnings from which we must set out, and look no farther backwards in our inquiries, as we have already observed. . . .

S. 3   But if any one will consider, he will (I guess) find that the great advancement and certainty of real knowledge, which men arrived to in these sciences, was not owing to the influence of these principles, nor derived from any peculiar advantage they received from two or three general maxims laid down in the beginning; but from the clear, distinct, complete ideas their thoughts were employed about, and the relation of equality and excess, so clear between some of them, that they had an intuitive knowledge, and by that a way to discover it in others, and this without help of those maxims. For I ask, is it not possible for a young lad to know that his whole body is bigger than his little finger, but by virtue of this axiom, "that the whole is bigger than a part"; nor be assured of it, until he has learned that maxim? . . .

S. 6   But since the knowledge of the certainty of principles, as well as of all other truths, depends only upon the perception we have of the agreement or disagreement of our ideas, the way to improve our knowledge, is not, I am sure, blindly, and with an implicit faith, to receive and swallow principles; but is, I think, to get and fix in our minds, clear, distinct, and complete ideas, as far as they are to be had, and annex to them proper and constant names. And thus, perhaps, without any other principles, but barely considering those ideas, and by comparing them one with another, finding their agreement and disagreement, and their several relations and habitudes, we shall get more true and clear knowledge by the conduct of this one rule, than by taking up principles, and thereby putting our minds into the disposal of others.

S. 7   We must therefore, if we will proceed as reason advises, adapt our methods of inquiry to the nature of the ideas we examine, and the truth we search after. General and certain truths are only founded in the habitudes and relations of abstract ideas. A sagacious and methodical application of our thoughts, for the finding out these relations, is the only way to discover all that can be put, with truth and certainty, concerning them, into general propositions. By what steps we are to proceed in these, is to be learned in the schools of the mathematicians, who, from very plain and easy beginnings, by gentle degrees, and a continued chain of reasonings, proceed to the discovery and demonstration of truths, that appear, at first sight, beyond human capacity. The art of finding proofs, and the admirable methods they have invented for the singling out, and laying in order, those intermediate ideas that demonstratively show the equality or inequality of unapplicable quantities, is that which has carried them so far, and produced such wonderful and unexpected discoveries: . . . .

S. 8   This gave me the confidence to advance that conjecture which I suggest, chap. 3, viz. "That morality is capable of demonstration, as well as mathematics." For the ideas that ethics are conversant about being all real essence, and such as, I imagine, have a discoverable connexion and agreement one with another; so far as we can find their habitudes and relations, so far we shall be possessed of certain, real, and general truths; and I doubt not, but, if a right method were taken, a great part of morality might be made out with that clearness, that could leave, to a considering man, no more reason to doubt, than he could have to doubt of the truth of propositions in mathematics, which have been demonstrated to him.

S. 9   In our search after the knowledge of substances, our want of ideas, that are suitable to such a way of proceeding, obliges us to a quite different method. We advance not here, as in the other (where our abstract ideas are real, as well as nominal, essences), by contemplating our ideas, and considering their relations and correspondencies; that helps us very little, for the reasons that in another place we have at large set down. By which, I think, it is evident, that substances afford matter of very little general knowledge; and the bare contemplation of their abstract ideas will carry us but a very little way in the search of truth and certainty. . . .

S. 10   I deny not, but a man, accustomed to rational and regular experiments, shall be able to see farther into the nature of bodies, and guess righter at their yet unknown properties, than one that is a stranger to them; but yet, as I have said, this is but judgment and opinion not knowledge and certainty. This way of getting and improving our knowledge in substances only by experience and history, which is all that the weakness of our faculties in this state of **mediocrity** . . . which we are in in this world, can attain to; make me suspect that natural philosophy is not capable of being made a science. We are able, I imagine, to reach very little general knowledge concerning the species of bodies, and their several properties. Experiments and historical observations we may have, from which we may draw advantages of ease and health, and thereby increase our stock of conveniences for this life; but beyond this, I fear our talents reach not, nor are our faculties, as I guess, able to advance.

S. 11   From whence it is obvious to conclude, that since our faculties are not fitted to penetrate into the internal fabric and real essences of bodies; but yet plainly discover to us the being of a God, and the knowledge of ourselves, enough to lead us into a full and clear discovery of our duty and great concernment; it will become us, as rational creatures, to employ those faculties we have, about what they are most adapted to, and follow the direction of nature, where it seems to point us out the way. For it is rational to conclude, that our proper employment lies in those inquiries, and in that sort of knowledge which is most suited to our natural capacities, and carries in it our greatest interest, i.e. the condition of our eternal estate. . . .

A Guide to Selections from *Second Treatise of Civil Government*

In the passages selected from Chapter VI of the *Second Treatise of Civil Government,* Locke gives a biblical explanation for parental responsibility for the education of children. In the passages selected from Chapter IX, he presents reasons for subjecting ourselves to government as opposed to living in the state of nature. Both chapters are so clear as to need no further explanation.

SELECTIONS FROM

Second Treatise of Civil Government

*An Essay Concerning the True Original, Extent
and End of Civil Government*

◄◆►

CHAPTER VI

Of Paternal Power

S. 56 Adam was created a perfect man, his body and mind in full possession of their strength and reason, and so was capable from the first instant of his being to provide for his own support and preservation, and govern his actions according to the dictates of the law of reason God had implanted in him. From him the world is peopled with his descendants, who are all born infants, weak and helpless, without knowledge or understanding. But to supply the defects of this imperfect state of maturity till the improvement of growth and age had removed them, Adam and Eve, and after them all parents were, by the law of nature, under an obligation to preserve, nourish, and educate the children they had begotten, not as their own workmanship, but the workmanship of their own Maker, the Almighty, to whom they were to be accountable for them.

S. 57 The law that was to govern Adam was the same that was to govern all his posterity, the law of reason. But his offspring having another way of entrance into the world, different from him, by a natural birth, that produced them ignorant, and without the use of reason, they were not presently under that law. For no body can be under a law that is not promulgated to him; and this law being promulgated or made known by reason only, he that is not come to the use of his reason cannot be said to be under this law; and Adam's children being not presently as soon as born under this law of reason, were not presently free. For law, in its true notion, is not so much the limitation as the direction of a free and intelligent agent to his proper interest and prescribes no farther than is for the general good of those under that law. Could they be happier without it, the law, as a useless thing, would of itself vanish. . . .

S. 58 The power, then, that parents have over their children arises from that duty which is incumbent on them, to take care of their offspring during the imperfect state of childhood. To inform the mind, and govern the actions of their yet ignorant nonage, till reason shall take its place and ease them of that trouble, is what the children want, and the parents are bound to. For God having given man an understanding to direct his actions, has allowed him a freedom of will and liberty of acting, as properly belonging thereunto, within the bounds of that law he is under. But whilst he is in an estate wherein he has no understanding of his own to direct his will, he is not to have any will of his own to follow. He that understands for him must will for him too; he must prescribe to his will, and regulate his actions, but when he comes to the estate that made his father a freeman, the son is a freeman too. . . .

CHAPTER IX

Of the Ends of Political Society and Government. . . .

S.123 If man in the state of nature be so free as has been said; if he be absolute lord of his own person and possessions; equal to the greatest and subject to no body, why will he part with his freedom? Why will he give up this empire, and subject himself to the dominion and control of any other power? To which 'tis obvious to answer, that though in the state of nature he hath such a right, yet the enjoyment of it is very uncertain and constantly exposed to the invasion of others; for all being kings as much as he, every man his equal, and the greater part no strict observers of equity and justice, the enjoyment of the property he has in this state is very unsafe, very unsecure. This makes him willing to quit this condition which, however free, is full of fears and continual dangers; and 'tis not without reason that he seeks out and is willing to join in society with others who are already united, or have a mind to unite for the mutual preservation of their lives, liberties, and estates, which I call by the general name, property.

S. 124 The great and chief end therefore, of men's uniting into commonwealths, and putting themselves under government, is the preservation of their property; to which in the state of nature there are many things wanting.

First, There wants an established, settled, known law, received and allowed by common consent to be the standard of right and wrong, and the common measure to decide all controversies between them. For though the law of nature be plain and intelligible to all rational creatures, yet men, being biased by their interest, as well as ignorant for want of study of it, are not apt to allow of it as a law binding to them in the application of it to their particular cases.

S. 125 Secondly, In the state of nature there wants a known and indifferent judge, with authority to determine all differences according to the established law. For everyone in that state being both judge and executioner of the law of nature, men being partial to themselves, passion and revenge is very apt to carry them too far, and with too much heat in their own cases, as well as negligence and unconcernedness, make them too remiss in other men's.

S. 126 *Thirdly,* In the state of nature there often wants power to back and support the sentence when right, and to give it due execution. They who by any injustice offended, will seldom fail where they are able by force to make good their injustice. Such resistance many times makes the punishment dangerous, and frequently destructive to those who attempt it. . . .

S. 128 For in the state of Nature to omit the liberty he has of innocent delights, a man has two powers.

The first is to do whatsoever he thinks fit for the preservation of himself and others within the permission of the law of nature; by which law, common to them all, he and all the rest of mankind are one community, make up one society distinct from all other creatures and were it not for the corruption and viciousness of degenerate men, there would be no need of any other, no necessity that men should separate from this great and natural community, and associate into less combinations.

The other power a man has in the state of nature is the power to punish the crimes committed against that law. Both these he gives up when he joins in a private, if I may so call it, or particular political society, and incorporates into any commonwealth separate from the rest of mankind.

S. 129 The first power, viz. of doing whatsoever he thought fit for the preservation of himself and the rest of mankind, he gives up to be regulated by laws made by the society, so far forth as the preservation of himself and the rest of that society shall require; which laws of the society in many things confine the liberty he had by the law of nature.

S. 130 *Secondly,* The power of punishing he wholly gives up, and engages his natural force (which he might before employ in the execution of the law of nature, by his own single authority, as he thought fit) to assist the executive power of the society as the law thereof shall require. For being now in a new state, wherein he is to enjoy many conveniences from the labour, assistance, and society of others in the same community, as well as protection from its whole strength, he is to part also with as much of his natural liberty, in providing for himself, as the good, prosperity, and safety of the society shall require, which is not only necessary but just, since the other members of the society do the like.

S. 131 But though men when they enter into society give up the equality, liberty, and executive power they had in the state of nature into the hands of the society, to be so far disposed of by the legislative as the good of the society shall require, yet it being only with an intention in everyone the better to preserve himself, his liberty and property (for no rational creature can be supposed to change his condition with an intention to be worse), the power of the society or legislative constituted by them can never be supposed to extend farther than the common good, but is obliged to secure everyone's property by providing against those three defects above-mentioned that made the state of nature so unsafe and uneasy. And so, whoever has the legislative or supreme power of any commonwealth, is bound to govern by established standing laws, promulgated and known to the people, and not by extemporary decrees, by indifferent and upright judges, who are to decide controversies by those laws; and to employ the force of the community at home only in the execution of such laws, or abroad to prevent or redress foreign injuries and secure the community from inroads and invasion. And all this to be directed to no other end but the peace, safety, and public good of the people.

Bibliography

BOYD, WILLIAM, *From Locke to Montessori*, London, G. G. Harrap and Co., 1914. Chapter I.

LAURIE, SIMON SOMERVILLE, *Studies in the History of Educational Opinion from the Renaissance*, Cambridge, Cambridge University Press, 1903. Chapters VIII-XV.

LEITCH, JAMES, *Practical Educationists and their Systems of Teaching*, Glasgow, J. Maclehose, 1876. Chapter I.

. . .

AARON, RICHARD I., *John Locke*, Oxford, Clarendon Press, 1955 (second edition). Originally published 1937.

FOWLER, THOMAS, *Locke*, New York, Harper and Bros., 1880.

FRASER, ALEXANDER CAMPBELL, *Locke*, Edinburgh and London, Blackwood, 1890.

GIBSON, JAMES, *Locke's Theory of Knowledge*, Cambridge, Cambridge University Press, 1917.

VIII

ROUSSEAU

J EAN JACQUES ROUSSEAU WAS BORN in 1712 to a French Protestant family of Geneva. His mother died in childbirth and he was reared until the age of ten by his father. At that time, his mother's relatives took over his education. After spending two years at school, he was given training first as a notary and then as an engraver. He succeeded in neither of these efforts. At the age of sixteen he left Geneva. According to his own account in the *Confessions,* he spent some time knocking about in the capacity of servant to various wealthy persons. He was converted to Catholicism. His adventures introduced him to Madame de Warens, a wealthy and liberated widow, who provided some training for him in music and the classics. He left her protection in Annecy to engage in the teaching and performance of music, travelled to Paris, and walked back to her in Chambéry. Here, in 1732, Madame de Warens installed him in her household as lover. His duties appear to have left him some time for reading. In 1738, another lady took his fancy, and Madame de Warens, another lover. He remained in her ménage, however, until 1740 when he accepted a post of a different sort—tutor to a family in Lyons. He enjoyed meagre success as a teacher; and in 1741 he went to Paris, hoping to interest the great world in a system of musical notation he had invented. This hope remained unfulfilled. He spent some time on the staff of the French ambassador in Venice, and in 1745 returned to Paris where he acted as secretary to an influential family, music copyist, and composer. Through his friendship with Diderot, he came to know the literary circles of Paris, and contributed to the *Encyclopédie*. He formed a union with a thoroughly uneducated woman, Thérèse Le Vasseur, whom he married near the end of his life. He claims to have had five children by her, and to have sent them all to an orphanage.

In 1749, Rousseau entered an essay in a contest supported by the academy of Dijon. He won the prize; and his *Discourse on the Arts and Sciences,* published the next year, brought him immediate fame. In 1752, another essay, the *Discourse upon Inequality,* failed to win a prize offered by the same academy, but attracted considerable attention when it was published in 1755. Rousseau continued to compose music and to write about it with some effect. In 1754, he went to Geneva, foreswore Catholicism, and took up again Protestantism along with Genevan citizenship. Two years later he returned to Paris and began writing in earnest. By 1762, he had published *La Nouvelle Héloïse, The Social Contract,* and *Emile,* and had acquired great literary reputation as well as sufficient notoriety to be threatened by arrest. Powerful circles considered his work immoral, anticlerical, and revolutionary. The Parlement of Paris had condemned *Emile.* He fled to Switzerland; and after the Council of Geneva joined Paris in its condemnation, he renounced Genevan citizenship and attacked the Council violently. He spent the next few years moving about from place to place in Switzerland, England, and France. In 1770, he returned to Paris where, not far from sanity, he worked again as a music copyist. He completed his famous *Confessions* and wrote several other major and many minor works including his *Considerations on the Government of Poland.* In 1778, he moved to the country where he died in July of that year.

It is difficult to give an adequate exposition of Rousseau's thought. His writing is frequently vivid, eloquent, and epigrammatic. Limited passages often express his ideas with great clarity, but their coherence with each other leaves much to be desired. Those ideas which are clear to the reader sometimes obviously bear upon one another; but often they fall into irrelevance or blatant incompatibility. Also, many passages are rhetorical, repetitious, and opaque, serving to mask rather than to reveal whatever thought inspired them. An adequate exposition would set forth the outline of Rousseau's thought, indicating where it falls into obscurity and incoherence as well as into cogency; but it would also constitute a very long book. In a short space, one cannot do such justice to Rousseau. Here, we have deliberately selected certain parts of his thought and made of them a system, less incoherent perhaps than his own, and inclusive of those ideas through which he influenced, probably as much as any thinker of modern times, the subsequent theory and practice of philosophy, politics, and education.

EDUCATIONAL THEORY

Rousseau's educational theory has three parts: one pertaining to private education of men, another to public education of men, and a third pertaining to women. The first is found chiefly in *Emile* with some recurrence in *La Nouvelle Héloïse,* in parts of his *Discourse upon Inequality,* and in *The Social Contract;* the second, in one part of his *Considerations on the Government of Poland;* and the third, in Book V of *Emile.* Private education of men absorbed by far the greater part of his attention. To it, we shall devote most of our attention, although we shall add a few statements concerning public education.

Rousseau's views concerning the education of women are of considerable historical importance. He believed that their psychological differences from men required education of quite a different sort. Limitations of space, however, make it impossible to present his views on that subject here.

STATEMENTS OF FACT

In Rousseau's educational theory, there are statements of fact about human nature and human history. With respect to the first he discusses human capacities and their emergence from infancy to maturity. With respect to human history he discusses the development of society from the life of primitive man to that of eighteenth-century Europe, especially France. Rousseau assures us that his statements concerning human nature are based upon his own observations of what is common to all men, regardless of rank and nation, and that others would agree with him if they troubled to investigate the matter.[1] Statements concerning the development of society occupy a somewhat unclear status in Rousseau's writing; but he seems to hold that while there is no direct evidence for them, they receive indirect support from the observable facts of human capacity and of its development in the individual person.[2]

[1] Jean Jacques Rousseau, *Emile,* translated by Barbara Foxley, Everyman's Library No. 518 J. M. Dent & Sons, Ltd., London, 1911, pp. 216–17.
[2] Cf. Rousseau, *A Discourse upon the Origin and Foundations of the Inequality among Mankind,* printed for R. and J. Dodsley in Pallmall, London, MDCCLXI. Rousseau clearly regards his discussion here as speculative history (pp. 94–95); but he seems to say (pp. 10–11) that it is based upon a distinction to which the contrast between the state of nature and the social state points, the distinction between nonsocial and social motives.

H u m a n   n a t u r e

CAPACITIES. Rousseau, like most of the authors hitherto treated, holds
that the human being is a combination of soul and body,[3]
and in working out his *theory* of human nature, devotes most of his attention to the soul. The latter, he holds, possesses five capacities: those of
sense, feeling, desire, will, and reason. His theory of human nature consists in a description of the way these capacities manifest themselves, and
in a hypothesis as to the order of their development in each person. Let
us consider these capacities.

The Senses. The soul's capacity for sense is, actually, a collection of six
capacities. Rousseau adopts a classic view that there are five distinct powers of sensation and a sixth which presides over them in a certain way.
The five are the capacities to smell, to taste, to touch, to hear, and to see.[4]
The sense organs, the nose, the tongue, the skin, the ear, and the eye, are
acted on by external objects; and we become aware of smells, tastes, touches,
sounds, and sights. We do not become aware, through these organs alone,
of external objects. We are all acquainted with situations in which we
smell, taste, touch, hear, or see something which is in fact not there. These
experiences show that between ourselves and external objects there is a
veil of sensations which we attend to directly as a result of the activation
of our powers to sense. Sensations are not parts of the objects which cause
them; and they occur, for the most part, when those external objects in-
teract with our sense organs.

The sixth sense, Rousseau calls the "common-sense" or "reasoning
of the senses." It presides over the other five by combining the sensations
which are caused by a given object into a single "percept" or idea of it.
A rose causes a particular smell, touch, sight, and (for the very curious)
sound and taste. But these sensations are totally distinct from one another
and cannot, as such, constitute the idea of a rose. In order to represent
the flower, they must be put together. The soul's power to combine them
is its common-sense. ". . . this sixth sense has no special organ, it has its
seat in the brain, and its sensations . . . are called percepts or ideas. . . .
Thus, what I call the reasoning of the senses . . . consists in the formation
of simple ideas through the associated experience of several ideas . . ."[5]
The power of common-sense, of sense reasoning, gives us our ideas of
particular external objects with their various kinds of sensory qualities,
tactual, auditory, visual, etc.

The ideas provided by common-sense are representatives of those
things which cause the sensations out of which they are formed. The

3 *Emile*, pp. 246–47, 256.
4 *Ibid.*, p. 122.
5 *Ibid.*

rose before us causes sensations of smell and of sight, and these remain with us as images. The common-sense fuses these images together into an idea which represents the rose. So it is for those groups of images which stem from the sensations of every object. The common-sense "teaches the nature of things by the sum-total of their external aspects."[6]

Feelings. Feelings are closely connected with sensations. When we direct our attention upon the sensation an object causes, disregarding the latter, we are aware of a feeling. Sensations are either pleasant or painful. The color and scent of the rose are pleasant; the pressure of the cutting knife is painful. When these sensations recur as images, they are also pleasant or painful. Feelings of pleasure and pain suffuse sensations as well as images of them; and the ideas of their causes, formed by the common-sense, are likewise pleasant or painful. The capacity to harbor these ideas is the capacity to feel toward the objects they represent.[7] The manifestation of this capacity is closely associated with the other capacities of the soul, especially with that of desire.

Desire. The capacity for desire is awakened by feelings of pleasure and pain. An object produces a sensation; and according as the latter is pleasant or painful, we endeavor to secure or avoid the object which causes it. Thus, being pleased by light, the young infant follows it with his eyes and cries if he is put in the dark. A desire is an endeavor to secure an object whose idea is pleasant and to avoid an object whose idea is painful. The capacity for desire is the capacity to engage in such endeavors.[8]

These endeavors fall into two groups: those desires which are instinctual, unlearned, or innate, and those which are learned, resulting from social experience. Unlearned desires fall under one or other of two headings: self-love (sometimes called "self-preservation") and pity. Rousseau contrasts self-love with selfishness. Selfishness is made up of tendencies to prefer ourselves over others or to prefer securing what we want when we know that our success excludes that of other persons. Moreover, it is learned. The man, learning that someone else wishes food that he himself wants, and that if he eats the other cannot, harbors a selfish desire if he wishes to eat it nonetheless. Self-love, on the other hand, involves no comparison of oneself with others whatever and is unlearned or innate. Thus, the man who desires food, but who does not consider whether his securing it will prevent another from eating, is acting from self-love. To the capacity for all our spontaneous and unlearned or innate desires,

---

[6] *Ibid.*
[7] *Ibid.,* pp. 7, 29–30, 253n.
[8] *Emile,* pp. 29–30.

except for pity, Rousseau gives the misleading name "self-love"—misleading because it suggests that men are innately egoistic.[9] His point concerning self-love is that it is neither egoistic nor altruistic.

Rousseau excludes certain desires from self-love. The desires for vengeance or punishment, for dominion or aggression, for servitude or submissiveness, and for personal property or possessions are all learned. They do not occur in primitive men and in young children who have not yet experienced those social situations which give rise to them. They make no part of self-love.[10]

Other desires, although not carefully treated, clearly must be included in self-love. Hunger, thirst, sleep, and perhaps crying when in pain are unlearned desires which Rousseau sometimes seems to countenance.[11] But there is one desire which he makes central among all others. This is the desire for sexual activity.

The desire for sexual activity is directed simply toward physical consummation. As such, it involves no love or affection for any object upon which it may focus. It is unlearned. A primitive man requires just some, no particular woman; and he forms no lasting unions. Affection is genuine, Rousseau holds; but it is not itself innate. It develops along with many other desires and emotions according as social institutions channel the desire for physical consummation.[12]

The other unlearned way of manifesting the capacity for desire is pity. It is the desire which ". . . inspires us with a natural Aversion to see any other Being, but especially any Being like ourselves, suffer or perish";[13] and its objective is the prevention of that suffering or destruction. Suppose we see someone in pain. The idea of this suffering is itself painful; and in some circumstances we might simply run away from the disagreeable situation. But if we pity the sufferer, we feel his pain through imaginative sympathy. We never pity those whom we suppose to lead a pleasant and happy existence. But our sympathy is not enough. At the same time that we feel the victim's pain, we know that the causes which led to it might quite as well have brought the same wretchedness to us; and we feel afraid. Without fear for oneself there can be no pity for others. Moreover, we believe that the victim is aware of the suffering which he is undergoing. We cannot feel pity for the burning log because we suppose that it does not feel the fire. Feeling the pains of others, realizing that their fears might be our own, and seeing that they are aware

9 *Discourse upon Inequality*, pp. lv–lvi, 65–66, 86–87; also *Emile*, pp. 56, 172–74. It should be noted, however, that Rousseau expresses the incompatible view that self-love is directed toward the welfare of the agent in explicit opposition to the welfare of others, i.e., the view that men are innately egoistic (see, for example, *Emile*, p. 61).
10 *Discourse upon Inequality*, pp. 78–79, 43–46, 89–92; also *Emile*, p. 33.
11 *Discourse upon Inequality*, pp. 48–52; *Emile*, pp. 30–32.
12 *Discourse upon Inequality*, pp. 78–86; also *Emile*, pp. 172–76.
13 *Discourse upon Inequality*, preface, p. lv.

of their suffering—under these conditions we pity them; we naturally desire to give assistance.[14] Unlike the goals of self-love, the objective of pity
involves other persons; it is the remedy for their ills. It is an innate desire;
and along with one component of self-love, the sexual, it forms the instinctive material out of which experience, reason, and will develop the
adult person.

The Will.   The capacity to will is closely connected in Rousseau's thought,
with that of desire. Every desire is the idea of an object, formed by the
common-sense along with an effort, inspired by its pleasantness or painfulness, to secure or avoid that object which the idea represents. As a
desire, it involves a course of action leading to a goal, the object to be
secured or avoided. It is clear that some desires are compatible with each
other; their goals and the courses of action which lead to them may all
be pursued by one person. It is equally clear that others are incompatible;
they cannot be realized in a single life. One may desire now to be in New
York and to be in London; but one can neither engage in both those
courses of action which would lead to these goals at the same time, nor
enjoy, at the same time, the life which both cities offer. Where we entertain such conflicting desires, it is necessary to choose between the goals
involved in them; and consequently between the courses of action which
lead to them. The will is that capacity of the soul which enables us to
choose between conflicting goals and to initiate one course of action as
opposed to another, i.e., the course which leads to the goal selected.[15]

   While Rousseau speaks of the will in this way, he also uses the
word "will" in a second sense. The goal of a desire may be more or less
comprehensive. It may be the welfare of the community as a whole, that
of some smaller part of the community, or that of a particular person.
Rousseau sometimes uses the word "will" to refer to the goal of desire;
and when he does so, he classifies wills into general, corporate or party,
and particular. The general will is the welfare of the community, the
corporate will that of some particular person.[16] Thus, the word "will"
sometimes refers to the capacity to select and act for goals while at others
it refers to those goals themselves.

Reason.   Reason consists of two capacities according to Rousseau. The
first is the capacity for sense reasoning or the common-sense which we
have already noticed. The second is the capacity for intellectual reasoning. This activity shows itself in three ways: in the formation of general

[14] *Discourse upon Inequality,* pp. 71–73; also *Emile,* pp. 184–86, 190–91.
[15] Cf. *Discourse upon Inequality,* pp. 92–93; *Emile,* pp. 256–57.
[16] Cf. *Social Contract,* Book III, Chapter II. In this passage, Rousseau is particularly
concerned with that subordinate group which constitutes the government; he uses the
word "corporate" to describe the welfare of the government.

ideas, in their application in judgment, and in inference from one judgment to another. Sense reasoning provides us with particular ideas of particular things—of this plum tree, that oak tree, *et alia*. The capacity for intellectual reasoning enables us to compare these particular ideas and to form the idea of a tree as such. This idea is not the idea of a precise shape or color of tree; such an idea would be an idea of a particular tree. It is a general idea, an idea of no particular shape or color whatever; and since it cannot be provided by the common-sense, it must spring from a different faculty. The judgment "this tree is a plant," similarly, cannot spring from the faculty of sense. It is the application of general ideas to particular things and consequently it involves ideas which the common-sense cannot yield. Also, it expresses an activity, that of joining a subject and predicate, which is totally foreign to the activity of sensing. Similarly, when we infer, from the judgment that this is a tree and all trees are plants, the further judgment that this is a plant, we are exercising the faculty of intellectual reason.[17]

Reason and Language.   The exercise of this capacity is intimately connected with the use of language. The common-sense provides us with no general ideas by which to understand the similarities and differences, the relations and disjunctions of particular objects. To become aware of the idea of a color in distinction from the surface which it covers, of a relation between things in distinction from the things themselves, of a tree as such in distinction from particular trees—all this requires words by which to center our attention upon such abstract things unrepresentable by sense. Without the use of proper names, we could not compare objects represented by the common-sense; but without the use of other names, we could not form the general ideas of properties and classes which result from that comparison. Moreover, without the use of sentences or propositions, we could not bring clearly before our minds the relations between particulars and between genera and species that we represent by general ideas and capture in the judgments and inferences we make with them. ". . . general Ideas cannot be conveyed to the Mind without the Assistance of Words, nor can the Understanding seize them without the Assistance of Propositions."[18]

The exercise of reason is instrumental to the organization of desires. It enables us to predict what consequences will follow from our actions, showing us, in this way, how to achieve the goals of desire. It also enables us to see which goals are good and which bad. It does not by itself make us choose the former; this is the function of will. But by discovering the good and by revealing the way to it, it enables the will to make an

17 *Discourse upon Inequality*, pp. 58–60; *Emile*, pp. 71, 122, 131.
18 *Discourse upon Inequality*, p. 58; also, pp. 47–48, 57–60; *Emile*, p. 131.

informed selection of goals, and to initiate those courses of action which lead to them.[19]

EMERGENCE OF CAPACITIES. Rousseau presents a hypothesis as to the times in which the various faculties of the soul begin to exercise themselves and as to the kinds of adult persons which their exercise constitutes. He divides life from infancy to maturity into five stages and asserts that each sees the emergence of one of the faculties into full-fledged operation. He presents the adult person endowed with all five and possessed of a character which varies according as they are exercised in different social environments. For the most part (sex is the notable exception), the exercise of each faculty is not presented as making a sudden appearance but, rather, as dominating in its stage. The adult personality appears as a function of the exercise of all and of the social institutions in which the person lives.

Infancy and Feeling. The first stage is infancy, from birth to about two. This stage is dominated by feeling, by the feeling of pleasure and pain. Of course, pleasure and pain cannot occur by themselves; they are responses to or qualities of (Rousseau does not say which) sensations received by the infant. The occurrence of these feelings leads to habits of securing and avoiding the objects which cause them. In later stages these habits manifest themselves as desires.[20] But the infant's life is chiefly one of pleasure and pain and habits relevant to each, e.g., that of nursing.

Boyhood and the Senses. The second stage extends roughly from two to twelve. Its beginning is marked by eating and walking. It is dominated by the exercise of the faculty of sense. The development of the appropriate sense organs coupled with independent movement brings into consciousness an enormous number of sights, touches, sounds, etc. The ability to speak and to remember enables the common-sense to compare the sensory and imaginal material thus discovered, and to form words and ideas for particular sensible objects. Moreover, imagination which comes into play with memory presents new objects for desire, thus increasing the relatively small stock of infantile wishes. But desire, imagination, memory, and language are all dominated by sense since they can extend to nothing which is not derived from it.[21]

Intellectual reason manifests itself only slightly in this second stage. Movement, along with sufficient strength to manipulate physical things, provides the child with an idea of himself, i.e., with an idea of something

[19] *Discourse upon Inequality,* pp. 139–41; also *Emile,* pp. 34, 196–97, 292, 423.
[20] *Emile,* pp. 7, 29.
[21] *Emile,* pp. 41, 44, 71, 89–90, 97, 104, 112, 113, 115, 122.

opposed to external objects; and in this self-consciousness, he finds desires for things which are sometimes satisfied and at others disappointed. This experience provides him with a notion as to his own well-being, i.e., with the notion of the satisfaction of his desires. But it does not extend far into the future. The child cannot think of his well-being as including or excluding the satisfaction of a desire which cannot occur until twenty years have elapsed. The contemplation of his limited well-being, however, requires the exercise of reason. The child must judge in two ways in order to conceive it. He must first judge that "this is a thing of a certain sort" and he must judge, secondly, that things of this sort, if dealt with in a certain way, bring about what he wishes to secure or to avoid. To desire a picnic tomorrow as part of one's well-being requires judging that something is food and that if one puts it there, one can find it tomorrow in the picnic basket. This exercise of reason, of course, is furthered by the development of speech.[22]

Preadolescence and Reason. Between twelve and fifteen, the intellectual reason emerges as dominant. At this stage of life, one possesses greatest strength; since the desires are few and physical energy great, there is an enormous superfluity of power over what is required to satisfy wants. This excess is devoted to the satisfaction of curiosity and eventuates in judgments concerning the relations of things. Its exercise enables the child to extend the notion of his well-being over a much longer period of time and to develop a comprehensive system of goals whose achievement constitutes his natural happiness. It enables him, also, to think of actions as instrumental to that happiness. He can distinguish, by virtue of the intellectual reason, between what is naturally good and what is useful to its accomplishment. At this stage, the enormous supply of unused energy is directed toward discovering what is true about the world, toward developing a comprehensive notion of well-being, and toward using those truths as instruments for achieving the latter.[23]

Adolescence, Desire, and Emotion. Between fifteen and twenty, the quality of life is altered enormously by the emergence of the sexual desire. It brings with it an interest in other persons and, coupled with pity, a genuine affection for them. In preceding stages the child lives in a state of psychological self-sufficiency. But now, the ideas awakened in the mind by other persons please or displease and the simple desire for physical consummation alerts one to their existence and importance. The natural inclination to pity fuses with the purely physical sexual desire and produces the desire to assist and cherish. This new desire is love or affection;

22 *Emile,* pp. 42, 56, 72.
23 *Emile,* pp. 82, 128–29, 130, 131, 140, 141.

and when one begins to feel it, he begins to watch for signs of a similar inclination on the part of others toward himself. Innately, it has no focus; but one who shows signs of reciprocation becomes the person upon which it is centered. Its physical sexual aspect then may become overt. It endows love for a particular person with a superfluity of driving urgency which overflows and awakens related desires, charging them with an emotional vitality they would not otherwise possess. Many of these related desires are directed toward persons other than the beloved. The desires thus started are of different sorts which are determined by the way in which those others are related to the situation. Thus, for example, friendship is felt for those who give no trouble, jealousy for those who interfere in one way, simple hatred for those who interfere in another. This is the time in which the simple feelings of pleasure and pain give rise to the complex life of desire and its emotions according to the ways in which the social situation of the person allows expression to the emerging desire for sex and the always present natural inclination to pity.[24]

Morality. Moreover, in this stage the youth begins to develop notions of right and wrong, and of kinds of behavior subject to moral judgment. He acquires the notion of extended well-being; this is, simply, all the objectives which will satisfy his desires. His new interest in others now enables him to distinguish between those objectives which consist in improving the lot of others from those whch consist in improving his own. He can act altruistically or selfishly; and he can, therefore, acquire the notion of the well-being of society as a whole. He can see that accomplishing the latter may be a different thing from realizing his own well-being, that doing his duty may be quite different from realizing his own particular interests. Sex coupled with pity makes one interested in securing the welfare of others and that of the community at large. They lay the basis for action from duty as opposed to action from simple inclination.[25]

Maturity and Will. The fifth stage of development is not clearly demarcated by Rousseau, but he seems to hold that it lasts from about twenty to about twenty-five. The faculty which comes into play during this period is the will. In the preceding stage, the person has developed the distinction between those objectives of his desires which constitute his own well-being and those which constitute the well-being of society as a whole. He now generalizes this distinction into that between the well-being of any particular person and that of society. He adds a third element to this twofold distinction of objectives—the well-being of a group less comprehensive than society, but more comprehensive than a particu-

---

[24] *Emile*, pp. 172–74, 175–76, 188, 190–91, 197.
[25] *Emile*, pp. 182, 195–96.

lar person. This is the well-being of a group, party, or class as opposed to that of an individual person and to that of an entire society. The person's desires now impel him toward three kinds of goals which may not lie along the same path: toward what will satisfy his personal interest, that of some group, or that of his society. For example, a landed proprietor may wish to impose a charge for use of a road running through his property; such a toll would be to his personal interest. He may also desire to preserve the power of the landed aristocracy, and the toll might operate to destroy this power by increasing the harassment of the poor. Moreover, he might desire to advance the well-being of the nation as a whole, and this well-being might require both the distribution of land and the abolition of all toll roads. Such a person must choose one from among the objectives toward which his desires move, and must initiate the action which expresses his choice. Moreover, this is the time appropriate for marriage, and marriage involves a decision of the same kind. From among possible mates, one must be chosen; and the course leading to marriage initiated. This is a decision to which a consideration of one's peculiar interests is not alone relevant. The well-being of one group at least, the family, if not that of society at large should be accounted for. The will comes into exercise as the basis for determining one's role in society and participation in the institution of marriage.[26]

In this fifth stage, men reach maturity. The institutions in which they grow up provide details of character. But disregarding these differences bound to nation, class, and party, Rousseau assures us that all men desire to secure or to avoid those things whose ideas give them pleasure or pain respectively, that these desires express themselves in uniform habitual ways of securing their objectives, that reason serves as a practical instrument in the enterprise of realizing desires, that their attitudes and emotions are governed by the ways in which other persons impinge upon their love (the natural growth of sex and pity), and that their wills exercise themselves from time to time in selecting one from among competing desires to be realized in action informed by whatever knowledge their reason can bring to it.

The development of society

One of Rousseau's chief concerns, as we shall see, is to give a justification for the political state, a reason for holding that men ought to live under government notwithstanding its restraints. His procedure like that of Locke is in part to show how men would live were there no government and to conclude from the unsatisfactoriness of that state of nature, along with certain other premises, that they ought to live under the aegis of civil institutions. Rousseau presents this moral justification for govern-

---

[26] *Emile*, pp. 419ff; *Social Contract*, I, VII; II, III, IV; III, II.

ment as if it involved an account of human life, growing from the state of nature into the political state. But he tells the reader, in effect, that his account should be understood not as a history but as a metaphor which represents something quite different from human life—the psychological distinction between asocial and social motives with the different kinds of consequences to which they lead. This elaborate figure of speech, however, very clearly gets lost and the reader sees that Rousseau undoubtedly regards his work in two ways, both as a speculative account of human development from a primitive condition to a civilized political society, and as an account of the natural as opposed to the social behavior of men.[27] In the preceding section we have drawn upon his speculative history in order to ascertain his views as to the asocial and social motives of men, and as to the behavior which expresses them. We shall now present the speculative history. The conclusion that men ought to live under government will be discussed later.

THE STATE OF NATURE: FIRST STAGE. Rousseau divides the history of mankind into four stages, the first three of which constitute his "state of nature." In the earliest, each man secured all his necessities only by virtue of his native strength and practical intelligence. His senses, vitally important to the pursuit of food and to self-protection, were subtle; his feeling of pleasure and pain seldom awakened; his knowledge of particular things confined to those of practical utility; his reason exclusively devoted to acquiring that knowledge; his desires and emotions, few and simple. Male and female formed no lasting union; and offspring remained with the mother only until self-reliant. The chief task was wresting food from the land over which he wandered, and which no one owned; and each pursued it in isolation from others. The best combination of brain and brawn led to the survival of the most fit. Language was scarcely more than the expressive cries of brutes. Life was peaceful because, exclusively and separately occupied with survival, men had neither time nor opportunity for pity and the desires, many of them destructive, to which it gives rise. In this stage, men lived in savage but scarcely noble independence and equality.[28]

SECOND STAGE. The second stage is marked by the discovery of the bow, the fishhook, and fire. These discoveries required but also improved man's reason. They made it possible to store up more food than was needed at any particular moment and in this way to guard against future want. Prudence for the future made man conscious of himself, for it made him proud of his accomplishment. But self-con-

[27] *Discourse upon Inequality*, pp. 10–11, 93–95.
[28] *Ibid.*, pp. 25–28, 43–46, 65–66, 79–82, 98–99.

sciousness and pride required that others recognize him—the object upon which both that consciousness and pride were directed. Man shortly became aware that other persons exist with thoughts to be controlled and energies to be directed toward the objectives he himself adopted. This desire to use others led to association with them; but the nomadic nature of life, the need to get as much as one can for himself, made the association only temporary. Thus, prudence reinforced by invention led to temporary groups, but as yet did not give rise to permanent social institutions. This was the stage of savagery which might claim nobility.

THIRD STAGE AND PROPERTY. The third stage is marked by the discovery of new techniques for economic production. Hook, arrow, and fire improved the life of the hunting nomad; but the use, first, of stone implements and, later, of metal changed it altogether. These instruments made agriculture possible, and brought the permanent family into existence. The families which tilled the soil claimed it as their own. Those who were not members of the family group were naturally excluded from use of its land; and having mixed his labor with the land, the leader of the family, the father, acquired a property-right over it. Owners employed those who owned nothing and those whose intelligence enabled them to amass great property acquired dominion over field laborers and over those who owned less. New techniques of production ushered in settled family life, property, class distinctions, and inequality of economic power coupled with economic dependence of owners and workers. The noble savage disappeared.[29]

DESIRE AND EMOTION. With economic inequality and interdependence came a complete alteration in the life of desire and emotion. Having always the same companions and becoming familiar with their problems, men came to pity them, most notably those of their own family; and pity, coupled with sex, gave rise to ties of love and affection between them. Language grew up as a necessity of cooperative existence. It enabled the expression of desire and, by this means, its continuing multiplication. Love and affection grew into that complex of desires and emotions which make up family loyalty. But from the generous conduct which expresses that loyalty many destructive desires also emerged. In order to advance the family welfare, one must diminish or destroy that of those who opposed it. Moreover, other vicious passions grew up toward persons both within and without the group. Love for others generated a need to be approved by them, and this need for public approbation gave rise to the notion that one was better than others. This idea made each person resent any questioning of his own excellence and

29 *Ibid.*, pp. 108–19.

gave rise to many hurtful inclinations such as ambition, vengeance, jealousy, hatred, and cruelty. New techniques gave rise to settled family life and inequality of economic power and these, in turn, gave rise to all those inequalities of value which people place upon themselves and others in light of their desire to be approved by those toward whom they direct their love and their affection.

JUSTICE. Near the end of the third stage, another idea emerges in human life, that of justice. Each landowner fears the loss of his property, for the desire to own is never satisfied. Small owners desire more land and large owners need to deprive the smaller of their holdings in order to remove the threat they offer. Those who hold no land constitute a danger to both. The idea of justice emerges as the idea of a set of rules which will assure stable ownership and orderly transfer of title. But in the third stage, there is no government to enforce justice, and consequently a constant fear of disorder not infrequently justified by the fact. From the holding of property, the idea of right or just action arises; but this new morality finds no enforcement other than the sporadic insistence of individuals upon its recognition.[30]

THE CONTRACT AND THE POLITICAL STATE. Government naturally emerges as an instrument for enforcing the morality of justice. Owners express to one another their common danger and convince those who possess nothing to join them in life under government. The latter, armed with the force of all derived from their agreement or contract, assure security to each member of society—to the owners their property or its transfer only by consent, and to those who own nothing, freedom from oppression. The business of government is, officially, to palliate the inequalities which spring from wealth and poverty by mutual duties which will secure ownership while satisfying, to some degree, the avarice of those who hope to become owners. But while this is its official purpose, government becomes, in fact, the instrument by which the wealthy strengthen the fetters of the poor and enhance their own power to exploit. Government and the laws emerge as an apparatus by which the inequality and interdependence of mankind, economic, social, and moral, might be crystallized and made irrevocable.[31]

We have seen how the capacities of human beings develop from one stage of life to another. We have also seen how the modern (eighteenth century) political state with all its inequalities and dependencies of one person and class upon another has risen from the most primitive human

30 *Ibid.*, pp. 116–19, 124–26.
31 *Ibid.*, pp. 133–38.

life. In the light of these two theories, we must now examine Rousseau's educational recommendations.

RECOMMENDATIONS—PRIVATE EDUCATION

Goal recommendation

The goal which Rousseau recommends for private education is peace with oneself. This tranquility is neither the untrammeled satisfaction of all desires, nor the puritanical abnegation of them. It lies, rather, in a harmony between power and desire which occurs when we want only what we are able to secure through exercise of our native abilities, and when such wants are satisfied through the latter. Enjoying it demands a minimal reliance upon society; for while its institutions—government, business, organized art and amusement, etc.—ought to operate to satisfy needs, they in fact exploit those whom they do not corrupt by multiplying their vicious desires, and are, in any case, threatened by social revolution.[32]

This internal peace is not a single kind of life yielded at the end of a successful education. Rather, a different kind of contentment belongs to each of the five stages through which the individual passes. The goal recommendation in Rousseau's educational theory, thus, splits into five parts, each of which we shall examine briefly.

Subordinate recommendations

Education consists in all the activities involved in achieving peace with oneself. They are of three kinds: activities carried on by nature herself— the growth of organs and faculties through the five stages outlined earlier; the activities of men in directing these natural processes; and those of things—the action of the environment upon the growing person. The activities of nature, the five stages of growth, limit what men can teach each other, and what their experience of the environment can teach them.[33] Consequently, Rousseau recommends a different method and curriculum, though not always a different administrative procedure, as useful for bringing about internal peace in each of the five stages.

There are three different ways for realizing the goal of education: one for private, one for public education, and one for the education of women which, here, must be disregarded. Within private and public education, one can distinguish recommendations concerning method, curriculum, and administration, which are subordinate to that of achieving peace with oneself at each stage of life. Let us consider the proposals concerning private education.

[32] *Emile,* pp. 6–7, 20, 197–98.
[33] *Ibid.,* pp. 6–7.

INFANCY.   In the first stage, one's life is chiefly that of pleasure and pain; but even in this rudimentary existence, there is a kind of calm to be achieved. It can be secured if pain is diminished so far as possible, and pleasure increased. To this end, Rousseau recommends that mothers care for their own children and not rely on servants, feed them at the breast and not employ wet nurses, and wrap them in loose rather than tight garments. Here Rousseau is objecting to practices among the wealthier classes of Europe. Moreover, habits should be discouraged so far as possible in order to prevent the pain of disappointment. But while these recommendations make for a more contented infancy, their validity stems also from their usefulness to later life. Maternal care provides a sound emotional basis for future development, loose garments allow for healthy bodily growth, and the absence of strong habits permits the deliberate establishment of others at a time when good ones can be fostered more readily. With an eye to the future, Rousseau recommends, also, not pampering the infant in order to prevent the habit of domination, not ordering his life rigorously in order to prevent that of submissiveness, and moving him about in order to give him the idea of himself and of space. Generally, the treatment of infants ought to be personal and highly permissive; and what ought or ought not to be done for them can be learned by watching and listening carefully to their expressive babble, the language of infancy, to ascertain when important needs require administrations and when caprices may be ignored.[34]

BOYHOOD.   The education of boyhood as of all later stages of life should be administered by the father or (if not possible) by a tutor. This tutor ought to remain with his student until the latter's education is completed, i.e., until he is about twenty-five. The child should be reared in the country, or at least removed from the vices of society.

Training the senses.   The senses, including the common-sense, dominate this period of life. The curriculum, therefore, ought to consist in the training of the senses and in such knowledge as they alone can offer. There should be no explicit teaching of any language, especially a foreign one, no fables, no books, no moral training; all these require experience which the child does not possess and meet needs which he does not harbor. He cannot learn a subject before equipped with the capacity for it, and he cannot assimilate what appears useless to him. What he wants to know is what the world of sensory observation contains; this is the need which it is possible to satisfy, and whose satisfaction makes the boy happy.[35]

The training of the senses takes the form of correcting the judg-

---

[34] *Ibid.*, pp. 11, 12, 14, 15, 30, 31, 33, 35.
[35] *Ibid.*, pp. 53–55, 73, 76, 77.

ments yielded by one sense with the help of those of others. Thus, immediate judgments concerning the distance and size of things derived from vision can be verified by judgments derived from others. The seen distance of a thing can be corrected or confirmed by walking to it; the seen size by touch. Audition should be trained in a similar way. The sound which bodies make can tell us that they are large or small, far or near, and moving rapidly or slowly. Rousseau notices that this information is not based on hearing alone, but also on a kind of touch, that stimulated by sound waves, chiefly in the face. These auditory and semitactual judgments should be verified by touch and sight. The sense of touch, though not far reaching, is the most accurate of the senses in its judgments of shape, size, texture, and the like; and as the crucial consideration in verifying other sensory judgments, it should be trained to the highest degree of accuracy possible. Rousseau is not concerned to train the child for accurate judgment of taste and smells. A highly developed taste is more than a child needs or wants, and a discriminating sense of smell makes the imagination wild. Rousseau suggests a training for the muscular sense also—a training which will develop accurate discrimination with respect to weight and resistance—even though this sense does not appear in our earlier classification. It would be trained as the others by comparison of its judgments with theirs.

The knowledge which this training should yield is of two kinds: the first is knowledge of particular things, and the training of the senses, if successful, naturally leads to it because that training provides precise sensations of various kinds out of which the common-sense creates an idea of the object causing them. Also, it should produce the ideas of space and time in which particular things may be found and, consequently, a second kind of knowledge, that of the observable relations between things in the natural world.

Methods. Three procedures are suggested for training the sense of vision. So far as possible, all should be applied in games. The first consists of games whose winning requires the most accurate visual judgment of distance. It involves correlating distances seen with distance experienced neuro-muscularly. The prize goes, for example, to the child who most accurately finds the shortest route over a distance estimated by the eye. The second procedure is drawing. Learning how to draw things related in space will increase the precision of ideas of their shapes and will clarify perspective relations. The third procedure is geometical construction. At this stage, the child cannot do mathematics; his intellectual reason is still dormant. But the compass and straightedge will give him an intuitive knowledge of geometrical relations which geometry can later formulate. The method for improving audition is twofold. First, the child should play games in the dark; the absence of light will compel him to rely upon audible relations and locations of bodies. Secondly, simple poetry and simple language often repeated together with reading music will make his feeling for pitch, rhythm, and meter much more acute. The recognition of things by touch and its use in finding one's way about are improved by games in the dark and by maintaining the finger-tips in a subtle condition.[36]

The Basis for Morality.   At this stage, the child cannot act morally. Moral conduct is conduct engaged in because of one's duty, and the child, at this stage, cannot understand what duty is. He tells the truth because it is natural to do so, not because it is a duty; but the notion of promise-keeping is unintelligible to him since he cannot foresee the future and bind himself by a promise to act in a certain way later. Duty, acting always in accord with a rule because one has promised to do so, is a notion irrelevant to the child's behavior. Nonethelesss, one can cultivate in the child those habits which will make right action easier at a later stage. Thus, one ought to encourage the habit of respect for other peoples' possessions; this will enable respect for property, that over whose use some person has legitimate control, at a later stage. Similarly, one ought to engender habits of obedience; not by exacting promises to obey, but by letting the child suffer the consequences of disobedience. If there is any danger that these consequences should not follow, the tutor can make them certain while letting them appear natural. Violent emotions should be discouraged by treating them as illness. The possibilities of doing harm should be kept at a minimum, for the habit of acting harmfully enables the intention to do harm which is necessary to immorality. Morality, at a later stage, may be made more certain by instilling the belief that it is a way of acting one cannot engage in before he is mature.[37]

Reading and Writing.   The child's life, in this stage, is one of no formal instruction, observation of nature, and a great deal of play and gymnastic activity. The closest he should come to formal instruction is learning how to read and write. Make it interesting and useful for him to learn these arts, and any method will accomplish the result.[38]

General Method.   Governing all the detailed procedures which the tutor should use with the boy, there is a single principle. It is: allow him to do

[36] The discussion of the training of the senses and of the ideas it should engender is distributed in *Emile* over a considerable area, but chiefly between pp. 97–121.
[37] *Emile,* pp. 57–68.
[38] *Ibid.,* pp. 80–81.

what he desires so long as that is within his power. Freedom consists in desiring what one is able to do and in doing what one desires. Thus, in allowing the child to do what he desires when it is in his power, one makes him free. This principle requires, first, that dependence upon others, especially parents, be maintained at a minimum. Uncontrolled affection for the child is likely to diminish his power by instilling a great number of desires in him, or to augment it improperly by making him dependent on others for the satisfaction of his needs. Freedom requires that the child should be made self-reliant. Second, the use of this principle means that learning will be agreeable, for the child will be doing what he desires to do. The principle that inspiring interest is the way to teach follows from the principles of freedom. Third, in order to determine what the child's powers are, he should be observed carefully. This supervision will show what desires ought and ought not to be encouraged. Fourth, the child ought to be made to believe that, in learning, he is doing what he desires to do. If necessary, he should be deceived into this belief. Fifth, he should learn what desires are harmful in their satisfaction by the punishment of natural consequences, not by commanding his freedom. Sixth, where desires are too dangerous, force should be used in restraining them. Seventh, imagination should be discouraged, since it leads to a multiplication of desires which would quickly exceed the boy's power to realize them.[39]

Use of the principle of freedom with its attendant maxims assures happiness for the child to the age of twelve. But it does something more. In the child's freedom and independence it lays the basis for knowledge and good conduct in maturity by acquainting him with the natural world and sequestering him from society; it prevents that early frustration of pity which hardens the heart, and that instilling of prejudice which stocks the mind with error, Rousseau calls these procedures "negative education." It teaches neither virtue nor knowledge, but it paves the way for both by preventing the early establishment of error and vice.[40]

PREADOLESCENCE: THE PROBLEM. The third stage of life, preadolescence, is marked by a sudden and great increase in strength. The child's desires remain few and simple, but his growth gives him much more strength than is required for satisfying them—a superfluity which at no other time of life is so ample. This strength naturally assumes two forms: one of working as opposed to playing, the other of wondering about the physical and social world. The child has developed the idea of himself and the idea of securing what he

[39] *Ibid.*, pp. 42–48, 50, 55, 58, 84.
[40] *Ibid.*, pp. 38–39.

wants. Consequently, he can subordinate means to ends and work to secure the latter. His energy also runs over into wondering or desiring to know. The pedagogical problem is to unify these two activities, that of working and that of wondering, into a single activity of learning.[41] We shall examine the curriculum and procedures of instruction first, and then see how this unification is achieved.

Curriculum. The preadolescent should study the natural environment, geometry, geography, astronomy, economy, and social institutions. In studying the natural environment, he ought, simply, to notice the natural objects it contains—forests, lakes, shrubs, animals, and the like. He cannot yet enjoy them, for the emotions which lend them the colors of interest have not yet emerged in his life, dependent as they are upon the sexual desire. But a careful attention to them lays the basis for the later appreciation of nature which Rousseau pointed to, in a very effective way, as among the chief enjoyments of life. Geometry, geography, and astronomy will satisfy his natural wonder about the physical world. The study of the economy and social institutions, especially those of economic production, will yield an idea of his place in society and of social inequality and interdependence. In this connection, he ought to learn a trade such as carpentry; a vocational skill will assure the gentleman a livelihood in case of social revolution—something which Rousseau anticipated and through his writings, perhaps unwittingly, helped to further in France.

Procedures. None of these subjects should be learned from books. Rather, the knowledge of each should grow out of the tutor's directing the observation of the student, and out of the student's exercise of his intellectual reason. Objects in nature should be carefully pointed out to him, their differences and similarities remarked upon and their peculiarities noted. Learning geometry should take the form of independent reasoning and this can be stimulated by posing practical problems whose geometrical solution is felt as important.

Where instruments for measuring are required the student should make them for himself. Geography and astronomy, similarly, should be learned by directed observation and independent thought. The student may learn that the earth is round by being made to notice that the sun rises in the East and sets in the West and by being asked to speculate on the question of how it happens to do so every day. When maps and globes become useful, he should make them for himself. The economy and its institutions should be observed directly by laboring in workshops. This will show him how commodities are produced and distributed, will give

[41] *Ibid.,* pp. 128–29, 140.

him the idea of property, and will show him the social inequalities and interdependencies based upon it. It will also enable him to learn a trade.[42]

General Method.   First, books ought not to be used to convey information to the preadolescent boy. They are made of symbols and symbols absorb the attention of the student, diverting him from the things they symbolize. Globes and maps, made by the student himself, are helpful even though symbols; for the very making of them is the expression and crystallization in the student's mind of the geographical and astronomical facts for which they stand. Books, on the other hand, are not his own creation. There is one exception to the stricture against books. *Robinson Crusoe* should be a constant companion. In it, the student will find an inspiration for the independence of mind, the self-reliant intellectual activity, and the bent toward doing what is practically useful on one's own which is requisite to knowledge of the world. It is not that the student will learn this from the statements in the book, but rather that he will be inspired by its hero's example to a similar individuality of thought and conduct. With the abolition of books, independent observation of things and reasoning about them is the only alternative for teaching.

Second, one should not try to teach the student many things. His interest in a few can lead him to genuine knowledge of them. But if many are forced upon him, he can learn none of them thoroughly and will end by being interested in learning nothing at all. Third, one should teach only those subjects around which center problems whose solution appears useful to him. His interest in learning will be aroused and maintained in this way; and without it no subject can be mastered. Fourth, although a subject is organized after a logical model, as is the case of geometry, one should never teach it by following that model. Interest in a subject, grounded on its utility, never can flow in deductive channels, but it is the student's only motive. Consequently, the only order to follow in instruction is that of association and suggestion. Fifth, one should never appeal, in instruction, to the student's desire to excel over others: this will lead to jealousy and hatred. The student should compete for excellence in learning; but his rival should be his own earlier record, not the activity of those few others with whom in his rural environment he may associate.[43]

The application of these five general principles results in an activity of teaching and learning which focuses wonder and work on a single objective. If employed, they satisfy the student's wonder about things by giving him a knowledge of them; and they afford him this knowledge by

---

[42] *Ibid.*, pp. 130–32, 134–35, 144, 147–48, 152–53, 155–58, 163, 165. These passages discuss both curriculum procedures.
[43] *Ibid.*, pp. 128–30, 133–35, 139, 140, 142, 147.

making it arise as a result of his own work to bring about what he regards as practically useful discovery.

ADOLESCENCE: THE PROBLEM. In this stage of life, love and affection with all their attendant desires and emotions emerge; and the student naturally wishes to associate with others and to learn more about the society they form. But social life ordinarily leads to the multiplication of desires beyond one's power to satisfy them and to the pursuit of selfish ends. Introducing the youth into it and teaching him about it ordinarily leads to the blunting of natural pity, libertinism, and economic exploitation. These prevent that inner peace, the just proportion between desire and power, which is the objective of education at every stage. But the demands of youth cannot be prevented; and the educational problem of this stage is that of providing a protection which will enable him to live in society without adopting its vices, to share a life with others without surrendering his independence, to develop the desires and emotions without submitting to those which are destructive. We shall examine the curriculum, its procedures, and general method in order to see how Rousseau would solve this problem.

Curriculum. During this period, the student should spend some time in Paris where he should read a great many books—ancient history and biography, Greek and Latin imaginative literature, French and Italian poetry, drama, grammar and rhetoric, fables, and contemporary literature. Habits of right conduct should be deliberately established. Natural religion, the belief that God governs the world but authorizes no particular institution, should be instilled; and the student who is not born into a religion should be required to choose some sect.[44]

Procedures. The procedure for dealing with the youth's reading is discussion. It should make three points. The first is that men suffer many sorrows, some natural, but the majority of them artificially induced by economic and social inequalities. The second is that, in society, the student will be threatened by them himself. History and biography, especially, help to make these points. If vanity makes him feel removed from this danger, its natural consequences should be allowed to diminish it; but the exhibition of human folly in fables may be even more useful, especially if he is allowed to draw the moral himself. The third point is that contemporary literature exhibits the artifice and corruption of contemporary society, i.e., the consuming interest in doing more than one is able and a thorough disregard of the simple, generous goods offered by

44 *Ibid.,* pp. 192–94, 199, 200–201, 201–202, 208–209, 209–10, 210, 214, 219–20, 222–23, 278, 298–99.

a more natural life; while a study of ancient literature shows what the good life is since it takes the life of nature as its model. The discussion of his books, along with attendance at the theater, will show the youth that in society men suffer from different degrees of unhappiness, that they are conscious of it, and that he is threatened by it. This knowledge will awaken his pity for others; but it will not blunt that desire as would a direct exposure to much evil. He will desire to be of assistance to others; and to avoid the cause of their unhappiness, i.e., their economic and social interdependence. Grammar and rhetoric will aid this purpose; but it should come late in the period since it would be of little use in view of the small number of associates he is at first allowed.

Habits of good conduct should be established, first, by bringing the student to work for the happiness of others. He cannot yet act rightly since he knows nothing of duty, but doing good deeds engenders the habits of good conduct which enable him to act rightly when he comes to knowledge of morality. Second, they will be established by deferring sexual activity as long as possible. Deferring it allows habits of helping others, independently of one's own emotions toward them, to become established—impartiality undiminished by the social ties incurred by sexual behavior and its attendant emotions. Rousseau is convinced also, that long postponement insures the physical and mental health of the person and his offspring. The postponement of sexual activity would be accomplished by directing the youth's attention into hunting and farming, by a round-the-clock surveillance of him, and by avoiding attractive and forward women.

The teaching of religion should not consist in reading theology; it is too abstract and difficult. It should consist, rather, in bringing the youth to observe the beauty and design of nature and to infer from it the existence of a deity governing the universe—an inference of reason whose conclusion would be reinforced by dictates of the heart. Teaching religion would consist in observation, inference, and attention to one's own intention—all clarified in conversation. It has the merit of assuring good character independent of the restraints of civil law.

General Method. There is no rule which tells the tutor exactly what to do at this stage. His objective is the cultivation of sentiments—of kindly interest in others springing from pity and sex, coupled with a high degree of independence; of willing submission to the Deity Whose recognition is largely a matter of intuition. There are no recipes for creating these emotions. But there is one general principle which is a guide, if not a guarantee, for the instructor. It is that of using one passion to control another. Reason is passive and cannot be used to this end. Passions which distract the student from learning what his books afford, from habits of good conduct, and from religious belief may be controlled by appeal to his loyalty, love, and gratitude toward the tutor, especially if the tutor does not destroy these emotions by letting the student know he expects them. Obedience may also be secured by appeal to the student's growing sense of individuality, by bringing him to see that he is now responsible for his own actions.[45]

This curriculum and these ways of dealing with the student will alert him to the vices of contemporary social life, and will endow him with the capacity to resist them. His insight into the human condition, his habits of good conduct, and his religious belief will make him helpful to others but independent of their caprices. They will keep his desires few, commendable, and within his ability to satisfy them. He will be able to live in society without conforming to its destructive patterns, independent of the fortunes of his station because, aside from wife and children shortly to be acquired, he relies for happiness chiefly upon his own inner resources.

EARLY MATURITY: PROBLEMS AND PROCEDURES. From twenty to twenty-five, the will comes into full play; and the chief decisions it must make concern marriage and the kind of life in society the student adopts. The problem is to enable the young man to make a useful decision on both scores.

The decision to marry should be fostered in the following way. The student should be removed from Paris, and while wandering with his tutor through the countryside, should come upon a family, in straightened circumstances and possessed of a daughter a little younger than he, modest, simple, and reared for the purpose of exercising the duties and enormous powers which Rousseau attributed to the female partner in marriage. He should fall in love with her, be removed from her for an extended period of travel, and return to marry at the age of about twenty-five. The period of travel will enable the student to decide whether his rural discovery is the person with whom he will spend his life and about whom he will center his new-found, but limited emotional dependence.

During the period of travel, the student should study the nature of government and the rights and duties of the citizen. He will learn the distinctions between the general, the corporate, and the particular will; and will observe the manner in which the nations of Europe fail to embody the general will or public good in their laws. He should decide against a life of business, finance, civil service, or the army; all these make him enormously dependent upon others. He should exert his will in favor of an agricultural life on his own land, remote from aggressive

45 *Ibid.*, pp. 190, 192–94, 195–96, 282, 287–88, 292.

neighbors, persecution by priests, and the corruption of cities and institutions of government. Such a life is the best one can find in a society whose governments are corrupt, acting to realize not the public good but their own welfare as a class. Full participation in public affairs where these are degenerate is impossible for the good man because they are not, while he is, motivated by the general will. The conclusion of private education ought to be the withdrawal of the student and his wife, of Emile and Sophy, from participation in public affairs.

Both the decision to marry and to live in society but independently of it require knowledge of morality. This is knowledge of one's duties. Any action is done from duty if it springs from a principle which controls the desires and emotions. Reason offers no such principle; rather, its role is to show the way to realize our desires. The sense of duty, the conscience, and the will decide which desires will be realized; and where reason is informed, the will chooses not merely rightly but also intelligently. The informed will issues commands to our desires which are in conformity with the general will; and since Emile's will develops fully at this time, he is able to act morally—to marry wisely and in conformity with duty, to withdraw from society from which the public good has been banished by governments acting as instruments for the class of the powerful and wealthy.[46] In earlier stages, the instructor controlled the student by pitting one passion or emotion against another; in maturity, the student's own will emerges as controller with the help of reason of those habits or desires which his experience of the world and his feeling-reaction to it have built up.

RECOMMENDATIONS—PUBLIC EDUCATION

Rousseau's consideration of private education culminates with the recommendation that the young adult seeing the corruption of contemporary society should retire from it so far as possible. In no way other than withdrawal can that genuine happiness be achieved which springs from desiring only what our unaided efforts can secure and from decisions made in the light of duty. But this recommendation was directed toward a society which Rousseau regarded as approaching dissolution. Reform was demanded in many nations of Europe; and near the end of Rousseau's lifetime, the chaotic history of Poland seemed to present the opportunity for it. A friend asked Rousseau to make suggestions for reform of the Polish government. His reply includes a section in which he recommends a system of public education—a system which would not exclude

[46] *Ibid.,* pp. 409–10, 420–21.

private education but which is considerably different from it.[47] We may assume that Rousseau would have made similar recommendations for public education in any country where reform seemed likely, i.e., where it seemed possible that actions of government might be brought to embody the general will or public good rather than the good of the wealthy and powerful classes.

Goal recommendation

The purpose of public education is to reproduce the national culture from one generation to another, to develop in the student the national character. This character expresses national manners, customs, and tastes; but its chief trait is that it provides for those who wear it a spontaneous inspiration to work for the general will or good of the nation. In subjecting one's own life to the welfare of the whole, one finds the only freedom which is genuine. He desires the public good, advancing it either by sacrificing his particular inclination in its favor or by contributing to it all his own positive force. Everything he desires is within his power to achieve and he is both happy and free. The promotion of freedom through submission to the general will is the goal recommendation for public education.

Subordinate recommendations

Rousseau orders the curriculum and administration of education to promote this adherence to the general will. Beginning at an early age children should be given intensive instruction in the geography, economy, history, and laws of Poland; the deeds of national heroes should be emphasized. All the public school students should participate in games regularly, and those given a private education should be compelled to take part also. These games should have a common goal, which all can aspire to achieve, and should be played in public. Rousseau justifies this recommendation of compulsory physical education on the grounds that it makes for health, discipline, equality, fraternity, competition, and a habit of living under public inspection and of needing public approval. Prizes would be awarded not by referees but by public acclamation. In short, it would produce a healthy stock and people who have little feeling of self-advancement but a great need for cooperative effort toward the welfare of the state. The public good would be further enhanced by a short period, to follow leaving school, spent in a kind of model government. Here the students would go through all the forms of actual admin-

[47] *The Political Writings of Jean Jacques Rousseau*, vol. II, edited by C. E. Vaughan. *Considérations sur le gouvernement de Pologne, et sur sa Réformation Projetée, Chapitre* IV, "Education." Cambridge University Press, Cambridge, 1915.

istration. It would both interest them in and prepare them for a public life.

The curriculum should be administered through schools whose teachers and administrators were public officials. Rousseau recommends that no foreigners be employed and that all priests should be excluded from the public schools—a drastic recommendation since Church schools were well established as the chief teaching agencies in Poland. Tuition should be low; there should be scholarships carrying much prestige and offered to those altogether unable to pay. Teaching, as such, is not a self-contained profession, but only one aspect of public administration. Consequently all teaching positions should be temporary; and teachers should expect advancement to more brilliant posts upon fulfilling their duties well. They should be married and distinguished for learning and common sense.

The schools should be administered by a central commission whose function it should be to inspect teachers, to make certain that the national objectives are being realized, and to advance or demote them as their performance warrants.

PHILOSOPHY OF EDUCATION

EPISTEMOLOGY

Rousseau holds that private education in societies whose institutions are corrupt should aim at providing an internal happiness in withdrawal from public affairs; and that in societies like that of Poland, where there is hope for reform, public education should aim at the same internal peace without withdrawal by fostering an inclination to serve the public good through institutions newly made responsive to it. In both cases, while knowledge is an important ingredient in the objective of education, its importance is not intrinsic to itself, but lies, rather, in its usefulness for realizing nonintellectual purposes and for the cultivation of good sentiments. It is important to know what is true because knowing it enables us to adjust our desires to our powers and to see which desires should be realized. Rousseau presents a theory as to the extent and method of knowledge which seems to support this view. Let us examine it, briefly, in order to see if it does so.

Extent of knowledge

To know is to be certain about something, to see that some statement is true about it and could not be otherwise. However, we are immediately aware only of sensations and ideas. It seemed to Rousseau that we could be certain of the truth of no statements except those describing our sensations and ideas, that we could never be certain of the truth of statements about the things our ideas represent. But he argues himself out of this subjectivist position by adopting the following rule: admit as self-evidently true all statements you cannot help believing, and as true, all which follow from them; disregard all others.[48] Let us see where this rule led him.

Rousseau, first, could not help believing that he had ideas of the various kinds of sensation and that by comparing them, he united many of them into compound ideas which served to represent physical things. It followed, he thought, that there must be something which carried on these activities of sensing, and of comparing and combining. This was his self—an immaterial substance whose characteristic trait is the capacity to think or be aware of things. Following his rule, and admitting the activities of sensing, comparing, and combining, he concluded, first, that he existed. Secondly, he could not help believing that some of the ideas formed by the common-sense corresponded to single physical objects which were their causes outside his mind. For the simple sensations out of which they were formed, the color, scent, and solidity of the rose, were involuntarily present to him; and it was clear that each, taken separately, could not be caused by a separate physical object. Those sensations and images which did not come at will, and which he combined into the idea of a single object, must be caused by a single physical substance—a substance different from any mind because characterized by a trait incompatible with the capacity to think, i.e., by extension. His rule, thus, enabled Rousseau to show that he could know that he existed, and that in perception he confronted a world other than himself. Every person might make this argument, and each such argument shows that there is a self making it who confronts a common physical environment.[49]

Rousseau drew a third conclusion which concerned what we can know about the physical environment and the self. The objects in the former are composed of matter. The properties essential to matter were those which he could deduce from the qualities it caused him to perceive in it and these were three in number. Material objects he sometimes perceived in motion and sometimes at rest; consequently, motion was not natural to them. Matter does not move spontaneously or of itself. Secondly, Rousseau could not help but experience his own act of will as the cause of some of the motions of his own body; only those material bodies move spontaneously which have wills. Consequently, the motion of material objects is given to them, ultimately, by some willing, voluntary agent. We can know that the physical universe is made of material sub-

[48] *Emile,* pp. 231–32.
[49] *Ibid.,* pp. 232–34, 241–42.

stances, that our souls are active immaterial substances, and that some active, willing agent gives material substances their motion.[50]

From experiment and observation, Rousseau tells us fourthly, we learn that bodies move according to general laws; and he supposed that this rule of law extends throughout nature that every event of every kind, physical, biological, and even psychological, may be described in terms of some law. According to this view nothing happens at any time past, present or future, which cannot be described as accompanied by an event of some particular kind. Laws tell us that things happen in uniform ways. Consequently, it is possible to predict what will happen in the future if we know the laws which describe all of nature.[51]

While everything we know, beyond what is immediately present to us, is known with the help of laws, we often make mistaken claims to knowledge. These mistakes have no basis in sensations. What we sense is clearly present to us and we are incapable of being in error concerning it. Mistakes arise in the judgments or inferences we make from our sensations, and are corrected most efficiently by more careful sensory observation of the same kind as that from which we drew the mistaken inference. Consider a stick partially submerged in water. It looks bent; and from this visual sensation, we infer that it really is bent. We correct this mistaken inference by more careful visual observation; we stir up the water, causing the stick to look as if it were following the ripples; we draw the water off, causing it to look as if it were growing straight. Certainly, the stick does not move with the ripples and does not grow straight as the water is removed. Our eyes did not deceive us in showing us a bent stick because they have shown us that it is not bent. The procedure followed for further visual observation gives a true idea of the object visually observed, i.e., that it is straight; consequently, it makes it impossible to infer anything erroneous concerning the shape of the stick from our visual idea of it.[52]

Method

Rousseau advocates and uses a method for securing knowledge which contains three elements. All three are not involved in every one of his claims to knowledge, nor does he hold that every procedure for acquiring knowledge need contain all three. Observation, experiment, generalization, and inference or reasoning are necessary to support any claim about the existence or occurrence of particular things and for asserting that particular laws describe nature. The "inner light," faith, or the dictate of

50 *Ibid.*, pp. 234–36.
51 *Ibid.*, p. 234.
52 Rousseau's position here is altogether confused. The inference that the stick is bent is corrected not merely by further visual experience, but also by appeal to judgments to the effect that sticks do not move with ripples of the water they are in, and do not grow straight as the water is removed.

one's heart are sufficient to support statements about the universe as a whole, particularly those of a religious kind. But a third element always governs both these procedures. We should not bother even to try to know what has no practical importance for us. Knowledge arises out of our hopes and fears as an instrument for realizing the former and allaying the latter. This practical need should direct all our empirical investigation of nature and all our speculation, based on what the inner light declares, concerning its origin and governance. While the statements in which we express our knowledge must be true or probable, by virtue of empirical evidence or of the evidence proffered by the inner light, what is important about their truth or probability is that it lends to action based upon them utility in satisfying our non-intellectual needs. All claims to know which have no practical importance, especially the metaphysical systems of philosophers, should be disregarded as vain and idle.[53]

Rousseau's discussion of the extent of knowledge seems to be intended to show that his recommendation of the student's personal exploration of nature can succeed. These explorations amount to, and in some cases are designed as, experiments; and the view that the world proceeds according to laws supports this recommendation by assuring us that the experiments can lead to the discovery of the laws. His discussion of the method for clarifying our sensory observations and for avoiding errors of inference is designed to justify his recommendation of the training of the senses and the deliberate formation of clear ideas of things, especially in boyhood and preadolescence. His statements concerning the empirical method seem to justify his recommendation that the student should rely on his own investigations rather than on those of others written down in books—his thoroughgoing de-emphasis of authority. His exaltation of the inner light is a justification for rejecting as legitimate parts of the curriculum all those philosophical systems which impugn natural religion. His emphasis on the pragmatic origin of knowledge and the instrumental character of reason justifies his exclusion from the curriculum of that large amount of traditional learning which he regards as of no practical importance. It should be noted, however, that Rousseau's discussion of the extent and method of knowledge is little more than a declaration, and that its guarantee of the recommendations mentioned is little more than the tone of conviction in which it is stated.

METAPHYSICS

Rousseau expresses a metaphysical theory which has a certain relevance to the general aim of education, both private and public, as he

[53] *Emile,* pp. 231–32, 240; *Discourse upon Inequality,* pp. 39–41.

understands it. In expressing it, his intent seems to be to show that it is possible to develop persons who can control their own lives. Let us see how he guarantees this possibility.

God and the physical universe

Rousseau's metaphysical theory contains four propositions of especial importance here. He holds,.first, that God exists and that the entire physical universe moves according to laws which express His will. This motion, we have seen, cannot be inherent in bodies; and since the only source of motion with which we are directly acquainted is our own will, we cannot but conclude that what moves all things is a will. Observation shows that the parts of the physical universe move according to law; the solar system, the circulation of the blood, the adaptation of different forms of life, one to another, are examples. It follows, Rousseau thought, that the will which makes things move in such ways is an intelligence. There are many ways in which bodies could move, but there is only one set of laws according to which they actually *do* move. The agent which controls their moving, consequently, must have selected the patterns they actually follow from among all those which are possible, and this awareness of possibilities requires intelligence.

This argument for the existence of an intelligence which controls the physical universe by its will, Rousseau finds reinforced by the inner light; he cannot help but feel that its conclusion is true and the systems of jargon constructed by metaphysicians neither enhance nor diminish his conviction.[54]

Secondly, the body which every human being possesses is governed by law as much as is any other. Some of its motions are given to it wholly from without—its motion with that of the earth, and its fall when not supported. Others are composed of both external and internal factors. Through the sense organs, external bodies cause sensations whose pleasure or pain brings about the motions of desire, attraction toward those bodies whose ideas are pleasant and repulsion from those whose ideas are painful. In cooperation with the instincts of pity and of sex, a complex of habitual desires and actions, with all their attendant emotions, comes into existence and constitutes the essential pattern of the individual personality. Both as a physical object and as a focus of sensations and attendant habits, the actions of the human body are quite as much determined by physical law as those of any other material substance.

God and the moral universe

Yet, we often know that those of our actions which express our desires are wrong. Injury is treated with revenge, misfortune with contempt, and

[54] *Emile*, pp. 235–38.

opportunity with self-aggrandizement rather than consideration for others. Still, we know that we should love our enemies, assist the unfortunate, and consider ourselves as no more important than others. We feel an opposition between the rules which ought to govern our conduct, and the inclinations toward personal satisfaction dictated by pleasure and pain which actually do so—a contradiction between moral laws and physical laws. This contradiction demonstrates that the human being is an immaterial substance or soul as well as a body. For there must be something which can act according to the duties we recognize; and since the body is governed by physical rather than moral law, there must be some other substance over which the latter holds dominion. This immaterial substance is a part of ourselves; and enmeshed in our senses, we frequently disregard its moral law in favor of the physical.[55]

Thirdly, the moral law expresses itself in our acts of will. The will is our ability to choose between desires and it involves, in each case of its exercise, a judgment that it is better to act on one desire rather than another. This judgment may be to act on a desire which is in accord with duty; then, the action springing from it is right. It may be, also, to act on one which is not; then, the action is either wrong or indifferent. But in both cases, the judgment and its action, the whole act of will, is free. It has no antecedent cause; there is no physical law which describes it. In their conduct, human beings are trapped in a system of universal, invariant, physical law willed by Providence; but having immaterial souls, they are also free and active agents whose wills introduce into nature actions which are "no part of the system marked out by Providence. . . ."[56]

Fourthly, the moral law which governs the free acts of the soul is sanctioned by God's will. The soul consists of no parts; hence, it cannot suffer dissolution. We are not, however, directly aware of it in ourselves. In memory, past consciousness presents itself to us, and in expectation future consciousness is anticipated. One's awareness of self is not that of an immaterial substance but, rather, that of a unity of conscious acts held together by this backward and forward glance. After death, the unity continues but expectation disappears, leaving only a recollection of our conduct during life. God's reward for virtue is our memory of it. His punishment of the wicked is not everlasting since that would be incompatible with His goodness; it is the torment for evil-doing, imposed by one's own conscience and by other persons, experienced during this life.[57]

Rousseau's metaphysical picture shows God as a willing intelligent agent whose existence and nature is represented in the universe in two ways: first, in the system of physical law which explains the motion of all

[55] *Ibid.,* pp. 240–41, 246–47, 256–57.
[56] *Ibid.,* p. 243.
[57] *Ibid.,* pp. 246–47.

bodies; and, secondly, in the system of moral law which all immaterial substances are free to obey and free to exemplify by control or denial of desires natural to the bodies with which they are connected.

The freedom which this metaphysical theory insures makes plausible the chief objective of both private and public education. If correct, it shows that the mature person is free to do what he ought, i.e., to act upon those desires which are not only within his power but which are also in accord with duty. In retirement from a corrupt society and in participation in a good one, this is the form which any life ought to exhibit. The metaphysical theory shows that it is possible despite the universal reign of physical law and thus gives foundation to the curriculum and method which is directed toward it.

ETHICS

Rousseau's ethical theory is not set down systematically, but in *Emile* and *The Social Contract* we find some ethical reflection which provides at least a sketch for it. This sketch yields a definition for "the good life," and a statement as to what some of its constituents are. It plays the role in Rousseau's thought of a justification for the objectives of education both private and public.

The good life

The good life, for Rouuseau, is one of happiness; but since the notion of happiness varies from one person to another and is frequently quite unclear, Rousseau's definition of the good life must be explained further by explaining his notion of happiness. In society under government by virtue of the organization of economic and other activities which it implies, men possess more power to control the world than is necessary to satisfy their fundamental needs. To use it, men have multiplied their desires far beyond necessity and, through the instrumentality of their institutions, have exploited one another for trivial or evil purposes—for the sake of shallowness and greed. The pursuit of such goals is unending because the power to satisfy new desires is always present. It is found in the lives of most men but it embodies the genuine character of none. The interdependence of human beings in society has made them discontented because, by increasing their power without improving the institutions through which it is expressed, it has generated a form of life which does not embody the most widespread and fundamental of human needs. Power to satisfy desire does not lead to happiness.

In the state of nature, life apart from government and its institutions, the power of men is insufficient to satisfy their fundamental needs. When there is independence rather than cooperation under government, there is insecurity for all. An excess of desire over power leads to misery and frustration. Here, too, the genuine character of no one can be expressed in his life since the power to express it does not exist. Discontent, again, is the result.

Happiness consists in an inner peace which we find when power and desire are in equilibrium and when power is exercised to realize good desires. We cannot be happy if we harbor more desires than we can realize, and if we have more energy than is required to satisfy them. But we also cannot be happy merely because our power to control the environment is exactly used up by the satisfaction of the desires we feel. We might enjoy such an equilibrium and yet suffer from discontentment because we recognize that our power is utilized for the realization of desires which are indifferent or evil rather than good. The inner peace which is happiness requires that power be exerted for the satisfaction of good desires.[58]

The important problem then is that of identifying those desires which are good. It is easy to suppose that the goodness of a desire is its conduciveness to an action which is pleasant, but this view Rousseau rejects. It is also easy to suppose that it consists in its leading to an action which is forced upon the agent by some other person, in its leading to an action which is compelled by civil or divine law. This view Rousseau rejects also. Pleasure does not make a desire good and conformity to law is prudence, at best. The goodness of a desire consists in our choosing to realize it rather than another and in our choosing correctly.[59] A desire is good because we will correctly realize it.

We must next ask what makes our act of will one which is correct. Here, Rousseau seems to invoke the distinction between the general, the corporate, and the individual will, i.e., the welfare of the whole, of a more limited group, and of a particular person. Ideally, the correctness of an act of will consists in the fact that the realization of the desire which it selects constitutes part of the general will or public welfare. Assuming that a road open to all is part of the public welfare while a toll road is not and that I desire both, my selection of the former desire for realization is a correct act of will. Class or private interests might be better served by selecting the desire for a toll road, but this act of will would be incorrect since the welfare of smaller groups and of individuals may be incompatible with that of the whole. Our desires frequently conflict, tending sometimes toward the public welfare and sometimes not. Those are good which are in conformity with duty, and duty consists in the general rule that we ought to will to realize the general welfare.

---

[58] *Ibid.,* pp. 44–47, 59, 298–99.
[59] *Ibid.,* pp. 256, 408–10; *Social Contract,* Book II, Chapter III.

The institutions of society (Rousseau had in mind that of the later eighteenth century) are devised and controlled in such a way that the general will cannot be embodied in them. They are inadequate for the realization of good desires. In these unfavorable circumstances, must we say that there can be no good desires, i.e., that there can be no act of will which is in conformity with duty? Rousseau seems to give two answers. The first is to repeat the view that good desires are those which are in conformity with duty or the general will and to recommend in consequence a reformation of social institutions, violent if necessary. The second is to assert a quite different view, i.e., that where we cannot act on desires sanctioned by duty or the general will, we should select for action those which are within our power and lead to our own welfare (the particular will).[60]

The good life, one of happiness, consists in an inner peace which proceeds from an equilibrium between power and desire and from a free and correct choice of those desires which we act to satisfy. This free choice is correct if the desire selected leads to action whose consequences make part of the general will; or, where the general will is precluded, if the desire selected makes for action whose consequences constitute part of the particular will. In general, the good life is tranquility which proceeds from the satisfaction of desires in accord with duty as both vary with concrete circumstances.

Criteria for the good life

What are the criteria by which we decide which of our desires should be realized? Many social situations are possible. How can we tell which of them is the public good or general will? Many personal lives are possible. How can we tell which of them is the individual good or particular will? We cannot say that reason affords the answer to either question; for while reason can show us the consequences of adopting this rule rather than that, of taking this rule to be our duty rather than that one, it cannot tell us that the consequences constitute the public or individual good. The dictates of conscience or of the heart are the ultimate resort. That a particular social arrangement constitutes the social good or general will is decided by noticing whether conscience gives approval to it and the same must be said for the individual good or particular will. The criterion for the good life, both social and individual, lies in the fact that the rules of duty which it embodies are acceptable to conscience; and this is the fact that the consequences yielded by following them are approved by that faculty.[61]

---

[60] *Emile,* pp. 10, 46, 59, 157, 198, 256, 298–99, 421.
[61] *Ibid.,* pp. 34, 68, 248–49, 250, 252–53.

Education and the good life

Rousseau holds that each stage of development carries with it its own good. But there are two kinds of good and the various stages of life cannot all be good in the same sense. The life which is naturally good is one which is tranquil because of an equilibrium between innocent desires and the capacity to satisfy them. Apart from institutions based upon private property and socialized techniques of production, the desires of men are innocent as are also the desires of children. This is the import of Rousseau's view that God made all things good and that man is born free, while it is human meddling which makes things evil and enslaves the meddler. The life which is morally good is that in which guilty desires are properly subject to the rule of duty. It is the good life as that has been outlined above.

In accord with this distinction between the naturally and the morally good life, Rousseau argues that the first four stages of life can be naturally good and that the business of education is to assure the achievement of it in each period. Thus, the infant should be permitted the pleasure which comes from fulfillment of all its desires provided such permissiveness does not lead to injuring it or establishment of harmful habits; the boy should be made happy by satisfying his curiosity about the sensible world; the preadolescent, by combining satisfaction of his dominant desires to know and to work; and the adolescent, by formation in him of those habits of feeling and acting which yield the greatest degree of tranquility toward newly emergent desires and emotions. In each case, the happiness which education should engender is only naturally good since prior to maturity, the person cannot understand a rule of duty, nor act upon it. Despite this truth, in the second, third, and fourth stages of development, the child can be brought to behave as if he were acting because of a rule of duty; and this establishment of habits of the right sort is a preparation in boyhood, preadolescence, and adolescence for the morally good life of maturity. The first four stages of education have their own natural good; but in each, the tutor should prepare the child for an adult life whose tranquility stems from the exercise of power in accord with duty for the realization of desires. The nature of duty, itself, as well as of concrete duties is the chief subject for mastery in the last stage of private education. We have seen that it is the goal which informs all of public education from its beginning to its end.

Duty and the political state

Only in the uncorrupted political state can the life which is morally good be fully realized. One's duty is always to act upon a rule whose obedience makes part of the general will or public good. In everyone, there are two tendencies: a tendency to adopt such rules and another to adopt those courses of action which make part of the corporate or particular will. Acting in the latter way, however, produces the insecurity and exploitation which characterizes both the latest stage in the state of nature and life in the corrupt political states of civilization. But the contract or agreement upon which political states rest, is an agreement between these two tendencies in oneself—an agreement that where there is incompatability between interest in the general will and interest in lesser goods, the former shall prevail. In this contract between the two parts of the self, Rousseau finds the force inherent in the rule of duty, and identifying this rule as commanding the general will, he identifies the morally good life with one conducted within uncorrupted political and social institutions—with a life in obedience to civil law.[62]

The agreement with ourselves, always to act in accord with duty, involves a complete abrogation of individual autonomy. In the state of nature, one has rights over his own life, property, speech, etc. The decision to live in a political state, however, is the decision to give up all these rights to that state. Consequently, the citizen can claim only those rights explicitly granted to him by the state. Thus, private property, freedom of speech, of thought, of association, *et alia,* are matters for the state to determine; and Rousseau quite clearly believed that a healthy state would limit the scope of some of these rights considerably—most notably the right to private property. Although his views on this subject were not consistent, he seems often to have argued that the use of state power for the protection and enhancement of the interests of the indolent and wealthy should be remedied; and the remedy was the reconstruction of the state in such a way as to destroy the power of parties and classes. This remedy involves an enormous limitation upon the private ownership, especially of land, which led to the inequality and corruption against which he inveighed. The social contract, or decision to act in accord with duty, makes personal rights a gift from the state rather than an individual endowment.[63]

For Rousseau, it was the business of private education to enable people to live independently of those societies which did not embody the general will and to survive their reconstruction. On the other hand, it was the business of public education to promote the good life by fostering an attitude of spontaneous submission to duty as the moral manifestation of the general will and as an instrument for its embodiment in the state.

---

[62] *The Social Contract,* I, vi, vii; II, iv; III, xvi; IV, ii.
[63] *Ibid.,* I, vi, xi; II, iv.

A Guide to Selections from *A Discourse upon the Origin and
Foundations of the Inequality among Mankind*

In the passage selected from the "Preface," Rousseau states that
the two natural motives of men are those of self-love or self-preservation
and of pity.

In the passages selected from the "First Part," Rousseau discusses
the state of nature. In the first stage, men are wholly independent of one
another, healthy, and utterly primitive. In the second stage language
develops out of instinctual cries; and it affords, together with the elements of love—pity and sex—a basis for social organization.

In the passages selected from the "Second Part," spontaneous social
organization is ascribed to the second stage. The third, marked by the
introduction of smelting and related agricultural techniques, consists in
the establishment of property, the development of civilized emotions and
tastes, and the introduction of conflict and inequality.

In the fourth stage, the social contract imposes law protecting
property. In this civilized state, men's vices pervade their lives, and stem
from their inability to live except in the opinion of others. The dependence of each on others—the inequality of men—is fixed by law,
and it is the source of misery. Primitive men, on the other hand, lead a
life of virtue. Governed by no law, they are equal to one another; and
since none has need of the good opinion of others, primitive men do not
engage in vice in order to secure it.

SELECTIONS FROM

A Discourse upon the Origin and Foundations of the Inequality among Mankind*

PREFACE

Laying aside therefore all the scientific Treatises, which teach us
merely to consider Men such as they have made themselves, and confining
myself to the first and most simple Operations of the human Soul, I

*Printed for R. and J. Dodsley, in Pallmall, London, MDCCLXI.

think I can distinguish in it two Principles prior to Reason, one of which interests us deeply in our Preservation and Welfare, and the other inspires us with a natural Aversion to see any other being, but especially any Being like ourselves, suffer or perish. It is from the Concurrence and the Combination our Mind is capable of forming between these two Principles, without there being the least Necessity for adding to them that of Sociability, that, in my Opinion, flow all the Rules of natural Right; Rules, which Reason is afterwards obliged to re-establish upon other Foundations, when by a gradual Exertion of its own Powers it has at last stifled the Authority of Nature. . . .

FIRST PART

What therefore is precisely the Subject of this Discourse? It is to point out, in the Progress of Things, that Moment, when, Right taking place of Violence, Nature became subject to Law; to display that Chain of surprising Events, in consequence of which the strong submitted to serve the weak, and the People to purchase imaginary Ease, at the Expense of real Happiness. . . .

Let us begin therefore, by laying aside Facts, for they do not affect the Question. The Researches, in which we may engage on this Occasion, are not to be taken for Historical Truths, but merely as hypothetical and conditional Reasonings, fitter to illustrate the Nature of Things, than to show their true Origin, like those Systems, which our Naturalists daily make of the Formation of the World. . . .

If I strip this Being [man], thus constituted, of all the supernatural Gifts which he may have received, and of all the artificial Faculties, which he could not have acquired but by slow Degrees; if I consider him, in a word, such as he must have issued from the Hands of Nature; I see an Animal less strong than some, and less active than others, but, upon the whole, the most advantageously organized of any: I see him satisfying the calls of Hunger under the first Oak, and those of Thirst at the first Rivulet; I see him laying himself down to sleep at the Foot of the same Tree, that afforded him his Meal; and behold, this done, all his Wants are completely supplied. . . .

Men, accustomed from their Infancy to the Inclemency of the Weather, and to the Rigour of the different Seasons; inured to Fatigue, and obliged to defend, naked and without Arms, their Life and their Prey against the other wild Inhabitants of the Forest, or at least to avoid their Fury by flight, acquire a robust and almost unalterable Habit of Body; the Children, bringing with them into the World the excellent Constitution of their Parents, and strengthening it by the same Exercises that first produced it, attain by this Means all the Vigour that the human Frame is capable of. . . .

The first Language of Man, the most universal and most energetic of all Languages, in short, the only Language he had Occasion for, before there was a Necessity of persuading assembled Multitudes, was the Cry of Nature. As this Cry was never extorted but by a Kind of Instinct in the most urgent Cases, to implore Assistance in great Danger, or Relief in great Sufferings, it was of little use in the common Occurrences of Life, where more moderate Sentiments generally prevail. When the Ideas of Men began to extend and multiply, and a closer Communication began to take place among them, they laboured to devise more numerous Signs, and a more extensive Language: they multiplied the Inflections of the Voice, and added to them Gestures, which are, in their own Nature, more expressive, and whose Meaning depends less on any prior Determination. They therefore expressed visible and moveable Objects by Gestures, and those which strike the Ear, by imitative Sounds: but as Gestures scarcely indicate any thing except Objects that are actually present or can be easily described, and visible Actions; as they are not of general Use, since Darkness or the Interposition of an opake Medium renders them useless; and as besides they require Attention rather than excite it: Men at length bethought themselves of substituting to them the Articulations of Voice, which, without having the same Relation to any determinate Object, are, in quality of instituted Signs, fitter to represent all our Ideas; a Substitution, which could only have been made by common Consent, and in a Manner pretty difficult to practise by Men, whose rude Organs were unimproved by Exercise; a Substitution, which is in itself still more difficult to be conceived, since the Motives to this unanimous Agreement must have been some how or another expressed, and Speech therefore appears to have been exceedingly requisite to establish the use of Speech.

We must allow, that the Words, first made use of by Men, had in their Minds a much more extensive Signification, than those employed in Languages of some standing, and that, considering how ignorant they were of the Division of Speech into its constituent Parts; they at first gave every Word the meaning of an entire Proposition. When afterwards they began to perceive the Difference between the Subject and Attribute, and between Verb and Noun, a Distinction which required no mean Effort of Genius, the Substantives for a time were only so many proper Names, the Infinitive was the only Tense, and as to Adjectives, great Difficulties must have attended the Development of the Idea that represents them, since every Adjective is an abstract Word, and Abstraction is an unnatural and very painful Operation.

At first they gave every Object a peculiar Name, without any regard to its Genus or Species, things which these first Institutors of Language were in no Condition to distinguish; and every Individual presented itself solitary to their Minds, as it stands in the Table of Nature. If they called an Oak A, they called another Oak B; so that their Dictionary must have been more extensive in Proportion as their Knowledge of Things was more confined. It could not but be a very difficult Task to get rid of so diffuse and embarrassing a Nomenclature; as in order to marshal the several Beings under common and generic Denominations, it was necessary to be first acquainted with their Properties, and their Differences; to be stocked with Observations and Definitions, that is to say, to understand Natural History and Metaphysics, Advantages which the Men of these Times could not have enjoyed.

Besides, general Ideas cannot be conveyed to the Mind without the Assistance of Words, nor can the Understanding seize them without the Assistance of Propositions. . . . Every general Idea is purely intellectual; let the Imagination tamper ever so little with it, it immediately becomes a particular Idea. Endeavour to present to yourself the Image of a Tree in general, you never will be able to do it; in spite of all your Efforts it will appear big or little, thin or tufted, of a bright or a deep Colour; and were you Master to see nothing in it, but what can be seen in every Tree, such a Picture would no longer resemble any Tree. Beings perfectly abstract are perceived in the same manner, or are only conceivable by the Assistance of Speech. . . . We must therefore make use of Propositions; we must therefore speak to have general Ideas; for the Moment the Imagination stops, the Mind must stop too, if not assisted by Speech. If therefore the first Inventors could give no Names to any Ideas but those they had already, it follows that the first Substantives could never have been any thing more than proper Names. . . .

I stop at these first Advances, and beseech my Judges to suspend their Lecture a little, in order to consider, what a great Way Language has still to go, in regard to the Invention of Physical Substantives alone, (tho' the easiest Part of Language is to invent,) to be able to express all the Sentiments of Man, to assume an invariable form, to bear being spoken in public, and to influence Society: I earnestly entreat them to consider how much Time and Knowledge must have been requisite to find out Numbers, abstract Words, the Aorists, and all the other Tenses of Verbs, the Particles, and Syntax, the Method of connecting Propositions and Arguments, of forming all the Logic of Discourse. For my own Part, I am so scared at the Difficulties that multiply at every Step, and so convinced of the almost demonstrated Impossibility of Languages owing their Birth and Establishment to Means that were merely human, that I must leave to whoever may please to take it up, the Task of discussing this difficult Problem, "Which was the most necessary, Society already formed to invent Languages, or Languages already invented to form Society?"

But be the Case of these Origins ever so mysterious, we may at least infer from the little care which Nature has taken to bring Men together by mutual Wants, and make the use of Speech easy to them, how little she has done towards making them sociable, and how little she has contributed to any thing which they themselves have done to become so. . . .

It is therefore certain that Pity is a natural Sentiment, which, by moderating in every Individual the Activity of Self-love, contributes to the mutual Preservation of the whole Species. It is this Pity which hurries us without Reflection to the Assistance of those we see in Distress; it is this pity which, in a State of Nature, stands for Laws, for Manners, for Virtue, with this Advantage, that no one is tempted to disobey her sweet and gentle Voice: . . . It is in a word, in this natural Sentiment, rather than in fine-spun Arguments, that we must look for the Cause of that Reluctance which every Man would experience to do Evil, even independently of the Maxims of Education. . . .

Let us begin by distinguishing between what is moral and what is physical in the Passion called Love. The physical Part of it is that general Desire which prompts the Sexes to unite with each other; the moral Part is that which determines this Desire, and fixes it upon a particular Object to the Exclusion of all others, or at least gives it a greater Degree of Energy for this preferred Object. Now it is easy to perceive that the moral Part of Love is a factitious Sentiment, engendered by Society, and cried up by the Women with great Care and Address in order to establish their Empire, and secure Command to that sex which ought to obey. This Sentiment, being founded on certain Notions of Beauty and Merit which a Savage is not capable of having, and upon Comparisons which he is not capable of making, can scarcely exist in him: for as his Mind was never in a Condition to form abstract Ideas of Regularity and Proportion, neither is his Heart susceptible to Sentiments of Admiration and Love, which, even without our perceiving it, are produced by our Application of these Ideas; he listens solely to the Dispositions implanted in him by Nature, and not to Taste which he never was in a Way of acquiring; and every Woman answers his Purpose. . . .

SECOND PART

Every thing now begins to wear a new Aspect. Those who heretofore wandered thro' the Woods, by taking to a more settled Way of Life, gradually flock together, coalesce into several separate Bodies, and at length form in every Country distinct Nations, united in Character and Manners, not by any Laws or Regulations, but by an uniform Manner of Life, a Sameness of Provisions, and the common Influence of the Climate. A permanent Neighbourhood must at last infallibly create some Connection between different Families. The transitory Commerce required by Nature soon produced, among the Youth of both Sexes living in Contiguous Cabins, another kind of Commerce, which besides being equally agreeable is rendered more durable by mutual Intercourse. Men begin to consider different Objects, and to make Comparisons; they insensibly acquire Ideas of Merit and Beauty, and these soon produce Sentiments of Preference. By seeing each other often they contract a habit, which makes it painful not to see each other always. Tender and agreeable Sentiments steal into the Soul, and are by the smallest Opposition wound up into the most impetuous Fury: Jealousy kindles with Love; Discord triumphs; and the gentlest of Passions requires Sacrifices of human Blood to appease it.

In Proportion as Ideas and Sentiments succeed each other, and the Head and the Heart exercise themselves, Men continue to shake off their original Wildness, and their Connections become more intimate and extensive. They now begin to assemble round a great Tree: Singing and Dancing, the genuine Offspring of Love and Leisure, become the Amusement or rather the Occupation of the Men and Women, free from Care, thus gathered together. Every one begins to survey the rest, and wishes to be surveyed himself; and public Esteem acquires a Value. He who sings or dances best; the handsomest, the strongest, the most dexterous, the most eloquent, comes to be the most respected: this was the first Step towards Inequality, and at the same time towards Vice. From these first Preferences there proceeded on one side Vanity and Contempt, on the other Envy and Shame; and the Fermentation raised by these new Levains at length produced Combinations fatal to Happiness and Innocence.

Men no sooner began to set a Value upon each other, and know what Esteem was, than each laid claim to it, and it was no longer safe for any Man to refuse it to another. Hence the first Duties of Civility and Politeness, even among Savages; and hence every voluntary Injury became an Affront, as besides the Mischief, which resulted from it as an Injury, the Party offended was sure to find in it a Contempt for his Person more intolerable than the Mischief itself. It is thus that every Man, punishing the Contempt expressed for him by others in proportion to the value he set upon himself, the Effects of Revenge became terrible, and Men learned to be sanguinary and cruel. Such precisely was the Degree attained by most of the savage Nations with whom we are acquainted. And it is for want of sufficiently distinguishing Ideas, and observing at how great a Distance these People were from the first state of Nature, that so many Authors have hastily concluded that Man is naturally cruel, and requires a regular System of Police to be reclaimed; whereas nothing can be more gentle than him in his primitive State, when placed by Nature at an equal Distance from the Stupidity of Brutes, and the pernicious good Sense of civilized Man; and equally confined by Instinct and Reason to the Care of providing against the Mischief which threatens him, he is withheld by natural Compassion from doing any Injury to others, so far from being ever so little prone even to return that which he has received. . . .

As long as Men remained satisfied with their rustic Cabins; as long as they confined themselves to the use of Clothes made of the Skins of other Animals, and the use of Thorns and Fish-bones, in putting these Skins together; as long as they continue to consider Feathers and Shells as sufficient Ornaments, and to paint their Bodies of different Colours, to improve or ornament their Bows and Arrows, to form and scoop out with sharp-edged Stones some little fishing Boats, or clumsy Instruments of Music; in a word, as long as they undertook such Works only as a single Person could finish, and stuck to such Arts as did not require the joint Endeavours of several Hands, they lived free, healthy, honest and happy, as much as their Nature would admit, and continued to enjoy with each other all the Pleasures of an independent Intercourse; but from the Moment one Man began to stand in need of another's Assistance; from the Moment it appeared an Advantage for one Man to possess the Quantity of Provisions requisite for two, all Equality vanished; Property started up; Labour became necessary; and boundless Forests became smiling Fields, which it was found necessary to water with human Sweat, and in which Slavery and Misery were soon seen to sprout out and grow with the Fruits of the Earth.

Metallurgy and Agriculture were the two Arts whose Invention produced this great Revolution. With the Poet, it is Gold and Silver, but with the Philosopher, it is Iron and Corn, which have civilized Men, and ruined Mankind. Accordingly both one and the other were unknown to the Savages of *America,* who for that very Reason have always continued Savages; nay other Nations seem to have continued in a State of Barbarism, as long as they continued to exercise one only of these Arts without the other; and perhaps one of the best Reasons that can be assigned, why *Europe* has been, if not earlier, at least more constantly and better civilized than the other Quarters of the World, is that she both abounds most in Iron and is best qualified to produce Corn.

To the tilling of the Earth the Distribution of it necessarily succeeded, and to Property once acknowledged the first Rules of Justice: for to secure every Man his own, every Man must have something. Moreover, as Men began to extend their Views to Futility, and all found themselves in possession of more or less Goods capable of being lost, every one in particular had Reason to fear, lest Reprizals should be made on him for any Injury he might do to others. This Origin is so much the more natural, as it is impossible to conceive how Property can flow from any other Source but Industry; for what can a Man add but his Labour to things which he has not made, in order to acquire a Property in them? 'Tis the

Labour of the Hands alone, which giving the Husbandman a Title to the Produce of the Land he has tilled gives him a Title to the Land itself, at least till he has gathered in the Fruits of it, and so on from Year to Year; and this Enjoyment forming a continued Possession is easily transformed into a Property. . . .

Behold then all our Faculties developed; our Memory and Imagination at work; Self-love interested; Reason rendered active and the Mind almost arrived at the utmost Bounds of that Perfection it is capable of. Behold all our natural Qualities put in Motion; the Rank and Condition of every Man established, not only as to the quantum of Property and the Power of serving or hurting others, but likewise as to Genius, Beauty, Strength or Address, Merit or Talents; and as these were the only Qualities which could command Respect, it was found necessary to have or at least to affect them. It was requisite for Men to be thought what they really were not. To be and to appear became two very different things, and from this Distinction sprang Pomp and Knavery, and all the Vices which form their Train. On the other hand, Man, heretofore free and independent, was now in consequence of a Multitude of new Wants brought under Subjection, as it were, to all Nature, and especially to his Fellows, whose Slave in some sense he became, even by becoming their Master; if rich, he stood in need of their Services, if poor, of their Assistance; even Mediocrity itself could not enable him to do without them. He must therefore have been continually at work to interest them in his happiness, and make them, if not really, at least apparently find their Advantage in labouring for his: this rendered him sly and artful in his dealings with some, imperious and cruel in his dealings with others, and laid him under the Necessity of using ill all those whom he stood in need of, as often as he could not awe them into a Compliance with his Will, and did not find it his Interest to purchase it at the Expence of real Services. . . . Such were the first Effects of Property, and the inseparable Attendants of Infant Inequality.

But it is impossible that Men should not sooner or later have made Reflections on so wretched a Situation, and upon the Calamities with which they were overwhelmed. The Rich in particular must have soon perceived how much they suffered by a perpetual War, of which they alone supported all the Expence, and in which, tho' all risked Life, they alone risked any Substance. Besides, whatever Colour they might pretend to give their Usurpations, they sufficiently saw that these Usurpations were in the main founded upon false and precarious Titles, and that what they had acquired by mere Force, others could again by mere Force wrest out of their Hands, without leaving them the least room to complain of such a Proceeding. Even those, who owed all their Riches to their own Industry, could scarcely ground their Acquisitions upon a better Title. It availed them nothing to say, 'Twas I built this Wall; I acquired this Spot by my Labour. Who traced it out for you, another might object, and what Right have you to expect Payment at our Expence for doing that we did not oblige you to do? . . . the rich Man, thus pressed by Necessity, at last conceived the deepest Project that ever entered the Human Mind: this was to employ in his favour the very Forces that attacked him, to make Allies of his Enemies, to inspire them with other Maxims, and make them adopt other Institutions as favourable to his Pretensions, as the Law of Nature was unfavourable to them.

"Let us unite, said he, to secure the Weak from Oppression, restrain the Ambitious, and secure to every Man the Possession of what belongs to him. Let us form Rules of Justice and of Peace, to which all may be obliged to conform, which shall not accept Persons, but may in some sort make amends for the Caprice of Fortune, by submitting alike the Powerful and the Weak to the observance of mutual Duties. In a word, instead of turning our Forces against ourselves, let us collect them into a sovereign Power, which may govern us by wise Laws, may protect and defend all the Members of the Association, repel common Enemies, and maintain a perpetual Concord and Harmony among us."

Much fewer Words of this kind were sufficient to draw in a Parcel of Rustics, whom it was an easy Matter to impose upon, who had besides too many Quarrels among themselves to live without Arbiters, and too much Avarice and Ambition to live long without Masters. . . . those among them, who were best qualified to foresee Abuses, were precisely those who expected to benefit by them; even the soberest judged it requisite to sacrifice one part of their Liberty to ensure the other, . . .

Such was, or must have been had Man been left to himself, the origin of Society and of the Laws, which increased the Fetters of the Weak and the Strength of the Rich; irretrievably destroyed natural Liberty; fixed for ever the Laws of Property and Inequality; changed an artful Usurpation into an irrevocable Title; and for the Benefit of a few ambitious Individuals subjected the rest of Mankind to perpetual Labour, Servitude, and Misery. . . .

By thus discovering and following the lost and forgotten Tracks, by which Man from the natural must have arrived at the civil State; by restoring, with the intermediate Positions which I have been just indicating, those which want of Leisure obliges me to suppress, or which my Imagination has not suggested, every attentive Reader must unavoidably be struck at the immense Space which separates these two States. . . . he will find himself in a Condition to understand how the Soul and the Passions of Men by insensible Alterations change as it were their Nature; how it comes to pass, that at the long run our Wants and our Pleasures change Objects; that, original Man vanishing by degrees, Society no longer offers to our Inspection but an assemblage of artificial Men and factitious Passions, which are the Work of all these new Relations, and have no Foundation in Nature. Reflection teaches us nothing on that Head, but what Experience perfectly confirms, Savage Man and civilized Man differ so much at bottom in point of Inclinations and Passions, that what constitutes the supreme Happiness of the one would reduce the other to despair. The first sighs for nothing but Repose and Liberty; he desires only to live, and to be exempt from Labour; may, the Ataraxy of the most confirmed Stoic falls short of his consummate Indifference for every other Object. On the contrary, the Citizen always in Motion, is perpetually sweating and toiling, and racking his Brains to find out Occupations still more laborious: He continues a Drudge to his last Minute; nay, he courts Death to be able to live, or renounces Life to acquire Immortality. He cringes to Men in Power whom he hates, and to rich Men whom he despises; he sticks at nothing to have the Honour of serving them; he is not ashamed to value himself on his own Weakness and the Protection they afford him; and proud of his Chains, he speaks with Disdain of those who have not the Honour of being the Partner of his Bondage. What a Spectacle must the painful and envied Labours of an *European* Minister of State form in the Eyes of a *Carribean!* How many cruel Deaths would not this indolent Savage prefer to such a horrid Life, which very often is not even sweetened by the Pleasure of doing good? But to see the drift of so many Cares, his Mind should first have affixed some Meaning to these Words *Power* and *Reputation;* he should be apprized that there are Men who consider as something the looks of the rest of Mankind, who know how to be happy and satisfied with themselves on the Testimony of others sooner than upon their own. In fact, the real Source of all those Differences, is that the Savage lives within himself, whereas the Citizen, constantly beside himself; knows only how to live in the Opinion of others; insomuch that it is, if I may say so, merely from their Judgement that he derives the Consciousness of his own Existence. It is foreign to my subject to shew how this Disposition engenders so much Indifference for good and evil, notwithstanding so many and such fine Discourses of Morality; now every thing, being reduced to Appearances, becomes mere Art and Mummery: Honour, Friendship, Virtue, and often Vice itself, which we at last learn the secret to boast of; how, in short, ever inquiring of others what we are, and never daring to question ourselves on so delicate a Point, in the midst of so much Philosophy, Humanity and Politeness, and so many sublime Maxims, we have nothing to shew for ourselves but a deceitful and frivolous Exterior, Honour without Virtue, Reason without Wisdom, and Pleasure without Happiness. It is sufficient that I have proved that this is not the original Condition of Man, and that it is merely the Spirit of Society, and the Inequality which Society engenders, that thus change and transform all our natural Inclinations. . . .

A Guide to Selections from *The Social Contract*

In these very brief selections, Rousseau presents the essence of what he regards as one of the most important problems that human beings face. This is the problem of finding some form of society (of 'association') that will protect each man against others, but also will not limit his freedom—the problem solved by the social contract. The inequality that has developed among men—the inequality of property—is the chief source of their conflict and their need for protection; the form of society that can prevent this conflict must cancel the effects of economic inequality by enforcing moral and legal equality. Freedom consists in obedience to good laws; and the form of society that incorporates these enables freedom as obedience to them. Good laws are those that embody the general will, which must not be confused with the totality of particular wills, purposes, or interests. The solution of the problem consists in giving our support —in surrendering all our natural rights and powers—to a society whose institutions are animated by the general will, whose laws proclaim moral and legal equality as a consequence, and which advances freedom by requiring obedience. This surrender of natural rights to such a society is the social contract; and however much Rousseau speaks of the social contract as an historical agreement between different men, or between different men and society, he must also regard it as a resolve, internal to each man, to use his powers to advance the general rather than any particular will.

SELECTIONS FROM

The Social Contract*

◄◆►

BOOK I

VI

Of the Social Pact

I assume, for the sake of argument, that a point was reached in the history of mankind when the obstacles to continuing in a state of Nature were stronger than the forces which each individual could employ to the end of continuing in it. The original state of Nature, therefore, could no longer endure, and the human race would have perished had it not changed its manner of existence.

Now, since men can by no means engender new powers, but can only unite and control those of which they are already possessed, there is no way in which they can maintain themselves save by coming together and pooling their strength in a way that will enable them to withstand any resistance exerted upon them from without. They must develop some sort of central direction anl learn to act in concert.

Such a concentration of powers can be brought about only as the consequence of an agreement reached between individuals. But the self-preservation of each single man derives primarily from his own strength and from his own freedom. How, then, can he limit these without, at the same time, doing himself an injury and neglecting that care which it is his duty to devote to his own concerns? This difficulty, in so far as it is relevant to my subject, can be expressed as follows:

"Some form of association must be found as a result of which the whole strength of the community will be enlisted for the protection of the person and property of each constituent member, in such a way that each, when united to his fellows, renders obedience to his own will, and remains as free as he was before." That is the basic problem of which the Social Contract provides the solution. . . .

*From *Social Contract: Essays by Locke, Hume, and Rousseau,* with an introduction by Sir Ernest Barker, New York: Oxford University Press, 1960, reprinted with the kind permission of the publisher. Footnotes omitted.

It must be clearly understood that the clauses in question can be reduced, in the last analysis, to one only; to wit, the complete alienation by each associate member to the community of *all his rights*. For, in the first place, since each has made surrender of himself without reservation, the resultant conditions are the same for all; and, because they are the same for all, it is in the interest of none to make them onerous to his fellows.

In short, whoso gives himself to all gives himself to none. And, since there is no member of the social group over whom we do not acquire precisely the same rights as those over ourselves which we have surrendered to him, it follows that we gain the exact equivalent of what we lose, as well as an added power to conserve what we already have.

If, then, we take from the social pact everything which is not essential to it, we shall find it to be reduced to the following terms: "Each of us contributes to the group his person and the powers which he wields as a person, and we receive into the body politic each individual as forming an indivisible part of the whole."

VIII

Of the Civil State

To the benefits conferred by the status of citizenship might be added that of Moral Freedom, which alone makes a man his own master. For to be subject to appetite is to be a slave, while to obey the laws laid down by society is to be free. But I have already said enough on this point, and am not concerned here with the philosophical meaning of the word *liberty.* . . .

IX

Of Real Property

I will conclude this chapter, and the present Book, with a remark which should serve as basis for every social system: that, so far from destroying natural equality, the primitive compact substitutes for it a moral and legal equality which compensates for all those physical inequalities from which men suffer. However unequal they may be in bodily strength or in intellectual gifts, they become equal in the eyes of the law, and as a result of the compact into which they have entered.

BOOK II

III

Whether the General Will Can Err

It follows from what has been said above that the general will is always right and ever tends to the public advantage. But it does not follow that the deliberations of the People are always equally beyond question. It is ever the way of men to wish their own good, but they do not at all times see where that good lies. The People are never corrupted though often deceived, and it is only when they are deceived that they appear to will what is evil.

There is often considerable difference between the will of all and the general will. The latter is concerned only with the common interest, the former with interests that are partial, being itself but the sum of individual wills. But take from the expression of these separate wills the pluses and minuses—which cancel out, the sum of the differences is left, and that is the general will. . . .

A Guide to Selections from *Considerations Concerning the Government of Poland and Its Projected Reform*

In these passages, Rousseau advances a view of education quite opposed to the one for which he is most famous. It is the view that the proper objective for public education in a good state is the development of selfless and intense—if not uncritical—patriotism. He proposes a highly centralized system of public schools for this purpose, and makes several practical and original suggestions that have been adopted in one form or another in educational practice.

SELECTIONS FROM

Considerations
Concerning the Government of
Poland and Its Projected Reforms*

———◄◆►———

IV

Education

This is the important topic. It is education which ought to give people the national mold, and direct their opinions and their tastes in such a way that they are patriots by inclination, by passion, by necessity. An infant in opening his eyes ought to see the fatherland, and until death ought to see nothing else. Every true republican imbibed along with the milk of his mother the love of the fatherland; that is, of laws and liberty. That love makes all his existence; he sees only the fatherland, he lives only for it; as soon as he is alone, he is nothing; as soon as he no longer has a fatherland, he is no more; and if he is not dead, he is worse.

National education belongs only to free men; they are the only ones who can have a communal life and who can be truly bound by Law. A Frenchman, an Englishman, a Spaniard, an Italian, a Russian are all pretty much the same man; he leaves school already wholly formed for licence, that is for servitude. At twenty, a Pole ought to be no other man; he ought to be a Pole. I desire that in learning to read he should read things about his own country; that at ten he should know all its products; at twelve all its provinces, all its roads, all its towns; that at fifteen he should know all its history; at sixteen all its laws; that there might not have been in all Poland a good deed or an illustrious man which his heart and memory does not acknowledge, and of which he could not render an account in an instant. One can judge from this that it is not ordinary studies directed by foreigners and priests that I should wish the children to pursue. The law ought to regulate the matter, the order,

*The selections are taken from *The Political Writings of Jean Jacques Rousseau,* edited by C. E. Vaughn, Cambridge University Press, 1915, vol. II. *Considérations sur le gouvernement de Cologne, et sur la Réformation Projetée, Chapitre IV,* "Education," reprinted with the kind permission of Basil Blackwell, publisher. Translated for this work by Kingsley Price.

and the form of their studies. They ought to have only Poles as teachers, all married, if that is possible, all distinguished by manners, integrity, common sense, enlightenment; and all destined for positions not more important or more honorable, because that is not possible, but less laborious and more brilliant, when they have performed well in these positions for a certain number of years. Be careful, above all, not to make a profession of the occupation of pedagogy. Every public official in Poland ought to have no other permanent occupation but that of citizen. All the posts that he fills, and especially those which are important, like this one, ought to be considered only as places for testing him and as steps for further promotion after having merited it. I exhort all Poles to pay attention to this maxim, on which I shall insist often; I believe it the key to great potential in the state. One will see later how it is possible in my opinion to apply it without exception.

I do not like at all these distinctions of schools and of academies which cause the rich nobility and the poor nobility to be reared differently and separately. All, being equal in the constitution of the state, ought to be reared together and in the same manner; and if it is not possible to establish public education completely without tuition, it is necessary at least to put a price on it that the poor can pay. Would it not be possible to establish in each school a certain number of places completely free, that is at the expense of the state, and which are called bourses in France. These places, given to the children of poor gentlemen who have deserved well of the fatherland, not as charity, but as a recompense for the good services of their parents, would become by this title, honorable and could create a double advantage which is not to be neglected. For that it would be necessary that the nomination not be arbitrary, but be made by a kind of judgment of which I shall speak later. Those who would fill these places would be called "Children of the State" and distinguished by some honorable token which would give them precedence over other children of their age, not excepting those of the great.

In all schools it is necessary to establish a gymnasium, or a place of bodily exercise, for children. This matter so neglected is, in my opinion, the most important part of education, not only to form a robust and wholesome temperament, but even more for the purpose of morality which one neglects or discharges with nothing but a parcel of precepts, pedantic and vain, which are so many lost words. I can never reiterate enough that good education should be negative. Prevent vices from being born, you will have done enough for virtue. Good public education provides the easier way to fulfill this purpose; it is to keep children active, not by boring studies where they understand nothing and which they hate only because they are forced to remain quiet; but by exercises which please, by satisfying the need to move, proper to growing bodies, and the delight of which for them will extend further.

One ought not to permit them to play separately at their caprice, but all together and in public, in such manner that there should be always a common goal toward which all aspire, and which excites competition, and emulation. Parents who prefer domestic education, and rear their children under their own supervision, ought none the less to send them to these exercises. Their instruction can be domestic and individual, but their games ought to be always public and shared with all; because here it is not merely a question of keeping them busy, of giving them a robust constitution, of making them agile and strapping, but of accustoming them early to discipline, equality, fraternity, competition, to living under the eyes of their fellow citizens, and desiring public approval. To accomplish this, the prizes and rewards for the winners ought not to be assigned by decision of the masters of the exercises, nor of the leaders of the schools, but by acclamation and judgment of the spectators, and one can reckon that these judgments will be always just, especially if one takes care to make these games attractive to the public, in arranging them with a little pomp and in a way that should constitute a spectacle. Then it is to be supposed that all respectable people and all good patriots will make it their duty and pleasure to attend.

In Berne, there is an annual training program for the young patricians who leave school. It is what they call *l'Etat extérieur*. It is a copy in miniature of all the elements that form the Government of the Republic: a senate, magistrates, officers, bailiffs, orators, law-suits, sentences, ceremonies. The *Etat extérieur* has even a little Government and some income; and this institution, authorized and protected by the sovereign, is the seed bed of statesmen, who will direct one day the public affairs in the very employments which they formerly practiced only in play.

Whatever form one gives to public education, the details of which I shall not take up here, it would be good to set up a college of magistrates of the first rank which would have the supreme administration, and which would appoint, discharge, and change at will the principles and heads of schools, who will be themselves, as I have already said, candidates for these high administrative positions, as well as the masters, whose zeal and vigilance one also will take care to excite, by means of higher posts open or closed to them according to the way in which they will have fulfilled their tasks. Since it is upon these institutions that the hope of the Republic depends, the glory and the destiny of the nation, I find them, I confess, of an importance which I am quite surprised no one anywhere has dreamed of according them. I sorrow for humanity because so many ideas which seem good and useful to me are found, although altogether practicable, always so remote from everything which is done.

Of course, I am only sketching the broad outlines here; but that suffices for those whom I address. These poorly developed ideas show from afar the ways, unknown to us, by which the ancients led men to that vigor of soul, to that patriotic zeal, to that esteem for the truly human qualities free from consideration of what is wholly alien to man, which are without example among us, but whose leavens in the hearts of all men require for fermentation nothing but the impetus of appropriate institutions. In this spirit, direct the education, the institutions, the customs, and the manners of the Poles; you will develop in them that leaven which is not yet deadened by corrupt principles, by out-worn institutions, by an egoistic philosophy which preaches and kills. The nation will date its second birth from the terrible crisis from which it is emerging; and seeing what its still undisciplined members have done, it will expect a great deal and will obtain more from a well balanced institution; it will cherish, it will respect laws which will gratify its noble pride, which render and maintain it happy and free; tearing from its breast the passions which evade them, it will nourish there those which cause them to be loved; in fine, renewing itself so to speak, it will regain in this new age all the vigor of a glowing nation. But, without these precautions, expect nothing of your laws. However wise, however foresighted they may be, they will be disregarded and idle; and you will have corrected some abuses which wound you, in order to introduce others which you will not have foreseen. These are preliminaries which I have believed to be indispensible. Let us glance now at the constitution.

A Guide to Selections from *Emile; or, Education*

In the passages selected from *Emile*, Rousseau asserts that a birth, the infant has few needs, and is incapable of satisfying them himself. He learns to possess many needs, however; and education is the process of enabling him to satisfy them through his own efforts. If education does not succeed, he has no secure way of satisfying his needs; and the mature person possesses desires he cannot realize. In that case, desire exceeds power; and the internal peace that constitutes ultimate happiness and the objective of education cannot be secured.

Education depends upon nature or the natural development of the body and mind, upon men or the ways they have learned for dealing with this development, and upon things or our experience of our surroundings. Nature cannot be altered; and in education, one must organize the second and third factors—dealing with others, and the experience of things—in ways that are allowed by it.

The remainder of the passages selected includes (1) a considerable part of Rousseau's discussion of the preadolescent stage in which reason emerges, together with his suggestions for ways in which men and things may be used to further development in it; (2) important parts of his discussion of the stage in which emotion and desire emerge, together with his suggestions for its proper cultivation; (3) those parts of his famous discussion of religion and theology (*The Creed of a Savoyard Priest*) that deal with morality and our ways of knowing it, and with metaphysical considerations he regards as involved in morality; and (4) a statement of the view that happiness consists in such a balance between desire and power that we desire nothing we cannot ourselves realize.

SELECTIONS FROM

*Emile; or, Education**

◄◆►

BOOK I

. . . . We are born weak, we need strength; helpless, we need aid; foolish, we need reason. All that we lack at birth, all that we need when we come to man's estate, is the gift of education.

This education comes to us from nature, from men, or from things. The inner growth of our organs and faculties is the education of nature, the use we learn to make of this growth is the education of men, what we gain by our experience or our surroundings is the education of things.

Thus we are each taught by three masters. If their teaching conflicts, the scholar is ill-educated and will never be at peace with himself; if their teaching agrees, he goes straight to his goal, he lives at peace with himself, he is well-educated.

Now of these three factors in education nature is wholly beyond our control, things are partly in our power; the education of men is the only one controlled by us; and even here our power is largely illusory, for who can hope to direct every word and deed of all with whom the child has to do.

Viewed as an art, the success of education is almost impossible, since the essential conditions of success are beyond our control. Our efforts may bring us within sight of the goal, but fortune must favour us if we are to reach it.

*From the book *Emile; or, Education* by Jean Jacques Rousseau, translated by Barbara Foxley. Everyman's Library, reprinted by permission of E. P. Dutton and Co., Inc., New York; and of J. M. Dent & Sons, Ltd., London. Footnotes omitted.

What is this goal? As we have shown, it is the goal of nature. Since all three modes of education must work together, the two that we can control must follow the lead that which is beyond our control. . . .

We are born sensitive and from our birth onwards we are affected in various ways by our environment. As soon as we become conscious of our sensations we tend to seek or shun the things that cause them, at first because they are pleasant or unpleasant, and then because they suit us or not, and at last because of judgments formed by means of the ideas of happiness and goodness which reason gives us. These tendencies gain strength and permanence with the growth of reason, but hindered by our habits they are more or less warped by our prejudices. Before this change they are what I call Nature within us. . . .

The natural man lives for himself; he is the unit, the whole, dependent only on himself and his like. The citizen is but the numerator of a fraction, whose value depends on its denominator, his value depends upon the whole, that is, on the community. Good social institutions are those best fitted to make a man unnatural, to exchange his independence for dependence, to merge his unit in the group, so that he no longer regards himself as one, but as a part of the whole, and is only conscious of the common life. . . .

In the natural order men are all equal and their common calling is that of manhood, so that a well-educated man cannot fail to do well in that calling and those related to it. It matters little to me whether my pupil is intended for the army, the church, or the law. Before his parents chose a calling for him nature called him to be a man. Life is the trade I would teach him. When he leaves me, I grant you, he will be neither a magistrate, a soldier, nor a priest; he will be a man. All that becomes a man he will learn as quickly as another. In vain will fate change his station, he will always be in his right place. . .

As soon as the child begins to take notice, what is shown him must be carefully chosen. The natural man is interested in all new things. He feels so feeble that he fears the unknown: the habit of seeing fresh things without ill effects destroys this fear. Children brought up in clean houses where there are no spiders are afraid of spiders, and this fear often lasts through life. I never saw peasants, man, woman, or child, afraid of spiders.

It is only by movement that we learn the difference between self and not self; it is only by our own movements that we gain the idea of space. The child has not this idea, so he stretches out his hand to seize the object within his reach or that which is a hundred paces from him. You take this as a sign of tyranny, an attempt to bid the thing to draw near, or to bid you to bring it. Nothing of the kind, it is merely that the object first seen in his brain, then before his eyes, now seems close to his arms, and he has no idea of space beyond his reach. Be careful, therefore, to take him about, to move him from place to place, and to let him perceive the change in his surroundings, so as to teach him to judge of distances.

BOOK III

About twelve or thirteen the child's strength increases far more rapidly than his needs. The strongest and fiercest of the passions is still unknown, his physical development is still imperfect and seems to await the call of the will. He is scarcely aware of extremes of heat and cold and braves them with impunity. He needs no coat, his blood is warm; no spices, hunger is his sauce, no food comes amiss at this age; if he is sleepy he stretches himself on the ground and goes to sleep; he finds all he needs within his reach; he is not tormented by any imaginary wants; he cares nothing what others think; his desires are not beyond his grasp; not only is he self-sufficing, but for the first and last time in his life he has more strength than he needs. . . .

He has, therefore, a surplus of strength and capacity which he will never have again. What use shall he make of it? He will strive to use it in tasks which will help at need. He will, so to speak, cast his present surplus into the storehouse of the future; the vigorous child will make provision for the feeble man; but he will not store his goods where thieves may break in, nor in barns which are not his own. To store them aright, they must be in the hands and the head, they must be stored within himself. This is the time for work, instruction, and inquiry. And not that this is no arbitrary choice of mine, it is the way of nature herself.

Human intelligence is finite, and not only can no man know everything, he cannot even acquire all the scanty knowledge of others. Since the contrary of every false proposition is a truth, there are as many truths as falsehoods. We must, therefore, choose what to teach as well as when to teach it. Some of the information within our reach is false, some is useless, some merely serves to puff up its possessor. The small store which really contributes to our welfare alone deserves the study of a wise man, and therefore of a child whom one would have wise. He must know not merely what is, but what is useful.

From this small stock we must also deduct those truths which require a full-grown mind for their understanding, those which suppose a knowledge of man's relations to his fellow-men—a knowledge which no child can acquire; these things, although in themselves true, lead an inexperienced mind into mistakes with regard to other matters. . . .

His progress in geometry may serve as a test and a true measure of the growth of his intelligence, but as soon as he can distinguish between what is useful and what is useless, much skill and discretion are required to lead him towards theoretical studies. For example, would you have him find a mean proportional between two lines, contrive that he should require to find a square equal to a given rectangle; if two mean proportionals are required, you must first contrive to interest him in the doubling of the cube. . . .

Man's diverse powers are stirred by the same instinct. The bodily activity, which seeks an outlet for its energies, is succeeded by the mental activity which seeks for knowledge. Children are first restless, then curious; and this curiosity, rightly directed, is the means of development for the age with which we are dealing. Always distinguish between natural and acquired tendencies. There is a zeal for learning which has no other foundation than a wish to appear learned, and there is another which springs from man's natural curiosity about all things far or near which may affect himself. The innate desire for comfort and the impossibility of its complete satisfaction impel him to the endless search for fresh means of contributing to its satisfaction. This is the first principle of curiosity; a principle natural to the human heart, though its growth is proportional to the development of our feeling and knowledge. . . .

Teach your scholar to observe the phenomena of nature; you will soon rouse his curiosity, but if you would have it grow, do not be in too great a hurry to satisfy this curiosity. Put the problems before him and let him solve them himself. Let him know nothing because you have told him, but because he has learnt it for himself. Let him not be taught science, let him discover it. If ever you substitute authority for reason he will cease to reason; he will be a mere plaything of other people's thoughts.

You wish to teach this child geography and you provide him with globes, spheres, and maps. What elaborate preparations! What is the use of all these symbols; why not begin by showing him the real thing so that he may at least know what you are talking about? . . .

As a general rule—never substitute the symbol for the thing signified, unless it is impossible to show the thing itself; for the child's attention is so taken up with the symbol that he will forget what it signifies. . . .

His geography will begin with the town he lives in and his father's country house, then the places between them, the rivers near them, and then the sun's aspect and how to find one's way by its aid. This is the meeting place. Let him make his own map, a very simple map, at first containing only two places; others may be added from time to time, as he is able to estimate their distance and position. You see at once what a good start we have given him by making his eye his compass. . . .

Remember that this is the essential point in my method—not to teach the child many things, but never to let him form inaccurate or confused ideas. I care not if he knows nothing provided he is not mistaken, and I only acquaint him with truths to guard him against the errors he might put in their place. Reason and judgment come slowly, prejudices flock to us in crowds, and from these he must be protected. But if you make science itself your object you embark on an unfathomable and shoreless ocean, an ocean strewn with reefs from which you will never return. When I see a man in love with knowledge, yielding to its charms and flitting from one branch to another unable to stay his steps, he seems to me like a child gathering shells on the sea-shore, now picking them up, then throwing them aside for others which he sees beyond them, then taking them again, till overwhelmed by their number and unable to choose between them, he flings them all away and returns empty handed. . . .

There is a series of abstract truths by means of which all the sciences are related to common principles and are developed each in its turn. This relationship is the method of the philosophers. We are not concerned with it at present. There is quite another method by which every concrete example suggests another and always points to the next in the series. This succession, which stimulates the curiosity and so arouses the attention required by every object in turn, is the order followed by most men, and it is the right order for all children. . . .

We shall make all our apparatus ourselves, and I would not make it beforehand, but having caught a glimpse of the experiment by chance we mean to invent step by step an instrument for its verification. I would rather our apparatus was somewhat clumsy and imperfect, but our ideas clear as to what the apparatus ought to be, and the results to be obtained by means of it. For my first lesson in statics, instead of fetching a balance I lay a stick across the back of a chair, I measure the two parts when it is balanced; add equal or unequal weights to either end; by pulling or pushing it as required, I find at last that equilibrium is the result of a reciprocal proportion between the amount of the weights and the length of the levers. Thus my little physicist is ready to rectify a balance before ever he sees one.

Undoubtedly the notions of things thus acquired for oneself are clearer and much more convincing than those acquired from the teaching of others; and not only is our reason not accustomed to a slavish submission to authority, but we develop greater ingenuity in discovering relations, connecting ideas, and inventing apparatus, than when we merely accept what is given us. . . .

As the child develops in intelligence other important considerations require us to be still more careful in our choice of his occupations. As soon as he has sufficient self-knowledge to understand what constitutes his well-being, as soon as he can grasp such far-reaching relations as to judge what is good for him and what is not, then he is able to discern the difference between work and play, and to consider the latter merely as relaxation. The objects of real utility may be introduced into his studies and may lead him to more prolonged attention than he gave to his games. The ever-recurring law of necessity soon teaches a man to do what he does not like, so as to avert evils which he would dislike still more. Such is the use of foresight, and this foresight, well or ill used, is the source of all the wisdom or the wretchedness of mankind. . . .

As soon as they foresee their needs before they feel them, their intelligence has made a great step forward, they are beginning to know the value of time. They must then be trained to devote this time to useful purposes, but this usefulness should be such as they can readily perceive and should be within the reach of their age and experience. What concerns the moral order and the customs of society should not yet be given them, for they are not in a condition to understand it. . . .

Emile is industrious, temperate, patient, stedfast, and full of courage. His imagination is still asleep, so he has no exaggerated ideas of danger; the few ills he feels he knows how to endure in patience, because he has not learnt to rebel against fate. As to death, he knows not what it means; but accustomed as he is to submit without resistance to the law of necessity, he will die, if die he must, without a groan and without a struggle; that is as much as we can demand of nature, in that hour which we all abhor. To live in freedom, and to be independent of human affairs, is the best way to learn how to die.

In a word Emile is possessed of all that portion of virtue which concerns himself. To acquire the social virtues he only needs a knowledge of the relations which make those virtues necessary; he only lacks knowledge which he is quite ready to receive.

He thinks not of others but of himself, and prefers that others should do the same. He makes no claim upon them, and acknowledges no debt to them. He is alone in the midst of human society, he depends on himself alone, for he is all that a boy can be at his age. He has no errors, or at least only such as are inevitable; he has no vices, or only those from which no man can escape. His body is healthy, his limbs are supple, his mind is accurate and unprejudiced, his heart is free and untroubled by passion. Pride, the earliest and the most natural of passions, has scarcely shown itself. Without disturbing the peace of others, he has passed his life contented, happy, and free, so far as nature allows. Do you think that the earlier years of a child who has reached his fifteenth year in this condition have been wasted? . . .

BOOK IV

As soon as a man needs a companion he is no longer an isolated creature, his heart is no longer alone. All his relations with his species, all the affections of his heart, come into being along with this. His first passion soon arouses the rest.

. . . the first desires are preceded by a long period of unrest, they are deceived by a prolonged ignorance, they know not what they want. The blood ferments and bubbles; overflowing vitality seeks to extend its sphere. The eye grows brighter and surveys others, we begin to be interested in those about us, we begin to feel that we are not meant to live alone; thus the heart is thrown open to human affection, and becomes capable of attachment. . . .

I think I can sum up the whole of the preceding reflections in two or three maxims, definite, straightforward, and easy to understand.

First Maxim—It is not in human nature to put ourselves in the place of those who are happier than ourselves, but only in the place of those who can claim our pity.

If you find exceptions to this rule, they are more apparent than real. Thus we do not put ourselves in the place of the rich or great when we become fond of them; even when our affection is real, we only appropriate to ourselves a part of their welfare. Sometimes we love the rich man in the midst of misfortunes; but so long as he prospers he has no real friend, except the man who is not deceived by appearances, who pities rather than envies him in spite of his prosperity.

The happiness belonging to certain states of life appeals to us; take, for instance, the life of a shepherd in the country. The charm of seeing these good people so happy is not poisoned by envy; we are genuinely interested in them. Why is this? Because we feel we can descend into this state of peace and innocence and enjoy the same happiness; it is an alternative which only calls up pleasant thoughts, so long as the wish is as good as the deed. It is always pleasant to examine our stores, to contemplate our own wealth, even when we do not mean to spend it.

From this we see that to incline a young man to humanity you must not make him admire the brilliant lot of others; you must show him life in its sorrowful aspects and arouse his fears. Thus it becomes clear that he must force his own way to happiness, without interfering with the happiness of others.

Second Maxim—We never pity another's woes unless we know we may suffer in like manner ourselves. . . .

Why have kings no pity on their people? Because they never expect to be ordinary men. Why are the rich so hard on the poor? Because they have no fear of becoming poor. . . .

So do not train your pupil to look down from the height of his glory upon the sufferings of the unfortunate, the labours of the wretched, and do not hope to teach him to pity them while he considers them as far removed from himself. Make him thoroughly aware of the fact that the fate of these unhappy persons may one day be his own, that his feet are standing on the edge of the abyss, into which he may be plunged at any moment by a thousand unexpected irresistible misfortunes. . . .

Third Maxim—The pity we feel for others is proportionate, not to the amount of the evil, but to the feelings we attribute to the sufferers. . . .

We only pity the wretched so far as we think they feel the need of pity. The bodily effect of our sufferings is less than one would suppose; it is memory that prolongs the pain, imagination which projects it into the future, and makes us really to be pitied. This is, I think, one of the reasons why we are more callous to the sufferings of animals than of men. . . . we . . . become callous to the fate of our fellow-men, and the rich console themselves for the harm done to the poor by the assumption that the poor are too stupid to feel. . . .

There is, so our wiseacres tell us, the same amount of happiness and sorrow in every station. This saying is as deadly in its effects as it is incapable of proof; if all are equally happy why should I trouble myself about any one? Let every one stay where he is; leave the slave to be ill-treated, the sick man to suffer, and the wretched to perish; they have nothing to gain by any change in their condition. . . . In a word, teach your pupil to love all men, even those who fail to appreciate him; act in such a way that he is not a member of any class, but takes his place in all alike; speak in his hearing of the human race with tenderness, and even with pity, but never with scorn. You are a man; do not dishonour mankind. . . .

Hitherto my Emile has thought only of himself, so his first glance at his equals leads him to compare himself with them; and the first feeling excited by this comparison is the desire to be first. It is here that self-love is transformed into selfishness, and this is the starting point of all the passions which spring from selfishness. But to determine whether the passions by which his life will be governed shall be humane and gentle or harsh and cruel, whether they shall be the passions of benevolence and pity or those of envy and covetousness, we must know what he believes his place among men to be, and what sort of obstacles he expects to have to overcome in order to attain to the positions he seeks.

To guide him in this inquiry, after we have shown him men by means of the accidents common to the species, we must now show him them by means of their differences. This is the tie for estimating inequality, natural and civil, and for the scheme of the whole social order. . . .

. . . to bring the human heart within his reach without risk of spoiling his own, I would show him men from afar, in other times or in other places, so that he may behold the scene but cannot take part in it. This is the time for history; with its help he will read the hearts of men without any lessons in philosophy; with its help he will view them as a mere spectator, dispassionate and without prejudice; he will view them as their judge, not as their accomplice or their accuser. . . .

Provided a man is not mad, he can be cured of any folly but vanity;

there is no cure for this but experience, if indeed there is any cure for it at all; when it first appears we can at least prevent its further growth. But do not on this account waste your breath on empty arguments to prove to the youth that he is like other men and subject to the same weaknesses. Make him feel it or he will never know it. . . . I shall let flatterers take advantage of him; if rash comrades draw him into some perilous adventure, I will let him run the risk; if he falls into the hands of sharpers at the card-table, I will abandon him to them as their dupe. . . .

The time of faults is the time of fables. When we blame the guilty under the cover of a story we instruct without offending him; and he then understands that the story is not untrue by means of the truth he finds in its application to himself. The child who has never been deceived by flattery understands nothing of the fable I recently examined; but the rash youth who has just become the dupe of a flatterer perceives only too readily that the crow was a fool. Thus he acquires a maxim from the fact, and the experience he would soon have forgotten is engraved on his mind by means of the fable. There is no knowledge of morals which cannot be acquired through our own experience or that of others. When there is danger, instead of letting him try the experiment himself, we have recourse to history. When the risk is comparatively slight, it is just as well that the youth should be exposed to it; then by means of the apologue the special cases with which the young man is now acquainted are transformed into maxims.

I am never weary of repeating: let all the lessons of young people take the form of doing rather than talking; let them learn nothing from books which they can learn from experience. How absurd to attempt to give them practice in speaking when they have nothing to say, to expect to make them feel, at their school desks, the vigour of the language of passion and all the force of the arts of persuasion when they have nothing and nobody to persuade! All the rules of rhetoric are mere waste of words to those who do not know how to use them for their own purposes. How does it concern a schoolboy to know how Hannibal encouraged his soldiers to cross the Alps? If instead of these grand speeches you showed him how to induce his prefect to give him a holiday, you may be sure he would pay more attention to your rules.

I am aware that many of my readers will be surprised to find me tracing the course of my scholar through his early years without speaking to him of religion. At fifteen he will not even know he has a soul, at eighteen even he may not be ready to learn about it. For if he learns about it too soon there is the risk of his never really knowing anything about it.

The obligation of faith assumes the possibility of belief. The philosopher who does not believe is wrong, for he misuses the reason he has cultivated, and he is able to understand the truths he rejects. But the child who professes the Christian faith—what does he believe? Just what he understands; and he understands so little of what he is made to repeat that if you tell him to say just the opposite he will be quite ready to do it. . . .

THE CREED OF A SAVOYARD PRIEST

. . . While I meditated upon man's nature, I seemed to discover two distinct principles in it; one of them raised him to the study of the eternal truths, to the love of justice, and of true morality, to the regions of the world of thought, which the wise delight to contemplate; the other led him downwards to himself, made him the slave of his senses, of the passions which are their instruments, and thus opposed everything suggested to him by the former principle. When I felt myself carried away, distracted by these conflicting motives, I said, No; man is not one; I will and I will not; I feel myself at once a slave and a free man; I perceive what is right, I love it, and I do what is wrong; I am active when I listen to the voice of reason; I am passive when I am carried away by my passions; and when I yield, my worst suffering is the knowledge that I might have resisted.

Young man, hear me with confidence. I will always be honest with you. If conscience is the creature of prejudice, I am certainly wrong, and there is no such thing as a proof of morality; but if to put oneself first is an inclination natural to man, and if the first sentiment of justice is moreover inborn in the human heart, let those who say man is a simple creature remove these contradictions and I will grant that there is but one substance.

You will note that by this term *substance* I understand generally the being endowed with some primitive quality, apart from all the special and secondary modifications. If then all the primitive qualities which are known to us can be united in one and the same being, we should only acknowledge one substance; but if there are qualities which are mutually exclusive, there are as many different substances as there are such exclusions. You will think this over; for my own part, . . . it is enough for me to recognize matter as having merely extension and divisibility to convince myself that it cannot think. . . .

A machine does not think, there is neither movement nor form which can produce reflection; something within thee tries to break the bands which confine it; space is not thy measure, the whole universe does not suffice to contain thee; thy sentiments, thy desires, thy anxiety, thy pride itself, have another origin than this small body in which thou art imprisoned.

I have a body which is acted upon by other bodies, and it acts in turn upon them; there is no doubt about this reciprocal action; but my will is independent of my senses; I consent or I resist; I yield or I win the victory, and I know very well in myself when I have done what I wanted and when I have merely given way to my passions. I have always the power to will, but not always the strength to do what I will. When I yield to temptation I surrender myself to the action of external objects. When I blame myself for this weakness, I listen to by own will alone; I am a slave in my vices, a free man in my remorse; the feeling of freedom is never effaced in me but when I myself do wrong, and when I at length prevent the voice of the soul from protesting against the authority of the body. . . .

No doubt I am not free not to desire my own welfare, I am not free to desire my own hurt; but my freedom consists in this very thing, that I can will what is for my own good, or what I esteem as such, without any external compulsion. . . .

The motive power of all action is in the will of a free creature; we can go no farther. It is not the word *freedom* that is meaningless, but the word *necessity*. To suppose some action which is not the effect of an active motive power is indeed to suppose effects without cause, to reason in a vicious circle. Either there is no original impulse, or every original impulse has no antecedent cause, and there is no will properly so-called without freedom. Man is therefore free to act, and as such he is animated by an immaterial substance; . . .

If man is at once active and free, he acts of his own accord; what he does freely is no part of the system marked out by Providence and it cannot be imputed to Providence. . . .

The morality of our actions consists entirely in the judgments we ourselves form with regard to them. If good is good, it must be good in the depth of our hearts as well as in our actions; and the first reward of justice is the consciousness that we are acting justly. If moral goodness is in accordance with our nature, man can only be healthy in mind and body when he is good. If it is not so, and if man is by nature evil, he cannot cease to be evil without corrupting his nature, and goodness in him is a crime against nature. . . .

There is therefore at the bottom of our hearts an innate principle of justice and virtue, by which, in spite of our maxims, we judge our own actions or those of others to be good or evil; and it is this principle that I call conscience. . . .

The decrees of conscience are not judgments but feelings. Although all our ideas come from without, the feelings by which they are weighed are within us, and it is by these feelings alone that we perceive fitness or unfitness of things in relation to ourselves, which leads us to seek or shun these things.   *(End of the Creed.)*

Now is the time to read pleasant books; now is the time to teach him to analyze speech and to appreciate all the beauties of eloquence and diction. It is a small matter to learn languages, they are less useful than people think; but the study of languages leads us on to that of grammar in general. We must learn Latin if we would have a thorough knowledge of French; these two languages must be studied and compared if we would understand the rules of the art of speaking.

There is, moreover, a certain simplicity of taste which goes straight to the heart; and this is only to be found in the classics. In oratory, poetry, and every kind of literature, Emile will find the classical authors as he found them in history, full of matter and sober in their judgment. The authors of our own time, on the contrary, say little and talk much. To take their judgment as our constant law is not the way to form our own judgment. . . .

After I have led Emile to the sources of pure literature, I will also show him the channels into the reservoirs of modern compilers; journals, translations, dictionaries, he shall cast a glance at them all, and then leave them for ever. To amuse him he shall hear the chatter of the academies; I will draw his attention to the fact that every member of them is worth more by himself than he is as a member of the society; he will then draw his own conclusions as to the utility of these fine institutions.

I take him to the theatre to study taste, not morals; for in the theatre above all taste is revealed to those who can think. Lay aside precepts and morality, I should say; this is not the place to study them. The stage is not made for truth; its object is to flatter and amuse; there is no place where one can learn so completely the art of pleasing and of interesting the human heart. The study of plays leads to the study of poetry; both have the same end in view. If he has the least glimmering of taste for poetry, how eagerly will he study the languages of the poets, Greek, Latin, and Italian! These studies will afford him unlimited amusement and will be none the less valuable; they will be a delight to him at an age and in circumstances when the heart finds so great a charm in every kind of beauty which affects it. . . .

BOOK V

When you reached the age of reason, I secured you from the influence of human prejudice; when your heart awoke, I preserved you from the sway of passion. Had I been able to prolong this inner tranquility till your life's end, my work would have been secure, and you would have been as happy as man can be; but, my dear Emile, in vain did I dip you in the waters of Styx, I could not make you everywhere invulnerable; a fresh enemy has appeared, whom you have not yet learnt to conquer, and from whom I cannot save you. That enemy is yourself. Nature and fortune had left you free. You could face poverty, you could bear bodily pain; the sufferings of the heart were unknown to you; you were then dependent on nothing but your position as a human being; now you depend on all the ties you have formed for yourself; you have learnt to desire, and you are now the slave of your desires. Without any change in yourself, without any insult, any injury to yourself, what sorrows may attack your soul, what pains may you suffer without sickness, how many deaths may you die and yet live! A lie, an error, a suspicion, may plunge you in despair. . . .

What is meant by a virtuous man? He who can conquer his affections; for then he follows his reason, his conscience; he does his duty; he is his own master and nothing can turn him from the right way. So far you have had only the semblance of liberty, the precarious liberty of the slave who has not received his orders. Now is the time for real freedom; learn to be your own master; control your heart, my Emile, and you will be virtuous.

Do not expect me to supply you with lengthy precepts of morality, I have only one rule to give you which sums up all the rest. Be a man; restrain your heart within the limits of your manhood. Study and know these limits; however narrow they may be, we are not unhappy within them; it is only when we wish to go beyond them that we are unhappy, only when, in our mad passions, we try to attain the impossible; we are unhappy when we forget our manhood to make an imaginary world for ourselves, from which we are always slipping back into our own. The only good things, whose loss really affects us, are those which we claim as our rights. If it is clear that we cannot obtain what we want, our mind turns away from it; wishes without hope cease to torture us. . . .

Would you live in wisdom and happiness, fix your heart on the beauty that is eternal; let your desire be limited by your position, let your duties take precedence of your wishes; extend the law of necessity into the region of morals; learn to lose what may be taken from you; learn to forsake all things at the command of virtue, to set yourself above the chances of life, to detach your heart before it is torn in pieces, to be brave in adversity so that you may never be wretched, to be steadfast in duty that you may never be guilty of a crime. Then you will be happy in spite of fortune, and good in spite of your passions. You will find a pleasure that cannot be destroyed, even in the possession of the most fragile things; you will possess them, they will not possess you, and you will realise that the man who loses everything, only enjoys what he knows how to resign. It is true you will not enjoy the illusions of imaginary pleasures, neither will you feel the sufferings which are their result. You will profit greatly by this exchange, for the sufferings are real and frequent, the pleasures are rare and empty. Victor over so many deceitful ideas, you will also vanquish the idea that attaches such an excessive value to life. You will spend your life in peace, and you will leave it without terror; you will detach yourself from life as from other things. Let others, horror-struck, believe that when this life is ended they cease to be; conscious of the nothingness of life, you will think that you are but entering upon the true life. To the wicked, death is the close of life; to the just it is its dawn.

Bibliography

Boyd, William, *The Educational Theory of Jean Jacques Rousseau,* London and New York, etc., Longman's Green and Co., 1911; reissued New York, Russell and Russell, 1963.

Compayré, Gabriel, *Jean Jacques Rousseau and Education from Nature,* translated by R. P. Jago, New York, T. Y. Crowell and Co., 1907. (*Jean-Jacques Rousseau et l'éducation de la nature,* Paris, 1901. Vol. I of series entitled "Les grands éducateurs.")

Davidson, Thomas, *Rousseau and Education According to Nature,* New York, Charles Scribner and Sons, 1898.

. . .

Green, Frederick Charles, *Rousseau and the Idea of Progress,* Oxford, Clarendon Press, 1950.

Hendel, Charles William, *Jean-Jacques Rousseau, Moralist,* 2 volumes, New York and London, Oxford University Press, 1934; second edition, Indianapolis, Bobbs-Merrill, 1962 (Library of Liberal Arts).

Morley, John, *Rousseau,* 2 volumes, London, 1915.

Wright, Ernest Hunter, *The Meaning of Rousseau,* London, Oxford University Press, 1929.

IX

KANT

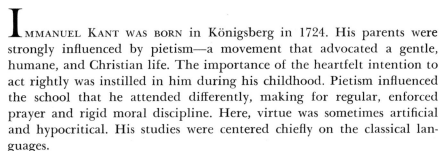

IMMANUEL KANT WAS BORN in Königsberg in 1724. His parents were strongly influenced by pietism—a movement that advocated a gentle, humane, and Christian life. The importance of the heartfelt intention to act rightly was instilled in him during his childhood. Pietism influenced the school that he attended differently, making for regular, enforced prayer and rigid moral discipline. Here, virtue was sometimes artificial and hypocritical. His studies were centered chiefly on the classical languages.

At sixteen, he entered the University of Königsberg as a student of theology but he worked chiefly on philosophy and physics. His family circumstances were by no means affluent (his father was a saddler) and he earned some income by tutoring.

At twenty-two, Kant left the University to spend the next few years as tutor to various noble families of East Prussia. He regarded himself as possessed of no great talent for teaching. In 1755, he returned to the University and took up that quiet, retired, academic existence for which he is famous and which occupied the rest of his life.

At the University of Königsberg, Kant wrote and lectured on geography, anthropology, education, and physics. In this last area he developed a nebular hypothesis of the origin of the solar system, anticipating the work of Laplace; but his chief interest lay in philosophy. During his academic life he wrote a great deal; and in the decade, 1781-91, he published three books which gave him an immediate reputation and which established him in the eyes of many as one of the great philosophers of European civilization. The *Critique of Pure Reason* demarcates the area (a very small one) in which pure reason, thought unaided by observation, can discover what is true. *The Critique of Practical Reason* shows how reason, again unmixed with materials drawn from sense, can reveal our duties and motivate us to perform them. The *Critique of Judgment* treats of certain philosophical problems centering in the natural occurrence of beauty and the appearance in nature of purposiveness. In shorter works, notably the *Idea of a Universal History* and *Perpetual Peace,* Kant applied principles developed in these other books to concrete historical and political problems.

After 1790, Kant centered his attention on the philosophy of religion, an area of thought which is involved to some extent in each of the three Critiques; and four years later he published *Religion within the Limits of Pure Reason.* The Ministry of Education and Religion had been worried for some time over the unorthodox views of the celebrated philosopher. There had been an attempt to prevent publication of his writings. And now, Frederick William II publicly disapproved his views, promising trouble if he continued to express them. Kant agreed not to write on the philosophy of religion "as subject of Frederick William II"; but after the death of that king, he took up the topic anew. He died in 1804 after several years of fragile mental health.

EDUCATIONAL THEORY

KANT OFFERED COURSES in education at the University of Königsberg on two occasions—in 1776-77, and 1786-87. A rule of the University required that a member of the philosophical faculty provide such courses,[1] and Kant took his turn. He made notes for his lectures but never wrote them up into a coherent essay. Some of his students, loath to lose his thoughts on any subject, brought about the publication of these notes in 1803, under the title *Immanuel Kant Ueber Pädagogik,* edited by Theodore Rink. The notes are repetitious and somewhat incoherent. We have developed here an educational theory based upon them rather than a faith-

---

[1] Edward Franklin Buchner, *The Educational Theory of Immanuel Kant,* J. B. Lippincott Company, Philadelphia, 1904, pp. 15–16. This book contains a careful scholarly analysis and translation of Kant's *Lecture-Notes on Pedagogy.* It has been of great assistance in understanding Kant's thought concerning education.

ful summary. The theory incorporates ideas drawn not only from the lecture notes but from other books of Kant as well.

STATEMENTS OF FACT

The statements of fact in Kant's educational theory are of three sorts. They are drawn from his views concerning psychology, universal history, and the practice of educational institutions. We shall set down his statements concerning psychology first.

Psychology

THE MENTAL FACULTIES: DESIRE. Human activities, Kant holds, depend upon three mental faculties or powers: the faculties of desire, of volition, and of cognition.[2] The faculty of desire is the power to try to bring into existence the object to which an idea refers.[3] Consider the idea of my being in New York. It refers to a possible location for me and as such, it is an idea merely, not a desire. But if I am prompted by this idea to make its object real, i.e., to go to New York, it ceases to be an idea merely, and becomes a desire. Kant's view concerning desire is very like that of Locke on the same subject. A re-examination of Lock's view will help to explain that of Kant for one who finds the latter obscure.

All desires are lured toward their fulfillment by the promise of pleasure. This is the feeling of agreeableness found in agreement between the idea involved in a desire and the actual consequences of the effort to bring its object into existence.[4] Thus, if my desire to be in New York succeeds, my whereabouts (my being in New York) agrees with my idea of my being there. What the idea represents actually exists by virtue of my

---

[2] In the *Critique of Practical Reason (Kant's Critique of Practical Reason and other Works on the Theory of Ethics,* translated by Thomas Kingsmill Abbott, Longmans, Green & Co., London, 1879), Kant speaks in one place (pp. 137–38) of two faculties of the mind, those of cognition and of desire. Elsewhere in the same work (pp. 167–68), he speaks of the will as a power different from that of desire or of cognition. On the other hand, in the *Critique of Judgment* (translated by J. H. Bernard, Haffner Publishing Company, New York, 1951, p. 13), he speaks of the three irreducible faculties: "the faculty of knowledge, the feeling of pleasure and pain, and the faculty of desire." He has, throughout his work, no single view as to the number of mental faculties necessary to explain human conduct. I have adopted the division into those of desire, of volition and of cognition because it seems most appropriate for his views concerning education and other topics related to it.

[3] *Critique of Practical Reason* (Abbott translation), pp. 134–35n.

[4] "Pleasure," Kant writes, "is the idea of the agreement of the object or the action with . . . the faculty of causality of an idea in respect to the actuality of its object . . ." (*ibid.,* pp. 134–35 n). But Kant adds to this notion of agreement that of the feeling of agreeableness; and he actually uses the word "pleasure" to refer to the feeling of agreeableness found in the agreement mentioned between our causal efforts or actions and their successful effects.

efforts. I harbor the feeling of agreeableness toward that agreement. If it does not succeed, if there is disagreement between my whereabouts and my idea of it, my desire to be in New York is frustrated and I feel displeasure or pain at the disagreement. The faculty of desire exercises itself only to secure pleasure.[5] This doctrine is Kant's psychological hedonism.

Our desires always occur according to natural laws. A natural law is a general statement to the effect that, given certain circumstances, whenever a thing of one kind occurs, one or more of another kind also occur. "If a body is heated, it will expand, provided it is not under pressure," typifies natural laws, and Kant holds that all desires occur because other things occur, just as the expansion of a body occurs because of a rise in its temperature. Men grow up in particular environments and within each, a desire of any particular person is uniformly the result of something else which happens in or to him—some other desire he harbors or some external event. Thus, given an environment of European civilization, a man may desire to be in London because he desires to visit relatives, or because of something external to him such as the advertising of tourist agencies. Kant holds that a similar desire is awakened by similar causes for all persons similarly circumstanced—indeed, that everything a person is, feels, and does may be described in terms of some natural law.[6]

There is one law of nature which describes all our desires. We have seen that each of them is a desire for pleasure; Kant argues that every desire is also a desire for the pleasure of the person who harbors it. On this view, I never desire your pleasure or happiness but only my own; and you suffer from an analogous limitation. This doctrine is egoistic hedonism and Kant advances it as a law of psychology.[7]

Kant regards some desires as instinctual and he singles out four of them for more or less extended treatment—sex, isolation, association, and wildness.[8] His view of the nature of the sexual instinct is not unusual and we will discuss his recommendations concerning its treatment later. The instinct of isolation is a complex affair. Nature endows men with a desire to dominate others and each man attributes to others the aggressive desire which he finds in himself. The resistance others offer to his own desire for domination makes each fear all others. The result is a natural disposition to withdraw from society. This instinctual desire for isolation goes hand in hand with an unlearned desire for association. This third instinct is required in order that the natural desire for domination should

---

[5] *Ibid.*, p. 150.
[6] *Ibid.*, pp. 226–27.
[7] *Ibid.*, p. 151.
[8] *Lecture-Notes on Pedagogy* (Buchner translation), pp. 4, 5, 111. *The Idea of a Universal History from a Cosmopolitical Point of View in Fourth Proposition, in Kant's Principles of Politics*, edited and translated by W. Hastie, T. & T. Clark, Edinburgh, 1891.

receive expression; one cannot dominate others unless he associates with them. Isolation and association are different aspects of a single instinct, that of domination over others. The fourth instinct, wildness (Kant sometimes calls it "freedom"), is a natural inclination to reject all laws which restrict our desires. Each of the latter is directed toward an objective, and the laws of society and of morality frequently enjoin us not to act to realize some of these objectives. The instinct to be wild is an unlearned desire to disobey all such injunctions.

The faculty of desire is the power of acting upon our ideas to make their objects real. We try to realize only those objects which are pleasant. Our harboring of desires is describable by laws of nature. The objective of all of our desires is private happiness or pleasure, and the objectives which we instinctually endeavor to realize include those of our ideas of sex, of isolation from others, of association with them, and of a wild life free from civil and moral laws.

VOLITION. The faculty of volition or will is a power possessed by all rational beings "to determine their causality by the conception of rules."[9] Their causality, as we have seen, is their desire and the determination of this causality is the decision to work for the realization of one such object as opposed to that of others. A rule is a command to do something, what Kant calls an "imperative." Suppose that, in the summer, I desire both to be in London and to be in New York. The rule, "never go to New York in the summer," enables me to determine which of these desires to select for action, i.e., to determine my causality; and the ability to use this rule is the faculty of volition or will. The exercise of this faculty is closely connected with that of desire. It consists in using rules to fix upon those desires whose objectives merit realization. It does not guarantee, we should notice, that our effort will succeed or even that a desire more urgent than the one selected will not prevail.

COGNITION. The faculty of cognition is our power to be aware of things. It consists of four subordinate powers: those of sense, of imagination, of understanding, and of reason. Each of these powers exercises itself upon material and while the latter varies from one to another exercise of each of the powers, the exercise of each power itself never varies. Our acts of sensing, imagining, understanding, and reasoning are each of the same sort, however different the materials upon which they are directed.

We exercise our faculty of sense upon materials of two radically different kinds. The sense organs provide us with colors, sounds, touches, and the like, and these sensory materials constitute the ingredients of

[9] *Critique of Practical Reason* (Abbott translation), p. 168.

external objects. On the other hand, the faculty of sense also reveals to us desires, acts of volition, thoughts, pleasures and pains, and the acts of sensing both these and the material ingredients of external objects. Exercising the power to sense yields awareness of the constituents of our own minds as well as of external objects.

But common to sensory materials of both these kinds is the fact that each bit of them occurs in time. The sensory ingredients of external objects and the constituents of our own minds come necessarily before and after each other as we sense them with the help of our organs and directly in introspection. To be in time is a property which all those things we sense must necessarily possess. The ingredients of external objects, moreover, are related spatially; the trunk, the branches, and the leaves of the plum tree which I now perceive are above and below, to the right and left, near to and far from one another. The materials of external objects as we come upon them through sense must be found in space. The exercise of the faculty of sense places all the objects upon which it is directed in time, and many of them in space. Apart from its exercise, i.e., apart from introspection and observation, the parts of one's mind cannot be related by temporal relations, nor the parts of physical things by spatial and temporal relations. The exercise of this power, Kant concludes, consists of locating the materials upon which it is directed in the frameworks of time and space.

Our power to combine the materials of sense is the faculty of imagination.[10] In retrospection we come upon ourselves only bit by bit. This desire, that thought, this feeling, that sensation, occur at different moments; but while we find them all in time, exercising our power of sensing them does not show us their connection, i.e., their unity as ingredients in one person or one self. Similarly, our sensing the plum tree reveals its constituents in different moments of time and different parts of space, but it does not show us their connection in one tree. The exercise of our power to imagine consists in combining the manifold items presented to sense; and in any act of imagination, there are four subordinate stages. First, we must retain or remember the items sensed from one moment to another; secondly, reproduce them as images of the original items; thirdly, associate them with others according to rules; and, fourthly, recognize the resultant unity as a thing of the kind constructed by following those rules. Our imagination combines desires, thoughts, feelings, etc., into a single person by retaining them, by reproducing them, by associating them with others, and by recognizing that they make up a person by virtue of the rules followed and derived from the kind of thing a person is. Similarly, our imagination combines branches, twigs, leaves, etc.,

[10] *Critique of Pure Reason,* translated by Norman Kemp Smith, St. Martins Press, Inc., New York, 1961, p. 144.

into the plum tree by retaining our sensations of them, reproducing them, associating them according to rules derived from what a plum tree is, and recognizing that the resultant complex is a thing of the kind (plum tree) that is constructed by applying those rules to appropriate sensory materials. Our power to imagine enables us, through memory, to add to any present moment's sensory item the past of a thing and, through expectation, its future. What its past and future are, it determines by the rules it follows in associating remembered and expected items with the present one. Further, it enables us to recognize what kind of thing results from its activity by enabling us to recognize the rules we have been following in organizing the sensory material.[11]

The understanding is the faculty which provides the rules,[12] and they are of two kinds. Some are learned by observation and introspection. The ways in which feelings and emotions wax and wane and give place one to another in our minds can be noticed by introspection and from this reflection we may derive general statements which function as rules for organizing the ingredients of ourselves around any given moment's content. Similarly, observation of plum trees yields general statements as to their changes—their blossoming and bearing, their budding and defoliation, by use of which we can organize the history of any particular tree around any given moment. There are other rules which are not discovered by introspection and observation. That the ingredients of ourselves and of the tree must be organized around a substance, that the various stages in each must cause those which follow, are rules whose foundation lies in reflection upon our knowledge rather than in empirical inquiry. The faculty of understanding is the power to discover empirical laws through introspection and observation and to propound others which cannot be discovered in this way. It is also the power to convert these latter laws into rules (what Kant describes as schemata for categories) that the imagination employs in organizing every object we can experience.

The faculty of reason is the power through whose exercise we arrive at ideas which unify the activities of the understanding and imagination.[13] These last, in conjunction with sense, yield selves and physical objects insofar as we can experience them. The notion of applying to all possible sensory material the rules and categories provided by the understanding yields the notion of the world of possible experience—of possible selves and physical objects. Each item in this world must be thought of as depending upon something—upon its cause or its condition; and we can explain any one of them, partially, by exhibiting that condition—an illness by its bacteria and an emotion by its incitement. But since

11 *Ibid.,* pp. 146–47.
12 *Ibid.,* p. 147.
13 *Ibid.,* p. 304.

every item possesses such a condition, we can make nothing completely intelligible by indicating it; the condition itself must always be explained in a similar fashion. There must be, then, a totality of conditions which provides the complete explanation for any particular item in the world of possible experience. This idea unifies the activity of applying rules to sensible things by pointing to a single thing, the totality, which includes that application to sense. But obviously such an idea can be produced neither by sense, imagination, nor understanding. The totality can be neither present to sense, since the latter is awareness of elements only, nor to imagination and understanding, since these enable only the construction of subordinate parts of the totality. The idea of it is produced by the faculty of reason in response to our demand for a complete explanation as to why each item in the world of possible experience is what it is.

This idea assumes three forms. The totality which explains the self is the soul. The totality which explains this particular train of physical objects or events is the entire physical world. The totality which explains all souls and all physical objects taken together is God. My soul makes me the person I am, determining that I should harbor just these feelings, thoughts, etc. The whole physical world makes it necessary that just this object should appear here and now. God's intent explains why both souls and the physical world are what they are. Reason produces or invents the ideas of the soul, of the physical world, and of God, and, by use of these ideas, it advances an explanation of why we find what we find in our experience.

The faculty of desire gives rise to activities similar in many respects to those of animals. Animals express their desires in ways predominantly instinctual; and unlearned desires—desires whose objectives are not illumined by cognition—serve their purposes well. Superhuman beings possess no faculty of volition; unable to harbor evil desires, they need not decide between good and evil with the help of rules. Man's life, on the other hand, is neither wholly instinctual, nor devoid of evil desires. The faculties of cognition and volition are, together, peculiar to him. Their exercise constitutes his humanity. But possessing these faculties does not guarantee their successful exercise, i.e., the achievement of knowledge, especially knowledge of one's duties, and the actual will to do the right. While animals live by instinct and superhuman beings by knowledge alone, man can realize his humanity only through knowledge of the right and that voluntary control of desire which enables him to follow it.

Human history

Kant holds that we can regard all nature, both animate and inanimate, as a mechanistic activity and as a purposeful one.[14] A mechanistic activity

---

[14] *Critique of Judgment* (Bernard translation), §§80–83.

(mechanism) is one which can be described by laws, stating spatio-temporal relations between its various stages. The working of a clock may be regarded as mechanistic. Each stage of its operation, the spring and the cogs being in a certain state, accompanies or precedes another stage, the hand pointing to certain numbers, etc. By describing the working of the clock in this way we make no reference to the purpose of the whole process, that of telling time, nor to that of any of its stages, e.g., the purpose of enabling the hands to point. We may think of all nature, similarly, as describable by a set of laws and, therefore, as a mechanistic activity. Kant suggests that there is a set of laws which describe the ways in which life arises from mere matter and higher forms from lower forms of animate existence—a pre-Darwinian evolutionary hypothesis.

A purposive activity is one which is done for the sake of something else, its goal or end. That the clock works in order to enable us to tell the time is a purposive (teleological) explanation of its activity. Thus, too, we might describe the parts of any whole as functioning in order to enable the functioning of the other parts and of the whole itself. All nature, in this way, may be conceived as progressing toward a goal or end. This is the teleological view of nature. Kant suggests that the proper way of regarding nature is both mechanistic and purposive—that there is a mechanism at work in nature and that it directs all her processes toward a single, inevitable goal.

This goal is a world-wide political state, and the mechanism which carries nature toward it is expressed in the laws of psychology and their extension into history. By instinct, men desire power, its use for egoistic hedonistic purposes, and a wild life; but their faculty of cognition enables them to see that an untrammeled expression of these instincts would amount to a state of insecurity for all. They voluntarily organize themselves into political states, adhering to a social contract. But between political states, the same egoistic desires break out anew, causing war which drives separate political entities together in gradually increasing extents, in order to avoid the insecurity of separate, sovereign existence. The mechanism of egoistic persons and states, expressed in personal and social conflict, leads inevitably toward the goal of a single international state, embracing all mankind.[15]

The international state is not merely the mechanistic result of historical processes; it is also the goal toward which they aim. "All the capacities implanted in a Creature by nature," Kant writes, "are destined to unfold themselves, completely and conformably to their end, in the course of time."[16] Observation shows that organs that persist in animal

15 *Idea of a Universal History,* Fifth Proposition and Seventh Proposition, and *Perpetual Peace,* First Supplement of the Articles; in *Kant's Principles of Politics* (Hastie translation).
16 *Idea of a Universal History,* First Proposition.

bodies play some role in their lives, that arrangements of parts have some end to accomplish. An organ or an arrangement which served no purpose would be a contradiction. Similarly, the faculties of volition and cognition must accomplish their purpose. That they do so is a teleological law; and the mechanism of human activity, describable by mechanistic laws, must be regarded as achieving a social order in which an enlightened and rational will controls desire, and humanity is fully realized in both personal and social existence.

In the present generation, however, this purpose cannot be accomplished. The objective inherent in volition is the fulfillment of duties, especially the duty to respect the rights of man and to obey the law of the local and the international state; and the objective inherent in cognition is perfect knowledge of the world we can experience and an explanation of it through use of the ideas which reason propounds. But the strength of desire breaks down the barriers of will, making for egoistic behavior rather than respect for others, for violation of civil law, and for international warfare. The shortness of life makes it impossible to discover all knowledge. Humanity can not have been achieved in any generation including the present one; but since it must be realized somehow, Kant concludes that it will be realized as a result of a collective effort in the life of the race as a whole. Each generation inherits and augments both the knowledge and the morality of the preceding, and the realization of humanity appears as a goal toward which the succession of generations tends. A law of progress follows from the teleological law that all faculties succeed in their exercise, and this progress is carried by a psychological mechanism of instinctive self-seeking and unlawfulness.

Administration of education

Kant considers the advantages and disadvantages of tutorial education, and of public and private schooling. The tutor can attend more carefully to the moral training of his charges but, under his care, as opposed to that of a school, it is easier for the child to reproduce family faults and to throw off all authority where it is divided between tutor and parents. Schools generally require that the child both recognize the rights of others and learn to make his own respected. They make for advancement only through merit and they are good instrumentalities for instruction. But publicly supported schools are subject to the biased intervention of the prince—poorly educated as a rule, and incapable of viewing his subjects as anything but instruments for making war. Private schools, on the other hand, run the risk of being controlled by parents who are interested only in the welfare of their particular children rather than in the objective proper to education. Education is most efficient where controlled by independent experts not supported by governments and uninfluenced by parents.[17]

RECOMMENDATIONS

Definition of ''education''

For Kant, "education" means care, discipline, and instruction.[18] Clearly, a child must be nourished and guarded if he is to survive; and the first element of the definition needs no explanation. Discipline is the eradication of wildness. Instruction is the cultivation of the volitional and cognitive faculties.

Goal recommendation

The goal which Kant recommends for education, i.e., what care, discipline, and instruction should promote, is the realization of humanity. We have seen that this is the goal toward which progress moves, and education appears in Kant's thought as an aid to the force of history. The concrete embodiment of humanity, we have also seen, is an international state which maintains peace. But this international state, Kant argues, requires that its local member states be republics, and, in turn, that their citizens possess character and intellectual attainment. Individual persons of this sort tend to organize themselves into republics, and republics, into the international state.

Subordinate recommendation

To form such persons is the subordinate goal of education. The person who possesses character is one who harbors the purpose of acting rightly and who actually engages in such action. A person has a purpose of acting in a certain way if whenever he finds himself in certain circumstances he makes a particular response. Thus, one who harbors a gluttonous purpose is one who, whenever he is confronted with food, endeavors to partake of it uncontrolledly. The purpose of acting rightly is the purpose of making the correct choice between two or more desires whenever they occur; and a person of character is one who harbors the purpose of acting rightly and who, in fact, does so.[19]

There are many different ways of acting rightly—as many as there are opposed desires, recurring in clusters, between whose members one must choose. Consequently, a man of character possesses many different

[17] *Lecture-Notes on Pedagogy* (Buchner translation), §§16, 17, 24, 25, 30.
[18] *Ibid.*, §1.
[19] *Ibid.*, §§77, 94.

purposes. Kant singles out three for special discussion. These are obedience, truth-telling, and sociability. Obedience is of two kinds. Obedience to a person is submission to his will and it is enforced by punishment or the threat of it. Obedience to moral law is submission to rules of duty. It is enforced by no physical sanction, but occurs voluntarily when conscience makes a rule of duty clear. When tempted by a contrary desire, a person of character decides in favor of the law of the state and actually obeys it. Where the state is not concerned, he decides to do what he ought to do and actually does it. Truth-telling is the purpose of saying what is true whenever asked and includes the purpose to keep one's promises. A promise is a statement of what one intends to do in the future, given certain circumstances, and the purpose of promise-keeping includes performing the action toward which the intention stated is directed. To state falsely what one intends to do, or to fail to do it given the circumstances, is to tell a lie; and consequently, incompatible with the purpose of truth-telling. Sociability is the purpose of making and preserving friendships. It is an important element in character and, along with obedience and truth-telling, should be fostered in children from the beginning.[20]

Kant emphasizes the importance of developing character; he pays much less attention to intellectual attainment. This results from exercising the faculty of cognition. The power of sensation should be developed so that fine discriminations can be made, especially with the eyes and ears. The exercise of the imagination, as we have seen, depends upon memory, and this should be trained to the greatest exactness possible. The development of the understanding consists in the acquisition of rules of various sorts. Rules for reading and writing assist in the acquisition of still others —the empirical or scientific laws of nature; the man who has learned such rules possesses culture. Prudential rules show us how to manage others for our own purposes, and rules of good manners reduce the friction inherent in society. One who has learned rules of these two kinds is civilized. Development of the power of reason consists in possessing the ideas which reason propounds and in applying them to the world possible for creatures of sense, imagination, and understanding.[21] Intellectual attainment consists in seeing exactly what our senses deliver and in understanding it by applying to it the correct rules. It consists in culture and civilization.

Persons of character and intellectual attainment tend to associate themselves in republics. In such states, the constitution provides that legislation, including foreign policy, must receive the consent of the people; and the power of making laws is separated from that of their en-

---

20 *Ibid.,* §§80, 87, 88.
21 *Ibid.,* §§18, 69–71, 74; also Buchner, *op. cit.,* pp. 263–64.

forcement. People of character regard it as their duty to respect the rights of man—his liberty and his equality—and consequently to live in states whose executives cannot abuse their power by both making and enforcing law. This dutiful respect lies at the basis of a genuine social contract. Moreover, persons in whom the faculty of cognition is developed will see that the republican constitution, as opposed to the autocratic, can guarantee liberty and equality or prevent the personal conflict that natural egoism engenders.[22]

Republican states, thus formed, are most likely to associate themselves in an international state. The duty to respect liberty and equality of others is flagrantly violated by international warfare; in the latter, other persons are regarded as instruments to one's own purposes, i.e., as properly subject to one's own will as expressed in state action, and possessed neither of liberty to determine their own lives nor of equality in importance to oneself. Where declaration of war requires the consent of citizens as in a republic, war is improbable; for, since it is contrary to duty, consent to its declaration will not be forthcoming. Moreover, the citizens in such a state will see that warfare offers the greatest threat to their private happiness and to the republican constitution, and for these egoistic reasons will demand an international state.

The subordinate task of education is to form persons of character and intellectual attainment in order to foster republicanism and consequently the international state which embodies humanity. How can this task be accomplished?

CURRICULUM. Kant says only a little as to the curriculum which furthers character and intellectual achievement. Character, he argues, is promoted by an early inculcation of rules of duty; and he suggests a moral catechism to be studied frequently, and fables, poems, and histories, in which shining examples of dutiful action are embodied.

When the sex instinct becomes manifest in boys, they should be taught the dutiful way to manage it; and, while some of Kant's views might make the queen herself describe them as Victorian, he is probably one of the first (perhaps taking his cue from Rousseau) to bring the subject openly into books on education.

Intellectual development can be fostered by games which train the senses; by maps which steady and regularize the imagination; by history, mathematics, botany, mineralogy, languages, geography, and geology, which cultivate the understanding. Children should not be permitted to read novels and fairy tales; for they disorder the imagination by training it to follow rules nowhere exhibited in the real world. Kant insists that the best way to further intellectual achievement is to train the faculties to

[22] *Perpetual Peace* (Hastie translation), §2, First Article.

a high capacity to acquire knowledge, not to give knowledge to the student directly as a part of instruction. He says nothing directly concerning the cultivation of reason; but he argues that children should be taught a few elementary religious doctrines. They concern God; and since the idea of Him is one of the ideas propounded by reason, religious education would cultivate that faculty to some degree.[23]

METHOD.   The method for cultivating character must be directed upon volition. It is this faculty which enables us to make correct choices between desires and consequently to act upon duty. There are two stages in the method. First, wildness must be eradicated. This instinct complicates every moral choice. The latter consists in deciding for one desire as opposed to another by using a rule or law; and since wildness encourages disobedience to all law, it makes for disregarding of every moral choice. Discipline is the method for eradicating wildness, and it consists in compelling children to sit still, be quiet, and "do exactly as they are told." Secondly, action upon duty must be positively fostered. Learning rules of duty, from a moral catechism, discussing and comparing actual examples of it drawn from history and biography, and seeing how the rules apply to them, will help to train volition to act dutifully. But character cannot be advanced by rewarding right actions with pleasure and punishing the wrong with pain. A right action is one done because it is right; and the attachment of pleasure and pain to it would turn a right action into one done, not for the purpose of doing right, but for securing pleasure or avoiding pain. This difficulty, Kant thought, might be circumvented by disapproval of wrong actions rather than approval of the right, which is a kind of pleasure, and by encouraging the child to adopt and to adhere to rules of duty on his own. This personal adherence to rules is furthered by bringing the child to compare his own behavior with the ideal human type. Consideration of this ideal shows him how he has fallen short in the past, and with it in mind, he should compete for improvement with his past performances. The instructor should never compare him with other students, nor foster competition with them. Such a procedure may encourage humility which is necessary to character, but it surely develops envy, which is an important root of corruption.[24]

The correct choice between desires, upon which character depends, requires that the faculty of volition be uninfluenced by external forces, i.e., that it be free. To this end Kant makes two negative recommenda-

---

[23] *Lecture-Notes on Pedagogy* (Buchner translation), §§68–74, 104–11.

[24] *Ibid.*, §§4, 77, 79, 83, 87, 99; but cf. also Kant, *Critique of Practical Reason*, Second Part, "Methodology of Pure Practical Reason," (Abbott translation), pp. 361–62. Here Kant holds that the beginning of character education, habits of right conduct must be established by use of the "leading strings" of pleasure and pain or reward and punishment.

tions, and one positive. One should prevent the growth of habitual behavior and abstain from shows of affection. Habits, at best, prevent acting on desires selected by volition where these oppose them and, at worst, mask the need for decision. Caresses foster dependence of the child on those who demonstrate affection for him, and this dependence discourages autonomous decisions on his part. A positive measure for teaching freedom is the requirement that children conform strictly to the rules of the school, but that these rules should be freely adopted by them—a suggestion of student government.[25]

The method for securing intellectual accomplishment may be expressed in seven principles. First, the faculty of sense should be trained for accuracy by games which, however, should not be pleasant since pleasure rather than sensory refinement may become their objective; and, also, by drawing, map-making, and the like, which require an accurate observation of things depicted. Secondly, the imagination should be perfected by cultivating the subordinate power of memory and this is done by drill in languages, names of places, and the like. Fairy tales and novels should be avoided because they distract the mind by violating all regular ways of behaving, and weaken the memory. Thirdly, the understanding is strengthened by appealing to different motives from those of learning the rules taught in concrete situations. Thus, reading and writing may be taught by appealing to the motive of hunger. The hungry child will draw a loaf of bread when asked, and this activity of drawing (making a private alphabet) may be converted shortly into that of writing, and that into reading. Similarly, the child should avoid instruments in learning the rules of geography and the like, relying on the motive toward sensory discrimination, or make his own maps, compasses, etc. Indeed, this indirect motivation suggests to Kant that children can teach themselves and that they learn by doing. Fourthly, the rules whose learning cultivates the understanding should be presented in an order which corresponds to the order of the different stages of the process of our coming to understand them. Thus, in learning geology, the student should be acquainted through observation with particular geological structures; next, with a true description of them; then, with the laws which explain those true descriptions; after that, with the way in which these descriptions may be derived from their laws; and last, with the way in which these laws may be derived from others more fundamental. This is the path of investigation of nature, and teaching should follow it if it is to be effective. Fifthly, reason should be strengthened by showing the way in which each law may be regarded as dependent in the totality of laws. Sixthly, this order for the cultivation of understanding and reason should be embodied in Socratic dialogue and discussion. Mere questioning shows what has been

[25] *Lecture-Notes* (Buchner translation), §§38, 44, 50.

learned but does not instruct; questioning along with discussion of answers accomplishes both. Seventhly, all teaching of the understanding and reason should allow time for meditation; such cultivation is best furthered by the student's exercising his own faculties in organizing the materials concerned.[26]

ADMINISTRATION. Education should proceed primarily in private schools under control of expert administrators and teachers. Domestic education, presided over by tutors and parents, perpetuates family faults; public education, influenced by the militaristic nationalism of the prince and by the parental bias of the relatives of children, is prevented from pursuing the future realization of humanity which is its proper objective. Training for character may be shared with parents and church, but intellectual attainment should be wholly the responsibility of the private school.[27]

Only boys should attend such schools. The faculty of cognition in girls is not capable of much development. Their training should aim at the cultivation of taste, the control of desire, and the management of the household; this training can be best offered by the mother at home.[28] Boys should attend school only to the age of sexual maturity. Then they are able themselves to beget children of their own; and therefore, should be teachers rather than pupils.

Supplementary recommendation

SCIENCE OF EDUCATION. It is evident that education, i.e., care, discipline, and instruction, should further the cultivation of character and intellect as efficiently as possible. Insofar as this subordinate goal is pursued in a haphazard way (Kant says "mechanically"), it is not very certain of success. Every event in all its recurrences, Kant believed, brings with its companions of particular sorts— every lightning flash precedes a thunderclap, every failure to support a body, its fall. Nature is uniform and her uniformity consists in the fact that each happening of a given kind occurs under the condition that some happening of another kind or kinds also occurs. The expression of any part of the uniformity of nature is a law of nature, and the laws about a subject make the science of it. The science of a subject is very useful, for each of its laws shows how to bring something into existence, i.e., an event of one of the kinds which the law correlates. We need merely introduce one of its companions. Kant believed that the achievement of character and intellectual development, like all other events, always is accom-

---

26 *Ibid.*, §§68–76; cf. also Buchner, *op. cit.,* pp. 261–63.
27 *Lecture-Notes,* §§16, 17, 19, 22, 25.
28 Buchner, *op. cit.*, pp. 84–86, pp. 226–27.

panied by an event of some other kind or kinds, and the statement of relevant uniformities is the science of education. It is clear that if we could discover the laws of this science, we could easily derive from them rules whose employment would make the achievement of character and intellectual development more certain than it now is. Kant recommends that schools be used not merely as training centers for teachers, but also as laboratories in which experiments should be conducted toward the discovery of the laws of education—a recommendation suggested to him by the Philanthropist Institute of Dessau, and carried out by Herbart, his successor at Königsberg.[29] The realization of humanity will be furthered by the development of character and intellect; this, by teachers who employ useful methods; and these, by careful training in rules for teaching derived from laws which state the conditions under which care, discipline, and instruction are most effective.

PHILOSOPHY OF EDUCATION

KANT DESCRIBED THE doctrines that resulted from his philosophical reflection as critical philosophy. By the word "critical," he intended to suggest that his philosophy is based upon a careful determination of the capacities of the human mind—of the faculties of reason, understanding, imagination, and sense; and that in light of this determination a great deal of traditional philosophy not so based must be rejected or re-interpreted. His criticism is couched in language which is very obscure, and his teaching embodied in an intellectual structure as elaborate as the language is dark. Here, I give only a sketch of his critical philosophy, setting down those dominant features of it which seem to pertain to his comments upon education and avoiding so far as possible his own difficult language.[30]

PRELIMINARY DISTINCTIONS

Kant's critical philosophy rests upon the distinctions between the realms of experience and of things-in-themselves and between matter and

---

[29] *Lecture-Notes* (Buchner translation), §§7, 20.

[30] In addition to the books mentioned at the beginning of this chapter, the reader may wish to consult Kant's *Prolegomena to Any Future Metaphysics*, translated by Lewis White Beck, The Liberal Arts Press, New York, 1950; and *Foundations of the Metaphysic of Morals*, translated by Lewis White Beck, The Liberal Arts Press, 1959. Among the many useful commentaries on Kant's philosophy we may mention *Commentary to Kant's "Critique of Pure Reason"* by Norman Kemp Smith, Macmillan and Co., Ltd., London, 1918; *Kant's Treatment of Causality* by A. C. Ewing, K. Paul, Trench, Trubner Co., Ltd., London, 1924; and *Kant's Theory of Knowledge* by H. A. Prichard, Oxford University Press, 1909.

form. The realm of experience is made up of those things and happenings which human beings are *actually* aware of and which they might *possibly* be aware of. It contains, for example, all the tables, mountains, and selves of which anyone, at any time, is aware as well as the processes of painting, eroding, and learning that we find they undergo. But it also contains all those things and happenings, before and after and spatially remote from us, of which we would be aware if we existed in places and times from which we are, in fact, absent. The realm of experience presupposes the realm of things-in-themselves. The latter is made up of things which we cannot possibly experience at all, but which are required, nonetheless, to explain things and happenings we do experience. A table, for example, could not be experienced as colored, shaped, and tangible in certain ways unless there were something apart from our experience of it which caused us to experience it in those ways. Nor could we find ourselves desiring, willing, and learning unless there were something apart from our experienced activities which determined them. The realm of things-in-themselves is not in our possible experience; but it harbors the explanation of the latter—in Kant's language, the "condition" or "ground" for it.[31]

The matter of a thing, Kant holds, is the elements which constitute it. The matter of a desk, for example, is its top, legs, and drawers; of a self, its desires, feelings, and thoughts; of a poem, its lines and larger units. The forms of things are the ways in which its elements are combined. In a desk, the legs are below and support the top; in a self, desires, feelings, and thoughts succeed and influence each other; in a poem, the lines rhyme, and the thoughts they carry fit together in certain coherent ways. The form of a desk is the pattern for all desks; of a self, the order of its parts; and of a poem, the sonnet, the epic, *et alia*.[32]

KNOWLEDGE

For Kant, "knowledge" means the experience of an object ("objective perception") embodied in judgments of whose truth we are certain. Some experiences have no objects. Melancholy and cheer, cold and heat, the sensation of red and smooth—these are experiences. But they are not experiences of objects; for within each, we can find no difference between the act of experiencing and the object upon which it is directed. These mental states cannot be cases of knowing, for knowledge is "experience related to an object." Moreover, objective experience, if it is also knowledge, must be embodied in judgments which we can hold to be true with perfect certainty. My present experience of the tree outside

[31] *Critique of Pure Reason* (Smith translation), e.g., pp. 23–24, 466.
[32] *Ibid.,* pp. 66, 280.

the window is an objective experience and not a mere mental state; but this does not make it knowledge. I can not know that the object of my experience is a tree, unless I judge that it is a tree and hold that judgment to be true in such a way that I cannot be mistaken.[33]

What kinds of things can we know or what kinds of things can we judge in such a way as to be certain of no mistake? Kant's answer to this question makes use of the distinctions we have explained above.

First, we cannot know what the matter is in any individual object, or what physical objects and selves the world contains. Matter is the sensible elements of things; and we have seen above that it varies from one time to another. As a consequence, we can never be certain that a judgment stating that a thing has certain elements or that things with certain elements are always related to each other in a certain way is true at any time other than the one in which these material elements are being experienced. We cannot be certain that this canary is yellow; for though yellowness may now be joined to the other material ingredients of the bird, it may be separated from them at some other time. The canary may turn white. For the same reason, we cannot be certain that all bodies are heavy, and that all lightning causes thunder, however certain these judgments may at first appear. Our experiences of individual objects and of things of one kind as causing things of another are objective, but our judgments about their objects cannot be made with certainty.

Secondly, we can be certain about some forms of the physical objects and of the selves we can experience, as well as of certain forms which, taken together, they compose. We have seen that exercise of the cognitive faculty consists in organizing the material elements of physical objects and selves in certain ways, and that its exercise is required for the experience of an object. Its ways of organizing material elements into objects, and objects into larger complexes, make up many of the forms into which experienced things fall; and the mind, thus impressing its own forms upon matter, leaves traces on everything we experience. Thus the spatio-temporal relations within individual objects and between them, and the temporal relations between the parts of our selves are given to them by our exercising the faculty of sense upon them. We can be certain of the judgment that every part of a physical object is related to others in space and time, and that every individual physical object is related to others by relations of the same sort; and we can also be certain that every self is made up of items related in time. But the things we experience are related to each other by other relations, and some of these reflect the imagination's activity in applying rules which the understanding originates. Lightning is continuous with thunder, in space and time, by virtue of the way our senses operate, but it is the cause of thunder by

33 *Ibid.*, pp. 314, 646.

virtue of the way the imagination and understanding operate. The former applies to the elements of lighting and of thunder the rule that every event must have a cause; and the understanding, carrying this form of things within it as part of its structure, gives it to the imagination as a rule for its organizing activity. Kant thought that besides the spatio-temporal forms of things inherent in sense, there are twelve others which are native to the understanding, and must, for that reason, be exhibited by all objects of experience. These include the forms of quantity or number of parts, of substance and quality or the relation between the enduring and the less enduring elements of a thing, of cause and effect, of reciprocal influence, and others which we cannot mention here. Judgments that things are related in these twelve ways as well as judgments concerning their spatio-temporal relations cannot be mistaken.[34]

What we can know is that all experienceable things possess certain forms such as those of space and time and of cause and effect. Our experience of these is objective, but it is not the experience of any individual object or group of them. Rather, it is the experience of forms of objects, and we can be certain that all objects exhibit these forms because every object is constructed according to them. We cannot know that an individual object will contain any particular material element; but we can know that no matter what its elements, they will be arrayed in space and time. We cannot know that any causal law, any statement like "things of this sort cause things of that sort" is true; but we can know that a thing of whatever sort must cause a thing of some other. Knowledge is experience of the forms for objects embodied in judgments about which we cannot be mistaken because we employ those forms to construct the objects which occupy them.

Thirdly, our knowledge, thus, does not extend to judgments of two important kinds. We cannot know that the judgments of common sense and the laws of science are true where they concern the matter of things. Our experience of the yellow canary and of lightning as causing thunder are objective. But it is not knowledge, for we cannot be certain that the judgments which embody it are true. Moreover, judgments about the realm of things-in-themselves cannot express knowledge. Such things cannot be the objects of experience at all and, consequently, we cannot embody experience of them in judgments of whose truth we are certain. We can only know that the things which occupy the realm of experience possess certain forms and that these are referred to by the judgments embodied in mathematics and logic, together with a very few abstract principles employed in physics. But the concrete judgments of science and everyday life cannot be known even though they pertain to the realm of

[34] *Ibid.*, pp. 180–87.

experience; and those which refer to things without that realm must, for that reason, forever remain beyond our cognitive competence.

METAPHYSICS

Kant's view of knowledge leads him to a rejection of traditional metaphysics. This discipline arose as an answer to some very natural questions. What explains the fact that I have just these particular thoughts, feelings, and desires? Why is there just this particular object, e.g., just this particular destructive storm, here and now, and not some better weather? Why is the entire world of nature and of man just what it is, and why does it exist at all? These questions are natural to the human mind; and as we have seen, it creates ideas by use of which to answer them. My soul explains why I harbor certain thoughts, feelings, and desires; the whole physical world makes it necessary that just this particular object should be here and now, and allows no other; God causes just this system of nature to exist, and permits no other. Metaphysics answers these demands for explanation by asserting that everything we find is determined by our souls, by the whole world and, ultimately, by God. But these judgments cannot embody knowledge. There is no objective experience corresponding to them. Such an experience, as we have seen, is the mind's organization of elements into some form. But our sense cannot deliver to us any material elements which could be the constituents of the soul, of the world as a whole, and of God. The soul lies behind sensory experience and never appears in it. The physical world as a whole is made up of objects we construct as we experience them; but it can never, as a whole, be in our experience since the latter is precisely the activity of organizing its parts. The elements of the Divine Being are never presented to the senses; consequently, we can never experience Him by organizing such elements. The ideas of the soul, of the whole world, and of God are about things we can never experience, i.e., they are ideas of things-in-themselves. The doctrines of traditional metaphysics arise out of a wonder native to man and are couched in ideas his reason creates; but an examination of his cognitive faculty shows that they are as invalid as they are inevitable.

Still, if Kant rejected traditional metaphysics, he helped introduce a new doctrine of a similar sort. The traditional view, as he understood it, held that everything in nature is an appearance to us of something we can not experience—of the soul, the world, and God. But on his view, everything we can experience is a result of the mind's activities of sensing, imagining, and understanding as they exercise themselves in forming objects out of matter given to the senses. Everything we experience, therefore, depends in part upon the human mind; we can imagine nothing existing independently of its activities. This leads to the view that every conceivable existence requires the existence of mind—to a kind of idealism; and this Kantian doctrine dominated many areas of thought long after the work of Kant, himself, was finished.

METAPHYSICS AND THE METHOD OF KNOWLEDGE

Traditional metaphysics gives us no knowledge but the ideas it employs are useful in developing the empirical sciences.

The ideas of reason prompt us to continue our search, through observation and introspection, for those unities which would guarantee our scientific statements about selves and external objects. The idea of the soul prompts us to search for a unified system of psychological laws; the idea of the physical world as a whole directs us toward a completely comprehensive system of laws describing physical events; and the idea of God as the perfect orderer and cause of both mental and physical nature leads us to believe that there are such comprehensive systems—a belief whose failure would render the entire enterprise of empirical investigation purposeless and vain. The ideas of reason lead us naturally into the illusions of traditional metaphysics, but they also regulate and foster the search for empirical knowledge.[35]

ETHICS

It is not the business of ethical philosophy, Kant holds, to discover moral truths. The religious seer, the social reformer, and the literary artist may add novel insights to the store of unreflective morality, but the task of the philosopher is simply that of clarifying and showing how to justify the judgments it contains. Kant advances a view as to the clarification of these judgments and as to the way of showing their validity.

The clarification put forward depends upon the distinction between matter and form. "One ought always to keep his promises, always to refrain from lying, and always to abstain from the property of others" —these typify moral judgments; and each refers to something which possesses both matter and form. This "something" is human conduct— promise-keeping, truth-telling, abstention from theft, or what not; and

[35] Kant frequently speaks of the sciences and of common sense as embodying empirical knowledge. This use of the word "knowledge" is different from that given the word when he is concerned to distinguish knowing from believing (Smith, *ibid.*, p. 646). According to it, "knowledge" means experience of an object, which, of course, involves judgment. But the judgment which such an experience involves is always a "synthetic *a posteriori* judgment," i.e., a judgment which, since its truth depends upon observation or introspection, can never be held with certainty.

the matter of human conduct is not simply the events which compose it. The mere motions involved in keeping a promise, e.g., placing in the hands of a lender a sum equivalent to the sum borrowed, have no moral significance; one might engage in them by some strange accident or as a part of some theatrical performance. In order that motions should possess moral significance, they must be expressive of some intention.

The intention cannot be an exercise merely of the faculty of desire. This exercise is the effort to realize some objective, and this objective is always a pleasure of the person acting. Thus, if the matter of moral judgment were action which expressed desire, all such judgments would refer to the consequences desired, and brought about by the action. If made quite explicit, they would be of the form: "If you want so-and-so, then do such-and-such"; they would all allow for not doing such-and-such where so-and-so is not the egoistic pleasure of the person addressed. But while we issue such hypothetical imperatives in many practical circumstances, moral judgments can never assume that form. The judgment, "One ought always to keep his promises," cannot be put in the form: "If one desires a pleasant life, one ought to keep his promises." Rather, it is put forward as universal and necessary for all men; and since it admits of no conceivable exception, the moral propriety of promise-keeping cannot depend upon its consequences. The form of all moral judgments is that of an unqualified command, a "categorical imperative" in Kant's language; and consequently, the matter referred to by such judgments cannot be actions expressive of the intention merely to fulfill desire.

The matter of moral judgment is action which expresses an intention of volition. This faculty puts forward rules for deciding between competing desires; and an intention of the will is an intention to act upon a desire thus selected, *because* thus selected.[36] The will, as we have seen, decides which of several desires we should act upon; and its deci-

---

[36] Some passages suggest a different view (*Critique of Practical Reason*, Abbott translation, pp. 233–40). Kant sometimes treats volition as if all its rules directed that one ought to do what he in no way desires. On this view, doing one's duty can have no empirically discoverable motive, and can embody no desire. Holding it, Kant draws the conclusion that dutiful action is motivated by a feeling known *a priori*, and embodies this respect for duty. But it is difficult, then, to see how respect for duty differs from desire to fulfill it, however much it may be known *a priori;* and in any case, it is obviously false that we never desire to do what we ought to do. Besides, the passages mentioned are incompatible with the central doctrine that all our actions have causes in the world of experience—causes which always involve our desires. Kant never forgets the opposition between volition and desire; but we can treat it as a tension between a governing rule and what it governs—between a rule for selecting a desire to be realized and the desires from which the selection is made. On this view, dutiful action always expresses desire, but never consists in the fact that it does so. Rather, it consists in the fact that it is an action, caused by a desire that has been selected according to rule, used because it is the right rule. Passages supporting this interpretation are numerous. Some of the clearest are found in *The Critique of Practical Reason* (Abbott translation), pp. 209–20.

sion consists in applying a rule according to which only one of the competing desires is right. Wherever, for example, one desires both to break and to keep a promise, it selects the latter desire for fulfillment according to the rule of promise-keeping. Moreover, the morality of promise-keeping consists not merely in accordance with that rule; such conformity could stem from a rule of mere legality, a rule for avoiding the pains of jail and securing the pleasures of freedom, or what not. Morality flows, rather, from the intention to act upon a desire selected by a rule *because* it is thus selected—from a respect for general rules or laws. It expresses, in this way, an intention of volition.

The action to which moral judgment refers always has a certain form—the form of the rule applied to desire in the intention of the will. This form is that of a universal law of nature. Thus, the moral judgment, "one ought always to keep his promises," refers to a certain way of acting on the part of all those who make promises; and the form (or way) of this matter (or action) is put by saying that every instance of making a promise is followed by keeping that promise. The will's employment of rules (Kant says "maxims") to select the desire we shall act upon gives to the matter judged in moral judgment the same form as that of a judgment which is not moral at all—the form of a law describing some aspect of nature.

Kant's clarification of moral judgments amounts to the assertion that they describe the kinds of action we would engage in if we acted according to the right rules. These actions are our duties, and they reflect the rules we ought to use in deciding which desires to act upon.

How do we decide which rules are right, i.e., determine our duties? How can we justify our moral judgments?

We cannot hold that an action is dutiful because it leads to happiness or pleasant consequences for the actor. These are not part of the matter of moral actions as we have seen. Rather, the validity of a moral judgment must be found in the form of the action to which it refers. The form must spring from a rule which is applicable to all persons, no matter what the circumstances. Some rules cannot have a universal application. Consider the rule, "one ought to break his promise if it is to his advantage to do so." It is possible to employ this rule for deciding between the desire to break and the desire to keep a promise only when the notion of promising can be applied to action. This notion can be applied only in a society where people expect the promiser to keep his word; and so long as some do so, the notion is applicable. In these circumstances, some can use the rule of promise-breaking; for the innocent expectation of fulfillment at once makes possible both the promise and the fraud. It is possible, therefore, for some to act upon desires selected by the rule of promise-breaking. But this rule cannot be a rule for all. Where no one expects promises to be kept, none could be either kept or broken; in such a case, the very notion of a promise would be inapplicable to action, i.e., altogether unusable. A generalized rule of promise-breaking is, thus, an irrational absurdity. On the other hand, the rule of promise-keeping can be generalized; and this general form of the rule gives the form of law to the action which flows from a desire selected by that rule.

Exhibiting its lawfulness by tracing it, thus, to a rule that may be generalized shows that promise-keeping is a duty. So it is for all our duties. They originate in rules for deciding between desires which our reason certifies by exhibiting the unreasonableness of their denials, i.e., the unreasonableness of accepting rules which cannot be applied to all. Abstaining from the property of others is a duty because allowing universal theft destroys the applicability of the notion of property; telling the truth is a duty because universal lying makes inapplicable the notion of language (the communication of truth). To justify a moral judgment is to show that the rule which gives form to the action judged is a rule for all since the denial of it is irrational when generalized. To justify a moral judgment is to show that whatever action it refers to, it fits into the formula: "Act so that the maxim of thy will can always at the same time hold good as a principle of universal legislation." This is Kant's famous "categorical imperative."[37]

Kant mentions very few of the kinds of actions which are dutiful. Promise-keeping, truth-telling, and a few others recur as examples of actions which fit the pattern of the categorical imperative. He describes two other kinds of action as reformulations of the categorical imperative; but even though thus presented, they seem actually to increase the number of duties mentioned. These are the principles: "One ought to treat every human being not merely as a means but as an end also," and "One ought to regard all, including himself, as members of a "kingdom of ends" in which each person makes the laws he obeys." The first enjoins us to refrain from using others as nothing but instruments for securing our own advantage; the second, to treat all persons as free to obey a single system of rules which bind all because each member of the community adopts it. These principles may be combined in the rule: "One ought to respect the values of all persons, including oneself, by treating them as important in their own right, and as able to adopt freely the laws by which they live." This duty springs from the unqualified value Kant finds in individuality.

ETHICS, METAPHYSICS, AND EPISTEMOLOGY

Our duties cannot be gainsaid. On a moment's reflection at most, the moral judgments which embody them are seen as true, universally

---

[37] *Critique of Practical Reason* (Abbott translation), p. 165.

and necessarily, by all men. But while conscience makes them evident, action frequently denies them. Everything in the world of possible experience, as we have seen, has a cause. Our desires are caused by earlier events, and themselves, cause the actions we engage in. When desires compete, volition uses the right rule if we are thoughtful to select one for fulfillment. But causal influences frequently intervene to make us act upon another. Still, since duty remains, we must be free to act upon it even though we do not do so; and since, as parts of the world of experience, all our actions have causes which run ultimately beyond ourselves, we must exist in the world of things-in-themselves as free agents—as souls possessed of independent and original causal power. Kant's theory of knowledge and his treatment of metaphysics have shown that we are caught in a mesh of causal laws which preludes our freedom and that we can never know anything about the world of things-in-themselves. But his ethics shows that we have souls which are free in the world of things-in-themselves, for we must be free to do what we ought to do. Their existence and freedom is implied by every duty—especially those which remain unfulfilled.

Conscience dictates the necessity of fulfilling every duty; but in this life, nature prevents so perfect a record. Since the necessity remains, we must believe that we exist eternally. In so long a time, it is possible for us to realize all the duties we lay upon ourselves by adopting the categorical imperative as the criterion employed to make them out. The soul is not only free, it is also immortal.

Moreover, conscience tells us that a life of duty, unrelieved by happiness, cannot be the lot of perfect virtue. Duty does not guarantee happiness; for, since they are completely separate from each other, one can achieve the former without possessing the latter. In this world of possible experience, there is no perfect judge or law-giver who compensates for their logical separateness by adding happiness to the lives of those who merit it. Indeed, those who most frequently enjoy happiness are unreflective knaves and deliberate scoundrels; taking it for the only good, devoting their energies to it, and disregarding their duties, they succeed in securing happiness which, by itself, is of no moral worth whatever. Still, the *summum bonum,* the greatest good, is a life of perfect duty also pervaded by the charms of happiness; and since it must exist, but does not in the world of possible experience, the perfectly dutiful soul also enjoys perfect happiness. Kant concludes, further, that since duty and happiness are completely separate, they must be put together in the *summum bonum.* This combination is performed by God—the lawgiver and governor who, recognizing that the virtuous should be happy, rewards merit with delight. Thus, the immortality of the soul and the existence of God, which epistemology and metaphysics show we cannot know, ethics compels us to believe.

In his critical philosophy Kant holds that we can know very little about the world of experience—only that it possesses certain forms; and that these forms make science possible. He holds, also, that traditional metaphysics is altogether impossible as a branch of knowledge. But in the ethical part of that philosophy, he adopts the view that denying metaphysical claims to know that there is a soul which is free and immortal, and a God which orders and governs the world, makes room for a faith in them, whose scope is determined by the moral judgments of ordinary life.

EDUCATION AND THE CRITICAL PHILOSOPHY

Kant recommends as the goal for education the elevation of man out of the disorderly life of egoistic desire into that of humanity. The latter is embodied in the international state which preserves peace and is established by agreement between local nation states, republican in character. It is the goal toward which history progresses, but it is also the objective toward which all the activities of education ought to be directed.

Kant's ethical reflection bears upon this goal recommendation in two ways. First, the international state is suggested by the ideal life or *summum bonum*. The latter is an immortal existence in which God adds happiness to moral worth; it is suffused with the consciousness of doing one's duty and of enjoying life as well. This ideal bears a strong resemblance to the goal of history which education should subserve. Under the international state, the abolition of warfare would increase happiness, and that happiness would be deserved by the citizens who enjoy it. For only because they have fulfilled their duties within the nation would it be republican in character, and only because national communities have this character would they unite in the international state. Critical reflection on morality certifies our belief in the *summum bonum;* and this ideal immortal life among things-in-themselves finds its counterpart among experienceable objects in the goal of progress which education should promote.·

Secondly, Kant's ethical theory shows that the actions which would lead to the happiness of this historical ideal are duties. Promise-keeping, truth-telling, respecting the individuality of men by treating them as important in themselves and as able freely to make the laws under which they live—all these are essential to exercise of the human rights to freedom and equality, or fraternity. Only where these duties are fulfilled, and these rights exercised, can the social contract upon which nation-states are based give them a republican character. Moreover, the same duties are necessary to the formation of the international state. For it is based upon the promises or treaties of its members and designed to enhance respect for individuality by abolition of warfare. The latter is immoral, for it treats the enemy as merely a means to the satisfaction of the purposes of one's nation; thus violating the duty to respect individuality. Its rule, also, cannot be generalized; for generalizing it into the rule, "all nations ought to make war when to their advantage," implies the dissolution of that stability necessary to the existence of any nation.

The means through which the international state may be achieved is the gradual improvement of individual human beings from one generation to another. This improvement results from a certain way of educating them, i.e., of caring for, disciplining, and instructing them.

Kant's critical philosophy bears upon this education in three ways. First it provides him with a method for instruction in intellectual subjects. This philosophy has shown that experiencing something consists in judging it, and that judging a thing consists in organizing sensible materials of various kinds in certain patterns or forms. We engage in this activity when we describe a particular thing in a certain way and when we explain our description of it by reference to laws. We also organize things when we explain one law by derivation from another. Knowledge and empirical science depend upon the mind and consist in its activities of providing form for matter by applying rules to the elements of sense. Kant derives, from his description of the activity of judging, a principle for instruction: all information should be learned through the procedure required for knowing it. He assumes that the experience of learning must be the same as the experience of knowing and, on that assumption, he borrows from his theory of knowledge an important principle for instruction. That we should observe and apply rules to things before claiming to know them is a pedagogical principle whose basis Kant finds in his analysis of knowledge.

Secondly, the critical philosophy shows what it is that intellectual instruction is directed upon. The schools should enhance knowledge by improving the faculties which give rise to it, not by communicating it directly. Anyone can learn things on his own and this learning may be of much importance for practical purposes. But the schools should develop the cognitive faculty in its four subordinate parts, thus providing a general education which exercises the faculties rather than a specialized one which requires no tutorial attention. What the cognitive faculty is, which should be thus exercised, is the question to which the critical philosophy makes the answer we have examined.

Thirdly, Kant's critical philosophy bears upon instruction in morality by showing what character is and what method cannot be used to achieve it. Independently of any ethical theory, one might hold that character consists in the embodiment of duty in action; but without reference to some ethical theory, one cannot know what it is which ought, thus, to be embodied. Kant's ethical theory provides an analysis of duty and by means of this analysis sets forth the nature of the objective of instruction in morality. This notion of what is to be sought governs the curriculum of moral instruction, for it determines what rules shall be learned and what examples presented. Moreover, by showing that reward and punishment are bound to fail, Kant's ethical theory plays a role, if only a negative one, in determining the method of moral instruction.

The subordinate recommendation of Kant's educational theory, that intellectual attainment (culture and civilization) and character should be fostered as a means toward the future realization of an international community is determined by his critical philosophy. This philosophy shows him how knowledge may be conveyed from teacher to learner, what character consists in, and what method to avoid in its cultivation.

The critical philosophy influences Kant's thought concerning education through one other channel—that of the function of reason. We can never discover that reason's idea as a unitary explanation of experience is true; nonetheless, we cannot help believing that experience proceeds within a systematic set of laws. We cannot help believing that some of these describe the conditions under which caring for, disciplining, and instructing are most effective. To discover them through scientific investigation is part of Kant's recommendation concerning education; and that such laws are there, waiting to be set forth as a science, is a part of the regulative function of reason without which the injunction to search for them would be idle.

A Guide to Selections from *Lecture-Notes on Pedagogy*

In these passages, Kant argues that education is necessary to make men human, and that we ought to develop a science of it in order to realize this purpose well. He discusses the objective of education—the future perfection of the race—and holds that that perfection will be furthered by eliminating wildness, by teaching skills, by instructing men in prudential ways of dealing with one another, and by cultivating morality. To promote intellectual skills, the faculties must be cultivated. The way of developing good moral character is discussed in some detail.

SELECTIONS FROM

Lecture-Notes on Pedagogy*

—◀●▶—

1.   Man is the only creature that must be educated. By education we mean care (maintenance), discipline (training), and instruction, including culture. Man is thus babe, pupil, and scholar. . . .

7.   Man can become man through education only. He is only what education makes him. It is to be noted that man is educated only by man, and by those men who are educated themselves. Defects, therefore, in the discipline and instruction of some men make them poor educators of their pupils. If a being of a superior nature were to assume the care of our education, we would then see what man could become. But, since education partly teaches man something and partly merely develops something within him, it cannot be known how far his natural qualities go. . . .

14.   Since the development of human capacities does not take place of its own accord, all education is an *art*. Nature has bestowed no instinct for that. The origin, as well as the progress, of this art is either *mechanical*, without plan, being arranged according to given circumstances, or *rational*. The art of education has a mechanical origin solely at those occasional times when we learn whether something is injurious or beneficial to man. Every art of education which arises merely mechanically must carry with it many faults and deficiencies, since it has no plan for its foundation. The art of education, or pedagogy, must therefore become rational if it is to develop human nature so that it attain its goal. Parents already educated are examples which the children imitate. In order to improve children, it is necessary that pedagogy become a study, otherwise there is nothing to hope from it, and he who has been educated corruptly trains others in a like manner. The mechanism in educational art must be transformed into science, otherwise there will never be a united effort, and one generation will pull down what its predecessor has built up.

15.   *One principle in the art of education,* which those men who devise educational plans should especially have in mind, is this: children should be educated, *not* with reference to their present condition, but rather with regard to a possibly improved future state of the human race—that is, according to *the idea of humanity* and its entire destiny. This principle

* The passages are taken from the translation by Edward Franklin Buchner, in his *The Educational Theory of Immanuel Kant,* with kind permission of the publisher, J. B. Lippincott Company, Philadelphia, 1904. Footnotes omitted.

is of great moment. Parents usually educate their children for the present world, corrupt though it be. They should, however, educate them *better,* that an improved future condition be thereby realized.

18. In his education man must therefore be:

(a) *Disciplined.* "To discipline" means to attempt to prevent the animal nature from becoming injurious to human nature in the individual as well as in the member of society. Discipline is, hence, only the taming of wildness.

(b) *Cultured.* Culture includes instruction and teaching. It furnishes skillfulness, which means the possession of a faculty sufficient for the execution of any desired purpose. It determines no goal whatever, but leaves that to circumstances.

Some kinds of skillfulness are good in all cases,—for example, reading and writing; others for a single purpose only, as music, which makes us agreeable in company. Because of the multitude of aims, skillfulness becomes, in a certain sense, indefinitely varied.

(c) *Civilized.* It must also be seen to that man acquire prudence, be a suitable member of the social community, be well liked, and have influence. To this end there is necessary a certain form of culture which we call "civilization." Essential thereto are manners, politeness, and a certain judiciousness by virtue of which all men may be used to one's own ultimate aims. This form of culture adjusts itself to the changeable taste of each age. Thus, a few decades ago people were still very fond of ceremonial in social intercourse.

(d) *Moralized.* Moralization must not be neglected. Man should not only be qualified for all sorts of purposes, but he should acquire that type of mind which chooses good aims only. These are such as are necessarily approved by everyone, and which at the same time can be the purpose of everyone.

67. It is of the greatest importance that children learn to work. Man is the only animal that must work. . . .

Man must be occupied in such a manner that, so engrossed by the purpose which he has in mind, he becomes oblivious of himself, and the best rest for him is that which follows labor; hence the child must be accustomed to labor. And where else than in the school is it possible to give the inclination to work a better cultivation? The school is a forced culture. To lead the child to look upon everything as play is very injurious. There must be a time for recreation, but there must also be a time for work. . . .

68. As for the free culture of the faculties of the mind, it must be observed that it is continuous. It has the higher powers particularly in view. The lower powers are cultivated at the same time, but only with reference to the higher; wit, for example, for reference to the understanding. The principal rule to be followed here is that no power of the mind shall be cultivated in isolation, but each with reference to the others; for example, the imagination only for the benefit of the understanding.

The lower faculties have no worth in themselves; for example, a man may have a great memory, but no judgment. Such a one is a living lexicon. But such pack-mules of Parnassus are necessary; for, although they themselves are unable to produce anything rational, they can drag along the material out of which others can bring something good. Wit becomes outright silliness if it is unaccompanied by judgment. Understanding is the knowledge of the universal. Judgment is the application of the universal to the particular. Reason is the faculty of perceiving the union of the universal with the particular. The free culture continues its course from childhood until the time when the youth is liberated from all education. If, for example, a youth adduces a universal rule, he should be permitted to cite instances in history or in fables in which it is concealed, and passages in poetry where it is already expressed, and thus induced to exercise his wit, memory, etc.

69. The maximum, *tantum scimus, quantum memoria tenemus*, is without a doubt quite correct, and that is why the culture of the memory is very necessary. All things are so made that the understanding first follows the sensuous impressions and the memory must retain them. Thus it is, for example, with languages. They can be learned either by formal memorizing or by conversation, and in the case of modern languages the latter is the best method. The acquisition of a vocabulary is really indispensable; but it is best to have the pupils learn those words which occur in reading an author. It is necessary that the pupils have a fixed and definite task. Geography also is best learned by a mechanical method. The memory especially loves this form of mechanism, and in a multitude of cases it is very useful. Up to the present time there has been contrived no mechanism to facilitate the study of history; the attempt has been made with tables, but these do not appear to have very good effects. History, however, is an excellent means of exercising the understanding in judging. Memorizing is very necessary, but as a mere exercise it has no value,— for example, memorizing a speech word for word. In any case, it only helps towards the encouragement of confidence; and, besides, declaiming is something for adults only. Here belong also all those things which are learned merely for a future examination, or *in futuram oblivionem*. The memory should be employed only with such things as are important for us to remember and which have relation to real life. Novel-reading is most injurious to children, since it only serves to amuse them for the time being. Such reading weakens the memory. It should be absurd to wish to remember romances and to repeat them to others. Thus all novels should

be taken out of the hands of children. While reading them they fashion for themselves in the story a new romance; for they rearrange the circumstances, and fall into reveries and become empty-minded. . . .

70.   The memory must be cultivated early, but care must be taken to cultivate the understanding at the same time.

The memory is cultivated:

(a) By retaining the names which appear in narratives.

(b) By reading and writing; the child must practice the former by mental effort without having recourse to spelling.

(c) By languages, which the child must learn first by hearing before he reads anything.

Then a suitably arranged *orbis pictus*, so called, would be of great use, and a beginning can be made with botany, mineralogy, and a description of nature in general. To make sketches of these objects gives occasion for drawing and modeling, for which a knowledge of mathematics is necessary. The earliest scientific instruction is connected most advantageously with geography, mathematical as well as physical. The narration of travels, illustrated by maps and engravings, leads to political geography. From a study of the present surface of the earth the student goes back to its former condition, and comes upon ancient geography, ancient history, etc.

In the instruction of children we must try to effect a gradual union of knowledge and power. Among all the sciences, mathematics appears to be the one which best accomplishes this purpose. Moreover, knowledge and language should be united (eloquence, rhetoric, and oratory). But the child must also learn to distinguish clearly between knowledge and mere opinion and belief. In this way there is formed a correct understanding, and a taste that is *correct* rather than *fine* or *delicate*. The taste which is to be cultivated first is that of the senses, especially that of the eye, and lastly that of ideas.

71.   Rules must appear in everything that is to cultivate the understanding. It is also very useful to abstract them, so that the understanding may not proceed in a merely mechanical fashion, but rather with a consciousness of the rule which it is following.

It is also very good to arrange the rules into certain formulas and to intrust them in this form to the memory. Then, if we remember a rule and have forgotten its application, we will not be long in recovering it. Here occurs the question: whether rules should first be given *in abstracto* and learned only when their application has been completed, or should rule and use go together. The latter course alone is advisable. In the other instance the use remains very uncertain until one reaches the rules. The rules should also occasionally be arranged into classes; for they are not retained if they have no relation to one another. Thus grammar must always be a little in advance in the study of languages. . . .

75.   The best method of cultivating the faculties of the mind is that each one himself do all that which he wishes to accomplish; for example, to put immediately into practice the grammatical rules which he has learned. A geographical map is best understood if one can draw it himself. The best way to understand is to do. That is most thoroughly learned and best remembered which one learns himself. There are, however, but few men who are capable of this. They are called self-taught men.

76.   In the culture of the reason, one must proceed according to the Socratic method. Socrates, who called himself the intellectual midwife of his hearers, gives in his dialogues, which Plato has in a certain sense preserved for us, examples of how one can lead even old people to produce considerable from their own reason. There are many points on which it is not necessary that children should exercise their reason. They must not reason about everything. They do not need to know the reasons of everything which is to contribute to their education; but as soon as duty comes into question, the principles must be made known to them. We must see to it, anyway, that rational knowledge be drawn out of them rather than introduced into them. The Socratic should furnish the rule for the catechetical method. It is, to be sure, rather slow; and it is difficult so to arrange it that at the same time that knowledge is being drawn out of one mind the others shall learn something. The mechanically catechetical method is also good in many of the sciences; for example, in the instruction in revealed religion. In universal religion, on the contrary, it is necessary to employ the Socratic method. In respect to that which must be learned historically, the mechanically catechetical method is found to be preferable.

MORAL EDUCATION

77.   Moral culture must be based upon maxims, not upon discipline. Discipline prevents defects; moral culture shapes the manner of thinking. One must see to it that the child accustom himself to act according to maxims and not according to certain impulses. Discipline leaves habits only, which fade away with years. The child should learn to act according to maxims whose justice he himself perceives. It is easily seen that it is very difficult to accomplish this in the case of young children, and that therefore moral education demands the utmost sagacity on the part of parents and teachers.

When the child is untruthful, for example, he should not be punished, but treated with contempt, and should be told that he will not be believed in the future, etc. But if he is punished when he does wrong and is rewarded when he does right, he does right in order to be treated well.

And when later he enters the world where things do not happen in that way, but where he can do right or wrong without receiving any reward or chastisement, he becomes a man who thinks only of how he can best make his way in the world, and will be good or bad just as he finds it most profitable.

78.   The maxims must spring from man himself. In moral education, the attempt to introduce into the child's mind the idea of what is good or evil must be made very early. If one wishes to establish morality, there must be no punishment. Morality is something so holy and sublime that it must not be degraded thus and placed in the same rank with discipline. The first endeavor in moral education is to establish a character. Character consists in the readiness to act according to maxims. At first these are the maxims of the school and later they are those of humanity. In the beginning the child obeys laws. Maxims also are laws, but subjective; they spring out of the human reason itself. No transgression of the law of the school should go unpunished; but, at the same time, the punishment must always be commensurate to the fault.

80.   Obedience, above all things, is an essential trait in the character of a child, particularly that of a pupil. It is twofold; first, it is an obedience to the *absolute* will of him who directs; but it is, secondly, an obedience to a *will regarded as rational and good.* Obedience can be derived from constraint, and then it is *absolute,* or from confidence, and then it is of the other kind. This *voluntary* obedience is very important; but the former is also externally necessary, since it prepares the child for the accomplishment of such laws as he will have to fulfil later as a citizen, even if they do not please him.

87.   A second chief trait in the formation of the child's character is *veracity.* Indeed, this is the principal feature and the essence of a character. A man who lies has no character at all, and if there be anything good in him, he owes it entirely to his temperament. Many children have a disposition to lie, which has no other cause than a vivacious imagination. It is the father's affairs to see to it that they break off this habit, for mothers usually consider it a thing of no, or at least very small, importance; they even look upon it as a flattering proof of the superior talents and capacities of their children. . . .

91.   Practical education includes:

  (a) Skill,
  (b) Worldly wisdom and
  (c) Morality.

  It is essential that skill be thorough and not transitory. An appearance of the possession of a knowledge of things which cannot be afterwards realized must not be assumed. Thoroughness should be a quality of skillfulness, and gradually become a habit of the mind. It is the essential point in the character of a man. Skill is essential to talent.

92.　Worldly wisdom consists in the art of applying our skill to man,—that is, to use men for our own ends. To acquire this, many conditions are necessary. It is really the last thing to be acquired; but, according to its worth, it occupies the second phase.

If the child is to be given over to worldly wisdom, he must dissemble, make himself impenetrable, and yet be able to penetrate others. Especially must he conceal his character. The art of external appearance is propriety, and this art must be possessed. It is difficult to penetrate others, but it is necessary to understand this art and at the same time to make one's self impenetrable. This includes dissimulation,—that is, concealing one's faults, and the above-mentioned external appearance. Dissimulation is not always hypocrisy, and can sometimes be permitted, but it borders very closely upon immorality. Simulation is a desperate means. Worldly wisdom requires that a man shall not fly into a sudden passion; but neither must he be altogether too indolent. Thus one must not be vehement, but yet strenuous, which is not the same thing. A strenuous (*strenuus*) man is he who has pleasure in willing. It is a question of the moderation of the emotions. Worldly wisdom is a matter of temperament.

94.　The final thing in practical education is the foundation of character. This consists in the firm resolution of the will to do something, and then in the actual execution of it. *Vir propositi tenax,* says Horace, and that is a good character. If, for example, I have promised anything, I must keep my promise, even if it does me harm. The man who forms a certain resolution, but does not carry it out, can no longer trust himself. If, for example, having taken the resolution always to arise early to study, or to do this or that, or to take a walk, one then excuse himself in the spring-time because the mornings are still too cold and it might be injurious to him; in summer because it is so favorable for sleeping, and sleep is particularly agreeable to him, and thus from day to day defer the execution of his resolution, he finally ends by destroying all confidence in himself.

That which is contrary to morals should be excluded from resolutions of this kind. The character of a wicked man is very bad, its chief quality being its perversity; yet we admire seeing him executing his resolutions and being firm, although one would prefer to see him display an equal persistency in good conduct.

There is not much to esteem in him who is constantly deferring the performance of his purposes. The so-called future conversion is of this sort. The man who has always been vicious, and who wishes to be converted in an instant, cannot possible succeed; for only a miracle could make him instantly like one who has conducted himself well during his whole life and has never had other than upright thoughts. For the same reason, there is nothing to be expected from pilgrimages, castigations, and fastings, since it is impossible to conceive how pilgrimages and other practices can contribute anything towards making, at a moment's notice, a virtuous man out of a vicious one.

What shall it profit for uprightness and improvement of character to fast during the day only to eat so much more during the night, or to inflict a penance on the body which can contribute nothing to a change of soul?

A Guide to Selections from *The Idea of a Universal History*

In these passages, Kant holds that conflict between individuals leads to their organization in a political state. In this state, each person finds the fulfillment of his capacities; but there is conflict between states, and Kant holds that it leads to an international society or community on which each state depends for its safety.

SELECTIONS FROM

*The Idea of a Universal History**

◄◆►

FOURTH PROPOSITION

The means which Nature employs to bring about the development of all the capacities implanted in men, in their mutual antagonism in society, but only so far as this antagonism becomes at length the cause of an Order among them that is regulated by Law.

By this Antagonism, I mean the "unsocial sociability" of men; that is, their tendency to enter into society, conjoined, however, with an accompanying resistance which continually threatens to dissolve this society. The disposition for this lies manifestly in human nature. Man has an inclination to "socialise" himself by associating with others, because in such a state he feels himself more than a natural man, in the

---

* The passages are taken from *The Natural Principle of the Political Order Considered in Connection with the Idea of a Universal Cosmopolitan History*, in *Kant's Principles of Politics*, edited and translated by W. Hastie, 1891; with kind permission of the publishers, T. & T. Clark, Edinburgh.

development of his natural capacities. He has, moreover, a great tendency to "individualise" himself by isolation from others, because he likewise finds in himself the unsocial disposition of wishing to direct everything merely according to his own mind; and hence he expects resistance everywhere just as he knows with regard to himself that he is inclined on his part to resist others. Now it is this resistance or mutual antagonism that awakens all the powers of man, that drives him to overcome all his propensity to indolence, and that impels him through the desire of honour or power or wealth, to strive after rank among his fellow-men—whom he can neither bear to interfere with himself, nor yet let alone. Then the first real steps are taken from the rudeness of barbarism to the culture of civilisation, which particularly lies in the social worth of man. All his talents are now gradually developed, and with the progress of enlightenment a beginning is made in the institution of a mode of thinking which can transform the crude natural capacity for moral distinctions, in the course of time, into definite practical principles of action; and thus a pathologically constrained combination into a form of society is developed at last to a "moral" and rational whole. . . . The natural impulses that urge man in this direction, the sources of that unsociableness and general antagonism from which so many evils arise, do yet at the same time impel him to new exertion of his powers, and consequently, to further development of his natural capacities. Hence they clearly manifest the arrangement of a wise Creator, and do not at all, as is often supposed, betray the hand of a malevolent spirit that has deteriorated His glorious creation, or spoiled it from envy. . . .

SEVENTH PROPOSITION

The problem of the establishment of a perfect Civil Constitution is dependent on the problem of the regulation of the external relations between the States conformably to Law; and without the solution of this latter problem it cannot be solved.

What avails it to labour at the arrangement of a Commonwealth as a Civil Constitution regulated by law among individual men? The same unsociableness which forced men to it becomes again the cause of each Commonwealth assuming the attitude of uncontrolled freedom in its external relations, that is, as one State in relation to other States; and consequenly, any one State must expect from any other the same sort of evils as oppressed individual men and compelled them to enter into a Civil Union regulated by law. Nature has accordingly again used the unsociableness of men, and even of great societies and political bodies, her creatures of this kind, as a means to work out through their mutual

Antagonism a condition of rest and security. She works through wars, through the strain of never relaxed preparation for them, and through the necessity which every State is at least compelled to feel within itself, even in the midst of peace, to begin some imperfect efforts to carry out her purpose. And, at last, after many devastations, overthrows, and even complete internal exhaustion of their powers, the nations are driven forward to the goal which Reason might have well impressed upon them, even without so much sad experience. This is none other than the advance out of the lawless state of savages and the entering into a Federation of Nations. It is thus brought about that every State, including even the smallest, may rely for its safety and its rights, not on its own power or its own judgment of Right, but only on this great International Federation (*Foedus Amphictionum*), on its combined power, and on the decision of the common will according to laws. . . .

A Guide to Selections from *Perpetual Peace*

In the passages presented here, Kant asserts that conflict between individuals naturally leads to national republics, and that conflict between these nations will give rise to an international community that will guarantee peace between its members. A mechanism of history assures what ought to exist—sovereign republics organized into a peaceful international community.

That men ought to construct republican states and a peaceful international order is shown by the fact that the statement that they should exhibits the form of the categorical imperative. Any statement of the form, "one ought to do so-and-so, if such-and-such" (other words like "because" might be substituted for "if"), cannot express a duty. Rather, it can tell us no more than that so-and-so ought to be done where the sentence involved in the if-clause is true. Such a statement can express only an obligation that depends upon taking some state of affairs as a goal or objective; the action referred to is an obligation because it leads to the goal adopted. Consequently, such an action need not be obligatory for those who reject the goal. The statements that refer to these actions, and that state such obligations Kant elsewhere calls "hypothetical imperatives," and describes here as capable of stating the solution to a merely technical problem—the problem of how to secure international peace provided one adopts it as a goal.

But duties are actions that ought to be performed no matter what goals are adopted or rejected. Consequently, they cannot be stated with qualifications. They can be expressed only in unqualified statements— statements of the form: Act in such-and-such a way. Elsewhere, Kant calls this form of statement *"the* categorical imperative" and suggests that only those statements fit it which express a will to act upon a principle that all could act upon—a principle that involves, consequently, no reference to a goal or end to be achieved. The realization and preservation of international peace must be a duty because the corresponding injunction exhibits the form of the categorical imperative.

SELECTIONS FROM

*Perpetual Peace**

━━◀◆▶━━

The question then arises, as to what is the essential meaning and aim of this design of a Perpetual Peace. It may be put thus: "What does Nature do in this respect with reference to the end which man's own reason presents to him as a duty; and, consequently, what does she do for the furtherance of his moral purpose in life? And, further, how does she guarantee that what man ought to do according to the laws of his freedom, and yet does not do, shall be done by him without prejudice to his freedom even by a certain constraint of nature; . . ."

1.   Even if a people were not compelled by internal discord to submit to the coercion of public laws, War as an external influence would effect this. For, according to the arrangement of nature already indicated, every people finds another pressing upon it in its neighbourhood, and it must form itself internally into a State in order to be equipped as a "Power" so as to defend itself. Now the Republican Constitution is the only one which perfectly corresponds to the Rights of man; but it is at the same time the most difficult to found, and still more so to maintain. So much is this the case that many have asserted that the realization of a true Republic would be like a State formed by angels, because men with their selfish inclinations are incapable of carrying out a constitution of so sublime a form. In these circumstances, then, nature comes to the aid of the rational and universal will of man, which, however honoured in itself, is impotent in practice; and it does this just by means of these selfish inclinations. . . .

Such a problem must be "capable of solution." For it does not turn directly upon the moral improvement of men, but only upon the

---

* The passages are taken from *Perpetual Peace,* in *Kant's Principles of Politics,* edited and translated by W. Hastie, 1891; with the kind permission of the publishers, T. & T. Clark, Edinburgh.

mechanism of nature; and the problem is to know how men can use the conditions of nature in order so to regulate the antagonism of the hostile sentiments at work among the people that the individuals composing it shall have to compel each other to submit to common compulsory laws, and that there shall thus be brought about a state of peace in which the laws will have full power. This process may be seen going on in the actually existing, although still very imperfectly organised States. For, in their external relations to one another, they already approach what the idea of Right prescribes, although the essential principle of Morality is certainly not the cause of it; and indeed a good political constitution is not so much to be expected from that principle but rather conversely the good moral culture of a people from such a constitution. Hence the mechanism of nature as it works through selfish inclinations which are externally and naturally antagonistic in their operation to each other, may be used by reason as a means of making way for the realisation of her own end by the application of a Rule of Right, and thereby of furthering and securing Peace both internal and external, so far as it may lie within the power of the State to do so. . . .

APPENDIX

I

On the Discordance between Morals and Politics in reference to Perpetual Peace

The Science of Morals relates directly to practice in the objective sense, inasmuch as it is a system of unconditionally authoritative laws, in accordance with which we *ought* to act. It is therefore a manifest absurdity, after admitting the authority of this conception of duty, to assert, notwithstanding, that we *cannot* so act; for, were it so, this conception would have no value. . . . Hence there can be no conflict between Political Philosophy as the practical science of right and Moral Philosophy as the theoretical science of right; and consequently there can be no opposition in this relation between practice and theory. . . .

But in order to bring practical philosophy into harmony with itself, it is necessary first of all to decide a preliminary question. That question is: Whether, in dealing with problems of the Practical Reason, we ought to begin from its "material" Principle, as the end which is the object of the activity of the will, or from its "formal" Principle, as that which is founded merely upon freedom in its external relation. This formal principle is expressed as follows: "Act so that thou canst will that thy maxim shall become a universal Law whatever may be its End."

It cannot be doubted that the latter principle must take the precedence; for, as a principle of right, it has unconditional necessity, whereas the former is obligatory only under the presupposition of the empirical conditions of the proposed end so existing that it can be realised; and if the end, as in the case of Perpetual Peace, should also be a duty, the duty would itself have to be deduced from the formal Principle which regulates external action.—Now the material principle is the principle of the "political moralist," and it reduces the questions of national, international, and universal Right to the level of a mere "technical" problem. On the other hand, the formal principle is the principle of the "moral politician," and the question of right becomes with him a "moral" problem. Their different methods of procedure are thus wide as the poles asunder, in regard to the problem of bringing about Perpetual Peace which, in the view of the moralist, is not merely to be desired as a physical good, but also as a state of things arising out of the recognition of duty. . . .

Bibliography

FRANKENA, WILLIAM K., *Three Historical Philosophies of Education: Aristotle, Kant, Dewey,* Chicago, Scott, Foresman and Co., 1965. (Keystones of Education Series.) Chapter III.

. . .

BECK, LEWIS WHITE, *A Commentary of Kant's 'Critique of Practical Reason',* Chicago, Chicago University Press, 1960.

PATON, H. J., *Kant's Metaphysic of Experience: a Commentary on the First Half of the 'Kritik der reinen Vernunft',* 2 volumes, London, G. Allen and Unwin, Ltd., 1952 (second edition); New York, Macmillan, 1936. (Muirhead Library.)

SMITH, NORMAN KEMP, *A Commentary to Kant's 'Critique of Pure Reason',* London, Macmillan, 1923 (second edition). Originally published 1918.

X

HERBART

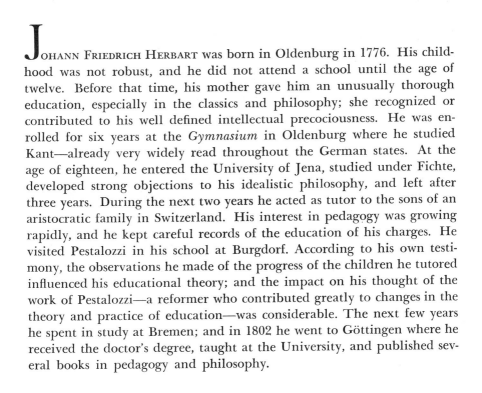

JOHANN FRIEDRICH HERBART was born in Oldenburg in 1776. His childhood was not robust, and he did not attend a school until the age of twelve. Before that time, his mother gave him an unusually thorough education, especially in the classics and philosophy; she recognized or contributed to his well defined intellectual precociousness. He was enrolled for six years at the *Gymnasium* in Oldenburg where he studied Kant—already very widely read throughout the German states. At the age of eighteen, he entered the University of Jena, studied under Fichte, developed strong objections to his idealistic philosophy, and left after three years. During the next two years he acted as tutor to the sons of an aristocratic family in Switzerland. His interest in pedagogy was growing rapidly, and he kept careful records of the education of his charges. He visited Pestalozzi in his school at Burgdorf. According to his own testimony, the observations he made of the progress of the children he tutored influenced his educational theory; and the impact on his thought of the work of Pestalozzi—a reformer who contributed greatly to changes in the theory and practice of education—was considerable. The next few years he spent in study at Bremen; and in 1802 he went to Göttingen where he received the doctor's degree, taught at the University, and published several books in pedagogy and philosophy.

In 1809, Herbart accepted the chair recently vacated by Immanuel Kant at the University of Königsberg. He spent twenty-four years lecturing there on pedagogy, psychology, and philosophy, publishing books in all three fields, and administering and teaching in a demonstration school and training college in which his psychological and pedagogical principles were illustrated. In 1833, he returned to the University of Göttingen where he continued a similar academic existence. He died in 1841, after having won for himself, through his writings, significant chapters in the history of pedagogy, of psychology, and of post-Kantian German philosophy; and through his lectures and numerous students, an enduring influence on educational practice—especially in the United States of America.

EDUCATIONAL THEORY

STATEMENTS OF FACT

Herbart includes in his educational theory statements of fact of three kinds.[1] He finds them in his psychology, in his views regarding the relation between individuals and the human race, and in his beliefs about society and the state. Those drawn from his psychology are by far the most numerous and most carefully elaborated; the others, he advances almost casually. We begin with the statements drawn from his psychology.

Psychology

MENTAL ACTIVITIES: IDEAS.   Herbart's psychology is concerned, chiefly, with mental activities. He holds that they are constituted by *ideas*[2] *arranged in series,* and that all ideas arise in experience although some transcend it. The external senses give us ideas such as those of shapes, of colors, and of sounds; the internal sense (introspection) yields ideas of desires, of volitions, of griefs and joys, etc. And we create ideas, such as those of substance and of force, that have no counterparts in our experience,[3] but apply to a world beyond the one

---

[1] In his *Outlines of Educational Doctrine,* Herbart says that his educational theory has a two-fold basis—a basis in psychology and in ethics. This assertion suggests that the only statements of fact required by that theory are those of psychology. However, he does in fact make reference to statements of the other kinds mentioned. Cf., e.g., *The Aesthetic Revelation of the World,* tr. Henry M. and Emmie Felkin, Heath's Pedagogical Library, D. C. Heath & Co., Boston, 1893, p. 75.

[2] Herbart, Johann Friedrich, *A Text-book in Psychology,* tr. Margaret K. Smith, D. Appleton and Company, New York, 1894, p. 2. The German word is *Vorstellung;* and it is translated sometimes by "concept," sometimes by "representation" as well as by "idea."

[3] *Ibid.,* p. 69.

revealed by sense and introspection. The activities of the mind—perceiving, remembering, imagining, thinking, desiring, and the like—consist in serial orders of ideas provided by experience. The perception of a tree is the sensing of trunk, branches, twigs, and leaves in a certain serial arrangement. The memory of yesterday's walk is a serial ordering of the ideas—the episodes—that constitute it. Imagining the adventures of Jack the Giant Killer amounts to running through the series of ideas that make up the story. Thinking a question through is observing a serial order in our ideas from premisses to conclusion. Desiring is a serial order of the idea that awakens desire, the desire itself, the objective toward which it presses, the factors that impede it, etc. The view that mental activities consist in such series of ideas, Herbart regards as clearly supported by introspection. His psychology is largely an explanation of the activities of the mind thus conceived.

REJECTION OF FACULTIES. Herbart rejects the view that mental activities are to be understood as the exercise of mental faculties. Psychology, in his time, explained the uniformity of mental activities as determined by faculties that always exercise themselves in the same way—remembering, etc. Herbart points out that such uniformities have always been observed in the minds of civilized men, and argues that they might result from social and cultural inheritance (from civilization) quite as well as from the exercise of faculties.[4] The faculties are not necessary because mental activities can be explained in other ways. Moreover, there is good reason to think they do not exist. Remembering, imagining, etc., occur very differently in the same mind where different materials are involved. The same person may remember easily the vocabulary of a science, but may be quite unable to remember village gossip.[5] Psychology, Herbart concludes, has no need of mental faculties.[6]

Psychologists have been captivated by the spurious notion of these faculties because they have asked the wrong question about the arrangement of ideas that constitute mental activity.[7] They have asked why, once experience has given us ideas, those ideas return to consciousness from time to time. This question takes quite naturally as its answer the proposition that the agency of a faculty causes them to return. A different question elicits a better answer. If we ask why ideas ever vanish from con-

[4] *Ibid.*, pp. 37–39, p. 103.
[5] *Ibid.*, p. 73.
[6] But Herbart does not reject the notion so firmly as one might suppose; and although he inveighs against the faculties, he devotes a long section of *A Text Book in Psychology* to a description of psychological phenomena "according to the hypothesis of mental faculties," and uses the word "faculty" frequently in other parts of his writing.
[7] *Ibid.*, pp. 70–71.

sciousness, the need for a faculty to summon them back does not arise. The disappearance of ideas cannot be the cessation of their existence; for, in memory, in imagination, in thought, they recur. Nor can their vanishing consist in change; it is nonsense to hold that one idea changes into another. The idea of red is unalterably red. What could one be saying who asserted that his idea of red was transformed into one of green, or into the number twelve? Herbart concludes that the withdrawal of ideas from consciousness can consist neither in their ceasing to exist nor in their change or transformation. He endeavors to explain their arrangement in series—the mental activity that introspection reveals—not by reference to the exercise of faculties, but by reference to properties inherent in the ideas themselves.

PROPERTIES OF IDEAS. There are three properties that every idea possesses, and that explain their vanishing from consciousness. Every idea has a quality entirely its own. Each shade of color, each shape, each tone, each desire is just the color or shape, the sound or urgency that it is. None could have a different quality from the one it possesses on pain of being different from what it is—a feat nothing can perform. And besides its quality, each idea must possess some degree of clarity or vividness. The lower degrees, we call "obscure" or "faint" or by some similar adjective. A shape may be obscure or clear; a color, weak or vivid; a sound, soft or loud; a desire, slight or overwhelming. But these traits fall on a single scale—a scale that runs from extreme clarity at the top to extreme obscurity at the bottom; and any idea is capable of occupying different places or degrees on this scale despite the unalterability of its quality, as the same shade of color may be more or less vivid, the same tone more or less loud. To the quality and its degree of clarity that every idea possesses, Herbart adds the property of striving, or, to use his word, force. Every idea strives to preserve itself against occupying a low degree of clarity, and this endeavor consists in its striving to exhibit its unique quality to the highest degree possible—in its endeavor to occupy the topmost place on the scale of clarity.

CONSCIOUSNESS. Herbart's answer to his question as to why ideas vanish from consciousness flows from his identification of the quality of an idea with the content of consciousness, and certain degrees of the clarity that ideas possess with consciousness itself. The content of consciousness is what we are directly aware of, and it is composed of shades of color, shapes, pitches, longings, etc. The degree of clarity of these ideas manifests the success of their striving, and a high degree of clarity constitutes consciousness of the idea to which it belongs. The striking vividness of a color, the sharp clarity of a shape, the loudness of a sound—all this is nothing but the consciousness with which such contents of the mental life are endowed. Their vanishing from consciousness consists in their becoming obscure or acquiring a low degree of clarity. The scale of clarity must be thought of as cut by a horizontal line; and in terms of this diagrammatic metaphor, the vanishing of ideas is their resting on, or passing below that division—their failure to preserve such a degree of clarity as would maintain their status above it. The mind, thus, has two parts, each of which is stored with ideas: a conscious part in which the striving of each of its occupants succeeds in showing its quality to a high degree, and an unconscious part in which the striving of its ideas exhibits their qualities in a relatively low degree. The two parts are separated by the "threshold of consciousness"[8]—a piece of apparatus Herbart introduced and made current in psychology. All ideas begin their existence in consciousness—in the high clarity of sensory perception, and their vanishing from it consists in their sinking below the threshold.

But no idea is contented to remain on or below the threshold. Each constantly strives toward a high degree of clarity or consciousness. Once it ascends to the threshold, it awaits the opportunity to rise above it that is afforded when conscious ideas assume the relations that permit such movement. We must now examine these relations.

By virtue of their qualities, ideas bear three[9] relations to one another; and where one of them holds, some of the ideas it relates become unconscious. This relation is extreme opposition. Ideas that come to us through a single avenue of experience may be extremely opposed to each other. Red, yellow, and green, which come through vision; hope, fear, and joy, which come through introspection—these are related in this way. Where there is extreme opposition, ideas cannot all possess consciousness at once; and where their strivings to be clear are unequal,[10] their extreme opposition forces those of weaker impulse below the threshold. Vivid ideas of red and yellow will make unconscious a weak idea of green, and vivid hope and joy will do the same for a feeble fear. The unconscious part of the mind, thus, is peopled with ideas whose striving for consciousness is weaker than that of those in it.

Extreme opposition in quality between ideas crowds some of those it relates into unconsciousness; but two other qualitative relations between ideas do not give rise to this consequence. One is the relation of irrelevance. Ideas that come to us through different avenues of experience are related in this way. There is no difficulty in fixing in consciousness an

---

8 *Ibid.*, pp. 12–13.
9 Herbart does not clearly distinguish these relations from one another. He speaks only of opposition and the lack of opposition between ideas. Cf. e.g., *ibid.*, pp. 9–10.
10 *Ibid.*, pp. 11–12. But two ideas whose strivings are equal both vanish into unconsciousness, while two whose strivings are unequal both remain with a lessened clarity in the combination they form.

idea of red, received through vision, and an idea of middle C, received through audition. The consciousness or clarity of one in no way diminishes that of the other. We are frequently clearly aware of a color and a tone simultaneously.

Like irrelevance, moderate opposition enables ideas to exist together in consciousness. The ideas of middle C and of E can perfectly well exist side by side in our awareness. And the ideas that are found in consciousness are those that are irrelevant and those that are opposed only moderately; their strivings toward clarity do not, in view of these qualitative relations, preclude the possibility that others should be conscious as well.

When ideas that encounter one another in consciousness are related by extreme opposition, some are driven down into unconsciousness; but some of those on the threshold are able to make their way up into the light. The ideas that arise must be related to the combatants that win in the encounter by qualitative irrelevance or by moderate qualitative opposition. Try to attend at once to the ideas of cranberry sauce, blackberry jelly, and of sauerkraut juice. The encounter of these ideas will lead to the suppression of the third since the striving of its saltiness is more feeble than the combined strivings of the sweet sauce and the sweet jelly. Its sinking into unconsciousness leaves a vacant place in the upper domain, but that place does not remain unfilled. If there is on the threshold the idea of candles at dinner, the qualitative irrelevance it bears to the sweetness of the sauce and the jelly will enable it to take the place left vacant. Moreover, the relation of moderate qualitative opposition would permit another idea to rise into clarity if it should be on the threshold; and the idea of roast turkey might join those of the sauce, the jelly, and the candles. Ideas vanish from consciousness because they fail in the combat of qualitative opposition that is extreme; they ascend into consciousness because there are places thus left open. Those that return are qualitatively irrelevant, or only moderately opposed in quality to the ideas that crowd others out.

APPERCEPTION. Herbart explains the connection of ideas in series by reference to the striving toward clarity, and the qualitative relations they bear to one another. All ideas originate in external sensation; and in their original appearance they are uncompounded or simple. The infant's consciousness is occupied by simple colors, small shapes, uncompounded tones, and the like. If the supply of sensory material quickly ceased, leaving the number of ideas very small, none would become unconscious, and mental activity would be confined to the consciousness of a few elements, statically arranged.[11] But it does

11 *Ibid.*, pp. 163–64.

not cease. A recurrent supply of new simple sensations leads to their combination in consciousness. Where the elements are qualitatively irrelevant to one another, they may combine into a "complication"; and where they are moderately opposed, they may "fuse" or "blend."[12] Thus, a color, a shape, and a fragrance may combine into a complication we call a "blossoming tree"; and three tones may "fuse" into a chord.

The encounter of several elementary ideas that are extremely opposed in quality leads to the suppression of the weaker; and the encounter of compound ideas, similarly related, bears the same consequence. But as others crowd down upon the occupants of unconsciousness, the ideas on the threshold make their way up to join the ideas to which they are qualitatively irrelevant or only moderately opposed.[13] Thus, the encounter of the idea of a plum tree, of its blossoms, and of a frosty day will lead to a combination of the first two whose combined striving will crowd the last into unconsciousness; and will permit other ideas, irrelevant or only moderately opposed to the combination of the first two, to join them in clear awareness. We forget the possibility that winter may not be quite past; and the consciousness of the blossoming tree initiates a series of memories of past springs, or the imagination of the one to come, or the thought that the blossoming tree will attract bees, will come to the time of harvest, etc. Similar reproduction of ideas in series may be initiated by memories, by images, and by mere thoughts. The process in which extreme opposition in quality forces some ideas into unconsciousness, thus allowing others on the threshold to join those that are conscious, Herbart calls apperception; and a series of ideas—itself made up of terms that may be either simple or compounded—produced by apperception, he calls an "apperceptive mass" or "circle of thought."[14]

Apperception is the process of forming elementary ideas into series or compounds, and of ordering these compounds, themselves, into series. It is explained in terms of the striving of every idea toward perfect clarity, and the qualitative relations of ideas that enable their combination. Its products, apperceptive masses, are series of ideas—some like the plum tree ordered in space, and others like trains of memory, imagination, thought, etc., organized in time. Mental activity is a continuous movement of ideas, up and down, across the threshold of consciousness accompanied by their continuous grouping and regrouping in consciousness according to the relations of the qualities they possess.

But this grouping and regrouping in consciousness, although it

12 *Ibid.*, pp. 16–17.
13 *Ibid.*, pp. 30–31.
14 These phrases quickly became a part of the language of psychology, and the notion they embody was seized upon by many psychologists to explain mental activity, and by educators to guide instruction.

involves recruitment from below, always is initiated by some conscious idea—simple or complex. This idea, at first, occupies consciousness exclusively or very nearly so. We are thoroughly engaged by it; and this intense noticing Herbart calls "absorption" ("Vertiefung"). A new sensation or complex of them may take up all or most of our awareness for a time. But this time is relatively short. If there are any conscious ideas simultaneous with, and irrelevant or only moderately opposed to it, they will shortly combine with it; and others, waiting on the threshold, will add to the combination in the way described above. This process of addition to ideas that formerly absorbed us, Herbart calls "reflection" ("Besinnung"). Thus the absorbing sight of the shape of a tree may soon combine with ideas of fragrance, of graveled walks, etc., into the conscious perception of a tree in the garden; and this idea, in turn, may be joined by others from unconsciousness—ideas of the tree in the garden in the winter just past, and in the summer yet to come. Ideas of the shape of a tree—present, past, and future—"fuse" with one another as do those of its fragrance in various times; and ideas of all the different kinds involved make the "complication" which is the idea of the tree and the garden throughout its whole career. The entire idea of the tree and the garden forms a series of elements whose members adhere closely to one another, and behaves like one unitary idea in relation to others. The visual experience of the three is absorption; the grouping of other ideas around it into the complication that is the tree in the garden with a career reaching into the past and future is reflection. When some new idea with great clarity is introduced—the idea of dinner, for example—that of the tree and the garden vanishes into unconsciousness, allowing the thought of food its brief moment of absorption and its subsequent reflection—thoughts of repairing to the dining room, etc. Herbart regards all mental activity as falling into a recurrent pattern of absorption and reflection—a continuous rhythmic pulsation of the mental life like that of respiration.[15]

ATTENTION AND INTEREST. This pattern of absorption and reflection applies to successive acts of attention. Ideas in which we are absorbed are those to which we attend; and an act of attention may be conceived as an act of forming new ideas.[16] Sometimes this act is spontaneous; we cannot help but attend to a bright flash, a loud sound, or sharp pain. We cannot learn to attend to ideas

[15] Herbart, Johann Friedrich, *A Textbook in Psychology,* tr. Margaret K. Smith, D. Appleton and Company, New York, 1894, N. pp. 165–66.
[16] *Ibid.,* pp. 167–68, also *Outlines of Educational Doctrine,* tr. Alexis F. Lange, The Macmillan Company, New York, 1901, pp. 62–64. Herbart defines "attention" as involving a "readiness" to form new ideas; but since the notion, readiness, suggests that of a mental faculty—a notion he rejects—I have refrained from using it in this exposition.

perceived through external sense and introspection, and attention of this kind is primitive. But primitive attention to ideas of perception and introspection quickly leads to reflection—to the summoning of those ideas we have learned to connect with those that come spontaneously; and Herbart calls our attention to them "apperceiving attention." Our primitive attention to a bright flash and a loud sound quickly gives place to the apperceived ideas of July the Fourth, the nation's founders, etc. Both primitive and apperceiving attention may be either involuntary or voluntary. We may attend to what we perceive and to the ideas it summons without effort and with no control, or we may control our perception and introspection and eliminate unwanted ideas from those summoned from unconsciousness. These distinctions between different kinds of attention are important to Herbart's discussion of the methods of instruction.

Attention and expectation account for interest.[17] A new idea may find itself quickly overwhelmed; extreme opposition to ideas simultaneously in consciousness, or to others it allows to rise from the threshold, may quickly force it into unconsciousness. A sharp pain combined with a vivid fear may make us forget a loud noise, and a train of past adventures may make us disregard the moonlit summer night that summoned them to mind. In these cases, the object of one act of primitive attention is made unconscious by another, or by the ideas it, itself, summons from unconsciousness in apperceiving attention. We have no interest in the noise or the moonlit night. But in other cases, both of primitive and of apperceiving attention, the idea we attend to summons others that combine with it to form a series, all of whose terms remain in consciousness. Attending to a loud sound may call up ideas of what is to follow, as attending to the report of a gun may lead to the idea of the race it initiates or as attending to the idea of the plum tree may lead to an expectation of the summer crop. And a mere thought, an object of apperceiving attention, also may arouse an expectation with which it combines; the thought of theaters may summon an expectation of social reform that will make possible or enhance theatrical performance. An interest is a series of ideas, each of which is attended to, in which the first term constitutes the object of interest, and in which the other terms constitute an expectation of, or plan to realize, that state of affairs to which the object of interest refers. Attending to the report leads us to expect the race it represents; attending to the idea of next summer's tree leads us to expect to secure its fruits; and attending to the thought of theaters leads us to expect a society in which plays can be enjoyed. And these combinations of ideas are interests in the report, the tree, and the theater.

The object of an interest, consequently, is not a future event.

[17] *Ibid.,* p. 168.

Rather, it is a present object of present attention. Nonetheless, every interest contains a reference to some future event; for the expectation that accompanies its object is a plan of action whose consequences appear as what will satisfy the plan if we put it into effect—as what will make real the reference of the idea that is the interest's object. An interest in the theater is the idea of a set of institutions including theaters, together with the expectation or plan of making such institutions real. And an interest, although it includes an expectation of the future, excludes the action to which that expectation points, holding in attention no more than its object and the mere plan for realizing what that object stands for.

DESIRE AND WILL. An interest, of course, may lead to action that will satisfy it; but when it does so, it is not an interest merely. But, it is also not a desire. An idea of red may summon a plan for painting things that color—may be the object of an interest in red; and we may realize this interest by actually engaging in the activity of painting. But so far, we do not desire to make things red, for we cannot desire to do what we are in fact doing. Still, a desire to make things red is not simply the interest in doing so. An interest focuses on a present object—the idea of red; but a desire focuses on a future object—on doing something in some future time. In so far as an idea is kept clear in attention, it may summon a plan for realizing what it stands for; and in so far as both it and its plan are held before the mind and not allowed to run into action, they constitute an interest. But the clarity of an interest may be diminished by extreme opposition to other ideas it encouners. The expectation, or plan, of using red may be diminished by the idea of difficulty in securing the shade represented. In so far as such expectations are held in consciousness by their union with some object of attention, they are pleasant, as is the prospect of applying the color we have selected. But in so far as they are also impeded—pressed down toward the threshold—by ideas that are extremely opposed in quality, they are painful, as is the doubtful expectation of using a red that is hard to find. Expectations—plans for making real what they represent—are desires provided that their combination with some object of attention assures them a place in consciousness, although at the same time, their opposition to other ideas there makes them more obscure than they would be if those ideas were absent. A desire is an expectation that is both pleasant and painful, both consciously directed toward realization and pressed down toward unconsciousness or impeded by competitors. It is a conscious interest in doing something in the future that remains none the less unsatisfied.

An act of will or volition is directed upon desires. On St. Helena, Napoleon still desired, no doubt, to rule the French; but he also desired to live peacefully in retirement. He choose the latter desire as the basis of his action rather than the former. He did not attempt a swim to the nearest loyal troops. He consigned his desire to rule, so far as he could, to unconsciousness. During his life as emperor, we may suppose that his mind was occupied by the same desires—the desire to live peacefully in retirement and the desire to rule the French. But in those more glorious days, it was the desire for a retired life that he relegated to obscurity. He chose to realize the desire to rule. The selection for realization of one desire from among others is an act of will;[18] and it is such an act that explains Napoleon's resignation on St. Helena as well as his enjoyment of imperial power in Paris.

DELIBERATION. Deliberation consists in attending to several interests, and in willing to realize the desire involved in one.[19] When one considers whether to take a walk or to continue to study, the idea of the walk allows into consciousness the attendant expectation or desire for changed surroundings, and the idea of continuing to study allows into consciousness the expectation or desire for increased confidence in examinations. But attention need not stop at this point. We attend to other consequences of fulfilling each desire in an "inner experiment." The consequences of the walk are seen to include a decreased confidence about examinations, and those of continuing to study, to include a prolonged dreariness of occupation. The choice of one alternative as opposed to the other requires the banishing of the latter to unconsciousness—the greater strength of one of the interests or apperceptive masses as opposed to the other. And this addition occurs when a principle is invoked that adds sufficient strength to one interest to insure its winning.

The principle invoked is a rule that we ought to choose to realize desires of a certain kind. Such rules depend upon memory of the way in which similar choices have been made in the past. At first, one interest wins over another by virtue of the feebleness of the latter, merely. In such cases, there is no deliberation; there is simply the *de facto* conquest of one interest by another. But as similar cases recur, we remember how the conflict of desires in opposing interests has been, in fact, resolved. And the apperceptive mass formed by the memories of these resolutions appears as a principle in dealing with cases of choice in the future as we have, spontaneously, in the past. The supposition that a desire can be fulfilled is this principle; and when it joins forces with one of the desires in a con-

---

18 But Herbart says: ". . . willing . . . is a desire combined with the supposition that it can be fulfilled" (*Ibid.*, p. 82). However, a desire that does not suffer from competitors—from suppositions that it might *not* be fulfilled cannot be a desire; and the supposition that a desire will be fulfilled can be nothing but the rejection of desires alternative to it. So that an act of will must be distinguished from the desire it favors as an act of choosing it for realization and of excluding its alternatives.
19 *Ibid.*, pp. 86–89.

flict, we choose to realize that desire rather than the others. Deliberation consists in attending to conflicting desires where one is finally chosen for realization by an act of will that applies the rule or principle that desires like it as opposed to those like its competitors should be allowed fulfillment.

MORAL DELIBERATION. Deliberation frequently consists in deciding between different means to the same end. If one is concerned merely to maintain health, deliberation about his dinner is of this sort. A sensible choice consists in fixing upon the desire for those dishes on the menu which preserve health, and in suppressing the desire for others. But sometimes our conflict does not consist in desiring to follow different paths to a single goal; on some occasions, the conflict consists in our harboring desires for different ends that cannot all be realized. The thought of the income tax brings with it a desire to reduce costly government services to a minimum, but the thought of widespread misery summons a desire for a socialized society. Here, we do not desire different means to a single end. Rather, we desire to achieve ends that are themselves incompatible. A society cannot both disregard and foster the welfare of its citizens. In such a case, we must choose between desires for different ends, and act to realize one as opposed to the other. Where choice is of this kind, the general principle that combines with the desire that wins is a moral principle—a rule for deciding what goal we ought to realize; and where we choose between desires to realize incompatible ends with the help of a moral principle, our deliberation must also be described as moral.

But while decision between desires for competing ends with the help of a general principle is moral, it is not, as such, right. We might, in our moral deliberation, choose to realize an end that ought not to be realized. There are certain traits that every proper objective exhibits. These are the criteria whose presence shows that our choosing the end is right, and whose absence from it shows that our choice of it is wrong. They are stated in principles that Herbart calls "moral ideas," and will be considered shortly. "Moral deliberation," thus, is a phrase that covers deliberation whose outcome is either right or wrong; and it must be distinguished from deliberation about different means to a single end which is neither.

PERSONALITY. Herbart regards every person as possessed of a soul; but the soul, he holds, is altogether inaccessible to observation. Hence, the belief in it cannot be expressed in a statement of fact. That there are souls connected with persons is part of his metaphysical doctrine shortly to be explained.

The person as observed in introspection is a collection of interests whose objects are constantly moving up and down, across the threshold of consciousness, constantly allowing the interests that attend them to travel similarly up and down, and continually influencing one another in various ways in consciousness itself. The young child's interests are few in number; but as new experience brings him more ideas, the apperceptive masses they form group themselves into additional interests. Desires for food and sleep come quickly to be supplemented with interests in colors and sounds, in toys, in other people, etc. But a mere collection of interests does not constitute a person. It does so only in so far as the interests that compose it are to some degree deliberately organized. If a principle organizes them—favoring the realization of some over others in certain circumstances, or of the latter over the former in others—they constitute a person; and the notion of personality applies not to a collection of interests as such, but to one in which fulfillment and restraint are determined by a rule[20]—to one in which interests are ordered by the desire that their satisfaction or frustration should fall into a certain pattern. "Character" is a word Herbart uses to mean this organization of interests.

The ego or the self is the person viewed as organized around present consciousness. At any moment of waking life, some idea occupies our awareness. But from it, interests extend toward the future; and memories, toward the past. The sight of the plum tree arouses the desire to tend it, and to enjoy its fruit in the future. It also calls to mind memories of last year's cultivation, of the crops it has yielded in the past, of climbing it in early childhood, etc. The organization of interests by principles and by expectations and memories that run from a continually advancing present into an indeterminate future and a continually growing past is the self of every person.

The self is individual or unique. The cluster of interests and memories that reach forward and backward from any present idea—the ego—is not exactly repeated for any other. Peter and Paul may each have desires and memories that center in the plum tree they now both see. But Peter is interested in sharing the crop with his neighbor, whereas Paul wishes to preserve it for himself; and Peter's memories include climbing in, while those of Paul include falling out of the plum tree as a child. The individuality of the cluster of interests and memories that make up each person marks out a system of possible behavior, unique to each. The diversity of these systems from one person to another means that no one will respond in quite the same way to his environment as does another; and a self or person, however much he may be like another, is always unlike all in some respect.[21]

[20] Herbart, Johann Friedrich, *Outlines of Educational Doctrine,* tr. Alexis F. Lange, The Macmillan Company, New York, 1901, pp. 146–50.
[21] *A Text-book in Psychology,* pp. 169–71.

Although each person is unlike all others, all possess interests of two major kinds: interests that do not depend upon sympathy with others, and those that presuppose it.[22] An idea of any individual thing awakens an interest in knowing more about that thing, in understanding what relations it bears to others, and in enjoying it aesthetically as it appears in its relations with them. These three interests require, only, that we be aware, by virtue of sense, reason, and our ability for enjoyment, of the things toward which they are directed. They are cognitive interests. Each person, also, is interested in the sentiments and feelings of other persons, in those of society at large, and in those of the complex formed by God and the human race. He feels impelled to improve the lot of other individuals, to enhance the life of society, and to achieve unity with God and humanity. These interests require not mere awareness of the ideas they involve, but also the sympathy with the feelings of other persons, both finite and divine, that enables us to have ideas of those feelings. They are sympathetic interests. The occurrence in each man of cognitive and sympathetic interests thus subdivided is of importance in deciding the constituents of the curriculum.

Two factors make up the source of personality. The place in which a person lives gives him ideas through the external senses; and his body, regarded as a part of his physical environment, provides others.[23] The forest gives to those who dwell in it the idea of trees; and his body gives to each person ideas around which instinctual interests like those of sleep, sex, etc., are organized. Besides the physical environment, the social environment also gives material to personality.[24] The nation, the stage of its development, the class, the family—all these and many other social influences determine the qualitative relations of ideas; and by making now some and now others irrelevant, or in some degree opposed to one another, they determine the kinds of interests that can be harbored by the persons they affect. National temperaments, ways of life peculiar to social classes, family ethos, etc.—all these amount to series of ideas formed, in part, by various social influences.

The Individual and the Race

Herbart appears to have held the view that the moral development of the individual and that of the race are parallel, and that the pattern exhibited by the latter must be exhibited, as well, by the moral growth of each individual person. Moral development is development of the capac-

[22] Herbart, Johann Friedrich, *The Science of Education: Its General Principles Deduced from Its Aims,* tr. Henry M. and Emmie Felkin, D. C. Heath & Co., Boston, 1893, Book II, Chapter 3.
[23] *A Text-book in Psychology,* pp. 104–05, p. 34.
[24] *Ibid.,* pp. 104–06.

ity to act rightly—the capacity to govern one's actions by principles of right willing. Its beginning is spontaneous choice out of which grow general principles of voluntary action. The life of early humanity was determined by these spontaneous choices; they dominated ancient Greece. And the human race, in those early times, enjoyed a moral boyhood out of which grew more advanced stages of the capacity for moral self-control. The present human condition—the capacity of the race to act voluntarily upon general principles or intentions—is the mature stage of its history, and is implicit in those of boyhood and youth. This pattern of development from spontaneous action to voluntary self-control also gives form to the life of each individual person; and each of us, from birth to maturity, runs through a series of stages, beginning with spontaneity and ending with the high capacity for moral self-control toward which earlier stages point. Providence imposes this parallelism on the career of each individual and that of the race.

This destiny, sprung solely out of the individuality of environment, which inevitably becomes special for each separate example of the race, in contradistinction to his (i.e. the separate example's) origin from the supreme plan of nature which was designed in the first instance for the race by an all-ordering Providence—this destiny is the necessity which impels men; . . .[25]
The obscurity of this passage—an obscurity typical of Herbart's writing— suggests the view just outlined; but it also makes clear that we cannot be altogether certain that he held it as opposed to any other that is somewhat similar to it.

Society and the State

The present moral condition of the race is manifested in the voluntary actions of societies and of the state. Societies are groups of persons whose members share a single purpose; and where there are several that contribute to a larger single purpose, that constitute a system of economic production and distribution, and that live under a single political authority, there is not a collection of societies merely, but a sovereign political state. The state has no life of its own, no purposes other than those of its members; but it is, nonetheless, the source of all the rights and duties they possess.[26] It is a good state to the degree that it distributes these rights and duties according to the right moral principles and in so far as it controls the relation of the smaller societies that make it up. The relations of societies within the state—of classes to one another, for example—and of individuals within the groups that make them up is analogous to the rela-

[25] Herbart, Johann Friedrich, *The Aesthetic Revelation of the World,* tr. Henry M. and Emmie Felkin, *Heath's Pedagogical Library,* D. C. Heath and Co., Boston, 1893, p. 75.
[26] Herbart, Johann Friedrich, *Algemeine Praktische Philosophie,* Buch II; Kapitel v., iv; also, *Encylopädie der Philosophie,* Kapitel ii, v.

tions between different apperceptive masses and different individual ideas within the person. Just as a government may control the degree of dominance that any social group possesses by juxtaposing it now to one, now to another group, so also, we can control the domination over our minds by this or that apperceptive mass by controlling those it encounters.[27]

RECOMMENDATIONS

Herbart's statements of fact provide part of the basis for his theory of the way in which children should be treated. The rest of that basis is supplied by certain moral principles. The moral principles outline the goal he recommends for all personal and social conduct; while the statements of fact yield a basis for recommending the paths that lead to its embodiment. In this section, Herbart's recommendations will not simply be stated; they will also be explained. In presenting an explanation of them, we are trespassing on the domain of his philosophy of education; but we must state part of his philosophy of education here since his educational recommendations would remain quite unintelligible without it.

Goal Recommendations

"The one and the whole work of education," Herbart writes, "may be summed up in the concept—Morality."[28] Morality (he also calls it "virtue") consists in the kind of life led by persons who are good, and Herbart's goal recommendation amounts to the view that the young should be treated in such a way as to make them good persons. A person, it will be recalled, is an organization of interests; and interests are ideas accompanied by plans for realizing the objects they represent. The plans involved in interests are desires, since the ideas that compose them are clearly insistent upon their realization, but also pressed down toward the obscurity of unconsciousness by other ideas to which they are extremely opposed. Where desires conflict because the ends toward which they are directed are incompatible—where they are in extreme opposition, a general moral principle, concerning the kind of ends that ought to be realized, must be invoked in order to resolve their conflict; and such a principle, constructed by apperception out of memories of earlier resolutions, is a principle of will.

The application of a principle of will is an act of will; and an act of will consists in the selection, in obedience to a principle, of some desires for realization and the relegation of those with which they are in conflict to unconsciousness. In this way, acts of will organize desires; they

[27] Herbart, Johann Friedrich, *A Text-book in Psychology*, pp. 190–91, 194–96.
[28] *The Aesthetic Revelation of the World*, p. 57; see also, *The Science of Education*, p. 108, and *Outlines of Educational Doctrine*, pp. 44, 143.

therefore organize, as well, the interests to which those desires belong. A person is made up of interests that are organized by acts of will, and a good person is one whose interests are organized by acts that apply the right principles. Herbart's goal recommendation may be understood as the recommendation to treat the young in such a way as to make them into persons whose component interests are organized by particular acts that apply the right principles to the conflict of desires—into persons who, since they are good, lead that kind of life in which virtue consists. In order to understand this recommendation, we must understand what it is that makes a principle of will a right one.

THE MORAL IDEAS. Herbart holds that there are five principles that are right, and that the rightness of each lies in its stating that a certain relation ought to hold between the will and other aspects of the person who harbors it, or between the will of one person and those of others.[29] An act of will in which any of these principles is applied in the selection of desires for realization is also right; and engaging in it confers goodness, in some degree, upon the actor. He calls these principles "moral ideas."

INNER FREEDOM. The first of these principles is inner freedom (*innern Freiheit*).[30] Herbart holds that all events are governed by laws, and that, consequently, every act of will has a cause —a cause that is an idea preceding it in the mind of the person who performs the act.[31] But the cause of any particular act of will is a link in a chain of causes that extends backward in time far beyond the person who engages in it. There are causes for our acts of will that are external to us, and no right principle of will can require that the acts in which it is applied be externally free. Such a principle would be futile because inapplicable.

Still, we cannot doubt that when we engage in acts of will, we possess freedom of some kind. The kind is suggested by the phrase "inner freedom." Imagine a person who, from habit, from political inheritance, or from rhetorical persuasion votes for candidates who support social legislation rather than for those who reject it. His acts of will apply the principle that the general welfare ought to be advanced, but he does not know that this is the principle he applies. By use of it, he resolves the conflict between his desire for social legislation and, say, that for lowered

29 Herbart, Johann Friedrich, *Algemeine Praktische Philosophie*, in *Sammtliche Werke*, Vol. II, ed. Karl Kehrbach, Verlag Von Veit & Comp., Leipzig, 1885, Buch I. Kapitel i–v. See also excerpts from the same in this chapter, tr. David A. McCullough.
30 *Ibid.*, Buch I, Kapitel i.
31 Herbart Johann Friedrich, *The Aesthetic Revelation of the World*, pp. 60–61.

taxes. But he does not know why he engages in this resolution of his conflict; he has no insight into the principle that governs his choice. He is inwardly compelled to employ a principle he is also externally caused to accept.

Imagine, now, a second person—one who believes that he adopts certain principles for application in his acts of will. He believes, for example, that he adopts the principle of the general welfare. But a belief may be mistaken. He may make choices that are applications of a principle quite different from the one he believes he adopts. He may, in fact, always choose candidates who favor lowered taxes, finding some rationale for selecting the desire to vote for them instead of for those who favor social legislation. In such a person, there is disagreement between the belief that he adopts a certain principle and the principle that, in fact, governs his acts of will. Such a person, also, is not inwardly free.

But imagine a third person who knows clearly that he adopts certain principles in making his choices. He has insight, as Herbart says, into his will. If he knows that his principle is the general welfare, then since knowledge cannot be mistaken, his acts of will never fail to select for realization desires that are directed toward that objective. There is always agreement between his insight and his will. Inner freedom is this agreement; and insight guarantees it even though our acceptance of the principles insight reveals is externally caused by historical circumstances. One who possesses insight always chooses to act upon a desire that obeys the principle he knows he follows. External circumstances may prevent his acting on this desire; but so long as the agreement between his insight and his will—his insight and the acts of applying the principle—is not impaired, he does not lose his inner freedom.

Any principle of will that is right is one known by the person who adopts it to govern his acts of will. This is the principle of inner freedom. But it is clear that our knowledge of the principles we adopt is not enough to guarantee that they are right; any principle whatever might be adopted with utter clarity and self-consciousness. Iago knew with utmost clarity that he adopted the principle of advancing his own preferment no matter what the means. However, a consideration of the remaining moral ideas enables us to see that many principles are wrong.

PERFECTION. The second principle of those that are right is the principle of perfection (*Vollkommenheit*), or many-sidedness.[32] The term "perfection," in this context, does not refer to good-

---

[32] *Outlines of Educational Doctrine*, Part II, Section II, Chapter ii. In this book, Herbart treats perfection and many-sidedness as the same trait, and clarifies the notion by speaking of the multiplicity of interests rather than of the multiplicity of wills—a phrase he makes central to his discussion of perfection in *Algemeine Praktische Philosophie*, Buch I, Kapitel ii. The latter work was published much earlier; and in the *Outlines*, he seems not to recognize the relation the later book bears to the earlier.

ness as the synonymous use of the term "many-sidedness" attests. It refers, rather, to the magnitude of our interests that are not yet satisfied, or, more briefly, to that of our desires.

Our desires have magnitude in three respects. First, any one of them has strength. Its strength is the clarity of the ideas in it; but Herbart includes, as well, the frequency with which it recurs. A very clear desire that occurred only once could not be strong, nor could one that recurred often if it were always close to unconsciousness. Secondly, our desires are numerous in kind. We desire to eat, to sleep, to read, to garden, to listen to music. It is clear that the desires we harbor are as numerous as the kinds of objectives that would fulfill them. Thirdly, our desires are harmonious or cooperative. The desire to study cooperates with the desire to be a lawyer, and the desire for tennis with the desire for health. But desires are not equally strong, equal in number from one time or person to another, and equally cooperative. Each is more or less strong on a scale, running from feebleness and infrequency to indefinite vividness and frequency. The number of desires we harbor, at one time, differs from that of another time; and the number of desires in any person exceeds, equals, or falls short of that in any other. The cooperativeness that one desire exhibits for another differs from time to time, and with respect to the other desires involved. The desire to study cooperates with the desire to be a lawyer less when it is weak than when it is strong; and with respect to the desire to be a lawyer, the desire to play tennis may be wholly uncooperative although it supports firmly the desire for health. The magnitude of our desires, taken all together, is a function of the magnitude of the strength of each, of the cooperativeness of each, and of their multiplicity; and its degree is a function of the degrees of these component magnitudes.

Herbart holds that the magnitude of the desires in any person—the magnitude of his active, unsatisfied interests—is their perfection, and that one principle of right willing is the rule that one ought always to choose for realization those particular desires that will make for the greatest magnitude or perfection over all. The reason for this view appears from a consideration of the consequences of rejecting it. If one adopted the principle opposed to that of perfection—the principle of keeping it at the lowest possible degree—he would will to bring about all of three conditions. He would choose to make his desires as weak as possible, as few as possible, and as chaotic as possible. But it is clear that one's desires ought not to be feeble, few, and chaotic.[33] And if one simply had no principle relevant to this topic, these three unfortunate conditions might occur quite as well as not. It follows that we ought to adopt the principle that every act of will should choose to realize the desire that advances perfection as opposed to one that does not.

---

[33] *Algemeine Praktische Philosophie,* Buch I, Kapitel ii; also, *Outlines of Educational Doctrine,* Part II, Section II, Chapter ii.

While the perfection of our desires ought to occupy the highest possible degree, it does not follow that any particular one of its component magnitudes need do so. The very great strength of a desire could diminish its cooperativeness, and could preclude the existence of any others; the very great multiplicity of desires could lessen the strength of each, and the organization of all; and the very great cooperativeness of each desire could decrease both multiplicity and strength. The principle of perfection does not require that we always select the strongest, the most novel, and the most cooperative desire. Rather it requires that no matter what the desire selected, it should allow that others selected be as strong, as numerous, and as cooperative as possible. It counsels us constantly to watch for needed readjustments of the different components of perfection in order that the degree of each should be as high as it can be in relation to that of the others. Where this condition holds, the perfection of the whole of our desires is at its height.

The kinds of things one can desire are determined by the ideas one has; and these are generated, in part, by one's physical and social environment. The highest possible degree of perfection, consequently, varies from one time and place and culture to another. It is affected, also, by one's own individuality; and Herbart suggests that knowledge and imagination give rise to an effort always to heighten the degree of perfection one presently enjoys. The second moral idea is the principle that every act of will ought to be the selecting of a desire that increases the perfection of the person who engages in it.

BENEVOLENCE. The third principle or moral idea is that of benevolence (*wohlwollens*).[34] Our acts of will are not always governed by this principle. Sometimes, we act from malevolence instead. One who believes that another is interested in swimming, but chooses to prevent his doing so simply for the sake of frustrating his wishes, is malevolent. He desires to keep another from achieving what he believes him to desire simply for the sake of that prevention, and he chooses that desire for realization. The principle of benevolence, on the other hand, directs us to select for realization those of our desires that are directed toward enabling others to secure what we believe them to desire simply for the sake of their securing it. A person is benevolent who believes that another wishes to swim, who desires to enable him to do so for that reason, and who chooses this desire for realization as opposed, say, to the desire not to pay his admission fee. The principle of benevolence is not concerned with enabling others to realize their actual desires. Belief may be mistaken; and others may not, in fact, entertain the desires our

[34] *Ibid.,* Buch I, Kapitel iii.

belief attributes to them. Still, one who enables another to do what he believes he desires to do simply for the sake of the realization of his desire, is treating him benevolently even though his belief as to the other's desire should be in error. Benevolence is a relation of agreement between our acts of will, and our beliefs about the desires of others. And it is expressed in the principle that one ought to choose for realization those of his desires that would enable others to realize the desires that he believes them to possess for the sake, only, of their realizing them.

JUSTICE. The fourth principle of right willing is that of justice (*Rechts*), and it must be understood in contrast to the first three.[35] Each of these three requires the relation of agreement between different aspects of the same person: inner freedom, between his knowledge and his principles of will; perfection, between those principles and the desires they select for realization; benevolence, between his principles of will and his own beliefs about the desires of other persons. The principle of justice prescribes agreement between one person's will and the wills of other members of his own society.

Imagine a situation in which there is no agreement between the wills of different persons. In it, each of them would resolve his own conflict of desires by making a selection from them that has no regard for the selection made by others. But the will to secure what one desires is equally strong in all men, and the complex of actions that different men would participate in would often come to chaos. If several persons desired to cultivate the same piece of land, and if each chose this desire for realization, the resulting complex of actions would be one of complete disorder; the cultivation of the land by each would make impossible that use of it by others.

The conflict we have imagined would be diminished or removed if there were an inequality of wills. Wills are unequal if in cases of such conflict, some of those who are parties to it choose to realize other desires than those that make for it. If several persons were to choose the same piece of land for cultivation, and if some (but not all), noticing the conflict to which their choices led, were to rescind those choices directing their desires elsewhere, there would be an inequality of wills. The conflict would be lessened. If it involved only two, inequality of will would remove it altogether; the withdrawal of one person would leave the other in undisputed possession of the land. But wills are not unequal and where they disagree in conflict, no one withdraws the desire his will selects in favor of others. In view of this equality of wills, the disorder that would arise in the situation we have imagined would be removed only if each

[35] *Ibid.*, Buch I, Kapitel iv.

party to it were to choose to realize some altogether different desire. The equity of wills is compatible with such a choice; for if each party to the conflict makes it, none withdraws in favor of another. It is clear, however, that the mere withdrawal of all the persons involved in conflict would create another problem. If all who wished to use a piece of land chose not to, there would be no conflict over that parcel; but since men must till the fields, there surely would be over another. And the decision on the part of each person not to realize desires that lead to conflict, in a particular case, cannot be enough to insure the stability of life. Persons must agree to accept some rule that decides whose selection of desire shall be honored, and whose disallowed. Such a rule is a civil law. Conflict of the kind we have imagined can be avoided if, and only if, the will of each person agrees with that of others in not choosing to realize desires that lead to conflict, and in accepting a law that decides who may legitimately act upon desires that would have this consequence if they were acted on.

Justice consists in engaging in acts of will that agree with those of other persons in such a way that each rejects desires that would lead to conflict, and obeys the law that all accept for orderly fulfillment of desire. The desires Herbart explicitly mentions are those directed toward control of things, and their just regulation consists in the laws that determine ownership. The principle of justice is the rule that one's acts of will ought always to exhibit such agreement. Herbart contends that the maintenance of a stable life requires denying that men have any rights against the state. Since all wills are equal, no one can assert a superior validity for his choice of desires. The consequence is that all rights, notably the right to property, must flow from the state, and can in no way depend upon the persons subject to it. Laws, he says, cannot improperly compel, since no one has a right against them; but they can confer favors. The favors they confer are the rights that citizens enjoy.

EQUITY. The fifth principle of right willing, that of equity (*Billigkeit*), Herbart explains as a rule for restoring the moral *status quo*.[36] To understand it, we must examine two concepts that play a role in determining its meaning. The first is the concept, *action*. An action is a motion of our bodies. The important thing to notice is that all such motions make a difference. The action of applying the brakes puts the car in a different place from where it would have been if they had not been applied, and the beating of the heart causes longer life than does its cessation. All the actions we engage in, all our motions, leave the world in a different state from the one it was in before.

---

36 *Ibid.*, Buch I, Kapitel v.

The second concept is that of *intentional action*. Some of our actions are not intentional. We are not aware of, nor do we try to accomplish them. Ordinarily, we are not conscious of the circulation of our blood, nor do we try to make it occur. Ordinarily, we make no effort at breathing. Actions not conscious and attempted, are not intentional. But others are. A move in a game of chess, the composition of a sonnet, the ordering of dinner from a menu are, all of them, actions we consciously engage in, and endeavor to perform. To be aware of doing something, and to try to do it, is to intend it; and while many of our actions are mistaken and automatic—not tried for, and neither conscious nor endeavored—many others are intentional.

Some intentional actions have no purpose beyond themselves. We may be conscious of, and endeavor to engage in the motions of a religious ritual, of writing a poem, and of merely sunning ourselves on the beach. But we need not do these things in order to be able to do others. Worship, poetic production, and sunbathing may be all that we intend to accomplish when we engage in them. Actions whose intentions are thus limited, Herbart sometimes calls simply "goals."[37]

But not all intentional actions are thus limited. Some men worship in order to improve their prospects. Some write poems in order to make money. Some lie in the sun in order to assure health. These actions look to others as objectives we would achieve by performing them. And intentional actions, viewed as means to others, Herbart sometimes calls simply "intentions."[38]

Actions we intend because of their consequences must be distinguished from intentional actions that have consequences not themselves intended. Two men who claim a single parcel of land may fall into conflict over it. But neither need intend to engage in that conflict. Each thinks of controlling the parcel, and endeavors to control it; but neither, so far, can be described as intending to engage in the dispute that, in fact, occurs. The conflict is a consequence of what each intends—the exclusive control of the land; but it is not a consequence aimed at by either until each assumes a position with respect to the land that he intends to defend against the other. In even this extreme case, each man aims, primarily, at exclusive control; and each intends to defeat the claim of the other only because its success would preclude that of his own. Some intentional actions aim at securing nothing beyond themselves; others are means in the sense that we engage in them in order to secure their consequences; others, still, have consequences not themselves intended.

Actions of the second kind just mentioned—those we intend to per-

---

[37] Cf below, selections from *General Practical Philosophy,* Book I, Chapter v.
[38] *Ibid.*

form because of their consequences—fall into two subordinate kinds. The consequences concerned sometimes are wholly extrapersonal, but sometimes they occur as alterations within persons. We may intentionally prune the plum tree in order to improve next year's crop. But we may also prune it in order to increase the happiness of its owner. In both cases, the pruning, like all actions, brings about a difference—a set of consequences the world would not contain if the action had not occurred. But the difference aimed at, in the first case, is the improvement of a crop; while the difference aimed at, in the second, is the enhanced happiness of a person.

Actions performed because of their consequences for persons also fall into two subordinate kinds. The consequences may occur in the actor himself or in another person or persons. The physician who treats himself engages in treatment because he wishes to improve his own health. But ordinarily, a physician treats others; and in doing so, his intentional actions are performed because of the effects they produce in other persons.

Intentional actions, performed because of their consequences for others, may be either good or bad. A good action is one whose intention is to bring about good, and one that actually accomplishes this objective. A physician who cured a patient by mistake could not have done a good action since he did not intend it; and one who intended such a cure, but failed, also could not have acted well. A bad action is one whose intention includes the production of bad consequences, and one which succeeds in that production. A physician cannot perform an action that is evil unless he intends to perform it, and unless he succeeds.

The principle of equity, Herbart holds, prescribes agreement between good and bad intentional actions, performed by one person, because of their consequences for others, and the way in which other persons deal with the actor. The way of dealing prescribed can be understood by observing what is involved in the success of good and bad actions. The intention that lies behind a good action is, itself, good; the effort to make someone more healthy is laudable. But the success of a good action is the transfer of goodness from the intention that lies behind it to the consequences it brings about. Successful medical treatment transfers goodness from the physician's intention to the patient's state of health. The difference made by a successful, good action directed toward another lies in the fact that before it there was a good intention in the actor, while after it there is a good condition in the life of someone else. Something of the same sort may be said for evil actions, directed against others. The successful action of a corrupt politician—the difference that he makes in the world—consists in his transferring evil from his own intentions to the lives of those whom he exploits. But this transfer of goodness and badness from one person to another may be cancelled; the goodness or badness may be returned to its place of origin. Where a physician is honored for his good treatment of patients other than himself, the goodness he gave away is returned to him—at least in some degree if not in the same form. So also, the defeat of an incumbent, but corrupt office seeker cancels, at least in part, the evil he intentionally visited upon his constituents. Equity consists in cancelling the good and evil done by good and evil actions, and this cancellation consists in visiting upon the doer, good or evil that is equal in amount to the good or evil he visited upon others in the actions he directed toward them.

The principle of equity requires that the good and evil actions that a person engages in should agree with the way in which others deal with him; it requires that they cancel the good and evil that he does to others in the manner described above. As a principle of will, it directs us always to choose for realization those of our desires that lead to this deliberate cancellation of the loss of good by its return, and the loss of evil by its restoration as opposed to other desires that lead, for example, to our refusal to concern ourselves with the moral condition of others. Like the principle of justice, it prescribes a relation between our own acts of will and some of those that others engage in—their intentions to perform actions that succeed in producing good or evil for others. It directs the preservation of the moral *status quo*.[39]

The first two moral ideas appear to be principles that tell us what relations other principles of willing ought to bear. The principle of inner freedom directs us to be clearly aware of the principles we, ourselves, adopt. The principle of perfection enjoins us to employ only principles that maximize the perfection of our own desires. The other three moral ideas appear to be principles that refer not to other principles, but to acts of will we ought to engage in. The principle of benevolence urges us to select those desires to act upon that conform to our beliefs about what others desire in such a way as to assure, for its own sake, what appears to us to be the happiness of others. The principle of justice demands that our acts of will agree with those of others concerning the establishment of, and obedience to laws—especially those that create property rights and provide for their transfer. The principle of equity enjoins us to act on the desire that others should be rewarded and punished for their good and bad deeds respectively. Although the first two principles refer to other principles of right willing directly, they refer indirectly to acts of will

39 Despite his presentation of the principle of equity as a rule our acts of will should observe, Herbart sees a difficulty in this view of it. The principle, thus regarded, requires that each man requite others for those of their good and bad actions that are externally directed. Such activity would lead to social chaos in which each man, recognizing the good and bad actions of others, spends his time in administering appropriate rewards and punishments to them. To avoid such disorder, Herbart enjoins God to make equity reign; but concludes, lamely, that each man ought to regard the goodness of his actions as his reward, and their evil as his punishment.

since the principles they describe are, themselves, principles that instruct us concerning those acts; and we can describe all the moral ideas as rules or principles that tell us what kinds of acts of will we ought to perform.

FORMAL CHARACTER OF THE IDEAS.   Since all the moral ideas are principles that direct our acts of will, they determine what desires we ought to try to realize; but it is important to notice that they are stated without reference to any desires in particular. We ought always, they tell us in substance, to act upon desires to enable others to realize what we believe to be their desires, to obey the laws, to requite others for their good and evil conduct, and to increase the perfection of our own desires. But the principle of benevolence affords no information either concerning what people do generally wish for, or what we might reasonably believe to be the content of their wishes. The principle of justice directs us to choose our desire to obey the laws rather than the desire to violate them; but it gives us no information as to the concrete nature of the objective of this desire, since it does not tell us which of many possible laws, concerning property, etc., we should agree to obey. The principle of equity requires that we choose to realize the desire to preserve the moral *status quo* in others. But since it provides no way of delimiting the goodness and badness that good and bad actions bring about, it does not specify concretely what we should desire to do in desiring to suit rewards and punishments of others to the character of their conduct. The principle of perfection urges us to develop within ourselves desires that are strong, numerous, and cooperative; but since any group of desires may possess these traits, the principle cannot inform us as to those we should cultivate.

All the principles of right willing determine the acts of will in which we should engage solely by reference to the relations that they bear to other aspects of the person in whom they occur (in the case of the first three), or to the acts of will of other persons (in the cases of justice and equity). They refer, Herbart says, only to the formal character of acts of will. He believes that to determine what desires one ought to act upon, one need not consider at all the objectives of those desires—their content. This view makes it possible for him to hold that many different kinds of life are good; for many, very different desires may be expressed in many, very different biographies—each of which, nonetheless, springs from acts of will that exhibit the same formal traits of inner freedom, perfection, benevolence, justice, and equity. The Christian and the pagan, the democrat and the totalitarian, the Platonist and the Epicurean—each of them, at least officially, desires to live in a way quite different from the way that would satisfy any of the others. But lives of these various kinds might all flow from acts of will governed by Herbart's five principles. Depending solely upon their formal traits to decide what acts of will are right, Herbart advances a moral ideal for individual conduct which, however rigorous it appears, leaves ample room for great variety.

THE DERIVED IDEAS: SOCIETY. The moral ideas clearly govern the acts of will of individual persons; but they also govern the acts of a society. A society is a group of persons, living in a limited domain, participating in a single economy, and governed by common rules. Families, churches, business corporations may fit this description. But the society that controls all others, and with which Herbart must be chiefly concerned, is the political state.

A society must often decide between alternative courses of conduct. Families must decide where to live; churches, whether to take part in political movements; manufacturing corporations, the question of diversification; and the state, its laws. Such choices may be regarded as social acts of will that choose for realization one of the society's desires as opposed to others. One may regard a plurality of persons, Herbart says, as one person if he wishes to do so; and if he does, ". . . their plural willing is comparable to the several efforts and resolves of one and the same rational being."[40] But the acts of will of a society, like those of an individual, are right or wrong according as they conform or fail to conform to certain principles. Herbart contends that the principles of right willing for societies are the same as those for individuals. But he speaks of them, in their social application, as "derived."

A society applies the moral ideas to itself—resolves its conflicts of desire—through the operation of groups or institutions subordinate to it. These institutions vary from one form of society to another. A democracy possesses a different structure from that of an aristocracy. But although the institutions through which society applies the moral ideas to itself differ, the same principles are applied in all.

Any society must resolve the conflict that arises when different persons will to engage in incompatible actions. It must prevent disorder by authorizing only one of the parties to express his will, or by denying such an expression to all of them. In the state, some groups of persons must make and enforce laws—especially those concerning property; there must be a set of institutions that function as legislature, judiciary, and legal administration. The conflict these institutions would prevent is inherent in the wills they regulate; and these wills, as we have seen, are not directed toward the creation of the conflict, but simply toward doing things all of which cannot be done. Such institutions, in their endeavor to prevent this conflict, constitute society's application of the principle of

---

40 Cf. below, selections from *General Practical Philosophy*, Buch I, Chapter vii.

justice. Herbart calls attention to their necessity for society by describing the latter as a "society of law."

Justice with its laws regulates the meeting of incompatible wills. But wills meet in a second, quite different fashion to whose regulation the idea of justice is irrelevant. Some men deliberately do good and bad deeds, visiting good and evil upon their fellows; and society must decide how they should be requited. It must provide institutions that assign good to those who act well toward others, and harm to those who act badly toward them. Scientific academies, titles of nobility, and social censure requite men for their good and bad actions. They exemplify society's application of the principle of equity. Its application must be distinguished from that of the principle of justice. Legislatures, courts, and administrative institutions endeavor to prevent disorder that arises unintentionally; but these other institutions requite men for actions that deliberately bring benefit or harm to others. Herbart calls the institutions that apply the principle of equity a "system of rewards."[41]

A society perfectly just and equitable, however, might lack an important trait. Property would be respected; good and bad actions would be requited; but there might be a very low degree of well-being. The people might live in the misery of ignorance, poverty, and disease. The social application of the principle of benevolence requires that social well-being be advanced as far as possible. There must be a set of institutions that administer educational, economic, medical and other resources. Herbart calls it an "administrative system."

A society in which well-being is widespread may also possess a high degree of perfection. In it, fundamental economic and social problems have disappeared; and individual persons are free to develop their more humane interests. These interests become strong and numerous in kind. And the creative energies of each person cooperate with similar tendencies in others to produce a system of culture. Herbart seems to have in mind, here, the harmonious flowering of art, science, and religion—as well as more humble activities such as those of sport—that many have thought would follow successful conquest of the more material problems of mankind.

A society that is just, equitable, benevolent, and perfect must be aware that its being so consists in its following the principles we have discussed. If it does not possess this knowledge, it will not possess all these

---

[41] Upon occasion, Herbart seems to identify society's application of the principle of justice and the principle of equity, perhaps thinking of punishment for the violation of law as requital for evil deeds. But this identification must be mistaken since justice is concerned with unintended conflict of wills, while equity is concerned with their intentional conflict—with wills to benefit or harm other persons.

traits; rather, at least on some and perhaps on many occasions, it will act in ways contrary to one or more of those principles. Ignorance of the rules that determine one's choice is one condition for choosing wrongly. Hence we can infer from the justice, equity, benevolence, and perfection of a society, the proposition that it knows that it follows these principles. Society's application to itself of the principle of inner freedom leads us to attribute this knowledge to a soul conceived of as that of society itself— not as that of any individual; and this location of society's knowledge of its own morality leads to the view that it is "animated" or (as the German may be translated) "ensouled."[42]

The goal Herbart recommends for education is the life of virtue, and a virtuous life is one governed by right principles. The right principles of willing are those of inner freedom, of perfection, of benevolence, of justice, and of equity. They tell us what kinds of desire should be realized by pointing to certain formal traits of the acts of will that choose them for realization—to certain relations between those acts and other aspects of the actor, or to the acts of will of other persons. The five moral ideas apply both to personal and social acts of will; and the objective appropriate to education is not merely an individual, but also a society (especially the state) whose desires are governed by acts determined by those principles.

Subordinate Recommendations

GOVERNMENT OF CHILDREN. Herbart recommends a three-fold way of dealing with children, on the grounds that it produces the personal and social ideal just outlined. First, they must be governed or disciplined, and the government of them consists in keeping them busy. They should be kept interested in what they are doing: amused with stories and games, etc.; assigned tasks or allowed to choose from them if they have preferences; assured success in the performance of them; and treated kindly but firmly. They should be assisted in finding jobs at appropriate ages. Proper government keeps children in order and out of trouble; and it makes instruction possible.

INSTRUCTION. Secondly, children must be instructed. Instruction should produce virtue; but Herbart discusses chiefly one part of this objective—the production of perfection or many-sidedness of interest.[43]

---

[42] But Herbart was loath to draw the conclusions that societies have souls of their own. He said that we may *regard* them in this way, not that they *possess* them. He also held that there are no purposes except those of individual persons—a view hard to reconcile with the notion that groups have souls. But the latter view was widespread among philosophers in his day.

[43] *Outlines of Educational Doctrine*, Part II, Section II, chaps. ii and iii.

Bringing the latter about consists in deliberately supplying the student with ideas, and in deliberately fostering plans for realizing the objects they stand for. Independently of instruction, the child acquires ideas directly through his own experience, and indirectly through communication with others. Ideas, thus acquired, form themselves into apperceptive masses whose qualities permit instruction to add to the student's mind ideas to which they have appropriate relations of quality, but prevent its adding those that are extremely opposed. The instructor should make use of the channels of experience and communication by showing his charges those items of which he wishes them to have ideas, and by discussing such novelties. These new ideas find a place in the student's mind determined by their relations of quality to the apperceptive masses already formed; and, in accord with the individuality of each child, they become desires—press upward, after a period of obscurity, toward the clarity of realization. Each child brings to them plans for realizing the objects they refer to. But such ideas or desires accompanied by plans to make their objects real, if not yet carried out, are interests. Instruction, thus, produces interests; and these interests should be as diverse in kind as is compatible with their being strong and harmonious.

Instruction creates interests; and since interests are the materials of which persons are composed, instruction is the means to personality. Good instruction, we may add, is the production of persons who possess a high degree of perfection. Possessing a body of interests of this kind enables the person to apply the principle which assures the continuance and enhancement of perfection.

Curriculum. Herbart holds that the curriculum—at least through the secondary level—ought to contain scientific and historical subjects, and he bases this recommendation on the division of all natural interests into cognitive and sympathetic. Cognitive interests lead one to attend to individual things, their relations to one another, and the aesthetic quality of the whole they form; and the sciences present opportunities for realizing these interests. Geography, for example, presents the child with his neighborhood, its relations with others extending to the entire globe, and enables him to enjoy the adaptation of part to part in the whole thus constituted. Sympathetic interest enables the child to understand biographies, the careers of nations, and the vicissitudes of the race recorded in religious documents. But Herbart's description of the courses of study as scientific or historical is not very precise, as is shown by the fact that literature and language study, which he regards as very important, fall clearly into neither classification.

Method. Herbart derives the method of instruction from his description of the process of apperception.[44] This process, as we have seen, exhibits a pattern of absorption and reflection—of the absorption of attention by a single idea, and of the spreading out of attention (*Besinnung*) from the one by which it was absorbed to those the latter permits to rise from unconsciousness. The method of instruction, of deliberately giving the student new ideas, must cause him, first, to be completely absorbed in them, one by one. The instructor, by vivid narration and description, by maps, pictures, etc.,[45] ought to endeavor to bring about this concentrated attention. Herbart describes this aspect of the method of instruction as purely presentative.[46] It presents the student with ideas of things as they are; and in presenting them, it in no way alters them.

The second aspect of method is analysis; and it consists in two kinds of alteration of ideas subsequent to absorption in them. Herbart uses the term "analysis" to refer to the procedure of deliberately allowing the student to express his thoughts in unregulated conversation which, however free, obliges the student to do things of two kinds. First, it should make him attend to the parts of the thing that earlier absorbed all his attention. Secondly, it should make him attend to ideas of things he believes to be related to the thing in which he was earlier absorbed. Its neighbors in space and time, its past and its future, its causes and its effects, its explanation and what it, itself, explains—some or all ideas of such related things, depending upon the purpose concerned, should be allowed to rise out of the student's unconsciousness and to share his attention with the idea in which it was absorbed. Instruction in its aspect of analysis clarifies ideas of things given to the student in pure presentation by pointing out their parts, and brings him to attend to his ideas of relations those things bear to others. The result of successful analytical instruction is the student's attention to a constellation of ideas, organized around one whose parts are clear, and extending to others related in various ways to the first.

The center of such a constellation of ideas is the object of an interest, and analysis brings to such an object many ways of dealing with it—both relevant and irrelevant. It is the task of instruction in its third aspect, *synthesis,* to enhance the relevant and to eradicate the irrelevant. This task is accomplished by the teacher's overtly managing conversation, lectures, pictures, etc., in such a way as to oblige the student to attend

[44] But it is also suggested to him by consideration of long established methods—methods which he combines into one. Cf. *ibid.,* pp. 52–55.
[45] In Herbart's day, there were few books in German schools, and few public or private libraries. The teacher was obliged to present orally a great deal of what students now, in Europe and the United States of America, read for themselves.
[46] *Ibid.,* p. 106.

only to ideas that are relevant to the object of his interest.[47] Instruction concerning the theater, for example, after presenting the idea to the student, should clarify its parts—stage, lines, actors, play as opposed to real action, etc., and should bring out the student's beliefs about its relations to other things—the church, social attitudes and movements, persons and societies, its history, etc. Pure presentation and analysis perform these tasks; but synthesis should eradicate false ideas from the mass the student brings to the idea of the theater—should bring him to attend only to relations the theater genuinely bears to other institutions, social attitudes and movements, etc.

The student should do more than attend to the object of his interest and to other items related to it in ways that are relevant. He should put the ideas of these things together for himself. The instructor should oblige him to do so in order that the student's self-activity should establish an enduring interest—a well organized apperceptive mass. An interest in the theater should be created not only by bringing the student to attend to the relations it has borne to institutions in the past, but by speculating as to its relations to things in imaginary, future, or idealized societies. Or, where the interest is in theatrical performance, it should be cultivated not by historical investigation and speculation, merely, but also by actual performances. Instruction concerning the Pythagorean theorem should consist not merely in explaining the parts of the idea of a right triangle, and in trying out all sorts of proofs in order to retain in consciousness the adequate, and to consign the inadequate to unconsciousness, but also in practicing the application of the theorem to right triangles of different shapes and sizes.

Instruction in the aspect of synthesis should observe certain rules. First, it should be applied to persons who have an interest, natural or learned, in the subject being taught.[48] Secondly, ideas should be added in the proper order of explanation—premises before conclusions, and ideas that are easy before the more difficult ideas they explain.[49] Thirdly, the addition of each new idea or item of information must be, and must appear to the student to be a step in the achievement of some goal. The student must be made to see how one step in instruction facilitates another, and how all make up a task that will succeed if each component step succeeds.[50]

Herbart's discussion of the method of instruction in terms of pure presentation, analysis, and synthesis is not so well known as his description

[47] *Ibid.*, pp. 106, 125.
[48] *Ibid.*, pp. 125–27. In this place, Herbart seems to assume that there are some interests that are natural or unlearned—presumably falling under the classifications, cognitive and sympathetic—and others that are learned—those instruction should foster.
[49] *Ibid.*, p. 127.
[50] *Ibid.*, pp. 127–28.

of it in terms of the four formal steps of clearness, association, system, and method. But although the terms are different, he says the same thing in both accounts. Clearness and pure presentation, both, consist in the effort to bring about the student's clear attention to an idea; association and analysis, in the effort to bring about awareness of the parts of the idea and of beliefs concerning its relations; system and method together with synthesis, in the elimination of irrelevant and enhancement of relevant beliefs as well as in the application of the idea to be understood to many different instances. Both these descriptions fit into the pattern of absorption and reflection. Absorption corresponds to pure presentation and clearness, reflection to analysis and synthesis, or to association, system, and method. The description in terms of pure presentation, analysis, and synthesis may have been preferred by Herbart; it occurs in the *Outlines*, one of his latest works. But the description in terms of the "four formal steps" obtained currency, and was developed in considerable detail by his followers.[51]

The purpose of instruction, according to Herbart, is the production of virtue as a whole—the production of persons, and presumably of societies, in which the application of all five moral principles or ideas to situations of choice assures the goodness of individual and social life.[52] Nonetheless, he discusses, almost exclusively, that part of virtue, only, which springs from the application of the principle of perfection. His reason for neglecting the other four is that perfection is the means to their possession. The production of many interests is, perhaps, relatively easy; and if instruction creates interests, the employment of the principle of perfection might well be furthered by it. But it is not clear that producing adherence to the principle of perfection is a means to virtue as a whole. Perfection is logically independent of the other four moral ideas; and inducing adherence to it would not *ipso facto* bring about adherence to the others. Of course, employing the principle of perfection might be connected psychologically with adopting the principles of inner freedom, justice, and the rest. But far from providing evidence for this connection, Herbart does not even discuss it.

At any rate, Herbart does hold that instruction should further perfection or many-sidedness. It consists in the student's application to his own choices of the principle that assures his possession of interests that are strong, varied, and cooperative, and in a consequent social application of the same principle. The curriculum should supply the objects around

51 They divided the first step, clearness, into preparation for the idea, and presentation of it, making the four steps into five. For a very brief description of this development, see Lange's comments in his translation and edition of *Outlines of Educational Doctrine,* especially pp. 53–59. Cf. also Rein, W., *Outlines of Pedagogics,* tr. C.C. and Ida J. Van Liew, E. L. Kellogg & Co., New York and Chicago, 1893.

52 *Outlines of Educational Doctrine,* p. 44.

which interests center, making them as varied as possible, and the three phases of the method of instruction should make them strong and co-operative.

TRAINING. Herbart calls the third part of the treatment of children "training," and he describes its objective as moral strength of character.[53] A character or person, it will be recalled, is a collection of interests organized by principles or rules, determining that some shall be satisfied and others consigned to unconsciousness. Strength of character is the degree to which these principles are established. A weak character is one in whom choices are incoherent; a strong character, one in whom there is a relatively high degree of adherence to principles. Moral strength of character is a relatively high degree of adherence to moral principles—the five rules we have examined. Training, therefore, is that way of dealing with children whose objective is establishment in them of the disposition to follow moral principles in making choices between incompatible ends. We have seen that the ultimate end of personal and social life is one that includes inner freedom as opposed to ignorance of the principles one employs, perfection as opposed to meagerness of interests, benevolence as opposed to malevolence or indifference, justice as opposed to injustice, and equity as opposed to inequity. The objective of training, then, is the establishment in the child of a disposition to choose in accord with the rules that lead to this end. There is no natural basis for this disposition, and the problem of training consists in determining how the psychological mechanism of apperception may be used to create it.

The solution to the problem consists of two stages. In the preliminary stage, three things must be done. First, the child must be put in a situation, imaginary or real, in which he must make a choice. Secondly, he must be given examples of right choices, and be made to see clearly what principles are followed by those who make the exemplary choices. Thirdly, he must imitate the examples, in his imagination or in reality.[54] If these three conditions are satisfied in any one case, the child will make a choice from among his desires which, though not itself moral, is the choice he would have made if moral principles had been already established in him. The idea of making it will pass into his unconsciousness; but when another similar situation arises, it will be permitted to rise from his unconsciousness by virtue of the qualitative relation of moderate opposition to that situation—by virtue of the mechanism of apperception.[55] Ultimately, an apperceptive mass will be formed consisting of

53 *Ibid.*, p. 143.
54 *Ibid.*, pp. 154, 172, 192.
55 *Ibid.*, pp. 160–61.

ideas of settling choices between incompatible ends in the right way. Such a mass is the same thing as the idea of employing the five moral principles to describe moral choices; and when it is established, the child will have the moral principles whose employment makes his choices right. The question, then, for the preliminary stage, is how to assure the satisfaction of the three conditions mentioned earlier.

In order that these conditions should be satisfied, the student must be treated in certain ways. He must be made to feel the approval of others for choices that run in the right, and their disapproval for those that run in the wrong direction. He must, nonetheless, always be treated kindly and sympathetically. He must be shown that it is necessary, often, to endure what is disagreeable in order to achieve what he longs for or likes. He must be allowed to enjoy both the good and bad consequences of his choices, excluding those that are seriously harmful. The entire process must be agreeable or pleasant if possible. Good conduct which the student is likely to ignore must be pointed out; but in order to avoid feelings of inadequacy, it must be the conduct of those not closely involved in the student's life.[56]

The life of the child provides many real examples of the necessity for choices—situations to be dealt with in the ways just indicated. Aggression from and against his fellows provides an opportunity for cultivating a disposition toward justice. It also enables the child to begin to see the need for requiting good and evil deeds according to the principle of equity although he should not be permitted, himself, to execute rewards and punishments. Quarrels and disputes, similarly, may arouse the feeling of benevolence, and may create a situation in which a choice based upon benevolence can be fostered. The feeling, frequently found among older children, that one has a firm commitment to a set of principles, should not be stifled, since it is the beginning of inner freedom; but since many who lack it feel inadequate for that reason, its presence should not be too publicly remarked.[57]

In the preliminary stage, the child who is treated in these ways may make choices or engage in acts of will that lead, through apperception, to the disposition to act rightly. And it seems quite clear that if he is not enabled to make choices, he will not develop the dispositions to choose rightly that constitute the material of virtue.

The second stage of training consists in making the student himself attend to his own choices. The teacher must point out to him how these choices were right and how they were wrong, neither exaggerating nor belittling their moral value. He should also engage in explicit appro-

56 *Ibid.*, pp. 142–45, 149–52, 154–56, 172, 191–92.
57 *Ibid.*, pp. 186–92.

bation and censure.⁵⁸ These procedures will cause the student to consign wrong principles to unconsciousness, leaving the right ones in a position to be employed in the future.

Training in these two stages is directed toward producing the disposition to choose rightly. If it succeeds, the student will be aware of the five moral principles, and will employ them in his acts of will. His contemplation of them, in the second stage, excites his moral taste; and his approbation of adopting them as his own endows them with such a moral beauty, while his disapprobation of rejecting them lends them such a moral ugliness that he refrains both from the drift which is obedience to no principles whatever, and from the spurious morality which is obedience to those that are wrong. Successful training produces the disposition to choose rightly, and excites that approbation, directed toward the five moral ideas, whose presence in a person is necessary to transform choices that are in accord with moral principles into those that are right⁵⁹ because made in order that those principles should be exemplified.

The distinction Herbart draws between government, instruction, and training is by no means clear-cut. We need not trouble with its unclarity, but we may notice that it suggests clear distinctions among three phases of education. It suggests that government of children is the use of power to keep them in order, that instruction is the effort to create interests with their component desires, and that training is the effort to instill dispositions to choose among one's desires in accord with the five moral principles, whose employment contributes to a life of virtue. A successful government, instruction, and training of children will lead to their approbation of the five moral principles, and to that conscious employment of them because of their rightness, which as we shall see, makes for right conduct and for virtuous persons and societies.

ADMINISTRATION. Herbart's discussion of the administration of education points out advantages and disadvantages of different procedures, and concludes with a recommendation for a combination of home and school education. The home is best fitted to instill morality; parents, siblings, and tutors have a vivid knowledge of the inner life of a child, and can adapt government, instruction, and training most usefully to produce virtue. But business, noise and the like diminish the efficiency that the home possesses in this regard. Private schools can prevent evils that come from environment; but the deliberate selection of students that confers this merit upon them brings with it the disadvantage that the child grows up with a limited social experience. The advantage of state schools lies in their superior ability to enable the student to

⁵⁸ *Ibid.*, pp. 193–97.
⁵⁹ Cf. below, the discussion of ethics and education.

acquire knowledge; their disadvantage is that not knowing the internal bent of the child, they cannot properly further the moral organization of interests in things that knowledge of them should lead to. Herbart urges that whenever possible, the home should provide education on the elementary level, and the schools—apparently state schools—on the secondary and higher. He praises the administration of American schools on the grounds that it permits any child to enter the schools at the lowest and to ascend to the highest rung of the educational ladder.[60]

PHILOSOPHY OF EDUCATION

ETHICS AND EDUCATION

We have already examined Herbart's discussion of the kinds of things that are right and good. Those that are right are acts of will that conform to the five moral ideas,[61] and those that are good or virtuous are persons and societies that engage in these acts. We shall now consider, very briefly, his answer to the question concerning the *nature* of rightness and goodness.

Herbart holds that the rightness of the five moral principles consists in their being approved by the person who adopts them. Some very general considerations serve to eliminate alternatives to this view; and most of his discussion in *General Practical Philosophy* is an exposition rather than a defense of it.

First, we cannot explain the notion of value, in general, by use of the notion of *desire*. Desires, themselves, are right or wrong; and for that reason, such an analysis of value, in general, would presuppose what it should explain. Secondly, value, in general, cannot consist in our willing or resolving upon what possesses it. The same difficulty arises. Willing, itself, possesses a value—is right or wrong; and the value of a thing cannot be analyzed by reference to the value of something else. Since value, in general, cannot be explained by use of notions of desire and will, the specific value, moral rightness, cannot be thus explained.

Moreover, the moral rightness of a will cannot consist in its conformity to *duty* or the categorical imperative. The categorical imperative is itself a command or will; and since what it would restrain is a will

---

[60] For Herbart's views concerning administration, cf. *Outlines of Educational Doctrine*, pp. 317–25.
[61] Herbart holds that an act of will may not conform precisely to the five moral principles; and consequently, he ought to regard rightness and goodness as possessed of degrees—the highest, in each case, consisting in, or depending upon, precise conformity to those principles. Cf., e.g., below, *General Practical Philosophy*, Introduction, Section II.

also, there is no better reason to suppose that moral value consists in obedience to it, than in the obedience of the categorical imperative to the will it would restrain. Besides, this view of the nature of moral rightness requires that each man possess two wills—a commanding will and a will that it commands; and this view is false. No theory of the nature of the rightness of actions that would explain it by reference to desire, will, or duty is correct; and Herbart concludes that the moral rightness of rules for choice consists in the fact that the person who employs them has a taste[62] for or approbation of them.

We should notice six characteristics of the rightness or approbation of moral principles. First, it always extends only to what is directly before it. In this respect, approbation or moral taste differs from desire. The object of our desire is always partly in the future; it is something that will be realized at a later date although to some degree present now, when the desire occurs. What we desire, then, cannot be completely before the mind. But what we approve is completely before us—not something to be realized in the future.

Secondly, it follows from this first point that we can never be mistaken about the characteristics of the thing we approve of. What we desire, when realized, may turn out to be different from what we had thought. Part of the desire, its realization, was not, at the earlier time, present to us. Hence we can be mistaken concerning it. But since the object of approbation is always completely present to it, that approbation cannot be mistaken about what it focuses on.

Thirdly, our moral approbation is an effect caused by the things toward which it is directed. In this respect, it differs from ideas of other kinds. Our thought of Julius Caesar, for example, is not an effect that gentleman exercises upon us; we can entertain and reject it at will. But our approbation of inner freedom, perfection, justice, and the other moral principles is an effect they call forth when we think of them, and is quite involuntary.

Fourthly, since approbation is an involuntary effect of things approved, every case of it is logically independent of every other. The judgment, "I approve of all students," seems to have a bearing on "I approve of this student"; if the first is true, it appears, the second must be also. It seems that we should be able to correct one approbation by appeal to others. However, we are not, in fact, able to treat them in this way. Since each approbation is an effect of its object, no one of them has a genuine logical bearing on another, and the truth or falsehood of one cannot re-

---

[62] Herbart regards ethics as part of aesthetics, and looks upon the task of aesthetics as that of dealing with things in so far as they appeal to our taste—with things that are beautiful.

quire that of another. Moral judgments are independent, and no one of them can give us a reason for, or justification of another.

Fifthly, since the object of approbation is always complete, we never approve of things universally. In order to do so, it would be necessary either to think of all the members of a class at once which is impossible, or to regard the object of moral taste as incomplete which is false.

Sixthly, the objects of moral approbation are never particulars. Just as the beauty of a musical composition lies in its form, and the pleasantness of a chord in the relations of the tones that compose it, so the object of moral approval or disapproval is always the form or structure of a thing. We approve of relations, not of particular things; and the relations we approve of are, as we have seen, relations of will.[63] Hence, moral approbations never exact anything in particular of us, but only that whatever acts of will we engage in, they should be related to other aspects of ourselves or to the acts of will of others by relations stated in the five moral ideas.

Herbart finds no difficulty in his view that moral judgments can be neither justified nor corrected. The moral chaos which it seems to imply is precluded by another fact. Men always respond in the same way when they contemplate the five moral principles with clarity. The ideas involved in the rules of inner freedom, perfection, benevolence, justice, and equity awaken in all minds the response of approbation. Consequently, the support or correction of moral judgments is not only not possible; it is also quite unnecessary. Since all men approve the same principles, no principle is in need of rational support or correction. Each man approves the moral principles, and consequently acts of his own will, that others approve of with the same consequence; and it is each man's approbation of *his* own acts, on the grounds that they exemplify the five moral principles, that confers rightness upon conduct, goodness upon the life of the actor, and, derivatively, upon a society that, itself, acts according to the same principles.

Herbart supports his recommendation that the government, instruction, and training of children be directed toward personal and social virtue through the creation of persons that adhere to the five moral ideas by the view that these moral ideas are right; and he explains the proposition that they are so by analyzing rightness in terms of approbation, and by holding that men always, in fact, approve of them.

---

[63] This phrase "relations of will" is taken from Herbart's language. As we have seen, it refers to the principles that prescribe certain relations between acts of will and other aspects of the same person, and acts of will of different persons.

METAPHYSICS AND EDUCATION.

Herbart bases his recommendations concerning the government, instruction, and training of children on his psychology, and makes them flow from his use of its description of mental activity to mark out paths through which teachers can guide children toward a goal provided by ethics. He holds, however, that his psychology is based on experience, on mathematics, and metaphysics. Mental activity, he resolves into series of ideas; and experience gives descriptions of these series to psychology. Mathematics provides a quantitative formulation of the relations of ideas in series. Metaphysics explains why there is mental activity at all. His recommendations concerning education, thus, ultimately rest, in part, on metaphysics. We shall state some salient aspects of his metaphysical doctrine, and endeavor to make out Herbart's view that psychology rests upon it.

Herbart holds that everything we experience is unreal. It must be so because it is contradictory. It is made up of substances that are either material or mental, and that are constantly changing. But all these concepts—"substance," "matter," "self," and "change"—contain contradictions; and contradictory concepts cannot apply to what is real.

The concept "substance" is that of something with properties. We use this concept when we say of a table, for example, that it is brown. But to say that it *is* brown is to identify the table with its property—to identify the table with its brownness. But it is contradictory to say of one thing that it *is* another—of the table that it *is* brown. The concept "substance" is contradictory; and however much things appear to have properties, they cannot really possess them. It does not help to say that a substance is identical not with one, but with all of its properties; for it is still different from and therefore not identical with them.

Similarly, the concept "matter" cannot really apply to anything; for what is material is spread out through space. Consequently, its parts occupy points. But points must be both completely separate from one another in order that several should make a line, a plane, or a volume, and must also interpenetrate in order that lines, planes, and volumes should be continuous. But nothing can be both discrete and continuous; and the concept "matter," being contradictory, can apply to nothing real.

The concept "self" also can apply to nothing real. We use it as if it referred to something which had our ideas. But this something must itself, appear to us as an idea—an idea of the thing that has our ideas. However, this idea, itself, brings with it the idea of something that has it; so that the concept of the self always presupposes that we have applied it to something before we have made that application. And our use of it, consequently, can never extend to anything real.

The proposition that everything changes, analogously, cannot describe reality. The concept "change" contains its own contradiction. Change is the acquisition by a thing either of a different place, or of a different property. The first kind of change is motion; the second, alteration. But a thing in one place cannot *move* to another unless it remains identical; otherwise, there would be simply two things—one here, and another there. Motion requires identity of the moving thing. But a thing in one place cannot be identical with a thing in another. Similarly, in order for an apple to become red, it must remain identical throughout its alteration. But a green apple cannot be identical with a red apple. So it is for all qualitative alteration; and the concept "change" can apply to nothing real.

Still, Herbart cannot believe that there is nothing real. He holds that the world we experience, as contradictory, is the appearance to us of what is real and not contradictory. Experience gives us no knowledge whatever of this real world. Nonetheless, independently of our experience of it, we can know that it is made up of many different things, each of which has its own character, and each of which is perfectly simple. He calls these things "Reals";[64] connected with each person, Herbart holds, there is one Real. The ideas that constitute the interests of which a person is composed are related to each other through the process of apperception we have examined. Each idea is the appearance of a Real; but if each were an appearance of a different Real, they could never be connected with one another. If the idea of red were an appearance of Real A, and if the idea of fragrance were the appearance of Real B, the two could never be "complicated" into the idea of a rose, and an interest in roses could not occur. But persons are interested in roses. It follows that each person is the appearance of a single Real; and this Real, Herbart identifies with the soul. Dwelling, as it does, in a realm where there is no change, it is indestrucible, and therefore immortal.

Since each Real is perfectly simple and changeless, Herbart must explain how persons appear as complex—have different ideas from time to time, lose old and acquire new interests, and appear to change in other ways. His explanation contains four steps. First, although the Reals are not related in space and time,[65] there are some unknowable relations that they bear to each other. Secondly, some of these relations disturb the Reals, and their disturbances consist in their engaging in acts of preserving their simplicity and changelessness—in acts of self-preservation. Thirdly

[64] This discussion of Herbart's metaphysics has relied on the treatment of it given by Wilhelm Windelband, *A History of Philosophy*, Vol. II, tr. Tufts, Harper & Brothers, publishers, New York, 1958, and Harold Höffding, *A History of Modern Philosophy*, Vol. II, tr. B. E. Meyer, Dover Publications, Inc., 1955.

[65] Herbart regards "time" as a contradictory concept for reasons similar to those that lead him to describe "space" in this way.

our ideas are appearances to us of these acts of self-preservation. In view of some unknown relation between Real A and Real B, Real A acts to preserve itself; and relying upon our experience, we say that person A, (whose soul is Real A) sees the plum tree (whose Real is Real B). Fourthly, the simplicity of the soul precludes its undergoing many disturbances or engaging in many acts of self-preservation simultaneously.[66] Consequently, only a few ideas can occupy consciousness at one time.

From his metaphysical doctrine that the real world is made up of unknowable, simple, changeless Reals related to one another in unknowable ways, but known to engage in acts of self-preservation, Herbart derives part of the conceptual framework of his psychology. Elementary ideas, he equates with the soul's acts of self-preservation, and their simple qualities with the simplicity of the soul. Their clarity or consciousness, he derives from the soul's inability, being simple, to engage in many acts of self-preservation; and their striving toward high clarity he seems to equate, also, with the soul's striving to preserve itself. Once we have these concepts to describe ideas, apperception can easily be developed as we have seen, and the way is left open for experience to provide a statement as to what particular ideas organize themselves into the interests that constitute persons.

For Herbart, metaphysics helps to explain psychology; and since psychology supplies the machinery for producing virtue, his metaphysics is a part of the justification of the goals he recommends that educators should try to achieve.

MATHEMATICS AND PSYCHOLOGY

Herbart's work in psychology is historically important in a way we have not yet indicated. He is the first to have used mathematics in the effort to describe psychological phenomena. He held that the clarity of one idea in relation to another can be described in quantitative terms, and that the amount of clarity that any combination has may be described quantitatively by reference to the relative degrees of clarity of its components. These degrees cannot be simply added to ascertain the clarity of the combination, since the clarity of one diminishes that of another. But by use of other mathematical operations, he advanced mathematical formulas that would describe the clarity of such combinations. But clarity and consciousness are the same quality of ideas, and consequently his formulas enabled him to describe exactly the kind of relations in which the emergence of one idea into consciousness would press others down

[66] I have found no passage in Herbart in which this step is made explicit. It should be noted that it is difficult to see how the concept "simultaneity" can apply to something that is not temporal.

toward or into unconsciousness. His mathematical laws of psychology did not become part of the operating inventory of that science, but his construction of them was an important influence in introducing the use of mathematics in psychology, which has become widespread.

A Guide to Selections from *General Practical Philosophy*

The reader should notice that the German word, here translated by "practical," means what we would commonly mean by moral. General practical philosophy is general moral philosophy, or ethics.

In the passages that follow, Herbart advances the view that moral philosophy consists in a clarification and explanation of moral judgments, and attempts their clarification and explanation. Some theorists have held that moral value consists in being desired; but since desire, itself, is either good or bad, this view cannot afford a satisfactory account of it. Others have held that moral value consists in being willed, but such an account possesses a difficulty of the same kind as that in terms of desire. Nor can it consist in conformity to duty where duty is understood in terms of the categorical imperative; for since duty enforces its will against what often wills to disobey it, it presupposes that we have two wills, which is false. Moral value cannot consist either in being desired, in being willed, or in being in conformity with the categorical imperative. Moral value consists in the approbation given to the thing that possesses it by the man who judges it. It is the taste each man has for rules that govern choices.

The objects of moral tastes, unlike those of desire, are complete and perfectly present to the act of taste or approbation. They are always forms of things rather than things themselves. The things to which they apply are acts of choosing one desire as against others; and the forms that we thus apply, and that cause our approbation of them, are relations that can hold between the will and other aspects of the same person, and between his will and those of others.

Moral judgments are not universal; they are not judgments about all the things in a class. They are also not particular since they are not about particular things. Each moral judgment is the expression of approbation felt by the person who makes it toward some relation of the kinds mentioned in the preceding paragraph.

In the excerpts from Book I, Herbart discusses these relations, treating them as expressed in the five moral ideas or principles we have examined. The reader may consult Chapter X of this volume, under the heading *Recommendations,* for an exposition that may help him to understand the passages mentioned.

SELECTIONS FROM

General Practical Philosophy*
(ALLGEMEINE PRAKTISCHE PHILOSOPHIE)

———◄•►———

INTRODUCTION

What is the good? Who is good? Better? Worse? With these words of
praise and blame, one makes judgments on others in conversations and on
himself in conscience. Is such judgment proper at all? If so, which judgments are right? As the pronouncement of praise or blame may be called
a practical judgment, practical philosophy may be expected to provide
the rectification of such judgments as its proper vocation—if it has a
vocation and if it is something itself.

*　　　*　　　*

If something is a good insofar as it is desired and striven for, then the
final reason for its preferability lies just in this desire and striving themselves. But the goodness of this desire, its preference over every bad desire
—should it come from this good [of being desired]? So we go around
in a circle; everything remains indefinite and practical philosophy has
neither a beginning nor content. Thus we must originally value either
the good independently of desire for it, or the desire independently of its
good. Perhaps each of the two can occur, albeit not at the same time.
There may be goods—and an evaluation of them *in virtue of which* they
are marked *as* goods—which are independent of all willing, wishing, striving, appropriating, and the like. And if such a *will-less*, involuntary evaluation is once assumed, a certain desire, a certain willing, resolving, and
acting may appear among its objects. Indeed, the latter case is the really
endemic fundamental presupposition of practical philosophy, whose critique should touch immediately on the will without bothering about
other things. So some sort of willing must now be reckoned among the
goods on their own account, leaving their objects out of the question; similarly, others must be accounted among the evils. Nevertheless, let us admit

---

* Translated by David A. McCullough, text after the original Göttingen edition of 1808,
ed. Justus fr. Danekwerts, from *Joh. Friedr. Herbart's Sämmtliche Werke,* ed. Karl
Kehrbach, (Verlag Von Veit & Comp. Leipzig: 1885). Words in brackets do not have
counterparts in the original German text, but are added by the translator in order to
clarify its meaning.

that ordinary language is violated here, as it was before when we assumed goods in general, demarcated as such by an involuntary evaluation. . . .

Here we are reminded of what seemed forgotten when it was asked: just what can practical philosophy present in order to make judgments on it? It provides nothing other than certain sketches of such and such a willing, so that in respect to some willing an involuntary approbation becomes active in the observer, in respect to others an involuntary condemnation. . . .

* * *

. . . It [the theory of duties] immediately seizes free will in every form and, with the expression "duty," announces its constraint.

. . . Duty proclaims the constraint of will. By what? If this question were to be answered by asserting an original and inner *obligation,* i.e., a self-given law (not to mention a would-be *external* authority, which could produce only servitude insofar as the authority did not enforce moral concepts already *presupposed*) ; if, in short, a categorical imperative appeared as the principle of theory of duty—which is in fact unavoidable —then there would be a split in the will of the willing person, an obeying will and a commanding will. For commanding is willing; and anything else would be easier to explain than the singular precedence of one will over the other in the same subject. Constraint of the will by the same person's will? Someone might say that the one will is stable, the other wavering; the former essential, the latter accidental. Then, for the sake of order, the flexible would have to submit to the inflexible. Yet, if one attempted to make this credible and even to see into the transcendental depths of rational nature, then (assuming the truth of these disclosures) nothing other than a *law of nature* would be brought to light. Indeed, it might be fulfilled sometime in the distant future—for up until now, experience has never heard that the ostensibly commanding will in men knows how to rule better than does the one marked for obedience. *Now laws of nature yield natural necessity.* But this is not what those had in mind who undertook to detect in duty a constraint of will by one's own constraining will. They hoped rather to remind each and every one—even the most stubbornly insubordinate—of his duties, without however bringing into question whether he in fact governs himself according to duty.

* * *

To be sure, duty proclaims the constraint of will and means silencing any glory attaching to goods and virtues which was prompted by gratification and the bravado of self-conscious energy. But the servitude of one will and the mastery of another—this remains foreign to duty, whether master and servant are two or are melted into one. . . . Physical power may work inhibitively on the strength of will, but duty well knows that it has not the ability to compel. Leave aside, then—totally aside—the strength of will, its actions, and all degrees of its potentially affecting and being affected in conflict with a counter-operative power and strength; give up the thought of actuality; which could make itself felt in reality. What remains? Its bare *what*, its *image* (Bild) !

The image of the will is bound, in the fashion of images, to the involuntary judgment which appears in the person who apprehends [it].

And the willing person is provided with his own view, in which his image and self-judgment are simultaneously produced.

Judgment is not will and cannot command. But it can be seen censuring again and again—until, perhaps, a newly produced will decides to alter the old will to suit it. This decision is a command and the altered will seems to obey; both together appear as self-regulation. Duties, virtues, and goods align themselves accordingly, together with the concepts of a higher will, which, if it is only useful as a model, does not need to assume the rôle of basic power in the human mind in order to mold it. But it would be an all too impudent venture to raise legitimate religious questions here in the vestibules of practical philosophy.

*   *   *

I.

On Moral Taste

Here we have to do with the sharp distinction between taste and desire, so that the source of all authority over desire and will does not itself give the appearance of identity with them. It comes immediately to our notice that *desire seeks the future while taste decides on what is before it.* Also, it is for just this reason that only desire can properly be *satisfied,* while observance and *adherence to its instructions* are much more appropriate to taste.

*   *   *

The old saying, *ignoti nulla cupido,* tells us already that desire must above all *know* its object. . . . Suppose, for example, that someone desires to see a familiar person or hear a familiar piece of music. To a lesser degree, the person or music is present to him in fantasy during the desire, but only the actual seeing or hearing *completes* the representation. . . . The inner activity of representation, beginning with the point where it arises from the background of countless slumbering thoughts, through all the levels to which it alternately rises and sinks, pressing against an inner inhibition, to the point where perception—or fantasy, research, calculation, effort—places it in the center of consciousness in completed form; this activity of representing the desired is itself the desiring. One would be quite mistaken to think of a general faculty of desire as a workshop in which representations arrived at by other means are transformed into objects of desire by an incomprehensible operation.

Wherever this activity of a representation occurs, that which is represented is something desired. And what *is not* to be desired must *not* be represented with such pressing activity; rather, it must stand quietly in a completed representation, neither needing nor being capable of elevation and filling-out through accident or fancy. Taste possesses what it judges clearly before it; it has and holds the image on which it pronounces approval or disapproval; and also its verdict has a lasting ring which does not become silent until the image is taken away.

Now it is easy to understand what can be *given* to desire for its satisfaction; namely, repeated productions of the same representation, by which those already present are reinforced and freed from inhibitions by the pressure of contrary perceptions, feeling, and recollections. But it may appear odd that taste, which is not given anything, itself *gives* something and, as it were, adds something out of its own riches *via* its judgment of the finished representation of its object. Was this addition already present in the mind? Was displeasure with an ugly object already in stock and now, since precisely this object presents itself to intuition, simply hauled out in order to be received by it? Suppose that one wanted to indulge in such a peculiar opinion; then, hopefully, displeasure with the object would at least *coincide* straight off *with the representation* of it and not—one does not know when or why—only later become available to it. Thus the judgment would not be at all separated or distinguished from the object on which it is made; one would have the same case which occurs with feelings of pleasure and pain, where in fact what is felt cannot be apprehended in isolation from the feeling of it. For no one would imagine, e.g., in the case of a toothache, that it is the tooth which is sensed in the pain itself; but also not one would be in a position to differentiate the representation from the hurting.

* * *

There could be a theory of pleasure and pain in which *what* is pleasant or unpleasant was registered; a theory which had nothing whatsoever to do with desires and their satisfaction, since it would not bother at all about the activity of representations but only about the quality of representations; a theory which, for precisely this reason, must have the greatest similarity to a true theory of taste. For certainly the task of the latter is to exhibit in its simplest terms that which pleases and displeases.

* * *

Two antitheses have been extracted; the specification of the conditions under which all objects of judgments of taste must fall can lean on these. What is represented in a judgment of taste must be represented as complete and uninhibited; this distinguishes it from desire, which struggles up against inhibitions. What is represented in judgments of taste must also be separate from these judgments, i.e. represented without approval or disapproval, merely theoretically as an object of knowledge, as that *to which* the supervening judgment is directed. In this way it is distinguished from the pleasant and the unpleasant, which can only be grasped in the feeling itself. Now the question arises, how is it conceivable that approval or disapproval pertains to what is represented—without something indifferent coming into the picture as well?

* * *

Every part of that which pleases or displeases as a composite is indifferent taken individually, in itself; in a word, the *material* is indifferent but the *form* is subjected to aesthetic judgment. The best examples here are the simplest. In music for example, what is a fifth, a third, or any given interval of definite musical value? We know that none of the *isolated* tones whose relation forms the interval have, by themselves, the least bit of the character which is yielded by their sounding together.

* * *

Thus taste is not properly speaking a faculty for *giving* approval or disapproval. Rather, those judgments which are commonly understood by the concept "taste," in order to distinguish them collectively from other mental expressions, are effects of the completed representation of relations constructed from a plurality of elements.

* * *

Moral taste, as taste in general, is no different from poetic, musical, or plastic taste. But the *contrast between* taste and desire is specifically different in morals from what it is in the arts. In the latter case, elements of relations which are subjected to aesthetic judgment are outside us; in the former, they are in ourselves. In the arts, they are only objects which we notice and which may interest us, perhaps to the point of partiality, but we can always part from them if necessary and they can always be exchanged for other, better, and more appropriate [elements]. But in moral judgments, taste—as our own verdict—turns against ourselves; it touches on desires which are our own mental states. And if it is to be obeyed, then we must not merely tolerate the escape of an external object, but must break off our own activity and alter our mental state internally. With this demand, we step forth against ourselves and appear as our own adversary whenever, glimpsing our own desire and impulses, we disapprove of them.

* * *

II.

To What Extent Can Practical Philosophy Be Universal?

Taste is confronted with a relation: will it pronounce its approval or disapproval in a proposition which can be brought under the logical formulae, all A is B, no A is B?

Assume that it can; then the universality of practical maxims, axioms, and principles would be obvious without any further explanation, since it would be immediately given in or with the judgment of relations of will. Yet it would remain inexplicable how one could try to impose an order on the sum of these maxims, axioms, and principles in virtue of which they would have to appear logically prior and posterior to one another and derivable from one another. For every judgment of taste either stands alone—immediately certain and absolute—or does not exist at all; it receives no certainty from any other source.

* * *

If universality were a characteristic of aesthetic judgment, then the completed representation of the relation on which it is made would be impossible. For the view into the logically universal is a view of the incalculable multiplicity of that which might fall within the *compass* (*Umfang*) of a concept.

* * *

Just as no judgment of taste can be universal in itself, it is equally impossible to construct something out of several of them by abstraction and still retain an appearance of aesthetic validity. If the dissimilarities of relations on which several judgments are made are stripped off and the common properties retained, where, after this stripping-off, is the completed representation—on which alone taste depends? The garbled remains have no value. . . .

* * *

Universal concepts lose a lot of incidental specifications when they are abstracted from the real, and among these also the quantitative specification of their validity in particular cases. The concept *bright* may be abstracted from moonlight, candlelight, sunlight; the variation in degree by which brighter light is distinguished from the less bright is no longer to be found. . . . In the same way, from an endlessly varied set of psychological phenomena—inclination, wish, endeavour, drive, yearning, mood, intention, purpose, resolve—the universal concept of desire and will is derived. . . . Now if relations of desires are to be presented in universal concepts, so that judgments of taste can be made on them, then for complete apprehension it is required that all incidental considerations of the differences in these psychological states be suppressed; only the activity of the representation of that which is desired—and is the desired precisely because of this activity—is to be thought of. Harmonious or disharmonious relations between such activities will hover before us in judgment; they will fill us and call to mind no possible "more" or "less" in their degree. To that which hovers before us we will gladly give the honourable name of *practical idea,* denoting something which is immediately represented and apprehended in the mind, needing no sensuous intuition or accidental data of consciousness. But if a *single, actual* desire comes together with another single desire into a relation and appears before the judging eye, they will never present a pure idea. Rather, every one will be laden with all sorts of modifications which belong to psychological investigation. Now here will be found differences of degree—*stronger or weaker wills* and, in conformity with them, *more or less strongly pronounced replication of the ideas!*

BOOK I

THEORY OF IDEAS

——◄●►——

CHAPTER I

IDEA OF INNER FREEDOM
(Idee der innern Freyheit)

*   *   *

Our investigation began with the presupposition that there is a kind of judgment concerned with the will. Before we look around further for the relations into which the will enters, there is a relation right here before us, that between representative taste and the will which either corresponds to the representation or fails to.

Judgment and will are not two separate, two distinct persons, one of which gives an instruction and the other of which receives it. Rather, it is one and the same rational being which wills and also judges—judges and wills.

Let us conceive this rational being. Suppose a desire or resolve arises in him; immediately a *representation* of his desire and resolve stands before him. Glimpsing it and judging it are one; the judgment hovers over the will; if the judgment persists, the will proceeds to the act. Now the person has either affirmed by will what he rejected in judgment; or he has willingly refrained from what he prescribed in judgment; or will and judgment have unanimously affirmed, unanimously denied. In any case, we see the elements of the relation interpenetrated by one another in that, representing and replicating, they either agree with one another or conflict.

In the case of agreement, one can regard the will positively on the one hand as *activity,* negatively on the other as maintaining a particular direction to the *exclusion* of all *other* possible directions. . . .

Where there is lack of agreement, it is either the activity or maintenance which is missing. If it is the former, then only replication is lacking. As opposed to this, conflict occurs in the stricter sense, with reciprocal negation, where the activity takes an opposite direction. Who fails to recognize here the judgments of everyday life which reproach now weak wills, now evil wills?

If one attempts to separate the elements of the relation, however, reproach and approbation are silenced. Taken alone, neither insight nor obedience are pleasing. Or does it win approval when someone brings down judgments on another without a corresponding adherence to them in *himself?* At most, the *justice* of the judgment and the spiritual *power* whence it issues would be praiseworthy. But all strength pleases—about which more later. Does it win approval if, reversing the case, a person seeks out the advice of another and then *blindly follows it?* Trust is to be praised here—if, that is, this trust originated previously from insight.

*   *   *

The specific property peculiar to that relation which we have allowed the appellation 'inner freedom' lies precisely in the fact that it ties together two quite heterogeneous expressions of a rational being—taste and desire. The strict disparity between the two holds the elements of the relation apart; they can flow together just as little as they can lose one another—given that the relation *as such* does not disappear and its aesthetic character along with it.

*   *   *

It cannot remain unnoticed that an essential reference inhibits the relation just traced, in virtue of which this relation encompasses all the other ideas without being dedicated to any one in particular. Obedience should correspond to insight. *What* does this insight see into? Here is revealed the presupposition that there are still other relations which share in the sanction of taste. Which, we do not need to know at this point. . . .

. . . But it is through the second element of the same relation— obedience—that the idea of inner freedom actually becomes practical, i.e. a guide for decisions. The will should be obedient; it could not be disobedient; usually, it hovers between obedience and disobedience: this, then, is the tractable element. The other element, however, is rather rigid; true insight, taste, does not change.

CHAPTER II

IDEA OF PERFECTION
(Idee der Vollkommenheit)

*　　*　　*

One's own will is manifold to the extent that it has manifold objects. And if one includes what is willed in the concept of will, he can be easily misled into mixing relations among objects in with the relations of will. Not only would an endless set of relations spring up then, but the chief mistake would lie in their not being at all characteristic of the will; and in judging *them* the will as such would not be judged. Hence we must abstract from that which is willed; this leaves a question as to what in the will, as mere activity and endeavour, is left for judgment.

As endeavours, all wills are alike; they only repeat the same concept of effort and excitement in different examples, except in respect to their *strength*. The quantities of various efforts are measured against each other; some are weaker, some are stronger, some are more lasting, others more fleeting. Let us leave aside completely the question of what value the weaker or stronger might possess according to criteria yet to be discovered. *Only the relation of magnitude* between 'more' and 'less' activity, between weaker and more powerful impulses, will be taken up.

The judgment which apprehension of more and less leads to is only too familiar to men. They are blinded by strength; their eye becomes dulled to injustice, inequity, and malevolence. It is not worth their trouble to notice precisely *what* the weaker is; it is inferior in fact, as in their opinion simply because it is the weaker.

No question about it: in pure relation of magnitude, the stronger pleases in comparison with the weaker, the weaker displeases compared to the stronger; one or the others, depending upon which member one begins with in his comparison.

*　　*　　*

Quantity, relative degrees of which afford an opening to judgment, lies either in individual impulses, or in their sum, or in the system of them.

In individual impulses, energy is pleasing; in their sum, multiplicity; in their system, co-operation. The great man is triply great: his power has strength, richness, and health. With the less great, the locus of weakness is partially in debility, partially in limitations, partially in the dissipation or conflict of powers.

As individual impulses are measured against one another in the individual man, so one man is the measure of another when the two are together. One overshadows the other; but who is it whom no one else can overshadow? Who is perfect? Perfection itself, it would seem, lies in infinity. But this is self-contradictory, for the full is the complete and infinity is beyond completeness. However, every finite measure is made full by that which is equal to it in magnitude. A man is perfect *according to his own measure* if his individual efforts equal one another; if further his individual efforts, taken together, fill out the sphere of concepts to which they point (satisfying the expectations which they arouse); if, finally, his individual efforts, working together, bring forth the greatest possible effort of which they are capable. The imperfect man is apparent as such whenever he is compared with another who excels him in some respect, or with the concept of that which would excel him.

. . . The man who is working towards his own cultivation—if he is not bent on social comparisons—is reluctant to part from the idea of a next higher stage which, beyond the present stage, he has yet to reach. In this manner, the forward-looking view which constantly accompanies him leads him ever further—into infinity, if his powers allow. Perfection is won at every step, but in the winning it is lost again.

*   *   *

CHAPTER III.

IDEA OF BENEVOLENCE
(Idee des Wohlwollens)

A rational being who continually perfects himself is constantly short of his self-imposed standard. But if he perseveres in a state which, in virtue of a thorough-going parity, meets his own measure (any external standard being accidental), then judgment, encountering no 'more' and 'less,' remains completely silent. And inner freedom becomes empty, for with the disappearance of the judgment to which it refers, it must disappear at the same time. If one were to allow room for the inadmissable thought that relations among the *objects* of manifold efforts could be ascribed to the rational being himself, such that a harmony in the former is imparted to the latter, nevertheless those persons who possess only inner freedom and perfection will cease to please as soon as we withdraw our notice from the contrast of members in the relations and attend to the person as an individual, i.e. as a single element lacking a second with which to form a relation.

The question now arises whether, as we move along, we shall encounter another idea according to which a rational being could appear as an enduring object of approval, if possible without changing our point of view.

In order to progress it is necessary to move beyond the will of one and the same being to the external wills of other rational beings. It would seem that the only relations which can arise in this manner are those which pertain to several persons *as several*. Hence no value *belonging exclusively* to a single person may be derived from them.

But a brief reflection reminds us that, if the relations between the wills of several persons are to be meaningful to them, then above all one must know about the other, one must represent to himself the will of the other. Now if a relation between a *represented,* external will and one's own will should exist, without also taking the *actual* external will into consideration, then this relation would occupy a middle position between those relations which assume only a single person and those—yet to be discovered—in which several persons may appear together. Such a relation would lie wholly contained in one person, since what is represented is certainly contained in the person who represents it. To this extent, it could help determine a value peculiar to this person. . . .

The relation of which we speak is quite well known to the common judgment of men in society. The expression "goodness" designates something which occasionally appears as kindliness, occasionally as *good will,* receiving much esteem in the second case and little in the first. Goodness itself, as pure moral beauty, hovers over both. Clearly, it is just this which assimilates external wills, dedicates itself to them, and accompanies them harmoniously with its own will. It is also clear that goodness is self-subsistent and does not depend on the success of its attempts, nor on the resultant sentiment, nor even on the conception, true or false, of what the other person might have actually wanted. There are times when goodness does not know the world; it may happen now and then that, meaning well, it did ill. . . .

But how can benevolence arise in the human spirit at all? How, as a phenomenon, is it connected with other phenomena? This question has nothing in common with exposition of the idea. To conceive of a relation between a represented, external will and the will of him who represents it, such that what the other wills, merely as such, is willed on his behalf; and to conceive of this with approval, is all but a single act of thought. Or are there spirits in whom approbation has become so weak that it is necessary, in order to bring it out, to oppose this idea to the ugliest of all relations—malevolence—perhaps in the form of envy or of gloating over the misfortunes of others? For these [emotions], at least, are so insulting to every eye and with such immediate force that no one will have the time to meditate on trivial speculative reasons for his displeasure. In comparison to benevolence, these unpleasant relations have the advantage, from the thinker's and observer's point of view, of clarity and lack of ambiguity. Their elements cannot dissolve into one another; the envious and the envied are undoubtably two. On the other hand, the benevolent man and the person to whom he is dedicated can often—where bonds of love, family, or even common interests enter in—appear as blended into one another, as one soul in two bodies. Thus, even the purest benevolence is usually object of suspicion among men. . . .

It has already been shown which place this idea assumes among the others. It is the only one in which an approval is voiced which rests on an apprehension without glances to the side. There is no question here of material for the form or of a reference point for a relation; there is no disappearing into enduring states, even with a change in viewpoint. For it would be false to regard the value of benevolence as dependent on the value of the external, represented will. Rather, it is obvious that this simple element of the relation, taken by itself, could have no value. Hence we should refrain from asking whether he—the object of our benevolence—has earned it. If he earned it and one showed an interest in him for that reason, then recognition of his merit might be praise-worthy: only there is no trace of benevolence in this. Now in order to forestall objections from the other side, it is necessary that the external, represented will be found blameless; otherwise, the innerly free man's benevolence would find itself inhibited in its expression. Goodness is goodness precisely because it is good to an external will immediately and without motives.

*　　*　　*

CHAPTER IV.

IDEA OF JUSTICE
(*Idee des Rechts*)

A new field is opened. Relations come forth which are not so conspicuous to the eye of those who are striving for their own improve-ment; but these appear the most interesting to the outward view of the worldly-minded. They do not recommend themselves much to the former because they awaken no approbation, only displeasure. But they mean a great deal to the latter because they touch on property and commerce.

*　　*　　*

It is no longer a question of represented, external wills, but of the actual wills of several rational beings. It is obvious right away that these wills cannot enter into actual relations without mediation. For whatever re-mained enclosed in the consciousness of each would be nothing to the other. The wills must break out into an external world common to all.

*　　*　　*

. . . The activity of a will may reach all the way over to another will so that the activity of the one injures the other—and not just accidentally as a consequence of change brought about in the sensible sphere, but due to an intention on the part of another which is carried out in an act. Then we have a connexion between two wills which may, perhaps, exhibit a relation, without having to think of the other will as if it, too, were expressing itself in action. On the other hand, if the activity of the first will remains stuck, as it were, in the sensible world, and does not penetrate through it to the will opposite—at least not *as* will, not intentionally—then something is lacking in order to connect them, a supplement which will have to come from the second will. This would be the case when both actively expressed themselves and, as they accidentally encountered one another in the sensible world, fell into a relation. The last of these possible cases is insofar the simplest, in that it does not require an expression of a will as far-reaching as does the first-mentioned. Thus it will be taken up first. It will lead to the idea of justice, the other to the idea of equity. . . .

According to our assumption, several rational beings—two, let us say—unintentionally and accidentally form a relation in that their wills assert themselves in the common, sensible world. That they must arrive at the same point is obvious; forces in the sensible world would not connect anything or mediate anything if they passed by one another without conflict. Now the same point, the meeting-place, may be assumed to be as simple as you like, as may the manner of disposing of this point from either side. For whatever either of the two persons might wish to undertake in respect to the third point, it is only relevant insofar as they mutually hinder one another. . . .

Now we assume that both know of each other and recognize each other as mutually hindering wills. . . . But if they know that they are hindering each other, they still desire their goal even with this knowledge; hence they desire the non-being of the hindrance; each wants the negation of the other's will. Thus they are in *conflict*. Conflict is distinct from malevolence. It is an unfortunate relation between several actual wills; the other, like benevolence, lies wholly in the mind of the individual who opposes himself internally to a *represented* external will, even if it is not an actual one. In pure conflict, the wills regard one another only as hindrances to their goals; thus if they did not meet at the external point in question, each would leave the other untouched. In malevolence, however, one will is the immediate object of the other. Hence malevolence is one-sided in itself. Conflict, on the other hand, is always two-sided and ceases as soon as one of the parties gives way. The individual contender can even please as a hero due to his strength and his bravery. In poetic descriptions of war, elevation of the greatness which is revealed in battle alternates constantly with imprecation of the relation itself *in* which the lauded persons put themselves. In men's everyday conversations both are found wondrously enough blended. But whoever grasps the mere relation between conflicting wills and ignores the quantities of powers will not hesitate to pronounce the judgment: *conflict displeases*.

What does this judgment point to? What must happen in order to avoid the displeasure? For no one will deny *that* a practical instruction is embedded in it, least of all the contenders themselves if they possess inner freedom and are not blinded by their own brilliance.

First, this much is clear: as the case stands before us, there is no difference between the contenders; everything is equal on both sides. Hence the practical instruction must apply equally to both.

Each conceives in his own will the will of the other which inhibits him. This negation must be negated, so that obedience complies with the displeasure. Thus, each allows for the will of the other, knowing that the other inhibits him; that is, he allows himself to be inhibited and foregoes his own disposal of the third [point], leaves it at the disposal of the other. This relinquishment is not benevolence but the assumption that the other will pursue his goal; precisely for this reason, one's own complaisance becomes a condition of avoiding conflict.

If everything goes right, this happens on both sides; each gives in to the other and conflict is avoided doubly. There is nothing in this now which can displease. Let us be wary of giving an ear too hastily to well-meaning desires which might regret somewhat that now neither accomplishes his goal, leaving the useful object lying unused in the middle. It may happen that one notices the relinquishment of the other and then appropriates the relinquishment AS *with the will of the other*. It can happen that, if both have already given ground, yet one perceives the concessions made *sooner* than the other and—since now he can do it without conflict—takes up his own again in order to pursue his original goal. Then a possession is established which cannot be immediately annulled, either by benevolence or any other practical idea. One has conceded; in consequence of this concession, the other perseveres in his original will. If the conflict is now to be renewed, it can only be raised by the first person as he takes back his concession; thus he promotes displeasure in the conflict. Accordingly, the practical instruction from this displeasure, which now applies to him alone, would have moved to his side. If he is not to be judged thus, his relinquishment, once it is done, must have the validity of a rule, a boundary which he may not step across and which excludes him from that which he has conceded to the other. In a word, there is a *lawful boundary* between the two.

Law *(Recht)* is the concordance of several wills, thought of as a rule, which avoids conflict.

Hopefully no one will ask by what sign recognition on the one side and seizure on the other might be declared. Human language does not belong to the theory of ideas. The relationship is simply between the wills themselves and they must be thought of as standing in it immediately, despite any mediation which might be indispensable between them as beings in nature. The person who has recognized that something belongs to the other knows best that, to the extent that he swerves from the attitude of concession, he would be inwardly renewing the conflict. On the other hand, whoever would ascribe a right to himself had better make sure that he is not mistaken about the apparent sign of the other's recognition which has taken place and on which alone he can base a right.

*   *   *

It is clear enough, then, that the origin of all rights is by no means to be sought in *material* rights which someone confers upon *himself* and in virtue of which he may exclude everyone else; it is to be sought instead in relations which are formed *between* two persons bilaterally, and which are valid *as such* only *in the way* they were formed.

*   *   *

All that is left now is discussion of the question, do rights inherently warrant protection by means of *force*? This may receive a short and definite "no." . . . The coercionist sees coercion merely as a means to recoup his own. Here he forgets that the other's rights, which his coercion breaches, subsist as rights in themselves, without regard to the aim for whose sake one allows himself to violate them. . . . Concessions must obviate conflict as often as it can be raised; every single object of a possible conflict is to be regarded as a demand for self-subsistent and complete relinquishment, one which cannot be cancelled by the breaking of other relations and which cannot be drawn into their ruins. The extent to which coercion is nevertheless permissible will be covered by other theories* in the sequel.

*   *   *

CHAPTER V.

IDEA OF EQUITY
(Idee der Billigkreit)

Unintentional encounters of several wills, when they conflict over the disposal of a third external point, lead, as has been shown, to the possibility of establishing a relation of justice. Also, it has already been said that if an *intentional act* by a rational being is assumed for the sake of contrast, then it would be premature to think of an active expression of the other will along with it. A connexion between both wills is already present insofar as the action of one rational being penetrates the common medium and intrudes on the will of the other, so that the one is affected and either welcomes the intention which affects him or the opposite. Having presupposed this connexion, we are in a region as yet untouched

* Ed. note. The theories referred to are not stated in the translated excerpts published below.

by the previous judgments. If there is an aesthetic relation to be found here then it is a new one, and judgment of it will stand out with an authority all its own.

But we can ask, is the connexion between the will which deliberately acts and the will which is affected by its intent really a relation? Suppose it is not; then we would have to look for an appropriate second member in order to build the relation. Suppose further that during the search we become aware of a judgment of taste; then, according to the principles of the Introduction, a relation is really at hand. . . .

First, not every intent is a goal, though every goal is an intent. Goals are willed immediately; intentions are often willed as means to other goals. An immediate act of will, if it refers to another rational being, can be willing of good or willing of ill. Intentions can include one or the other or neither. Thus they can please or displease or be indifferent in themselves, as dispositions. These differences in judgment have to be set completely aside for now, at least in abstraction. For here we are not talking about the inner relations of a rational being to itself, only about an external relation which obtains among several wills. Our concern is with intention *as act;* if the intention, as a disposition, is also a goal and, as such, praiseworthy or blameworthy, then this is to be ignored for the time being.

Now intention as act connects both wills; nevertheless, it *does not* establish a relation in which *the two wills* are to be regarded as members. Rather, both wills go together as criteria to determine the single concept of *this* act. Act in general refers both to the doer and what is done; it is *what* it is thanks to both. In our case, the agent is that will which intends to affect the other. And what is done is the good or ill which the affected will sustains and which is only *really* good or ill by measure of how it is really sustained. An act is a good act if it *both* intends and produces good, an evil act if it has evil as *both* intent and consequence. Whenever the result diverges from the intention, and to the degree that it does so, it is neither one nor the other and our presupposition is not satisfied. For if the intent is present only in the mind and may be judged as such, the consequence lies wholly in the feelings of the person affected and may awaken our sympathy. But the requisite connexion of both wills is missing; the medium has not provided the conditions for it; it has substituted a mere natural phenomenon for the aesthetic relation.

If on the other hand the medium faithfully conveys the good or ill which the intention imparted to it, if what was willed is realized in the rational being affected, as movements decided upon are realized in the hand or foot . . . then, to be sure, we have an intentional act which is simultaneously determined by the doing and the done; but it must seem next that, with this act, we still have no *relation,* only a member of some

future relation, perhaps, if a second appropriate member can be discovered. And how shall the second be found? It might easily happen that
if someone set out to look, the requital which is called for by deliberate
doing of good or ill would present itself to him. For no one, if he stops to
think of the concepts of *reward* and *punishment,* will hesitate to affirm
that the unrequited act displeases. . . .

*   *   *

If the deliberate good deed or misdeed is not indifferent, then it is dis-
pleasing, so long as it stands there unrequited; thus it provides a whole
relation with no more missing members, since there is material for judgment. In order to find the hidden second member, one may not analyse
the previously constructed concept back into its properties, which are
well bound together in it; this could only destroy it. *Another* concept will
have to be found which does not enter into the content of the previous
one at all, but which is infallibly thought along with it due to a necessary
connexion—a truly second, purely separated member of a relation which
always accompanies the first all the same. And it doubtless will be found,
for the judgment of taste guarantees its presence.

An act cannot be thought of as an act if something is not *done
through* it which, *without* it, *would not* have happened. This negation
points to the *contrary state of affairs* which, *before* the act, might have
really existed. To be sure, there is no way of specifying this more accurately; still, there is a concept of a situation in which, independent of
the act, two mere wills oppose one another; and this bare concept suffices to form the contrast through which the act appears *as act* by cutting
the situation short by interrupting and wounding it, as it were. And it is
this contrast which serves the judgment of taste as an object, as surely
as the judgment of taste is produced from the apprehension of the concept of the act.

The act, as an intervention, displeases. The magnitude of the act
determines the magnitude of the displeasure. Where no good or ill is
intended, or where none is sensed, no will intervenes in another; there is
no act here, and displeasure just as little. But displeasure grows with the
good or ill which is met with in both intention and result, and indeed
in the same manner with benefaction as with malefaction. The disposition
of the benefactor may please as well and the well-beng of the recipient
may gladden us; even the strength of the active power may please. It is not
too easy to abstract from this and to retain simply the act as act, but it
becomes easier as there appears, from a practical instruction extracted
from judgment, the symbol in which displeasure with the act finds its
expression.

If displeasure could work on the act as a force works, then it would
inhibit it. As does every resistance, it would work on it in an opposite

direction, endeavouring by retrogression to cancel the act's progress. Now displeasure is not a power; the act, however, actually happens. But after it is completed, there remains the thought of the regress by which it would have been cancelled. A positive which displeases drives one to the concept of the negative equal to it; together they come to zero. Thus, return of the same quantum of good or ill from the recipient to the agent is what the judgment indicates. Requital is the symbol in which displeasure is expressed: an apparent positive in which a negation is veiled.

* * *

CHAPTER VII.

TRANSITION FROM THE ORIGINAL TO THE DERIVED IDEAS
(Uebergang von den ursprünglichen zu den abgeleiteten Ideen)

As called for by the first principles, the conceivable relations of will have been sought out up until now such that a progression was observed from the simplest presuppositions to others increasingly composite. The first relation was that between judgment itself and the will in general, which either corresponds to it or not; the second was between several efforts which, already in one and the same rational being, measure one another by magnitude; the third lay so to speak on the edge of progress to a plurality of rational beings, comprehending a merely *represented* external will together with the will of the person who represents it; the fourth arose from the encounter of several actual wills at an external object; the fifth followed from the deliberate act whereby one will does good or harm to another. Can this progression be carried further? If so, what would come up for judgment?

* * *

For the sake of progress, more than two wills had to be assumed. But it is quite clear that among these, any two which meet with or without intent will always repeat the previous relations; accordingly, we could only expect further ramifications of what has already been specified by justice and equity. Thus it is apparent that the sequence of simple ideas is closed.

On the other hand, a more composite judgment now enters in, one which will proceed with greater certainty after its single elements have been properly clarified.

* * *

In order at least to open the field of this investigation as wide as possible, we will permit ourselves an assumption which at first may seem to be a mere fiction, but which is largely realized in human existence. The assumption is: one can regard the plurality of rational beings as many or as one, as one wishes, and in the latter case, their plural willing is comparable to the several efforts and resolves of one and the same rational being.

. . . Perfect communication is not the first and most natural assumption which accompanies the idea of a *plurality* of rational beings. Rather, the kind of mediation which was sufficient to allow the appearance of justice and equity deserves first place in the sequence of presuppositions which we have to make. Hence there will be a different ordering of ideas as they are applied from that in which they first occurred. Justice will precede and equity will come next; then the first three ideas will be added in reverse order, so that the idea of inner freedom finishes and, appropriately, completes the retrogression from the relations of several wills to those which require a single center of consciousness.

When we think of a group of willing beings gathered on common ground which attracts them and busies them with its many products, and offers *each* of these products to *all*, then we can expect first that they will fall into frequent conflicts. Fulfillment of this thought yields the idea of a *society of law* (Rechtsgesellschaft).

Yet even if legal boundaries were drawn and the activity of the one were enclosed in greater, of the other in smaller spheres, the activity and inactivity of those enclosed would still have effects beyond the boundaries, and any intent or negligence which lay in this efficacy would summon up a displeasure in the unrequited acts. If the displeasure is to be obliterated, and the group undertakes to see after this, then they would find themselves united in an institution which one may call a *system of rewards* (Lohnsystem).

Now if the affairs of the group were ordered like this beyond reproach, there would still be little joy in their contemplation. The benevolent observer would ask for quite another arrangement than the bulwark of law, merely thrown up to preclude conflict. He would want to see the greatest possible sum of well-being achieved and an administration of resources established which was the most expedient to this end. And he would be sure of his own approval of these benevolent wishes. . . . Thus the idea of an *administrative system* (Verwaltungssystem) arises.

The increase of well being tends to elicit manifestations of energy; their propagation, their cooperation or conflict shows. The judgment that must be applied according to the idea of perfection in its turn. Concern for living up to this idea will unite the many into a *cultural system* (Cultursystem).

But where efforts to further the adequate realization of justice, equity, and benevolence have become a communal matter, there is communal obedience to communal insight, there is the inner freedom of many who seem to have a single spirit. The split between one and the other, each of whom only follows *his* judgment and wants to be left to *his* conscience—this empty, dead opposition has disappeared: the united people compose an *ensouled society* (beseelte Gesellschaft).

It may be that every state should become an ensouled society. But that is not our concern here. The state is characterized by its coercive power. Ideas have no power. It is all the more important to avoid confusion of the state with the social ideas just indicated because these apply not only to the large agglomeration of men, but to every small and smallest association as well, familial no less than civic. To put it the other way around, associations, no matter what they might be, cannot acquire any moral value except by realization of the ideas. It can be quite necessary and even momentous to consider what means are proper to each type in order to do this. But the judgment of the relations of will does not change with the means; it does not know these means, but arises only with respect to the end; and approval will only grow as imitation of the models approaches completeness.

Bibliography

ADAMS, SIR JOHN, *The Herbartian Psychology Applied to Education,* London, Isbister and Co., Ltd., 1898.

COMPAYRÉ, GABRIEL, *Herbart and Education by Instruction: a Criticism,* New York, T. Y. Crowell and Co., 1907. (*Herbart et l'éducation par l'instruction,* Paris, P. Delaplane, 1903.)

DARROCH, ALEXANDER, *Herbart and the Herbartian Theory of Education,* London, New York and Bombay, Longmans, Green and Co., 1903.

DE GARMO, CHARLES, *Herbart and the Herbartians,* New York, Charles Scribner and Sons, 1895.

MACVANNEL, JOHN ANGUS, *The Educational Theories of Herbart and Froebel,* New York, Columbia University Press, 1905.

XI

J. S. MILL

J OHN STUART MILL WAS THE ELDEST CHILD of a famous father. The latter, James Mill, made an important contribution to the history of British India; played a leading role in the movement for social reform in Britain, headed by Jeremy Bentham; and wrote an influential book which has a permanent place in the history of psychology, *Analysis of the Phæ-nomena of the Human Mind.* Its thesis is that all mental phænomena which are not impressions are copies or ideas of them, and that the occurrence of ideas is explained by laws of association. He employed his psychology to produce in his son a person devoted to the general happiness, and the son reports that his friends sometimes referred to him as an artificial man. The artificer was his father, and the rearing provided by so eminent a parent for so important a son is certainly one of the more remarkable episodes in the practice of that art.

In his *Autobiography,* especially the first three chapters, John Stuart Mill describes the content and method James Mill gave to his education. At the age of three, he was learning Greek, and only a little later, arithmetic and history; from eight to twelve, Greek and Latin literature in the original, poetry in English, history, algebra, geometry, differential calculus, other branches of mathematics, and the natural sciences; from twelve to fourteen, logic, economics, and rhetoric—as well as the earlier subjects in more detail. These studies were pursued under the careful tutelage of James Mill. Each was carried out in such a way as to assure strong associative bonds between the ideas involved in it. Mill says that his purpose in describing his education is to demonstrate how much time is wasted in childhood. Since, according to his own statement, he was rather below than above the average in mental ability, he was sure that any child could do as well as he.

At the age of fourteen, Mill left England for travel on the Continent where, among the French, he was deeply impressed with the importance of untrammelled spontaneity and individuality—traits of character he found lacking among the English. After a year, he returned to England; and, for a short while, continued studying under the direction but not the tutelage of his father. In 1823, at an early age, he took a job as clerk with the East India Company; and remained with it, rising to a position of great responsibility, until the government took over direct control of relations with India some thirty-five years later. Mill's position with the East India Company allowed considerable leisure. He employed it in discussion of intellectual and social problems with his friends, writing for journals, and composing *A System of Logic* (1843) and *Principles of Political Economy* (1848). Sometime after the dissolution of the East India Company, he spent one term in Parliament where he was particularly concerned to represent the interests of the workers whom, along with women, he regarded as greatly oppressed.

In 1826, at the age of twenty, Mill went through a mental and emotional crisis. He suddenly came to feel that the realization of the social ideal to which he had been so clearly consecrated would not make him in the least happy. His analytical turn of mind had destroyed the associative bond which had made him feel pleasure at the thought of the happiness of all. The education provided by his father could not compensate for the lack of a spontaneous desire for the welfare of society. He began to read poetry and other imaginative literature, and the emotional life he found there seems to have restored his physical equilibrium.

In 1830, he met Harriet Taylor, an accomplished, intellectually inclined, married woman with whom he formed a close friendship. Some regarded it as scandalous, but Mill explicitly insists that such a view had no basis in fact. Mrs. Taylor played an important part in his thought and in the writing of many of his articles and books. They were married some 21 years later—after the death of Mr. Taylor for whom they both entertained affection and respect. Their marriage concluded with her death seven years later; and, except for his term in Parliament, Mill spent the rest of his life in semi-retirement, chiefly at Avignon in the company of his stepdaughter, Helen Taylor. He published *On Liberty* in

1859, *Utilitarianism* and *Representative Government* in 1861, and *An Examination of Sir William Hamilton's Philosophy* in 1865. He carried on a large correspondence; and with it, as with these books, Helen Taylor was a constant and devoted assistant. He was born in London in 1806, and he died at Avignon in 1873.

EDUCATIONAL THEORY

MILL DEVOTES NO LARGE work to education. He discusses it, however, in parts of several of his books, and at length in a good many essays. In one of the latter, "The Inaugural Address," delivered to the University of St. Andrews, on his installation as rector in 1867, he tells us that by "education" in a large sense he means both the deliberate effort to perfect human nature and the effect upon human beings of their cultural and physical environment.[2] Here I shall bring together his thought on this subject and present it as a theory concerning this deliberate effort and this unintended effect.

STATEMENTS OF FACT

According to Mill, all statements are about observable facts, and holding them to be true or false is always a matter of empirical evidence. His educational theory includes assertions about human nature, society, historical progress, and the condition of schools. Let us consider his description of the facts of human nature.

H u m a n   n a t u r e

Mill holds that a human being is a mind and a body. The mind is composed of mental states, of sensations, ideas, thoughts, desires, emo-

[1] The reader with general interest in Mill's thought about education may wish to read the following essays: "Inaugural Address Delivered to the University of St. Andrews," *Dissertations and Discussions*, Vol. I, Henry Holt & Co., New York, 1874; "Professor Sedgwick's Discourse on the Studies of the University of Cambridge," *Dissertations and Discussions*, Vol. I, John W. Parker & Son, London, 1859; "On Genius," *Monthly Repository*, Vol. VI, 1832 (signed "Antiquus"); "Miss Austin's Translation of M. Cousin's Report on the State of Public Instruction in Prussia," *Monthly Repository*, Vol. VIII, Charles Fox, London; an unheaded article in the *Globe* (October 23, 1835), p. 3. Those with more specific interests may consult "Whately's Elements of Logic," *Westminster Review*, Vol. IX (January, 1828); and (for Mill's view on India's need for education) "Minutes of Evidence Taken before the Select Committee on the Affairs of the East India Company" (*Parliamentary Papers*, 1831–32, Vol. IX). For more detailed references to these and other aspects of Mill's thought, the reader may look at *Bibliography of the Published Writings of John Stuart Mill*, by MacMinn, Hainds & McCrimmon, Northwestern University, Evanston, Illinois, 1945. Much about education may be found also in Mill's *Autobiography*, *On Liberty*, *Utilitarianism*, and *A System of Logic* (Book VI).
[2] "Inaugural Address," *Dissertations and Discussions*, Vol. IV, pp. 332–34.

tions, and the like. Mental states and their relations to each other are the only things we can observe in the mind; and statements about the latter can be no more than descriptions of these states and relations.[3] Some such statements are found in common sense; and others, of a more general kind, make up the science of psychology.

P s y c h o l o g y

This science contains five laws which govern the relations between mental states. First, whenever any sensation or impression has once occurred in a mind, another state exactly like it, but less intense, may also occur in that mind independently of the cause of the former. Thus, once we have seen the plum tree, we are capable of entertaining an idea of it—something we do whenever we remember or think of it. The plum tree causes the first state of mind, but is not present to us when we attend to it in recollection or thought. And any mind contains, in addition to sensations, only those states which sensations thus allow.

LAWS OF ASSOCIATION. The other four laws are laws of association and govern the relations between impressions and ideas as well as between ideas only. The first is that an impression or idea tends to excite an idea of something similar to it; the impression or idea of the plum tree may usher in an idea of the cherry tree in the garden of one's childhood. The second is that any one impression or idea of a group whose members have been frequently conjoined in our experience, either simultaneously or in immediate succession, tends to excite the ideas of the other members; the sound or thought of thunder introduces the idea of lightning. The third is that the more intense an idea or impression is when it first occurs to us along with others, the less frequently the group need recur in order that one member should bring others to mind; the mere thought of a wound experienced only once suffices to call up its entire setting.[4] These three laws are stated in the *Logic*.

In *An Examination of Sir William Hamilton's Philosophy* Mill adds a fourth law.[5] It is that of two phænomena which have never appeared separately to us, and which have frequently appeared together, the idea of one always excites that of the other; so that they, themselves, are inseparable and lead us to believe that the facts they represent are likewise inseparable. Everything we can be aware of is either a sensation or an idea derived from it; and ideas are ushered into the mind on particular occasions through association with the sensations or other ideas.

[3] John Stuart Mill, *A System of Logic*, Eighth Edition, Harper & Brothers, New York, 1874, I, II, §8, pp. 56–57.
[4] *Ibid.*, VI, IV, §3.
[5] John Stuart Mill, *An Examination of Sir William Hamilton's Philosophy*, Henry Holt and Company, New York, 1874, vol. I, pp. 83, 234–36, 310–11.

This association occurs under the conditions that we have frequently experienced things as similar, as contiguous, as intense, or as always conjoined.

SENSATIONS AND INSTINCTS. Some mental states are not the products of association. These are sensations and instincts.[6] We know that they are caused by states of the body, i.e., of the brain and nervous system. The *idea* of red and the *idea* of hunger can occur to us only if we have had *impressions* of red and hunger; and while they may possess some causal basis in bodily states, the only explanation for their occurrence presently tenable, lies in their association with other mental states, and in their being conditioned by impressions. These latter, sensations and instincts, depend on states of the body; and are not produced in experience by association. They are, thus, prior to it; and as such, they constitute the materials out of which, through association, the mind comes into existence.

ACQUIRED DESIRE. A characteristic of some of these native impressions helps to fill out the mind. We speak of a person as more or less sensitive; in doing so, we refer to the vividness of his sensations. And this vividness determines what mental states will be associated. It puts them forcibly to the fore in consciousness; and given their similarity, contiguity, or constant conjunction, makes their ideas more likely of association than would their dim presence in the background. Now, instincts constitute a species of desire. Desire is the pleasantness of an idea, as aversion is its painfulness;[7] and instincts are unlearned desires and aversions. The desire to secure one's own pleasure and avoid one's own pain is an instinct, and a corresponding interest in the welfare of others is not. Nonetheless, one who is vividly conscious of the pleasure or pain of others associates it by similarity with his own; and in this way, the thought of the welfare of anyone whatever awakens a desire for it as spontaneous as the unlearned desire for one's own. Association creates a desire for the welfare of others out of the material of instinctual egoism. The laws of physiology together with the accidents of history determine what sensations and instincts the mind contains prior to experience. The vividness of sensations together with the laws of association and the accidents of experience add acquired desires to the stock of instincts native to the mind, and determine the cluster of mental states in which it presents itself.[8]

6 Mill, *Logic,* VI, IV, §4.
7 J. S. Mill, *Utilitarianism,* The Liberal Arts Press, Inc., N.Y., 1948, p. 49.
8 *Ibid.,* pp. 19, 40–41. Mill does not seem to recognize (*Logic,* VI, IV, §4) that his sensitivity is nothing more than vividness of sensation; and that in speaking of it as enabling certain kinds of association, he is simply saying that one law of association, that of intensity, enhances the working of others.

WILL AND HABIT. The will is closely related to desire, but different from it. Desire both instinctual and learned is passive; in desire we do nothing but feel pleasure or pain and act as they command. On the other hand, will is an active phænomenon. In willing, we endeavor to secure only those things whose ideas are pleasant. But through the force of habit, will can become dependent of desire; and we often find ourselves willing out of habit what we no longer desire at all.[9] Mill accounts for the conative aspects of the mind in terms of sensation, instincts, and association, together with the concepts of acquired desire, habit, and will.

EMOTION. Although he believes that there is not yet conclusive evidence for it, Mill thinks the feelings and emotions are probably produced through association.[10] In instinct and acquired desire, pleasure and pain attach themselves to certain ideas. For the hungry man an idea of food is pleasant. But when these ideas are associated with certain others, other emotions and feelings arise. For the hungry man, the idea of food associated with the idea of place close by produces hope; with that of others who desire it, fear; with that of certainty of securing it, joy; with that of his inability to do so, despair, etc. Thus, with the assumption that all ideas are derived from impressions and combined through association, Mill endeavors to account for the way in which mental states come and go, appear and disappear, in a series which constitutes a mind.

The complexes of mental states produced by association are sometimes like machines, sometimes like chemical compounds. The idea of the plum tree calls up the idea of a cherry tree; and this, the idea of the swing which hangs in it. Every part of this complex is manifest in it, as are, also, the transitions from one part to another. It is like a machine. The idea of the visual shape of an object, on the other hand, is produced by association of ideas which are not manifest in it. Some of its components are ideas derived from impressions of touch. Similarly, joy bears within it no traces of the components whose association gives rise to it—no sign of personal gratification of some desire, or of confidence about the means to its satisfaction. Visual shape and joy are more like chemical compounds than they are like machines; and Mill thinks the analogy between psychology and chemistry more useful in developing explanation by association with the analogy with mechanics, drawn by earlier associationists.

CHARACTER. The mind is a series of mental states held together, sometimes mechanically and sometimes chemically, by the laws of association; and no mind is quite like any other. No person is stocked with instincts precisely identical in direction and vivacity with those of

[9] *Ibid.*, pp. 49–50.
[10] *Logic*, VI, ɪᴠ, §§3, 4.

others; nor do sensations present themselves alike to all. Consequently, the cluster of desires, habits, resolutions, tastes, and emotions which, from moment to moment, and out of materials prior to experience, association is bringing into existence, is never precisely repeated from one person to another. Character is uniqueness of interest; and since all possess it, every person possesses character. But the expression of character is a matter of degree; and the well developed character is a person who deliberately endeavors to fulfil his unique impulses, while the ill developed character hides his uniqueness behind the mask of conventional propriety. There is no such thing as a single nature manifested by all human beings. Rather, it is the nature of a human being to be a unique cluster of interests, arising out of universal laws of association working upon native instincts and sensations.[11]

Society

Within society, individuality has always struggled for expression. At first, its opponent was the authority of the king or ruler. The Greek city, Rome, the mediæval polity—all advanced the view that individual rights did not depend upon his will. In England, the community limited the royal power by requiring cooperation with it of some other element in the constitution. Later still, the government came to be regarded as exercising the power of the people, as possessed of no independent authority whatever. In all this, individuality or character was struggling to establish an area within which it might be free, i.e., within which authority could not legitimately oppose it.

Government is not the only force opposed to liberty. In democracies like the United States of America and Great Britain, it is opposed by the authority of the majority view on any subject. The latter reigns in matters of legislation and can easily invade the liberty of the minority by improper use of legislature and courts. It possesses, in any case, great informal power. There is a wide-spread fear to be oneself. It is manifest in the eagerness to conform to the majority view in all matters—from religion, through science and art, to convention in dress and sports. It feeds upon the rewards offered to propriety and joins the majority in order to destroy that unique self of which it is a secret part. A powerful class, e.g., the middle class of Great Britain, may serve as well as the majority; and its inculcation of respectability has served to destroy the individuality of those who have put on its sentiments in order to advance in the world. The majority opinion, and that of a dominant class, have net yet become identified with government policy; but there is great danger that the demand for uniformity may become identified with that

---

11 *Ibid.*, VI, II, §§2, 3; also, *On Liberty*, pp. 59–60.

policy wherever democracies exist to express the majority view, or to be controlled by a dominant class.[12]

Concerning economic problems, Mill advocated the development of socialism in the form of industrial cooperation. When he wrote, some held that the class which owned the means of production naturally adopted the responsibility for caring for workers. Mill noticed that this adoption was not widespread, and argued that by the time it should become so, the workers would no longer need to be improved by others. Workers, like all other men, demand 'self-dependence,' not dependence on others; and the problem of improving the material well-being of all would be solved by reforming capitalism, part by part, as its strains become manifest, in the direction of industrial cooperation. The idleness of owners is unjust; and the wage arrangement unsatisfactory on both sides. And where workers own and manage the capital of an enterprise there is added to material well-being the moral advantage for all of contributing to a common purpose.[13]

In every age, Mill believes, men need to feel at one with their societies; and in all but the most primitive they tend to regard them as made up of their equals.[14] This civilizing impulse propels them toward democracy and a socialized economy, but it also drives them toward a tyranny of the majority or of a dominant class—a tyranny especially easy to enforce where democratic institutions are well established. The fear of this tyranny lies side by side, in Mill's thought, with advocacy of the conditions which he thought gave rise to it.

Progress

Progress does not characterize all history. It consists in increases of knowledge, and in its increasing use to improve the mental, moral, and physical well being of mankind. This increase presupposes man's feeling of unity with others, "which, if perfect, would make him never think of, or desire, any beneficial condition for himself in the benefits of which they are not included."[15] It requires an active interest in discovering truth, and therefore freedom, to investigate all opinions, both true and false.[16] The feeling of unity which leads to the social use of knowledge and the freedom of investigation of opinion which brings knowledge about are lacking in the nations of the East—some of which were, at one time, highly civilized. Their progress was stopped by the rule of custom. When feeling, thought, and action run wholly in the channels of custom, progress can not take place. For individuality or character cannot express itself in freedom of

---

[12] Mill, *On Liberty*, Chapter I.
[13] Anschutz, *The Philosophy of J. S. Mill*, Clarendon Press, Oxford, 1953. Chapter III; also John Stuart Mill, *Principles of Political Economy IV, VII*, §§4, 6, and IV, III, §1.
[14] Mill, *Utilitarianism*, pp. 40–41.
[15] Mill, *Utilitarianism*, Chapter III, pp. 41–42.
[16] Mill, *On Liberty*, Chapter II.

inquiry; nor, finding itself reflected in others, can it feel a unity of interest with them. Individuality is the antithesis of custom;[17] and where it reigns, as in the nations of modern Europe, progress occurs. The greatest threat to this progress lies in the enormous increase of customary feeling, thought, and action brought about by mass communications, rapid transit, and the tendency toward universal state-controlled education.

Condition of the schools

Education proceeds chiefly through the schools. They constitute the most important medium in which the effort to perfect human nature is expressed, and through which the development of human beings is affected by their physical and cultural environment. Until very near the end of Mill's life (The Forster Act of 1870), English schools were administered by private agencies—both religious and non-sectarian; Parliament supported them only in part, and enrollment was neither universal nor compulsory. In large measure, school education went to those children whose parents could both afford and desire it for them. The infant schools have sprung from a good motive Mill thinks—that of awakening in the very young a love for what is good; but they have been converted into agencies which, at best, advance infantile parroting of wholly intellectualistic themes. This encouragement of mere rote learning characterizes all the schools and universities. It is furthered in the lower schools by the Lancasterian monitors whose immaturity does not distinguish between repetition and insight, and by rewards for saying and doing 'the right thing.' There, as well as in the universities, to teach is to indoctrinate, and to learn is to cram oneself with ideas to be mechanically remembered. The mind of the learner is filled with ideas of others, not with its own. The schools promote "cram," not knowledge. For most, the period of education is a time of useless labor or 'criminal idleness.' In the schools, this is the effect of the environment on childhood and youth; and for many, the deliberate use of the schools to perfect human nature degenerates into an aim at a universal pretence of learning rather than a unique grasp of truth.[18]

RECOMMENDATIONS

Goal recommendation

Mill holds that the only thing good in itself is pleasure or happiness, and that the greatest good is the pleasure or happiness of all persons.[19] This is the goal which justifies every other—the Utilitarian ideal.

[17] Mill, *On Liberty*, Chapter III, pp. 71–73.
[18] J. S. Mill, "Inaugural Address," *Dissertations and Discussions*, Vol. IV; "Miss Austin's Translation of M. Cousin's Report on the State of Public Instruction in Prussia," *Monthly Repository* (July, 1834); "On Genius," *Monthly Repository* (October, 1832).
[19] But sometimes, "so far as the nature of things admits, of the whole sentient creation." Mill, *Utilitarianism*, Chap. II, p. 16.

Subordinate recommendations

There are various ways of reaching it. They constitute those actions which are virtuous, right, or obligatory; and the schools should play an important role in bringing men to such conduct. There is a natural tendency to act for one's personal interest merely;[20] and as such, this natural tendency leads to wrong action. Education ought to use its power ". . . to establish in the mind of every individual an indissoluble association between his own happiness and the good of the whole . . . so that he may be unable to conceive the possibility of happiness to himself, consistently with conduct opposed to the general good, but also that a direct impulse to promote the general good may be in every individual one of the habitual motives of action, . . ." [21] Education ought to form good character by fostering this association, i.e., persons whose interests are directed in unique ways toward securing the general welfare.

ADMINISTRATION. Three other recommendations attend this one concerning character. First, the administration of the schools should remain, generally, in private hands; state control would lead to that stultification of thought and extinction of individuality which constitute the general misery rather than the general welfare. Those who can afford it should pay for the education of their children. But all should attend elementary schools, and since some parents cannot pay the costs, there should be as much public support for these schools as is required by compulsory and universal attendance. State support of private schools together with compulsory universal attendance on the lower levels of education would help the schools in their task of forming good character.[22]

CURRICULUM. Mill's treatment of the content of elementary and secondary education is rather sketchy.[23] History and geography should be offered in the elementary schools only; and there, only to children of workers who are unable to own their own books. These studies are inherently delightful, wholly dependent on memory, and especially pertinent to the life of a man or woman possessed of a personal library. But teaching can add nothing to the reading of the materials involved. Also, modern languages should not be learned in school; they should be learned while sojourning in the countries where they are

[20] *Ibid.*, Chapter II, pp. 19–22. But Mill also seems to say that interest in the welfare of society is natural or instinctual, cf. *ibid.*, Chapter III, p. 40.
[21] *Ibid.*, Chapter II, pp. 22–23.
[22] Mill, *Principles of Political Economy*, Longmans, Green and Co., London, 1909, V. XI, §8; also, *On Liberty*, Chapter V.
[23] It is found chiefly in *Dissertations and Discussions*, Vol. IV, "Inaugural Address"; but the suggestions there **should** be compared with the *Autobiography*, especially the first five chapters.

spoken. Science, including mathematics, should be introduced on the elementary level; and later, deductive logic along with Greek and Latin literature. Logic enables one to detect fallacies and to draw correct inferences; while the study of Greek and Latin shows clearly that words are not things—an error which knowing one language, only, can easily lead one into.

The university curriculum should include courses in the classical languages, the sciences, philosophy, and the arts. The literatures of Greece and Rome are indispensable. They show us the thought of other cultures, and prevent provincialism. Their syntax sets forth the form of thought, and acquainting ourselves with it enables us to avoid intellectual error. Their wisdom is profound; and their style, the unsurpassed model for writers. Their dialectic trains the intellect; and best of all, they are a delight to read.

The university should offer courses in mathematics, and in the sciences, both natural and social. Mathematics gives a model for discovering truth by purely logical or deductive procedures; and besides, being necessary to the sciences, it improves our thought about nonmathematical subjects. The natural sciences, chemistry and physics, are valuable both intrinsically and instrumentally. As activities and as products, as laboratroy pursuits and as theories develop, they embody the delight taken in knowing. Also, they are useful in the daily work of the world; while they possess, as well, two other kinds of instrumental value. Knowledge of them prevents our falling prey to charlatans and to scientists who would misuse the prestige of esoteric wisdom for harmful social ends. Moreover, their study cures intellectual weakness. This consists in the inability to perceive how one thing bears upon another, i.e., how it does or does not constitute evidence for it. The natural sciences offer a model for this relation of evidence, rules for discovering it, and practice in applying them. Physiology should be studied since it helps to solve problems of public health, and makes it clear that toleration in matters of morality is necessary in light of predisposing causes for temperamental differences. Social subjects should be taught to the extent that they have been organized in a scientific way; and this principle ushers into the curriculum psychology, economics (political economy), jurisprudence, and international law.

Philosophy should play an important part in the university. Deductive or 'ratiocinative' logic, derived from Aristotle, should be started earlier; but inductive logic, the logic of the empirical sciences, should be introduced on the university level. The former yields rules by which purely rational inferences may be correctly guided. Inductive logic, to which Mill made an important contribution in his famous *A System of Logic,* yields rules for guiding our inferences from observation. Together, they constitute a field of study which Mill regarded as important for reasons already stated. The philosophy of mind, ethics, theory of knowledge, and metaphysics should be offered. The first two are helpful in giving guidance to practical life; and if theory of knowledge and metaphysics can give us no conclusive answers, they at least deal with questions which everyone asks, which many find interesting, and which each man will do well to know that others have worried over. The philosophy of history will present principles for understanding events otherwise disparate and disconnected; and the philosophy of religion, together with its history, will reveal an important aspect of human life without persuading for or against any creed or sect.

The arts should occupy an important place in the university curriculum. As activities, they flow from the effort to perfect execution; and as artifacts, they reveal ideal forms of life created by that impetus. The task of each man is to improve the life of all. The arts show in vivid, concrete detail what that improved life consists in. The charm of their beauty adds to this didactic function the important one of bringing men to love the virtue they ought to practice. And Mill seems to say that by use of the vividness of the impressions of art, one can establish that indissoluble association between the welfare of all and egoistic personal interest which he advances as the chief subordinate task of education.

The student should emerge from the university with a detailed knowledge of one or several fields, an acquaintance with all important general truths, and an insight into the way in which his specialties fit into the system of all knowledge. Every thing he learns should be treated with a view to its consequences for improving human welfare; but the university must be kept clearly separate, as a place for general education, form professional schools of all sorts. Those who attend the latter will be improved for having attended the university; but the university should be devoted to the classics, the sciences, philosophy, and the arts— all of which civilize and form good character before they create scholars and practitioners.

TEACHING METHODS. Mill objects strongly, as we have seen, to the method of "cram" which, he thinks, characterizes most teaching. In his essay, "On Genius,"[24] he argues that learning comes from within, and that teaching consists in whatever assists learning. In learning from someone else, to avoid mere parroting, we must put ourselves in a position to experience what he experienced—to feel the problem he felt, to devise the solution he experienced—to feel the problem he felt, to devise the solution he devised, etc. But discovering something independently of others, not learning from them, requires consulting our own experience in the same way. To learn the proof of the Pythagorean the-

[24] *Monthly Repository,* 1832, signed by pseudonym "Antiquus."

orem, as that of Pythagoras, requires that we do what Pythagoras did; but to discover a new proof would not be significantly different. Genius is the ability to discover the truth for ourselves with or without the help of others, by consulting our own experience, both inner and outer; and to teach is to help one to exercise his genius.

Mill says little concerning effective methods of teaching. In the "Inaugural Address," he tells us that in teaching languages, vocabulary should be given first, and rules later. Elsewhere,[25] he tells us that the teacher ought to present all possible views on any topic with equal vividness. This procedure will prevent a true doctrine from becoming a lifeless dogma; and, by stimulating thought, will enable correction of false views. The first of these suggestions is familiar. The second accords with Mill's notion that genius is an ability to deal carefully with our own experience; it urges that that experience cannot be adequately dealt with unless it incorporates all possible candidates for knowledge with respect to a given topic. His recommendations are not numerous; but whatever methods of teaching ought to be employed, they will bring many, in some degree at least, to a knowledge of classical literature, science, philosophy, and art—the meaning of all of which includes their direction of human activities toward the Utilitarian ideal. For genius is widespread, and the proper teaching methods are those which enable its exercise wherever it occurs.

PHILOSOPHY OF EDUCATION

METAPHYSICS

Mill holds that psychology lies at the basis of education; and he also holds that at the basis of psychology, as of all science, lies metaphysics.[26] It elaborates upon the distinction between appearance and reality. Appearances are states of consciousness. Every thing we can observe is, or is made of these phænomena. Behind phænomena lies reality, but Mill expresses several different views as to its relation to phænomena. In the *Logic*, he contends, first, that it is composed of substances possessed of powers to produce states of consciousness. Some of these underlie bodies; and, by exercising their powers upon minds, produce the states of consciousness (sensations) we think of as the properties of bodies. Others are minds; and possess the power to receive the sensations thus attributed to bodies. But while all this is true, Mill holds that the substantial causes of which reality is composed must remain forever unknown;

25 Mill, *On Liberty*, Chapter II, pp. 43–44.
26 Mill, *An Examination of Sir William Hamilton's Philosophy*, Vol. I, pp. 10–11.

they lie beyond the limit of experience.[27] Later in the *Logic,* however, the substances which produce states of consciousness are spoken of as mere forces;[28] and in the discussion of Hamilton, the reality behind appearances has become nothing more than a set of permanent possibilities of experience—a real body, the permanent possibility of sensations of certain sorts; a real mind, perhaps the permanent possibility of sensations also, but of inward states of consciousness as well, such as feelings and emotions.[29]

Mill's thought concerning reality exhibits several phases; but each is characterized by the notion that reality is, or is characterized by, a multiplicity of tendencies toward, or possibilities of experience, states of consciousness, or appearances. These tendencies or possibilities need not be directly manifest in experience. The states of consciousness in which any one of them might appear to us may be partly cancelled by the working of another tendency or realization of another possibility, or altogether offset by it. The tendency or possibility of fall in which gravitation consists is not manifested in those states of consciousness which are the observed flights of birds; nonetheless, it is a permanent tendency in things.

At any moment, there are many states of consciousness; and each of these appearances results from the exercise of some force, or realization of some possibility, in the world of reality. However, each phænomenon also possesses a necessary antecedent among the phænomena in the moment immediately preceding; and each antecedent phænomenon, a necessary consequent in the moment which follows. Appearances proceed in a temporal series of fields, each element of which has one and only one antecedent and consequent in the field immediately preceding and succeeding its own; and according to which each phænomenon is produced by a cooperation between some one or more of the forces in reality and the antecedent phænomena which constitute its historical circumstances.

EPISTEMOLOGY

This metaphysical view provides a framework for Mill's epistemology. Knowledge, for him, consists in being aware with perfect certainty that something is true; and there are three kinds of universal propositions in which knowledge is expressed. The first state sequences between successive appearances, i.e., between antecedents and consequents. That age *precedes* prudence, and youth impetuousness, are such propositions; and they may be verified as true by observation. But ob-

---

27 Mill, *A System of Logic,* I, III, §§3, 4, 6, 7, 8, 13, 14, 15.
28 *Ibid.* e.g., III, VI, §3.
29 Mill, *Examination,* Vol. I, pp. 238, 242, 253. But he is not quite certain that minds thus conceived could be conscious of their parts and of themselves.

servation alone can not guarantee that they hold for cases beyond its reach; it can give no reason why age should *cause* wisdom and youth folly. For the antecedent and consequent observed in experience may be, both of them together, the effect of some real tendency or possibility not yet discovered which might not operate behind unobserved appearance; or each may be a composite appearance whose parts manifest many different real forces which, again, may cooperate differently or fail completely beyond our experience. Universal statements concerning successive appearances, verified in experience but in need of explanation, are merely empirical laws; as such they do not embody knowledge.[30] Rather, they embody it only when explained.

Universal propositions of the second sort provide the explanation for empirical laws. The latter are explained when they are seen as instances of more general and abstract propositions from which, given certain circumstances, they can be deduced. The laws of association, for example, refer directly, not to concrete states of consciousness, but to certain *sorts* of them—those, whatever they may be, which are similar, inseparably conjoined, intense, etc.; the circumstances of society and biography provide the concrete impressions and ideas associated in any particular case, in the way stated by those laws. That pink is associated with girls in an empirical law; but it is explained by the more general law of frequent association. It is an instance of the latter; and its truth follows from the truth of that law together with the social circumstance that pink objects are frequently conjoined with girls, and the biographical circumstance that the conjunction is observed by someone.[31]

Propositions of the second sort themselves require explanation; and they receive it from laws of a third kind. These state the existence of a force or the coexistence of forces and their action upon one another. They are typified by the law of gravitation and by the law of planetary motion according to which planets are both attracted by, and propelled away from the sun and, hence, describe elliptical orbits around it. These are laws of causation; for together with concrete historical circumstances they state the causes whose effects, like the motions of the planets, we observe as appearances. They themselves admit of no explanation; there is nothing more ultimate from which such forces and their interaction can be derived. But ideally, at least, laws of the second kind can be deduced from them. Ideally, at least, the laws of psychology can be deduced from those of physiology; and these, ultimately, from the laws of causation statable in the science of physics. In turn, empirical laws can be deduced from laws of the second sort. In the end, the reason for adopting as certainly true any universal proposition lies in the fact that

[30] Mill, *Logic*, VI, v, §§1, 2.
[31] *Ibid.*, VI, v, §§3, 4.

our observation of appearances verifies it as true; but the discovery of empirical or of descriptive laws may depend upon our discovery that they are deducible from laws of causation together with statements of more particular circumstances. Knowing that a universal statement is true depends upon observation of appearances and, unless it is a law of causation, a capacity to derive it from, or explain it by those which are more ultimate.[32]

Knowledge is not exhausted by our certainty of the truth of propositions of these three kinds; we also possess knowledge of things immediately experienced, and expressed in singular propositions about them. We are perfectly certain, for example, that this is a plum tree; and this certainly depends in no way upon that proposition's being deducible from a universal one. Rather, its truth is guaranteed by what we now immediately experience or observe. Immediate experience is the model for what we mean by "knowledge," and anything else is knowledge only because it is like the model in being perfectly certain. "The tree in the garden next door is a plum" means simply that if anyone were there to observe it, he would have an immediate experience guaranteeing the truth of that proposition, like the immediate experience which guarantees the truth of the proposition, "This is a plum tree." The words "knowledge," "know," and their fellows refer most clearly to immediate experience; it follows that we know all singular propositions which embody it.[33]

Immediate experience consists in consciousness of attributes or universals. A sensation of blue is the consciousness of something which is repeatable and, in fact, repeated in all other sensations and ideas of blue. Something similar may be said for the consciousness of inward phænomena such as emotions. The things of immediate experience, bodies and minds, are clusters of such universals, ranged through moments of time. An orange, for example, is all the universals that anyone is now sensing or might now sense when looking at it, tasting it, touching it, etc.; but it is, also, those universals, both actually observed and possible of observation, which cluster together in all the moments of its career. On some occasions, Mill says that these universals or attributes qualify an individual [34]—that it is an individual (perhaps he means a substance) which holds them together. On others, he says that there is nothing to a thing of immediate experience but universals held together by the force of association—a principle which fastens remembrance of past and expectation of future to an idea or sensation in the present and,

[32] R. P. Anschutz, The Philosophy of J. S. Mill, Clarendon Press, Oxford, 1953, Chapter V.
[33] Mill, Examination, Vol. I, pp. 159–62.
[34] Mill, Logic I, v, §4.

in this chemical way, composes out of chaos a biography of actualities and possibilities.[35] But he always holds that the immediate experience of things, knowledge of them *par excellence,* is the consciousness of universals combined in one way or other. These are appearances, the conscious effects, which flow from reality, and which serve to verify all propositions both universal and singular.

Meaning

Mill holds that words may possess either or both of two kinds of meaning. They may denote something, merely; "John" denotes the person, i.e., it shows what thing its user refers to. Other words denote something, but also connote some attribute of it. "Tall" denotes tall things, but it connotes a certain universal or attribute possessed by all of them, i.e., height greater than the usual. The meaning of propositions is information about what is denoted by their subject terms—namely, that they possess the attributes connoted by their predicate terms. Thus, "John is tall' informs us that tallness is a universal exhibited by (or constituent in) John; and "All men are mortal," that the things which possess humanity also contain mortality.[36]

But Mill suggests a theory of the meaning of propositions which does not explain it in terms of denotation and connotation alone. The information which constitutes the meaning of many propositions concerns the coexistence and sequence of universals in immediate experience or consciousness. The predicate "plum tree," when combined with a subject, informs us that certain universals, e.g., "having leaves" and "having branches," coexist in immediate experience; while others, e.g., "having bare branches" and "showing blossoms," succeed each other there. And such information may always be formulated in a hypothetical way. "This is a plum tree" means a whole set of operations connected by the observation of certain universals—that if one looks in the direction of the plum tree, touches it, etc., he will be conscious of leaves and branches coexisting; if he performs similar operations in appropriate seasons, he will observe branches that are bare preceding branches in blossom; and a great number of other hypothetical statements. Mill suggests that the meaning of singular propositions is found in a set of operations together with the consequences to which these operations lead. The predicates of such propositions connote universals; and the propositions, themselves, mean the operations which lead to the experience of those universals. The meaning of general propositions, i.e., the information they carry, may be described in a similar way. Mill holds that some propositions carry information about the existence, the coexistence, or

---

[35] Mill, *Logic,* I, v, §5; *Examination,* Vol. I, pp. 234–41.
[36] Mill, *Logic,* I, ii, §5; I, v, §§4–5.

the succession of real forces or tendencies; but since these agencies can be understood only by reference to the experiences they generate, the meaning of the propositions which state them must be given, again, in terms of operations which they suggest and the consciousness of universals to which those operations lead. The law of gravitation, thus, means a whole set of operations and consequences. But the meaning of a proposition, clearly, does not depend upon the actual performance of the operations and consequent experiences in which it consists. And Mill's argument tends toward the conclusion that the meaning of a proposition is a set of operations and their consequences which need be no more than possible.[37] This is the important view that the meaning of any statement whatever is found in possible action, and it carries with it the additional view that the validity of any statement lies in some property of the consequences produced by that action.

Methods of knowledge

There are two methods by which knowledge may be secured. The purely rational method of deduction, described by traditional logic, is a procedure by which we come upon statements that are true provided that the premises for the inference are also true. This method is invaluable, for it enables us to discover many statements which, without it, would remain unknown. But it does not show that any statement thus discovered is in fact true. To find this out, we must engage in observation, and Mill advances four procedures (his famous methods or canons of induction)[38] for dealing with observation in such a way as to show what statements it verifies as true.

These procedures are designed to solve the problem of induction, of ". . . inferring from some individual instances in which a phænomenon is observed to occur, that it occurs in all instances of a certain class; namely, in all which *resemble* the former, in what are regarded as the material circumstances."[39] Mere uncriticized observation cannot warrant any such inference. The conclusion asserts that all the members of a class exhibit a phænomenon, and uncriticized observation of some members can afford no reason for this extension to all. To warrant a generalization, our observation of particulars must be of such a sort that it gives us some reason to apply to all what it immediately shows to be true of only some members of the class.

Each particular thing or event, as we have seen, is a cluster of universals (or phænomena) coexisting in each moment and succeeding each other from one moment to the next; and Mill interprets his prob-

---

37 Mill, *Logic*, I, v, §5; *Examination*, Vol. I, pp. 236–40; *On Liberty*, pp. 34–35, 42–43, 52.
38 Mill, *Logic*, III, viii–ix.
39 Mill, *Logic*, III, iii, §1.

lem as that of discovering procedures which, by showing how one universal is connected with others, will show what phænomena always coexist or succeed each other. On the assumption that all appearances are universals, and that from moment to moment there is a uniform sequence in experience, his inductive procedures present themselves as guarantees that the coexistence or succession of universals found in some instances characterize all. Suppose that we observe a temperature of 32° F. along with a frozen condition of the plum blossoms. We are tempted to infer from this uncriticized observation that a freezing temperature in their neighborhood always coexists with or precedes destruction of the blossoms. Mill's inductive procedures tell us how to make more critical observations, both passively and through active experiment, in such a way as to show whether these universals will always be found in that relation of coexistence or sequence, i.e., whether it is always true that freezing weather freezes plum blossoms.

The generalization to laws supported by observations of this deliberate and critical kind is the discovery of a causal pattern; for while uniform coexistence or sequence of attributes in experience may seem to be something more superficial, his metaphysical theory assures us that there is some more abstract law from which the empirical law follows, and some set of real forces or tendencies which cause the appearance to us of uniformity in experience. The knowledge acquired by inductive and deductive procedures is, thus, always made to rest on the knowledge of immediate experience; but on immediate experience or observation carefully made, arranged, and sorted to show us what inferences it allows.

ETHICS

The good

Mill holds, as we have seen, that the only thing good in itself is pleasure or happiness, and that the greatest good is the pleasure or happiness of all persons. He advances considerations designed to support this view.[40] "To be good" means to be desirable, and "to be desirable" means to be desired upon some occasion. The considerations in question are that ". . . each person, as far as he believes it to be obtainable, desires his own happiness," and that "this . . . being a fact, we have not only all the proof which the case admits of, but all which it is possible to require, that happiness is a good, that each person's happiness is a good to that person, and the general happiness, therefore, a good to the aggregate of all persons."[41] From a definition of "good" in terms of desire, from an analysis of desire in terms of pleasure, and from psychological egoism, Mill de-

---

[40] Mill, *Utilitarianism*, Chapter IV.
[41] *Ibid.*, Chapter IV, pp. 44–45.

velops the view that the general happiness or pleasure is the good for all. As such, it justifies all other objectives; and Mill recommends it as the ultimate goal for all human activity.

Kinds of happiness

There are at least four different kinds of activity in which men find happiness. The "higher pleasures" include the search for knowledge, the creation and enjoyment of the arts, and the elimination of social and personal misery; the "lower pleasures" consist in the satisfaction of egoistic and bodily desires. The "higher pleasures" are better, for those who are acquainted with activities of both sorts prefer them. But the "lower pleasures" are good so long as they do not dominate all activity. Where they do so, they are transformed from minor virtues into the major vices of selfishness, profligacy, and the like. In tranquility and excitement men also find great pleasure. Tranquil activities lead to a desire for the exciting; and those which are stirring to a need for the tranquil. Engaging in each leads to a desire to engage in the other; and since every activity falls somewhere between the extremes, all men desire both. The higher and the lower pleasures, tranquil and exciting activities, give us the classification of most of the activities which embody the general happiness.[42].

Duty

A duty is something one ought to do, and Mill defines "ought" by reference to his conception of the greatest good. To say that one ought to do so-and-so is to say that that action is conducive to, a cause or part of the cause of, the general welfare. It is clear that a good person is one who does his duty.

Excellence of character

There are two constituents in the moral excellence of personal existence. One whose life possesses it must, first, succeed in realizing the unique cluster of interests which constitutes his individuality; he must secure happiness. But happiness is not enough; for individuality might find its fulfillment only in activities which, however pleasant, were wholly egocentric—in pleasure of body and mind, of tranquility and excitement, which ignored the welfare of others. A morally excellent person enjoys happiness; but he also does his duty. Perfection of conduct is a second constituent in moral excellence. Mill fuses these two constituents. The social feelings make each man desire the happiness of all; and since this desire becomes his settled will, the perfection of duty appears as an ingredient in the happiness of individuality.[43]

[42] *Ibid.,* Chapter ii, pp. 16–18.
[43] *Ibid.,* Chapter iii, pp. 40–43.

One whose personal existence is morally excellent is a good character. A mind, as we have seen, is a series of mental states—of sensations and ideas, of desires, emotions, feelings, etc.—organized by the laws of association; and since each mind contains something unique, it is in some degree a character. A character, Mill holds, is good in so far as its happiness expresses individuality, and its individuality includes a desire to act for the general welfare where this desire has become a will or purpose.

The best society

The best society is one in which there is the greatest amount of good character, i.e., of happiness and perfection. Since happiness requires the expression of uniqueness, it must also be a society which guarantees to each person freedom to think and to express himself as he pleases, in speech, writing, and association. All men desire freedom of this sort; the activities which embody it are among those in which happiness consists. It has an instrumental value as well. It enables the discovery of truth and, therefore, its use to improve the material, mental, and moral well-being of mankind. It must be extended to the actions foreshadowed by thought and its expression. For since the meaning of propositions is found in the actions to which they lead, their meaning and their truth will be lost where their consequences are not enacted. Freedom is an essential part of happiness; and since it is also a means to happiness, to allow it is a duty imposed upon all. It ought to surround each mature person, and infringing upon it is a chief source of the evils traceable to governments and other institutions.

But while individuality requires freedom, duty requires that it be limited. The actions one desires to perform sometime involve harm to others. One may enjoy expressing his thoughts concerning social reform, and such expression may be a part of, or a means to progress. But in particular circumstances, it may lead to actions which harm others; and where this is true, duty requires that freedom be restricted—that expression of thought be curtailed. Mill's book, *On Liberty*, offers one of the classic defences of the view that the general happiness requires freedom of thought, expression, and association; and that the only legitimate check on freedom springs from the duty borne by each to refrain from actions injurious to others and to engage in those which advance the welfare of the generality.

The best society both allows and requires a representative government. In it, each person is free to work out not only his own personal life but the solutions to social problems as well; and by virtue of this freedom of thought, he naturally demands representation in a government which would embody them. A democratic government, in turn, is most conducive to a maximum of moral excellence in the citizenry. Each person endeavors to realize his own individuality; and, consequently, through a government responsive to his wishes, he is most likely to secure it. Even despots who are benevolent easily neglect the interests of their subjects. Moreover, the persons who, in the best society, are self-dependent present a great variety of interests; and a representative government, consequently, will distribute happiness most widely.[44] It prevents a single interest from silencing the less powerful, and assures the latter an opportunity to modify the former for the greater happiness. Besides, participation in government imposes responsibility and thus fosters the perfection of character involved in the execution of duty.[45] The best government is representative democracy, for it most efficiently advances and promotes that excellence of character in whose greatest quantity society finds its ideal.

EDUCATION AS SCIENCE AND AS ART

Mill's philosophy assures us that there is a science upon which to base an art of education. A mind, he tells us, is a series of states of consciousness. Each item in it falls into a uniform pattern of phænomena or appearances—of states of consciousness both actual and possible. If a complex item, it falls into a pattern composed of many subordinate patterns. A feeling of hope, for example, is compounded of pleasure and the thought of some future event; and each of these elements occurs in all the lines of uniformity in which we find the antecedents and consequences of the pleasure and the thought. As a series of appearances, a mind is like the path of a moving point, many of whose positions are, in turn, intersections in the paths of other motions. Moreover, each item in a mind could not have been other than it is; for the many uniformities into which it fits are the uniform sequences in consciousness caused by the real forces or possibilities which underlie appearances. Each mind is unique. The peculiarities of biographical circumstance introduce into any such series elements not found in others, even where a single culture may impose a considerable similarity. The American may tend to be optimistic or hopeful. Still, each American is unique; for the future event whose thought makes all hopeful differs from one to another. This is the nature of mind as Mill's metaphysics portrays it, and each mind is a character.

[44] I should add that Mill regards the whole and more even distribution of physical well-being as a problem demanding attention from nineteenth century European governments; but he seems also to hold that such a distribution would result more efficiently from voluntary industrial cooperation than from thoroughgoing state ownership and control of the means of production.

[45] Mill, *Utilitarianism, Liberty, and Representative Government,* Everyman's Library, no. 482, Editor Ernest Rhys, London, J. M. Dent and Sons, Ltd., New York, E. P. Dutton and Co., 1910; *Representative Government,* Chapter III, pp. 206–8, 216–17.

Mill's epistemology tells us how to understand character. Immediate experience, expressed in singular propositions, gives us the clearest example of knowing; but we can also know those successively more abstract patterns which surround immediate experience, expressed in successively more general propositions. Moreover, we can know that certain forces cause the patterns in which immediate experience appears, and can express them in causal laws. Where feasible, we can learn the abstract patterns by induction—by analyzing, sorting, and arranging immediate experience in ways which show the patterns that surround it; where not, we can know real forces and abstract patterns by deduction—by deducing the patterns from the forces, and the immediate experiences from the patterns, and verifying our statements concerning them by critical observation. In these ways, we can explain empirical and descriptive laws as well as the singular propositions expressive of immediate experience.

This experience assures us of many truths about particular persons or characters. We know, for example, that Jones is old and prudent. And the common sense of our culture embodies an empirical law which seems to explain this proposition. "The old are prudent," if true, explains Jones' behavior; it sets forth a pattern into which his age and prudence seem to fit. Historical growth gives empirical laws of character to all cultures; they are spontaneously accepted as parts of common sense. These patterns, themselves, may fit into patterns which are more abstract. Thus, "Experience engenders caution" is a pattern whose elements, in turn, may be age and prudence. These more abstract patterns are laws which explain empirical laws; but they do so only if we are entitled to add to them specifying cultural circumstances. Thus, a culture in which age yields experience will be one in which age is prudent, provided that the more abstract law about experience and caution is true. And it explains our immediate experience of Jones, by way of the empirical law, if his life has not been unduly sheltered. The more abstract laws which thus explain empirical laws about character must be applicable to all persons; but they admit of different empirical laws, since the latter hold true according as cultural circumstances allow. There must be a good many such laws; in addition to the one suggested, others may be "Inexperience accompanies rashness," and "Deceit accompanies distrust." Thus, one might explain the empirical laws that youth is foolish, and that all men tend to lie. These laws constitute a science waiting to be discovered. Mill called it "ethology," and described it as the science of character formation.[46] He looked upon it as an important chapter in the science of society which he hoped would be established. The laws of ethology do not describe particular characters; they set forth

---

[46] Mill, *Logic*, VI, v, §§1–2, 6.

a set of more abstract uniformities or patterns within which, according to particular circumstances, characters or minds grow and develop.

The laws of ethology cannot be discovered by induction. Passive observation cannot reveal the more abstract patterns of coexistence and sequence into which the elements of a character fall; the latter is too complex and too carefully guarded from the public by the person who bears it. Nor can we experiment to find them out; technical difficulties, let alone considerations of humanity, preclude tampering with personality. Deduction is the procedure which must be employed. The laws of association, as we have seen, present abstract patterns of coexistence and of temporal sequence according to which the elements of mind organize themselves; from them, together with more concrete cultural circumstances, we can discover what kinds of elements a mind includes. Thus, psychology tells us that when phænomena of two kinds have been frequently conjoined in our experience, an idea of one tends to excite an idea of the other. It tells us nothing about what precise idea excites any other. However, when we combine with this more abstract pattern the cultural circumstance that people frequently experience conjoined phænomena, some of which are pleasant and others painful, we can derive the law of character concerning experience and caution. As a person acquires more experience of pleasant things conjoined with painful, he will begin to look carefully into the consequences of doing what is pleasant, i.e., he acquires a cautious character. "The laws of the formation of character are, in short, derivative laws, resulting from the general laws of mind, and are to be obtained by deducing them from those general laws by supposing any given set of circumstances, and then considering what, according to the laws of mind, will be the influence of those circumstances on the formation of character."[47] These laws of ethology are verified as true or false by the empirical laws of character built up by common sense. They explain singular propositions about particular characters such as that concerning Jones' age and prudence in light of concrete biographical circumstances.

Ethology, the science of character formation, is also the science of education. We have seen that Mill includes in the meaning of the latter term the effect on human beings of their physical and cultural environment. Each character contains a physiological basis in the brain and nervous system; and this, together with its physical environment, provides the stock of sensations and instincts prior to experience. On it, experience of the cultural environment raises that unique edifice, constructed of acquired desire, will, and knowledge—that unique series of states of consciousness—in which character consists. Ethology is constituted by those laws which describe the patterns in which this char-

[47] Mill, *Logic*, VI, v, §4; also §§3, 5.

acter falls, i.e., the ways in which culture and nature cooperate to form a person of a particular sort. This is a description of the effect on human beings of their environment—the science of education.

From this science, it is easy to derive an art. Education also is the deliberate effort to perfect human nature; and this effort succeeds only in so far as those circumstances are supplied in which, according to ethological laws, character of the best sort will occur. To perfect human nature, we need to introduce circumstances which, according to the patterns of phænomena exhibited by ethology, introduce others which together constitute character of the sort we want. The laws of ethology may be converted into rules which guide the perfection of human nature; and when it is developed, the art of education ". . . will be the mere transformation of those principles into a parallel system of precepts, and the adaptation of these to the sum total of the individual circumstances which exist in each particular case.[48]

ETHICS AND EDUCATION

In his ethics, Mill advances two cardinal principles. The first is that "good" means pleasant, and that what is good is happiness or welfare, while what is best is the welfare of all. His Utilitarianism consists, in part, in reasons designed to persuade us to accept this principle. He holds the view that the general welfare is composed of happiness of two kinds: of pleasure in the realization of individuality, and in that of perfection or the fulfillment of duty toward the whole. He recommends the general welfare, thus conceived, as the ultimate goal for all teaching. For him, education's goal objective finds justification in the proof, contained in his ethics, for the first principle of that theory. The art of education must solve the problem of forming persons who constitute an ideal society, i.e., one of persons of moral excellence or good character; and since such a society constitutes the general welfare, education inherits this problem from the first principle of Utilitarianism and its proof.

The second principle in Mill's ethics is that "ought" means conducive to the general welfare, and that our duties are all those actions which, in fact, contribute to it. The moral force of this second principle is largely borrowed from adopting the general welfare as the greatest good. The first subordinate recommendation of Mill's educational theory is that the schools (and teaching generally) should be employed to create an indissoluble association in the student's mind between the thought of his own happiness and that of all persons. This recommendation would solve the problem, inherited from Utilitarian ethics.

[48] Mill, *Logic*, VI, v, §6.

Acting upon it would result in amalgamating the instinct for individuality with the desire for perfection, ie., in producing persons motivated toward the moral excellence in which general welfare consists. Mill's first educational recommendation is related to his ethics as an instance of its second principle, i.e., as one kind of action teachers ought to engage in.

Mill seems to regard some of the subordinate recommendations in his educational theory as ways of following out the first. Compulsory universal enrollment in the lower schools, together with state support where parents cannot afford the costs, would assure teachers a chance at trying to produce motivation toward good character in almost all children. Private control of schools would tend to prevent the use of state power by powerful groups (majorities or minorities) to crush individuality in favor of conformity—advancing, at the same time, the motivation to do one's duty. On the other hand, the curriculum of the classics, the sciences (both natural and social), philosophy, and the arts, foreshadowed in the lower schools and embodied fully in the university, is not obviously a way of associating individuality and perfection. Mill does suggest that the idealized existence portrayed by the arts shows us moral excellence and that the charm of fulfilling duty exhibited by them might cause us to identify individual satisfaction with fulfillment of obligation. But it is a suggestion, not a view he explicitly puts forward. The recommendation that teaching methods should make use of full discussion of all views, both true and false, shows also nothing but a very loose relation to his chief subordinate recommendation. To make use of the laws of association, of psychological statements of fact, to produce the motive toward moral excellence in all is the teacher's primary duty, because widespread moral excellence constitute the general happiness. But Mill never makes it clear how his other subordinate recommendations concerning curriculum and method point to actions which would constitute the fulfillment of the first subordinate recommendation.

The reason, Mill might have said, lies in the undeveloped state of ethology. If we knew how the abstract patterns or laws of psychology are specified in laws of character formation, we would know quite precisely what actions to institute, i.e., we would know how to establish the circumstances which would utilize the laws of psychology to produce good character. Until ethology is developed, teachers must employ precepts derived from laws which are merely empirical. That knowledge of the classics, of the sciences, of philosophy, and of the arts makes for good character; that full discussion of a topic makes for good character— these may be such empirical laws. Perhaps Mill believed that the practice of education can do no better than to make use of this common sense wisdom so long as ethology does not provide it with a more certain basis for its art.

Mill's ethics does provide an explicit justification for his recommendations concerning curriculum and method, but it short-cuts the first of his subordinate recommendations. He argues that the traditional curriculum, supplemented by laboratory study of the sciences, and devoid of religious indoctrination, should be offered because a society thus educated will embody the general happiness. Widespread knowledge will make the people demand, and enable them to preserve, the best society i.e., one in which public opinion is represented in government, in which personal freedoms are guaranteed, and in which there is continuing progress toward moral, mental, and physical well-being for all. Assuming that this general welfare is good and attainable only in democracy, assuming, also, that such knowledge does promote it, then if the curriculum advocated does guarantee this knowledge, its recommendation is clearly a proper part of educational theory; and if the methods Mill advocates for teaching make the curriculum succeed, they must appear, also, among the recommendations of education.

METAPHYSICS, EPISTEMOLOGY, AND EDUCATION

If our knowledge were complete, we would know all the facts involved in the growth and development of human beings; and in light of the cardinal principles of Utilitarian ethics, we would transform the statements which describe some of these facts into precepts for deliberately perfecting human nature. We would not treat all of them in this way; some would give us rules for achieving something less than perfection. The statements we would put to that employment yield the duties which Mill's ethics establishes as proper subordinate recommendations in his educational theory. So far, this is the burden of our discussion of the relation between Mill's metaphysics, epistemology, and ethics, on one hand, and his theory of education on the other.

Two points remain to be noticed. Knowledge, Mill argues, consists partly in being aware that certain universals are always connected in the same ways or patterns, and that these ways or patterns may be inferred from immediate experience where the latter is critically arranged. The canons of induction are rules for this critical arrangement. They show us what we can infer where immediate experiences are arranged to agree in exhibiting a single pattern, to differ with respect to a single pattern, or to agree in respect of a single pattern some of whose elements differ (or vary), from instance to instance, concomitantly with others. Whether we come upon a pattern by deduction or by induction, it must always be verified by experiences secured by use of these canons. Mill's epistemology justifies the procedure of referring to critically arranged immediate experience by arguing that it is implied by the metaphysical doctrine of real forces or tendencies causing uniformities in appearance.[49]

The meaning of a proposition, for Mill, is the information it carries; and ultimately, this information consists in possible operations and their consequences. The latter constitute the immediate experience which verifies the proposition as true or false; and the operations, the ways in which that experience is arranged. That freezing weather freezes plum blossoms means that if the weather in the neighborhood of blossoms is below 32°F., the blossoms freeze. This meteorological and arboreal operation, when made actual, arranges the immediate experience of freezing weather and freezing blossoms. And this pattern, thus arranged, is one in which many immediate experiences agree, with respect to which other immediate experiences (those of springs without frost) differ. The meaning of propositions about immediate experience cannot be understood in this way; but that of all others amounts to a set of possible ways in which immediate experiences of certain kinds are ushered in. To discover the meaning of most propositions, to learn what activities lead to what consequences, and to know that such propositions are true is to see that the immediate experiences to which those activities lead, in fact, occur.

The first point to notice concerns Mill's recommendation that the teaching of any topic should proceed through full discussion of all views, both true and false, with respect to it. This procedure is required by his doctrine of meaning. Except for those about his own immediate experience, a student can not, on that doctrine, perceive the meaning of any proposition apart from the possible ways of acting and possible experiences it involves. Newton's law of gravitation means what we would experience if we acted to observe things in certain ways and if forces continued to act as they have; while moral principles, analogously, mean what human beings would experience (e.g., happiness) if they acted in certain ways (e.g., with toleration for others, Christian love for them, etc.). Mill contends that the full discussion of a proposition, in fact, makes its meaning more clear to the participants than any other procedure—that, in particular, the dialectical clash of conflicting opinion concerning its truth renders more vivid than any other activity the operations and their experiential consequences which constitute that meaning. It shows the meaning of a proposition clearly by showing what immediate experiences would verify it as true or false, and through what operations these experiences can be arranged. The free discussion of Christianity, during its early history, made its doctrines meaningful; for it kept clearly before the minds of those concerned the ways in which a Christian, as such, acts

---

[49] Mill also argues (*Logic*, VI, v, §1.) that it is the procedure which scientists have always actually followed and, therefore, the only valid one.

and the immediate experiences (frequently of social import) attributable to such action only, i.e., how the Christian life agrees from one instance to another, how its pattern differs from that of the pagan, etc. This recommendation concerning teaching method depends on the truth of the statement of fact concerned, i.e., that full discussion does, in fact, enhance meaning; but it depends, also, on the doctrine of the meaning of propositions of which it is an instance, and upon the theory of knowledge from which that doctrine is, in turn, derived. To understand the meaning of most propositions is to understand what is involved in knowing them to be true or false; and it is in light of his theory of meaning and of his methodology that Mill regards full discussion of all topics as one of the teacher's duties.

The second point to notice concerns Mill's recommendation that the sciences be included in the curriculum. They improve one's intellectual ability, i.e., one's ability to make correct inferences; and therefore, further the pursuit of knowledge and the general welfare. Mill regards this as a fact; and, relying on his ethical principles, recommends the sciences accordingly. But it is from his theory of knowledge that we learn what a science is. The immediate experience which verifies a proposition as true or false may be experimentally or passively arranged. In the first case, we alter the elements of immediate experience; in the second, we refuse to do so. In the first, the operations involved are not only subjective (i.e., the deliberate and careful use of our sense organs to observe), but also objective (i.e., alterations of the objective materials experimented upon). In the second case, the operations involved are merely subjective. To verify a proposition as true or false is to discover that a critically arranged immediate experience does or does not exhibit the pattern of elements asserted by the proposition to be verified. The canons of induction tell us how this experience may be arranged, experimentally or passively, if it is to verify some proposition. In the first case, we have experimental science; in the second, non-experimental. But in either case, a science is a body of propositions whose meaning consists in operations leading to immediate experience arranged according to these canons. Mill holds that studying science of either kind will enable us more quickly to perceive the meaning of a proposition, i.e., the operations and consequent experience which it carries; and this conception of clear thinking he derives from his doctrine of meaning and of method.

Education is, in one sense, the deliberate effort to perfect human nature. The nature of the human being is the ability to generate out of sensation and instinct a series of states of consciousness which is, in each case, unique in some respect. The realization of this nature is a life of happiness coupled with duty—a life which helps to form the general welfare; and education should use precepts, derived from psychology and ethology, to direct people toward that realization. At least part of the means to realizing human nature is the cultivation of each man's genius —his ability to discover truth for himself; a full discussion of all views and a study of the sciences is part of the cultivation of genius. But why this should be so is a question which Mill answers by epistemological and metaphysical considerations.

A Guide to Selections from *Utilitarianism*.

In Chapter II of *Utilitarianism*, Mill states his views concerning the nature of rightness, and of the kinds of action that possess it.

The nature of rightness, he insists, is the productiveness of happiness or pleasure. But pleasures differ in quality. Some pleasures are higher—those of the higher faculties—and others are lower—those of the lower faculties. The rightness of action consists in its tending to produce the happiness that includes higher pleasures.

Pleasures also differ in quantity. Some are intense or widespread; others, feeble or enjoyed only by a few. The rightness of action consists not merely in its productiveness of happiness that includes higher pleasures, but of happiness that also is great in quantity.

The kinds of actions that are right are those of tranquility and excitement. They are prevented by poverty, disease, and loneliness. To the extent that the latter three conditions are diminished, right actions can be performed, and happiness achieved.

Mill holds that the happiness that right actions tend to produce is not that of the actor as such (though the latter need not be excluded from it), but of the entire sentient creation. He holds that while general happiness must be produced by any action that is right, the actor need not consciously aim at it, but only at making someone or something happy. He adds, nonetheless, that social institutions, including education, should be used so that each man comes to identify his own happiness with, and so far as possible to aim at, the happiness or good of the whole. He urges that religion and theology, far from being incompatible with Utilitarianism, sometimes suggest it by holding that God created man in order that they should be happy.

SELECTIONS FROM

Utilitarianism*

━━◄◆►━━

CHAPTER II

What Utilitarianism Is

The creed which accepts as the foundation of morals, Utility, or the Greatest Happiness Principle, holds that actions are right in proportion as they tend to promote happiness, wrong as they tend to produce the reverse of happiness. . . .

.   .   .

Now, such a theory of life excites in many minds, and among them in some of the most estimable in feeling and purpose, inveterate dislike. To suppose that life has (as they express it) no higher end than pleasure—no better and nobler object of desire and pursuit—they designate as utterly mean and grovelling; as a doctrine worthy only of swine, to whom the followers of Epicurus were, at a very early period, contemptuously likened; and modern holders of the doctrine are occasionally made the subject of equally polite comparisons by its German, French, and English assailants.

When thus attacked, the Epicureans have always answered, that it is not they, but their accusers, who represent nature in a degrading light; since the accusation supposes human beings to be capable of no pleasures except those of which swine are capable. . . . Human beings have faculties more elevated than the animal appetites, and when once made conscious of them, do not regard anything as happiness which does not include their gratification. . . . It is quite compatible with the principle of utility to recognize the fact, that some *kinds* of pleasure are more desirable and more valuable than others. It would be absurd that while, in estimating all other things, quality is considered as well as quantity, the estimation of pleasures should be supposed to depend on quantity alone.

If I am asked, what I mean by difference of quality in pleasures, or what makes one pleasure more valuable than another, merely as a pleasure, except its being greater in amount, there is but one possible answer. Of two pleasures, if there be one to which all or almost all who have ex-

*Fraser's Magazine, Vol. XLIV, No. CCCLXXXII, CCCLXXXIII,CCCLXXXIV, London, Parker, Son, and Bourn, 1861.

perience of both give a decided preference, irrespective of any feeling of moral obligation to prefer it, that is the more desirable pleasure. If one of the two is, by those who are competently acquainted with both, placed so far above the other that they prefer it, even though knowing it to be attended with a greater amount of discontent, and would not resign it for any quantity of the other pleasure which their nature is capable of, we are justified in ascribing to the preferred enjoyment a superiority in quality, so far outweighing quantity as to render it, in comparison, of small account.

Now it is an unquestionable fact that those who are equally acquainted with, and equally capable of appreciating and enjoying, both, do give a most marked preference to the manner of existence which employs their higher faculties. Few human creatures would consent to be changed into any of the lower animals, for a promise of the fullest allowance of a beast's pleasures; no intelligent human being would consent to be a fool, no instructed person would be an ignoramus, no person of feeling and conscience would be selfish and base, even though they should be persuaded that the fool, the dunce, or the rascal is better satisfied with his lot than they are with theirs. . . . We may give what explanation we please of this unwillingness; we may attribute it to pride, a name which is given indiscriminately to some of the most, and to some of the least estimable feelings of which mankind are capable: we may refer it to the love of liberty and personal independence, an appeal to which was with the Stoics one of the most effective means for the inculcation of it; to the love of power, or to the love of excitement, both of which do really enter into and contribute to it; but its most appropriate appellation is a sense of dignity, which all human beings possess in one form or other, and in some, though by no means in exact, proportion to their higher faculties, and which is so essential a part of the happiness of those in whom it is strong, that nothing which conflicts with it could be, otherwise than momentarily, an object of desire to them. . . . It is better to be a human being dissatisfied than a pig satisfied; better to be Socrates dissatisfied than a fool satisfied. And if the fool, or the pig, are of a different opinion, it is because they only know their own side of the question. The other party to the comparison knows both sides.

· · ·

According to the Greatest Happiness Principle, as above explained, the ultimate end, with reference to and for the sake of which all other things are desirable (whether we are considering our own good or that of other people), is an existence exempt as far as possible from pain, and as rich as possible in enjoyments, both in point of quantity and quality; the test of quality, and the rule for measuring it against quantity, being the preference felt by those who in their opportunities of experience, to which must be added their habits of self-consciousness and self-observation, are best furnished with the means of comparison. This being, according to the utilitarian opinion, the end of human action, is necessarily also the standard of morality; which may accordingly be defined, the rules and precepts for human conduct, by the observance of which an existence such as has been described might be, to the greatest extent possible, secured to all mankind; and not to them only, but so far as the nature of things admits, to the whole sentient creation.

·　　·　　·

. . . The main constituents of a satisfied life appear to be two, either of which by itself is often found sufficient for the purpose: tranquillity, and excitement. With much tranquillity, many find that they can be content with very little pleasure: with much excitement, many can reconcile themselves to a considerable quantity of pain. There is assuredly no inherent impossibility in enabling even the mass of mankind to unite both; since the two are so far from being incompatible that they are in natural alliance, the prolongation of either being a preparation for, and exciting a wish for, the other. It is only those in whom indolence amounts to a vice, that do not desire excitement after an interval of repose: it is only those in whom the need of excitement is a disease, that feel the tranquillity which follows excitement dull and insipid, instead of pleasurable in direct proportion to the excitement which preceded it. . . . Next to selfishness, the principal cause which makes life unsatisfactory is want of mental cultivation. A cultivated mind—I do not mean that of a philosopher, but any mind to which the fountains of knowledge have been opened, and which have been taught, in any tolerable degree, to exercise its faculties—finds sources of inexhaustible interest in all that surrounds it; in the objects of nature, the achievements of art, the imaginations of poetry, the incidents of history, the ways of mankind, past and present, and their prospects in the future. . . .
. . . In a world in which there is so much to interest, so much to enjoy, and so much also to correct and improve, every one who has this moderate amount of moral and intellectual requisites is capable of an existence which may be called enviable; and unless such a person, through bad laws, or subjection to the will of others, is denied the liberty to use the sources of happiness within his reach, he will not fail to find this enviable existence, if he escape the positive evils of life, the great sources of physical and mental suffering—such as indigence, disease, and the unkindness, worthlessness, or premature loss of objects of affection. The main stress of the problem lies, therefore, in the contest with these calamities, from which it is a rare good fortune entirely to escape; which, as things now are, cannot be obviated, and often cannot be in any material degree mitigated. Yet no one whose opinion deserves a moment's

consideration can doubt that most of the great positive evils of the world are in themselves removable, and will, if human affairs continue to improve, be in the end reduced within narrow limits. Poverty, in any sense implying suffering, may be completely extinguished by the wisdom of society, combined with the good sense and providence of individuals. Even that most intractable of enemies, disease, may be indefinitely reduced in dimensions by good physical and moral education, and proper control of noxious influences; while the progress of science holds out a promise for the future of still more direct conquests over this detestable foe. And every advance in that direction relieves us from some, not only of the chances which cut short our own lives, but, what concerns us still more, which deprive us of those in whom our happiness is wrapt up. As for vicissitudes of fortune, and other disappointments connected with worldly circumstances, these are principally the effect either of gross imprudence, of ill-regulated desires, or of bad or imperfect social institutions. . . .

.   .   .

. . . the happiness which forms the utilitarian standard of what is right in conduct, is not the agent's own happiness, but that of all concerned. As between his own happiness and that of others, utilitarianism requires him to be as strictly impartial as a disinterested and benevolent spectator. In the golden rule of Jesus of Nazareth, we read the complete spirit of the ethics of utility. To do as you would be done by, and to love your neighbor as yourself, constitute the ideal perfection of utilitarian morality. As the means of making the nearest approach to this ideal, utility would enjoin, first, that laws and social arrangements should place the happiness, or (as speaking practically it may be called) the interest, of every individual, as nearly as possible in harmony with the interest of the whole; and secondly, that education and opinion, which have so vast a power over human character, should so use that power as to establish in the mind of every individual an indissoluble association between his own happiness and the good of the whole; especially between his own happiness and the practice of such modes of conduct, negative and positive, as regard for the universal happiness prescribes; so that not only he may be unable to conceive the possibility of happiness to himself, consistently with conduct opposed to the general good, but also that a direct impulse to promote the general good may be in every individual one of the habitual motives of action, and the sentiments connected therewith may fill a large and prominent place in every human being's sentient existence. . . .

. . . It is the business of ethics to tell us what are our duties, or by what test we may know them; but no system of ethics requires that the sole motive of all we do shall be a feeling of duty; on the contrary, ninety-nine hundredths of all our actions are done from other motives, and rightly so done, if the rule of duty does not condemn them. . . . He who saves a fellow creature from drowning does what is morally right, whether his motive be duty, or the hope of being paid for his trouble; he who betrays the friend that trusts him is guilty of a crime, even if his object be to serve another friend to whom he is under greater obligations. But to speak only of actions done from the motive of duty, and in direct obedience to principle: it is a misapprehension of the utilitarian mode of thought, to conceive it as implying that people should fix their minds upon so wide a generality as the world, or society at large. The great majority of good actions are intended not for the benefit of the world, but for that of individuals, of which the good of the world is made up; and the thoughts of the most virtuous man need not on these occasions travel beyond the particular persons concerned, except so far as is necessary to assure himself that in benefiting them he is not violating the rights, that is, the legitimate and authorized expectations, of any one else. . . .

.   .   .

. . . We not uncommonly hear the doctrine of utility inveighed against as a *godless* doctrine. If it be necessary to say anything at all against so mere an assumption, we may say that the question depends upon what idea we have formed of the moral character of the Deity. If it be a true belief that God desires, above all things, the happiness of his creatures, and that this was his purpose in their creation, utility is not only not a godless doctrine, but more profoundly religious than any other. If it be meant that utilitarianism does not recognise the revealed will of God as the supreme law of morals, I answer, that an utilitarian who believes in the perfect goodness and wisdom of God, necessarily believes that whatever God has thought fit to reveal on the subject of morals, must fulfil the requirements of utility in a supreme degree. But others besides utilitarians have been of opinion that the Christian revelation was intended, and is fitted, to inform the hearts and minds of mankind with a spirit which should enable them to find for themselves what is right, and incline them to do it when found, rather than to tell them, except in a very general way, what it is; and that we need a doctrine of ethics, carefully followed out, to *interpret* to us the will of God. Whether this opinion is correct or not, it is superfluous here to discuss; since whatever aid religion, either natural or revealed, can afford to ethical investigation, is as open to the utilitarian moralists as to any other. . . .

.   .   .

A Guide to Selections from *On Liberty*

In Chapter I, Mill defends the principle that it is right for society to regulate the conduct of individuals only if its failure to do so would permit them to engage in actions harmful to others. All other social compulsion against individuals is wrong. All those actions that pertain to thought and feeling, together with their expression in speech and writing, to tastes and pursuits, and to association with other persons ought to be subject only to the control of the actor.

In Chapter V, Mill argues that people ought not be free with respect to the education of children, that there ought to be compulsory education through the lower levels, and that it should be administered through private schools where possible, but state schools where not—and always through the setting of compulsory state examinations.

SELECTIONS FROM

*On Liberty**

━━◀◆▶━━

CHAPTER I

Introductory

The object of this Essay is to assert one very simple principle, as entitled to govern absolutely the dealings of society with the individual in the way of compulsion and control, whether the means used be physical force in the form of legal penalties, or the moral coercion of public opinion. That principle is, that the sole end for which mankind are warranted, individually or collectively, in interfering with the liberty of action of any of their number, is self-protection. That the only purpose for which power can be rightly exercised over any member of a civilized community, against his will, is to prevent harm to others. His own good, either physical or moral, is not a sufficient warrant. He cannot rightfully be compelled to do or forbear because it will be better for him to do so, because it will make him happier, because, in the opinions of others, to do so would be wise, or even right. . . . The only part of the conduct of any

* New York: Appleton-Century-Crofts, Inc., 1947, reprinted with the kind permission of the publisher. Footnotes omitted.

one, for which he is amenable to society, is that which concerns others.

It is, perhaps, hardly necessary to say that this doctrine is meant to apply only to human beings in the maturity of their faculties. We are not speaking of children, or of young persons below the age which the law may fix as to manhood or womanhood. . . . For the same reason, we may leave out of consideration those backward states of society in which the race itself may be considered as in its nonage. . . . Despotism is a legitimate mode of government in dealing with barbarians, provided the end be their improvement, and the means justified by actually effecting that end. Liberty, as a principle, has no application to any state of things anterior to the time when mankind have become capable of being improved by free and equal discussion. . . .

It is proper to state that I forego any advantage which could be derived to my argument from the idea of abstract right, as a thing independent of utility. I regard utility as the ultimate appeal on all ethical questions; but it must be utility in the largest sense, grounded on the permanent interests of man as a progressive being. Those interests, I contend, authorize the subjection of individual spontaneity to external control, only in respect to those actions of each, which concern the interest of other people. . . .

But there is a sphere of action in which society, as distinguished from the individual, has, if any, only an indirect interest; comprehending all that porton of a person's life and conduct which affects only himself, or if it also affects others, only with their free, voluntary, and undeceived consent and participation. When I say only himself, I mean directly, and in the first instance: for whatever affects himself, may affect others through himself; and the objection which may be grounded on this contingency will receive consideration in the sequel. This, then, is the appropriate region of human liberty. It comprises, first, the inward domain of consciousness; demanding liberty of conscience, in the most comprehensive sense; liberty of thought and feeling; absolute freedom of opinion and sentiment on all subjects, practical or speculative, scientific, moral, or theological. The liberty of expressing and publishing opinions may seem to fall under a different principle, since it belongs to that part of the conduct of an individual which concerns other people; but, being almost of as much importance as the liberty of thought itself, and resting in great part on the same reasons, is practically inseparable from it. Secondly, the principle requires liberty of tastes and pursuits; of framing the plan of our life to suit our own character; of doing as we like, subject to such consequences as may follow: without impediment from our fellow creatures, so long as what we do does not harm them, even though they should think our conduct foolish, perverse, or wrong. Thirdly, from this liberty of each individual, follows the liberty, within the same limits, of combination among individuals; freedom to unite, for any purpose not involving harm to others: the persons combining being supposed to be of full age, and not forced or deceived.

No society in which these liberties are not, on the whole, respected, is free, whatever may be its form of government; and none is completely free in which they do not exist absolute and unqualified. . . .

Though this doctrine is anything but new, and, to some persons, may have the air of a truism, there is no doctrine which stands more directly opposed to the general tendency of existing opinion and practice. Society has expended fully as much effort in the attempt (according to its lights) to compel people to conform to its notions of personal, as of social excellence. The ancient commonwealths thought themselves entitled to practice, and the ancient philosophers countenanced, the regulation of every part of private conduct by public authority, on the ground that the State had a deep interest in the whole bodily and mental discipline of every one of its citizens; a mode of thinking which may have been admissible in small republics surrounded by powerful enemies, in constant peril of being subverted by foreign attack or internal commotion, and to which even a short interval of relaxed energy and self-command might so easily be fatal, that they could not afford to wait for the salutary permanent effects of freedom. In the modern world, the greater size of political communities, and, above all, the separation between spiritual and temporal authority (which placed the direction of men's consciences in other hands than those which controlled their worldly affairs), prevented so great an interference by law. . . .

Apart from the peculiar tenets of individual thinkers, there is also in the world at large an increasing inclination to stretch unduly the powers of society over the individual, both by the force of opinion and even by that of legislation: and as the tendency of all the changes taking place in the world is to strengthen society, and diminish the power of the individual, this encroachment is not one of the evils which tend spontaneously to disappear, but, on the contrary, to grow more and more formidable. . . .

.　　.　　.

CHAPTER V

Applications

I have already observed that, owing to the absence of any recognized general principles, liberty is often granted where it should be withheld, as well as withheld where it should be granted; and one of the cases in which, in the modern European world, the sentiment of liberty is the strongest, is a case where, in my view, it is altogether misplaced. . . . One would almost think that a man's children were supposed to be literally, and not metaphorically, a part of himself, so jealous is opinion of the smallest interference of law with his absolute and exclusive control over them; more jealous than of almost any interference with his own freedom of action: so much less do the generality of mankind value liberty than power. Consider, for example, the case of education. Is it not almost a self-evident axiom, that the State should require and compel the education, up to a certain standard, of every human being who is born its citizen? Yet who is there that is not afraid to recognize and assert this truth? Hardly any one indeed will deny that it is one of the most sacred duties of the parents (or, as law and usage now stand, the father), after summoning a human being into the world, to give to that being an education fitting him to perform his part well in life towards others and towards himself. But while this is unanimously declared to be the father's duty, scarcely anybody, in this country, will bear to hear of obliging him to perform it. Instead of his being required to make any exertion or sacrifice for securing education to the child, it is left to his choice to accept it or not when it is provided gratis! It still remains unrecognized, that to bring a child into existence without a fair prospect of being able, not only to provide food for its body, but instruction and training for its mind, is a moral crime, both against the unfortunate offspring and against society; and that if the parent does not fulfill this obligation, the State ought to see it fulfilled, at the charge, as far as possible, of the parent.

Were the duty of enforcing universal education once admitted, there would be an end to the difficulties about what the State should teach, and how it should teach, which now convert the subject into a mere battle-field for sects and parties, causing the time and labor which should have been spent in educating, to be wasted in quarreling about education. If the government would make up its mind to *require* for every child a good education, it might save itself the trouble of *providing* one. It might leave to parents to obtain the education where and how they pleased, and content itself with helping to pay the school fees of the poorer classes of children, and defraying the entire school expenses of those who have no one else to pay for them. The objections which are urged with reason against State education, do not apply to the enforcement of education by the State, but to the State's taking upon iself to direct that education: which is a totally different thing. That the whole or any part of the education of the people should be in State hands, I go as far as any one in deprecating. All that has been said of the importance of individuality of character, and diversity in opinions and modes of conduct, involves, as of the same unspeakable importance, diversity of education. A general State education is a mere contrivance for molding people to be exactly like one another: and as the mold in which it casts them is that which pleases the predominant power in the government, whether this be a monarch, a priesthood, an aristocracy, or the majority of the existing generation in proportion as it is efficient and successful, it establishes a despotism over the mind, leading by natural tendency to one over the body. An education established and controlled by the State should only exist, if it exist at all, as one among many competing experiments, carried on for the purpose of example and stimulus, to keep the others up to a certain standard of excellence. Unless, indeed, when society in general is in so backward a state that it could not or would not provide for itself any proper institutions of education, unless the government undertook the task: then, indeed, the government may, as the less of two great evils, take upon itself the business of schools and universities, as it may that of joint-stock companies, when private enterprise, in a shape fitted for undertaking great works of industry, does not exist in the country. But in general, if the country contains a sufficient number of persons qualified to provide education under government auspices, the same persons would be able and willing to give an equally good education on the voluntary principle, under the assurance of remuneration afforded by a law rendering education compulsory, combined with the state aid to those unable to defray the expense.

The instrument for enforcing the law could be no other than public examinations, extending to all children, and beginning at an early age. . . . To prevent the State from exercising, through these arrangements, an improper influence over opinion, the knowledge required for passing an examination (beyond the merely instrumental parts of knowledge, such as languages and their use) should, even in the higher classes of examinations, be confined to facts and positive science exclusively. The examinations on religion, politics, or other disputed topics, should not turn on the truth or falsehood of opinions, but on the matter of fact that such and such an opinion is held, on such grounds, by such authors, or schools, or churches. . . . There would be nothing to hinder them from being taught religion, if their parents chose, at the same schools where they were taught other things. All attempts by the State to bias the conclusions of its citizens on disputed subjects, are evil; but it may very properly offer to ascertain and certify that a person possesses the knowledge, requisite to make his conclusions, on any given subject, worth attending to. A student of philosophy would be the better for being able to stand an examination both in Locke and in Kant, whichever of the two he takes up with, or even if with neither: and there is no reasonble objection to examining an atheist in the evidences of Christianity, provided he is not required to profess a belief in them. The examinations, however, in the higher branches of knowledge should, I conceive, be entirely voluntary. It would be giving too dangerous a power to governments, were they allowed to exclude any one from professions, even from the profession of teacher, for alleged deficiency of qualifications: and I think, with Wilhelm von Humboldt, that degrees, or other public certificates of scientific or professional acquirements, should be given to all who present themselves for examination, and stand the test; but that such certificates should confer no advantage over competitors, other than the weight which may be attached to their testimony by public opinion.

A Guide to Selections from *On Genius.*

In these passages, Mill asserts the view that knowledge must be based upon one's own experience. Knowledge of general truths, once they are discovered, at any rate, is no exception. Nor is that of truths depending upon mathematical arguments although their discovery is more difficult than their learning. Especially, truths concerning morals require to be verified in one's own introspection.

Genius as the capacity to succeed in the discovery of truth can be very widespread. So also can be another kind of genius—the capacity to appreciate works of art; genius of this kind must exist wherever a work of art is created or understood.

The ancient Greeks fostered genius in their method of instruction by demanding independent thought, and by reducing rote memorization (cram) to a minimum. But after the comprehensive work of Aristotle and Plato, knowledge came to look like a finished product; and people began to regard it as something to be acquired from others—by memorizing the propositions which embodied it. The teachings of Jesus enjoyed a similar formalization which gave them a dogmatism that made them easy to remember, and deprived them of their spiritual power. The treatment of knowledge as something to be gotten by memory (by cramming things into the mind) has now deprived most of the propositions we learn of their meaning.

This trait of modern education has led to a decline in genius. Mill argues that the decline might be stopped by teaching not for memory, but for independent reasoning, imagining, analysis, and empirical investigation.

SELECTIONS FROM

*On Genius**

———◄●►———

There is a language very generally current in the world, which implies that knowledge can be *vicarious;* that when a truth has become known to *any one,* all who follow have nothing to do but passively to receive it; as if one man, by reading or listening, could transport another man's knowledge ready manufactured into his own skull. As well might he try the experiment upon another man's eyesight. Those who have no eyesight of their own, or who are so placed that they cannot conveniently use it, must believe upon trust; they cannot *know.* A man who knows may tell me what he knows, as far as words go, and I may learn to parrot it after him; but if I would *know* it, I must place my mind in the same state in which he has placed his; I must make the thought my own thought; I must verify by my own observation, or by interrogating my own consciousness.

The exceptions and qualifications with which this doctrine must be taken, and which are more apparent than real, will readily present themselves. For example, it will suggest itself at once that the truth of which I am now speaking is *general* truth. To know an *individual* fact may be no exercise of mind at all; merely an exercise of the senses. The sole exercise of mind may have been in bringing the fact sufficiently close for the senses to judge of it; and *that* merit may be peculiar to the first discoverer: there may be talent in finding where the thief is hid, but none at all in being able to see him when found. The same observation applies in a less degree to some *general* truths. To know a general truth is, indeed, always an operation of the *mind:* but some physical truths may be brought to the test of sensation by an experiment so simple, and the conclusiveness of which is so immediately apparent, that the trifling degree of mental power implied in drawing the proper inference from it, is altogether eclipsed by the ingenuity which contrived the experiment, and the sagacious forecast of an undiscovered truth which set that ingenuity to work: qualities, the place of which may now be supplied by mere imitation.

So, again, in a case of mere *reasoning* from assumed premises, as, for instance, in mathematics, the process bears so strong an analogy to a

* Published in *Monthly Repository*, Volume VI, 1832, pp. 649–59.

merely mechanical operation, that the first discoverer alone has any real difficulty to contend against; the second may follow the first with very little besides patience and continued attention. But these seeming exceptions do not trench in the least upon the principle which I have ventured to lay down. If the first discovery alone requires genius, it is because the first discovery alone requires any but the simplest and most commonplace exercise of thought. Though genius be no particular mental power, but only mental power possessed in a peculiar degree, what implies no mental power at all, requires to be sure no genius.

But can this be said of the conviction which comes by the comparison and appreciation of numerous and scattered proofs? Can it, above all, be said of the knowledge of supersensual things, of man's mental and moral nature, where the appeal is to internal consciousness and self-observation, or to the experience of our common life interpreted by means of the key which self-knowledge alone can supply? The most important phenomena of human nature cannot even be conceived, except by a mind which has actively studied itself. Believed they may be, but as a blind man believes the existence and properties of colour. To *know* these truths is always to *discover* them. Every one, I suppose, of adult years, who has any capacity of knowledge, can remember the impression which he experienced when he *discovered* some truths which he thought he had known for years before. He had only believed them; they were not the fruits of his own consciousness, or of his own observation; he had taken them upon trust, or he had taken upon trust the premises from which they were inferred. If he had happened to forget them, they had been lost altogether; whereas the truths which we *know* we can discover again and again *ad libitum*.

It is with truths of this order as with the ascent of a mountain. Every person who climbs Mont Blanc exerts the same identical muscles as the first man who reached the summit; all that the first climber can do is to encourage the others and lend them a helping hand. What he has partly saved them the necessity of, is *courage:* it requires less hardihood to attempt to do what somebody has done before. It is an advantage also to have some one to point out the way and stop us when we are going wrong. Though one man cannot *teach* another, one man may *suggest* to another. I may be indebted to my predecessor for setting my own faculties to work; for hinting to me what questions to ask myself, and in what order; but it is not given to one man to *answer* those questions for another. Each person's own reason must work upon the materials afforded by that same person's own experience. Knowledge comes only from within; all that comes from without is but *questioning,* or else it is mere *authority*.

Now, the capacity of extracting the knowledge of general truth from our own consciousness, whether it be by simple *observation,* by that kind of self-observation which is called *imagination,* or by a more complicated process of analysis and induction, is *originality;* and where truth is the result, whoever says Originality says Genius. The man of the greatest philosophic genius does not more than this, evinces no higher faculty; whoever thinks at all, thinks to that extent, originally. Whoever knows anything of his own knowledge, not immediately obvious to the senses, manifests more or less of the same faculty which made a Newton or a Locke. Whosoever does this same thing systematically—whosoever, to the extent of his opportunity, gets at his convictions by his own faculties, and not by reliance on any other person whatever—that man, in proportion as his conclusions have truth in them, is an *original thinker,* and is, as much as anybody ever was, a *man* of *genius;* nor matters it though he should never chance to find out anything which somebody had not found out before him. There may be no hidden truths left for him to find, or he may accidentally miss them; but if he have courage and opportunity he *can* find hidden truths; for he has found all those which he knows, many of which were as hidden to *him* as those which are still unknown.

If the genius which *discovers* is no peculiar faculty, neither is the genius which *creates.* It was genius which produced the Prometheus Vinctus, the Oration on the Crown, the Minerva, or the Transfiguration; and is it not genius which *comprehends* them? Without genius, a work of genius may be *felt,* but it cannot possibly be understood.

The property which distinguishes every work of genius in poetry and art from incoherency and vain caprice is, that it is *one, harmonious,* and a *whole:* that its parts are connected together as standing in a common relation to some leading and central idea or purpose. This idea or purpose it is not possible to extract from the work by any mechanical rules. To transport ourselves from the point of view of a spectator or reader, or that of the poet or artist himself, and from that central point to look around and see how the details of the work all conspire to the same end, all contribute to body forth the same general conception, is an exercise of the same powers of imagination, abstraction, and discrimination (though in an inferior degree) which would have enabled ourselves to produce the selfsame work. Do we not accordingly see that as much genius is often displayed in explaining the design and bringing out the hidden significance of a work of art, as in creating it? I have sometimes thought that *conceptive* genius is, in certain cases, even a higher faculty than *creative.* From the data afforded by a person's conversation and life, to frame a connected outline of the inward structure of that person's mind, so as to know and feel what the man is, and how life and the world paint themselves to his conceptions; still more to decipher in that same manner the mind of an age or a nation, and gain from history or travelling a vivid conception of the mind of a Greek or Roman, a Spanish peasant, an American, or a Hindu, is an effort of genius, superior, I must needs believe, to any which was ever shown in the creation of a fictitious character, inasmuch as the imagination is limited by a particular set of conditions, instead of ranging at pleasure within the bounds of human nature. . . . According to my view, genius stands not in need of access to new truths, but is always where knowledge is, being itself nothing by a mind with capacity to know. There will be as much room and as much necessity for genius when mankind shall have found out everything attainable by their faculties, as there is now; it will still remain to distinguish the man who knows from the man who takes upon trust—the man who can feel and understand truth, from the man who merely assents to it, the active from the merely passive mind. Nor needs genius be a rare gift bestowed on few. By the aid of suitable culture all might possess it, although in unequal degrees.

.   .   .

The ancients, in this particular, were very differently circumstanced. When the range of human experience was still narrow—when, as yet, few facts had been observed and recorded, and there was nothing or but little to learn by rote, those who had curiosity to gratify, or who desired to acquaint themselves with nature and life, were fain to look into things, and not pay themselves with opinions; to see the objects themselves, and not their mere images reflected from the minds of those who had formerly seen them. Education *then* consisted not in giving what is called knowledge, that is, grinding down other men's ideas to a convenient size, and administering them in the form of *cram*—it was a series of exercises to form the thinking faculty itself, that the mind, being active and vigorous, might go forth and know.

Such was the education of Greece and Rome, especially Greece. Her philosophers were not formed, nor did they form their scholars, by placing a suit of ready-made truths before them, and helping them to put it on. They helped the disciple to form to himself an intellect fitted to seek truth for itself and to find it. No Greek or Roman schoolboy learnt anything by rote, unless it were verses of Homer or songs in honour of the gods. Modern superciliousness and superficiality have treated the disputations of the sophists as they have those of the schoolmen, with unbounded contempt: the contempt would be better bestowed on the tuition of Eton or Westminster. Those disputations were a kind of mental gymnastics, eminently conducive to acuteness in detecting fallacies; consistency and circumspection in tracing to its consequences; and a faculty of penetrating and searching analysis. They became ridiculous only when, like all other successful systems, they were imitated by persons incapable of entering into their spirit, and degenerated into foppery and *charlata-*

nerie. With powers thus formed, and no possibility of parroting where there was scarcely anything to parrot, what a man knew was his own, got at by using his own senses or his own reason; and every new acquisition strengthened the powers, by the exercise of which it had been gained.

Nor must we forget to notice the fact . . . that the life of a Greek was a perpetual conflict of adverse intellects, struggling with each other, or struggling with difficulty and necessity. Every man had to play his part upon a stage where *cram* was of no use—nothing but genuine *power* would serve his turn. The studies of the closet were combined with, and were intended as, a preparation for the pursuits of active life. There was no *littérature des salons,* no dilettantism in ancient Greece: wisdom was not something to be prattled about, but something to be done. It was this which, during the bright days of Greece, prevented theory from degenerating into vain and idle refinements, and produced that rare combination which distinguishes the great minds of that glorious people,—of profound speculation, and business-like matter-of-fact common sense. It was not the least of the effects of this union of theory and practice, that in the good times of Greece there is no vestige of anything like sentimentality. Bred to action, and passing their lives in the midst of it, all the speculations of the Greeks were for the sake of action, all their conceptions of excellence had a direct reference to it.

This was the education to form great statesmen, great orators, great warriors, great poets, great architects, great sculptors, great philosophers; because, once for all, it formed *men,* and not mere knowledge-boxes; and the men, being men, had minds, and could apply them to the work, whatever it might be, which circumstances had given them to perform. But this lasted not long: demolishing the comparatively weak attempts of their predecessors, two vast intellects arose, the one the greatest observer of his own or any age, the other the greatest dialectician, and both almost unrivalled in their powers of metaphysical analysis,—Aristotle and Plato. No sooner, by the exertions of these gigantic minds, and of others their disciples or rivals, was a considerable body of truth, or at least of opinion, got together—no sooner did it become *possible* by mere memory to seem to know something, and to be able for some purposes even to use that knowledge, as men use the rules of arithmetic who have not the slightest notion of the grounds of them, than men found out how much easier it is to remember than to think, and abandoned the pursuit of intellectual power itself for the attempt, without possessing it, to appropriate its results. Even the reverence which mankind had for these great men became a hindrance to following their example. Nature was studied not in nature, but in Plato or Aristotle, in Zeno or Epicurus. Discussion became the mere rehearsal of a lesson got by rote. The attempt to think for oneself fell into disuse; and, by ceasing to exercise the power, mankind ceased to possess it.

It was in this spirit that, on the rise of Christianity, the doctrines and precepts of Scripture began to be studied. For this there was somewhat greater excuse, as, where the authority was that of the Omniscient, the confirmation of fallible reason might appear less necessary. Yet the effect was fatal. The interpretation of the Gospel was handed over to grammarians and language-grinders. The words of him whose speech was in figures and parables were iron-bound and petrified into inanimate and inflexible *formulae*. Jesus was likened to a logician, framing a rule to meet all cases, and provide against all possible evasions, instead of a poet, orator, and *vates,* whose object was to purify and spiritualize the mind, so that, under the guidance of its purity, its own lights might suffice to find the law of which he only supplied the spirit, and suggested the general scope. Hence, out of the least dogmatical of books, have been generated so many dogmatical religions—each claiming to be found in the book, and none in the mind of man; they are above thought, and thought is to have nothing to do with them; until religion, instead of a spirit pervading the mind, becomes a crust encircling it, nowise penetrating the obdurate mass within, but only keeping out such rays of precious light or genial heat as might haply have come from elsewhere.

And after all which has been done to break down these vitiating, soul-debasing prejudices, against which every great mind of the last two centuries has protested, where are we now? Are not the very first general propositions that are presented for a child's acceptance, theological dogmas, presented not as truths believed by others, and which the child will hereafter be encouraged to know for itself, but as doctrines which it is to believe before it can attach any meaning to them, or be chargeable with the greatest guilt? At school, what is the child taught, except to repeat by rote, or at most to apply technical rules, which are lodged, not in his reason, but in his memory? When he leaves school, does not everything which a young person sees and hears conspire to tell him, that it is not expected he shall think, but only that he shall profess no opinion on any subject different from that professed by other people? Is there anything a man can do, short of swindling or forgery, (*à fortiori* a woman,) which will so surely gain him the reputation of a dangerous, or, at least, an unaccountable person, as daring, without either rank or reputation as a warrant for the eccentricity, to make a practice of forming his opinions for himself?

Modern education is all *cram*—Latin cram, mathematical cram, literary cram, political cram, theological cram, moral cram. The world already knows everything, and has only to tell it to its children, who, on their part, have only to hear, and lay it to rote (not to *heart*). Any purpose, any idea of training the mind itself, has gone out of the world. Nor can I yet perceive many symptoms of amendment. Those who dislike what is taught, mostly—if I may trust my own experience—dislike it not for being *cram*, but for being other people's cram, and not theirs. Were they the teachers, they would teach different doctrines, but they would teach them *as* doctrines, not as subjects for impartial inquiry. Those studies which only train the faculties, and produce no fruits obvious to the sense, are fallen into neglect. The most valuable kind of mental gymnastics, logic and metaphysics, have been more neglected and undervalued for the last thirty years, than at any time since the revival of letters. Even the ancient languages, which, when rationally taught, are, from their regular and complicated structure, to a certain extent a lesson of logical classification and analysis, and which give access to a literature more rich than any other, in all that forms a vigorous intellect and a manly character, are insensibly falling into disrepute as a branch of liberal education. Instead of them, we are getting the ready current coin of modern languages, and physical science taught empirically, by committing to memory its results. Whatever assists in feeding the body, we can see the use of; not so if it serves the body only by forming the mind.

Is it any wonder that, thus educated, we should decline in genius? That the ten centuries of England or France cannot produce as many illustrious names as the hundred and fifty years of little Greece? The wonder is, that we should have produced so many as we have, amidst such adverse circumstances. We have had some true philosophers, and a few genuine poets; two or three great intellects have revolutionized physical science; but in almost every branch of literature and art we are deplorably behind the earlier ages of the world. In art, we hardly attempt anything except spoiled copies of antiquity and the middle ages. We are content to copy them, because that requires less trouble and less cultivated faculties than to comprehend them. If we had genius to enter into the *spirit* of ancient art, the same genius would enable us to clothe that spirit in ever-new forms.

Where, then, is the remedy? It is in the knowledge and clear comprehension of the evil. It is in the distinct recognition, that the end of education is not to *teach*, but to fit the mind for learning from its own consciousness and observation; that we have occasion for this power under ever-varying circumstances, for which no routine or rule of thumb can possibly make provision. As the memory is trained by remembering, so is the reasoning power by reasoning; the imaginative by imagining; the analytic by analysing; the inventive by finding out. Let the education of the mind consist in calling out and exercising these faculties: never trouble yourself about giving knowledge—train the *mind*—keep it supplied with materials, and knowledge will come of itself. Let all *cram* be ruthlessly discarded. Let each person be made to feel that in other things he may believe upon trust—if he find a trustworthy authority—but that in the line of his peculiar duty, and in the line of the duties common to all men, it is his business to *know*. Let the feelings of society cease to stigmatize independent thinking, and divide its censure between a lazy derelection of the duty and privilege of thought, and the overweening self-conceit of a half-thinker, who rushes to his conclusions without taking the trouble to understand the thoughts of other men. Were all this done, there would be no complaint of any want of genius in modern times. But when will that hour come? Though it come not at all, yet is it not less your duty and mine to strive for it,—and first to do what is certainly and absolutely in our power, to realize it in our own persons.

Bibliography

ANSCHUTZ, R. P., *The Philosophy of J. S. Mill*, Oxford, Clarendon Press, 1953.

PLAMENATZ, JOHN P., *The English Utilitarians*, Oxford, Blackwell's, 1958 (second revised edition). Chapter VIII.

STEPHEN, SIR LESLIE, *The English Utilitarians*, Volume III, John Stuart Mill," London, Duckworth, 1900; London, London School of Economics, 1950.

XII

JOHN DEWEY

JOHN DEWEY WAS BORN IN 1859 in Burlington, Vermont; he died in 1952. After his graduation from the University of Vermont, he spent two years teaching school. In 1882, he entered upon graduate study of philosophy at The Johns Hopkins University and received the Ph.D. degree in 1884. From that time until his retirement in 1930, he taught philosophy at several institutions—from 1904 onward, at Columbia University in its Teachers College and Department of Philosophy.

Throughout Dewey's mature life, the nature, the importance, and the reform of education were major interests. In 1889, he published a book with J. A. McLellan entitled *Applied Psychology: An Introduction to the Principles and Practice of Education*. He had already written his *Psychology* in which he argued that that discipline was properly a natural science, not a subject for speculation. In 1896, while teaching at the University of Chicago, he established an experimental school in which the

1 Large portions of this chapter are reproduced here from: *The Year Book of Education 1957*, edited by George Z. F. Bereday and Joseph A. Lauwerys; published in association with The Institute of Education, University of London, and Teachers College, Columbia University, by Evans Brothers Ltd., London, and Harcourt, Brace and World, Inc., New York; §1, "The Great Traditions," Chapter III, "American Thinking: Some Doctrines of John Dewey," pp. 52–64, by Kingsley Price. I wish to express sincere appreciation to both publishers for their generous permission to use these materials.

science of psychology and the principles of education might be investigated and children taught well. It lacked the traditional procedures, techniques, and curriculum; and it enjoyed a considerable success. The school incurred the disfavor of powerful University officials, however; and, after seven years, it closed. Dewey resigned from the University of Chicago and took up his membership in Columbia University. A series of articles and books on philosophy of education (the series extended to the end of his life) followed the books already mentioned—notably the famous *School and Society* (1899), *Democracy and Education* (1916), *Experience and Education* (1938), and *Education Today* (1940).

Dewey's interest in education cannot be separated from his interest in philosophy at large. The business of philosophy is the solution of human problems; and, since education consists in training people to solve them, philosophy and education cannot be thought apart. Interspersed with his writings on philosophy of education, there are many others on metaphysics, epistemology, ethics, æsthetics, and logic—especially, *The Quest for Certainty* (1929), *Experience and Nature* (1925), *Ethics* (with Tufts, 1908), *Art as Experience* (1934), *Logic: The Theory of Inquiry* (1938), and *Essays in Experimental Logic* (1916). In all these books and others, too, Dewey emphasizes the point that philosophy and education are close allies, even though education is not his immediate concern in them.

The continual reconstruction of experience at which philosophy properly aims is not achieved solely through the formal instrumentalities of education. Other efforts assist it; and Dewey wrote many books and articles not explicitly concerned with the schools and not narrowly philosophical—notably, *Reconstruction in Philosophy* (1920), *Human Nature and Conduct* (1922), and *The Public and its Problems* (1927). His ultimate interests were primarily social, not academic, despite his long career in teaching and the ample quantity of his literary production. His life, as clearly as his writings, exhibits this reforming zeal. Not long after the close of World War I, he began a series of visits to other countries that extended into the early 30's—visits to Japan, China, Turkey, Mexico, The Union of Soviet Socialist Republics, and South Africa. These visits made him an unofficial spokesman for American thought to other parts of the world, but they also reflected the interest on the part of other nations in his educational theory—an interest which led most, if not all of them to endeavor to put that theory to work. This theory was already extremely influential in the United States and was especially evident in the Progressive movement.

Dewey's efforts at reform were not directed at the schools alone. He was influential in organizations of teachers, first in the Teachers Union, then in the Teachers Guild in New York, and in the American Association of University Professors. He was active in the American Civil Liberties Union, and he headed the unofficial American investigation into the charges against Trotsky. He defended Bertrand Russell when he was removed from his teaching post in the College of the City of New York, and he protested the decision against Sacco and Vanzetti. He endeavored to organize a third party which would deal seriously with the question of social and economic reform—a question which, he thought, the two major political parties only skirted at best. He publicly endeavored to prevent war. And all these activities he supplemented not only by his books, but also by a long tenure as contributing editor to the *New Republic*.

Dewey's life was as much a public career as it was a private biography. His social and political views still serve, in this country, to distinguish liberals from others; but many of his views concerning education are so widely accepted as to bear no impress of his name. Those which are not coin of the educational realm are still sufficiently vital and important throughout the world to incur frequent refutations whose style exhibits as much heat as cogency.

EDUCATIONAL THEORY

THE WRITINGS OF JOHN DEWEY extend over a period of some sixty years and embody many different statements on particular topics. An exhaustive study of his work would consider whether, and in what respects, his views altered during the course of his long philosophical and literary career; but here there is not time for that consideration. I shall set down in brief compass the essential points in Dewey's theory of education and certain parts of his philosophy which are pertinent to that theory. I shall omit exposition of much that is important for other purposes. In view of his profound influence on philosophy generally, and on the theory and practice of education in the United States and throughout the world, my treatment of his work may seem somewhat perfunctory. I can plead only that his views are more familiar to many readers than those of other philosophers represented in this book and that, in any case, space is growing short.

STATEMENTS OF FACT

The statements involved in Dewey's educational theory are not easy to classify. Many seem intended as statements of fact, but some might regard them, actually, as expressing Dewey's evaluation of facts. Others seem intended as value statements, but many readers would regard them, actually, as Dewey's descriptions only of what he took the facts to be. Others, still, seem intended both as statements of fact and as statements of value, but it is not clear that they are not, instead, analyses of the ideas of the facts and values they seem intended to state.

Here, with some trepidation, I present as statements of fact those I believe Dewey would regard as such. They are of three kinds, and they concern human nature, society, and the condition of the schools. We shall consider them in that order.

Human nature

Factors of two kinds, according to Dewey, constitute the nature of every human being—force and pattern. Force (Dewey calls it "impulse") is the fluorescence of living tissue; and as a consequence of it, the human being is constantly active.[2] There is no direction immanent in this activity; the behavior of the infant is random and aimless. But very quickly, a pattern is assumed by impulse; and in that pattern, impulse finds a direction and a goal. This impulse is innate to the human creature, but the pattern in which impulse is manifested (Dewey calls it "habit") is entirely acquired.

A habit is a disposition to respond in a certain way to environmental stimuli.[3] A person acts habitually provided that, given certain circumstances, he responds in a given fashion to certain stimulating conditions. The motor response is an objective; it affords a release for impulse. The mode of release is taught by experience, and the smooth release of impulse which the organism learns is its adjustment to its world. In adjustment, impulse finds its objective; and adjustment is what results from the articulation of impulse by habit. Thus, when habit is superimposed on impulse, the latter receives a direction and a goal from the banks which channel it. Dewey's point is that all human behavior (except perhaps for reflex action) is composed of innate impulse organized by acquired habit.

Intelligence is a habit which is actuated when other habits break down. A habit breaks down when its change lags behind changes in the environment and when habits conflict. A way of responding to environmental stimuli may persist after the environment has changed in such a way as to make the response no longer effective in securing the smooth release of impulse, i.e., in securing adjustment. Thus, for exercise, one may continue to play football after the time of life during which it is safe. This is a lag in habit. Also, one may try to respond to the same environmental stimuli in two or more ways, i.e., habits may conflict. This

[2] John Dewey, *Human Nature and Conduct,* Modern Library, New York, 1930, pp. 89–90.
[3] *Ibid.,* pp. 41, 89.

occurs when money in one's environment stimulates the patterns both of generosity and of miserliness. In both lag and conflict, impulse is impeded or blocked, smooth release is prevented, and adjustment is not achieved. On these occasions, intelligence comes into play. It is the habit of observing the facts which give rise to the blocking of impulse, of entertaining hypotheses as to what conduct might serve to secure adjustment by altering these facts, of selecting one of those hypotheses for verification because of the apparent capacity of the consequences foreseen to institute desirable adjustment, of acting upon it, of observing whether the actual consequences of acting upon it are those desirable ones foreseen, of verifying another hypothesis if they are not, and so on, until some satisfactory state of affairs is reached. This is, as Dewey understands it, the method of science, and it is common to all intelligent behavior, since it is its very nature. But where intelligence is securely established, to act intelligently is a habitual response to a problem, and is a provisional way of channeling impulse between the non-intelligent courses in which it flows before and after. Thus, we may say that impulse from time to time demands reform of its pattern, that these times are those of lag or conflict, and that intelligence is a pattern through which impulse runs when its old patterns are unsatisfactory until intelligence finds for it another non-intelligent but still habitual course.

There is, then, no such thing as a universal human nature. There is no single enduring substance which acts and undergoes. There are no instincts whose unlearned objectives might provide a basis for a universally compelling goal for all individual and collective endeavor.[4] There are no innate faculties whose exercise would constitute a nature common to our race. There is, in the human being, only impulse, in various ways shaped by learned habits to find its directions and its goals in whatever activities provide adjustment for it from one place and time to another. What man is, is what he does here and there, now and then.

Society

A society, according to Dewey, is a system of institutions whose subordinate parts fit together, and which as a whole can fit together with other societies. We can understand this statement by understanding the concepts employed in making it. Let us consider, first, that of "institution."

An institution is a group habit, i.e., a way in which a group of persons responds to environmental stimuli. It is, first, a pattern which involves the impulse of several persons. In the family, for example, the impulse of several persons is directed toward sexual fulfillment and toward the care of the young. But, secondly, the several persons involved are

---

4 *Ibid.*, pp. 149 f.

united in a certain fashion. In a family, each person foresees, or at least comes to foresee, the effects of his action upon other members, and acts to secure only those consequences which, taken all together, advance the adjustment of each. The parents and the children have a common interest in a shared goal. The result is group behavior. The behavior of individuals constitutes that of a group, provided that the consequences aimed at by each are selected in the light of their influence upon, and their possible influence by activities of the others. The entire set of consequences of possible activities thus determined is a shared goal, and the entire set of impulses toward the various members of this set is a common interest. In group behavior, there must be a common interest in a shared goal. Thus, in team play, each person determines his actions in the light of their influence upon other persons and of theirs upon his; and from such determination on the part of each, the action of the team as a whole results. The activities of persons who make up an institution, like those of the members of a team or of a family, must fit together in this way; if they do not, they compose no institution, although they may form a collection of merely disparate or conflicting activities.[5]

The subordinate parts of a society are institutions, and to say that they form a society is to say that they fit together in a way similar to that through which the activities of individuals determine an institution. A society for the protection of birds, for example, is made up of the executive committee, the committees on membership, on legislation, on publicity, etc. The activities of these committees fit together, and this fitting together consists in the foreseeing, by members of the subordinate institutions, of the effects of the conduct of one group on that of the others and the attempt to make these foreseen consequences such that the members of all the institutions may work for them or share them. If there were not this shared goal, there would not be a single society for the benefit of birds, but several independent or conflicting committees. In the same way, a city is composed of many institutions—the board of aldermen, the mayor, the city manager, and what not—the behavior of all of which must emanate from a common interest and flow toward a common goal as long as the city is constituted by their joint action.

A society, while made up of institutions which fit together in the way described, also can fit together with other societies. A city can share the consequences it endeavors to secure with a county, a province, or a nation; and a nation, by working for results which can supplement those aimed at by other nations, can fit together with them.

5 *Ibid., passim; Experience and Education,* Chapter iv; *The Public and Its Problems,* Chapters i and ii.

Condition of schools

Dewey began his work when the spirit of the schools was highly authoritarian. The teacher ordered, drilled, and commanded; and while in the United States, attendance well into adolescence was becoming universal and compulsory, relatively few people, Dewey thought, learned much in school. The three R's and the classical humanistic subjects still dominated the curriculum, and their failure to call forth the interest of many students made authoritarian methods for teaching them seem more necessary still. Everyone was going to school to learn much the same thing in much the same way; but many, in fact, learned nothing. The old curriculum was being administered to everyone, and the result was a failure that, starting with method, pervaded all aspects of education. Dewey pointed to the remedy in a new notion of education, of its goal objective, and of the methods through which that goal might be realized.

RECOMMENDATIONS

Goal recommendation

Dewey tells us that "education," in its broadest sense, means the process by which any society perpetuates itself.[6] The vital impulse of infants demands expression, but contains within itself no pattern for it. The process of supplying this pattern, of shaping infantile vitality, is education; and the shape imposed is the system of institutions which compose society. Education is, thus, a necessary condition for the survival of any group. For if there were no such shaping, the energies of the young, expressing themselves haphazard, would develop habits of individual and social activity at odds with the system of institutions into which they were born and would break with rather than continue it. All the young must be formed in this way; otherwise, some will develop independently of their society. Education is the process of giving form to impulse; its goal objective is the perpetuation in all the younger generation of the society which educates.

Subordinate recommendations

Dewey makes many recommendations concerning the pursuit of this goal. They pertain to its methods, i.e., the manner of forming the young, and to its curriculum, i.e., the kinds of things that method ought to teach. We shall consider the recommendations which are central in each class.

---

6 John Dewey, *Democracy and Education*, The Macmillan Co., New York, 1916, pp. 3–4.

METHOD. The method of education, Dewey argues, ought to be one of discipline, but not of authority. The latter is control of the young by external force and is bound to fail. It is based on the assumption that there are some objectively good or right goals of conduct and that a child might be compelled to achieve them. If these assumptions were true, the teacher might, legitimately, exercise authority; for through it, he could produce a good state of affairs in his charges. But these assumptions are both false. No thing is good and no action is right objectively, i.e., in total independence of the desires of human beings; all value is subjective. Moreover, no action can be an achievement unless the doer desires to do it and unless he foresees its existence as a consequence of some other action of his own. Where a deed is not desired or not foreseen, even though a person does it, it cannot be one of his accomplishments. The energetic anticipation necessary to achievement cannot be forced upon one from without. But authority is precisely the process of applying pressure to compel the child to achieve what he neither desires nor foresees doing and is, therefore, always futile. Since goods are subjective and desire incapable of compulsion, external force can never be a method for producing good results. Discipline in education, if it is effective, cannot consist in the exercise of authority.

Discipline is a persistent effort to learn, and it cannot occur unless the student has a desire for, and an anticipation of, the thing to be learned.[7] But desire, or as Dewey also says, "interest," can arise only when impulse is impeded. One cannot desire to learn arithmetic unless he feels a problem in not knowing it—unless his impulse, by virtue of his lack of arithmetical knowledge, is blocked and hampered. A persistent effort to learn cannot arise unless the student feels a problem in his ignorance; and in this way, discipline emanates from within the learner.

But to feel a problem about subject-matter, while a necessary condition for discipline in education, is not enough. In addition, persistent effort to learn requires that others be involved in the same process. One will not try to solve a problem, even though he feels it, if doing so isolates him from his group; and cooperation, i.e., the determination of one's own action in the light of a goal shared with others, is necessary for persistent effort. Discipline in education emanates from within the student but requires, as well, a place for the activity of each student in a collective effort to achieve a common goal of knowledge.[8]

If the method of learning is disciplined, it will also be one of intelligence. The problem felt will naturally lead to searching for hypotheses for its solution—a process greatly facilitated by the pooling of rele-

[7] *Ibid.,* p. 151.
[8] John Dewey, *Experience and Education,* Chapter iv.

vant experience of preceding events. Cooperative thought will readily work out the consequences of each hypothesis. Testing will occur, and the best solution will be discovered. Indeed, all disciplined learning must be intelligent behavior because learning of any sort consists in such behavior.[9]

A disciplined method of instruction is one which promotes disciplined learning. While one cannot say, independently of particular contexts of learning and teaching, what a teacher ought to do, one can lay down certain guiding injunctions. First, all compulsion should be avoided. The problem it creates in the student's mind is that of evading the force rather than of learning the subject matter. Mechanical drill, flogging (gross or subtle), competition for grades, the threat of nonpromotion—all such devices, except those necessary for protection of the school, are to be eschewed as methods of instruction. Secondly, the teacher ought to do whatever is necessary to make the student feel a problem in not knowing the subject matter at hand. He should proffer objectives upon which the student's impulse may focus; and, by thus fostering desire, should arouse the internal force of impulse toward mastery. Thirdly, in order to arouse interest, the teacher ought to familiarize himself thoroughly with capacities and interests of each student. There are no universal interests and, consequently no universally desirable or interesting subjects. Disciplined learning requires of the instructor attention to the individual student. Without it, the proffered objectives may call forth no answering response of impulse. Moreover, the subjects taught must vary in accord with the varying interests and capacities of different students. Otherwise, no genuine learning will occur. Fourthly, the teacher ought to create a situation in the classroom in which every person present, including himself, cooperates with the others in the process of learning. As a cooperating member of such a group, he himself has, at best, the advantages only of greater experience, not of greater authority over the pupils. These are the general conditions for discipline in instruction, because they are the conditions of disciplined learning; and any method of instruction which conforms to them can succeed, because it will provide for the student a way of learning by his own doing.

CURRICULUM. Dewey's recommendations concerning curriculum depend upon his definition of "education" and his view of its goal. The term education refers to the process of shaping impulse, and the goal objective of that process should be the perpetuation of the institutions that compose the society in question. The content of education, consequently, wherever it is complete, should include all subjects required

[9] John Dewey, *Democracy and Education*, pp. 180–82.

for shaping the impulse of the young in the pattern of the parent society.[10] The management and operation of business and industry, the natural and social sciences, the professions, the liberal, humanistic classical subjects, and the arts both practical and fine—all, equally, ought to be taught. The widespread view that for Dewey all education ought to be practical, in some narrow and exclusive sense of that term, is mistaken. He urges, however, that the subjects taught to each child should be determined in the light of the objectives upon which his impulse focuses. There are no subjects which are interesting to all; consequently, no single kind of subject matter, such as the classical languages, ought to be mastered by all. But all subjects should be available, since any student might prove interested in, and therefore capable of learning any. Many more might be interested in the liberal subjects than have hitherto mastered them; but while available to all, they, like all the others, should be imposed upon none.

Dewey's recommendations concerning method and curriculum were espoused by many followers; and, acting upon them, the latter brought about considerable changes in the schools. The injunctions to avoid compulsion, to present the subject as a real problem, to arouse interest by appeal to proclivities of individual students, and to carry on study in groups of which the teacher is a participating member were directed against the spirit of authority. No doubt they altered it greatly. His recommendation that all subjects be taught also won wide acceptance, and his followers used it to introduce into the schools many subjects of a practical and enjoyable kind that had been alien to them. The concepts of "the whole child," the "child centered" school, "life adjustment," *et alia,* are distortions of Dewey's opinions; but they represent the enthusiasm with which many accepted his recommendations.

PHILOSOPHY OF EDUCATION

EPISTEMOLOGY

Dewey holds that traditional views concerning knowledge are quite wrong. Their error springs from likening a knower to a spectator. The latter confronts an object which he does not alter. If what he watches were not independent in this way, he would not be its spectator; he would be, at least in part, its creator instead. The method of the spectator is passive recognition of what is there, and his objective is perfect certainty

---

10 *Ibid.,* p. 226. "The subject-matter of education consists primarily of the meanings which supply content to existing social life. The continuity of social life means that many of these meanings are contributed by past collective experience."

or assurance concerning it.[11] Thinking of a knower as a spectator, philosophers have required that the objects known be independent of our knowing them, that the method of knowing them be mere recognition, and that the purpose of knowing be perfect certainty concerning the objects known. With these requirements in mind, they have constructed different metaphysical theories as to the world we can know. That everything is really forms or universals, that everything is really the forces discussed by scientists, that everything is really everyday objects, that everything is really sense-data—these are all theories of the knowable world designed to meet the requirements of knowledge just mentioned.[12] Philosophers have sought for certainty that springs from nothing more than passive recognition of independent objects, and they have invented metaphysics to assure success. The difficulty is that the certainty they thus guarantee is certainty about a world completely unimportant—and unimportant no matter which metaphysical theory one takes as true.

The unimportance of the world of metaphysics lies in its incapacity to be altered by our action. Thought concerning knowledge has separated it too far from action. If the objects we know cannot be altered by us, then the world we know cannot be controlled for our benefit. It is the business of philosophy to remove this separation, and it can be done by showing that knowledge is a species of activity.[13]

Dewey tries to show that knowing is a kind of action; and to do so he makes use of his theory of human nature. Impulse must find a goal, and it finds it in habit. The organism whose impulse is thus channelled is adjusted. Still, habit sometimes breaks down. Intelligence is a way in which adjustment is re-established in these circumstances. Dewey understands knowing by reference to intelligence and, consequently, by reference to human nature.

Intelligence begins in consciousness. When there is no need for readjustment, we notice nothing. The familiar left-hand turn, we execute without being aware of doing so; but a roadblock springs immediately to attention. Consciousness occurs only where habits break down, and it consists in the awareness of problems. Its objects are things to be done.

The consciousness of problems in our environment leads to thought. This is the use of symbols—of words and sentences; and symbols represent actions to be performed, together with the consequences to which those actions lead.[14] Thus, "rose" means a certain set of operations together with certain experiences (of color, shape, of fragrance, etc.) to which they give rise; while "red" means a certain set of operations to-

11 John Dewey, *The Quest for Certainty*, Capricorn Books, G. P. Putnam's Sons, New York, 1960, pp. 71, 171, 196.
12 *Ibid.*, p. 195.
13 *Ibid.*, p. 284.
14 *Ibid.*, pp. 111, 137, 151, 221.

gether with a consequent particular color experience. A sentence, thus, always means something hypothetical in character. "That rose is red," means that *if* certain operations are performed by normal persons, they will experience a certain color. To think is to use symbols; and to use symbols is to imagine certain operations and the consequences which they yield. To think about a problem is to imagine a solution for it, i.e., to hold before our minds a set of operations not yet performed, together with their consequences not yet realized, where these operations and these consequences constitute a solution of a problem or a readjustment of habits broken down. The consciousness of problems gives rise, in this way, to thoughts which may embody their solutions.

Noticing the problematic features in our environment causes us to think of ways in which like problems have been solved before. Out of the confusion engendered by the discovery that our road is closed, a landmark soon stands out in consciousness. It reminds us of another road which took us to our destination on some earlier occasion. We find it and arrive only a little late. In this case, earlier experience brings to mind a set of possible operations which, in imagination, lead us to our destination. They are the meaning of the thought carried by the sentence, "If we take the other road, we shall arrive." Making these operations real in actual performance does, in fact, yield the consequence we used them to foresee. Solving a problem amounts, in this way, to acting upon the environment in order to bring about some consequence—to a rearrangement of our habits so that impulse can achieve its goal of smooth release. Where the first hypothesis fails, we try others until we find success. The solution of a problem is an overt action which is continuous with its possibility—with the meaning of its thought. In this way, thought and action appear as different phases of the same process—one earlier, the other later; thought the vision, action its embodiment.[15]

Intelligence is the habit of responding in this way to problematic situations. An intelligent person is one who always acts to solve his problems by thinking about the courses of conduct which might remove them and by acting upon them until he finds success. Such a person has knowledge. In what does his knowledge consist?

The knowledge which intelligence creates is not passive recognition of an unalterable world. Rather, it is a relation between a meaning or a thought and an overt action.[16] What we know is not something already existing; it is, rather, the knowledge that if we make certain possible actions real, the consequences we desire will follow. The knowable world is a set of activities leading to consequences which lead to other operations and consequences, etc. The method of knowing is not mere

15 *Ibid.*, pp. 166–67, 181.
16 *Ibid.*, pp. 198, 221, 242.

passive recognition of this relation between possible and actual actions; rather, it is the procedure of acting to verify the possibilities expressed in thought. The purpose of knowing is never perfect certainty; rather, it is the establishment of new habits which will bring impulse to its goal. Since what we know is not something independent of our alteration of it, the truth of our knowledge cannot consist in a mere transcription of reality; rather, it amounts to the ability of the operations we envision in meaning to bring us to the condition we desire in act. The truth of knowledge is the utility a thought possesses for showing us the way to the solution of a problem.[17] Knowing is a kind of acting, and the world we know is a set of problems together with the ways for solving them.

This conception of knowledge leads Dewey to argue that it is the source of freedom. To be free is to possess the instruments by use of which we may alter the environment to bring it closer to our needs. The free man knows how to institute changes which enable him to secure adjustment to the world. Knowledge, as Dewey understands it, is a set of such instruments—all the operations which experience shows are useful to human life. Knowledge is power, and in the ability to control which power implies lies the only freedom man can exercise.[18]

Dewey holds that his view concerning the origin, the method, and the objects of knowing brings the philosophical treatment of knowledge into line with the present state of science—the activity where we find the best examples of knowledge. Science is concerned to answer questions or solve problems. It solves them by developing hypotheses, deducing consequences from them, verifying those consequences, and retaining, rejecting, or modifying its hypotheses as the consequences verified direct. Its hypotheses are true if they thus yield the consequences desired and foreseen or predicted; if they do not, they are false. The control which the scientist exercises over his world is based upon his deliberate use of statements that have been subjected to this empirical test, and those statements are arrived at by acting on them according to the pattern of the hypothetico-deductive method. Not all knowledge is narrowly scientific—physical, biological, or chemical. The painter and the poet know the clouds and storms quite as well as does the meteorologist; and they know quite different truths about them. But the knowledge of all three consists in following paths which, however they may diverge, exhibit a single pattern—one which starts at clouds and storms, proceeds through verification of some hypothesis about them, and terminates in solutions to problems that arise in situations in which men and climate come together in consciousness.[19]

---

17 *Ibid.*, p. 245.
18 *Ibid.*, p. 250.
19 *Ibid.*, pp. 217–22.

ETHICS

Dewey wrote a great deal on ethical topics—much more than can be discussed here. For our purposes, there are four doctrines which must be stated. They are his views concerning value in general, the relation of means to ends, the criterion of moral value, and the nature of the best society and the best individual.

Value in general

Dewey contends that value or goodness is not a property or set of properties which delimits a single class in which we find all the things called "good." There are, on the contrary, at least two generically distinct references for the term. One is the class of unanticipated goods which Dewey sometimes calls "gratifications"; and the other is the class of goods properly so-called.[20] The members of the first class do not depend upon the directed activity of the one who enjoys them; pleasure in the prospect of a valley does not result from the directed activity of a hiker who comes upon it by chance. The members of the second class do depend upon such directed activity. We must examine this view a little more closely.

MEANS AND ENDS. Goods of the second sort are those temporal wholes of which the earlier parts are means to the later. The relation of means to ends is a causal relation, but it is also more than this. Taking food is a cause of survival, but it is not a means thereto unless some other feature is present. The other feature is the desirability of the cause and the effect taken together. Desire arises where impulse is blocked, and intelligence reveals a possibility of adjustment together with steps to be taken in its pursuit. Where these steps (the cause) together with their effect (the possibility of adjustment) constitute a whole which is desired, there is a relation of means to ends. Thus, eating is a means to survival, provided that a life which includes eating food and surviving is desired. Desiring a cause alone does not make it a means, and desiring an effect alone does not make it an end. It is, rather, the desirability of both in their entirety which makes one a means to the other; and the means-end relation is identical with the part-whole relation where the whole is desired by someone, and where the parts are related causally.[21]

Any whole of this sort is a good, properly speaking; but as such, it is only a candidate for moral value. A moral value is such a whole of conduct that has been judged by the person acting as preferable to other alternative possible wholes of conduct. A moral evil is such a whole, but one

---

[20] John Dewey, "Theory of Valuation" in *International Encyclopedia of Unified Science*, Vol. II, No. 4, p. 37.
[21] *Ibid.*, p. 41; *Human Nature and Conduct*, pp. 225–32, 269.

which has been rejected in the process of deciding what to do.[22] Thus, voting for A as a cause of bringing about one political condition and voting for B as a cause of another may both be desirable; but voting for A rather than B with similar effects in mind is an action which possesses moral value.

CRITERION OF MORAL VALUE. Dewey proposes as the criterion for moral value the possibility of growth contained in the whole desired. Growth is "cumulative movement of action toward a later result."[23] And by this definition Dewey seems to mean that it consists in a constant "formation of new purposes and new responses."[24] It is a good to engage in any action which is a cause of another thing, where both are desired in their causal connection. Burglary, if desired, along with the steps that further it, is a good. But it permits little or no opportunity for continuing formation of new goals for the burglar and others, and is, therefore, not so good an action as others, e.g., as rationally conducted social welfare work. It would, therefore, be incorrect to elect burglary as one's profession in preference to social work. The definition of "good" serves to mark out what is valuable; but the criterion of moral value—growth—serves to show us which of the numerous competing values are the correct ones for the choice which transforms them into moral values.

The best individual and the best society

Any individual life may be good, for any individual life may be one in which ends that release impulse are held in view and successful steps taken to accomplish them. But the best life, one in which there is a maximum of growth, can be achieved only by those who are intelligent. For the habits of every person, from time to time, begin to lag or to conflict; and if intelligence does not operate to remove the consequent blocking of impulse, the formation of new purposes and new responses does not occur. Intelligent behavior is the best guarantee of continuing growth; and continuity in growth is the best guarantee of moral excellence.

To some extent, any society is good; for so long as it endures, the institutions which compose it must anticipate in desire, and endeavor to secure a concert of the consequences of their activities. But a democracy is the best society.[25] In it there is an equality of opportunity for all, i.e., there is no class stratification. Equality of opportunity is the guarantee that each person can share in foreseeing and achieving the activities of the

---

22 John Dewey, "Theory of Valuation," pp. 23–24, 41, 59.
23 John Dewey, *Democracy and Education,* p. 49.
24 *Ibid.,* p. 206.
25 *Ibid.,* pp. 94–102.

institutions to which he belongs. This condition requires the maximum use of intelligence and, consequently, permits a maximum of individual growth. Moreover, democracy is characterized by the minimum of restriction upon the conduct of individuals and institutions; and this condition permits the maximum of growth in cooperation between societies.

EPISTEMOLOGY AND ETHICS

The burden of Dewey's discussion of knowledge is that we can know only what lies within our experience and the method of knowing it is that of hypothesis and verification. This view rejects all doctrines, like those of Plato, which hold that knowing requires a reference to something non-natural and non-experiential. It also rejects a view opposed to this one, namely, that if we make no reference to something fixed and eternal, we have no knowledge at all. Between metaphysics and scepticism, Dewey holds, there lies the correct view concerning knowledge: knowing is the active experimental use of things to verify in consequent experience the hypotheses which foretell it.

The outcome of Dewey's ethical reflection is that valid moral statements embody knowledge. When I state that something is good, I say that it is desired; and my statement may be tested in the same way as any other by discovering whether what it foresees does occur, i.e., whether anyone does, in fact, desire it. And when I state that something is morally good, I state that it is a means-end complex of conduct which someone desires more than some other whole, because it contains the possibility of greater growth. This statement, too, can be tested like any other, i.e., by acting to see whether the consequences it aims to do, in fact, ensue—whether the thing referred to is a means-end complex preferred to some other because it does, in fact, contain greater growth. And Dewey's moral statement in favor of the individual life of intelligence and democratic social existence may be verified in the same way. There is no need, in all this, to refer to non-natural things in order to account for the validity of our moral statements; nor, failing such reference, can we hold that moral statements have no validity whatever. Between an impracticable morality based on a meaningless metaphysics and a corrupt scepticism based on the view that moral statements tell us nothing, lies, in Dewey's opinion, the true view that moral statements, like all others, find their truth in their utility for bringing us to foreseen consequences in experience—consequences which lead continually to greater growth.

The view that to know is to think out and verify hypotheses, and that moral statements may embody knowledge, gives the key to freedom and control over the content of our lives. Our freedom is our ability to do what we prefer and is manifested in our choice of alternative courses of conduct. The statement that something is morally good expresses such a choice, and its validity enables us to control our lives by determining what experiences they shall contain. We possess this freedom and may exercise this control despite the fact that all our knowledge of the good life develops from past experience and concludes in future experience. In thought, we entertain the possibilities of operations and their future consequences. And since we think before we act, we can compare, exclude, and combine these possibilities in order to create anew—in order to foresee ends better than the past has known. Thought alone cannot show us their superiority; only knowledge, action which brings in fact the ends we hold in view, can issue us that warrant. But thought does, in this way, create splendid pictures of a life that never was on land or sea; and in light of ideals formulated from reflection on past experience and directed toward future experience, we can act to reconstruct and to improve both individual lives and social institutions. These ideals are not static; they change continually as old problems are solved and new ones emerge. They are continually reformed by the freedom thought affords and continually tested by man's effort to reconstruct experience in their image. They do not descend ready-made from a supernatural domain; man creates them for himself by his critical intelligence out of materials offered by the past. Freedom is the ability to act upon our own ideals, and control is the knowledge action brings that these comprehensive moral statements are true or useful.

ETHICS AND EDUCATION

According to Dewey, education is the process of giving habits to the impulse of the young; and its goal objective ought to be the perpetuation in them of the society into which they are born. His ethical theory offers a justification for this goal. Any society permits of greater growth than does chaotic anarchy, and all prefer the former to the latter. Consequently, a society which educates the young to reproduce its institutions performs an action which is morally good.

But merely to perpetuate society is not the best goal objective education can adopt. The best life for individuals is the life of intelligence—of freedom and control over one's own experience; and the best society is democratic—one in which there is no enduring class stratification. The greatest growth for persons and societies lies in this democracy, and to form the young in such a way as to assure it is the best goal objective education can embrace. Societies which are not democratic cannot become so overnight, but all can reform their ways of dealing with the young in such a way as to make a general progress toward this ideal.

The subordinate recommendations Dewey offers concern the methods of teaching and administration and the curriculum. He holds that teachers should not use compulsion, should make students feel the problem of being ignorant of subject matter, should discover and appeal to individual interests, and should work with students on the basis of equality in a social situation. He recommends that each class should constitute a society—i.e., a group in which the activities of each person aim at a goal shared by all—and that the school as a whole of such societies should itself form a single one. This requires some participation by students in the conduct or administration of the class and school. He recommends that all subjects be available to all, that prevocational, vocational, and academic subjects be taught to anyone whose interest lies in their direction, and not exclusively to particular groups within the population.

All these subordinate recommendations rest upon the facts of human nature and society as Dewey sees them; these facts show that any society will be reproduced and will gradually become more democratic if teachers and administrators institute the methods and curriculum recommended.

But Dewey's subordinate recommendations rest, as well, upon his ethical theory. First, the denial of authority in which his recommendations consists stems from the view that no value is objective, that all goods depend upon desire. Dewey's ethics shows, if he is correct, that no actions are universally and eternally good. Consequently, no student should be compelled to engage in them. This ethical denial clears the path for that rejection of authoritarian discipline essential to Dewey's notion of self-discipline. In the same way, it clears the way for that highly varied curriculum which he would substitute for the exclusive 3 R's and liberal humanistic subjects.

Dewey's ethics justifies his subordinate recommendations in a more positive way. Following them will lead to a life in school which is, itself, morally good. The student, in learning through his own activity or discipline, will solve problems he encounters, work for consequences he foresees and desires, and study what he prefers in a situation where the goal is a set of foreseen and desired consequences shared with others. His freedom to control his own school life makes all his school activities means-end wholes; each study is arranged so that the earlier parts cause the later, and each is freely chosen. All the student's experience in school will be organized in the light of those consequences which, in his own view, offer the greatest possibility of growth. Dewey's schools would, in this way, assure the moral value of childhood and youth as such, recognizing that they are not periods for preparation only.

Dewey's ethics, nonetheless, justifies his subordinate recommendations, thirdly, on the grounds that following them will lead to mature persons of the best sort who form societies of the best sort. The point of all his recommendations is that they establish the habit of intelligence, and one who can act intelligently leads the morally best existence—one which contains the greatest amount of growth. Such persons will not form a stratified society. Rather, they will form a democracy within which they cooperate freely with others, and which, itself, freely cooperates with other societies toward the better moral state of the entire race.

Dewey rejects all orthodox religion. He holds that it is based on metaphysical doctrines which are meaningless. But there is experience which is religious. It is characterized by a high degree of organization in light of, and a high degree of enthusiasm for, some goal or objective. He often speaks as if schools conducted in accord with his recommendations would produce persons of intelligence whose attitude toward this social and international ideal would constitute a religious experience.

EPISTEMOLOGY AND EDUCATION

Dewey's educational theory recommends to us the goal objective of democratic society and the subordinate objectives of self-discipline within a group and a highly varied curriculum. The latter, it holds to be necessary because of the facts of human nature and society. Given those facts, no other roads can lead to genuine learning; and given genuine learning, democracy will, as a matter of fact, result. But these objectives are influenced, also by Dewey's epistemological theory. That theory holds that all metaphysical entities lie beyond the ken of experience and can never be referred to in any way. This serves to exclude from the objectives which educational theory might recommend all those views concerning it which spring from a metaphysical source. A totalitarian state and authoritarian methods and curriculum cannot be parts of an educational theory because, in Dewey's view, the source from which they are derived cannot be known.

Dewey's objectives for education are influenced by his theory of knowledge in a second way. All moral statements can be seen to be true or false by discovering their utility or inutility through the process of verification. In light of this general principle, Dewey argues that the recommendations of his educational theory are supported by the test of utility. It would be futile, because meaningless, to recommend that teaching aim at imitation, in some degree, of the form of justice. But it is necessary to hold that the life of intelligence and democracy is best, and that the ways of reaching it in education which Dewey recommends are morally good, because these are the relevant judgments which can be supported in the way his epistemology requires.

There is a third way in which Dewey's epistomology is related to his theory of education. Its subordinate recommendations all rest on the assumption that knowing cannot occur except as a phase of intelligent activity and that the creation of problems, the appeal to interest, and group activity are all ways of releasing intelligence upon the subject-matter to be learned. The pattern of problem, hypothesis, consequence derived, verification, etc. is, according to Dewey, the only pattern from which knowing can emerge. It is the method which a scientist always pursues, and science is knowledge *par excellence*. He concludes that learning must follow it quite as precisely as does the process of discovery. The subordinate recommendations of his educational theory are, thus, injunctions derived from his philosophical conceptions of the way in which scientific knowledge proceeds.

A Guide to Selections from *Democracy and Education*

In the passages that follow, Dewey is concerned to advance his view of the nature of growth, and of its relation to education. "Growth" he defines as "the cumulative movement of action toward a later result." He explains this definition in terms of the passage from immaturity to maturity; and immaturity, as consisting in dependence and plasticity. Dependence is the ability to be helped by others in one's society; and plasticity, the adjustment to natural conditions that includes a knowledge of them which enables not merely an acceptance of them, but also their use as means to ends. But since there is no single set of ends appropriate to all persons and terminal to all change—no "static" end—adjustment is not a fixed state, but is rather a capacity to use natural conditions as means to many different ends. It requires intelligence in order to be effectively exercised; without it, habits of adjustment become mechanical and unuseful. Plasticity, consequently, is intelligent flexibility in using natural conditions for different purposes. Thus conceived, immaturty naturally leads to maturity, and the definition of "growth" that Dewey offers— the cumulative movement of action toward a later result—may be understood as meaning that growth is the passage from immaturity to maturity. But the child has certain native powers or instincts; and since there is no set of them universal to all persons, the maturity toward which immaturity directs itself may be quite properly different from one person to another. Moreover, since there is no temporally final condition in life, there is no final stage in growth; and Dewey regards growth as advance toward more growth.

Dewey identifies education with growth, and concludes that education is its own end, and that it is a process of continually transforming and re-organizing the stage in which one end is achieved into a means for achieving another. Formal education requires that teachers help students to grow toward the realization of their own individuality in order, as adults, that they be able to continue to grow independently. The end of education is more education, and the effect of it is the reproduction of society in a new generation transformed to solve new problems by continually re-organizing the conditions of growth.

Dewey's view of growth, it should be noted, involves some elements that are incompatible with the view of human nature we have attributed to him in foregoing pages. He holds, in these passages, that the child possesses certain native powers or instincts—a proposition which, as we have seen, he rejects in other writings.

SELECTIONS FROM

Democracy and Education*

————◀●▶————

CHAPTER IV

Education as growth

THE CONDITIONS OF GROWTH

In directing the activities of the young, society determines its own future in determining that of the young. Since the young at a given time will at some later date compose the society of that period, the latter's nature will largely turn upon the direction children's activities were given at an earlier period. This cumulative movement of action toward a later result is what is meant by growth.

The primary condition of growth is immaturity. This may seem to be a mere truism—saying that a being can develop only in some point in which he is undeveloped. But the prefix 'im' of the word immaturity means something positive, not a mere void or lack. It is noteworthy that the terms 'capacity' and 'potentiality' have a double meaning, one sense being negative, the other positive. Capacity may denote mere receptivity, like the capacity of a quart measure. We may mean by potentiality a merely dormant or quiescent state—a capacity to become something different under external influences. But we also mean by capacity an ability, a power; and by potentiality potency, force. Now when we say that immaturity means the possibility of growth, we are not referring to absence of powers which may exist at a later time; we express a force positively present—the *ability* to develop.

Our tendency to take immaturity as mere lack, and growth as something which fills up the gap between the immature and the mature is due to regarding childhood *comparatively*, instead of intrinsically. We treat it simply as a privation because we are measuring it by adulthood as a fixed standard. This fixes attention upon what the child has not, and will not have till he becomes a man. This comparative standpoint is legitimate enough for some purposes, but if we make it final, the question arises whether we are not guilty of an overweening presumption. Children, if they could express themselves articulately and sincerely, would tell a different tale; and there is excellent adult authority for the conviction that for certain moral and intellectual purposes adults must become as little children.

The seriousness of the assumption of the negative quality of the possibilities of immaturity is apparent when we reflect that it sets up as an ideal and standard a static end. The fulfillment of growing is taken to mean an *accomplished* growth: that is to say, an Ungrowth, something which is no longer growing. The futility of the assumption is seen in the fact that every adult resents the imputation of having no further possibilities of growth; and so far as he finds that they are closed to him mourns the fact as evidence of loss, instead of falling back on the achieved as adequate manifestation of power. Why an unequal measure for child and man?

Taken absolutely, instead of comparatively, immaturity designates a positive force or ability,—the *power* to grow. We do not have to draw out or educe positive activities from a child, as some educational doctrines would have it. Where there is life, there are already eager and impassioned activities. Growth is not something done to them; it is something they do. The positive and constructive aspect of possibility gives the key to understanding the two chief traits of immaturity, dependence and plasticity. (1) It sounds absurd to hear dependence spoken of as something positive, still more absurd as a power. Yet if helplessness were all there were in dependence, no development could ever take place. A merely impotent being has to be carried, forever, by others. The fact that dependence is accomplished by growth in ability, not by an ever increasing lapse into parasitism, suggests that it is already something constructive. Being merely sheltered by others would not promote growth. For (2) it would only build a wall around impotence. With reference to the physical world, the child is helpless. He lacks at birth and for a long time thereafter power to make his way physically, to make his own living. If he had to do that by himself, he would hardly survive an hour. On this side his helplessness is almost complete. The young of the brutes are immeasurably his superiors. He is physically weak and not able to turn the strength which he possesses to coping with the physical environment.

1. The thoroughgoing character of this helplessness suggests, however, some compensating power. The relative ability of the young of brute animals to adapt themselves fairly well to physical conditions from an early period suggests the fact that their life is not intimately bound up with the life of those about them. They are compelled, so to speak, to have physical gifts because they are lacking in social gifts. Human infants, on the other hand, can get along with physical incapacity just because of their social capacity. We sometimes talk and think as if they simply happened to be *physically* in a social environment; as if social forces exclusively existed in the adults who take care of them, they being passive recipients. If it were said that children are themselves marvelously endowed with *power* to enlist the cooperative attention of others, this would be thought to be a backhanded way of saying that others are marvelously attentive to the needs of children. But observation shows that children are gifted with an equipment of the first order for social intercourse. Few grown-up persons retain all of the flexible and sensitive ability of children to vibrate sympathetically with the attitudes and doings of those about them. Inattention to physical things (going with incapacity to control them) is accompanied by a corresponding intensification of interest and attention as to the doings of people. The native mechanism of the child and his impulses all tend to facile social responsiveness. The statement that children, before adolescence, are egotistically self-centered, even if it were true, would not contradict the truth of this statement. It would simply indicate that their social responsiveness is employed on their own behalf, not that it does not exist. But the statement is not true as matter of fact. The facts which are cited in support of the alleged pure egoism of children really show the intensity and directness with which they go to their mark. If the ends which form the mark seem narrow and selfish to adults, it is only because adults (by means of a similar engrossment in their day) have mastered these ends, which have consequently ceased to interest them. Most of the remainder of children's alleged native egoism is simply an egoism which runs counter to an adult's egoism. To a grown-up person who is too absorbed in his own affairs to take an interest in children's affairs, children doubtless seem unreasonably engrossed in *their* own affairs.

From a social standpoint, dependence denotes a power rather than a weakness; it involves interdependence. There is always a danger that increased personal independence will decrease the social capacity of an individual. In making him more self-reliant, it may make him more self-sufficient; it may lead to aloofness and indifference. It often makes an individual so insensitive in his relations to others as to develop an illusion of being really able to stand and act alone—an unnamed form of insanity which is responsible for a large part of the remediable suffering of the world.

2. The specific adaptability of an immature creature for growth constitutes his *plasticity*. This is something quite different from the plasticity of putty or wax. It is not a capacity to take on change of form in accord with external pressure. It lies near the pliable elasticity by which some persons take on the color of their surroundings while retaining their own bent. But it is something deeper than this. It is essentially the ability to learn from experience; the power to retain from one experience something which is of avail in coping with the difficulties of a later situation. This means power to modify actions on the basis of the results of prior experiences, the power to *develop dispositions*. Without it, the acquisition of habits is impossible.

It is a familiar fact that the young of the higher animals, and especially the human young, have to *learn* to utilize their instinctive reactions. The human being is born with a greater number of instinctive tendencies than other animals. But the instincts of the lower animals perfect themselves for appropriate action at an early period after birth, while most of those of the human infant are of little account just as they stand. An original specialized power of adjustment secures immediate efficiency, but, like a railway ticket, it is good for one route only. A being who, in order to use his eyes, ears, hands, and legs, has to experiment in making varied combinations of their reactions, achieves a control that is flexible and varied. A chick, for example, pecks accurately at a bit of food in a few hours after hatching. This means that definite coordinations of activities of the eyes in seeing and of the body and head in striking are perfected in a few trials. An infant requires about six months to be able to gauge with approximate accuracy the action in reaching which will coordinate with his visual activities; to be able, that is, to tell whether he can reach a seen object and just how to execute the reaching. As a result, the chick is limited by the relative perfection of its original endowment. The infant has the advantage of the *multitude* of instinctive tentative reactions and of the experiences that accompany them, even though he is at a temporary disadvantage because they cross one another. In learning an action, instead of having it given ready-made, one of necessity learns to vary its factors, to make varied combinations of them, according to change of circumstances. A possibility of continuing progress is opened up by the fact that in learning one act, methods are developed good for use in other situations. Still more important is the fact that the human being acquires a habit of learning. He learns to learn.

The importance for human life of the two facts of dependence

and variable control has been summed up in the doctrine of the significance of prolonged infancy.[1] This prolongation is significant from the
standpoint of the adult members of the group as well as from that of
the young. The presence of dependent and learning beings is a stimulus
to nurture and affection. The need for constant continued care was
probably a chief means in transforming temporary cohabitations into
permanent unions. It certainly was a chief influence in forming habits of
affectionate and sympathetic watchfulness; that constructive interest in
the well-being of others which is essential to associated life. Intellectually,
this moral development meant the introduction of many new objects of
attention; it stimulated foresight and planning for the future. Thus there
is a reciprocal influence. Increasing complexity of social life requires a
longer period of infancy in which to acquire the needed powers; this prolongation of dependence means prolongation of plasticity, or power of
acquiring variable and novel modes of control. Hence it provides a
futher push to social progress.

HABITS AS EXPRESSIONS OF GROWTH

We have already noted that plasticity is the capacity to retain
and carry over from prior experience factors which modify subsequent activities. This signifies the capacity to acquire habits, or develop definite
dispositions. We have now to consider the salient features of habits. In the
first place, a habit is a form of executive skill, of efficiency in doing. A
habit means an ability to use natural conditions as means to ends. It is
an active control of the environment through control of the organs of
action. We are perhaps apt to emphasize the control of the body at the
expense of control of the environment. We think of walking, talking,
playing the piano, the specialized skills characteristic of the etcher, the
surgeon, the bridge-builder, as if they were simply ease, deftness, and
accuracy on the part of the organism. They are that, of course; but the
measure of the value of these qualities lies in the economical and
effective control of the environment which they secure. To be able to
walk is to have certain properties of nature at our disposal—and so
with all other habits.

Education is not infrequently defined as consisting in the acquisition of those habits that effect an adjustment of an individual and his
environment. The definition expresses an essential phase of growth. But
it is essential that adjustment be understood in its active sense of *control*
of means of achieving ends. If we think of a habit simply as a change
wrought in the organism, ignoring the fact that this change consists in

---

[1] Intimations of its significance are found in a number of writers, but John Fiske, in
his "Excursions of an Evolutionist," is accredited with its first systematic exposition.

ability to effect subsequent changes in the environment, we shall be led to think of 'adjustment' as a conformity to environment as wax conforms to the seal which impresses it. The environment is thought of as something fixed, providing in its fixity the end and standard of changes taking place in the organism; adjustment is just fitting ourselves to this fixity of external conditions.[2] Habit as *habituation* is indeed something *relatively* passive; we get used to our surroundings—to our clothing, our shoes, and gloves; to the atmosphere as long as it is fairly equable; to our daily associates, etc. Conformity to the environment, a change wrought in the organism without reference to ability to modify surroundings, is a marked trait of such habituations. Aside from the fact that we are not entitled to carry over the traits of such adjustments (which might well be called *accommodations,* to mark them off from active adjustments) into habits of active use of our surroundings, two features of habituations are worth notice. In the first place, we get used to things by *first* using them.

Consider getting used to a strange city. At first, there is excessive stimulation and excessive and ill-adapted response. Gradually certain stimuli are selected because of their relevancy, and others are degraded. We can say either that we do not respond to them any longer, or more truly that we have effected a persistent response to them—an equilibrium of adjustment. This means, in the second place, that this enduring adjustment supplies the background upon which are made specific adjustments, as occasion arises. We are never interested in changing the *whole* environment; there is much that we take for granted and accept just as it already is. Upon this background our activities focus at certain points in an endeavor to introduce needed changes. Habituation is thus our adjustment to an environment which at the time we are not concerned with modifying, and which supplies a leverage to our active habits.

Adaptation, in fine, is quite as much adaptation *of* the environment to our own activities as of our activities *to* the environment. A savage tribe manages to live on a desert plain. It adapts itself. But its adaptation involves a maximum of accepting, tolerating, putting up with things as they are, a maximum of passive acquiescence, and a minimum of active control, of subjection to use. A civilized people enters upon the scene. It also adapts itself. It introduces irrigation; it searches the world for plants and animals that will flourish under such conditions; it improves, by careful selection, those which are growing there. As a consequence, the wilderness blossoms as a rose. The savage is

2 This conception is, of course, a logical correlation of the conception of the external relation of stimulus and response, considered in the last chapter, and of the negative conceptions of immaturity and plasticity noted in this chapter.

merely habituated; the civilized man has habits which transform the environment.

The significance of habit is not exhausted, however, in its executive and motor phase. It means formation of intellectual and emotional disposition as well as an increase in ease, economy, and efficiency of action. Any habit marks an *inclination*—an active preference and choice for the conditions involved in its exercise. A habit does not wait, Micawberlike, for a stimulus to turn up so that it may get busy; it actively seeks for occasions to pass into full operation. If its expression is unduly blocked, inclination shows itself in uneasiness and intense craving. A habit also marks an intellectual disposition. Where there is a habit, there is acquaintance with the materials and equipment to which action is applied. There is a definite way of understanding the situations in which the habit operates. Modes of thought, of observation and reflection, enter as forms of skill and of desire into the habits that make a man an engineer, an architect, a physician, or a merchant. In unskilled forms of labor, the intellectual factors are at minimum precisely because the habits involved are not of a high grade. But there are habits of judging and reasoning as truly as of handling a tool, painting a picture, or conducting an experiment.

Such statements are, however, understatements. The habits of mind involved in habits of the eye and hand supply the latter with their significance. Above all, the intellectual element in a habit fixes the relation of the habit to varied and elastic use, and hence to continued growth. We speak of *fixed* habits. Well, the phrase may mean powers so well established that their possessor always has them as resources when needed. But the phrase is also used to mean ruts, routine ways, with loss of freshness, openmindedness, and originality. Fixity of habit may mean that something has a fixed hold upon us, instead of our having a free hold upon things. This fact explains two points in a common notion about habits: their identification with mechanical and external modes of action to the neglect of mental and moral attitudes, and the tendency to give them a bad meaning, an identification with "bad habits." Many a person would feel surprised to have his aptitude in his chosen profession called a habit, and would naturally think of his use of tobacco, liquor, or profane language as typical of the meaning of habit. A habit is to him something which has a hold on him, something not easily thrown off even though judgment condemn it.

Habits reduce themselves to routine ways of acting, or degenerate into ways of action to which we are enslaved just in the degree in which intelligence is disconnected from them. Routine habits are unthinking habits; "bad" habits are habits so severed from reason that they are opposed to the conclusions of conscious deliberation and decision. As we have seen, the acquiring of habits is due to an original plasticity of our natures: to our ability to vary responses till we find an appropriate and efficient way of acting. Routine habits, and habits that possess us instead of our possessing them, are habits which put an end to plasticity. They mark the close of power to vary. There can be no doubt of the tendency of organic plasticity, of the physiological basis, to lessen with growing years. The instinctively mobile and eagerly varying action of childhood, the love of new stimuli and new developments, too easily passes into a "settling down," which means aversion to change and a resting on past achievements. Only an environment which secures the full use of intelligence in the process of forming habits can counteract this tendency. Of course, the same hardening of the organic conditions affects the physiological structures which are involved in thinking. But this fact only indicates the need of persistent care to see to it that the function of intelligence is invoked to its maximum possibility. The short-sighted method which falls back on mechanical routine and repetition to secure external efficiency of habit, motor skill without accompanying thought, marks a deliberate closing in of surroundings upon growth.

THE EDUCATIONAL BEARINGS OF THE CONCEPTION OF DEVELOPMENT

We have had so far but little to say in this chapter about education. We have been occupied with the conditions and implications of growth. If our conclusions are justified, they carry with them, however, definite educational consequences. When it is said that education is development, everything depends upon *how* development is conceived, Our net conclusion is that life is development, and that developing, growing, is life. Translated into its educational equivalents, this means (i) that the educational process has no end beyond itself; it is its own end; and that (ii) the educational process is one of continual reorganizing, reconstructing, transforming.

1. Development when it is interpreted in *comparative* terms, that is, with respect to the special traits of child and adult life, means the direction of power into special channels: the formation of habits involving executive skill, definiteness of interest, and specific objects of observation and thought. But the comparative view is not final. The child has specific powers; to ignore that fact is to stunt or distort the organs upon which his growth depends. The adult uses his powers to transform his environment, thereby occasioning new stimuli which redirect his powers and keep them developing. Ignoring this fact means arrested development, a passive accommodation. Normal child and normal adult alike,

in other words, are engaged in growing. The difference between them is not the difference between growth and no growth, but between the modes of growth appropriate to different conditions. With respect to the development of powers devoted to coping with specific scientific and economic problems we may say the child should be growing in manhood. With respect to sympathetic curiosity, unbiased responsiveness, and openness of mind, we may say that the adult should be growing in childlikeness. One statement is as true as the other.

Three ideas which have been criticized, namely, the merely privative nature of immaturity, static adjustment to a fixed environment, and rigidity of habit, are all connected with a false idea of growth or development,—that it is a movement toward a fixed goal. Growth is regarded as *having* an end, instead of *being* an end. The educational counterparts of the three fallacious ideas are first, failure to take account of the instinctive or native powers of the young; secondly, failure to develop initiative in coping with novel situations; thirdly, an undue emphasis upon drill and other devices which secure automatic skill at the expense of personal perception. In all cases, the adult environment is accepted as a standard for the child. He is to be brought up *to* it.

Natural instincts are either disregarded or treated as nuisances— as obnoxious traits to be suppressed, or at all events to be brought into conformity with external standards. Since conformity is the aim, what is distinctively individual in a young person is brushed aside, or regarded as a source of mischief or anarchy. Conformity is made equivalent to uniformity. Consequently, there are induced lack of interest in the novel, aversion to progress, and dread of the uncertain and the unknown. Since the end of growth is outside of and beyond the process of growing, external agents have to be resorted to to induce movement towards it. Whenever a method of education is stigmatized as mechanical, we may be sure that external pressure is brought to bear to reach an external end.

2. Since in reality there is nothing to which growth is relative save more growth, there is nothing to which education is subordinate save more education. It is a commonplace to say that education should not cease when one leaves school. The point of this commonplace is that the purpose of school education is to insure the continuance of education by organizing the powers that insure growth. The inclination to learn from life itself and to make the conditions of life such that all will learn in the process of living is the finest product of schooling.

When we abandon the attempt to define immaturity by means of fixed comparison with adult accomplishments, we are compelled to give up thinking of it as denoting lack of desired traits. Abandoning this notion, we are also forced to surrender our habit of thinking of instruction as a method of supplying this lack by pouring knowledge into a mental and moral hole which awaits filling. Since life means growth, a living creature lives as truly and positively at one stage as at another, with the same intrinsic fullness and the same absolute claims. Hence education means the enterprise of supplying the conditions which insure growth, or adequacy of life, irrespective of age. We first look with impatience upon immaturity, regarding it as something to be got over as rapidly as possible. Then the adult formed by such educative methods looks back with impatient regret upon childhood and youth as a scene of lost opportunities and wasted powers. This ironical situation will endure till it is recognized that living has its own intrinsic quality and that the business of education is with that quality.

Realization that life is growth protects us from that so-called idealizing of childhood which in effect is nothing but lazy indulgence. Life is not to be identified with every superficial act and interest. Even though it is not always easy to tell whether what appears to be mere surface fooling is a sign of some nascent as yet untrained power, we must remember that manifestations are not to be accepted as ends in themselves. They are signs of possible growth. They are to be turned into means of development, of carrying power forward, not indulged or cultivated for their own sake. Excessive attention to surface phenomena (even in the way of rebuke as well as of encouragement) may lead to their fixation and thus to arrested development. What impulses are moving toward, not what they have been, is the important thing for parent and teacher. The true principle of respect for immaturity cannot be better put than in the words of Emerson:

Respect the child. Be not too much his parent. Trespass not on his solitude. But I hear the outcry which replies to this suggestion: Would you verily throw up the reins of public and private discipline; would you leave the young child to the mad career of his own passions and whimsies, and call this anarchy a respect for the child's nature? I answer,—Respect the child, respect him to the end, but also respect yourself. . . . The two points in a boy's training are, to keep his *naturel* and train off all but that; to keep his *naturel,* but stop off his uproar, fooling, and horseplay; keep his nature *and arm it with knowledge in the very direction in which it points.*

And as Emerson goes on to show this reverence for childhood and youth instead of opening up an easy and easy-going path to the instructors, "involves at once, immense claims on the time, the thought, on the life of the teacher. It requires time, use, insight, event, all the great lessons and assistances of God; and only to think of using it implies character and profoundness."

SUMMARY

Power to grow depends upon need for others and plasticity. Both of these conditions are at their height in childhood and youth. Plasticity or the power to learn from experience means the formation of habits. Habits give control over the environment, power to utilize it for human purposes. Habits take the form both of habituation, or a general and persistent balance of organic activities with the surroundings, and of active capacities to readjust activity to meet new conditions. The former furnishes the background of growth; the latter constitute growing. Active habits involve thought, invention, and initiative in applying capacities to new aims. They are opposed to routine which marks an arrest of growth. Since growth is the characteristic of life, education is all one with growing; it has no end beyond itself. The criterion of the value of school education is the extent in which it creates a desire for continued growth and supplies means for making the desire effective in fact.

Bibliography

BAKER, MELVIN C., *Foundations of Dewey's Educational Theory*, New York, King's Crown Press, Columbia University, 1955.

FRANKENA, WILLIAM K., *Three Historical Philosophies of Education: Aristotle, Kant, Dewey*, Chicago, Scott, Foresman and Co., 1965. (Keystones of Education Series.) Chapter IV.

HORNE, HERMAN HARRELL, *The Democratic Philosophy of Education: Companion to John Dewey's* DEMOCRACY AND EDUCATION, New York, Macmillan, 1932.

BENNE, KENNETH D. and STANLEY, WILLIAM O., editors, *Conference on Education and Philosophy: Essays for John Dewey's 90th Birthday*, University of Illinois, 1949.

.   .   .

FELDMAN, WILLIAM TAFT, *The Philosophy of John Dewey, a Critical Analysis*, Baltimore, Johns Hopkins Press, 1934.

SCHILPP, PAUL A., *The Philosophy of John Dewey*, New York, Tudor Publishing Co., 1937 (The Library of Living Philosophers).

THAYER, HORACE STANDISH, *The Logic of Pragmatism*, New York, Humanities Press, 1952.

WHITE, MORTON, *The Origin of Dewey's Instrumentalism*, New York, Columbia University Press, 1943.

XIII

IN RETROSPECT

THE AUTHORS WHOSE WORKS have been presented and interpreted here advance eleven different theories of education and their philosophical reflections on them. All of these systems have common elements; yet few of them are obviously or remarkably similar. The theories of education they contain and the philosophies advanced to buttress them present a rich variety of teachings. Here we shall review these eleven philosophies of education, pointing to some of their similarities and differences. This procedure may bring some unity to the variety, and may facilitate understanding the book as a whole.

GOAL OBJECTIVES

ALL OUR THOUGHTS of education hold that training should yield a good life for those who undergo it. Some among them hold that the important quality of this life is religious. As the goal for all training, St. Augustine advances repentance for sin and conversion to Christianity in hope of the blessed life in eternal union with God. St. Thomas puts forward a similar goal for education—the direct vision of God; but, perhaps through the influence of Aristotle, he argues that a terrestrial knowledge of nature and divinity engendered by education is an imperfect approach to that eternal and perfect happiness. Comenius advocates an analogous goal: all training should direct the person toward immortal blessedness; but since immortal blessedness is warranted especially by a good life on earth, training should also direct the student toward good conduct within his state and toward the establishment of peace between states. These goal objectives are religious in the sense that the life they would embody is one of adoration of the Divine Being; their goodness is found in that worshipful union.

The other authors represented in this book advance goal objectives which are non-religious. The life these objectives advocate is not primarily one of religious adoration, either terrestrial or Heavenly, although its goodness in some cases involves a reference to the Divine Being. Some of these non-religious theories place the goodness of the goals they advocate in the life of the individual, while others place it in society.

Quintilian holds that training should be directed toward producing the orator. The goodness of his life consists in the calm or equability that springs from consciousness of having done one's duty. Rousseau holds that private education should guarantee the good life in every period of individual development from infancy to maturity. This goodness consists in an inner peace which springs from the ability to desire only what we can secure through our own efforts; each of the five stages of individual development, by virtue of the dominance of different capacities in it, has its own inner peace or goodness. The mature life toward which tutorial training should be directed possesses inner peace or freedom because it is independent of the decadent social institutions (those of eighteenth-century Europe) which surround it. For Herbart, the goal of education is the development of the capacity for approval and disapproval. He holds that this sensitivity reacts always to the same moral principles in the same way, and that although it alone constitutes the rightness of the choice it colors, each man finds himself in agreement with all others as to the moral principles he accepts or rejects. The development of morally sensitive individuals, he holds, leads to morally sensitive societies; but since the goodness of societies is a function of the rightness of the actions of their members, the social goal of education, he regards as derivative—not as ultimate. The goal objectives of Quintilian, of the tutorial education outlined by Rousseau, and of Herbart are individualistic.

Other authors recommend goal objectives that place goodness in the life of the individual, holding, at the same time, that such a life can occur only in a society of a particular sort. Thus, Locke puts forward the happiness and prosperity of the community as the goal for all training. He understands happiness in terms of the pleasure of individuals and seems to restrict it to the pleasure of desire satisfied in accord with a will to obey the natural law and civil laws which embody it. The goodness of life is within the individual, but the individual finds genuine happiness only in a society whose laws he can willingly obey because they protect his natural rights to life, liberty, and estate. Gentlemen find their happiness, partly, in serving society as their stations require; and the poor find theirs by engaging in productive employment. The training of each should lead in the appropriate direction. Kant holds that training should realize the ideal human being—one of perfect character and intellectual attainment. But he also contends that this realization both requires and, in turn, is required by societies republican in form and organized into a peaceful, international community. Mill contends that all training should aim at producing the general welfare. This consists in the maximum amount of happiness and perfection enjoyed by the greatest number of people. It can occur only if the government guarantees free expression to individuality—a freedom limited only by prevention of injury to others. Only in a representative democracy where people are free to protect their own interests by electing those who know how to insure their fulfillment will this individuality, this happiness and perfection, and this general welfare take place. Similarly, Dewey directs training toward the development of a non-stratified, classless society—toward democracy as he conceives it. Only in such a society can individuals find the greatest opportunity for that personal growth in which the good life consists.

Locke, Kant, Mill, and Dewey modify the individualism of their goal objectives by holding that the good life for individuals that all training ought to further involves a particular kind of society. Their goal objectives, therefore, are not only objectives for the training of individuals; the attainment of each requires a reconstruction of society into that shape within which the individuality recommended can flourish.

The goal objectives advanced by a third group of philosophers are societarian. All training, Plato argues, should produce persons who make up a just society. People should be treated differently according to their capacities, but the way they are treated should be determined by the way their talents can be utilized to produce the ideal social order. Creating the just person is an objective of education; but only because, in turn, he is a means to the just social order. Rousseau, writing about public education, advances as its goal objective the preservation and enhancement of national character and culture. Private training will provide the lady and gentleman with an independence of society—an independence which will enable them to survive its complete and revolutionary reform. But where the general will has not forsaken social instituitions, public education will assure their preservation and improvement by producing citizens who gladly express the general will and willingly submit to it, finding their own importance in the enhancement of their nation.

HUMAN NATURE

OUR FIRST AUTHORS, those who advance religious goal objectives, hold views of human nature that are similar in some ways, although different in others. St. Augustine, St. Thomas, and Comenius all assert that a person is (or at any rate involves) an immaterial substance, mind, or soul; and human nature, for each, appears as a set of activities common and peculiar to human beings because manifestations of the faculties they possess. These are the faculties of knowing, of feeling or desiring, and of willing; and if we remember the way in which these faculties are exercised according to each author, we shall understand why each maintains that all human beings act alike in certain respects. For St. Augustine, despite its knowledge and its better feeling, the soul freely exercises its will in favor of egoistic and bodily desires. This is original sin, and no man can escape it altogether. Comenius agrees, except for the last point. He holds that men can be completely perfected in knowledge, in virtue, and in piety; they will, in fact, achieve perfection at the end of history. For St. Thomas, a rational person cannot desire something without judging it to be good, and cannot judge something to be good that is not either itself the last end—the direct vision of God—or conducive to it. Men, of course, are not always rational. Their judgments are often mistaken; their actions misguided. For him, sin results from the faulty operation of reason, and looks as much like involuntary ignorance as like deliberate violation of God's law. Although these three religious authors do not attribute quite the same nature to humanity, the nature each does allot to that race consists in a single set of activities conceived as expressive of faculties common and peculiar to all its members.

The authors who advance the good life of the individual as goal objective, with little emphasis on religious contemplation and no dependence on society, hold views of human nature which differ considerably, one from another. For Quintilian, there need be no specific content common to the lives of all human beings. Each is made up of activities compounded of impulse running toward objectives supplied by passive cognition, and criticized by reason. But the objectives supplied to impulse may differ from one person to another and, consequently, so may the pattern which reason allows in any particular life. For Rousseau, the nature of a human being consists in those activities which the five capacities of the soul permit. And while all persons need not feel or sense or reason or will in the same way, there are instinctual desires which are common to them all. The adult person receives the material of his life from feeling and sense, orders it according to reason and will, and transforms it in ways determined by the interaction between his natural desires of pity and sex, and the familial institutions which surround and channel them. According to Herbart, there are no faculties; consequently, there can be no human nature which is their expression. There are souls; but since they are unknowable, we can apprehend no human nature that can be traced to their presence throughout the race. Each person, so far as he can be understood, is an organization of interests composed of ideas derived from his experience; but since experience varies, it need supply no common content for the ideas and desires, the volitions and thoughts of men. Psychological laws describe the organization of interests that constitutes each person, and the five moral principles are invoked by all in making moral choices. And Herbart might have attributed to humanity a nature understood in terms of the laws of psychology and universal agreement, for individual reasons, on the five moral principles.

Those goal objectives which hold that individuality is good, but that it can flourish only in societies of a certain sort, grow from conceptions of human nature which differ considerably. Locke holds that the human being is an immaterial substance dwelling in a material body, and possessed of two faculties—those of understanding and of will. However, except for epistemological reflection, he forgets the substance. The life of a human being can be understood as a texture of ideas which may be desires as well as cognitions, of acts of willing or preferring one desire to another, and of bodily actions consequent upon such choices. Even the identity of a person must be thought of as the consciousness of this series of ideas and acts, not as the duration of a substance. Kant thought of human nature as those acts of cognition, of desire, and of volition in which a mental substance can engage by virtue of its possessing those three faculties. But substance, for him, was a way of thinking about (or organizing) phænomena—not a thing, but a way of organizing the items of experience. And this makes it difficult to consider the faculties of the mind as anything more than a classification of mental occurrences. Mill ended by regarding human nature as consisting in a series of mental states in which ideas are related to each other and to impressions by association, and impressions only to physical objects by non-associative relations. Some elements in such a series must be inner feelings—possible or actual. Otherwise, a mind could not be distinguished from a physical object. And while what makes a series of phænomena a mind is its possession of inner feelings, what distinguishes each mind from every other is an interest or group of them which is unique to it. Certain instincts may be common, but every person desires in some way to be different from others. It is human nature to want to be one's unique self. For Dewey, there is no substance beneath human nature, and there is no activity common to all human beings— not even a desire to be different from the rest. Every human being is a compound of impulse and habit, and one of these habits is that of acting intelligently when others break down. But since there are no instincts, a person may acquire any habits whatever; and the nature of humanity dissolves into purely formal properties—those involved in acting intelligently to remove problems arising out of the breakdown of habits of no peculiarly human sort.

The societarian goal objectives we have studied involve doctrines of human nature which are similar to each other. Plato does not clearly hold that the soul is a single substance. He does insist, however, that the soul has three parts; and the capacities with which these parts endow the human being mark off his nature as that of reasoning, of acting energetically in favor of the good, and of bodily appetite. All human beings act in these three ways because they possess these three powers. Rousseau seems to hold that the soul is a mental substance, but he emphasizes the capacities rather than the substance in which they inhere. Human beings act as they do because of their capacities for feeling, sense, reason, desire, and will. For Plato, the just state depends upon the capacities of men; for Rousseau, the uncorrupted nation, similarly, takes its rise from the capacities which characterize the souls of all.

The religious philosophers we have examined advance views of human nature which make their goal objectives possible of attainment. Immortal blessedness is a possible goal for St. Augustine and Comenius because the substance which engages in the sin of incorrect choice also can choose to accept redemption, and because the same substance endures throughout life and after death. If man were not a substance or did not possess the faculty of volition, the notion of union with God would fail altogether as a goal, or would take on a very different character. For Comenius, also, man's nature must be found in a substance which uses its faculties well. Otherwise, the reward of immortal blessedness for terrestrial improvement would collapse. In order to be rewarded, it is apparent that one must endure—a single, persistent substance—from the time of the meritorius action to the time of the reward. The direct vision of God is a possible goal, for St. Thomas, because it is possible for men to be rational—to judge correctly as to its ultimate goodness, and to use terrestrial knowledge to achieve it. This possibility, of course, includes divine assistance in acquiring some of the virtues that make for the last end. But the possibility offered by human nature of achieving the direct vision of God appears as one instance of St. Thomas' comprehensive metaphysical scheme—the scheme according to which the potentiality of each substance directs itself toward actuality on a higher level.

The doctrines of human nature advanced by Quintilian and Rousseau make possible the individualistic goal objective of internal peace. Quintilian holds that reason can show the difference between better and worse desires, and that we can act accordingly. He who does so act achieves equability of spirit. Rousseau holds that there is a native bent toward internal peace involved in each capacity of the soul—the natural goodness with which men are born. Where civilization does not corrupt this natural tendency, internal peace may be achieved. Herbart's view of human nature as describable by the laws of psychology, and devoid of limiting faculties, enables him to urge the use of those laws to develop individuality; and the moral principles upon which men agree are sufficiently abstract not to limit seriously the content of the desires they govern.

The goal objectives of individualism which requires society of a particular sort are possible to the degree that human nature does not, itself exclusively, suffice to determine all goals. Locke begins to question a permanent immaterial substance whose nature might determine all ideals, and rests the latter on the nature of God and His creatures, together with the natural desire for power or possessions which, when made legitimate by mixing one's own labor with them, natural law guarantees and a good civil order protects. Kant transforms the notion of substance and faculties into a way of organizing and classifying our experiences, and views the goal objective for education as a kind of life in which cognition, desire (especially the egoistic instincts of isolation and association), and volition work together harmoniously in each person because he lives in a republic at peace with other states. Mill's general welfare, composed of individualistic happiness expressive of character and genius, together with perfection, requires a representative democracy; but it is a possible ideal to the degree that no immaterial substance with limiting capacities lies beneath humanity. His individualism is haunted, however, by the notion of instincts common to the race whose frustration would exclude some states of affairs from the content of happiness. Dewey, although inconsistent on this point (he sometimes recognizes instincts), holds that since human nature consists only in impulse formed by habit, including the habit of intelligence, its goal objective may be any kind of adjustment whatever. No instincts limit this objective. The only criterion by which to choose between objectives is the greatest possibility of growth contained in those we should prefer.

Societarian goal objectives accompany views of human nature which would enable their achievement. Plato's view of the three faculties, developed to varying degrees of perfection, generates the conception of persons who would naturally compose a just society; and Rousseau's citizen possesses in his faculty of will and in his unspoiled feeling, desire, and reason, an ability to choose in accord with the general will as opposed to his particular will or that of some sub-national group.

PROGRAMS OF TRAINING

THE RELIGIOUS PHILOSOPHIES we have examined have similar views of the problem of training. For St. Augustine, the original sin of man has brought about his declining history; and his misfortunes are, like the careers of other things, part of the Divine order of God's Providence implicit in the first moment. Unlike other parts of nature, however, man is free to alter his place in the order. The function of training in the schools and in the Church is to secure the exercise of man's freedom in the direction of repentance and conversion. Saint Thomas does not deny this function to training, but he emphasizes the importance of arranging the environment in such a way as to remove from it hindrances to the natural development of man. Inherent in reason and desire is the potentiality for the direct vision of God, and intellectual as well as moral training should enable this potentiality to become actual. Comenius sees nature as falling into a Divine order. Each thing develops toward the realization of its own purpose and toward the realization of a more comprehensive purpose that it shares with its fellows. Man is the only exception. His history is one of broad fluctuations between cosmic good and evil, and of a narrow but steady current of intellectual advance. Unlike other things, man is free to alter his place in nature and to make use of that current to realize both his own purpose and the purpose he shares with others. The problem of training is that of imposing on the development of men the kind of order which controls all other natural development, thereby enabling them to live peaceably in a good society, both national and international, and to justify the blessedness of immortality.

The administration, curriculum, and methods of teaching advocated by St. Augustine and Comenius are considerably different. St. Augustine does not argue that everyone should attend school, although he certainly holds that everyone should receive religious instruction either there or through the Church. He may have thought of schools largely as ecclesiastical agencies. Their curriculum—the liberal arts and religious doctrine—would be taught in an authoritative way on lower levels; these courses, thus taught, would culminate in repentance and conversion— belief in, and union with God. On higher levels, theology and philosophy would supplement more elaborate study of the liberal arts; and the method would be one of reason and discussion—one of discovering truth by introspection, one directed upon experience preserved in memory and organized by principles native to the mind. But while reason would transform belief into knowledge, it could not strengthen the union with God for which belief suffices. St. Augustine makes no mention of teaching and learning through empirical inquiry conceived as a deliberate effort to augment experience for the purpose of increasing knowledge.

According to Comenius, since the members of every other species develop in exactly the same way, all children (both boys and girls) should attend publicly supported, uniform lower schools. They should all undergo the same curriculum. The classics, the vernacular languages, and the empirical sciences (still in their beginnings), religion and the arts should all be taught from the lowest through the highest levels in a highly ordered way, with details being filled in gradually, and with the help of empirical materials such as pictures, maps, and real things when possible. In the training advocated, Comenius rejects authority and emphasizes an appeal to experience ordered by reason, while St. Augustine emphasizes authority on the lower levels and rational inquiry on the higher.

St. Thomas says very little about the administration of education, and about its curriculum. His discussion of teaching also contains no explicit statements concerning the methods of instruction. Nonetheless, from his analysis of the notion of teaching, we can conclude that he agrees with Saint Augustine that any proper method must enable the student to make actual and explicit for himself what he already knows potentially and implicitly. On the higher levels, this method is one of rational discussion.

The non-religious, individualistic writers we have studied see the problem of training in quite different ways. For Quintilian, the problem is that of providing objectives for impulse, content for critical absorption into the student's personality, and training in oratory. For Herbart, the problem is that of supplying ideas that may come to constitute good persons, not through their fitting in with pre-existing impulses or faculties, but through their own inherent ability to constitute interests—the mechanism of apperception that grows out of the inherent force of ideas. In Rousseau's view of private training, the problem is that of protecting the student's natural tendencies from the distortive influence of corrupt social institutions and, at the same time, cultivating the five capacities of the soul. Quintilian trains for his internal equability in schools, through lectures and rhetorical performances by the students themselves. This administration and these methods provide humanistic goals for impulse to seek, and the practice in speaking that develops the ideal orator. Herbart assures the development of the morally sensitive person by using the procedure of the four steps of clearness, association, system, and method; embodies his procedure in discussion or lectures, in homes or in schools; and makes use of materials drawn, when appropriate, from those parts of human history that correspond to the stage of individual life in which the student finds himself. Rousseau solves his problem by advocating tutorial training, establishment of an environment for the student like that of society before its corruption by the shallow and selfish desires for private property and related forms of superiority, and the consequent cultivation of reliance on one's own senses, reason, emotions, and will.

Those writers we have studied who advance individualistic goal objectives but hold that they require certain kinds of society advocate programs of training which vary considerably, one from another. Locke advocates tutorial training for the gentleman and lady, and working schools for the poor. The method of teaching depends upon the principle of utilizing some natural desires to frustrate others and to give life to the student's interest in learning. The curriculum should be arranged so that what is necessary for a given subject is learned before it, and it includes a politely general study of most of the classical liberal subjects and the modern arts and sciences, with certain exceptions. The poor, of course, would benefit from extremely little of this curriculum. From such a training, gentlemen and ladies would emerge who enjoy their own lives and their responsibilities as citizens of a democracy devoted to the protection of rights to property; from the working schools would emerge persons who equally enjoy their own less prominent lives and less distinguished responsibilities in that democracy.

Kant recommends private schools, but only for boys. Girls (not overly endowed with the cognitive faculty) may be trained at home for domestic responsibilities and in the arts. For boys, rigid discipline eradicates wildness and untempered egoism. Examples of morality in history and present conduct, discussion of them, and the memorizing of moral rules train the will in choosing rightly. The rest of the curriculum cultivates the senses, the application of rules by the imagination, the discovery of them by the understanding, and the unification of them by the reason. The result is a man who approaches the ideal of humanity, living in a republic at peace within an international state—the goal of human history toward which this training cooperates.

Mill holds that all children, both boys and girls, should be compelled to attend the lower schools. These schools should be privately controlled, except where the state can do a better job; but those who cannot afford tuition should receive public money for scholarships. The chief method of teaching is that of using the laws of association to bring the student to identify instinctive personal interest with an interest in the general welfare. This procedure helps to assure good character. The teacher should foster learning by encouraging the student to work through the material by himself, seeing how propositions are verified by working them out in thought or in the laboratory—by appeal to his own critical experience. The curriculum of the classics and of the sciences, presented in these ways, will help to establish the general welfare—a society of highly developed, free individuals, each of whom assures progress toward his own and the general happiness through a representative democracy, socialized as that becomes necessary for the enhancement of individuality.

According to Dewey, training in the lower schools should be universal. The chief principle of teaching should be the awakening of the consciousness of a problem in not knowing the subject. The solution of the problems he feels cultivates the child's intelligence and teaches him the subject. This method of inducing self-discipline does not succeed with respect to materials in which the student has no interest, but neither does any other. Since there is no universal interest in a subject and no universal nature to be developed, any subject should be taught to all who are interested. This method and this curriculum produce individuals who lead lives of intelligent adjustment, constantly in growth, and a democratic or classless society which guarantees that growth both for individuals and for the institutions within which they live.

Our societarian writers advocate programs of training much more similar to each other than those we have just discussed. Plato urges that all children of citizens attend public schools, that the schools be employed to decide what classes particular persons should be assigned to, and that the entire curriculum, from that of the lower schools for all through that of higher education for the few, be arranged so that an improved society is the paramount objective for all those who study it. Knowing is an intrinsically good activity; but the chief reason for installing it as the objective of public training institutions is that it is useful for advancing society toward the ideal condition. Rousseau, when he considers public education, advocates that all children be compelled to engage in public games, that the curriculum and methods of the public schools be deliberately directed toward eradicating feelings of the importance of individuals in favor of identification with the national welfare.

PHILOSOPHY OF EDUCATION

OUR RELIGIOUS WRITERS find a supernaturalistic philosophical support for the goal objectives and programs of training they advocate. St. Augustine, St. Thomas, and Comenius explain the value of created things as the degree to which they fulfill God's intention in creating them. The exemplar and the purpose of man is his nature as manifested by life in Eden; the misfortunes of his existence consist in his deviation from that life. But Saint Thomas adds, by use of the Aristotelian distinction between potentiality and actually, the notion that this life as a goal intended by God is also potentially present in all men as what they strive to make actual. Each philosopher argues that his program of training will improve humanity by bringing it closer to that perfection which is immediately derivative from God. For each, also, knowing depends upon God's existence. For St. Augustine, sensation and introspection (broadly conceived) yield knowledge; but only with the help of Divine illumination. For Saint Thomas, the light of reason enables the teacher and the student to deduce particular conclusions from innate, general principles; but it is a light that flows from a divine source. For Comenius, everything we know is discovered by introspection: since the mind is an image of God, it contains everything within it and knows whatever of its contents it explicitly considers. Teaching and learning are, for all three, largely matters of using language not to convey truth, but to bring the student to direct his attention to it as a matter of his own activity.

Like St. Augustine, St. Thomas, and Comenius, one of the individualistic writers we have described here as non-religious (to indicate the dominant tendency of his thought) nonetheless brings a supernatural standard to bear upon his educational theory. Rousseau argues that God's existence is guaranteed by the dictates of the heart as well as by several metaphysical arguments, and that He certifies the rightness of those choices that training should foster and that yield inner peace or happiness. God also explains the distinction between the world of nature and the moral world in which alone man can find genuine happiness. In his treatment of knowledge, however, nothing supernatural is found. We know what we cannot help but believe; and this includes what we discover by sense and experimental generalization from sense, what the heart reveals, and what is useful. We can know that God exists, but His existence is no guarantee of knowledge. While the individualistic objective of private education and the societarian objective of public education are both guaranteed by a metaphysically oriented ethics, the methods of teaching and learning are guaranteed by an epistemology which provides no supernatural basis for knowledge. A second individualistic writer, Quintilian, seems to suppose that internal equability has some relation to the order of nature, but one cannot tell with any certainty whether, for him, this order stems from a supernatural source. Our third individualistic author, Herbart, advocates religious teaching as a means to moral improvement, and accepts a fairly orthodox theology—an aspect of his thought we have not examined; but he rejects a supernatural foundation for the goal, the method, and the administration of education, making their value rest wholly on the individual person's approval of them.

The advocates of individualism, regarded as possible only in societies of certain kinds, have come to dismiss all reference to supernatural and to metaphysical existence in philosophical reflection upon their educational theories. For Locke, the rules of morality follow from the relation between the idea of God and the idea of His creature. Natural law embodies them, as does the civil law of good societies. His epistemology shows that we can know these rules and that God exists as the reference of His idea. This justifies the curriculum and methods which produce a happy life for individuals who assume their proper responsibilities in a society.

In Kant's view, our ideas of supernatural and metaphysical beings, since they refer to what cannot be experienced, cannot be known to be true or false. Metaphysical beings such as God may be postulated, however; and postulation of them helps to explain certain moral beliefs. But it is a natural occurrence—the future establishment of the ideal of humanity—which justifies moral and intellectual instruction; and it is the purely rational character of moral laws, expressed in the categorical imperative, which explains the moral value of that goal and of the training subordinate to it.

Mill's thought concerning supernatural and metaphysical entities exhibits great variety. In his essays on religion (not considered here), he argues that a limited God may exist; but whether this is so is wholly a cognitive matter, not a matter that concerns the value of life or the emotion of worship. The reality manifested by all states of consciousness is variously material and mental substance, forces and tendencies, or the mere possibilities of those states. Mill's theory that the meaning of propositions consists in sets of hypothetical operations which, given immediate experiences, lead to consequent experiences militates against the meaningfulness of any metaphysical proposition or any proposition about a supernatural being. Nonetheless, from metaphysical considerations he derives the necessary uniformity of the sequences of states of consciousness; and from that uniformity he derives his notion of critical and sorted experience as the conclusive test for all general propositions. By reference to it, he justifies the view that in teaching, however mild or controversial, all positions on any topic should be freely expressed; and by reference to that same uniformity he constructs the laws of association whose use transforms personal interest into social interest, giving the group a significance he overtly calls "religious." The ethical theory by which he justifies his goal objective is, on the other hand, wholly naturalistic. The principle of utility is explicitly derived from natural, egoistic desire; and the principle of obligation is made to depend wholly upon the utilitarian notion of good. The general welfare which education should advance has no metaphysical support; but Mill does provide one for the method and curriculum through which that objective would be achieved.

Dewey's philosophical support of his educational theory is avowedly naturalistic and empirical. All propositions can mean only experiences connected by operations; we can have no ideas of supernatural or metaphysical beings. Human nature, therefore, can not be said to be a copy of them; nor can human knowledge. To know is to relate the meaning of a proposition to the consequences that proposition foresees in useful action. This account of knowing affords a general description for the method of learning. Similarly, the good life can not consist in anything that involves metaphysical or supernatural reference. It is simply the continual realization of preferred desires in those personal and social activities that, as the doer himself correctly judges, contain the greatest possibility of growth. This is the naturalistic justification for the method of self-discipline and for the varied curriculum Dewey recommends.

Unlike Dewey, the societarian writers we have considered provide a metaphysical and supernaturalistic basis for their educational theories. For Plato, the forms or ideas exist nowhere in the natural world and are not discoverable by empirical methods of inquiry. They show what the just society is and the path by which it may be most nearly approached by the program of training which Plato recommends. The general will which, according to Rousseau, informs the institutions of a good society, and which national education ought to further, finds its origin in the will of God and in the nature with which His will has endowed the human soul.

Among the authors we have examined, the religious writers view education as the training of a common human nature, dependent on a substance. They justify this training through supernatural and metaphysical reflection. The non-religious, individualistic authors do not exclude supernatural and metaphysical justification of their educational theories. Those individualistic writers who modify their individualism with a recommendation of a social context of some sort range from emphasizing supernatural and metaphysical foundations for human nature and morality, and consequently for their educational theory, to denying the possibility of such foundations and adopting a straightforward naturalistic view. Those who emphasize the kind of society, as opposed to the individual, depend upon a supernatural and metaphysical source.

One theme cannot be dealt with here. It is the way in which analysis of educational terms, ideas, or concepts is interwoven with the activity of answering the questions of metaphysics, ethics, etc., in the writings we have examined. It is not very difficult to recognize analysis when we come upon it, if we are bearing it in mind at the time; but it is very easy to write analytical philosophy as if it were some other kind of statement if one is not thinking about the distinction at the time of writing. Most of our philosophers were not thinking about the distinction; and if there were space and time, it would be useful to examine their works (perhaps especially those of Locke, Kant, Mill, and Dewey) with a view to disentangling their analyses of educational terms from statements of other sorts. But there is not space and time; and in any case, the reader might like to do that on his own.

In this retrospect, we have considered only a few of the important themes our authors deal with. It is not intended as an exhaustive summary, but rather as a framework within which the reader may clarify and organize the ideas they express. The preceding chapters may help him in this enterprise, and the bibliographies provided suggest more material that may be of use to him. A critical evaluation of the systems of philosophy of education presented here—including the question of the significance of each for life in the second half of the twentieth century—is a problem to which this book may not be irrelevant, but whose solution can be sought only by each reader for himself.

Bibliography

BOYD, WILLIAM, *The History of Western Education,* London, A. and C. Black, Ltd., 1921. Revised and enlarged by Edmund J. King, New York, Barnes and Noble, 1965.

BROWNING, OSCAR, *Introduction to the History of Educational Theories,* New York, Harper and Bros., 1882. (Chapters 2: Quintilian; 4: Comenius; 7: Locke; 9: Rousseau; 11: Kant and Herbart.)

BRUMBAUGH, ROBERT S., and LAWRENCE, NATHANIEL M., *Philosophers on Education: Six Essays on the Foundations of Western Thought,* Boston, Houghton Mifflin, 1963. (Chapters 2: Plato; 4: Rousseau; 5: Kant; 6: Dewey.)

BUTTS, ROBERT FREEMAN, *A Cultural History of Western Education; Its Social and Intellectual Foundations,* New York and London, McGraw-Hill, 1947.

COMPAYRÉ, GABRIEL, *The History of Pedagogy,* translated by W. H. Payne, Boston, D. C. Heath and Co., 1888. (*Histoire de la pedagogie,* Paris, 1883.)

CUBBERLY, ELLWOOD PATTERSON, *The History of Education; Educational Practice and Progress Considered as a Phase of the Development and Spread of Western Civilization,* Boston, Houghton Mifflin, 1948.

HOYT, CHARLES OLIVER, *Studies in the History of Modern Education,* Boston, New York, and Chicago: Silver, Burdett and Co., 1910. (Chapters 1: Comenius; 2: Rousseau; 4: Herbart.)

MONROE, PAUL, *Source Book of the History of Education for the Greek and Roman Period,* London, Macmillan and Co., Ltd., c. 1929. (Chapter 7: Quintilian.)

QUICK, ROBERT HERBERT, *Essays on Educational Reformers,* Cincinnati, 1874; New York and London, D. Appleton, 1924. (Chapters 10: Comenius; 13: Locke; 14: Rousseau.)

INDEX